KT-466-105

Macromedia®
Dreamweaver® MX
UNLEASHED

Matthew Pizzi
Zak Ruvalcaba

 201 West 103rd Street, Indianapolis, Indiana 46290

Macromedia® Dreamweaver® MX Unleashed

Copyright © 2003 by Sams Publishing

All rights reserved. No part of this book shall be reproduced, stored in a retrieval system, or transmitted by any means, electronic, mechanical, photocopying, recording, or otherwise, without written permission from the publisher. No patent liability is assumed with respect to the use of the information contained herein. Although every precaution has been taken in the preparation of this book, the publisher and author assume no responsibility for errors or omissions. Nor is any liability assumed for damages resulting from the use of the information contained herein.

International Standard Book Number: 0-672-32446-6

Library of Congress Catalog Card Number: 2002110477

Printed in the United States of America

First Printing: December 2002

05   04   03   4 3 2

Trademarks

All terms mentioned in this book that are known to be trademarks or service marks have been appropriately capitalized. Sams Publishing cannot attest to the accuracy of this information. Use of a term in this book should not be regarded as affecting the validity of any trademark or service mark.

Warning and Disclaimer

Every effort has been made to make this book as complete and as accurate as possible, but no warranty or fitness is implied. The information provided is on an "as is" basis.

Acquisitions Editor
Jill Reed

Development Editor
Damon Jordan

Managing Editor
Charlotte Clapp

Project Editor
George E. Nedeff

Copy Editor
Barbara Hacha

Indexer
Heather McNeill

Proofreader
Leslie Joseph

Technical Editor
Anne Groves

Team Coordinator
Pamalee Nelson

Multimedia Developer
Dan Scherf

Interior Designer
Gary Adair

Cover Designer
Alan Clements

Page Layout
Susan Geiselman

Contents at a Glance

Table of Contents

Lead Authors

Matthew Pizzi is the Training Director at Train Simple (www.trainsimple.com), a software training company specializing in multimedia products, located in Santa Monica, California. Matthew has been teaching Macromedia products for several years and is the author of *Flash MX Unleashed* by Sams Publishing. He has also authored multiple training CDs. Matthew now heads up Train Simple online training efforts with their revolutionary Web-based training system.

Train Simple offers a robust training experience by means of qualified instructors, and top-quality curriculum delivered though small, intensive workshops. As a Macromedia Certified training provider, a Quark Certified Training Center, Discreet Authorized Training Center, as well as an Apple Authorized Training Center, Train Simple offers the most complete, up-to-date software training for all levels. Training levels range from the private enthusiast to the multimedia professional. For more information on classes, or training CDs, please visit www.trainsimple.com.

Zak Ruvalcaba has been researching, designing, and developing for the Web since 1995. He holds a Bachelor's Degree from San Diego State University and a Master of Science in Instructional Technology from National University in San Diego. He served as Creative Director with EPIC Solutions until 1998. His expertise in developing Web applications led him to a position as Manager of Web Development at SkyDesk, Inc., where he developed Web solutions for such companies as Gateway, HP, Toshiba, IBM, Intuit, Peachtree, Dell, Covad Communications, and Microsoft. He has worked at ADCS Inc. and Wireless Knowledge as a software engineer, developing .NET solutions for Mellon Financial, Goldman Saks, TV Guide, Healthbanks, The Gartner Group, and Commerce One.

His skill set includes technologies and languages from HTML, XHTML, XML/XSLT, WML, ASP, ASP.NET, Visual Basic.NET, Web Services, JavaScript, CSS, SQL, and ActionScript. Utilizing these technologies he is the founder and president of Module Media, a new media development and training firm in San Diego.

Aside from teaching and holding design lectures on various technologies and tools, including Dreamweaver MX, Flash MX, and ASP.NET for the San Diego Community College District, Zak Ruvalcaba is the author of the *10 Minute Guide to Dreamweaver 4* by Que Publishing, and is a Macromedia Certified Professional.

Contributing Authors

Kynn Bartlett has been working on the Web since 1994 and is especially interested in universal accessibility. As president of the HTML Writers Guild, Kynn founded the AWARE

Center in 1999 to promote accessible Web design, and he teaches online courses in Web accessibility. In addition to writing, speaking at conferences, and teaching online courses, Kynn is the cofounder of Idyll Mountain Internet, a Web development company. In his free time, he has an assortment of geek hobbies, documented in detail at http://kynn.com/. Kynn lives somewhere in southern California with his wife Liz and three large black dogs. His first book, Sams *Teach Yourself CSS in 24 Hours* was published in July 2002.

Hugh Livingstone is a Web developer and trainer, living in London, England. As well as running his own training company, he also works freelance for a wide variety of clients. He has been using Internet technologies since the beginning of the Web and training and writing about Web development for almost as long. He can be contacted at hugh@hughlivingstone.com.

Thomas Myer is the cofounder of Triple Dog Dare Media, a Web applications development group in Austin, Texas. Thomas has been a Web developer, information architect, technical communicator, and project manager for the past seven years. He lives in Austin, TX with his wife Hope, and dogs Kafka and Vladimir.

Dedication

I would like to dedicate this book to my fiancée Katy, for all her love and support.

—*Matthew Pizzi*

I would like to dedicate this book to my daughter Makenzie, my wife Jessica, and my mom and grandmother for their support.

—*Zak Ruvalcaba*

Acknowledgments

Writing a book is a tremendous effort and takes dedication and patience from all that are involved. I would like to thank all my co-authors, especially Zak Ruvalcaba for his expertise in ASP.NET, and his contributions to this book. I would also like to thank everyone at Sams Publishing for making this book possible. Jill Reed and Damon Jordan have been a pleasure to work with.

I would also like to thank the development and beta-testing teams at Macromedia, for putting together the best version of Dreamweaver yet. A huge thank you goes out to Jessica Kutash, for all encouragement as well. —Matthew Pizzi

Thanks to all of the co-authors of this book, especially Matthew Pizzi for allowing me to work with him on this project. —Zak Ruvalcaba

We Want to Hear from You!

As the reader of this book, *you* are our most important critic and commentator. We value your opinion and want to know what we're doing right, what we could do better, what areas you'd like to see us publish in, and any other words of wisdom you're willing to pass our way.

You can email or write me directly to let me know what you did or didn't like about this book—as well as what we can do to make our books stronger.

Please note that I cannot help you with technical problems related to the topic of this book, and that due to the high volume of mail I receive, I might not be able to reply to every message.

When you write, please be sure to include this book's title and author as well as your name and phone or email address. I will carefully review your comments and share them with the author and editors who worked on the book.

Email: webdev@samspublishing.com

Mail: Mark Taber
            Associate Publisher
            Sams Publishing
            201 West 103rd Street
            Indianapolis, IN 46290 USA

Reader Services

For more information about this book or others from Sams Publishing, visit our Web site at www.samspublishing.com. Type the ISBN (excluding hyphens) or the title of the book in the Search box to find the book you're looking for.

Introduction

If you've picked up this book, you're interested in the world of Web design and development and, more specifically, in how Dreamweaver MX can help you succeed in these endeavors.

For those of you who have used Dreamweaver in the past, you'll be glad to know that Dreamweaver MX comes with a lot of support for all the things you could do in the past—HTML code lookup, a useful design view, all the functions for building tables, forms, and other elements that take so much time if you do them by hand. You'll also be glad to know that Dreamweaver MX supports those of you who code in various middleware languages, such as ColdFusion, PHP, JSP, and ASP. You can even preview pages that get their content from ODBC and JDBC sources, streamlining development even more.

What's Inside, Part by Part

If you're new to Dreamweaver MX, read Part I, "Getting Up to Speed with Dreamweaver MX." In this part of the book, Chapters 1, 2, 3, and 4 provide a solid foundation for understanding other concepts in the book.

Part II, "Static Web Page Creation," covers some advanced topics, such as tables, forms, and framesets. If you're a programmer, understanding the basics of forms (see Chapter 6, "HTML Forms") in particular will be very handy to know. Whether you're a designer or a developer, understanding Dreamweaver MX's productivity tools—and especially templates and layers—is also covered in Chapter 8, "Dreamweaver Templates," and Chapter 11, "Layers in Dreamweaver."

Developers and designers who are building media-rich sites should concentrate on Part III, "Adding Interactivity." The chapters in this part of the book cover DHTML, Flash, Shockwave, and integrating images and other media into the Web sites you're building.

New and experienced developers alike will benefit from Part IV, "Introduction to Web Applications." Although there is some introductory material (such as Chapter 16, "Introduction to Web Applications"), Chapter 17, "Web Application Preparation," provides detailed installation and configuration instructions for popular Web servers and middleware/database packages.

After you've read the material in Part IV, deepen your understanding of development in Dreamweaver MX by reading Part V, "Behaviors and Middleware." Chapters cover ASP (Chapter 22, "ASP and ASP.NET"), JSP (Chapter 23, "JSP"), and PHP (Chapter 24, "PHP and MySQL").

After you understand how Dreamweaver MX works with a development environment, read Part VI, "Database-Driven Pages," for further understanding of database technologies and how they operate in a Web application environment.

Part VII, "Appendixes," consists of various detailed appendixes on accessibility and other topics that are at the forefront of today's Web development world.

What's Inside, Chapter by Chapter

Chapter 1, "What's New in Dreamweaver MX," introduces you to what's new in Dreamweaver MX, some of which I've already listed, and some I haven't: JavaBean intro-spection, Code Snippets, enhanced templates, and better toolbars.

Chapter 2, "The Dreamweaver MX Interface," covers the Dreamweaver interface: docu-ment views, toolbars, inspectors, panels, and status bars. By the end of the chapter, you should feel fairly comfortable with the Dreamweaver MX environment.

Chapter 3, "Dreamweaver MX Site Management," covers site management, including defining a site, file check in and check out, and defining a local root folder.

Chapter 4, "Dreamweaver MX Essentials," covers the essentials of HTML: page properties, HTML elements, JavaScript, typography, and graphics.

Chapter 5, "Creating Tables," and Chapter 6, "HTML Forms," cover HTML tables and forms—two parts of HTML that will make your design and development life much easier.

Chapter 7, "Framesets," covers framesets, including when to use frames and how to use them properly.

Chapter 8, "Dreamweaver Templates," covers Dreamweaver templates in depth. A good understanding of templates and the workflow surrounding them can make you more effi-cient.

Chapter 9, "Assets and the Library," covers the library, another time-saving tool. You'll learn how to create and store assets for a site, how to use those assets, and how to update all library assets from a centralized location.

Chapter 10, "Cascading Style Sheets," covers the different types of style sheets, how to apply them, and the different properties for text, backgrounds, borders, lists, positioning, and more.

Chapter 11, "Layers in Dreamweaver," covers layers. Layers are a key component of DHTML—and for those of you who have concerns about cross-platform compatibility, the chapter also covers conversion of layers to tables.

Chapter 12, "DHTML," covers DHTML, including timelines, layers, and creating slideshows.

Chapter 13, "Adding Video and Audio," provides an overview of media and includes how to link or embed media, as well as a discussion of ActiveX controls.

Chapter 14, "Inserting Flash and Shockwave," covers Flash and Shockwave—the differences between the two, what parameters they accept, and how to trigger different aspects with JavaScript.

Chapter 15, "Integration with Complementary Programs," shows you how to do roundtrip editing of graphics with Fireworks MX, as well as roundtrip editing of Flash MX. The chapter also covers importing Photoshop/ImageReady-generated HTML.

Chapter 16, "Introduction to Web Applications," begins a series of chapters on Web application development. The chapter covers basic concepts such as server-side scripting, databases, and SQL.

Chapter 17, "Web Application Preparation," covers how to set up and configure IIS and Apache; PHP/MySQL, Tomcat, SQL Server, and ColdFusion; and Data Source Names (DSNs).

Chapter 18, "Dreamweaver MX for Application Development," covers application development in a Dreamweaver MX environment: defining a site and connecting to a data source.

Chapter 19, "Behaviors," includes material that will make it easier to understand actions and events.

Chapter 20, "Extending Dreamweaver MX," covers extending Dreamweaver MX with objects, behaviors, and the menus.xml file. It also covers sharing those extensions with others.

Chapter 21, "Working with CGI and Java Applets," covers CGI and Java applets, with sample guest book applications and a Java-based chat room.

Chapter 22, "ASP and ASP.NET," provides a complete overview of the ASP object model and the .NET Framework.

Chapter 23, "JSP," covers the Tag Chooser, JSP directives, actions, scriptlets, expressions, declarations, cookies, and JavaBeans.

Chapter 24, "PHP and MySQL," provides a look at how PHP compares to CGI, how to use the Tag Chooser, and hand coding PHP.

Chapter 25, "Looking Ahead," covers emerging technologies, including XHTML, XML, XLST, WNL, and .NET mobile Web controls.

Chapter 26, "Database Primer," covers the basics (tables, rows, columns) and more advanced topics such as stored procedures, triggers, views, keys, and normalization. The chapter concludes with a Web store database example.

Chapter 27, "SQL Primer," covers selecting, inserting, updating, and deleting data. It also breaks down SQL into the different clauses and covers joins and subqueries.

Chapters 28 through 32 conclude the book with an in-depth tutorial on building a Web store application with ASP.NET. The chapters include real-life detailed code for catalogs, shopping carts, user registration, personalization, search functionality, and security.

The appendixes cover other important information, such as

- **Accessibility**   The standards, applying those standards, and the impact of accessibility on design and development efforts.

- **Third-party shopping cart products**   How to choose a shopping cart technology, some technology options, and integrating the shopping cart with Dreamweaver MX.

- **Server behavior builder**   Using server behaviors to write cookies, build custom code, and more.

- **Integration with Flash MX**   Create dynamic, media-rich sites by integrating Flash with middleware and database packages.

- **Dreamweaver MX and language resources**   Learn more about multimedia development, application integration, PHP, JSP, ASP, ColdFusion, and XML.

- **ColdFusion MX tags**   Learn how to use the Tag Chooser to implement ColdFusion tags, hand code ColdFusion, and debug your ColdFusion code.

It is our hope that Dreamweaver MX Unleashed can be your one-stop resource for all things related to Dreamweaver MX.

PART I

Getting Up to Speed with Dreamweaver MX

IN THIS PART

CHAPTER **1**

What's New in Dreamweaver MX

By Matt Pizzi

This chapter is for Dreamweaver designers and developers who are upgrading. If you are fairly new to Dreamweaver or you're not too comfortable with it, you may want to skip this chapter and move ahead to Chapter 2, "The Dreamweaver MX Interface."

Dreamweaver MX marks a new generation of Web development. Macromedia's latest effort on its flagship product hosts a series of new features and integrates several other applications within this product. Dreamweaver MX provides an authoring environment that personal designers or Web development teams can use to streamline their workflow. Designers, developers, and programmers can all benefit equally from this one product to quickly design, produce, deliver, and manage Web sites and Internet applications.

This chapter is designed for those who upgraded to Dreamweaver MX and are itching to learn and use the new feature set of this powerful release. I would like to take this time to clear up any prejudices that anyone may have or think I have. My co-authors and I are all bilingual and intend to share the screenshots between the Macintosh and Windows operating systems. All Web developers should have each machine in their studios anyway to completely and thoroughly check each site that they deploy. This version of Dreamweaver offers few differences between these two platforms, although more than the previous edition did. The most dramatic differences between the two happen in the Web application development portion of this book. All differences are noted.

I would also like to point out that with Dreamweaver MX, several Macromedia products have been integrated into

Dreamweaver, making it one of the most exciting releases in a while. Dreamweaver UltraDev, HomeSite, and ColdFusion Studio have all been brought together in Dreamweaver MX.

So now, without further ado, here are the key new features of Dreamweaver MX—enjoy!

New Interface Enhancements

If you've been using Studio MX, or intend to, the applications provide a consistent user interface to keep the learning curve of each product to a minimum and to increase productivity. Dreamweaver MX offers a cleaner, integrated UI in comparison to previous versions of the product. This is one of the key differences between Macintosh and Windows. The Mac offers integrated panels, consistent with the MX product line for the Mac. This version for the Mac is also carbonized to take full advantage of Mac OS X. The Windows version is more integrated and features a unique docking system while remaining true to the MX product line on Windows. Figures 1.1 and 1.2 show examples of the UI in each environment.

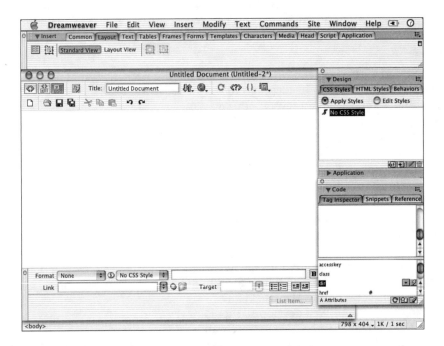

FIGURE 1.1   The Dreamweaver MX user interface on Mac OS X.

Windows offers an option to set the style of the interface to a floating panel arrangement, reminiscent of Dreamweaver 4. This option appears the first time you open Dreamweaver MX on a Windows machine in the form of Workspace Setup dialog box, as shown in Figure 1.3.

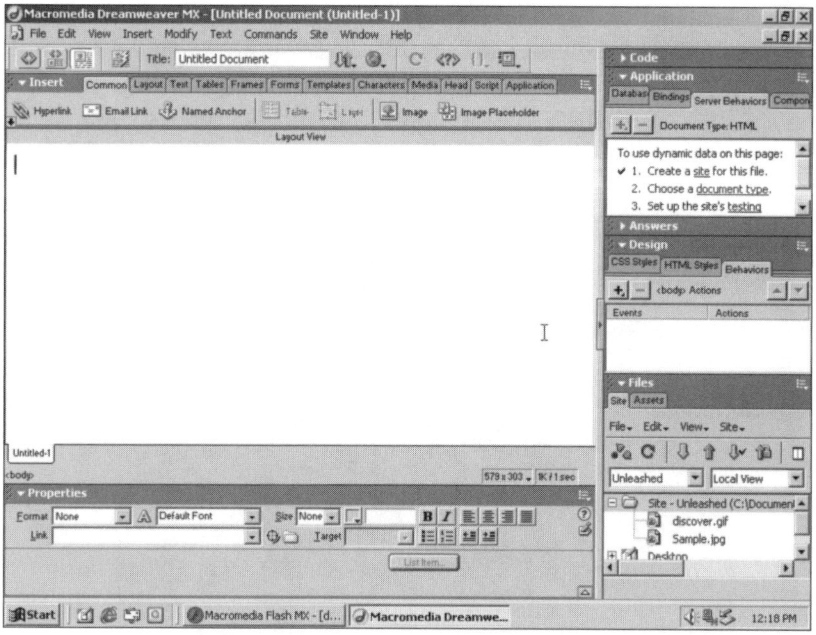

FIGURE 1.2   The Dreamweaver MX user interface in Windows.

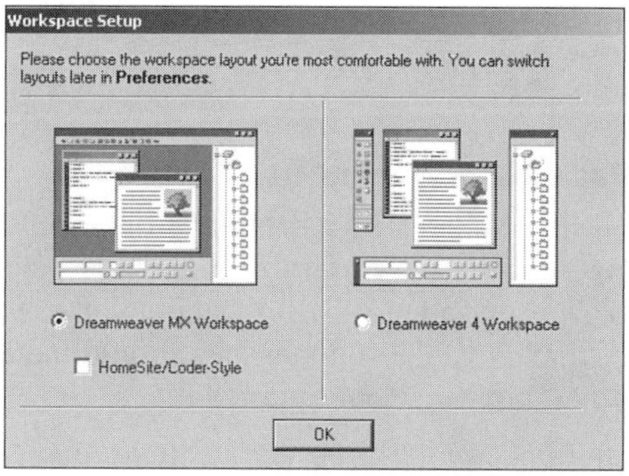

FIGURE 1.3   The Workspace Setup dialog box.

This dialog box offers three options: Dreamweaver MX Workspace (integrated workspace), Dreamweaver 4 Workspace (floating panel), and HomeSite/Coder-Style workspace. I personally recommend that if you are designing in a WYSIWYG environment, choose the integrated workspace. However, if you have a smaller screen, the floating panel option may offer more screen real estate than its new integrated counterpart. If you want to hand code when developing, the best choice is the HomeSite/Coder-Style option. In any case, you can always change those options after you've set them up by choosing Edit, Preferences. This launches the Preferences dialog box as shown in Figure 1.4. In this dialog box, be sure to choose the General category on the left side. In the center of the dialog box, click the Change Workspace button to open the Workspace Setup dialog box again. When the Workspace Setup dialog box is open, choose the style of your choice.

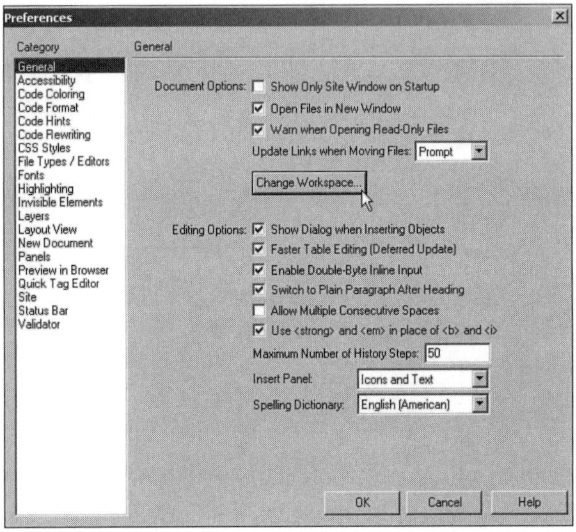

FIGURE 1.4   The Preferences dialog box.

Dreamweaver MX Panel Management

The behaviors of the panels have changed slightly in comparison to previous versions of Dreamweaver. These changes mostly have to do with lawsuits against Macromedia from Adobe. Both companies have been in court battling about copyright infringement, and each won some cases. When all is said and done, they should have gotten together and just shared their technologies, but hey, Adobe started it!

If you have a tabbed panel open and decide to drag it to another panel, you'll get an alert message telling you to contextual-click to move the panel to the desired location, as shown in Figure 1.5.

The contextual menu offers options to group the selected panel to a series of other predefined grouped panels, including creating a new group, renaming the panel group, minimizing the group, or expanding the group. This new way of organizing the panels isn't quite as elegant; however, it still serves its purpose and remains a useful feature for customizing the workspace to better suit your work habits.

FIGURE 1.5   An alert message appears when you try to drag panels.

Integrated File Explorer

A welcome new feature of Dreamweaver MX is the new integrated file explorer. This, however, is a feature that shows up only in the Windows OS, docked with the Assets panel. This panel offers quick access to the site files, whether local files, remote files, files on the testing server, or even a map of files. Essentially the entire Site Files window has been compacted into a docked panel. You can put and get files from this location as well as check in and check out files. A handy toggle button enables you to switch between the collapsed view (panel view) and the standard window view, called the expanded view, as shown in Figures 1.6 and 1.7.

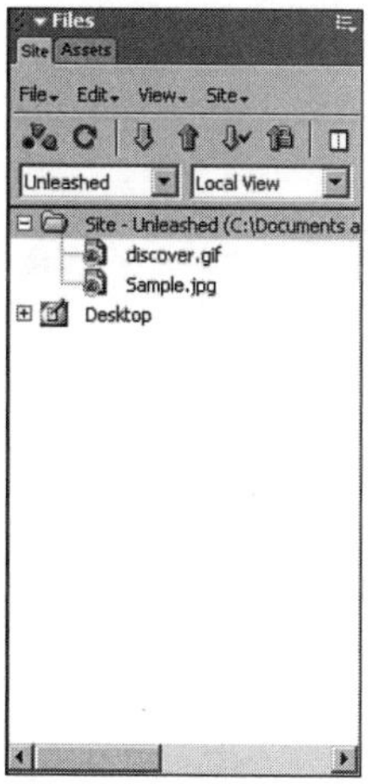

FIGURE 1.6   The file explorer in collapsed view.

Also notice in Figure 1.6 that the collapsed view offers the standard File, Edit, View, and Site menus.

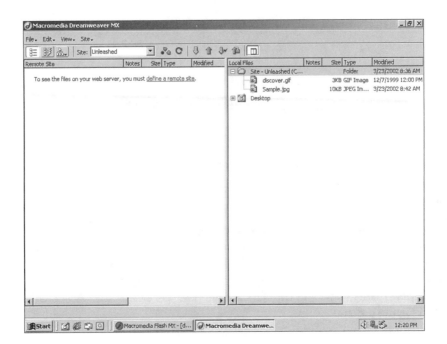

FIGURE 1.7   The file explorer in expanded view.

Standard Toolbar

Dreamweaver MX offers a standard toolbar to expedite common tasks such as New, Open, Save, Copy, Paste, Undo, and Redo. The toolbar, by default, is not visible; however, you can make it visible by choosing View, Toolbars, Standard. It will appear under the document toolbar as shown in Figure 1.8.

FIGURE 1.8   The new standard toolbar in Dreamweaver MX.

Of course, you can always position the toolbars anywhere you like. You can even undock them and turn them into their own free-floating panels.

Customizable Insert Panel

Dreamweaver MX changed the Object panel's name to the Insert panel. Macromedia also decided to place the Insert panel across the top of the page, as shown in Figure 1.9. To many people upgrading, this may not entirely make sense; however, it does clarify some of the interface redundancy. The Insert panel and the Insert menu offer many of the same features.

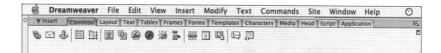

FIGURE 1.9   The Insert panel in Dreamweaver MX replaces the Objects panel.

Some of the Insert panel's options will change depending on which type of document you are editing or developing. For example, if you were editing a PHP page, you would see a PHP tab visible in the Insert panel. This is true for all middleware you may develop with.

The Insert panel is completely customizable using XML technologies in which it was developed.

Dreamweaver Workflow Enhancements

With the new release of Dreamweaver MX, Macromedia added some features to really improve workflow. One example, which is targeted toward the less-technical or less-experienced Web developer, is the Site Set-Up Wizard. Other new features target seasoned developers and experienced Dreamweaver users. Features offered are the JavaScript drop-down menu behavior, Pre-built Components, and enhanced Dream Templates.

There is something for everyone in terms of improving work performance. Dreamweaver MX is truly the most efficient tool in Web development.

Site Set-Up Wizard

My opinion is that Macromedia included this feature to help converted FrontPage users get up and running in Dreamweaver as quickly and as effortlessly as possible. Let's take a glance at what the wizard can do for you.

The wizard walks you through step-by-step in setting up the crucial fundamentals of Dreamweaver Web development. To access this wizard, choose Site, New Site. Be sure to have the Basic tab selected, as shown in Figure 1.10.

- The first question asks you to name your site. This name is simply a way for you to refer to the site within Dreamweaver and has no real bearing on the Web site itself. For that reason, this is the only place in Dreamweaver where spaces and special characters are acceptable in your naming conventions. Click the Next button to continue.

- After you click the Next button, you are presented with another question. Dreamweaver needs to know if you intend to build Web pages that include middleware code, such as ColdFusion, ASP, ASP.NET, JSP, or PHP. If you choose Yes, a drop-down menu appears, asking you to choose the middleware. After you choose Yes or No, click the Next button. A new section appears.

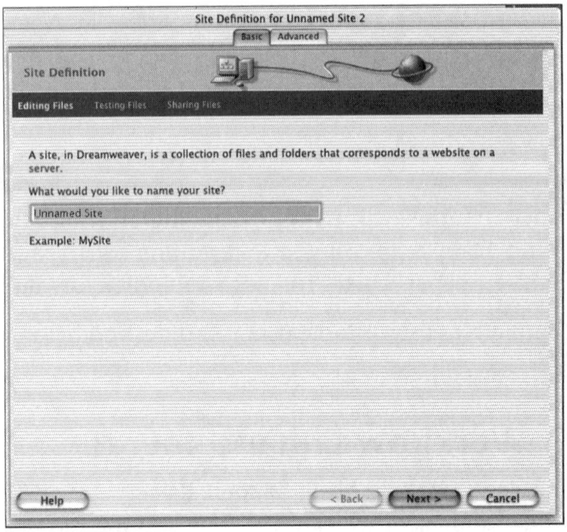

FIGURE 1.10   The Basic Site Definition dialog box, now warmly called the Site Set-Up Wizard.

- In this next section, you need to determine how you are going to edit (create) your pages. The first choice is on your local machine, which is recommended. If you must create pages over a local network, choose that option. Finally the last option, edit on server through FTP or RDS, makes sense only if you do not have access to a local Web server and you have high bandwidth. Click Next to bring up the next screen.

- On this page, fill out information on how you connect to your Web server. Your choices are None, FTP, Local Network, RDS, SourceSafe Database, and WebDav. After choosing your type of connection, you must determine what folder on the server you want to upload your files to. Click Next to advance to the final screen.

- The final screen provides the information that you have filled out throughout this process. One of the key things to be aware of is that Dreamweaver is automatically creating a local root folder for you. This folder will be saved in My Documents in Windows or on the desktop of a Macintosh. The local folder that the wizard creates for you will be named the same as what you named the site in step 1.

Again, I think this feature is best suited for new users of Dreamweaver or someone who is converting over from a lesser program. If you're a seasoned Dreamweaver user, the Site Definition dialog box you know and love is located under the Advanced tab.

Layout and Code Quickstarts

Creating a new document in Dreamweaver MX is no longer like your typical application. When creating a new document, you are presented with a series of choices in the New Document dialog box, as displayed in Figure 1.11.

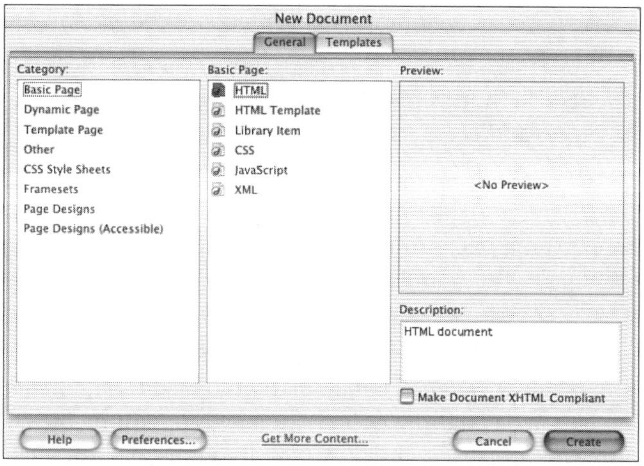

FIGURE 1.11   The New Document dialog box—new in Dreamweaver MX.

I will be honest with you—the first time I saw this, I said out loud, "Come on. You've gotta be kidding, right?" After the Set-Up Wizard and now this, you may have thought that Microsoft was playing a role in the development of Dreamweaver MX. Well, after using the application for a bit, this actually grew on me. This dialog box offers a few options to actually increase production time.

If you refer to Figure 1.11, you'll notice that this dialog box has two tabs. The first is for someone creating a brand new document. The other is to select a template already designed and used in all the local or defined sites within Dreamweaver. So if you are working a site you just set up, but you also have four or five other sites defined within Dreamweaver, you would have access to any of those templates within this New Document dialog box.

The General tab offers eight categories:

- **Basic Page**   Here you have the option of setting up a standard HTML document, an HTML Template document, a library item, a cascading style sheet, a JavaScript document, and an XML document.

- **Dynamic Page**   This section creates a document for different types of coding to create Web applications. Included are ASP/JavaScript, ASP/VBScript, ASP.NET/C#, ASP.NET/VBScript, ColdFusion, ColdFusion Component, JSP, and PHP.

- **Template Page**   This offers the capability to create any one of the dynamic standards listed in the previous bullet as a template.

- **Other**   This category is perfect for creating ActionScript, VBScript, XML, Java, JavaScript, and a host of other programming documents. Because of the tight integration with HomeSite and ColdFusion Studio, Dreamweaver MX is not only the leader is WYSIWYG Web development, but offers the coding environment of choice for professional programmers.

- **CSS Style Sheets**   With this option you can choose to create style sheets with predefined typefaces and color schemes.

- **Framesets**   The frameset option makes the most sense to me. If you have a design in mind and plan to use framesets, your best bet is to use them, or create them from the get go, by choosing one of the predefined frameset configurations. Of course, you are not limited to these configurations; you can always customize them after you get into Dreamweaver. For more information on framesets, see Chapter 7, "Framesets."

- **Page Designs**   This option can be handy if you need to rapidly build a Web page. These page designs act as starting points, intended for editing by a designer. You'll notice there are Greek text placeholders as well as image placeholders. You can tweak any element of this in initial layout.

- **Page Designs (Accessible)**   This category is much like the preceding one, with the exception of complete compliance with the accessibility standards for people with disabilities. Often, this compliance offers a disabled person a more informative session with a screen reader.

Enhanced Dream Templates

Macromedia spared no expense with its new enhancements in the template category. You can now effectively nest templates, allowing contributors a wider span of options without compromising the design and layout of the site.

However, with too many new features to list in this one category, I created an entire chapter just for Dream Templates. If this sounds like your cup of tea, or if your boss forced this cup of tea upon you, please read on and enjoy Chapter 8, appropriately titled "Dreamweaver Templates."

JavaScript Drop-Down/Pop-Up Menus

The wildly popular, yet sometimes buggy, feature of Fireworks 4 has found its way into this version of Dreamweaver. I must say the enhancements are wonderful, and most bugs have been squashed. This newer version of the behavior is a first for Dreamweaver, but it comes with some handy options not available in the Fireworks 4 counterpart. My favorite new addition is the alignment options, which can save a bundle of time in your own Web projects.

The following steps will help you to build a pop-up menu using the new behavior in Dreamweaver. It's quite clear and concise, but there are a few tricks along the way. (Besides, being only a few pages within this book, this will offer instant gratification.)

1. Download the premenu.html document from the Dreamweaver MX Unleashed companion Web site located at http://www.dreamweavermxunleashed.com. Be sure to navigate to the Chapter 1 section after you're on the site.

2. After you've downloaded the document, open it inside Dreamweaver. Highlight the text in the gray cell as shown in Figure 1.12.

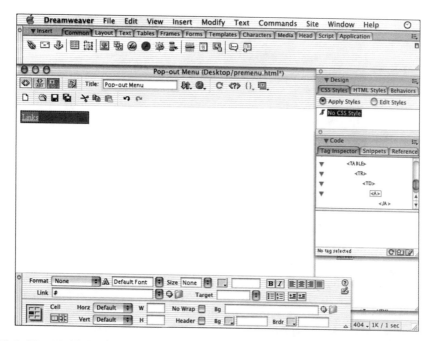

FIGURE 1.12   Highlight the text in the small cell in the top-right corner of the document.

3. With the text highlighted, notice the pound (#) sign in the Link text field of the Properties Inspector. This is necessary because you can't apply a behavior to text; however, it is possible to apply behaviors to hyperlinks. The pound sign transforms static text into hyperlinked text. With the text still highlighted, open the Behaviors panel. By default, the Behaviors panel is nested within the Design panel group. Click the plus (+) sign to access the drop-down menu, and in the drop-down menu choose Show Pop-out menu. This launches the Show Pop-out Menu dialog box as shown in Figure 1.13.

> **NOTE**
>
> To apply the Show Pop-out menu, you must have the document saved.

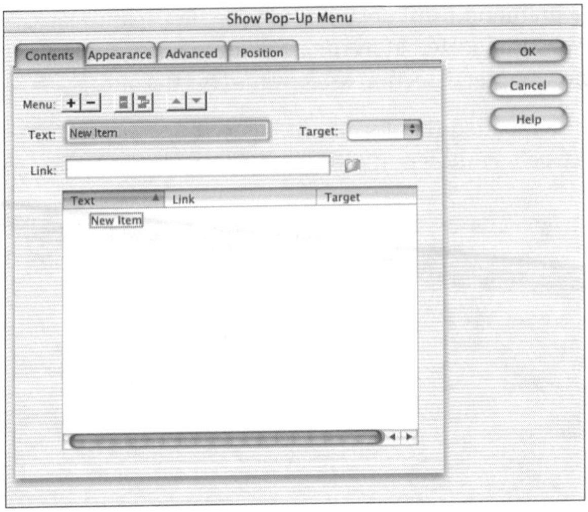

FIGURE 1.13   The Show Pop-out Menu dialog box.

4. Notice that the Contents tab is the initially selected option. Here in the text field, type the label or name of your hyperlink, the way you want it to physically appear in the drop-down menu. For this example, type **Train Simple**.

5. After typing the words **Train Simple**, we'll hyperlink it to Train Simple's Web site. In the hyperlink text field, type the absolute URL, `http://www.trainsimple.com`. After typing the hyperlink, press the Tab key. Notice that the text and the link have been added to the menu, as shown in Figure 1.14. The large portion of the dialog box, where the text and the link have been added, represents what will appear in the pop-out menu.

6. Click the plus sign in the top-right corner to add additional text to the pop-out menu. For this menu item, type **Macromedia** into the text box and press Tab to advance the cursor to the Link text box. Notice that the last hyperlink is still visible in the hyperlink text field. Change the existing link to read `http://www.macromedia.com`.

7. Repeat step 6 three more times with Web sites of your choice.

   Now that you have five menu items and hyperlinks corresponding to those menu items, you can create submenus for any one of those items. For example, Train Simple is well known for its Up to Speed training CDs, and many people visit the site for that reason alone. We can add a submenu of the Train Simple menu item to read Up to Speed, with a hyperlink pointing to that exact portion of the Train Simple Web site.

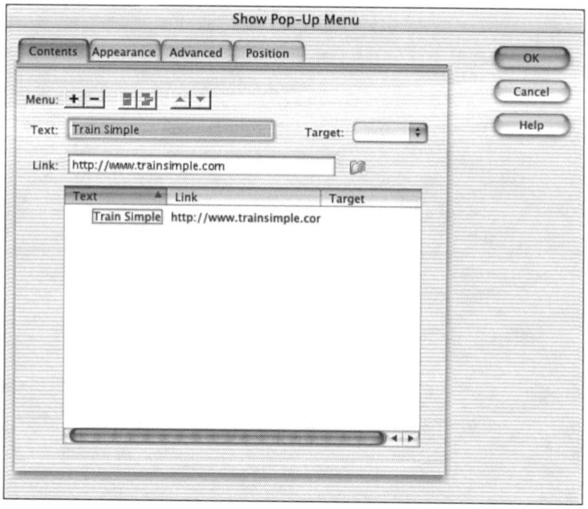

FIGURE 1.14   The text and hyperlink you entered in the top portion of the dialog box is now displayed in the menu area.

8. As in step 6, type **Up to Speed** into the text field. Tab to the hyperlink text field and type in the correct path to the Web site; for this example, type `http://www.trainsimple.com/products.htm`. Press the Tab key to add it to the menu.

9. In the body of the dialog box, highlight the Up to Speed option; using the Up arrow, move it so it is placed underneath the Train Simple option, as displayed in Figure 1.15.

10. With the Up to Speed option now placed properly, click the Indent Item button to force this option to be a submenu to the item above it. The Up arrow is in the top portion of the dialog box.

11. Click the Appearance tab toward the top of the dialog box to move to the next section. This section is the fun part—you get to choose what your menu will look like, in terms of color, size, typeface, alignment, and vertical or horizontal orientation. Notice the font list contains common fonts shared across different computer platforms. For this section, you need no instruction. Pick the colors and fonts of your choice.

12. Now that you have had the chance to show off your artistic side, it's back to business. Click the Advanced tab to move the dialog box to the next screen, as shown in Figure 1.16. Here you choose how big and what the cells will look like.

13. I'm going to leave everything set to default values. Feel free to make any adjustments you want. If you're unclear as to what these options are, refer to Chapter 19, "Behaviors."

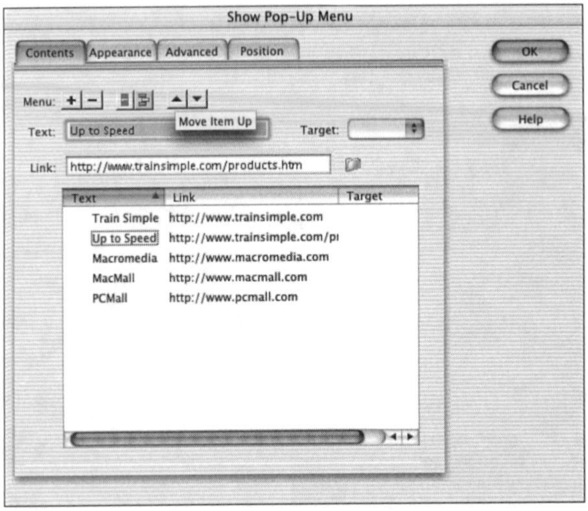

FIGURE 1.15   In this example, you move the Up to Speed option beneath the Train Simple option to prepare the submenu.

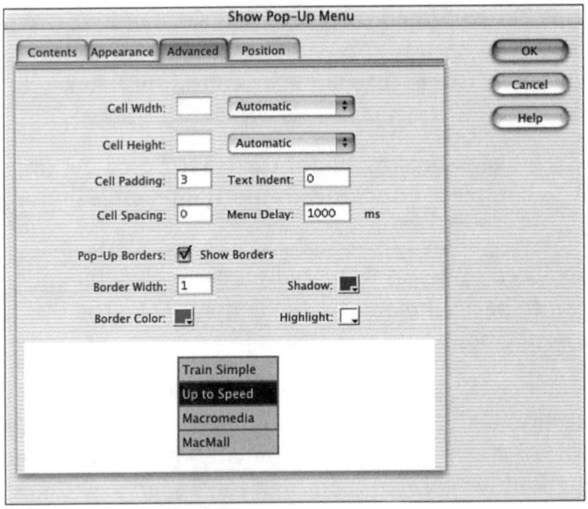

FIGURE 1.16   The Advanced portion of the Show Pop-Up menu offers many options for cell sizing and style.

14. Next, click the Position tab. You'll see a series of buttons. In these buttons are small blue boxes, which represent which way the menu will pop out. If you move your mouse over any of the buttons and pause for a moment, a ToolTip will be revealed,

offering a brief description about how the menu will pop out. For our purposes now, I'm going to choose Below and at Left Edge of Trigger.

15. When you're happy with the settings, choose OK. This will place you back inside the document. Press F12 on your keyboard or choose File, Preview in Browser, and choose the browser of your choice. This launches the browser specified.

16. Inside the browser, mouse over the button to reveal the menu as shown in Figure 1.17. If you mouse away from the menu, it will disappear.

FIGURE 1.17   The drop-down menu works great in many browsers and browser versions.

The Set Pop-Out menu behavior is new to Dreamweaver MX, and as you can see, in just a few short seconds you can create a functional, bug-free drop-down menu, which would otherwise take you hours to hand code.

Enhanced CSS Styles

This book contains a comprehensive chapter on CSS styles; however, if you're looking for some new tips on how to improve your workflow when using CSS styles, you're in the right place.

Macromedia has made accessing CSS styles a whole lot easier. In fact, you can access some of your styles from within the Properties Inspector. Simply highlight the text that you want to change within your document. Click the Toggle CSS/HTML Code button in the Properties Inspector, as pictured in Figure 1.18. Notice that your CSS styles are available right within the drop-down menu, as shown in Figure 1.19.

The Toggle CSS/HTML Code button

FIGURE 1.18   The Toggle CSS/HTML Code button.

FIGURE 1.19   The CSS style options are available within the drop-down menu.

Accessibility

Accessibility on the Web is one of the latest challenges to face Web developers. When creating an accessible document, you're broadening your audience to include people with disabilities. Dreamweaver MX offers a host of features to make sure your documents are in compliance with the accessibility guidelines.

In this upcoming exercise, you're going to look at how you can check to see whether a page is accessible. This gives you an idea as to how this option works inside of Dreamweaver MX. If you need specific or detailed information on the topic, an entire section of this book is dedicated to accessibility (see Appendix A, "Accessibility").

Checking Accessibility Compliance of an Existing Document

In this exercise, you're going to see if a page I created in 2001 is in compliance with the accessibility standards. If you'd like to follow along, download this exercise's corresponding files off this book's companion Web site located at http://www.dreamweavermxunleashed.com.

1. Open the 2001.html file in Dreamweaver as shown in Figure 1.20.

2. With the document open, choose File, Check Pages, Accessibility. This runs a command to check to see whether the page you have open is accessible. A report is generated in the Reports panel as displayed in Figure 1.21, providing information about elements that are not accessible.

3. If you'd like more information about one of the items in the report and learn how to correct it, contextual-click the item, and in the contextual menu, choose More Info. This brings you to the Accessibility Reference panel. The panel describes the error and then offers a remedy, as shown in Figure 1.22.

4. Finally, you can double-click the error in the Report window, which will bring you to the appropriate location in the HTML code. By doing this, you can make any necessary adjustments to make that particular item compliant with the accessibility standards.

When creating a new page, you may also want to make sure you're in compliance with the guidelines right from the beginning. Dreamweaver MX makes this a simple task.

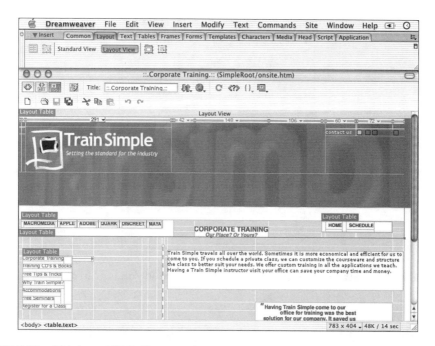

FIGURE 1.20   This is an HTML file created in 1999, which is not accessible.

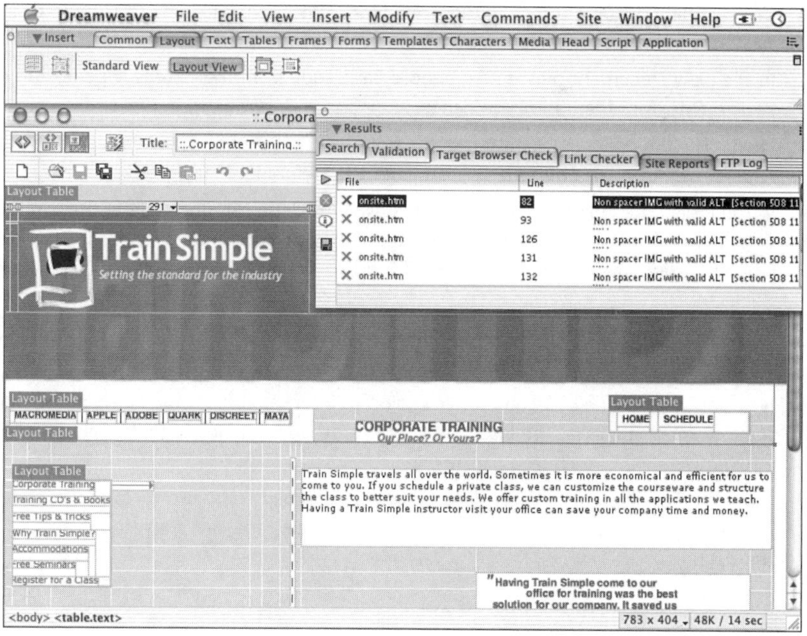

FIGURE 1.21   When you check the page for accessibility, Dreamweaver generates a report listing all the problematic areas of the page.

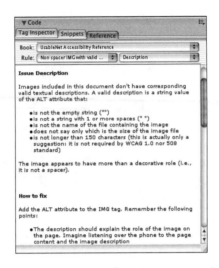

FIGURE 1.22   The accessibility reference provides information on how to correct inaccessible items.

Creating New Pages That Meet the Accessibility Guidelines

To make sure your pages are accessible right from the point of creation, follow these simple steps.

1. Create a new document by choosing File, New. This opens the New Document dialog box as shown in Figure 1.23.

2. In the New Document dialog box, choose Basic Page from the Category pane, and choose Basic HTML from the Basic Page pane.

3. Next, click the Preferences button in the bottom-left corner of the dialog box. Refer to Figure 1.23 to see the button. This launches the Preferences dialog box.

4. In the Preferences dialog box, click Accessibility from the category side of the window. Check off any of the options to have Dreamweaver prompt you for accessibility criteria when inserting any one of these items. I'm going to check Tables, Images, and Media. Click OK.

5. This brings you back to the New Document dialog box. Click the Create button to open the new document.

6. Now inside of my new document, I'm going to insert a table. In the Insert panel, under the Common tab, press the Insert Table button to open the Insert table dialog box. Enter in whatever values make you happy.

7. Click OK. This launches a second dialog box, Accessibility Options for Tables, as shown in Figure 1.24. Fill out the information in the way which you want a screen reader to handle the data.

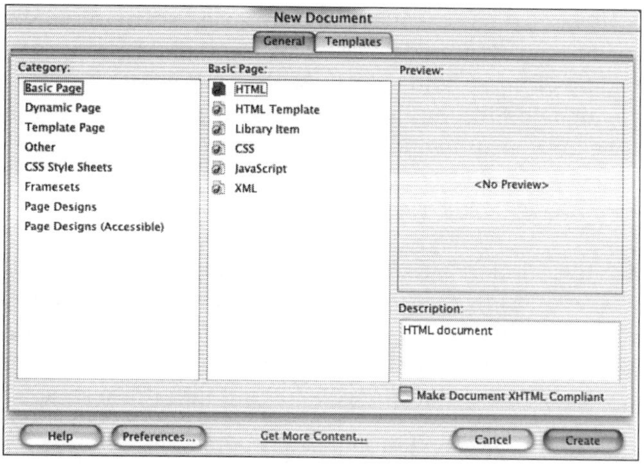

FIGURE 1.23   The New Document dialog box.

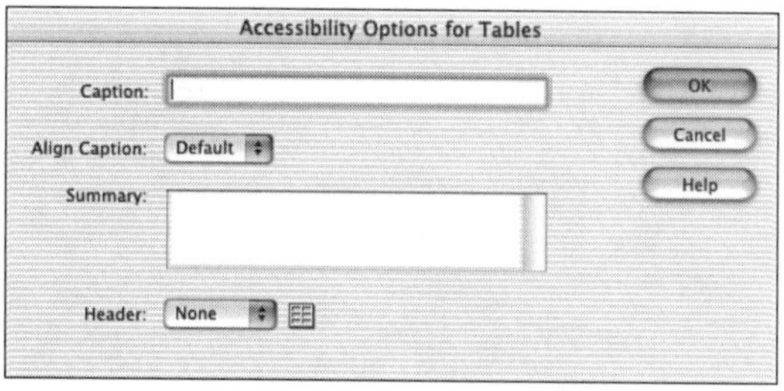

FIGURE 1.24   The Accessibility Options for Tables dialog box.

Remember these exercises are designed to get you up to speed in the accessibility-standard features inside of Dreamweaver MX. If you're looking for detailed and more specific information on accessibility refer to the accessibility section of this book (Appendix A).

Dreamweaver MX Offers Rapid Application Development

One of the most significant changes to the latest version of Dreamweaver is the capability to build database-driven Web applications. Not only is Dreamweaver an HTML editor, but it is also an ASP, ASP.NET, JSP, ColdFusion, and PHP editor.

Macromedia has essentially made Dreamweaver a one-stop Web development tool. Programs such as HomeSite, ColdFusion Studio, and UltraDev have all been incorporated into Dreamweaver MX. This easily makes Dreamweaver the most flexible, powerful tool for Web development and site management.

Dreamweaver MX Unleashed has chapters on how to get started in building Web applications and lays a solid foundation on databases, SQL, and middleware. If you've never thought about building or never built a database-driven Web site, this book offers the essentials to get you up and running. This book should also help you decide which of the middleware language fits you and your project.

Summary

Dreamweaver MX is the solution for Web developers creating and deploying any type of Web site. Dreamweaver offers tight integration with its MX siblings, as well as popular graphics applications manufactured by other companies. If you're upgrading to Dreamweaver MX from a previous version of the product, you'll be pleased with the interface and workflow enhancements Macromedia has put into this release.

If you are new to Dreamweaver, you'll immediately appreciate its professional level of tools and services. This book documents features and qualities of this product in exhaustive detail—from static page creation and extending Dreamweaver's functionality to application development and site management.

## CHAPTER 2

Welcome to the Dreamweaver MX Interface

by Matthew Pizzi

The Dreamweaver MX interface is clean and refined. Although the Dreamweaver 4 interface felt a bit clunky, your experience with MX will be one of organization and productivity. I must say that the improvements Macromedia made really shine through on the Windows side with its integrated MX offering. The overall interface on the Mac is also quite nice. Macromedia has carbonized this version of Dreamweaver to run natively on OS X and take full advantage of the operating system's resources. Please refer to Figure 2.1 to see Dreamweaver MX in Windows; Figure 2.2 shows the Macintosh counterpart.

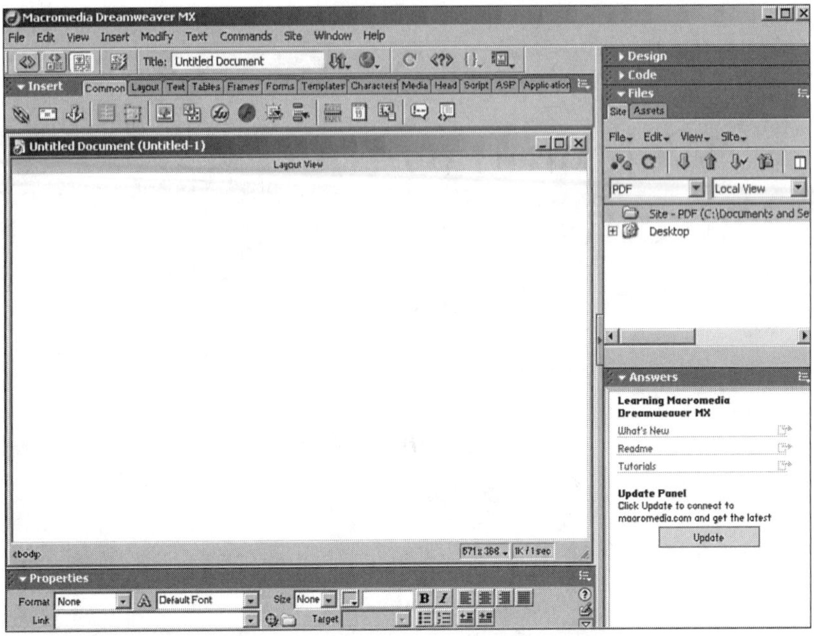

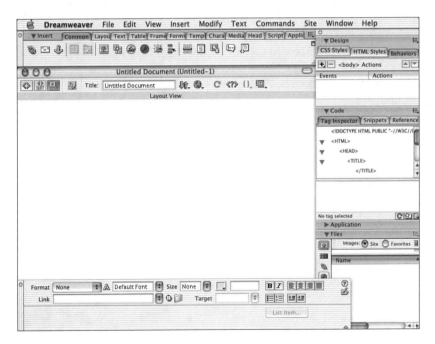

FIGURE 2.1   Dreamweaver MX in Windows XP.

FIGURE 2.2   Dreamweaver MX in Mac OS X.

Panels and Inspectors

As the title of this chapter suggests, I'm going to deconstruct what I think are the most important components of the Dreamweaver interface. I won't point out every crazy detail of each panel at this point, but I will certainly cover them in other chapters, especially in some of the projects where it'll make more sense to do so.

Properties Inspector

The Properties Inspector is one of the most important panels inside of Dreamweaver. It provides information about different items within your HTML document, which cannot be found anywhere else within the interface.

You might have heard that this panel is context sensitive, or at least that's what most authors or teachers end up calling it. That means it literally changes its appearance by providing detailed information about the item selected. For example, if you select a cell in a table it would offer options for background color, dimensions, horizontal, and vertical alignment, and so on. If I then select an image in the document, it would change to give me feedback on the dimension of the image, an option to hyperlink it, image mapping, and so. Therefore, I don't call it context sensitive, I call it Dreamweaver's little well in information. You, of course, can come up with your own nickname.

The capability to display various options for different items inside of Dreamweaver is what makes the Properties Inspector so powerful and convenient; it's many panels all rolled up into one. There is no way to offer screen shots or pictures of each characteristic of this panel. However, as you begin to develop and work more and more with the product, you'll see all that the Properties Inspector has to offer. Refer to Figures 2.3, 2.4, and 2.5 to get a feel about how the Properties Inspector will behave. It's also a good idea to experiment a bit yourself, insert a table, an image, and even a Flash button, and then select these different elements and watch the Properties Inspector change.

> **NOTE**
> Please visit the companion Web site at http://www.dreamweavermxunleashed.com and find a QuickTime movie further explaining the use of the Properties Inspector.

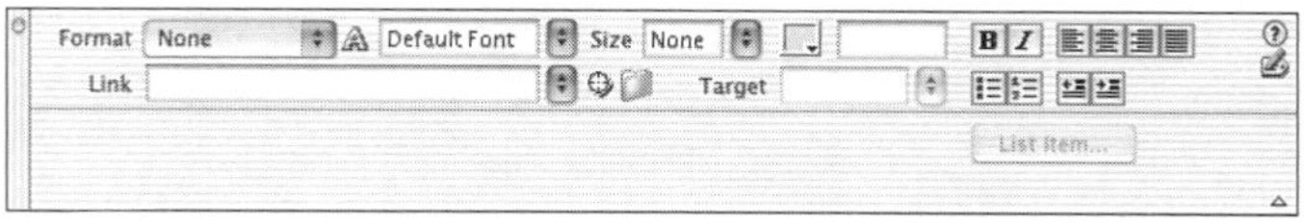

FIGURE 2.3   The Properties Inspector with nothing selected in the document provides typing options such as the typeface and font size.

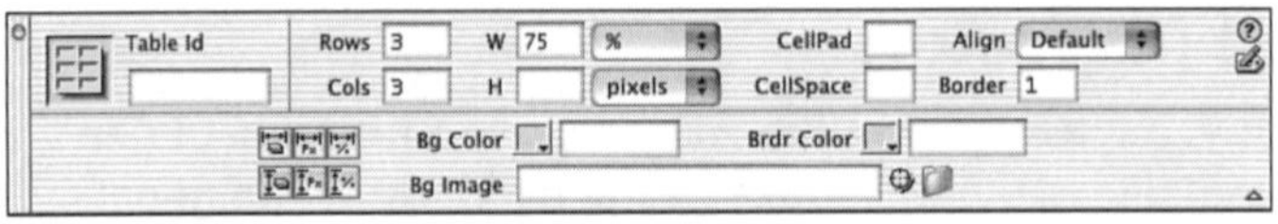

FIGURE 2.4   The Properties Inspector with a table selected offers feedback and options for the table such as dimensions and background color.

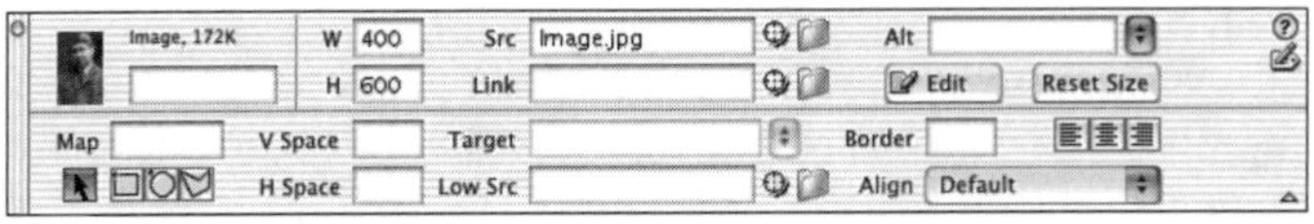

FIGURE 2.5   The Properties Inspector with an image selected provides information on the image's dimensions, file size, and path to where the file is located.

The Insert Panel

If there were a second-most important panel in the Dreamweaver interface, perhaps the Insert panel would claim the honors. The Insert panel is now properly named, previous versions of Dreamweaver referred to it as the Objects panel. Essentially, it is the same thing with a new name and position on the screen. The Insert panel is docked (Windows) or located at the top of the window (Mac), as opposed to being displayed vertically as in previous versions. Refer to Figure 2.6 to see the Insert Panel.

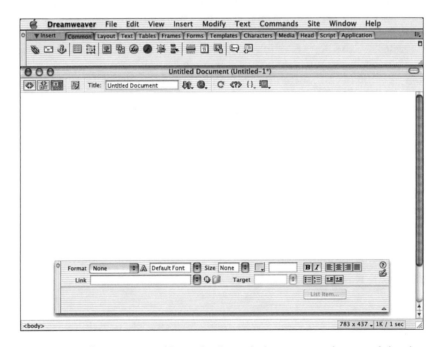

FIGURE 2.6   Notice the Insert panel has a horizontal placement at the top of the document.

With a click of the mouse, the Insert panel enables you to insert any item into your Dreamweaver document. To clear up any confusion, there is redundancy within Dreamweaver regarding this panel. Most of the options in the Insert panel can also be found under the Insert menu.

In Figure 2.6 notice the Insert panel has several tabs, each offering additional objects under that topic. Each topic has several icons, which depending on how long you've been using Dreamweaver, may mean nothing to you. So, if you are new to Dreamweaver may I suggest a tip to make working with this panel a bit more user friendly. Under the Dreamweaver menu on the Mac, or under the File menu on Windows, choose Preferences. This will open the Preferences dialog box as displayed in Figure 2.7. Be sure to have the General tab selected. Notice toward the bottom portion of the dialog is a drop-down menu for appearance choices for the Insert panel. In the drop-down choose Icons and Text. Then, choose OK. Notice the Insert panel increases in size, but it also offers the name of the object to the right of the icon. This makes it easier for individuals not too familiar with this panel. However, as time goes by and your proficiency with Dreamweaver increases, you might want to set the style back to Icons Only to save space.

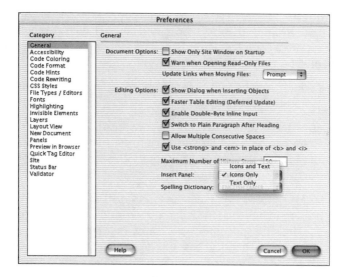

FIGURE 2.7   The Preferences dialog box offers a series of options to cater the functionality of Dreamweaver to suit your needs.

Here's a list that provides a breakdown of each object for each tab in the Insert panel. You might find this to be a useful resource when you're stumped and can't figure out what a particular object is.

Common Objects

The objects under the common tab of the Insert Panel allow you to perform common tasks in Dreamweaver with a single click of the mouse.

- **Hyperlink**—This object provides a dialog box, which contains options for creating hyperlinks within your HTML document. The dialog box also offers options for targets.

- **Email**—This option also launches a dialog box. The dialog box provides two text fields, one to type some text to be hyperlinked, and the other to type the actual link.

- **Named Anchor**—The Named Anchor object enables you to create HTML anchors. These anchors generally act as reference points for hyperlinks to link to an exact location on the page.

- **Table**—To use this option you must be in the standard mode. The Table object will open a dialog providing options for how many rows and columns you want your table to be, as well as options for table width, border size, cell spacing, and cell padding. These tables are best used for simple linear designs and layouts.

- **Layer**—As with the Table object, this option is only available in the standard view. Layers offer more freedom than regular HTML tables. Layers, like everything else in HTML, have certain advantages and disadvantages, which will be covered in more detail in Chapter 11, "Layers in Dreamweaver."

- **Image**—This option enables you to insert an image into your document. That's it, nothing fancy, nothing special.

- **Image Placeholder**—New to Dreamweaver MX is the option of inserting a place-holder image. This can be handy if you have to start laying out a page when all the graphics haven't been designed yet. This object does nothing more than insert an empty image tag with specified dimensions.

- **Fireworks HTML**—If you ever create graphics or Web content in Fireworks, and you create a button, image map, or whatever within Fireworks, to preserve the functionality of that Fireworks document, you must export the HTML code along with the graphics. After doing that, the best way to get that Fireworks content into Dreamweaver is to use the insert Fireworks HTML object. With this object all you have to do is source the HTML document created by Fireworks, and all the functionality of the artwork is preserved in Dreamweaver. This topic is covered in greater detail in Chapter 15, "Integration with Complementing Programs."

- **Flash**—This object enables you to insert .swf files created by any application capable of creating an .swf file, including Macromedia Flash, and Adobe Livemotion. This object works in much the same way as the insert image object.

- **Rollover Image**—Easily create JavaScript rollovers without any coding. Simply choose an up-and-over state in the Rollover image dialog box. Remember this uses JavaScript, so avoid spacing and special characters in your naming conventions.

- **Navigation Bar**—If you are disappointed by the limitations of the insert rollover object, the navigation bar might be the answer to your prayer. Create up to four states per button and create as many buttons as you would like all using an Up, Over, Down, and Over While Down states. You can position the navigation bar horizontally or vertically. You can only have one navigation bar per document.

- **Horizontal Rule**—This object inserts a horizontal rule. Horizontal rules are used to divide content in HTML documents.

- **Insert Date**—This object will open a dialog box providing options for day, date, and time formatting. There is also an option for automatically updating every time you save a document. This object is good for creating sections of your Web site that read "This page was last updated on _____."

- **Insert Tabular Data**—This is the solution if you ever need to import a table from a database or a spreadsheet to your Web site. Rapidly create tables based on tabular data from applications such as Excel, Access, File Maker Pro, and the list goes on.

- **Comment**—Insert comment enables you to place comments within your HTML code. This can come in handy for HTML programmers.

- **Tag Chooser**—This is another new feature for Dreamweaver MX. It enables you to pick tags from any of the Markup or server-side languages. This chooser seems to provide solid information on HTML, ASP.NET, and ColdFusion, but lacks depth in the other categories.

Layout Objects

The layout objects really have only two options, which can be grayed out if in the standard view. The options are layout table and layout cell, as shown in Figure 2.8. They're pretty self-explanatory, however, to see these options in action please refer to Chapter 5, "Creating Tables."

FIGURE 2.8 The Layout tab of the Insert panel offers options to help you design the layout of your document.

Text Objects

Text Objects provides an area on the Insert panel to format text. The majority of these options are also available through the Properties Inspector when typing inside of Dreamweaver. The most interesting feature, as displayed in Figure 2.9, is the new Font Tag Editor. The Font Tag Editor is best used when hand coding in Dreamweaver, it allows single-click access to commonly typed tags and attributes. Instead of having to type tag attributes you can select them from the Font Tag Editor in a GUI interface.

FIGURE 2.9   The Text Objects in the Insert panel contain objects for modifying text.

Table Objects

Table Objects, much like Text Objects, provides single-click access to commonly typed tags when hand coding in Dreamweaver. All but the Table Object are grayed out in the design view as displayed in Figure 2.10.

FIGURE 2.10   Notice all but the table objects are grayed when in the WYSIWYG design view.

Frame Objects

You'll notice in Figure 2.11 the Frame Objects offer single-click access for creating any one of the predefined framesets. Dreamweaver is in no way limited to those framesets, but they can offer a great place to start. New in Dreamweaver MX are options for inserting tags for creating frames when hand coding, including the newly popular iFrames. I discuss framesets in further detail in Chapter 7, "Framesets."

FIGURE 2.11   The Frame objects offer options for creating predefined frameset configurations, with a single click of the mouse.

Form Objects

As Figure 2.12 suggests, there are many objects you can use when creating forms. All these objects in some way can add functionality to an HTML form. Again, to avoid repeating myself, I'm not going discuss all the options that appear in this chapter, I do however use them all in Chapter 6, "HTML Forms."

FIGURE 2.12 The Form objects in the Insert panel contain objects used to build HTML forms.

Template Objects

These objects offer options for creating, editing, and working with templates inside of Dreamweaver. This will not be the last time I say this, but I cover templates in Chapter 8, "Dreamweaver Templates," so I don't want to discuss all the options here. However, if you refer to Figure 2.13, the first button in the top-left corner allows you to create a template by simply clicking the button. The template objects are new to Dreamweaver MX.

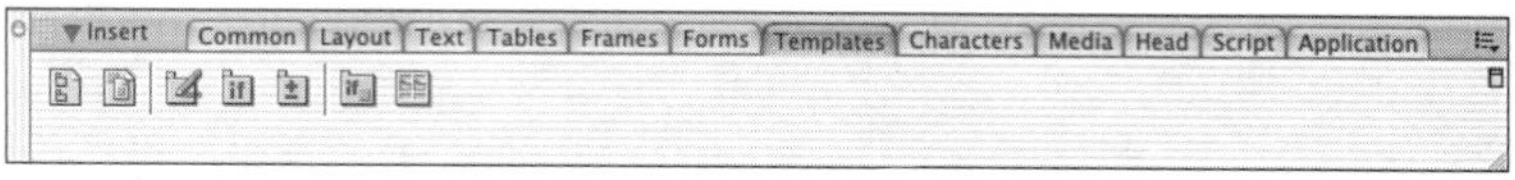

FIGURE 2.13 The Template objects in the Insert Panel contain objects for creating templates in Dreamweaver.

Character Objects

As you will see in Figure 2.14, the characters object provides you with options for creating special characters within Dreamweaver. The main reason this can be so important is because HTML cannot render many special characters you use on a regular basis. For example, HTML has no idea what © means. However, if you write in the HTML code &copy, a Web browser will render the copyright character on the screen. So, all the special characters listed here when pressed, will type some special tag in the HTML document. So, when you view it in a Web browser, the end user will see the character you intended them to see it.

Also, notice in Figure 2.14 that there are characters called Line-Break and Non-Breaking Space. These characters are used constantly in Web development. Line-Break is exactly that. Have you ever typed something in Dreamweaver and wondered why when you hit the Return (Mac) or Enter (Windows) key your cursor moved down two lines instead of one? That's because you are really inserting a paragraph <p> tag into the HTML, which creates a paragraph break, never allowing you to get text to advance to the line underneath the current one.

That's where Line-Break comes in. To insert a soft return or to advance the text line to the line directly beneath the current one, simply insert a line break. The line break will not give you a paragraph space. The keyboard shortcuts for line breaks are Shift+Return (Mac) or Shift+Enter (Windows).

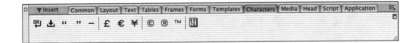

FIGURE 2.14   The Character Objects in the Insert panel contain characters that require special HTML code for a browser to render.

Media Objects

The Media Objects tab enables you to insert different multimedia files into your HTML documents. These media files can produce more engaging, interactive Web sites. As you can see in Figure 2.15 the Media tab contains eight different objects.

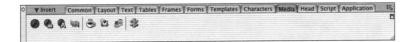

FIGURE 2.15   The Media Objects in the Insert Panel contain items for inserting plug-in type style media.

- **Flash**—This Flash object is essentially the exact same object found in the Common objects. Why does Macromedia do this? So you buy books from people like me or possibly some training videos, it makes the world go around.

- **Flash Button**—Well, if you need to create a quick Flash button, this might do the trick. My advice to you is this, don't use them. I know it might seem harsh, but here are my reasons. If you're not using Flash anywhere else within your Web site, why start requiring the end user to have a plug-in to view one silly button? Every other Dreamweaver developer knows what these buttons look like, so you look kind of lame using them in professional work. If you're a new user, or working on a personal project, they are a-okay with me. In fact, you can even download more styles off the Dreamweaver Exchange. Of course, all this is my opinion, which you might not agree with, you might love these buttons and there is nothing wrong with that.

- **Flash Text**—This is a similar option to the Flash button object. This also enables you to create Flash text inside of Dreamweaver. An advantage of Flash text is that it is vector-based, which offers smoother, crisper lines. The disadvantage is the same as the Flash button object. If you're not already using Flash within your HTML document, don't start by using just this Flash text. You will be requiring a plug-in just to view text. The best bet in that situation is to create text in Fireworks and save it as a .gif.

- **Shockwave**—The Shockwave object will enable you to insert files created in Macromedia Director and any other application capable of exporting a Shockwave file. The functionality of this object behaves much like the insert Flash object.

- **Applet**—This object enables you to insert Java applets, which are small programs written in Java. This object also behaves much like the insert Flash object. We have an entire chapter dedicated to inserting Java applets in this book.

- **Param**—New to Dreamweaver MX is the capability to insert a parameter tag using the Insert Panel. This tag is used by Netscape to handle plug-ins.

- **Active X**—You can also easily add the Object tag by clicking the Active X button. This is typically required by Microsoft's Internet Explorer when dealing with media.

- **Plug-in**—The Plug-in object is best for inserting other types of media that don't have specific buttons. Technologies such as QuickTime are commonly inserted using the plug-in object. Note that with the plug-in object, this will not write the necessary Active X controls for QuickTime to work properly in Internet Explorer 6. I discuss this in greater detail in Chapter 13, "Adding Video and Audio."

Head Objects

The Head objects can play a crucial role in your Web site; from marketing to functionality. I like to think of it as the smart section of an HTML document; after all it is the head! Anyway, the Head objects enable you to create refreshes or meta tags. As shown in Figure 2.16, there are six different Head objects.

FIGURE 2.16   The Head objects in the Insert Panel offer options for placing information within the head portion of an HTML document.

- **Meta**—Meta tags can be used for a variety of different reasons. Typically, Meta tags consist of information about the document or add functionality to the document.

- **Keywords**—Keywords are also meta tags, however, the keywords are typically picked up by the search engine's spiders. If you create a site and never register or submit it to any search engine or Web directory, you might still get a listing. The reason for that is because search engines run programs called spiders, which gather meta information from different Web sites. However, Internet searching has kind of turned into a professional sports arena. Have you ever noticed how you can't go to a ball game without visiting complexes named after big companies: Coors Field, Staples Center, United Center, and so on. To get the best visibility and listings on the Internet, you're going to have to pay for it.

- **Description**—After you're lucky enough, or broke, and your URL gets a listing, what are the end users going to see? Well, you decide. The description you type will show up underneath your hyperlink in the results page of the search, as shown in Figure 2.17. Keep your descriptions short, but make them interesting. Often times the description determines whether the user clicks your link.

- **Refresh**—The refresh object is a meta tag as well. This option will either refresh the current page, or refresh to a different page. Why would you do such a thing? Let's say you have a page displaying baseball scores, the catch is the scores are live, but it will display the current score on the load of the document. So, to get updates the end user will have to click the Reload or Refresh button on his browser. You can do this for him by placing a refresh tag in the document. The refresh object has options for how many seconds to wait before refreshing and what page to refresh to. Or, if you created some new pages on your Web site to replace some old ones, but you named them differently. Well, if you have a listing in a search engine, they'll have the link to your old page. All you have to do is place a refresh command in the linked document to have the page refresh to the new page just a few seconds after the page has been downloaded.

- **Base**—You can change the directory of files with the base object when using relative addressing. Relative addressing is covered in greater detail in Chapter 4, "Dreamweaver Essentials." You can even link your files to a different Web site, all using this one command. There is also an option for changing the target for the linked documents.

- **Link**—Even though there are a variety of reasons to use the link object, it is most commonly used with Cascading Style Sheets. It is used to point to a link between the current page and another page or file.

Script Objects

The Script tab contains three objects, which are pictured in Figure 2.18. These objects are designed to add functionality within the Web page by the use of JavaScript and VBScript. Now unfortunately, you'll have to master one of these scripting languages to find these objects useful. There are some practical applications we can create without a great deal of knowledge of these scripting languages. Refer to Chapter 19, "Behaviors," to get more detailed information.

Application Objects

The objects will only matter to you if you plan to do Web application development. These objects replace the Live objects in UltraDev 4. These objects enable you to quickly insert common tasks handled by a middleware as well as common page structures. As displayed in Figure 2.19, you can see that the Application Tab houses 10 different objects.

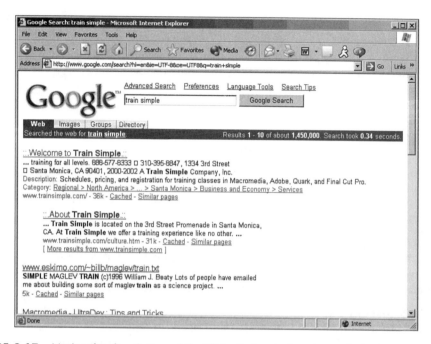

FIGURE 2.17   Notice the description of the Web site located underneath the hyperlink when a search is performed with a search engine or Web directory.

FIGURE 2.18   The Script Objects in the Insert Panel offers the ability to place scripts in your HTML documents.

FIGURE 2.19   The Application Objects in the Insert Panel are used for Web application development.

- **Recordset**—When creating database-driven Web sites, like everything else on the Web, speed is key. Taking all the information out of the database when a user requests information is a time consuming, daunting, unrealistic, and unnecessary task, therefore, you can extract information out of certain tables to make the data more manageable. Recordsets are often referred to as database queries.

- **Repeated Region**—This object is similar to that of the Repeat Region behavior found in the server behaviors panel. This object enables you to repeat the contents of a table. A good example of this is a results page from a search. See Chapter 31, "Adding Shopping Cart Functionality," for more detailed information.

- **Dynamic Table**—This object allows you to insert a table populated with dynamic content. It can speed up the process of binding data to a static table.

- **Recordset Navigation**—With the Recordset Navigation bar you can browse through the different records within a query. Dreamweaver will automatically place first, next, previous, and last buttons on your document, either in the form of text or images, with show if behaviors already applied to them. For more information on the Show If and Recordset Navigation bars, please refer to Chapter 28, "Working with Dynamic Data."

- **Recordset Statistics**—The Recordset Statistics object enables your end user to have an indication as to what record they are viewing. For example, if they were looking at records 10 through 15 of 30 records within the Recordset, by using the Recorset Statistics object, they would see text displaying "Records 10 to 15 of 30."

- **Master-Detail Page Set**—The object enables you to create a master-detail page relationship without any previously established content on a page. After using this object, it's very easy to modify the appearance of the page that gets created for you. For detailed information on master and detail pages, see Chapter 31.

- **Record Insertion Form**—The Recordset Insertion Form creates a form document with all the necessary functionality to insert a record into an existing table with the database. Go to http://www.dreamweavermxunleashed.com for a QuickTime video explaining this object. Also refer to Chapter 27, "SQL Primer," for more information.

- **Record Update Form**—Again this object is much like its cousin the Recordset Insertion Form object. The differences between the two are this: The Insertion Form object will write data to a specified table within the database. The Update Form does the same, but instead of creating a new record, you write over an existing one, thus updating it.

Middleware Tab

You will get an additional tab if your are creating dynamic Web sites (database-driven). The middleware you are using will determine if you get an ASP, PHP, ColdFusion, JSP, or ASP.NET tab. Each of these tabs will add functionality to the middleware you are working with. As you can see in Figure 2.20, I have a PHP tab active when creating PHP pages.

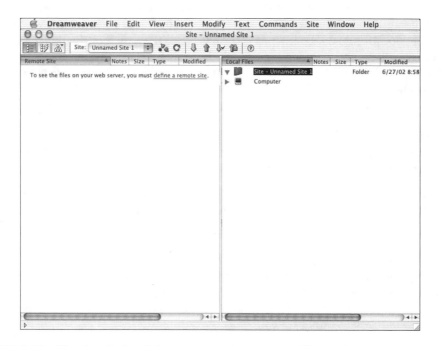

FIGURE 2.20 If I start off by creating a PHP page, I automatically get the PHP objects in the Insert Panel.

Site Window/Site Panel

This is one of the interface elements inside of Dreamweaver that really differs between the Macintosh and Windows operating systems. This might make some Mac users jealous, but hey Mac users have Steve Jobs. With all kidding aside, the site window or panel is a key component of the Dreamweaver MX interface. In Figure 2.21 you'll see the site window on the Mac, and in Figure 2.22 you'll see the site panel in Windows. Remember, the site panel in Windows can be undocked and treated like a free-floating window, just like it is by default on the Mac. I think this window/panel is so important because this is where all the files are organized and, if needed, even linked. This is also where you manage your site to get and put files. There are a lot of features to review in this panel, and we'll look at them all in Chapter 3, "Dreamweaver MX Site Management."

FIGURE 2.21 The site window is how you can view your site files on the Mac.

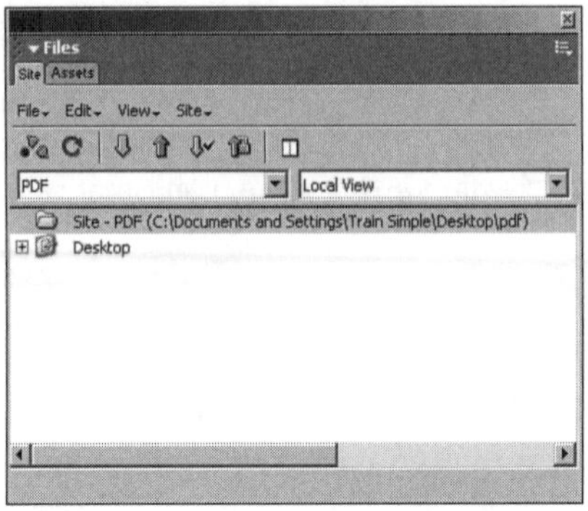

FIGURE 2.22   The site panel in Windows can be expanded or collapsed. The expanded view offers an easier look when managing your site.

Interacting with Panels

The way you interact with panels in Dreamweaver MX is a bit different from what you might expect. You see, Adobe and Macromedia have been tangled in lawsuits for copyright infringement. Each company, as of this writing, have each won some lawsuits. I'm telling you this because one of the lawsuits that Adobe won, or you could say that Macromedia lost, has to do with the dockable panels. The change to the panels in the new version of Dreamweaver is simply a method for offering the same functionality, but in a way that isn't on par with the Adobe way. I think they made this change a few nights before the release of the product.

Here's how they work:

1. If you attempt to click and drag one of the panel tabs to a different location you get a dialog box alerting that if you want to move the panel, you must contextual click and choose Group *name of panel* With, as shown in Figure 2.23.

2. In the contextual menu, you will get options for placing the panel with other panel groups, creating a new panel group, renaming a panel group, maximize the panel, and close the panel.

The panel groups do, however, make up for any inconveniences you find with new panel docking behaviors. The beauty of these new panel sets is the workflow enhancements. If a panel set is in your way simply click the arrow in the right corner of the panel and collapse it instead of closing it. After working with Dreamweaver's new enhancements, I can't image developing without them.

FIGURE 2.23   Notice the dialog box when you try to drag and drop a panel into another panel set.

Assets Panel

The Assets panel made its debut in Dreamweaver 4. It's a tremendous organizational tool, which enables you to manage your assets. As you add different content and media to your HTML documents keeping tabs on all your stuff can turn out to be a job in itself. Luckily, with Assets panel you can see all the content that you've used so far in your site, and you can even mark commonly used ones as favorites for even speedier file management.

The Assets panel contains all your images, links, colors, Flash files, Shockwave files, Movies, Scripts, templates, and library items all in one central location. Figure 2.24 displays all the different components of the Assets panel. The Assets Panel on the Mac is grouped with the File panel set. The strange thing is there is nothing else grouped within that set, so the Assets panel may look like its named "Files." Just a small oversight on behalf of the Dreamweaver development team.

FIGURE 2.24   The Assets panel is where all the assets in the site are stored. It offers quick access to files.

To add an asset to the Favorite portion of the panel, simply have the asset highlighted within the panel and in the submenu in the top-left corner choose Add to Favorites.

Design Panel Set

The design panel set contains three panels by default. It Contains the CSS Styles panel, HTML Styles, and the Behaviors panel. Each of these panel features will be deconstructed and used in projects in the upcoming chapters.

Code Panel Set

The Code panel is a great resource when you're writing code inside of Dreamweaver. The Reference panel includes the O'Reilly HTML and CSS reference as well as references on JSP and ASP by Wrox. There are also references on the UsableNet Accessibility standards, Sitespring project site reference, and a great ColdFusion reference. These can come in handy when you need specific information about a particular tag, for example, what it means, and how it works.

The Snippets panel is an area where you can store scripts or "snippets" of code. This can be ideal in situations where you need to repeat content in different pages, but you don't necessarily want to create a library item or template. We use the snippets panel in Chapter 22, "ASP/ASP.NET."

The Tag Inspector offers a visual representation of the code that you or Dreamweaver is writing. What's nice is that it lays the code out in a file tree format, enabling you to expand or collapse any tag to show or hide specific information. This panel is split in two, the top displaying what I call the code tree, and the bottom displaying the details as shown in Figure 2.25

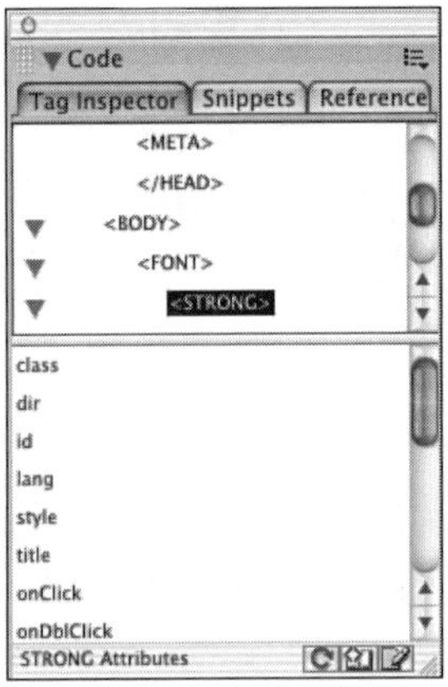

FIGURE 2.25   The tag inspector is divided into two portions, the code tree and the bottom details.

Application Panel

Again, the Application panel is specifically for Web application development. In Figure 2.26, you'll notice that the Application panel has four tabs. The Database tab enables you to set connection between Dreamweaver and the database. Your choices are creating a connection based on a DSN and a custom string. We'll look at each of those connections in Chapter 17, "Web Application Preparation."

The bindings tab enables you to query the database or create a Recordset. After creating a Recordset, you'll see database information in the body of this panel. Typically, Recordsets contain data bindings, which reflect different columns of the table you are querying.

Server Behaviors are server-side scripts, which add functionality to your page. These scripts generally work in conjunction with whatever data bindings you have created. There is great deal of detail about the data bindings and the server behaviors in Chapter 28.

The Components panel can add functionality to your site when developing Web applications. This topic is covered in detail in Chapter 31, " Adding Shopping Cart Functionality."

Answer Panel

The Answers panel behaves as a dock of current and helpful information. If you're looking to see if there are any updates to Dreamweaver, or if you need to go through a tutorial, the Answer panel is your answer so to speak.

Document Window

The Document window is where all the production of your Web page will happen. Dreamweaver tries to mimic what a Web browser looks like, so you have an idea as to what the page will look like on the Web in the development environment. Often times, however, you will want to check your work in an actual browser. Macromedia made the process of previewing the documents a snap. All you have to do is choose File, Preview in Browser, with Internet Explorer or any other browser; F12 is the keyboard shortcut. The document window consists of several different elements in its structure, as shown in Figure 2.26.

Toolbar

The toolbar is constructed of several different options. We'll look at each of these options, moving from left to right. Refer to Figure 2.27.

- **Code View**—The Code view, as pictured in Figure 2.28, is a full-featured code editor, reminiscent of Allaire/Macromedia HomeSite. It offers the essentials such as code coloring, auto indenting, and line numbering.

- **Split View**—The Split view provides developers the opportunity to experience the best of both worlds. Not only can you move things physically in the document and work in a very visual way, but you can also see and work in a more technical way at the same time. Dreamweaver also has a feature called Roundtrip HTML, whatever you do in the design view, will automatically be reflected in the code view and vice versa. If you don't know HTML this is a great way to learn. It can also be very handy for debugging. If something is positioned properly in your document, you might have an unnecessary tag. Select the item you're moving in the design view, notice that the code view is also highlighted, reflecting the area of the document you're working with. Refer to Figure 2.29 to see the split view window.

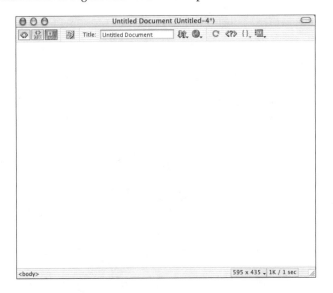

FIGURE 2.26   The Dreamweaver MX document window is the centerpiece of the Dreamweaver interface.

FIGURE 2.27   The Dreamweaver MX Toolbar contains buttons to perform standard tasks such as Copy and Paste.

- **Design View**—The Design view is the default view in Dreamweaver, which we looked at earlier in the Document Window section of this chapter. The design view is a visual design environment, also know as WYSIWYG HTML editing.

- **Live Data View**—This can be a time-saving feature for Web application developers. Typically, to see dynamic content you must upload it to the server, and then test it by calling the page from the server. Dreamweaver MX carries over a feature found in UltraDev 4, which is the live data view. In this view, Dreamweaver calls the server to process the scripts and display the information within the Dreamweaver authoring environment. The exception here is navigation, and passing parameters. It's helpful for quick previews, just to check if the dynamic content is working.

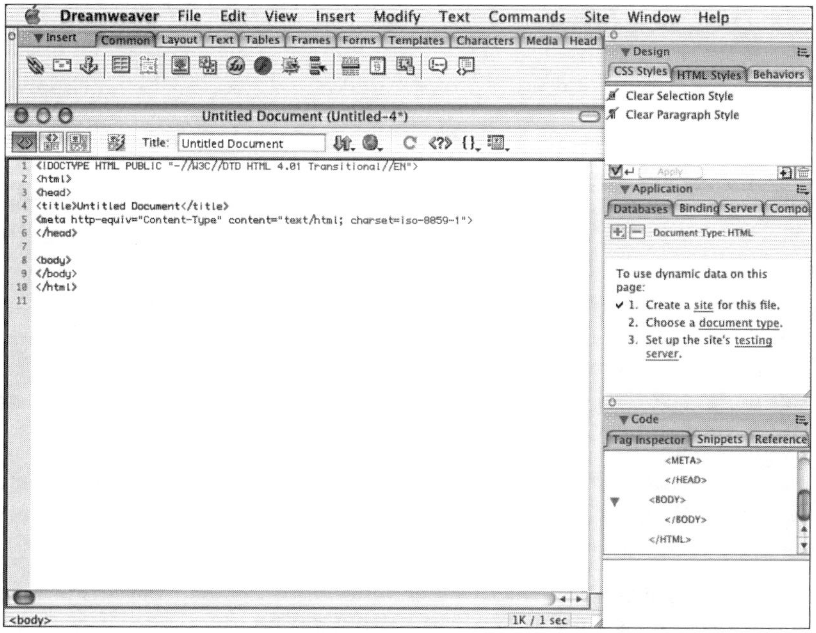

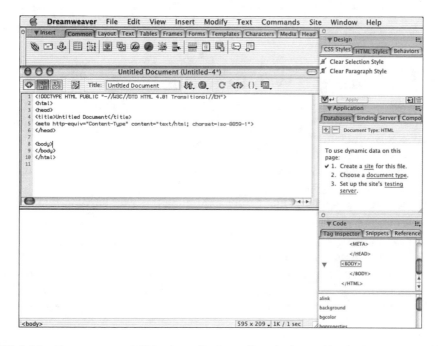

FIGURE 2.28   Dreamweaver MX in the code view is ideal for hand coding Web documents.

FIGURE 2.29   Dreamweaver MX in the split view offers the best of both the coding world and the WYSISWYG design world.

You add an HTML title to your document by typing in the title text field in the toolbar. The title shows up in the title bar of the browser window. It's a good idea to title your page for a couple of reasons, but one of the most important is search engines take titles into consideration when listing possible results for searches.

Referring back to Figure 2.27, you'll notice there are also options on the toolbar for managing local and remote files. Especially when doing application development, using the File Management menu can save time, more so on the Mac, because of its missing site panel.

Testing pages is common practice in Web development; it's also common to test using more than one browser. It's generally a good idea to test on the latest three versions of Internet Explorer and Netscape. Also, testing across platforms will ensure good performance and functionality. If you want ultimate control over the appearance of your site, you can also test other, less common browsers.

The Refresh button, well, refreshes. Sometimes when writing in the code any new changes will not be reflected in the document window in design view. This would be a good time to use the Refresh button.

There is also a reference button, which will either bring the code panel forward, appearing in front of all other panels, or it will open the panel if it is closed.

The Code button will enable you to set or remove breaking points within your code. This button is grayed out and not available when in the design view.

View Options enables you to change the view and characteristics of the code panel. Things like line numbers, word wrap, auto indent, and syntax coloring can all be applied here.

Document Size and Web Page Dimension

There are ways to set a target size to constrain your page to a specified dimension. This is important, remember everybody's computer is a bit different. Monitor size, resolution, how many colors, and what platform they have, are all factors that play into how your Web site will be displayed. To decide what the dimensions will be for your pages, consider who your audience will be. Most companies try to design for the lowest common denominator, which for computers on the Web is a screen resolution of 800x600. It's a good rule of thumb to design a site that will be visible and function when viewed at that resolution size.

Figure 2.30 shows that you can set the dimensions of your page by using the window size pop-up menu. Notice that each option has two dimensions. The dimensions on the left represent the actual size of the document, whereas the numbers on the right and in parentheses represent the resolution size the monitor has to be for the value to be acceptable. If you're designing a site to fit in a screen resolution size of 800x600, remember the whole screen is not your workspace. You have to allot room for the button bar, location bar, and other toolbars.

> **NOTE**
>
> It's important to know that if you choose a dimension in the window size pop-up menu, there is nothing locking the window to that size. If you resize, minimize, or maximize the window you're changing the window dimension. So it's good practice to keep your eye on it. Also, it doesn't have to be exact, just have a general idea of how large the space is that you're adding content to within a page.

```
592w
536 x 196   (640 x 480, Default)
600 x 300   (640 x 480, Maximized)
760 x 420   (800 x 600, Maximized)
795 x 470   (832 x 624, Maximized)
955 x 600   (1024 x 768, Maximized)
544 x 378   (WebTV)
Edit Sizes...
```

FIGURE 2.30   The window size pop-up menu offers common Web page dimensions

Status Bar

The Status bar is simply an indicator telling you the overall size of the document, and how long it will take that document to download with someone using a 28 kbps modem.

Summary

The Dreamweaver MX interface is clean and stays out of your way when developing. Macromedia has made many improvements to the interface with the release of MX. The expandable/collapsible panel sets will go a long way when it comes to speeding up your workflow.

## CHAPTER 3

Dreamweaver MX Site Management

by Matthew Pizzi

One of the crucial elements in Dreamweaver, or in any Web production, is site management. Dreamweaver excels at managing files on both the local and remote sides. Whether you're an independent designer/developer or one in an entire Web team, Dreamweaver excels at file management and organization.

It's important to note that this chapter provides complete information on managing a static site, which is to say that sites containing middleware or database connectivity will be covered in future chapters. So if you want to start working on a static site, read on.

Setting Up a Web Site in Dreamweaver MX

One of the most important steps in site management is defining a site within Dreamweaver. There are two ways to accomplish this, using either the Basic Site Definition dialog box or the Advanced Definition dialog box. Both offer similar features; however, the Basic version walks you through in a more methodical way. The Basic tab, as shown in Figure 3.1, is less cluttered than the Advanced tab, shown in Figure 3.2. Developers new to Dreamweaver may prefer the Basic tab, whereas the Advanced tab offers features and options better suited to Web professionals and seasoned Dreamweaver developers.

There are several ways to activate the Site Definition dialog box.

- Choose Site, New Site. This brings you directly into the New Site Definition dialog box.

- Choose Site, Edit Site. This launches the Edit Sites dialog box. Here you have the option of editing an existing site, or you can click the New button to define a new site.

- In the Site Files window, choose Edit sites from the site's drop-down menu located in the toolbar. This opens the Edit Sites dialog box. Here you can highlight an existing site and click Edit to modify its definition, or you can click New to define a new site.

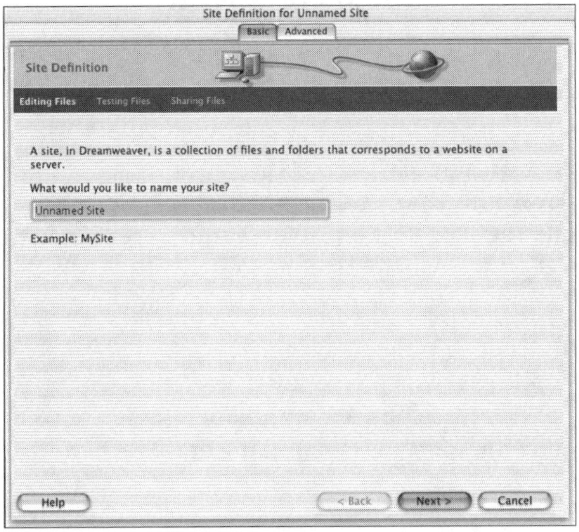

FIGURE 3.1   The Basic Site Definition dialog box.

The Local Info Category

In this chapter we'll spend more time looking at the Advanced tab, and then provide a recap of the Basic tab. The Advanced tab is probably where most Dreamweaver developers will do the majority of the site definition. We'll start by looking at the local info category.

The Site Name and Local Root Folder

The first thing you must do is name your site. This is simply a way to locate the site you're defining within Dreamweaver. Dreamweaver is a professional development tool, and because of that, it offers the capability to have several sites defined at the same time. The only way to distinguish between the different sites is to give each site a unique name.

This name has nothing to do with the Web site, in terms of functionality or anything else. It's simply a way to identify which site you're working with in Dreamweaver at a particular point in time. Spaces and special characters are acceptable here; however, it is one of the few places where it is appropriate in Web development.

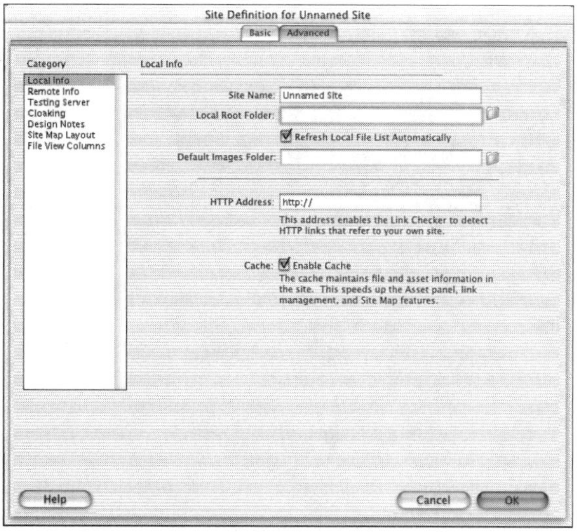

FIGURE 3.2   The Advanced Site Definition dialog box.

Referring back to Figure 3.2, you'll notice that the next text field is to define a local root folder. The local root folder plays a key role in file management and structure. Every file in your Web site should reside within the local root folder, unless it is absolutely linked to something in a different location. What I mean by an absolute link is one that contains the entire path to a particular location on a Web server. The reason that it plays such a pivotal role is the nature of an HTML document. Everything in a Web page is hyperlinked in some way or another, with the exclusion of a few things, such as type.

It is also very important because eventually the site that you are designing will leave your computer and be transferred to a Web server somewhere. Let's look at an HTML tag that sources an image that will be placed in the document. In Figure 3.3, you'll see that the source is pointing to the picture file, based on its location, in this case, within my computer. Notice how the img src tag is looking for a picture within my hard drive. The problem with this is that when the site is moved from my computer and then uploaded to a Web server, my hard drive is not moving over the server with the rest of my site files. Therefore, when the HTML document on the Web server sources a picture on my hard drive, it won't be able to find it. Because my hard drive is not on the server; the result is a broken image link in the Web browser, as shown in Figure 3.4.

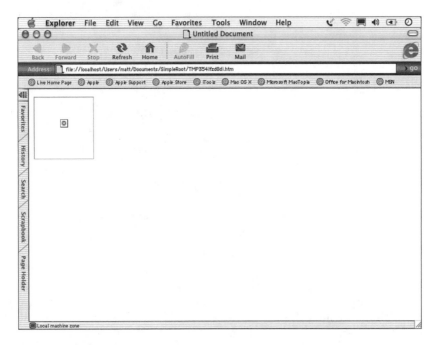

FIGURE 3.3   An HTML image source tag.

FIGURE 3.4   A broken image link appears in the browser if the image is not sourced to something within a root folder or is not sourced with an absolute path.

This example is one illustration of the importance of a local root folder. Your local root folder is ultimately a mirror image of your root folder on your Web server.

You can use either an existing folder on your computer or you can create a new one. The best way to define your local root folder is to click the little folder icon to the right of the text field to launch the Choose Local Root Folder dialog box as shown in Figure 3.5.

In the dialog box, highlight the folder; on Macintosh, click Choose, and on Windows, click the Open button, which then turns into a Select button. This action defines the selected folder as the local root folder for this site.

You'll also notice that a check box in the dialog box offers the option to refresh the local file list automatically. If you have this box checked, anytime you add a file to your page, the local file list will immediately reflect that. If you uncheck it, you will increase performance; however, to see the changes, you will have to refresh the list manually. You can refresh the list manually by clicking the Refresh button on the Site window toolbar, as shown in Figure 3.6.

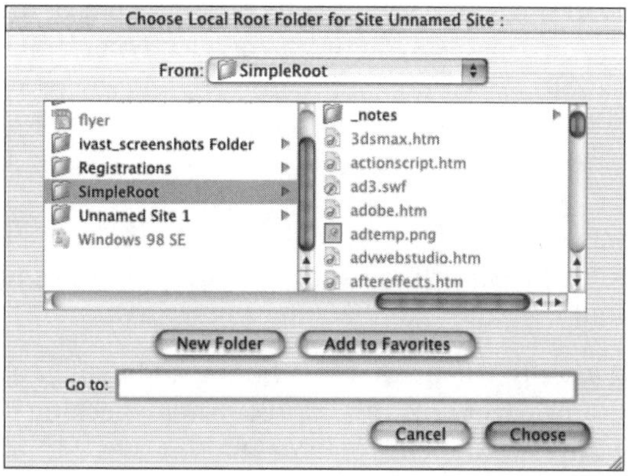

FIGURE 3.5   The Choose Local Folder dialog box.

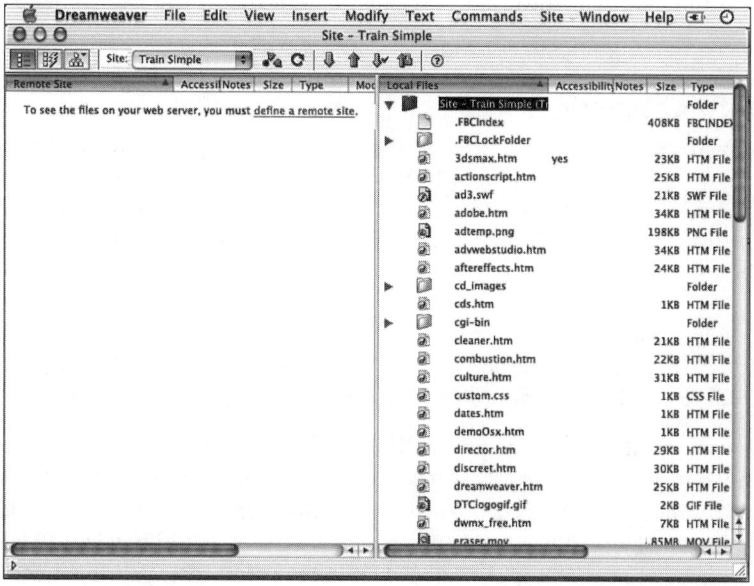

FIGURE 3.6   The Refresh button on the toolbar will refresh the local files in the Site window.

Unless you have a slow Internet connection, I recommend leaving the Refresh Local File Automatically option checked.

Default Images Folder

This text field is new to Dreamweaver MX. This is a simple way that Dreamweaver encourages site organization. This new feature is not only a time-saver, but a way to avoid broken image links. Earlier in this chapter, I showed you an image source link to an image file on my hard drive. Now in Dreamweaver MX, if you choose an image file outside your local root folder, Dreamweaver automatically makes a copy in the default images folder and sources it from that location, preserving all link integrity. If you're a long-time Dreamweaver user, you can definitely see the benefits of this new feature. If you're new to Dreamweaver, trust me—this feature is handy.

HTTP Address and Cache

These options are a bit more abstract than the previous ones we've just looked at. They also are not as crucial, but they can offer benefits when used.

The HTTP address matters only when you use absolute addressing. If you are using absolute addressing, Dreamweaver uses this address when checking links in your site to determine whether the links are sourcing external files or files within your site.

Cache offers speed enhancements when creating link updates. When you cache, the links are stored in your computer's memory, offering faster access, much like when a Web page is cached to your computer—it doesn't take nearly as long for the page to load within your browser.

Remote Info Category

This section of the dialog box enables you to define properties of your remote site—in other words, your Web server. The first thing you need to do is choose how you connect to your Web server. The information you fill out here will be used when connecting to the Web server through the Site window. The access drop-down menu offers many features, each described in more detail here.

FTP Host

The first choice, is the most common—FTP. FTP stands for File Transfer Protocol. When you choose FTP, a whole series of options are revealed, as shown in Figure 3.7.

- **FTP Host**   In this text field you will plug in the address to your Web server. If you are paying a company to host your Web site, the company gives you the specific address to fill out in this text box. An FTP address can vary in appearance, but generally looks something like `ftp.webserver.com`; or they could have an IP address, which appears like this: `ftp.127.0.0.1`. Whatever the case, you'll get the specific information from your host.

- **Host Directory**   The text field offers the option of inserting a path to your public documents on the server. Paths generally look like `http://www.traisimple.com/web1/htdocs`, or something along those lines. Check with your Web administrator for the exact information. Sometimes, if this text field is left blank, it will automatically connect to the appropriate location.

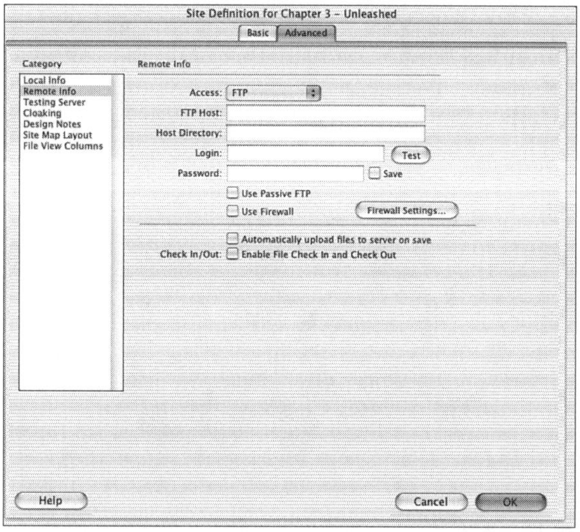

FIGURE 3.7   After you choose FTP from the drop-down menu, a variety of options become available in the Site Definition dialog box.

- **Login**   This field should contain your username or login name for the Web server. That's it, nothing special.

- **Password**   This option is simply your password to gain access to the Web server. It is, however, important to note that many Web servers are Unix based, which makes your login and password case sensitive.

- **Use Passive FTP**   Depending on your network, you may be required to connect through passive ftp. Passive ftp establishes a local software-based connection, rather than a remote-server-based connection. Check with your network administrator to see how you should be connecting, if you're using ftp.

- **Use Firewall**   If you are behind a firewall, set the appropriate port and host information in the Preferences dialog box. After filling that information out in Preferences, this option is automatically selected.

- **Use SHH Encrypted Login (Windows Only)**   This option uses a Secure Shell (SHH) for a secure FTP authentication.

- **Automatically Upload Files on Save**   I think this option explains itself; however, I do not recommend using it. What if you are experimenting? It's a bit too risky for me.

- **Enable File Check In and Check Out**   I'll discuss this option in further detail a bit later in this chapter. What it does is allow you to check in and check out files, which is a great Dreamweaver feature to use if you have more than one developer on your team. If you are the only one, leave this option unchecked.

Local Network

The Local Network option has fewer options than FTP does, as shown in Figure 3.8. This option is selected if you have a Web server running on your local machine or network. For this option you simply enter the correct path and name of the root folder of the Web server.

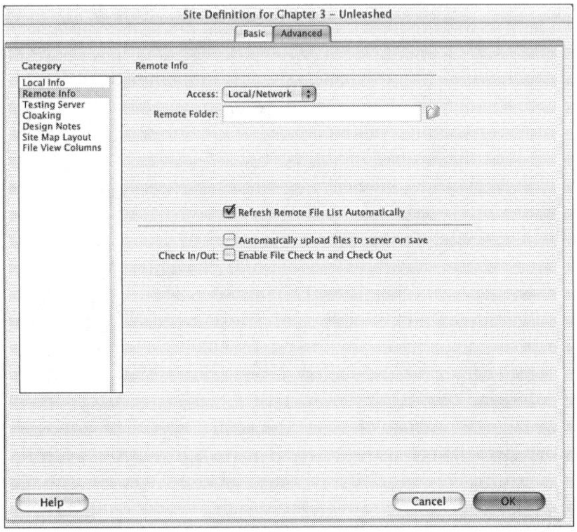

FIGURE 3.8   The Local Network tab has only a few options.

This section of the Site Definition dialog box also has options for enabling check in and check out, as well as Automatically Update Files to Server on Save. A different option from the previous screen gives you the capability to refresh remote file list automatically. This option is the same as the local option in the ftp remote info portion. Your connection to the server would determine whether you want this checked.

RDS

You should use this option if your host uses Remote Development Services. Click the options button to specify a Host Name, Port, Host Directory, User Name, and Password.

WebDav

This option should be used if you or your company uses the collaborative Web-based Distributed Authoring and Versioning standards.

Testing Server Category

This category is used only when developing database-driven Web sites. If you plan to create pages with middleware scripts, it is important to fill this section out properly. As displayed in Figure 3.9, there are three options—the server model, the type of pages the site will contain, and how you're going to access the application server—which must be filled out correctly. The testing server category is new to Dreamweaver MX, but similar to the application server option in UltraDev 4.

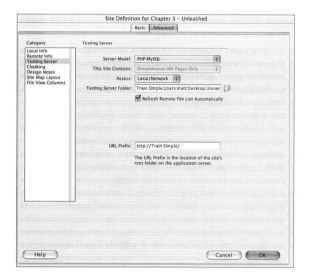

FIGURE 3.9 The testing server category in the Site Definitions dialog box.

Server Model

The server model drop-down box offers several options:

- **None**   Choose none if you do not need any database connectivity, or if you do not plan to create a Web application.

- **ASP JavaScript**   This option enables you to create pages that utilize Active Server Pages scripts. ASP alone cannot provide all the functionality of a database-driven Web site; it needs the help of another scripting language. Your choices here are JavaScript or VBScript. I typically recommend VBScript because both technologies are Microsoft solutions; however, if you know JavaScript and not VBScript, I would recommend using JavaScript for debugging purposes.

- **ASP VBScript**   This option is essentially the same as the previous one, with the exception of the client-side scripting language being VBScript instead of JavaScript.

- **ASP.NET C#**   The options for ASP.NET are similar to ASP. Again, this has to do with the scripting language. Depending on your knowledge of scripts, if you know C# but not VBScript, then the choice has been made for you. However, if you do not know either scripting language, choose Asp.NET C#. The capability to develop ASP.NET Web applications in a WYSIWYG environment is a first in Dreamweaver MX.

- **ASP.NET VB**   This option is similar to the preceding one. If you plan to build a site using ASP.NET with VBScript, this is an appropriate option to select.

- **ColdFusion**   Choose this option if you plan to deliver your Web applications with a ColdFusion server. This option enables you to take full advantage of the ColdFusion Markup Language.

- **JSP**   Select JSP if you plan to develop pages that use Java Server Page scripts.

- **PHP MySQL**   Equally as exciting as building ASP.NET Web applications is the capability to create PHP Web applications with a MySQL database. This is an important feature for anyone wanting to develop Web applications or database-driven Web sites on a Macintosh. You can develop and test all on the same machine, which was not possible in UltraDev 4.

This Site Contains

This area is active only when you select ColdFusion for the server model. The drop-down menu gives you the option to specify whether all the pages in your site were developed in UltraDev 4, Dreamweaver MX, or both. The reason for this is because Dreamweaver MX writes ColdFusion MX code, whereas UltraDev 4 writes ColdFusion 5 code. No big deal, just make Dreamweaver aware of the situation.

Access

This area of the testing server category is identical for the remote info categories options for FTP or local network connections to your application server.

Cloaking Category

Cloaking files simply hides the selected files from the Get, Put, Check In, and Check Out options. For example, you may have a folder containing your source files, such as FLAs, PNGs, or even PSDs. These files don't need to be transferred to the Web server. Any file format that you cloak will remain in your local folder and will not be uploaded unless you manually override the cloak setting. Cloaking hides files from the following operations:

- Put and Get

- Check In and Check Out

- Reports

- Synchronization

- Select Newer Remote and Select Newer Local

- Link Checking

- Find and Replace

In addition to those operations, the cloaked files will not appear in the Assets panel. You can specify which file types you'd like to cloak by checking off the Enable Cloaking check box and checking the Cloak Files Ending With option. In the text field, type in all the file extensions you'd like to appear cloaked.

CAUTION

When typing in the extensions you'd like to cloak, do not separate the file extensions with commas or semicolons; separate them with spaces.

You can also cloak a single file or folder, regardless of the extension. Simply highlight the file or folder within the site files and right-click (Windows) or Control+Click (Mac) to access the contextual menu. In the menu, choose Cloaking, Cloak. After you choose Cloak from the contextual menu, a red line appears through the icon of the file. You can uncloak a file the same way—by contextual clicking and choosing Cloaking, Uncloak.

Finally you can also cloak by using the Site menu and choosing the cloak option from there.

Design Notes Category

The design notes category offers only a few features, as shown in Figure 3.10.

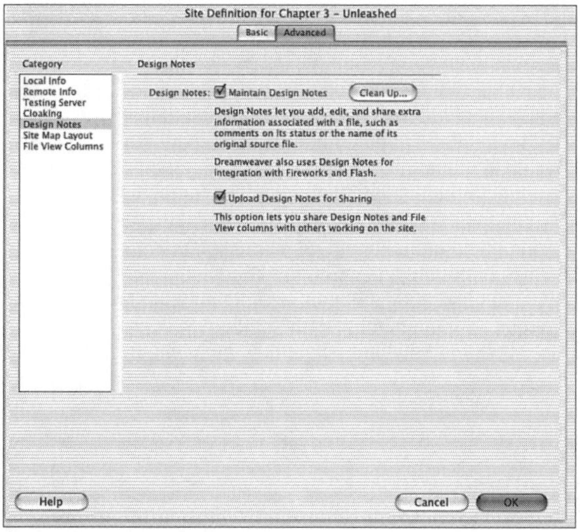

FIGURE 3.10   The design notes category.

When developing a Web site across several contributors and team members, it is important to keep everything straight among the designers, coders, and content providers. This is why Macromedia built in the Design Notes feature, to make this collaborative effort less painful and to make communication easier among the various team members. As you may have already been able to gather from this first paragraph, design notes are best used when more than one person is working on a project.

Design notes can be attached to any document created in Dreamweaver, as well as to any media inserted in a Dreamweaver document.

For design notes to be useful, everyone involved in the development of the Web site has to be able to view the most current version of the design note. Dreamweaver allows you to maintain the design notes on the remote server as a separate file. This way, the design notes are dependant files to the document. In Figure 3.10, you'll notice you can set these options in the Design Notes Preferences panel. This will also help you to remove unused notes as well.

Site Map Layout

One of the most important things in Web development is good usability and site structure. You want your site navigation to be easy to understand. You don't want visitors struggling with navigation or becoming lost in your site. Sometimes the challenge to a developer is to remember the structure you set up. Dreamweaver offers a Site Map view, which enables you to see not only the overall structure of your site, but the file hierarchy as well. Figure 3.11 illustrates the different options available in the Site Map Layout dialog box.

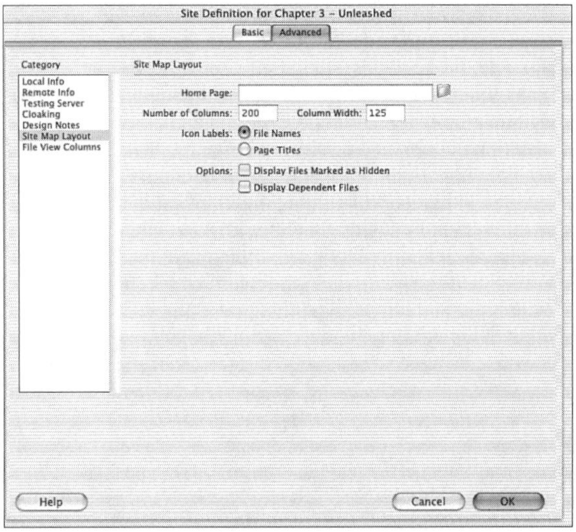

FIGURE 3.11   The Site Map Layout category of the Site Definition dialog box.

- **Home Page**   This text field looks for what is going to be the home page for your Web site. If you do not have one yet, Dreamweaver automatically looks for index.html, index.htm, or default.html. If it finds a file named that way, it will use it as the home page. For the map to create the file structure, it needs a starting point, and the starting point for all Web sites is the home page.

- **Number of Columns and Column Width**   These options determine how the map appears on a computer screen. If you need to print your map on a standard 8 1/2" by 11" document, you will have to reduce these numbers for the map to fit on the page.

- **Icon Labels**   This option determines how the icon will be displayed in your site map. You can choose File Name or Page Titles. I generally prefer the icons to display the filename. You link to files by name, you open files by name, it makes sense to display them with the name you interact with the most. However, in some situations the file names may be a bit ambiguous. The titles are a more accurate repesentation of the page or file for which you are looking. If you find yourself in a situation similar to that, then you may consider using titles.

- **Options**   Here you can decide to display hidden HTML files by choosing Display Files Marked as Hidden. You can choose to display dependent files in your site map as well. Files such as images, external scripts, and other types of media will be displayed within the map when this option is checked.

File View Columns

As you can see in Figure 3.12, the File View Columns will change what and how files are displayed within the Site Files window on the Mac or the Site Files Panel on Windows.

FIGURE 3.12   The File View Columns category in the Site Definition dialog box.

In this section of the Define Sites dialog box, you have the option of showing or hiding some of the predefined columns. You might want to hide some of the columns because their meanings do not pertain to the particular project that you're working on. You also can create your own custom columns. This can become important, depending on the project that you are working on. If one of the sites that you are working on has to meet accessibility guidelines, for example, you can create a column that reads "accessible", and simply fill that column out with a yes or a no. This will enable you to sort by the Accessible column and you'll quickly be able to detect which pages are accessible and which ones are not.

Creating a Custom Column

In this exercise I'm going to walk you through step-by-step, so you can see how to create your own custom columns and how you enter information into those columns.

1. Choose Site, Edit Sites to open the Edit Sites dialog box.

2. In the Edit Sites dialog box, highlight the site you want to edit by clicking it. With the name of the site highlighted, click the Edit button. This launches the Site Definition dialog box.

3. In the Site Definition dialog box, click the Advanced Tab, if it isn't already selected to display the Site Definition dialog box in the advanced view. Notice the categories section on the left.

4. In the categories section, click the File View Columns section. This moves the Site Definition dialog box to display options for the Site window on the Mac and the Site panel for Windows.

5. Click the plus sign under the File View Section of the dialog box to get a new column labeled Untitled.

6. Toward the bottom portion of the dialog box, there are some text fields in which you can relabel the name of the column and what to associate that column name to in the design notes.

7. In the Column Name text field, type in the word **Accessibility**. After typing the word, press the Tab key on your keyboard to move to the section. Notice that after you press the Tab key, the name of the column appears in the list above and you now have a blinking cursor in the Associate with Design Note text field.

8. In the Associate with Design Note field, you can either enter a custom value, or you can choose from one of the defaults in the drop-down menu. For this situation, you're going to create a custom value. In the text field, type in the word **Accessibility**. Press the Tab key to apply this value.

9. Choose an alignment in the Align drop-down menu. The default is left, and for this purposes, that will be just fine. Unless, of course, you want change—then feel free.

10. If you want to reorganize how the columns appear, with respect to their alignment from left to right, the column in the top of the list will appear closer to the aligned side that you chose in the previous step.

11. You want Accessibility to appear after the name column. To get this effect, highlight the Accessibility column name in the File View section of the dialog box. With it selected, press the up arrow in the right corner as many times as necessary until it appears beneath the name column. Notice you can't place anything above the name column. The name column always appears first.

12. When you're happy with the name and placement of your new column, press the OK button. This brings you back to the Edit Sites dialog box, where you can press the Done button. After you press Done, the Site Window on the Mac automatically launches.

Notice in Figure 3.13, the accessibility column appears next to the name column in the Site window on the Mac and the Site panel on Windows.

FIGURE 3.13   Notice the Accessibility column in the Site window.

You will however, notice no values appear in that new column area. In the next exercise, you'll see how you can add values to that column.

Entering Information into a Custom Column

This exercise shows you with the necessary steps to add values into custom columns.

1. Right-click (Windows) or Control+Click (Mac) the filename of one of the documents inside the site files view. This offers access to a contextual menu.

2. In the contextual menu, choose Design Notes. This launches the Design Notes dialog box.

3. With the Design Notes dialog box open, click the All Info tab and enter the data for the column you want to populate with data. After you've finished entering the data, click OK.

4. Inside the Site Files window (Mac) or panel (Windows), notice in the Accessibility column the text "yes" shows up, as in Figure 3.14.

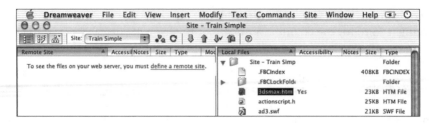

FIGURE 3.14   The Accessibility column now contains a value of yes.

There is one other way to add or change the content in a particular column. In the Site window or Site panel, double-click to place an insertion point, which will allow you to type in any value you want.

Managing a Web Site in Dreamweaver MX

Now that you know how to define a site within Dreamweaver, how do you manage your files? This section of the chapter is going to discuss exactly that. After designing and testing the Web site you've created, you're going to want to move that site from your local computer to a Web server somewhere. Furthermore, if you happen to be at a different computer and yet need to edit some portion of the site, how do you download files from your server?

We'll also take a look at version control with the synchronize feature, which compares files on the remote server and your local machine. Dreamweaver MX also offers several unique features that enable you to collaborate better with team or development editors.

Working with the Site Window/Panel

The Site window and panel act as the control center for managing your site. If your Site window is not visible, choose Site, Site Files. This launches the Site Files window, also known as the Site window. F8 is the keyboard shortcut to access this window. If you look at Figure 3.15, you'll notice the Site window has a toolbar; each option on the toolbar adds functionality toward managing your site.

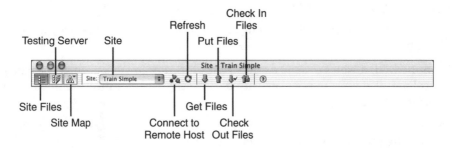

FIGURE 3.15   The Site window's toolbar has options for managing Web site files.

- **Site Files**   This button enables you to view the Site window in its default view, which is displaying all the files on the local side and remote side. Remember that the remote files are the files located on your Web server. You will see files on the remote side only if you are connected to the server.

- **Testing Server**   The testing server is a way for you to view your files located within the root folder of your testing server. Today the majority of operating systems ship with a built-in Web server. Windows XP Professional ships with Microsoft's IIS, and Mac OS X ships with an Apache Web server. Often, developers will use these local Web servers to test their pages. After they've tested okay, they'll move them to the remote Web server. When the Testing Server option is selected, the local files are still visible on the opposite side.

- **Site Map**   To view the site map of your Web site, click this button. Notice that this button offers two choices: You can either view only the map or you can view the map and the local files at the same time. If your site has any size to it, you may want to opt for Map Only. The site map can become large very quickly.

- **Site**   The Site drop-down menu is filled with all the different sites that you have defined within Dreamweaver. This affords quick access to any site and lets you move between them with ease. Notice toward the bottom the option of Edit Sites. If you choose Edit Sites, it launches the Edit Sites dialog box.

- **Connect to Remote Host**   This button connects to the remote host you specified in the Site Definition dialog box. You must have a connection to the Internet to make a live connection. After you've made a successful connection, the remote side of the Site Files will be populated with all the files on the server. The Connect button also appears to have green circles in it, indicating a connection. When you're connected, the Connect button becomes a Disconnect button.

- **Refresh**   What you specified in the Site Definition dialog box determines whether this button has any meaning. If you chose not to have the file list to automatically refresh, you will have to press this button to see the results of any files being moved from the remote side to the local side, or vice versa. Sometimes when you're moving files, you may have to refresh regardless of whether the FTP utility is acting buggy.

- **Get File(s)**   The Get button retrieves files from the remote server by downloading them to your computer. There are a couple of ways to get files from the server to the local files, and one is to press this button. You can also drag and drop between the two sides, and you can highlight the file you want to transfer and press Command+Shift+D (Mac) or Ctrl+Shift+D (Windows).

- **Put File(s)**   This is the opposite of the Get button. This will allow you to Put, or upload, files during an active session with the remote server. Like its Get counterpart, there are a couple of ways that you can upload files. You can highlight the file on the local side and press the Put button. Drag and drop is also supported when transferring files from the local side to the remote side. Finally, you can highlight the files and use the keyboard shortcuts of Command+Shift+U (Mac) or Ctrl+Shift+U (Windows).

> **NOTE**
>
> When getting and putting files, an alert message pops up. The dialog box asks if you would like to include all dependent files. Although this may seem obvious, you may not want to include the dependent files. For example, if you uploaded a page and all of its files, you may notice something wrong in the title of the page. You can easily correct that by changing it in Dreamweaver; however, you've changed the HTML only in the document. It would be necessary to upload only the HTML file and not all the images associated with it, because they're already on the server. If you check Don't Ask Again, it will assume you want to upload the dependent files. If you did check this earlier and now decide that you want the alert to appear, you can change that in the Preferences dialog box under the Site category.

- **Check Out Files/Check In Files** The Check In and Check Out buttons are active only when you have check in and check out selected in the Site Definition dialog box. These options let you officially check in and check out files, offering a visual cue to all the development team members that you are working on a particular file or files.

When transferring files, you will receive transfer information via a dialog box on the Mac or a progress bar, both on the Mac and PC. This progress bar indicates how long something will take to upload or download. In the bottom-right corner of the window or panel is a Stop Current Task button. This button enables you to terminate the active task of moving files.

Synchronizing Local and Remote Files

In Web development, sometimes it can get confusing managing versions of files. Where is the most recent file? This question is one that you'll probably ask yourself more than once throughout the development of a site. Fortunately, Macromedia has built a great feature into Dreamweaver called File Synchronization. This feature basically compares files between the local and remote side and will determine which is the latest version. If the latest version lives on the local side, it will upload that file accordingly.

File Synchronization can also delete files on either the local or remote side, if the file doesn't appear in both versions of the site. You can apply the synchronize command to selected files, or apply it site-wide.

Follow these steps to synchronize your files. In this example we are only going to synchronize a few files, however the process is the same if you want to synchronize an entire Web site.

1. Make sure your Site Window or Site Panel is open. Press F8 on your keyboard if it is not visible. Select a couple of different files that you want to synchronize.

2. Choose Site, Synchronize. The Synchronize dialog box will open.

3. Here in the synchronize dialog box, if you wanted to sync the entire Web site you would enter *Site Name* from the list. In our case we are going to choose Selected Local Files Only.

4. Set the direction of synchronization. Your choices are Put Newer Files to Remote, which evaluates which files are newer on the local side, and uploads whichever files Dreamweaver evaluated as being newer. The second choice is Get Newer Files from Remote; this option examines the files on the remote side, the files that are newer on the remote side get downloaded to the local side.

5. You can also choose Delete File Not on Local Drive, which will remove any local files that do have a counterpart on the remote side when using the Get Newer Files from Remote Side option. If you are using the Put Newer Files to remote side option, then the files on the remote side without a local equivalent will be removed.

6. When you are ready, click the Preview button. This will start the process of comparing files. This will be displayed in a Site dialog box for confirmation. If no files are mismatched, Dreamweaver informs you that no synchronization is necessary.

7. You have the opportunity to uncheck the action that Dreamweaver will perform if you want to override what Dreamweaver found to synchronize.

8. Once you are happy with the settings click OK. You will see a progress bar indicating the progress Dreamweaver is making with the synchronization.

9. Once the synchronization is complete you can save a log of the actions performed by pressing the Save Log button.

CAUTION

One suggestion is to have all the developers and team members set their system clocks to equal the time of the server. This can be important if the server is Boston, and some team members are in Los Angeles. It's been my experience that Dreamweaver doesn't factor time zones.

File synchronization is a powerful way to automate the organization of your site files. It's especially useful when there is more than one person working on a site. I would also recommend, use the Delete option with discretion, because it is an undoable act.

Working with the Site Map

Being able to customize the site map is what will allow you to get the most out of this Dreamweaver feature. The map gives you a visual representation of the navigation system and structure of your Web site. This can be very important because Web sites quickly become complex in their navigation structure.

The Site Map will always use the index page as the top-level page and display pages linked two levels deep. You can always see additional linked pages by pressing the plus/minus signs. To see the Site Map, press F8 on your keyboard.

In the toolbar of the site window or panel press the Show Map button. Notice the button has two choices, to display either the map by itself or the map along side of the files. To get the most use out of the map, I would recommend displaying the map and files. The only downside to the site panel in Windows, is it really doesn't yield enough room to display the map in an appropriate size. Your best bet is to click the expand button in the far right corner of the panel's toolbar, as shown in Figure 3.16.

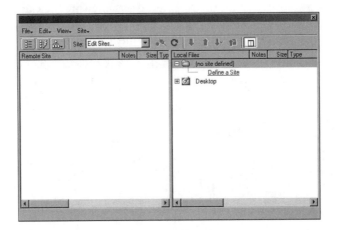

FIGURE 3.16   After clicking the expand button the site panel transforms into a site window reminiscent of Dreamweaver 4, or the site window on the Macintosh.

The site map offers the ability to change and manipulate files and links. If you want to add or delete links, you can do so in the site map view. You can also manipulate new files—this can be handy if you're looking to storyboard the structure of your Web site.

> **TIP**
>
> You can easily convert the site map into a bitmap file. Inside the Site window/panel, choose File, Save Site Map. Navigate to the location on your computer where you want it to be saved, type in a filename, and choose what type of file you would like to save it as: BMP or PNG. This is perfect if you want to email the map to colleagues. You may want to optimize it first in Fireworks to reduce the file size.

In this exercise you're going to look at how you can link an existing file to a new file.

1. Open your site map by pressing F8 on your keyboard. Be sure to display the site map and files by clicking the Site Map button in the toolbar. Notice the site map is now visible.

2. Click the index or home page icon of your Web site to highlight it.

3. Choose Site, Site Map View, Link to New File. This launches the Link to New File dialog box as shown in Figure 3.17. You can also contextual-click the selected icon and choose Link to New File from the contextual menu.

4. Enter in a name for the document with the appropriate extension: HTML, HTM, ASP, and so on.

5. Type in a title for the page, which will show up in the title bar of the browser window.

6. Enter in a name for the link. This name will be displayed in the document the way you type it here, in the form of a hyperlink.

7. After you're happy with the information you typed in, click the OK button or press Return (Mac) or Enter (Windows). A new icon is created in the map with a line connected to the home page, or whatever icon you had selected.

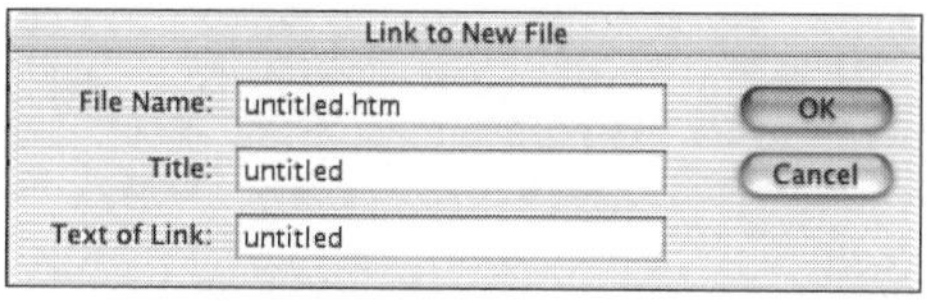

FIGURE 3.17   The Link to New File dialog box.

Linking to a new file is one way to storyboard, or to start a structure or filing system to a Web site. It can also be good to create new files this way, keeping your navigation clean and intact. You can also do the same thing for existing documents within your Web site. You can follow the steps in the previous exercises, just switching the option from Link to New File to Link to Existing File. You can also follow the steps in the next exercise.

In this exercise, you'll look at how you can use a shortcut by displaying both the site files and the site map. Linking documents is as simple as clicking and dragging.

1. In the Site window, be sure to display both the site files and the site map. Press F8 on your keyboard to make the site files visible. In the site files drop-down list located in the toolbar, choose Show Map and Files. Make sure, in Windows, that you're working with the expanded, undocked view of the Site panel.

2. With both the map and file views visible, select the file icon in the site map that you want to link. Notice a small icon that looks like a riffle scope just above the file icon in the top-right corner. This riffle scope is the point-to-file icon, and it allows you to do just that.

3. Click and drag the point-to-file icon and place it on top of the file you want to link to in the site files portion of the window, as shown in Figure 3.18.

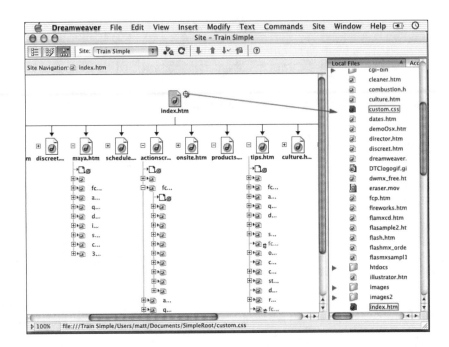

FIGURE 3.18   Use the point–to-file icon to quickly add links to documents.

4. Open the document that you dragged the point-to-file icon from in the site map. You'll notice a text hyperlink at the bottom of the page named the same as the file that you linked it to.

Modifying Page Titles

You can easily modify the titles of documents as well. Just be sure to view the files in the map by title name instead of filename. To show the title name, choose View, Show Page Title, or press Command+Shift+T (Mac) or Ctrl+Shift+T (Windows) to toggle the views.

With the title view active, click once to highlight the file, and then click a second time in the text area. This makes the text editable with a blinking cursor. Simply type in the new title for the document.

Maintaining Files

As with any Web production, moving and renaming files will be a necessity at some point. It is important to follow certain guidelines to preserve site and link integrity. You should make all such changes within the Site window or panel. This ensures that Dreamweaver will make the appropriate adjustments or modifications to any document a link or name change will affect. In contrast, if you make this change outside of the Site window and make the adjustments in Windows Explorer (Windows) or the Finder (Mac), Dreamweaver will not be aware of these changes, resulting in broken hyperlinks.

This exercise will show you how to rename files within Dreamweaver.

1. Be sure to have the Site window/panel visible. If you can't see the site files, press F8 on your keyboard to open the window/panel.

2. Inside the Site window, select a file by clicking in it, and then click a second time on the name of the icon to see a blinking cursor.

3. With the blinking cursor in the name of the file, press the Delete (Mac) key or Backspace (Windows) key to remove all the text for that file. Now that the icon does not have a name, type in a new one. Press Return (Mac) or Enter (Windows).

4. After pressing Return or Enter, the Update Files dialog box launches, asking you to scan the documents within the site, as displayed in Figure 3.19. After you press Scan, Dreamweaver searches the site for related files. When the scan is complete, the dialog box indicates what files need to be updated in your Web site, as shown in Figure 3.20. Click Update.

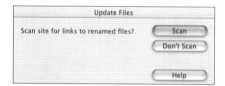

FIGURE 3.19   The Update Files dialog box asks to scan the site for related documents.

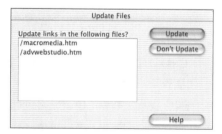

FIGURE 3.20   The Update dialog box displays files that will be updated.

5. Dreamweaver will open each file on the list, make the necessary change, save it, and close it.

The Update feature in Dreamweaver proves to be quite the timesaver. Image if you had to make all the changes manually to all the separate documents.

Changing Links

Moving files works much in the same way. If you need to move a file out of or into a different directory, be sure to do it in the Site window. Again, if documents are linked to the one you are moving, broken hyperlinks occur if Dreamweaver isn't aware of the change. If you move the file within the Site window, you will get the Update Files dialog box, just like in the previous exercise.

You can also easily change where links point to by using the change link command.

Change Links by Using the Change Link Command

To change a link by using the change link command, follow these steps:

1. Highlight the file for the link you want to change.

2. Select Site, Change Link to access the Select HTML File dialog box. You can also press Command+L (Mac) or Ctrl+L (Windows) to access the dialog box, or you can contextual click the icon and choose Change Link from the contextual menu.

3. Locate the HTML file you want the old link to point to. When you're happy with your selection, click the Done button.

4. After you choose the new file, the Update Files dialog box will appear, displaying all the files that need to be updated.

5. If you want all the files to be updated, click Update. However, if you want only certain files to be updated, highlight the files by clicking them. When clicking more than one, be sure to hold down the Command key (Mac) or Control Key (Windows).

6. If you don't want any of the files to be updated, choose Don't Update.

Change Link Sitewide

A very similar command to the Change Link command is the Change Link Sitewide command. With this command you essentially redirect all links from one page to another.

To use the change link sitewide command, follow these steps.

1. In the Site window/panel, select the file that you want to change.

2. Choose Site, Change Link Sitewide. You can also contextual click the icon and choose the Change Link Sitewide command from the contextual menu. This launches the Change Link Sitewide dialog box, as pictured in Figure 3.21.

3. You can also select the Change Link Sitewide command without a file select; however, the top text field in the dialog box will be empty, requiring you to fill it out. In the second text field (the one labeled Into Link To) either type in the path to the new file you want the link to point to, or click the folder icon at the end of the

text field to search for a file. If you search for a file within your local root folder, the correct addressing will be added to the filename.

4. When you're happy with the new file, click OK to bring up the Update Files dialog box. Refer to step 5 of the previous exercise for more information on how to handle this dialog box.

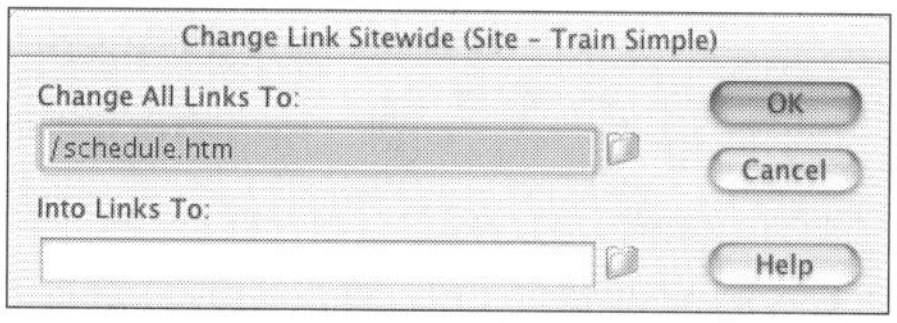

FIGURE 3.21   The Change Link Sitewide dialog box.

Deleting Links

Sometimes in Web site development, you may want to remove a link between different pages. You would accomplish this again in the Site window/panel. Because you want to change an attribute of a link, you want to make sure that Dreamweaver is fully aware of the situation, so it can make any necessary adjustments to other pages to preserve the link integrity of the Web site.

To remove or delete a link, highlight the file that you want to delete and either press the Delete key on your keyboard or choose Site, Remove Link, or contextual click and choose Remove Link from the contextual menu.

Checking Links

The check links command will report three problems within the site. They are the following:

- **Broken Links**   Broken links are hyperlinks that are not sourced properly. They generally will be linked to a file that does not exist in a particular directory.

- **External Links**   This report is simply expressing that file or site that the link is pointing to is outside Dreamweaver's link scope. It does not mean that these links are bad or broken; it simply means that Dreamweaver has no way of checking them, and you may want to consider checking them manually yourself.

- **Orphaned Files**   These files have no incoming links pointing them. This does not mean they do not add functionality to the site—so be sure not to delete them until you know exactly where they came from and what the file's purpose is. For example, Train Simple's Web site had an UltraDev page explaining the course outline of our UltraDev class. Now with Dreamweaver MX incorporating all the UltraDev functionality, the page is no longer needed, nor is anything linked to it. However, this page still appears prominently on search engines, and if an end user does a search and finds that page and clicks to visit it, Train Simple does not want the end user to get a 404—File Not Found error. On the other hand, Train Simple no longer teaches UltraDev. So what I did on the UltraDev page is add a refresh in the meta tag, which refreshes the page after five seconds to go to the advanced Dreamweaver MX page. So, even though nothing is linked to this page, it still has a purpose within the Web site; therefore, I would not want to delete this orphaned file.

There are two ways to check links—you can either check a single file, or you can check the entire site.

To check the links in a single document:

1. In the Site Window, highlight the file in which you want to check links. Choose File, Check Links, or press Shift+F8 for the keyboard shortcut. You can also contextual click the selected document and choose Check Links from the contextual menu. This launches the Link Checker dialog box as shown in Figure 3.22.

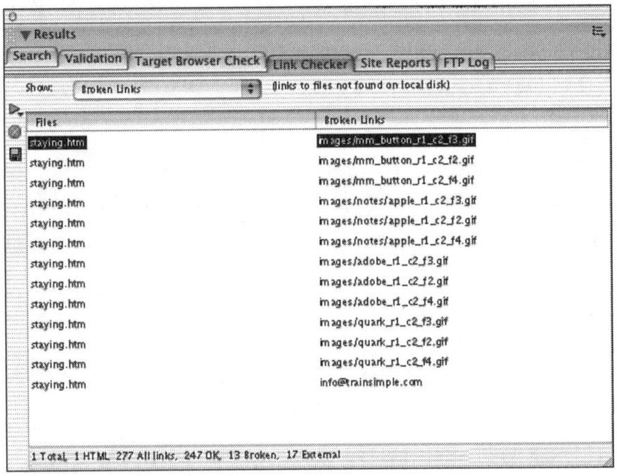

FIGURE 3.22   The Link Checker dialog box.

2. If you wanted to check more than one file, use Command+Click (Mac) or Ctrl+Click (Windows) to select multiple files and access the check links command the same as in step 1.

In the top-left corner of the Link Checker dialog box is a drop-down menu offering the results for the three options for link reports. You'll notice that the dialog box is divided into two columns, the left side is the problematic link, and on the right is the link that is causing the problem. The orphaned link files do not have the right columns, because there are no links associated with them.

You have two options for fixing the links:

- To fix the broken links, double-click the troubled document on the left side of the dialog box. This opens the document and highlights the problematic link. Make sure the Properties Inspector is visible and change the link in the Link text field of the Inspector.

- The second way to change the link is a bit easier. Click the troubled link on the right side of the dialog box. Here you can either type in the link manually or click the folder icon to search for the appropriate file. After the file is found, the correct path is added to the filename.

NOTE

Visit this book's companion Web site at http://www.dreamweavermxunleashed.com to watch a QuickTime movie on how the link checker works.

As you can see, Dreamweaver offers many options for managing links and files. It's of the utmost importance that you make link/file changes within the Dreamweaver Site window—not in Windows Explorer or the Mac Finder.

Using Site Reports

In Chapter 4, "Dreamweaver Essentials," you look at HTML a bit and learn how you can clean up different types of HTML. With the Site Reports option, you get a chance to double-check your work, and you also have the opportunity to see design notes and checked out files. Refer to Figure 3.23 to see all the options for what you can run Site Reports on. Refer to Table 3.1 to see what the different options mean and how they can help you.

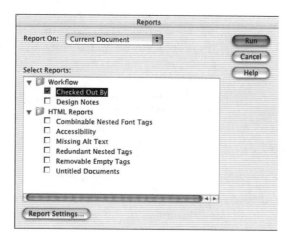

FIGURE 3.23 The Site Reports dialog box offers many report options.

TABLE 3.1   Site Report Options and Definitions

Report	Definition
Checked Out By	When Checked Out By is selected, the Report Settings button in the bottom-left corner of the dialog box is active. Click the button to search for an individual who may have files checked out. It's important to know that it is case sensitive; however, you do not need to type in someone's entire name. For example, if you were looking for Kathryn Olah, you could simply type in Kathryn, Kath, or even Olah.
Design Notes	With this option selected, it too will activate the Report settings button in the bottom-left corner of the dialog box. Click it to bring up a new dialog box where you can enter the design note to search for and how to search for it. When searching for a design note, you must enter in a condition for the search to meet.
Combinable Nested FONT Tags	This searches for unnecessary use of multiple FONT tags. If for some reason there is more than one FONT tag around a particular area of text, most likely it's because each FONT tag has a different attribute. For example, the following FONT tags could be combined: `<font size="3"><font face="Arial">` could read `<font face="Arial" size="3">`.
Missing Alt Tags	This option searches all the alt tags within your document to find any with missing alt tags. An alt tag is beneficial when end users are using text-only browsers. The user will get information about the image that they are not seeing by whatever is typed within in the alt tag. This will also keep you in compliance with the accessibility standards set for people with disabilities.
Redundant Nested Tags	This option checks to see if tags are nested inside themselves and removes them as necessary. The following code is an example: `<i>Visit Train Simple's Web site <i>today!</i></i>`.
Removable Empty Tags	If tags within your HTML document do not contain anything, you can build a report based on this option to remove them. An example of an empty tag looks like this: `<form></form>`.
Untitled Documents	This option is very handy. You'd hate to publish a Web page with the title set to "Untitled Document." If you build a report based on this option, it will return any duplicate titled document, as well as non-titled ones, and documents titled as the Dreamweaver default of Untitled Document.

To run a site report, follow these steps:

1. Choose Site, Reports to open the Site Reports dialog box.

2. In the Report On drop-down menu, you can choose from either the current document (if a document is open), the entire local site, any file you may have selected in

the Site window/panel, or finally, you can run a report on a selected folder. In this
case, I'm going to choose the entire local site.

> **NOTE**
>
> Reports can be run only on the local side. You cannot run reports on the remote side.

3. Now that you've selected what you're going to report on, the next thing to choose is
   what report you want to build. You can choose from any one of the options
   discussed in Table 3.1. Check any of the categories you're interested in Dreamweaver
   reporting on.

4. Click the Run button to generate the report. Notice, Dreamweaver creates a report
   based on the criteria you set up in step 3.

5. You can modify the pages or save the report for later use. To modify the page,
   double-click it within the Results dialog box to open the file.

6. To save the report for later use, click the Save Report button. This saves the file in an
   XML format, allowing you to later format the report into a Web page, a spreadsheet,
   or a database table.

Checking Browser Compatibility

Your target audience will determine what browser versions you should check to make sure
all the pages within your site are compatible with a certain browser version. In most cases,
you want to make sure that they are at least compatible with a 4.0 browser or later. Very
few people use a 2.0 browser, and for that matter, very little on the Web today is even
compatible with a 2.0 browser. You may want to make sure your site is compatible with a
3.0, however, if you have a very broad, general audience.

That's why it's very important as a Web developer to test your site in many browsers and
on different browser versions. Instead of installing every version on your computer and
testing them manually, there is a command within Dreamweaver to perform this task for
you. This Dreamweaver command, called Check Target Browsers, has a series of profiles
that you test your pages against. Dreamweaver ships with profiles for Netscape Navigator
2.0, 3.0, 4.0, 5.0, and 6.0. It also ships with profiles for Internet Explorer 2.0, 3.0, 4.0, 5.0,
6.0 and Opera (Mac) 2.1, 3.0, 3.5, 4.0, 5.0, and 6.0. You can also download additional
profiles from the Macromedia Exchange.

Dreamweaver will either check a single document or an entire folder. It's important to
know that Dreamweaver will not check scripts in the documents; however, you can debug
script within each browser, which is covered in Chapter 19, "Behaviors."

To run the Check Target Browser Command to ensure compatibility across browsers, follow these steps:

1. Select which file or folder you want to check by highlighting it within the Site window/panel. You can also perform this command on an individual file when it is open.

2. Choose File, Check Page, Check Target Browser. This opens the Check Target Browser dialog box, as displayed in Figure 3.24.

3. Inside the dialog box, highlight all the Web browsers you'd like to check to make sure your page is compatible with that version. You can select more than one by holding down the Command key (Mac) or the Control (Windows) key. If you hold down the Shift key, you can select a range of browser versions.

4. Press the Check button. After the checking process is complete, Dreamweaver will return results inside the Results panel shown in Figure 3.25. For a better look, click the Browser Report button on the left side to view the report in a Web page, as shown in Figure 3.26.

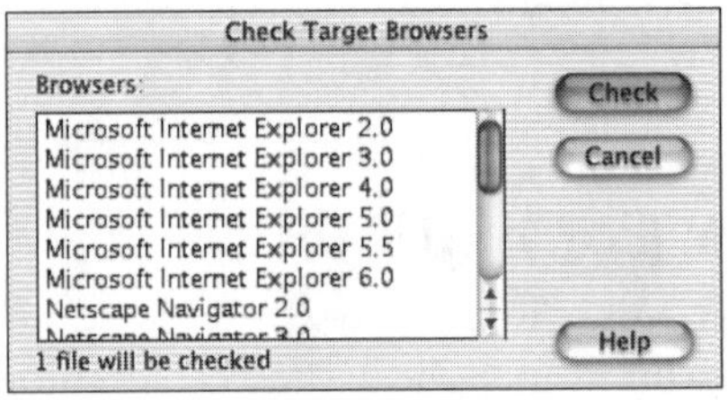

FIGURE 3.24   The Check Target Browser dialog box offers the option of checking compatibility with various browsers.

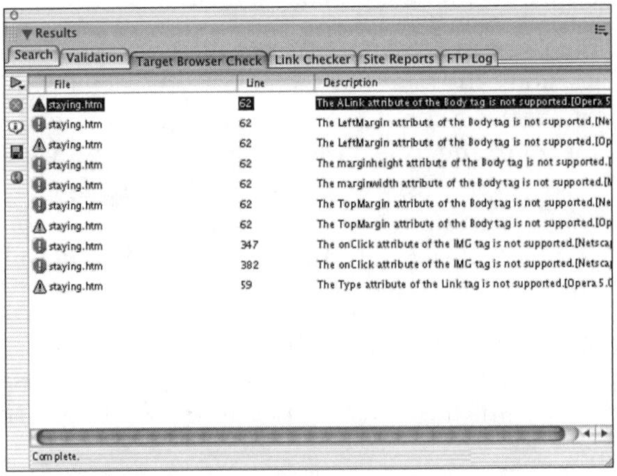

FIGURE 3.25   The results appear inside the Results panel.

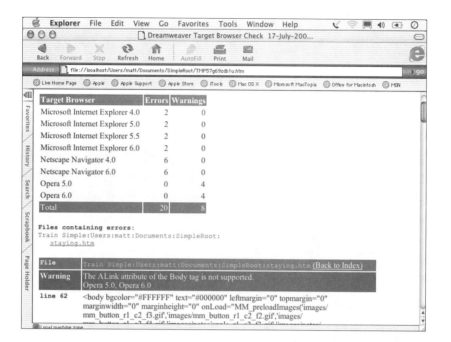

FIGURE 3.26 The HTML document provides feedback about the check performed by the Check Target Browser Command.

Summary

Managing your Web site's files without Dreamweaver is a monumental task. Luckily, the folks at Macromedia realized how important site management was and built wonderful features and aids right into Dreamweaver.

This chapter illustrates that Dreamweaver is just as much a Web development tool as it is a site management tool.

## CHAPTER 4

Dreamweaver MX Essentials

By Matt Pizzi

Working with Dreamweaver MX

Dreamweaver MX is the industry standard for creating and managing Web sites. One thing I always point out to students in my Dreamweaver classes is that Dreamweaver is an HTML editor. Dreamweaver writes HTML when you work in a visual way, much like print designers. The great thing is that Dreamweaver is doing all the coding for you in the background. It is important to remember that any limitations that you have in HTML, you'll also have in Dreamweaver. Dreamweaver does not offer any special code; it is 100% compliant with the guidelines established by the World Wide Web Consortium (W3C.com).

Now with the release of Dreamweaver MX, the stakes are a bit higher, in the sense that Dreamweaver's capabilities are more powerful and abundant. Dreamweaver is no longer just an HTML editor; it also offers a WYSIWYG Web application development experience. The application offers a very robust coding environment for hand coding HTML, JavaScript, ColdFusion, or any other language associated with the Web.

This chapter specifically looks at the details associated with the HTML editing capabilities of Dreamweaver MX. Of course, later in this book we dive into database-driven Web applications. For now, I just want to look at the coding environment for HTML as well as some of the basic features of the WYSIWYG HTML editing environment.

Working with an HTML Document

Dreamweaver has a central location where you can change documentwide attributes. These attributes affect the entire HTML document, from font and background color to hyperlink appearance and margin sizes. This central location is called the Page Properties. To access the Page Properties choose Modify, Page Properties to launch the Page Properties dialog box, as shown in Figure 4.1.

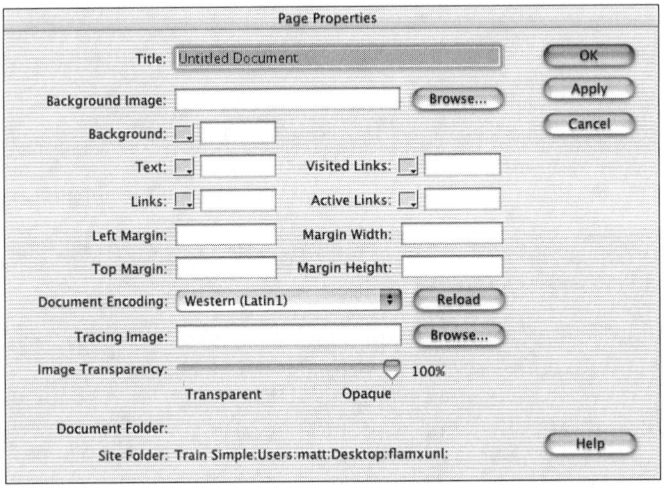

FIGURE 4.1   The Page Properties dialog box.

The Page Properties dialog box has several settings, which you can change to meet your liking.

- **Title**   Type the title of the document into this text field. Whatever you type will appear between the <title> tags in the head of the HTML document. After the page is published, this title appears in the title bar of the browser window.

- **Background Image**   Here you can type in the path to an image file that you want to tile in the background of the document. If you don't remember the path, you can always click the Browse button and search for the file on your computer. After you find the file, select it and Dreamweaver will capture the path to where it is located.

- **Background**   This is an inkwell that opens to a swatch containing the 216 Web-safe colors. You can select any one of the colors in the swatch or choose the color wheel in the top-right corner of the swatches to open a custom color picker. If you move the cursor out of the swatch pop-out, your cursor changes into an eye dropper tool, enabling you to sample colors from any location on the screen. You can also type in a hexadecimal value in the text field. The default color is white.

- **Text**   This offers an inkwell much like the Background option above it. Choose any color to set the global color of text in the document. The default color is black.

4

> **WARNING**
>
> Do not choose a black background color and white text if you want the end user to have the ability to print the page. Background colors do not print, which would then leave you with white text to be printed in a printer that is most likely using white paper and probably can't print white anyway. It makes for a less-than-optimal situation.

- **Links** You can also change the global text color for hyperlinks within the document. The default color is blue. Try to avoid changing the default color; most people recognize blue, underlined text as a hyperlink. Unless, of course, you have a blue background.

- **Visited Links** A visited link occurs when the end user clicks the hyperlink and visits the page, but then returns to the original page. By default, the hyperlink appears purple, again a color that most people recognize as a visited link, but here's your chance to change the color.

- **Active Links** An active link is the brief moment in time when the end user is actually clicking the link. The default color, depending on browser and version, is black. Change the color if you want, but I doubt anyone will notice.

- **Left Margin, Top Margin, Margin Height, and Margin Width** Every Web browser has a default of a few pixels of margins surrounding the document. Here you can adjust the size—or eliminate the margins altogether by entering values of zero. Left and Top margin values are used by Internet Explorer, and Margin Height and Width are used by Netscape.

- **Document Encoding** This is the character set in which you want your Web page to be displayed. The default is Western (Latin1).

- **Tracing Image** This option enables you to place an image in the background of the document. This will not be part of the exported piece; in fact, if you add a tracing image and test the page in a browser, the tracing image does not appear. This option is strictly for development purposes, offering you the capability to trace around a composite or mock-up of your site.

- **Image Transparency** When you use a tracing image, it often has a tendency to compete with foreground elements you are using to design the page. Here you can control the opacity of the tracing image. It's usually best to drop the transparency so it's easier to distinguish between the tracing image and actual elements of the design.

After you're happy with the settings, click the Apply button to see the changes you've made. If they look good, choose OK to exit the Document Properties dialog box. I generally recommend clicking the Apply button before OK to give you the chance to make any changes without having to relaunch the dialog box. It's a good workflow habit.

Creating a Color Scheme

Sometimes picking different colors for these options can become a tedious task. Fortunately, Dreamweaver features a command that enables you to select an entire color setup with a single click of the mouse. All the colors available in this color scheme command contain Web-safe colors. Web-safe colors will appear the same across different browsers, but more importantly—different platforms. Most computers on the Web today display at least thousands of colors, if not millions. Some try to trump up the importance of Web-safe colors, but the truth of the matter is that it's not nearly as important today as it was a few years ago. You can bet it won't even be issue in a few years.

Using the color scheme command is quite simple. Follow these steps:

1. Choose Commands, Set Color Scheme. This opens the Color Scheme dialog box, as shown in Figure 4.2.

2. Select a background color from the background category. The text and links category will change to offer appropriate options for a particular background color.

3. Choose a color scheme from the Text and Links category. Notice that the dialog box offers a preview at the far-right side of what the different text and link colors will look like up against the background color you specified.

4. After you're satisfied with a selection, click OK to apply the settings to your document properties. If you want to see the new color values placed in the appropriate corresponding location, open the Document Properties dialog box.

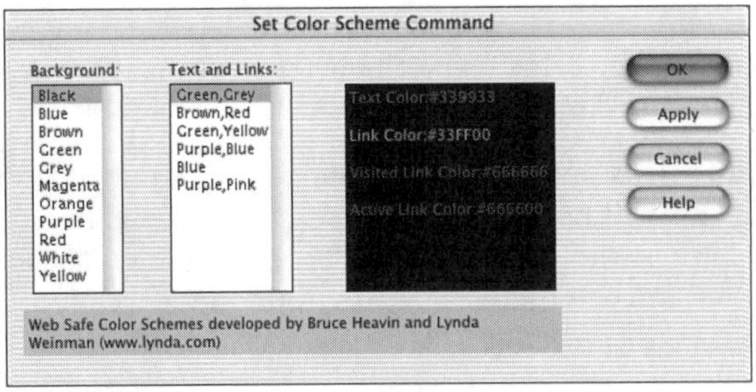

FIGURE 4.2   The Color Scheme Command dialog box enables you to choose a collection of complementing colors.

Working in the Coding Environment

One of the great strengths of Dreamweaver MX is its capability to offer a robust, professional coding environment. In this section of the chapter, you'll learn how you can use the code view to debug and enhance your development experience with Dreamweaver.

Figure 4.3 displays how you can view both the source code of the document as well as the visual layout. If you don't know HTML, Dreamweaver can act as a great learning tool.

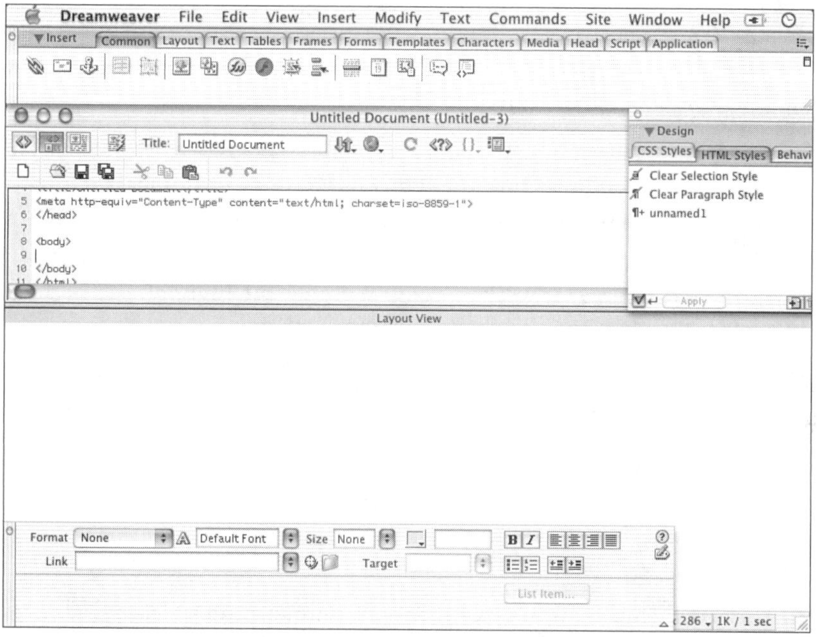

FIGURE 4.3   Dreamweaver's code and design view offers a unique look at both the visual layout of the page as well as the source code.

RoundTrip HTML

Unlike other competing HTML editors, Dreamweaver writes exceptionally clean HTML code. Dreamweaver does not add any proprietary tags that mean something only to Dreamweaver. Every HTML tag Dreamweaver writes is in line with W3C guidelines.

If that weren't enough, Dreamweaver also offers a wonderful feature called RoundTrip HTML. What is so great about this feature is you can work seamlessly between the HTML code and the design environments, and updates will be made accordingly and on-the-fly. For example, if you were to change the background color in the HTML code, after you return to the design environment, Dreamweaver would automatically update the background color to reflect the color value you added in manually.

The same is true in the opposite situation. If you make an adjustment to something in the layout view, the code automatically updates to reflect the changes. This is why it's easy to learn HTML and learn what some of the different tags are by watching what changes are made to the code as you lay out the page visually in the design view.

Code View

The code view has several preferences that define its appearance. These options can help create a more productive coding environment. To access the options, choose View, Code View Options to see the list of features.

- **Word Wrap**   This wraps all the code within the confines of the code window, making horizontal scrolling unnecessary.

- **Line Numbers**   Line numbers display a number for every line of code. This can help a great deal when you're trying to debug code. For example, when you are testing a page, if it returns an error, it will reference a line number where it encountered problems.

- **Highlight Invalid HTML**   This option switches the highlighting of invalid tags in the code view when the design view is refreshed.

- **Syntax Coloring**   This offers options in terms of what color certain code will appear. Again, this mostly helps with debugging issues. In the Preferences dialog box, under the Code Color category, you can choose different code color types for the different document formats. Whether you're writing HTML, ColdFusion, ASP.NET, JavaScript, or the like, different default color schemes are available. You change any aspect of these color schemes as well as make certain tags and code appear in a specified color.

- **Auto Indent**   This helps with writing code and keeping a clean, legible format, which helps later on in debugging, because the code is easier to read. If you want to remove an indent, just press the delete key (Mac) or Backspace key (Win). You can set how many characters to indent in the Preferences dialog box.

Quick Tag Editor

Another great thing about Dreamweaver is the Quick Tag Editor. This option enables you to move to the exact location of the code and edit the appropriate tag, as shown in Figure 4.4. You can access the Quick Tag Editor in several ways.

- Choose Modify, Quick Tag Editor. This brings up the Quick Tag editor; what you have selected in the design view determines what tag appears in the Quick Tag Editor.

- Use a keyboard shortcut to access the Quick Tag Editor: Command+T (Mac) or Ctrl+T (Win).

- Select the Quick Tag icon in the Properties Inspector; it is displayed as a small piece of paper with a pencil on top of it.

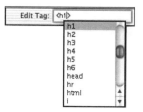

FIGURE 4.4   The Quick Tag Editor.

HTML Reference

Dreamweaver has an entire HTML reference built in to the program. This can be very useful when hand coding or debugging. The Reference panel, by default, is grouped with the Tag Inspector and the Snippets panel, as shown in Figure 4.5. You can look up any HTML tag that is considered appropriate by the HTML 3.2 or HTML 4 recommendation. The Reference panel also contains additional references on other mark-up and scripting languages. Complete references by O'Reilly, Wrox, and Macromedia provide detailed information on ColdFusion tags, JavaScript, Cascading Style Sheets, Accessibility standards, and Sitespring tags.

FIGURE 4.5   The Reference panel by default is grouped with the Tag Inspector and the Snippets panel.

Tag Inspector

The Tag Inspector is best used to edit code in a property sheet. It offers an interface and experience similar to that of an Integrated Development Environment (IDE). Any tag that you have selected in the code view will automatically offer options for the attributes of that particular tag. Refer to Figure 4.6 to see the anatomy of the Tag Inspector.

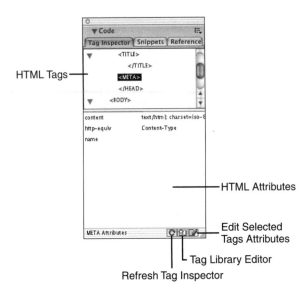

HTML Tags

HTML Attributes

Edit Selected
Tags Attributes

Tag Library Editor

Refresh Tag Inspector

FIGURE 4.6   The Tag Inspector.

Editing Tag Attributes with the Tag Inspector

This exercise offers a clear example as to how to use the Tag Inspector to change attributes of tags inside your HTML code.

1. Open a new document by choosing File, New. This launches the New Document dialog box. In the dialog box choose HTML for the type of document and click OK. This creates a new, untitled document.

2. After the new document is open, click the code view button inside the toolbar of the document. This switches the view to display the HTML code.

3. Place a blinking cursor inside the opening body tag. Next, open the Tag Inspector panel, if it's not already visible, by choosing Window, Tag Inspector. F9 is the keyboard shortcut.

4. Notice that the Tag Inspector provides options for all the possible attributes for the body tag, as shown in Figure 4.7.

5. Click to the right of the bgcolor attribute and notice that you can type in a hexadecimal value, or you can choose a color from the swatch.

6. This view sometimes provides a cluttered feeling, especially on monitors displaying smaller resolutions. If you click the Edit Tag button, found in the bottom-right corner of the panel, it launches the Tag Editor dialog box, as shown in Figure 4.8. This dialog box offers an organized, legible way to edit any tag's attributes.

7. Modify any attribute in the dialog box and click OK. If you switch to the design view you'll see that all the changes have taken place.

You can watch a QuickTime movie on how to use the Tag Inspector on the companion Web site at http://www.dreamweavermxunleashed.com.

FIGURE 4.7   The Tag Inspector offers options to modify the selected tag's attributes.

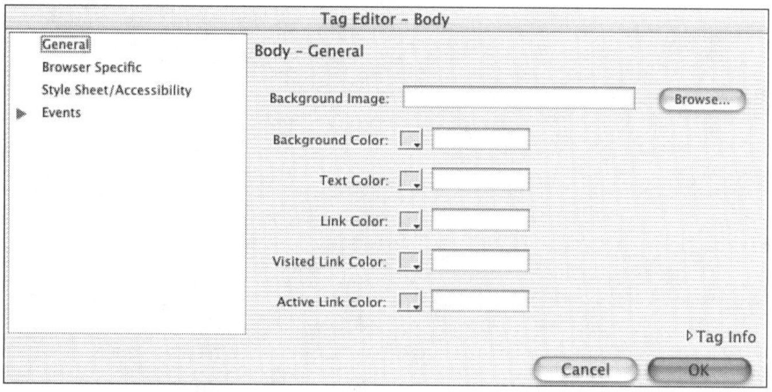

FIGURE 4.8   The Tag editor dialog box offers a clean, easy way to edit attributes of the selected tag.

Web Typography

Type on the Web is as tricky as it gets. It's unpredictable, you have minimal control, and if you're a designer, it's enough to drive you mad. The problem with type is that the Web browser will render it, based on your suggestions, if you're not happy with the default typeface of Times New Roman. However, there is a glitch—end users can specify to their browsers how they want the fonts to appear when they visit Web sites. There are also issues with type size; for example, type on a Macintosh is about 75% of the size of type on Windows.

The best way to control text, to have it appear the way that you want it to appear, is to use a cascading style sheet. Ultimately, it does help to understand how type on the Web works without a style sheet, but if you're already familiar with that, you may want to move on to Chapter 10, "Cascading Style Sheets," which covers Dreamweaver's CSS styles in exhaustive detail.

Text Formats

You can format text in an HTML document in several ways. The first is a heading format, which you can choose in the format drop-down menu in the Properties Inspector. A heading is created in the HTML code by using an <h1> through an <h6> tag, which is selected by choosing heading 1 to heading 6 in the Properties Inspector. These tags define type to appear in a different size; the text will appear bold and will automatically have a space or carriage return associated with it. There is no way to reduce the leading of text formatted with the heading tag. As you can see in Figure 4.9, the heading sizes gradually become smaller in size as the heading number gets larger. For example, a heading 1 tag is much larger than a heading 4 tag.

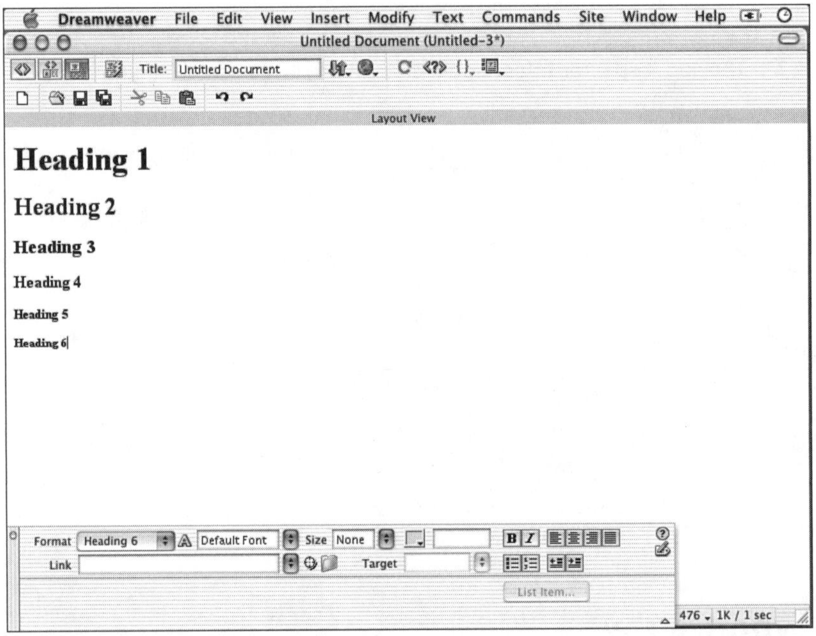

FIGURE 4.9   Notice how the headings vary in size, although most take on a boldface attribute.

Another thing that is important to understand about headings is they don't necessarily have a font size associated with them. The typeface you are using will appear either smaller or larger, in comparison to other typefaces, when a particular heading format has been applied to it.

You can set text to a heading format in two ways. The first is to highlight whatever text you want to format and in the Properties Inspector choose a heading size, as shown in Figure 4.10.

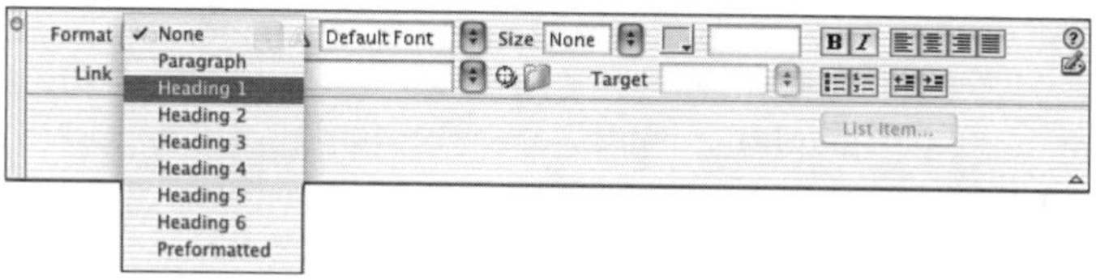

FIGURE 4.10   You can easily apply a heading format to text using the Format drop-down menu in the Properties Inspector.

The second way to apply a heading format to text is to select the text within the document and choose Text, Paragraph Format, Heading. In the menu, you can choose any heading size from 1 through 6. In that menu, you'll also notice keyboard shortcuts, as shown in Figure 4.11.

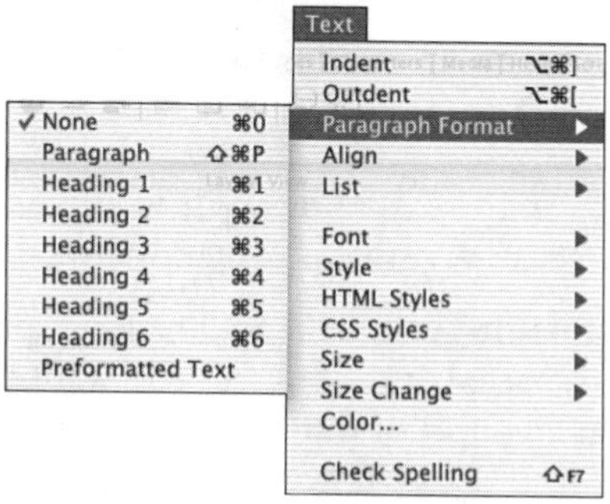

FIGURE 4.11   In the Text, Paragraph Format submenu are choices for heading sizes and their associated keyboard shortcuts.

Formatting Text Using Paragraph

Like the heading format, the paragraph format within Dreamweaver uses a common HTML tag. In this case Dreamweaver uses the <p>, or paragraph tag. This tag is placed within the HTML whenever the Return (Mac) or Enter (Windows) key is pressed. Anything between an open <p> paragraph tag and a closing </p> paragraph tag is considered by the Web browser as a paragraph. As the browser resizes, you'll notice the only thing to change within the paragraph is how the text wraps around the body of the browser.

> **NOTE**
>
> Often, developers do not want to create a new paragraph, but perhaps a new line. If you wanted to create a line return, but not a paragraph return, press Shift+Return (Mac) or Shift+Enter (Windows). This creates a break, which is accessible also through the Insert Panel under the Characters tab. This will insert a <br>, or break tag.

When you press Return or Enter, Dreamweaver automatically adds a paragraph tag. However, if you press Return or Enter more than once, Dreamweaver adds not only a paragraph tag, but with the paragraph tag will be a nonbreaking space special character, as shown in Figure 4.12.

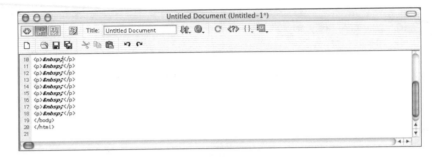

FIGURE 4.12   In the HTML, Dreamweaver adds a nonbreaking space special character within the paragraph tags.

Without this nonbreaking space, the extra line space would not appear in a Web browser, despite the fact that the line space is visible in Dreamweaver.

Which brings me to my next point—what is a nonbreaking space? A Web browser does not recognize more than one space. For example, if you want to add more space between words, you press the spacebar a couple of times. A Web browser recognizes only one of those spaces and ignores the rest. Often, however, you might want to add more than one space. You can insert a nonbreaking space, which is located in the Insert panel Characters tab, as shown in Figure 4.13. The keyboard shortcut to insert a nonbreaking space is Shift+Command+Space (Macintosh) or Shift+Ctrl+Space (Windows).

FIGURE 4.13   You can add a nonbreaking space by clicking the Nonbreaking Space button in the Insert panel, under the Characters tab.

However, a new feature inside Dreamweaver MX allows multiple spaces as you type, so if you press the spacebar more than once, Dreamweaver automatically inserts a nonbreaking space tag for you in the HTML code. You can set this option in the Preferences. Choose Edit, Preferences. This launches the Preferences dialog box. Inside the dialog box, be sure to have the General category selected. In the center of the dialog box in the Editing Options section, check the option Allow Multiple Consecutive Spaces, as shown in Figure 4.14.

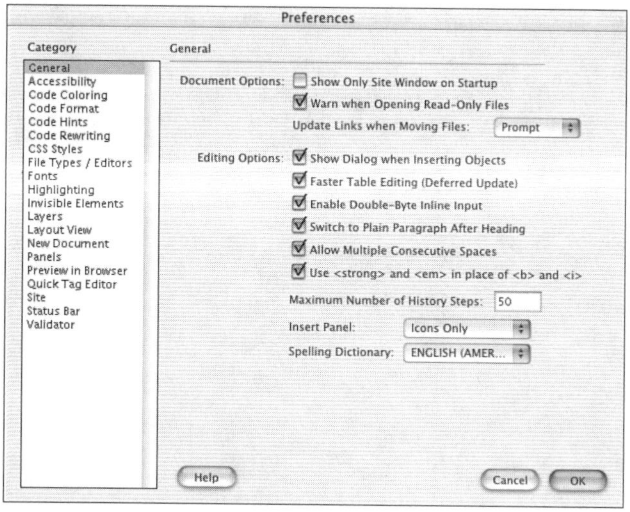

FIGURE 4.14   The Preferences allow for multiple spaces.

Preformatted

This format is a bit old school, and I don't recommend it too much. However, you may find it useful in some project, which is why I include it here. Basically what it does is allow you to type in HTML with as many spaces as you want, in terms of pressing the spacebar several times, and the browser will recognize and render those spaces. It's a bit unpredictable, but sometimes it can be good enough to yield results that you're looking for. Figure 4.15 is an example of how the preformat can be used; notice the code as well as what is displaying in the design view.

Choosing Typefaces

The way typefaces or fonts work on the Web is very different from type in print. Again, many of the same problems, such as the appearance of text on other computers, will come into play when you're dealing with type on the Web. Remember, the machine you're developing on can be very different from another machine that will actually be viewing your Web site. The first thing you must realize is that for an end user to view a specific typeface, it must be installed on that person's machine. If you're using an obscure font that most people won't have when developing your site, the ultimate outcome will be a page that doesn't look like the design you intended. It's always better to use common typefaces such as Arial, Helvetica, Times, Verdana—typefaces that ship with operating systems.

As Figure 4.16 illustrates, you can choose from a group of fonts in the Font drop-down menu in the Properties Inspector.

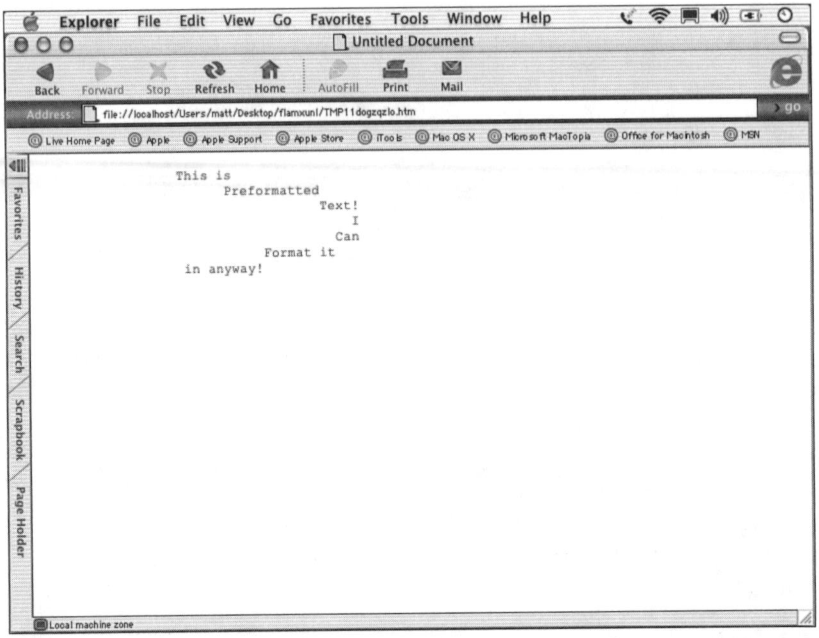

FIGURE 4.15 You can use the preformatted format option in the Properties Inspector to have browsers render spaces in your HTML code.

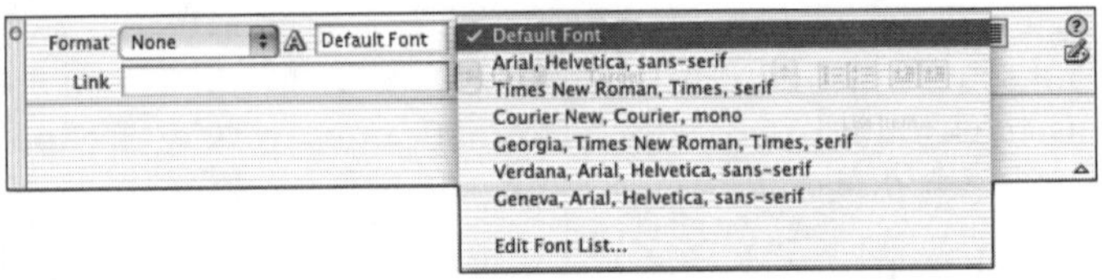

FIGURE 4.16 The default font list in the Properties Inspector.

In these font options, when you pick a typeface, you really end up picking more than one. For example, if you pick Arial, you also choose Helvetica and Sans Serif. What gives? Well, this is protection for the Web developer. If you want your type to appear in an Arial typeface, and if the end user does not have Arial installed, the Web browser will look for Helvetica, and if that is not available, it will use a default machine Sans Serif typeface. You can, of course, create your own or edit the existing font list. This next exercise will demonstrate how.

Notice that the first selected font is called the Default Font. If you choose Default Font, the text will be rendered by the default font set by the end user's Web browser's preferences. The default font normally is set to Times New Roman, but it can easily be changed by an individual by accessing the font preferences of the Web browser.

Edit the Font List in the Properties Inspector

In this exercise, you'll edit the existing font list by adding your own typefaces to the list of options. I encourage you to use caution when selecting typefaces to add to the font list. It's very important to remember that end users will need the typefaces you select on their machines. This Edit Font List feature is best suited to developers creating intranet sites, where the developer has a better idea as to what the clients have installed in their systems.

1. Open or create a new document. When the document is open, be sure to have the Properties Inspector open. If the Properties Inspector is not visible, choose Window, Properties.

2. In the Properties Inspector's Font drop-down menu, choose Edit Font List. This launches the Edit Font List dialog box as displayed in Figure 4.17.

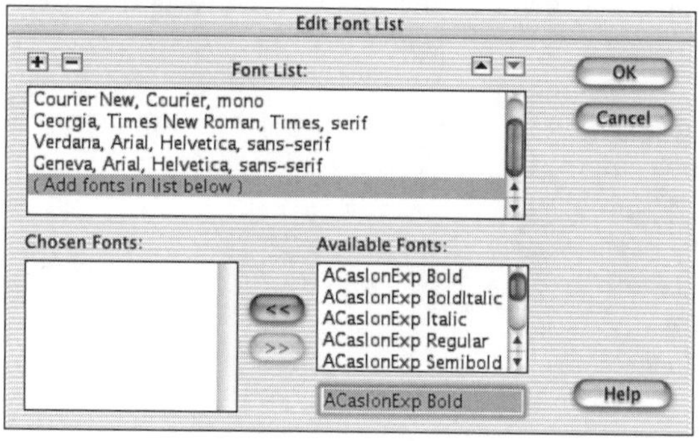

FIGURE 4.17 You can easily access the Edit Font List dialog box by choosing the Edit Font List option in the Font drop-down menu in the Properties Inspector.

3. To create your own addition to the font list, select a typeface from the available fonts selection box in the bottom-right corner. After the font of your choice is highlighted, press the left arrow button to add the font to the Chosen Fonts box. You can add as many fonts as you like, but three or four should be enough.

4. If you're happy with your font selection and would like to make additional options, click the plus sign (+) in the top-left corner. This will create a new, empty chosen fonts box, enabling you to create another option to add to the list.

5. If you're unhappy with a list option, you can select it, and with it highlighted click the subtraction button to remove it from the list.

6. When you are done editing, click the OK button. This will return you to the document; in the Properties Inspector, access the Font drop-down list. You'll see that your modifications have taken place, as shown in Figure 4.18.

Font Size

Font size is another great challenge in Web site development. With all the different factors of platforms and Web browsers, managing the size of type is no easy task. Remember that the end user determines how large or how small fonts appear in the browser. In many cases, at least in my experience, most people don't know they can change the default font attributes of a Web browser. The ones who do know tend not to change things, except that 12-year-old girls figure out they can use a crazy looking typeface.

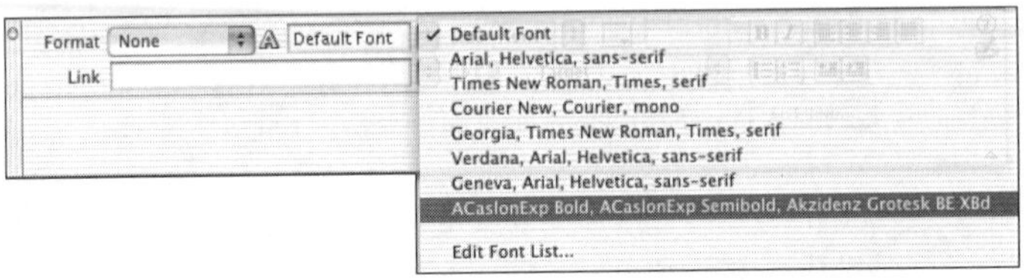

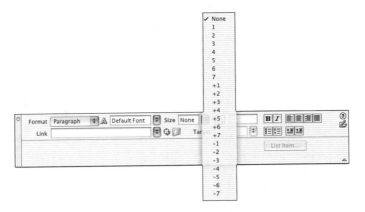

FIGURE 4.18   All changes made within the Edit Font List dialog box are immediately available.

If you decide you want to increase or decrease the size of the type, you can adjust it by using the Size drop-down menu in the Properties Inspector, as displayed in Figure 4.19.

FIGURE 4.19   You can change the type font size in the Properties Inspector by using the Size drop-down menu.

As you can see, the options in the drop-down menu do not resemble point sizes—they refer to HTML sizes. The default size for HTML text is 3, so you have the option of selecting an absolute size or a relative size. The absolute size is a straight number from 1 through 7; 1 is the smallest and 7 is the largest. With relative sizes, you can either add to or subtract from the default font size of the document. For example, if the default size is 3, you can add or choose +1, and the type will appear as an equivalent to an absolute size 4. Refer to Figure 4.20 for an example of the font sizes and how they relate.

Why? That must be the question you're asking right now. There is a tag called <basefont>. The <basefont> tag will allow you to change the default of the browser, which is generally

3. If you change the base font to 5, you can use sizes to adjust the size of the text relative to the base font value. Sound messy? It can be. If you find yourself bewildered and frustrated because of the lack of text control, move on to CSS styles.

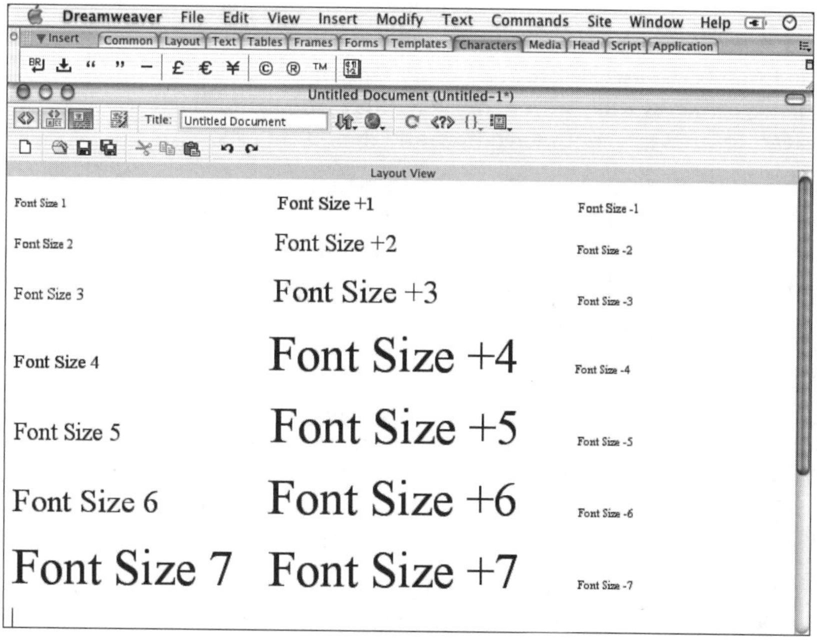

FIGURE 4.20   Notice the different font size options—some yield the same results.

Bold, Italic, and Alignment

This is about as easy as it gets. If you've ever used a word processor, you're probably familiar with how these options work. If you use the bold and italic options, Dreamweaver, by default, surrounds the text with <strong> and <em>, respectively. If you prefer Dreamweaver to use the <b> and <i> tags, you can change that in the Preferences. The Preferences dialog box, which is accessible under the Edit menu, offers an option under the General category to use <strong> and <em> in place of <b> and <i>. Simply uncheck that option.

The basic alignment options are also available inside of Dreamweaver. You can align the text to the left, center, right, or justify it. The buttons on the Properties look the same as every other program in the world.

However, there are a couple of buttons you're probably not familiar with—the Indent and Outdent buttons. These buttons are located directly underneath the Align Left and Align Center buttons. The Indent button changes the "margins" of how the text appears in the browser. It increases space between the text and the left and right sides of the browser. The Outdent button typically is used to remove any indents you might have added to your text.

Creating Lists

Bulleted and numbered lists are created quite simply in Dreamweaver. It is a long-time HTML practice, which is still used often, even today. You can make three types of lists in Dreamweaver: ordered lists, unordered lists, and definition lists.

Unordered and Ordered Lists

Unordered lists are commonly called bulleted lists. They create a circle by default to the left of the list item. You can change the appearance of a bulleted list circle to a square.

Ordered lists apply a number instead of a bullet to the left of the item and follow in sequential order.

You can create ordered and unordered lists in a couple of ways. In the design view, you can click the Ordered or Unordered List buttons in the Properties Inspector. With the button depressed, every time you press Return (Mac) or Enter (Windows), a new number or bullet appears. If you press Return (Mac) or Enter (Windows) twice, you will exit the list format. You also can choose Text, List, Ordered List or Text, List, Unordered List.

It is also quite simple to change the appearance of the number or bullets. You can change the appearance of the numbers in an ordered list from Arabic, which is the default, to Roman Numerals (Large or Small) or Alphabet (Large or Small).

For an unordered list the default is a solid circle, but you can change it to a square. To change the appearance of a list, place a blinking cursor somewhere within the list, and then press the List Item button in the Properties Inspector, as shown in Figure 4.21.

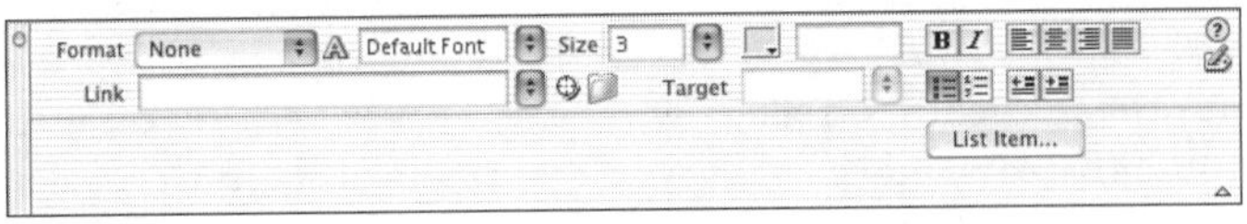

FIGURE 4.21   Click the List Item button to bring up the List Properties dialog box.

After you click the List Item button, the List Properties dialog box launches. In the List Properties dialog box, as pictured in Figure 4.22, use the Style drop-down menu to choose Square for an unordered list, or a Roman or Alphabet style for an ordered list.

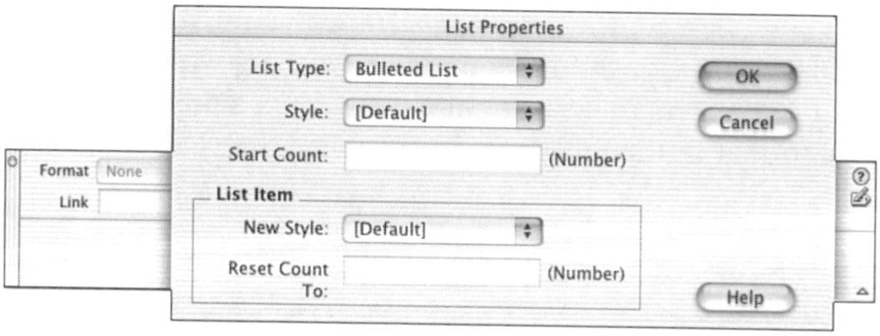

FIGURE 4.22   The List Properties dialog box.

If you are creating a list and it's not appearing or coming out the way you expected, double-check the HTML code. Often when you're working in Dreamweaver, if you cut or paste text into the list or if you delete some text, some HTML tags can get left behind. Clean HTML for an ordered list should resemble the following:

```
<ol>
 <li>list item</li>
 <li>list item</li>
</ol>
```

Or for unordered lists:

```
<ul>
 <li>list item</li>
 <li>list item</li>
</ul>
```

Definition Lists

Definition lists do not apply any bullets or numbering. Essentially a definition list indents text on every other Return (Macintosh) or Enter (Windows). Type a term, which will appear normal, press Return (Macintosh) or Enter (Windows), and the text will be indented until you press Return or Enter again. To see an example of a definition list, refer to Figure 4.23.

To apply a definition list, choose Text, List, Definition List, or choose the Insert Definition List icon from the Text tab of the Insert panel.

Nested Lists

You can nest lists within lists. You can combine the same style list when nesting, or you can alternate between different styles. To create a nested list, press the Indent button on the Properties Inspector, as shown in Figure 4.24. After pressing the button, notice that the bullets or numbers are indented, thus creating a nested list. If you want the nested list to use the opposite formatting—for example, if you're working with an unordered list and want the nested list to have numbers— highlight the nested portion of the list and press the appropriate list format in the Properties Inspector. Figure 4.25 is an example of a nested list.

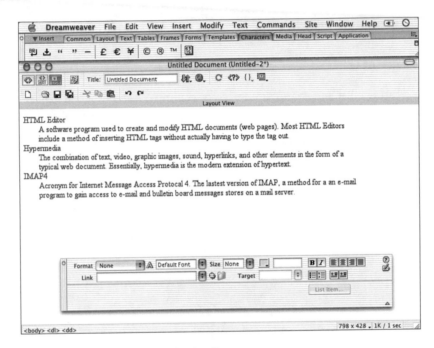

FIGURE 4.23   Text formatted as a definition list.

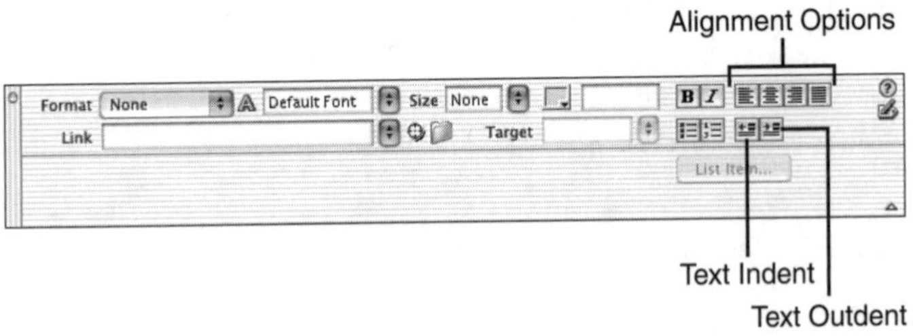

FIGURE 4.24   The Indent and Outdent buttons on the Properties Inspector.

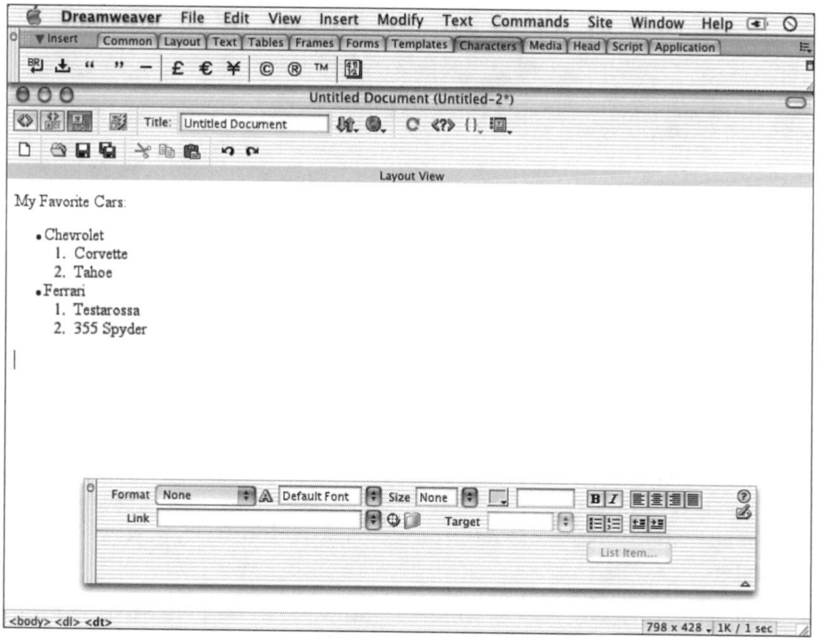

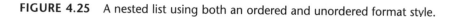

FIGURE 4.25   A nested list using both an ordered and unordered format style.

HTML Styles

When using HTML styles, you can offer a consistent look throughout your Web site by applying formats that you've set up in the HTML Styles panel. It's important to note that HTML styles are not nearly as powerful as cascading style sheets, nor as style sheets in desktop publishing programs such as Quark or InDesign.

The HTML Styles panel is an area where you can store HTML formats. A downside to this panel is that text or documents have no links associated with them. Therefore, if you apply a style to a body of text and then later update the style to a different color, the body of text will not be updated automatically. Instead, you have to reapply the format to the body of text to reflect the new changes.

Notice in Figure 4.26 that four possible icons can appear in the Styles panel. Each has a different meaning, and those meanings will basically describe how the HTML Styles panel works. The top two, however, are always present, whereas the others appear only if you define them.

- **Clear Selection Style**   This option removes a style that you created to be applied to selected text.

- **Clear Paragraph Style**   This enables you to remove any style that you may have applied to a paragraph.

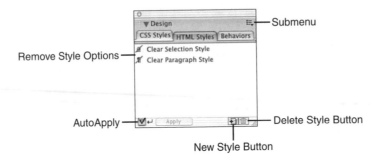

FIGURE 4.26   The HTML Styles panel.

Creating Styles

When creating styles, you have a couple of choices. You can either create a style that will be applied to a selection of text or to text that appears between opening and closing <p> paragraph tags. One style, oddly enough, is called a selection style, and the other is called a paragraph style.

The other choice you must consider is whether you want to remove existing format attributes to text before you apply the HTML style or add to the existing style and formatting of the text. You can add to an existing style only if the existing style does not conflict with an HTML style. For example, if the text you're about to apply the style to is the color green, but the HTML style is set to change the text to red, the HTML style will override the existing color, even though the HTML style is set to add to an existing style.

Creating HTML Styles

In this exercise we'll be going through the necessary steps to create an HTML style. You can download the HTML file called newsletter, located on our companion Web site at http://www.dreamweavermxunleashed.com, to use in this exercise.

1. Open the document newletter.html. You'll notice there are several lines and paragraphs of text, as pictured in Figure 4.27. What you're going to do is set up some style to format the text in this document.

2. The first thing to make consistent is the font and color of the headings. To do this, open the HTML Styles panel by choosing Window, HTML Styles. In the HTML Styles panel, click the New Style button located at the bottom-right corner of the panel. You can also create a new style by choosing New Style from the panel submenu. Notice this launches the Define HTML Style dialog box, as shown in Figure 4.28.

3. The Define HTML Style dialog box has several options. First, name the style. Let's name this **subheadings**.

4. Next, determine whether this is going to be a style that will be applied to a selection or a paragraph. For this exercise, choose the Selection option button.

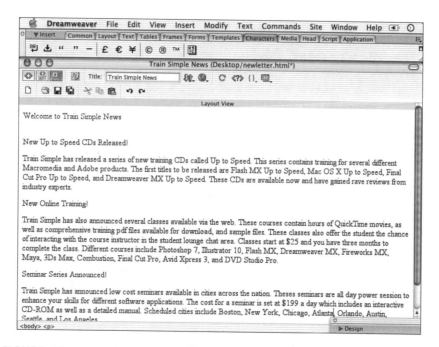

FIGURE 4.27 The document newsletter.html is a document filled with unformatted text.

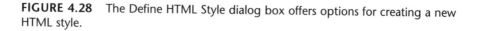

FIGURE 4.28 The Define HTML Style dialog box offers options for creating a new HTML style.

5. The next decision you have to make when defining a style is whether you prefer to add to the existing style of the text as you apply this HTML style or if you want to remove any formatting to the text before your HTML style is applied. For this exercise, add to an existing style.

6. You now have to configure the font attributes. Here, you decide what typeface you want to use and the size and color. There are also options for style, such as bold and italic. If you press the other button next to the style section, you'll get a drop-down menu with additional styling options, such as strikethrough and underline. For this exercise I'm going to choose Arial, Helvetica, sans-serif for the font. I'm then going to choose a size of 3, but I'm not going to select color. I want you to see the advantage of using the Add to Existing Style option. Feel free to choose your own styles.

7. Finally I'm going to press OK to exit the Define HTML Style dialog box. Notice back in the document, in the HTML Style panel, your style named subheadings.

8. To apply this style to some text, simply highlight a word or section text, and with it selected click the subheadings style located in the HTML Styles panel. Notice in Figure 4.29 the text has been modified, but the original color has been preserved because we chose Add to Ex.

9. If for some reason you decide you no longer want the style applied to a particular piece of text, highlight the text you want to remove the style from and click the Clear Selection Style option in the HTML Styles panel.

Creating and applying HTML Styles is simple. You can also create a paragraph style, which give you the capability to change the text in the same way you just did in this exercise to an entire paragraph of text. You create a paragraph style in the same way, but you have the additional options for alignment and format (Heading, Paragraph, or Preformat styles).

When applying a paragraph style, it is not necessary to select the entire paragraph; simply have a blinking cursor within the paragraph you want to apply the style to when you click the style in the HTML Styles panel. You can remove a paragraph style in the same way, but by using the Remove Paragraph Style option.

Editing HTML Styles

HTML Styles do not behave like CSS Styles in the sense that there is no connection between the Styles panel and the text you've applied a style to. When applying an HTML style, you're more or less adding a <font> tag with attributes around the selected text. You can edit an HTML style, but after editing it, the text you've applied the style to previously will not be updated; it's up to you to update it manually by reapplying the style.

Nevertheless, it is possible to change or edit the style you have setup in the HTML Styles panel. Simply highlight the style in the panel and choose from the submenu on the top-right corner of the panel, and in that menu choose Edit. This launches the Define HTML Styles dialog box.

Even though you can remove styles from text, you may want to delete them completely from the panel. To do this, highlight the style in the panel and click the Trash Can button in the bottom-right corner of the panel. You can also choose Delete from the panel's submenu.

Finally, you can also move HTML styles to other Web sites. CSS styles will often use an external file, which is easy to locate and share. HTML styles are a bit different, but it is possible to move the styles you set up in one site to another. To share HTML styles, locate the Library folder inside your local root folder. There you'll see a file called styles.xml. This is the file you can copy and move to different sites to move your HTML styles to another location.

Inserting the Time and Date

You can put the time and date on your page to let your viewers know how current the information is that they're looking at. It's quite simple to insert the date. Click the Insert Date button in the Common Objects of the Insert panel, or you choose Insert, Date. This launches the Insert Date dialog box, as shown in Figure 4.29.

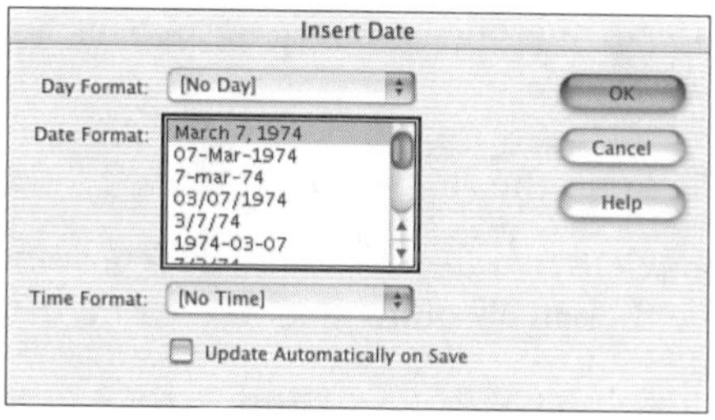

FIGURE 4.29   The Insert Date dialog box offers formatting options for the date and time.

In this dialog box, you can choose whether you want the day to appear and how you want it to be formatted, as well as how you want the date to appear. You also have the option of showing the time on your page. A drop-down menu provides you with options on how you want the time to be formatted as well.

An option is also available for updating the time and date automatically when saving the document. This can be convenient if you're interested in letting your viewers know when the last time an update has been made to the page. To activate this option simply place a check in the check box.

Inserting a Horizontal Rule

Frankly, I recommend from a design point of view not to use horizontal rules. Surely you can be creative enough to make a visual division in a document without resorting to a horizontal rule. However, you bought this book to understand the different Dreamweaver components; therefore, I will tell you how you can use a horizontal rule and what options are available.

To insert a horizontal rule, click the Insert Horizontal Rule button under the Common Objects in the Insert panel, or choose Insert, Horizontal Rule. After the horizontal rule is inserted into the document, select it, and then a series of options becomes available in the Properties Inspector, as shown in Figure 4.30.

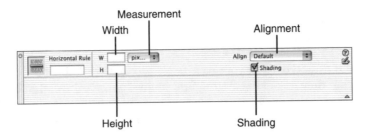

FIGURE 4.30   When you have a horizontal rule in a document, the options for the rule appear in the Properties Inspector.

These are the options available for the Horizontal Rule:

- **Width (W)**   The value entered in this text field determines the width of the horizontal rule, based on either an absolute pixel value or a percentage value.

- **Height (H)**   The value entered here determines the size or thickness of the horizontal rule. This value is measured in pixels.

- **Align**   This drop-down menu offers options for how the horizontal rule will align on the HTML page.

- **Shading**   When shading is selected, the horizontal rule will have a 3-D appearance. If it is not selected, the horizontal rule will appear as a solid bar.

There are no coloring options for the Horizontal Rule inside of Dreamweaver. It is not supported because the color attribute of the <hr> tag is supported only by Internet Explorer. If you want to add color to the horizontal rule simply select it, and inside the Properties Inspector click the QuickTag Editor to bring you to the <hr> tag of the HTML code. Here add a color attribute and have it equal a hexadecimal value. The horizontal rule will not appear colored in the Dreamweaver authoring environment; instead, you must preview it in Internet Explorer. To preview it, choose File, Preview In Browser, Internet Explorer.

Working with Hyperlinks

There are a couple of different ways to create hyperlinks. A hyperlink is how pages are connected on the Web. You'll look at how you can link to other files within your site as well as how to link to external Web pages and Web sites.

Creating a Link Using the Browse to File Method

To hyperlink existing text within your document, highlight the text, and in the Properties Inspector you'll notice a text field labeled Link. The first option is to type in the name of the file you want to hyperlink, including the full path. The full path is usually the most difficult part to remember. Instead, you can click the small folder icon at the end of the link text field, which opens a Select File dialog box. In the dialog box, you can search your local root folder for the file you want the text to link to. When you find it, highlight it and click the Choose (Mac) or Select (Windows) button. Dreamweaver will not only link to the appropriate file, but it will also append the correct path. It's a good idea to save your work and test the link by previewing the page in a Web browser. The best way to do that is to choose File, Preview In Browser, and then select the browser of your choice.

After setting up links this way, the Link text field turns into a drop-down menu where you can pick from a list of links you've used in the site. You can also access links from the Assets panel, which is covered in detail in Chapter 9, "Assets and the Library."

Linking to an External Web Site

Linking to external Web site is also very simple. The important thing to remember is that you must address the link by using the absolute URL. For example, if you highlighted some text in your document that needed to be linked to an external site, in the Link text field of the Properties Inspector you would have to address the link as follows: http://www.websitename.com. It is very important to include the http://, which sometimes new developers forget.

Targeting Links

In the Properties Inspector, there is a drop-down menu for targeting options. All but one of the options apply only if you're working with framesets, which I cover in a later chapter. The one option I'd like to share with you here is the _blank option. If you choose _blank in this drop-down menu, when the end user clicks the hyperlink, it will open that link in a new browser window. You typically want to do this when sending visitors to other sites so they don't leave yours entirely. However, you want to use this option wisely. Opening new browser windows can sometimes be confusing for the end user, and additional windows require additional RAM for the end user's computer.

Insert Link Object

The Insert Link object is found under the Common tab of the Insert panel. This object launches a dialog box offering options to create a hyperlink. You can insert text, links, and targets from within this dialog box.

Email Links

Adding email links to your pages is a way to offer your end users an easy way to email you without having to remember a specific email address. An email link, when clicked, will launch the end user's default email program. When it launches, it will be in the compose mode addressed to an email address specified by the link.

You can add an email link to existing text, or you can create text on-the-fly by using the Insert E-mail Link object located under the Common tab of the Insert Panel. If you want to add the link text, make sure you have it selected when clicking the E-mail link button. You can also choose Insert, E-mail Link. Both of these options launch the E-mail Link dialog box, as shown in Figure 4.31.

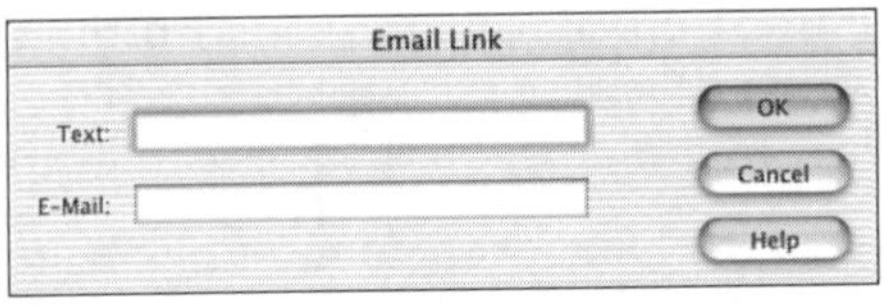

FIGURE 4.31   The E-mail Link dialog box enables you to create a hyperlink that will launch an email program.

If you have text selected, it will appear in the first text box labeled Text. Otherwise, you can type whatever you like and that text will appear wherever your blinking cursor is on the document. The second text field is where you type in the email address you want the end user to send the email to. When you're happy, click OK. If you highlight the new email link, in the Properties Inspector in the link text field, you'll see that Dreamweaver added a link that looks something like this: `mailto:email@address.com`. That code is what activates a browser to launch an email program.

Named Anchors

With named anchors, you can link to specific areas of a document. A named anchor is an invisible element you can insert into an HTML document. You can then hyperlink something in your document to that specific anchor, moving the document to display the area around the anchor.

Linking to a Named Anchor

Follow these steps to link elements on a Web page to a named anchor. You can download the file used in this exercise from this book's companion Web site located at `http://www.dreamweaver-mxunleashed.com`.

1. Open the anchor.html file you downloaded from the companion Web site. Notice the different headings and paragraphs. Toward the bottom of the page, you'll notice I set up a simple text navigation bar, as shown in Figure 4.32.

2. Place a blinking cursor next to the Introduction subheading. The blinking cursor represents the location where the named anchor will be placed. Click the Insert Named Anchor button under the Common object in the Insert Panel, or choose Insert, Named Anchor. This launches the Named Anchor dialog box, as shown in Figure 4.33.

3. Type in the name of the anchor. Avoid spacing and special characters in your naming conventions. Additionally, named anchors are case sensitive, so you must remain consistent when naming. Click OK when you've completed typing in the name. You'll notice a small anchor shield appear on your document. This symbol represents an invisible element. This icon will not appear in a browser. You can move this element wherever you think it will cater to the functionality of the link. Do not place an anchor within a layer; the anchor will fail in Netscape browsers.

WARNING

If you do not see the named anchor appear, choose View, Visual Aids, Invisible Elements; this will make the icon appear in the document.

---

4. Move to the bottom of the page. Highlight the Intro text in the navigation bar. You want to link this Intro text to the named anchor toward the top of the page. With the text selected, notice there is the link text field in the Properties Inspector. Click and drag the Point-to-File icon on the right side of the link text field. Drag until the icon is about a quarter of an inch from the top of the document window and the document will begin to autoscroll. When the top of the page is visible, move the Point-to-File icon on top of the named anchor. Notice the link is automatically filled out in the Properties Inspector, as shown in Figure 4.34.

5. You can also just type the name of the anchor into the link text field, as long as you place the pound sign (#) in front of the named anchor's name. The pound sign converts an item in a Dreamweaver document into a hyperlink.

You can even link to a named anchor from another page. Simply add #anchorname to any normal hyperlink.

TIP

Visit the companion Web site at http://www.dreamweavermxunleashed.com for a QuickTime movie tutorial on how to use named anchors.

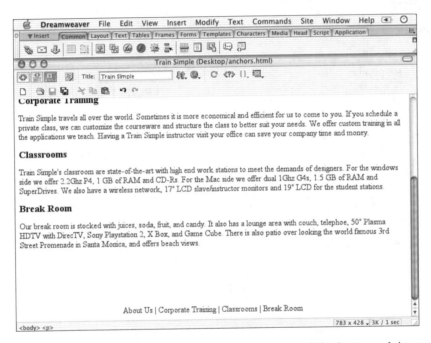

FIGURE 4.32 This document has a navigation bar set up toward the bottom of the page.

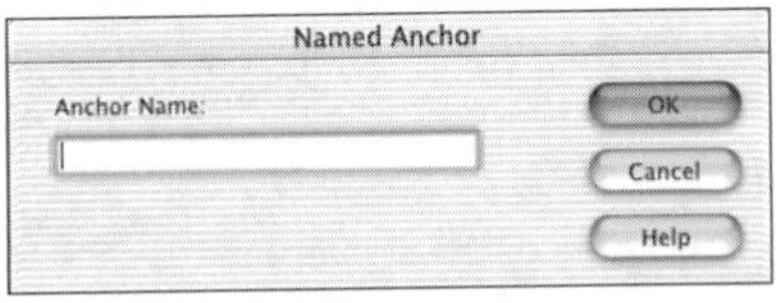

FIGURE 4.33 The Name Anchor dialog box offers the capability to name your named anchors.

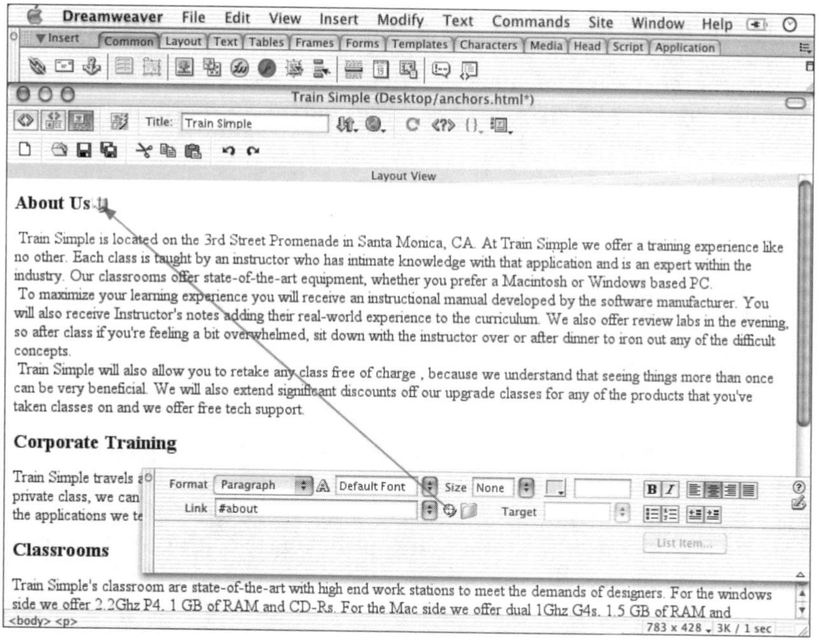

FIGURE 4.34   You can drag the Point-to-File icon over the named anchor and Dreamweaver will complete all the hyperlink information in the Properties Inspector.

Images on the Web

In my experience teaching Dreamweaver, I've found that some people new to Web design don't understand how graphics used in Dreamweaver were created. It's important to understand that Dreamweaver has no image-editing capabilities as a standalone application. Dreamweaver integrates well with some image editing programs such as Fireworks and Photoshop, but you cannot create or edit graphics inside of Dreamweaver. Dreamweaver is strictly the application for laying out content in an HTML form.

Therefore, let's briefly discuss what image formats are acceptable for the Web.

GIFs

GIF stands for Graphical Interchange Format and is used for images or graphics with smaller amounts of color and graphics without much tonal range. The reason is that because GIFs read color in a horizontal line, the more color it encounters when reading, the larger the file size. GIFs also have a color table attached to them. The color table dictates to the graphic how many colors and which color can be used in the artwork. More colors in the color table yield higher file sizes.

GIFs can also store transparency; for example, if you have an image with a solid background color, yet you didn't want to see that background, you can make it transparent. Creating GIFs with transparency requires you to master a few tricks, but that topic is out of the scope of this book. If you're new to creating content for the Web, I suggest visiting Web sites such as www.Webmonkey.com.

GIFs create the smallest file sizes and are best used for flat, lower-colored graphics.

JPEGs

JPEG stands for Joint Photographic Experts Group and is a lossy compression standard used on bitmap graphics with great tonal range, such as photographs. This compression standard removes pixels from an image to reduce the file size. Too much compression can result in a blurry, unclear image.

If you're moving over from the print world, the notion of removing pixels may seem like a sin. Remember that people will be viewing the artwork on a computer monitor, and it isn't intended to be viewed in any other format. If the image looks good on a monitor, that's all you need to be concerned with. Many of the image-editing applications have great features for compressing bitmaps.

PNGs

PNG stands for Portable Network Graphics, and a big buzz was associated with them a year or two ago. They were supposed to replace GIFs for a number of reasons, but the main one was the capability for PNG to be saved in many bit-depths. GIFs are limited to a bit-depth of 8, whereas PNGs can be saved from anywhere between 8-bit to 32-bit color. They never really caught on. Maybe they will in the future, but if you decide to use them, be aware that only Internet Explorer 4 and later can view them.

Inserting Images into a Dreamweaver Document

Placing an image into a document is one of the most common tasks you'll be performing in your Web development. Luckily, the task is also one of the easiest to perform inside the application.

Inserting an Image into a Document

Follow these steps to see how you can insert an image into your Web page. You can use any image you'd like for this exercise, or you can download the file from this book's companion Web site at http://www.dreamweavermxunleashed.com. Use the logo for the file called logo_gato.gif in the Chapter 4 section of the site.

1. After downloading the file, save it to the desktop of your computer.

2. Create a new basic HTML document. Choose File, Save As and save it as first_image.html in your local root folder.

3. Click the Insert Image button in the Common Tab of the Insert Panel. You can also choose Insert, Image. This launches the Select Image Source dialog box. It defaults to your Default Images folder for your Web site, but you can select files from other locations.

4. In the Select Image Source dialog box, navigate to the desktop and highlight the logo_gato.gif file. Click Choose (Mac) or Select (Windows) to select the file. Notice the image now appears in the document, as shown in Figure 4.35.

5. When an image is placed within an HTML document, an `<img src>` tag is used, and it will source the location of the image you want to have appear in the document. Notice that Dreamweaver made a copy of the image we sourced from the desktop and placed it inside the default images folder. This way, if we ever move our file onto a server, the HTML won't be sourcing an image that's outside the root folder.

If you do not have a default images folder defined in your site, you will get a dialog box indicating that the file is outside the local root folder and asking you to make a copy there. Make a copy into your local root folder.

Figure 4.36 shows several options within the Properties Inspector for modifying and altering the image.

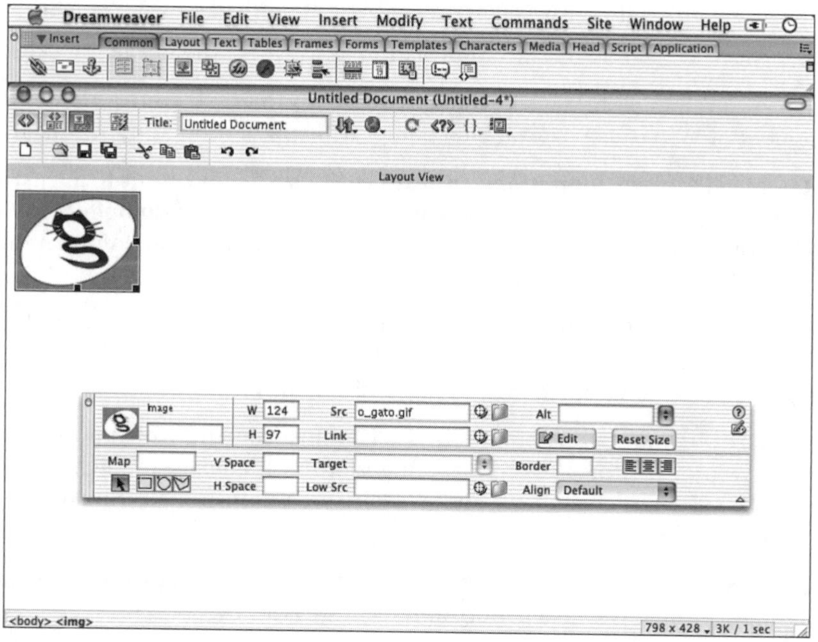

FIGURE 4.35   After you select an image from the Select Image Source dialog box, the image appears in the document.

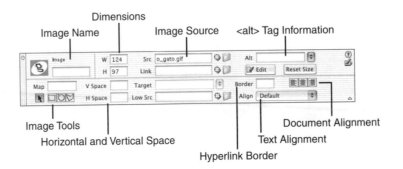

FIGURE 4.36   The Properties Inspector offers several options for altering the appearance of the image.

- **Name**   In this text field, you can name the image. This can be important when applying certain behaviors or working with DHTML.

- **Width and Height**   These text fields represent the width and height of the image in pixels. You can resize the image by typing in a new value; however, it is recommended that you import your image already sized properly.

- **SRC**   This text field offers path information as to where the image is located.

- **Link**   You can enter in a relative or absolute path to link the image to another document or Web site. A 1-pixel blue border will appear around hyperlinked images.

- **ALT**   Type in information in the alt text field that you may want to appear in a ToolTip. The alt information will also appear in browsers that do not display images, and it provides information to screen readers. You can find more information on the alt tag in Appendix A, "Accessibility."

- **Edit**   This button launches an external bitmap editor for you to modify the image without having to reimport it. For more information on editing and application integration, refer to Chapter 13, "Adding Video and Audio."

- **Reset Size**   If you resize an image in the HTML document, which is not recommended, you can restore the original dimensions of the image by clicking this button. You also can click the W and H where the numbers appear bold to restore the image's original size.

- **V and H space**   With this option you can enter in a pixel value to create an invisible cushion around the image, horizontally and vertically.

- **Target**   If you create a hyperlink for an image, you can target the link to open in a specific frame in a frameset or in a new browser window.

- **Low SRC**   This text field gives the option of targeting an image that, in an ideal situation, would be the same as the image link above it, but in a more compressed, lower-quality format. The low src image will load first, letting the end user know something is happening. This is a good idea if you have a chunky Web site or if you anticipate an audience with slower Internet connections.

- **Border**   When you create a hyperlink on an image, a 1-pixel blue border appears around the image. You can increase the border size by typing in a pixel value greater than 1, or you can remove it by typing in 0.

- **Alignment buttons**   These buttons work the same as they do for text. You can align the image to the left of the document, center it, or align it to the right side of the page.

- **Align Drop-Down Menu**   The options in this drop-down menu are not for the alignment of the image within the document, but around text. In Figure 4.37 I have aligned the text to appear toward the top of the image.

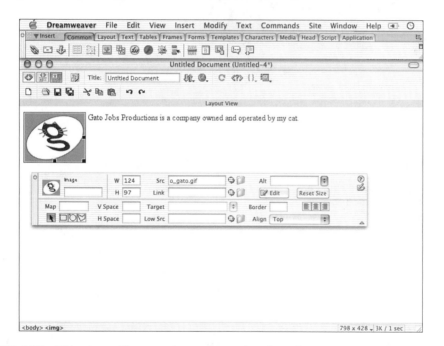

FIGURE 4.37   This picture illustrates how text can be aligned next to an image when using the Align drop-down menu in the Properties Inspector when an image is selected.

Image Maps

The one section I did not include in the preceding list is the map area. The map area is used to create image maps. Image maps are pretty straightforward; you can activate different regions of a single bitmap graphic to link to different pages and sites. To do so, choose the Map tool of choice and draw a shape, also known as a hot spot, over a particular region of the image. After you've drawn a shape, you can type a link into the Link text field of the Properties Inspector, as shown in Figure 4.38.

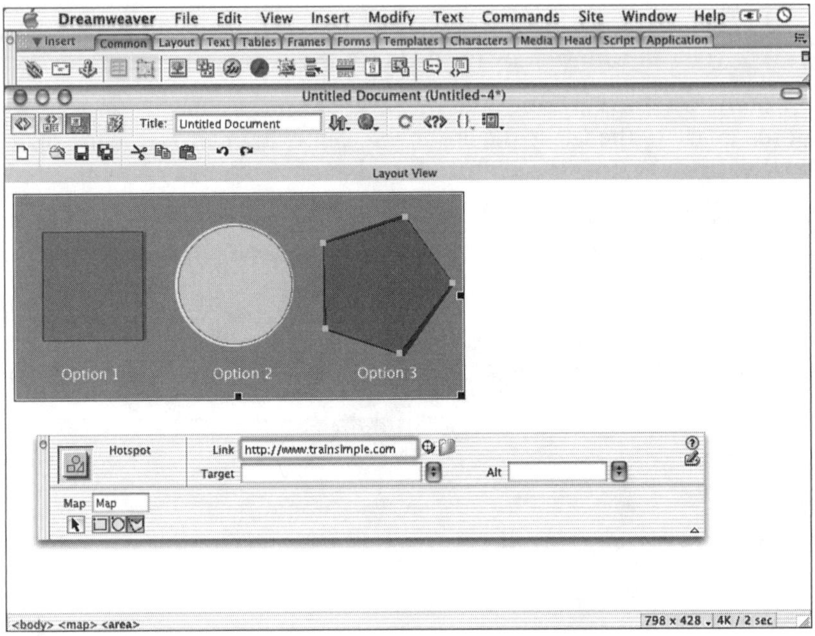

FIGURE 4.38   After drawing a hot spot shape, you can easily link the hot spot to a page or a Web site by using the Properties Inspector.

The rectangle map tool is used for drawing squares and rectangles, the oval tool is used for drawing circles (it can't draw ovals—go figure), and the polygon tool is a free-form shape drawing tool.

Rollover Images

Rollover images are commonly used in Web development and are a piece of cake in Dreamweaver. For a rollover to occur in a Web browser, JavaScript must be present in the HTML document—after all, the entire effect is JavaScript. If you don't know JavaScript, it's no big deal; Dreamweaver writes it for you.

Inserting a Rollover Image

Follow this exercise and complete the following steps to insert a rollover image into an HTML document.

1. Download the file called rollover.zip from the companion Web site located at `http://www.dreamweavermxunleashed.com`. After you've downloaded the file, unzip it to extract the two file images: button_up.gif and button_over.gif.

2. Inside of Dreamweaver, in any document, place a blinking cursor in the area you want the images to appear. Click the Insert Rollover Image button under the Common tab in the Insert panel. This launches the Insert Rollover Image dialog box, as shown in Figure 4.39.

3. In the first text field, name the image. This is typically used for the JavaScript, so avoid spacing and special characters in your naming conventions.

4. Browse for the file button_up.gif, which you downloaded to your computer for the original image. You can do this by clicking the Browse button and selecting the file from wherever it is located on your computer.

5. Do the same for the rollover image text field. Browse for the button_over.gif.

6. Type in some alternative text to appear within the alt tag. Again, this can play a role in how accessible your Web site is.

7. Finally, you can link the button. You can either browse for a local file, or you can type in an absolute URL. If you leave the link blank, you can always fill it in later in the Properties Inspector. Click Done.

8. You will return to the document with an image placed wherever your blinking cursor was. Choose File, Preview in Browser, Internet Explorer to see the new rollover image. Notice when you mouse over the image, it changes to the button_over.gif file as shown in Figure 4.40.

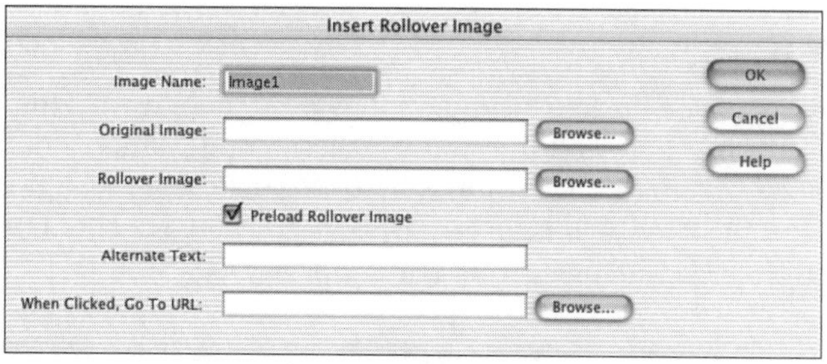

Insert Rollover Image

Image Name: Image1   OK
Original Image: Browse...   Cancel
Rollover Image: Browse...   Help
         ☑ Preload Rollover Image
Alternate Text:
When Clicked, Go To URL: Browse...

FIGURE 4.39   The Insert Rollover dialog box has an option for creating graphics that change their appearance when moused over.

NOTE

It's important to note that you cannot modify the rollover image after you exit the Insert Rollover Image dialog box. If you want to change the artwork, you can do it manually through the code, or you can delete the rollover and reinsert it.

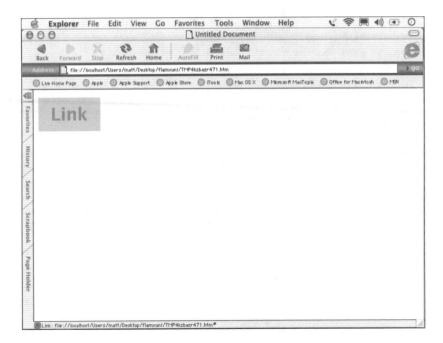

FIGURE 4.40   Notice that the graphic changes its appearance when moused over.

Navigation Bars

In the previous exercise, you created a simple rollover graphic. It was simple in the sense that it had an up and over state and that was it. What if you wanted a down state as well, and what if you had more than one button to create? That's when you use the Navigation Bar feature. This feature allows you to have four states as well as many buttons. The only catch is, you can have only one navigation bar per page.

Inserting a Navigation Bar into your Document

Follow these steps if you want to place more than one button with several states into your document. It's important to download the nav_buttons.zip file from this books companion Web site at http://www.dreamweavermxunleashed.com. Be sure to navigate to the Chapter 4 section of the site. Unzip the files and leave the Buttons folder on your desktop.

1. Open a new document by choosing File, New. This launches the New Document dialog box. Choose Basic HTML and click OK.

2. After the new document is open, choose File, Save As to launch the Save As dialog box. Name the file navigation.html and save it in the local root folder for whatever site you're working on.

3. Inside the document, click Insert Navigation Bar under the Common tab of the Insert Panel or choose Insert, Interactive Image, Navigation Bar. This launches the Insert Navigation Bar dialog box as shown in Figure 4.41.

4. Type **About** into the Element Name text field.

5. Next, browse for an up image. Locate the file called about_up.gif inside the Buttons folder you downloaded from the Web site. You can locate it by clicking the Browse button to launch the Select File dialog box.

6. After the up image is in place, click the Browse button for the over state. Find the image named about_over.gif.

7. After the over state is inserted, click the Browse button for the down state. Locate the file named about_down.gif.

8. The last state is the over-while-down state, which can be confusing. The way to activate the over-while-down state is also a bit strange, but here it is. If the end user clicks the button and moves the mouse away from the button without releasing the mouse and then moves the mouse back over the button, still without having released the mouse, it triggers the over-while-down state. It's such natural behavior to do that, isn't it? If you think it's stupid, you can leave this state blank. There is a graphic named about_over-down.gif; if you want this state, browse for that file.

9. Next, you must fill out the link. Because you don't have any local files, you can send it to Train Simple's About page. In the text field next to the label When Clicked, Go To URL: type in the following URL: `http://www.trainsimple.com/culture.htm`.

10. Use the drop-down menu to determine which window you want it to open in. The default is Main Window, which works at this point.

11. Make sure the Preload Images option is checked. Your rollover will not become active until all the images have been downloaded. If you don't have this checked, you run the risk of having the end user mouse over one of the images before the other states download, and they'll get a broken image icon.

12. Repeat steps 4 through 11 to include the Products, Locations, News, and Search set of graphics.

13. Also, make sure you insert this horizontally and that you use tables.

14. Choose OK, and test it out in a browser by pressing F12 on your keyboard. Notice in Figure 4.42 that the image changes on mouse over and down.

Some final notes about the navigation bar: if you want to modify it in any way, choose Modify, Navigation Bar. When you modify it, you'll no longer have options for inserting horizontally or vertically, nor will the table option be available. Finally, you must have an element name and an up image to add additional content to the navigation bar.

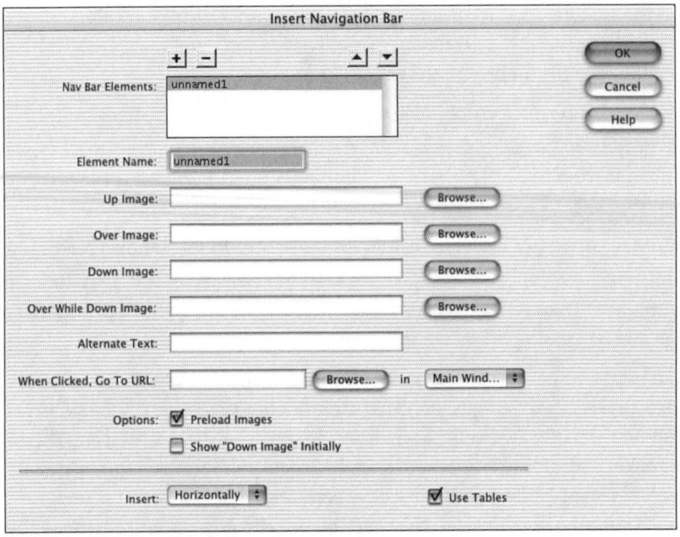

FIGURE 4.41   The Insert Navigation Bar dialog box.

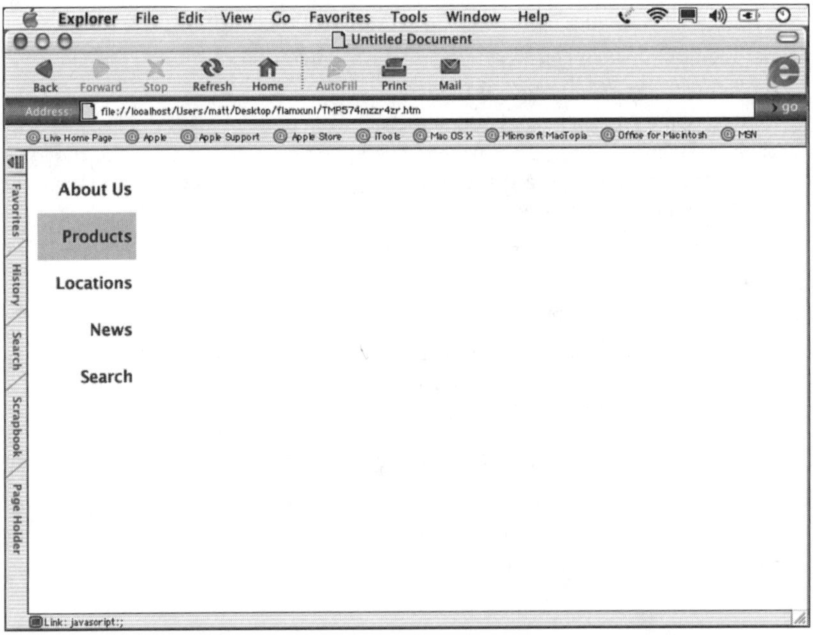

FIGURE 4.42   Notice that the navigation bar is placed into the document and when you preview it in the browser, you can see the different events for each button.

Background Images

Often, designers like to insert images into the background. These images tile, which means they repeat to fill the entire background. If you're clever enough when creating your background image in Fireworks, Photoshop, or any other image editing tool, you can set the dimensions and pattern of the image in a way that it won't appear to the user that it is tiling. You also can avoid tiling when using CSS styles.

To apply a background image, choose Modify, Page Properties. This launches the Page Properties dialog box. In the text field for the background image, click the Browse button and search for a file. After you've chosen one, click OK, and you'll see that graphic tile in the background, as shown in Figure 4.43.

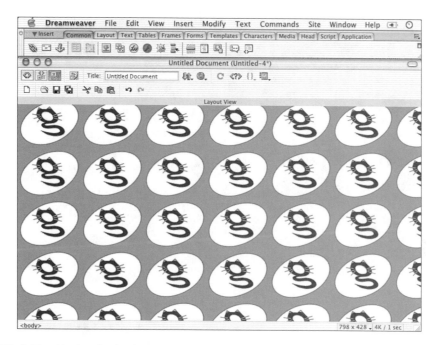

FIGURE 4.43   Notice the background image I've inserted tiles in the background to fill the document.

Image Placeholders

Image placeholders are new to Dreamweaver MX, and they come in handy. They allow you to space things out in your Web site before the actual content is available. Maybe the design team got backed up; now you can continue designing just by inserting an image placeholder. To insert an image placeholder, click the Image Placeholder button under the Common tab of the Insert Panel. This launches the Image Placeholder dialog box, as shown in Figure 4.44. Here you can specify dimensions, color, name, and even alt tag information. After you complete the necessary information and click OK, a placeholder is inserted into the document, as shown in Figure 4.45.

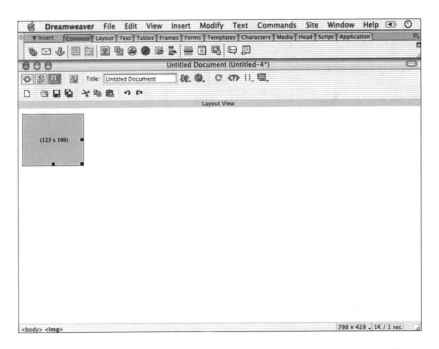

FIGURE 4.44   The Insert Image Placeholder dialog box offers options for dimension, size, color, and name.

FIGURE 4.45   The Image Placeholder is a generic image holding a spot for a real image.

To replace the image placeholder with the real image, highlight the image placeholder and in the Properties Inspector, in the SRC text field, either type in the path to the image or click the folder icon to browse for the file.

Summary

This chapter reviewed some of the basics of Dreamweaver. These concepts lay the foundation for a more compelling, interesting body of work. In the chapters that follow, you learn about tables and frames, which offer more flexibility in your Web designs.

PART II

Static Web Page Creation

IN THIS PART

CHAPTER **5**

Creating Tables

By Matthew Pizzi

Using Tables in Dreamweaver MX

Tables often serve as the backbone of any Web page layout or design. In the previous chapters, you've looked at text and learned how to insert images into a document; however, you had no real control as to how these items appeared on the page. The best way to manage content within a particular document is to place different items into tables. Tables introduce structure into an HTML document, regardless of what you're trying to organize. Whether it is text data, images, or even Flash content, tables will afford you the flexibility to control placement of these elements.

Tables have been the dominant tool for Web layout for many years, and continue to be the layout choice for most Web professionals. Just recently, with the edition of layers and CSS, there are now emerging options for precise placement of content. The W3C recommends using the CSS markup to position and layout your designs on the Web. As it starts to catch on, tables will lose popularity, giving way to these new standards.

With that aside, tables still play a crucial role in site development and design.

There are two modes in Dreamweaver when it comes to creating tables: the standard view and the layout view. These modes behave in different ways, and in different situations you may find one mode more effective than the other. This chapter starts by discussing tables in general and then moves on to the standard view. After you have a solid foundation of tables, you'll learn about the layout view.

Table Terminology

A table is nothing more than a grid to display data, much like a spreadsheet. In fact, tables originally were intended to display spreadsheet type data, but Web designers found them useful to lay out content within HTML.

Some basic options are associated with all tables and I'd like to briefly review some of the common elements and terms you'll encounter when working with them. As I talk about these different elements, be sure to refer to Figure 5.1. This figure is the Insert Table dialog box that you can activate by clicking the Insert Table button under the Common tab of the Insert panel. This dialog box asks you to define the different parameters associated with a table.

> **WARNING**
>
> If the table object under the Common tab is grayed out, you're in layout view. Click the Layout tab in the Insert panel and choose Standard View. This activates the table object under the Common tab.

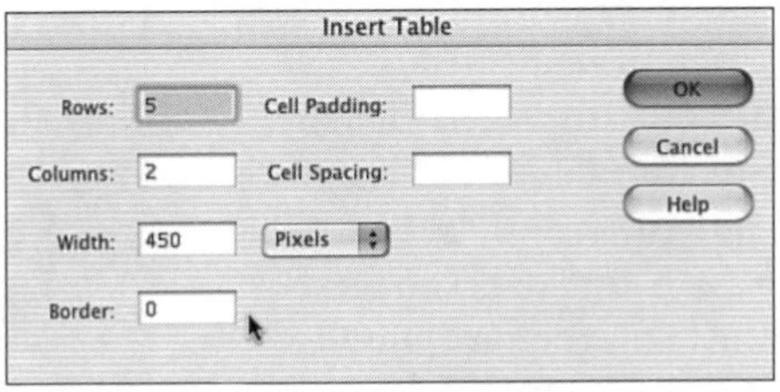

FIGURE 5.1   Set up the initial parameters of the table by filling out the criteria in the Insert Table dialog box.

Following is a breakdown of the different elements in the Insert Table dialog box.

- **Rows**   A row is the horizontal divider in a table. Type in a number value for how many rows you want to appear in your table.

- **Columns**   A column is the vertical divider in a table. When columns and rows intersect, a cell is formed. Type in a number for how many columns you want in your table.

- **Width**   This option determines how wide the table will be. Use the drop-down menu to choose between a pixel value and a percentage.

- **Border**   Here you can determine at what pixel size your table border should appear. If you prefer not to have a border, type in **0** for the value. Keep in mind that borders are displayed differently in different Web browsers, so perform adequate testing when creating tables with borders.

- **Cell Padding**   Cell padding is much like a cushion around the interior wall of the cell. Enter in a pixel value for how much space you want between the cell wall and the cell's contents.

- **Cell Spacing**   Type in a value to determine how many pixels each cell will be spaced.

You'll be using this dialog box later in this chapter when you begin inserting tables into your documents.

How the HTML Works

Yes, I know the beauty of Dreamweaver is not having to know how the HTML works. However, when it comes to debugging strange behavior, or undesired effects, the best way to fix it is to look at and adjust the HTML code. Now you don't have to master HTML; you just need to know what tags to look for if you are debugging the code.

When tables are created, several tags are associated with it. The first and possibly the most obvious is the <table> tag. The table tag lets the browser know that a table needs to be rendered on the screen and can contain attributes such as border and width. Then each component of the table also needs tags. The components I'm talking about are columns, rows, and cells. After the <table> tag has been established, the next thing a table needs is a row. A row is created by the <tr> or table row tag. Attributes exist that can be placed within the table row tag, such as horizontal and vertical alignment as well as background color. After a row has been established, cells can be formed with the use of the <td> table data tag. A table data tag is a bit more abstract; it's not a column tag. A table column is generated based on the number of <td> tags within a set of <tr> table row tags. Look at the following code for a table with three columns and three rows:

```
<table border="1" width =100%>
 <tr>
 <td> </td>
 <td> </td>
 <td> </td>
 </tr>
 <tr>
 <td> </td>
 <td> </td>
 <td> </td>
 </tr>
 <tr>
 <td> </td>
 <td> </td>
 <td> </td>
 </tr>
</table>
```

> **NOTE**
>
> The nonbreaking space code between the `<td>` table data tags is to prevent browsers from collapsing the column.

The table generated by this code is pictured in Figure 5.2.

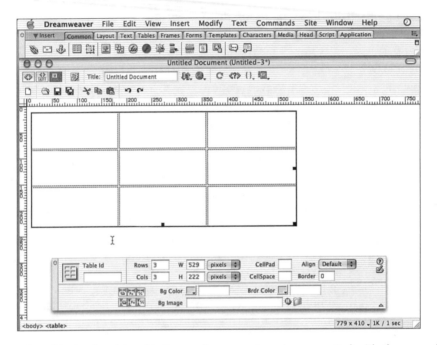

FIGURE 5.2   This simple table with three columns and rows was created with the preceding code.

Headings and Captions

A few more tags are associated with tables that you should be aware of: the caption and heading tags. Caption tags enable you to create a small caption underneath the table. Dreamweaver doesn't offer a caption option, so if you want to create a table caption, you'll have to manually type the code in code view. The tag should be placed after the initial `<table>` tag. The `<caption>` tag can have attributes for horizontal and vertical alignment.

A table header is denoted by a special table tag called the `<th>` table header tag. It is designed to automatically format the cell with bold centered text.

Inserting and Working with Tables

Now that you have a good idea as to what a table is and what it's used for, let's start working with them. I want to talk specifics when it comes to working with the different options and how these options will affect the appearance of your table. You can insert a table by choosing Insert, Table to launch the Insert Table dialog box—the same one you looked at earlier. Most of the settings are self-explanatory; however, what's not self-explanatory is how they directly affect the table. This is very important because if you get undesired effects with your table, your entire design can be compromised. You can enter in how many rows and columns you want your table to have. If you're not sure, just guess; it's an easy change later on. Border, cell spacing, and cell padding are all personal preferences. How much space do you need in and around your cell? Do you want a border, and if so, how big or thick do you want the border lines to be? Again, these are easy changes later on if you're not sure right now. All these options—borders, spacing, padding, number of columns, and number of rows—are inside the Properties Inspector; to get there, choose OK and exit this dialog box and then enter the document. Refer to Figure 5.3 to see the options inside the Properties Inspector.

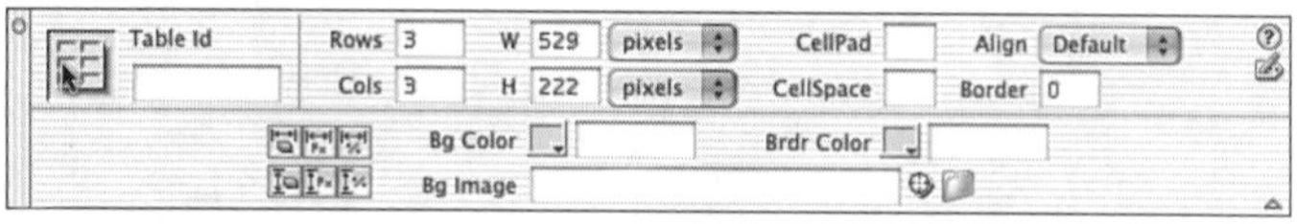

FIGURE 5.3   Many of the initial table setup options are available in the Properties Inspector.

The option I haven't talked about yet is the width. This is the one that can be tricky.

Pixel or Percentage-Based Width?

This is a decision you'll have to make. There is no right or wrong answer, but it will help if you set up some goals for how you want your site to appear in a Web browser. Then you can determine whether you want to use pixel or percentage-based tables. Let's look at one versus the other; each has great advantages and disadvantages. There may even be cases where you use a combination of both.

Percentage-Based Tables

Percentage-based tables are often referred to as stretchy tables or relative-sizes tables because the table will maintain a percentage of the browser size. The table literally resizes itself to always be the percentage you specify of the browser size. If you type in 100%, the table will always be the exact size as the browser window, or if you choose 60%, it will always be 60% of the browser window size. As with any rule, there is always the exception. There are a couple of times when percentage-based tables ignore the value you set for it. If you have an image that is too large to be displayed in a scaled-down browser window, the percentage is ignored. Or if you have No Wrap selected in the Properties Inspector and some text is too long for the browser window, the percentage gets ignored again. Refer to Figure 5.4 to see a table fitting in the browser window at 60%. Look at Figure 5.5 to see the same table not being able to scale to the 60% because of the large graphic.

FIGURE 5.4   The table is 60% of the browser window.

FIGURE 5.5   The table cannot resize to be only 60% of the browser window because of the large graphic.

Percentage-based tables have some advantages. They're ideal if you want your Web page to take up a larger portion of the screen when an end user has a large monitor. It's also less likely for an element to not show up on different browsers because it automatically resizes to fit within the browser window.

Percentage-based tables also carry some substantial disadvantages. It's difficult to control the design and placement of content because the table it's contained within can move and resize, thereby moving and resizing your design. That's why its important to have clear goals and a good vision as to what you want your Web site or page to look like.

Pixel-Based Tables

Pixel-based tables are often called absolute-size tables. With a pixel-based table, you can specify an exact size, in pixels, as to how wide your table will appear. This offers an easier design environment because you're working with an absolute value. You also have a higher comfort level knowing that the design will pretty much look the same in most browsers.

Much like percentage-based tables, if you have content—whether it is an image or no-wrap text—if it is too large for the specified dimensions, it will push out the table to accommodate it.

For the most part, problems like the one just mentioned can be avoided with planning. If you create a table with certain parameters, just be sure you have images and other content sized accordingly before inserting them into your table. Refer to Figure 5.6 to see an example of a pixel-based, or absolute-sized table.

FIGURE 5.6   This table is set to an absolute pixel size and will not change dimensions based on the size of the Web browser.

Modifying Tables

After you insert a table, how do you change different properties of it? Most of the options are available through the Properties Inspector, as mentioned earlier. So you know that you can change elements in the Properties Inspector, but let's dig a bit deeper and see how it all works. Because tables are constructed of different elements, namely columns and rows, selecting the table or certain table attributes can be a bit tricky. Next, let's look at how you can select the table.

Selecting Table Elements

There are several ways to select different table elements, but it sometimes can be a hassle. It's not always clear as to what you're selecting. You may think you're selecting the entire table when, in actuality, you're only selecting a cell. Macromedia gives several selection options, which, even though they can be annoying, once you master them, it becomes very helpful.

In Dreamweaver, you can select an entire table, a single row, a single column, multiple rows, multiple columns, a single cell, or multiple cells. Phew! Let's look at the different options in detail.

Selecting an Entire Table

There are numerous ways to select a table with your document. You can tell the table is selected by the options available in the Properties Inspector and if the <table> tag in the tag inspector in the bottom-left corner of the window is bold.

1. Select Modify, Table, Select Table. The table is selected.

2. Contextual-click by right-clicking (Windows) or Ctrl+Clicking (Mac) in the table area to gain access to the contextual menu. In the contextual menu choose Table, Select Table.

3. With a blinking cursor placed somewhere within the table, choose Edit, Select All or press Command+A (Mac) or Ctrl+A (Windows).

4. Click the <table> tag in the tag inspector, located on the bottom-left corner of the window.

5. Click any side of the table when the cursor appears as a hand (Mac) or four-way arrow (Windows). Sometimes it can be difficult to get the hand or four-way arrow; you may get an arrow pointing one direction, or even a two-way arrow. These cursors are for selecting and resizing columns and rows. Sometimes it is easier to get the hand or four-way arrow if you move up to the top-left corner and click.

6. Click outside the table and drag over it.

Remember that a table is selected when it appears to have a bold border, as shown in Figure 5.7. The border will also contain three resize handles, which enable you to resize the table by clicking and dragging one of the handles.

Selecting a Row or Column

You can also easily select columns and rows inside of Dreamweaver. Unlike selecting a table, there are no menu commands for selecting rows and columns. However, Macromedia did a great job of keeping this task simple.

To select an entire row, move the cursor outside the table. As you move the cursor closer to the edge of the table, you should get an arrow pointing in the direction of the table, as shown in Figure 5.8. When that cursor is visible, click the mouse once and the entire row or column will be highlighted.

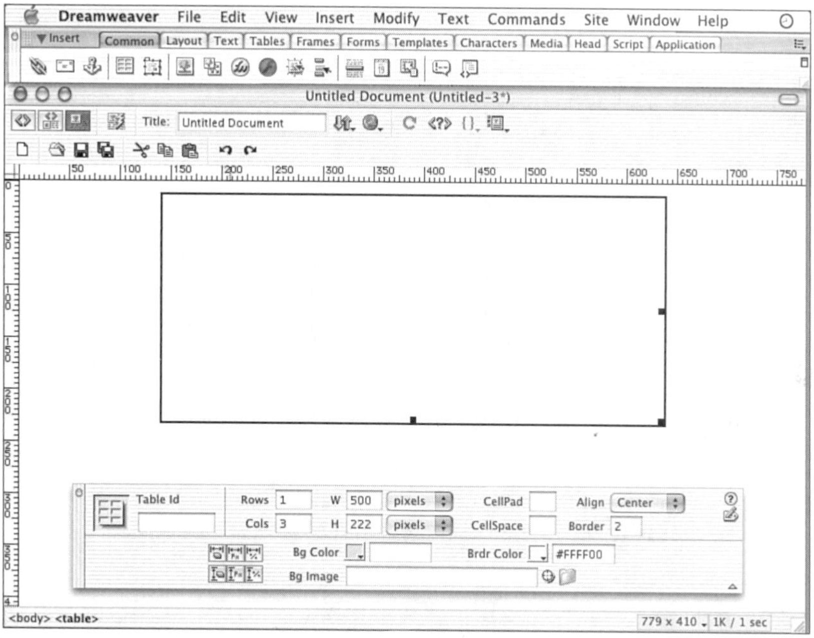

FIGURE 5.7   It's easy to tell when a table is selected; it will appear with a bold border surrounding it. Also, the table tag is bold in the tag inspector.

You can also select an entire row or column by clicking the mouse with your cursor in either the first or last cell in the row or column and dragging to the opposite side of the row or column until the entire section is highlighted, as shown in Figure 5.9.

Finally, you can select an entire row or column by placing a blinking cursor in the first cell of the row or column and then holding down the Command key (Mac) or Ctrl key (Windows) and clicking in the last cell.

Selecting Cells

You may want to modify a certain cell within your table but not the whole table or an entire row or column. Anytime you have a blinking cursor inside a cell, it essentially is selected. If you want to select more than one cell, whether they are adjacent or separated, simply hold down the Command key on the Mac or the Ctrl key on Windows.

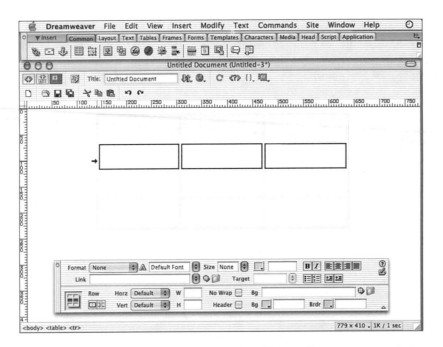

FIGURE 5.8   When you move the cursor outside the table, you'll get a cursor pointing toward the table. Click the mouse to select the desired column or row.

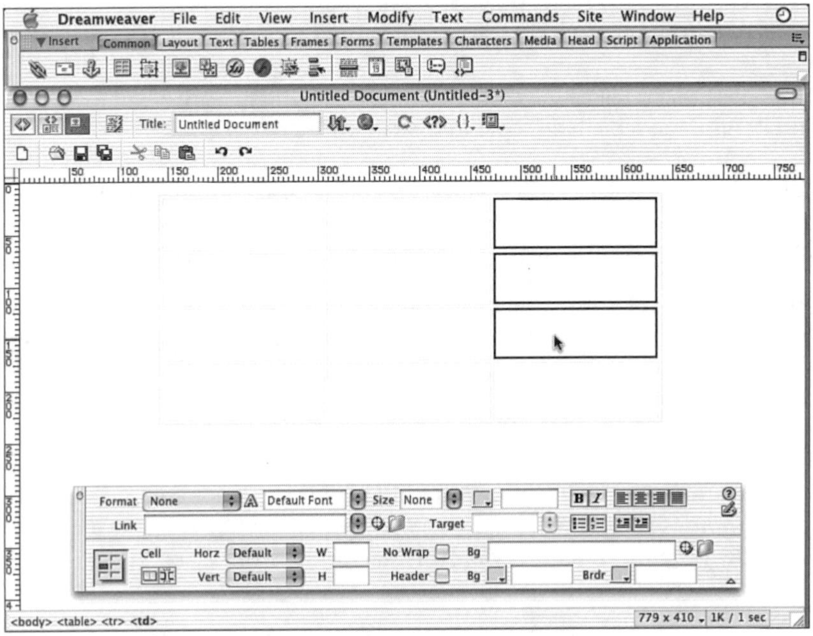

FIGURE 5.9   You can click and drag your mouse across a column or row to select the entire thing.

Modifying Table Properties

After initially setting up your table, you may want to modify it in certain ways. For example, perhaps you'd like another row or perhaps a different background color for the table. All these options are available to you through the Properties Inspector.

Table Alignment

There are three basic choices when aligning tables, which are the same choices you have for aligning anything in HTML. Align left, align center, or align right. There is also a default option, which aligns your table to the browser's default, which is normally left. Remember it helps if you have an idea or goal that you're try to achieve with your Web design. That will determine how your table should be aligned. To align a table, select it, and in the Properties Inspector choose the alignment option in the Align drop-down menu. Notice in Figure 5.10 how the table looks in a browser when aligned differently.

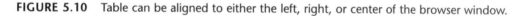

FIGURE 5.10   Table can be aligned to either the left, right, or center of the browser window.

Working with Table Borders

Table borders can be modified from the original size and color. The border thickness is a global attribute; however, you can change the border color of any particular cell.

To change the border size, select the table by choosing Modify, Table, Select Table. In the Properties Inspector, type in a value for the border size and keep in mind the value is based on pixels. Type in **0** if you don't want a border. If you plan on using a border with your tables, keep in mind that Netscape and Internet Explorer each render the border a bit differently. Refer to Figure 5.11 to see the difference between the border's appearance. In this example, I'm using a border size 15, which is really big; I want the borders to be clear in the figures.

With the table still selected, notice in the Properties Inspector that there is an option for border color. If you use the swatch to select a color, the entire table's border changes to reflect the color that you selected.

You can also change the border around an individual cell. Simply place a blinking cursor within that cell, and you'll notice a border color option as well in the Properties Inspector. Choose a different color by using the swatch. After you select a new color, it will automatically be reflected in your document. The cell border color overrides the table border color.

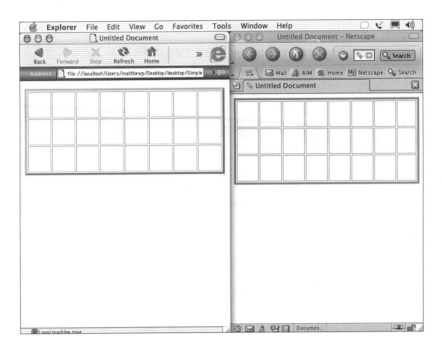

FIGURE 5.11   Notice how the border appears differently in Netscape from the way it appears in Internet Explorer.

Background Color and Images

You can set a color or background image for the background of the entire table or for individual cells. You may find that either of these techniques will help with the design of your page.

Setting the Background of a Table

With the table selected, in the Properties Inspector notice an area labeled Bg Color with a small inkwell next to it. If you click in the inkwell, a Web-safe color swatch pops open. Choose any one of the colors within the swatch, or type a hexadecimal value into the text field located toward the top of the swatch. After it's been selected, you'll see the background of your table automatically reflect the new color.

With the table still selected, notice that underneath the Bg Color option is a Bg Image option. In this text field, you can type in a path to an image in your local root folder or click the folder icon to search for an image. After you've completed that task, the image you selected will tile across the background of the table, as shown in Figure 5.12.

Setting the Background of a Cell

You can also set the background color or a background image of individual cells. Place a blinking cursor inside the cell you want to modify to select it. With the blinking cursor in the cell, you'll see the Bg Color option in the Properties Inspector. Use this swatch to select a color. After you select a color, it automatically overrides any background settings of the table, as shown in Figure 5.13.

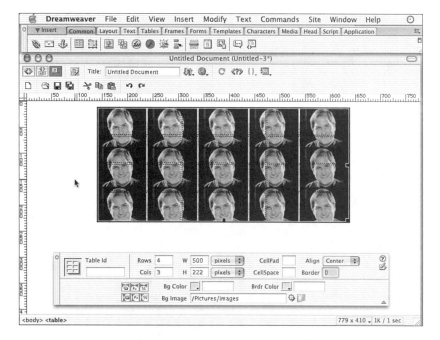

FIGURE 5.12 You can place an image into the background of the table.

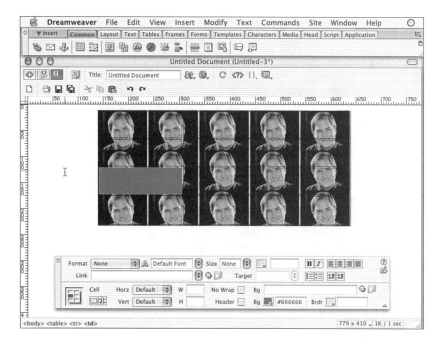

FIGURE 5.13 After you set a background color for a cell, it appears over any background color or image the table uses.

The same goes for background images. You can easily set a background image for a cell by using the Properties Inspector. You can either type in a path to the image file, or you can click the folder icon to the right of the text field and search the hard drive for the image. The image used by the cell will appear over any background settings used by the entire table.

Adding and Deleting Rows and Columns

After inserting your table initially into the document, you may decide you want to change the number of columns and rows your table has. If you were hand coding, this could end up being a nightmare, but with Dreamweaver it's a breeze.

The way you add and delete columns is very similar. Suppose, for example, you wanted to add an additional row or column. One thing you could do is select the table and in the Properties Inspector, type in a new value for how many rows and columns you want. This automatically adds the amount of rows you wanted to the bottom of the table and the amount of columns to the right of the table. If you had an extra row or column at either the bottom or right side of the table, all you have to do is decrease the number of rows and columns by the extra number and they'll automatically be removed. Well, this is great—but what if the columns and rows you wanted to add weren't at the bottom or right of the table; what if you wanted to add a column straight down the middle of the table? Fear not, the process is just as easy.

Inserting Rows and Columns

Suppose, for example, you had a table with six columns and you wanted to add a seventh. When you add the new column, you want it to appear between the third and forth column. To do this, place a blinking cursor in any cell of the third column. Next, choose Modify, Table, Insert Column, which automatically inserts a column to the right of the selected cell. You can also choose Modify, Table, Insert Rows or Columns. This launches the Insert Rows or Columns dialog box, as pictured in Figure 5.14. This dialog box offers the option of inserting more than one column or row at a time and placing the new columns in the cells in relationship to the selected cell.

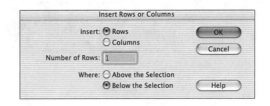

FIGURE 5.14   The Insert Rows or Columns dialog box offers the flexibility to insert more than one column or row at a time.

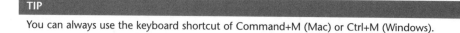

TIP

You can always use the keyboard shortcut of Command+M (Mac) or Ctrl+M (Windows).

Deleting Rows and Columns

If you need to delete a row or a column, it's a bit more straightforward. Place a blinking cursor in the cell of the column or row you want to delete and choose Modify, Table, Delete Row or Delete Column. You can also contextual-click in a cell and in the context menu choose Table, Delete Row or Delete Column.

You can highlight multiple rows or columns and press the Delete key to remove them from the table as well.

TIP

You can easily delete a row by using the keyboard shortcut of Command+Shift+M (Mac) or Ctrl+Shift+M (Windows).

Resizing Tables

You can easily resize any attribute of a table. As you mouse over column and row borders, you might have noticed a two-way arrow. If you click and drag with the two-way arrow you can shift around the column or row.

You can also change the size of a table by selecting it and entering in values for the width and height. Normally, developers don't specify a height unless their design requires it. If you do need to specify a height for the table, keep in mind that the table will resize the height if you add content that will not fit into your specified table size. HTML tables always add room vertically before they resize horizontally.

Clearing Cell Heights and Widths

Sometimes after resizing the table a bit, you may get undesired sizing and effects. This happens to the best of us, but there is a way to deal with it in Dreamweaver. When you resize certain elements within the table, Dreamweaver is assigning values for the width and height of the table cells. Remember that the cells all need to equal the entire width value of your table. If that's not the case, you will run into situations where content is not being line up properly. The best way to deal with this is to clear all values from your <td> table data tags, which are generating your cells. The easiest way to do that in Dreamweaver is through the Properties Inspector. With your table selected, click the Clear Cell Heights and Clear Cell Width buttons, as shown in Figure 5.15. You can also access these options by choosing Modify, Table, Clear Cell Heights or Clear Cell Widths.

Clear Cell Widths

Clear Cell Heights

FIGURE 5.15   Notice the Clear Cell Heights and Clear Cell Widths buttons will remove any values for the width and height of a cell.

Converting Pixels to Percentages

There's a chance when you initially set up your table that you wanted to work in pixels instead of percentages, or vice versa. If you designed or laid out some content, you may think it's too late to switch from either pixels or percentages to the other. One thing you do not want to do is switch what is in the drop-down menu next to the Width text field in the Properties Inspector. If you do that, you could be changing your table from 90% to 90 pixels, which is a dramatic change in the size of your table, thereby ruining any design that you may have. Instead, convert the percent value into an equivalent pixel value. Press the Convert Table Widths to Pixels button in the Properties Inspector, as shown in Figure 5.16. You can also choose Modify, Table, Convert Widths to Pixels. Dreamweaver will do the calculation and change the size of the table to the appropriate pixel value. With the new edition of Dreamweaver MX, you have the option of converting cell heights as well.

Percentage

Pixels

FIGURE 5.16   You can convert the height and width dimensions of a table from pixels to percentage, or vice versa.

Spanning Table Cells

When you're creating tables, you can use an option called Column Span and Row Span. These two attributes enable you to stretch a single table cell across one or more columns or rows. You may want to this because when you're laying out content and mixing images with text, different size elements will require different size cells. You can have a particular cell span across multiple columns or rows, as shown in Figure 5.17.

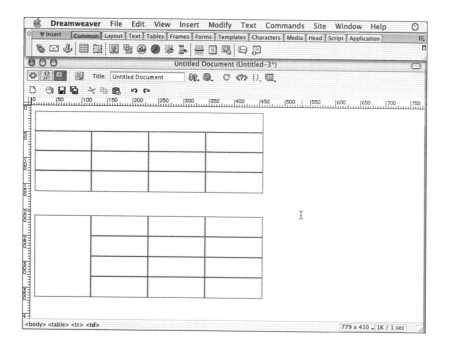

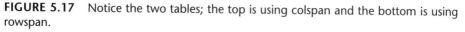

FIGURE 5.17 Notice the two tables; the top is using colspan and the bottom is using rowspan.

To create a Row Span, follow these steps:

1. Place a blinking cursor in the topmost cell of the column you want to Row Span. Row Span essentially combines cells vertically.

2. Choose Modify, Table, Increase Row Span. Notice that the cell you had selected and the cell underneath it are now combined.

3. Repeat steps 1 and 2 as many times you want to increase the Row Span. The keyboard shortcut is Command+Y (Mac) or Ctrl+Y (Win).

Creating a Column Span is very similar to creating a Row Span. To create a Column Span, follow these steps:

1. Place a blinking cursor in a table cell to the left of the cell you want to Column Span.

2. Select Modify, Table, Increase Column Span. The cell you had selected and the cell to the right have been united to create one cell.

3. Repeat steps 1 and 2 as many times as you want to increase the Column Span.

If you decide you want to remove a span, choose Modify, Table, Decrease Column or Row Span. Repeat that as many times as you would like to decrease the span.

Splitting and Merging Cells

You can also make adjustments to spans by splitting and merging cells. This way, you can divide or multiply the number of cells within your table. You can split a cell into different columns or rows. Again this is beneficial when designing pages with content that varies in size or dimension.

To merge two or more cells, follow these steps:

1. Place a blinking cursor into a cell of your choice.

2. Hold down the Shift key and click in an adjacent cell. Continue to do this until all the desired cells are selected.

3. Click the Merge Cell button in the Properties Inspector, as pictured in Figure 5.18. Notice that the selected cells become one.

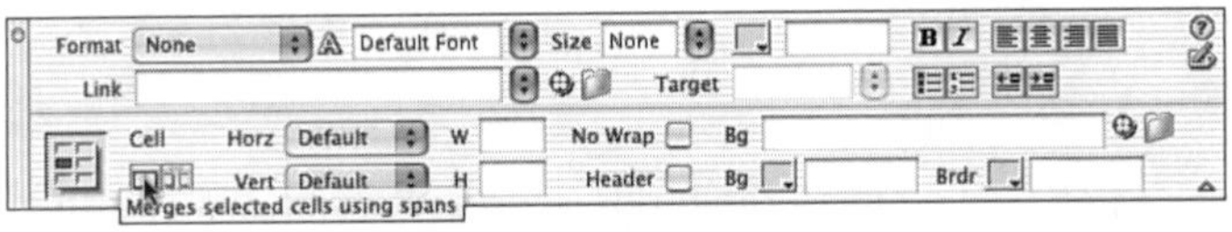

FIGURE 5.18   The Merge Cell button is located in the Properties Inspector.

Splitting cells is pretty much the same process; however, it yields the opposite result. Instead of transforming many cells into one, this option transforms one cell into many.

To split a cell into more than one column or row, follow these steps:

1. Place a blinking cursor into the cell you want to split to select it.

2. With the desired cell selected, click the Split Cell button in the Properties Inspector. This launches the Split Cell dialog box, as pictured in Figure 5.19.

3. Type in a number to indicate how many times you want the cell to split. Also, choose whether you want Rows or Columns.

4. Click OK. Notice the cell has been divided into as many cells as you specified.

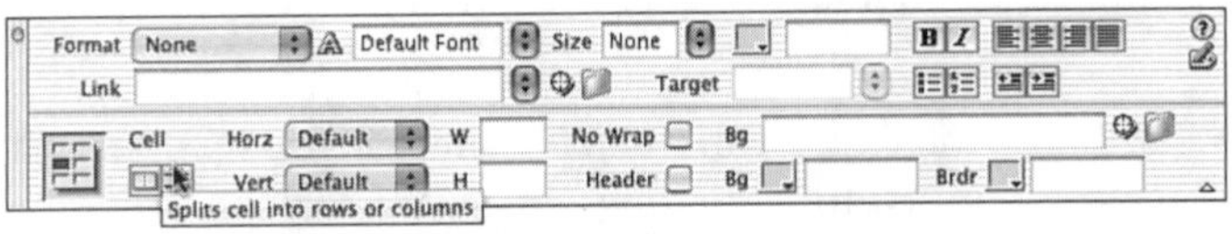

FIGURE 5.19   The Split Cell dialog box offers options for splitting the cell into rows, columns, and how many times to split the cell.

As you add more and more content to your Web page, splitting and merging cells will play a larger role. However, when you start splitting and merging a lot, the table may be a bit more difficult to control. Then you can use a combination of splitting, merging, and *nesting*, which is discussed next.

Nesting Tables

As previously mentioned, splitting and merging cells often can make managing a table difficult. That's why it sometimes makes sense to insert a table within a cell, offering a new set of columns and rows. This technique is called nesting. You can nest as many tables as necessary to get the results you're looking for.

Additional Table Properties

There are some additional table attributes that can help you get results that you're looking for. You have control over the horizontal and vertical placement of content within a cell. Notice in Figure 5.20 that you can use the drop-down menu to the right of the Horz and Vert options. You can align the cell content to the Left, Center, and Right horizontally or Top, Middle, or Bottom for vertical alignment.

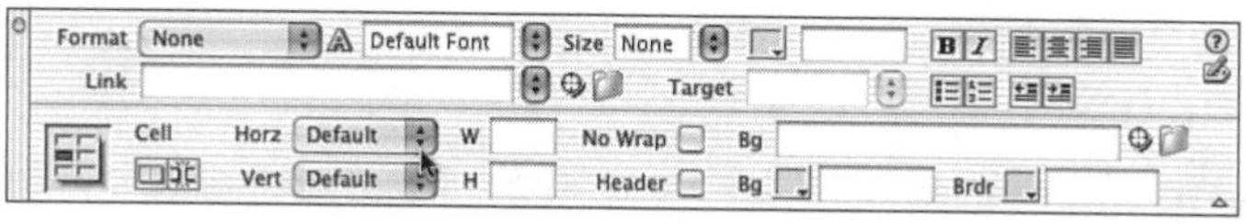

FIGURE 5.20   The alignment options for content found within a cell are available through the Properties Inspector.

Working with Table Formats

When working with tables, you may want to create a consistent design that presents the information in an easy-to-read manner. Often this requires creating a color scheme for your table to follow. Creating color and organizational schemes can become a time-consuming proposition; however, a Table Format feature inside of Dreamweaver offers a quick solution.

Table formats enable you to choose from several presets: Simple, AltRows, and DblRows. The simple format maintains the same background color throughout the entire table, but changes the top row and the left column. The AltRows format alternates the background color of each row in the table. You can choose from eight different color combinations. The last category, DblRows, alternates the background color of every two rows.

As you can see in Figure 5.21, the Table Format dialog box offers several choices for each of the formats. You have the freedom to choose row colors, alternate colors, alignment, text style, text color, and much more.

You can access the Format Table dialog box by choosing Commands, Format Table.

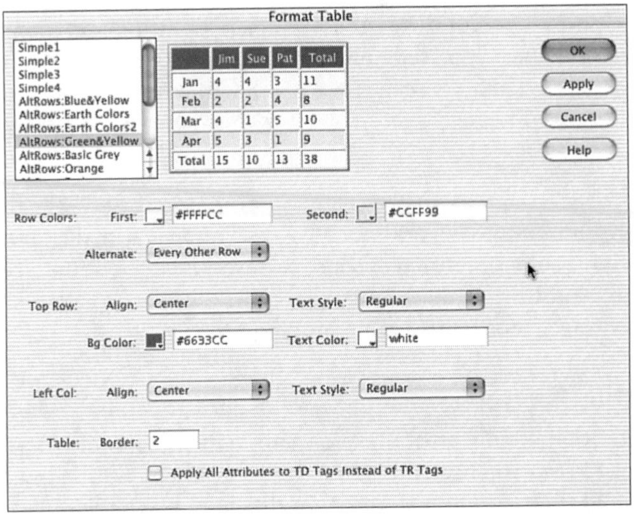

FIGURE 5.21   You can select several options for customizing the appearance of a table through the Format Table command.

Sorting Tables

Many times in Web development, tables are used to display data. Perhaps you have an interest in arranging the data in alphabetic order, or maybe you want to have numbers appear in an ascending or descending list. All this is possible with the Sort Tables command. To sort a table, use the Sort Table command, as shown in the following steps:

1. Select the table you want to sort. The best way to select a table is to place a blinking cursor in one of the cells and either Ctrl+Click (Mac) or right-click and choose Select Table from the context menu.

2. Choose Commands, Sort Table. This opens the Sort Table dialog box, as shown in Figure 5.22.

3. Choose the primary column that you wish to sort.

4. Next set the primary sorting option to either numeric or alphabetic sorting.

5. Choose which order you want the sort to be performed, either ascending or descending order.

6. If you want to perform additional sorts, repeat steps 3 through 5 for the Then section of the dialog box.

7. You might want to select the check box for including the first row, if your table doesn't have a header section. If you formatted your table with alternating row colors, you should check the Keep TR attribute option.

8. Choose OK to perform the sort.

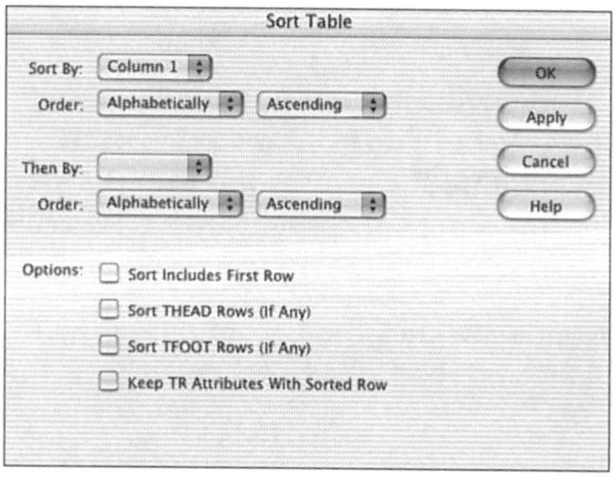

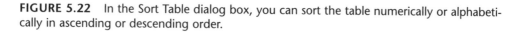

FIGURE 5.22   In the Sort Table dialog box, you can sort the table numerically or alphabetically in ascending or descending order.

Importing Tabular Data

If you have a spreadsheet or database table you'd like to convert to a Web page, you can easily do this with a command in Dreamweaver called Insert Tabular Data. All you have to do is export the data out of the database or spreadsheet application as a comma- or tab-delimited file.

After you've created a delimited file, you can import it by clicking the Insert Tabular Data button in the Insert panel under the Common tab. You can also choose Insert, Table Object, Tabular Data. This launches the Insert Tabular Data dialog box as shown in Figure 5.23. Browse for the data file and set the delimited preferences to either comma or tab and specify how you want the table to appear. Choose OK. All your data will be placed inside an HTML table.

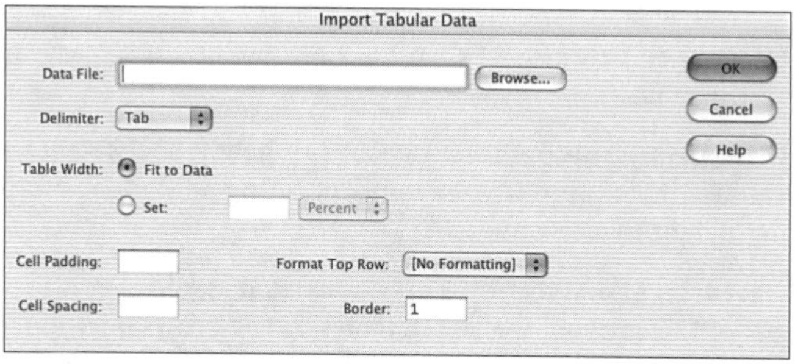

FIGURE 5.23   You can easily import spreadsheet or database files in Dreamweaver through the Import Tabular Data command.

Layout View

If creating tables seems like a tedious, time-consuming task, there is an easier way inside of Dreamweaver to create tables. As I teach Dreamweaver classes, I notice this is one of the top features for people moving from the print world into the Web world. It offers a more intuitive, less restrictive way of laying out content with tables. You can literally draw and position tables and cells wherever and however you want.

To start working in the layout view, click the Layout tab in the Insert panel. This activates two buttons: the Layout Table and the Layout Cell buttons, as shown in Figure 5.24.

Drawing Tables

To draw a table, select the Layout Table button. Your cursor changes into a crosshair. Click and drag out a table in the general size that you want it to appear. After drawing the table, you have a series of options in the top portion of the table window; click the down arrow to access the drop-down menu, as shown in Figure 5.24.

FIGURE 5.24   Several options are available for each column in the design view.

- **Make Column Auto Stretch**   By choosing Auto Stretch, you'll force the column to span across the browser when there is room in the window.

- **Add Spacer Image**   This choice places a transparent GIF image in a cell, which will prevent certain browsers from collapsing the table.

- **Remove All Spacer Images**   This option removes all the spacer images you inserted into the table.

- **Clear Cell Heights**   This option clears all cell height specifications set for the table. You can use this option if you're encountering alignment problems or if you set the wrong height by accident.

- **Make Cell Widths Consistent**   This choice makes all cell widths the same size, which is a benefit when you're resizing tables in the browser window.

Drawing Cells

When drawing cells in the layout view, it's a good idea to have a direction in the layout of your page. The reason I say this is because it's very easy to become sloppy with the layout view. You do want to make sure you're making as few spaces between columns as possible. The cleaner your table, the more predictable your page will look in a variety of browsers.

To draw a cell, click the Layout Cell button under the Layout tab of the Insert panel. Your cursor changes to a crosshair. You can now draw out a cell in any dimensions within the layout table.

When you select a cell it appears blue, in contrast to the table, which appears green. You can resize the cell by dragging any one of the resize handles. You can also drag and move the cell into a new location by clicking and dragging the border, without dragging a handle.

You cannot draw a cell in or on top of another cell; however, you can draw a table within the cell. You may want to create a nested table and that's the best way to do it.

Modifying Layouts

When you want to modify layout cells, in terms of Height and Width alignment, you'll find that it's a good idea to use both the standard view as well as the design view when creating tables. Some of the alignment options are available only in the standard view.

You may also want to consider merging a series of empty cells in the standard view to make a cleaner table than what the design view is generating.

Tracing Images

Many times you will need to create a Web page based on an existing design. Sometimes this design will be in print, and you'll have to make a Web version of it, or someone, or yourself could make a mock site in Photoshop. Whatever the case may be, Dreamweaver will enable you to place an image in the background that does not export, but enables you to literally trace over the existing design.

To create a tracing image, choose Modify, Page Properties. In the Page Properties dialog box, browse for a file in the Tracing Image text field, as shown in Figure 5.25.

After choosing a tracing image, you may want to take down the transparency of the tracing image so it won't compete with the foreground graphics that you'll be inserting into the document.

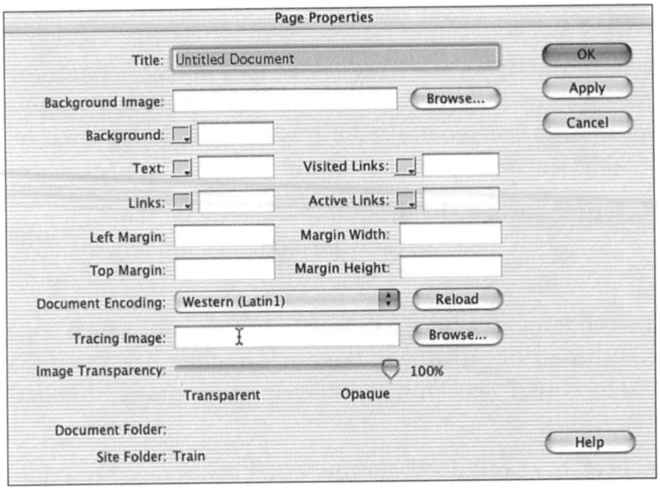

FIGURE 5.25   In the lower area of the Page Properties dialog box, you can specify a tracing image.

Summary

Tables are the key to designing Web pages. Although other techniques, such as layers, are emerging, tables seem to be the de facto standard for Web layout. Dreamweaver offers two very powerful tools for designing pages, and even though one doesn't offer any special benefits over the other, you may find yourself more comfortable with one of the techniques.

CHAPTER **6**

HTML Forms

By Matt Pizzi

Forms are everywhere on the Web; they push development to a higher level, which includes the beginning of interaction with the client or end user. Forms allow the end user to send information, whether it is a registration form, a request to be on a mailing list, or an online order. Forms are the backbone for moving data from a client machine to a server. Forms can get more involved when you're dealing with secure transactions or sending data to a database; these concepts mark a more advanced level of Web production called *Web application development*. Developing Web applications with a variety of middleware is covered in several chapters in this book. If this topic sparks an interest, check out Part IV and Part V of this book. If you haven't dealt with database-driven Web sites before, I urge you to read each chapter in these sections because they provide a solid foundation for these more advanced topics. For now however, we'll keep it on the easier side, but I will discuss interaction with a Web server because ultimately you're going to want to retrieve the data that the end user submits through the form.

Inserting a Form in Dreamweaver MX

You can insert a form into your document just like any other Dreamweaver object. Be sure to have the Forms tab selected in the Insert panel. You can also choose Insert, Form. When you're inserting a form, a set of red, dashed lines should appear across your document, as shown in Figure 6.1. These dashed lines are called the *form delimiter*. They are a visual representation of the form tag in the design view.

If you do not see the red, dashed lines, choose View, Visual Aids, Invisible Elements. If Invisible Elements is already checked, you may have this visual aid turned off in the Preferences. Choose Edit, Preferences to launch the

Preferences dialog box. Be sure to have the Invisible Elements category selected. With this category selected, make sure the Form Delimiter option is checked, as shown in Figure 6.2.

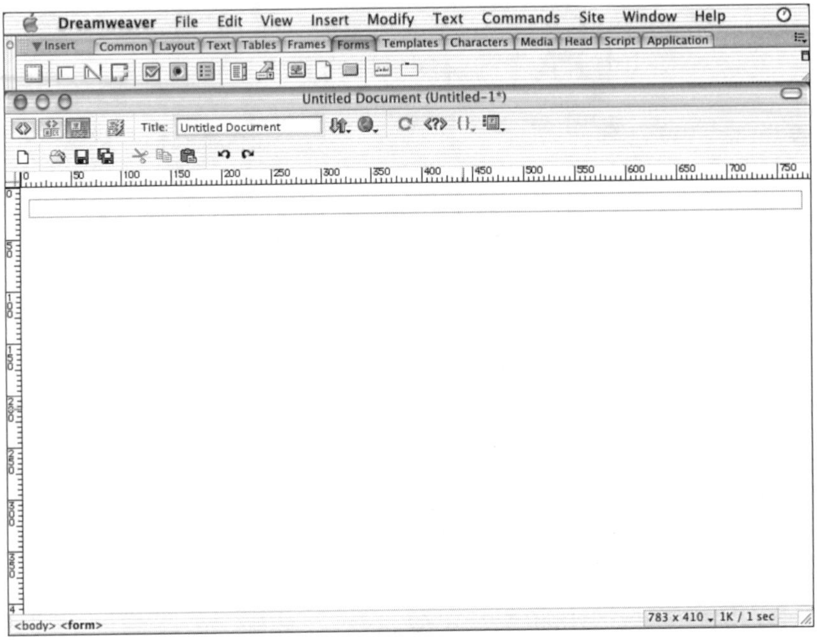

FIGURE 6.1   After you insert a form into your document, red, dashed lines indicate where the HTML form tag is located.

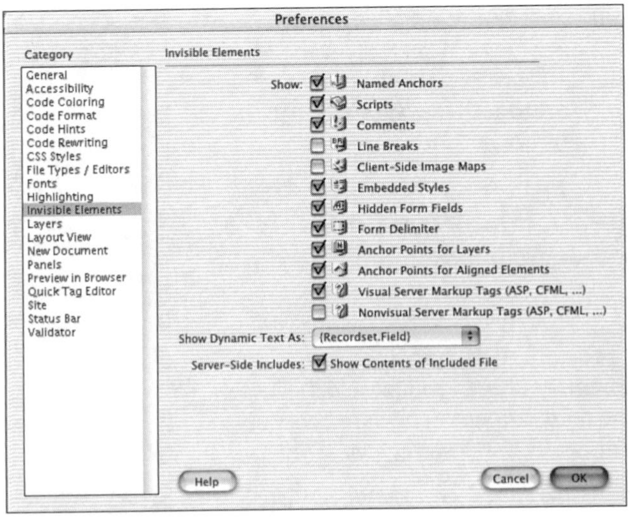

FIGURE 6.2   The Preferences dialog box offers options to show or not show specific invisible elements.

If the Properties Inspector is visible, you should see options for the form. If you're not seeing form options, this means you do not have the form selected. Selecting the form on occasion can be a bit tricky. You can click the dashed red lines, and if that doesn't do the trick, place a blinking cursor within the dashed lines and click the `<form>` tag in the tag selector located at the bottom-left corner of the document.

After you have the form selected, you'll notice that some options become available through the Properties Inspector. The first thing you should do is name your form. By naming your form, it can be referenced by JavaScript or other scripting languages. Because forms provide information and are a way to interact with the end user, developers often use a feature like that to gather information.

There are also options for the form action as well as the method. These topics are discussed toward the end of this chapter. They deal with taking the data from the Web browser and moving it somewhere else.

Inserting Form Objects

When you insert form objects into your HTML document, it is important to keep the objects within the red, dashed lines. If you have several sets of red, dashed lines in your document, that means you have several forms in your document, which will need to have their own Submit buttons. So as you add form objects to the page, if your intent is to have one form, it is extremely important to have only one form delimiter on your page.

You cannot resize the form delimiter; the delimiter expands as form objects are inserted between them. It's also worth noting that the delimiter or red, dashed lines will not appear in the browser. Remember it is a visual aid, so that you as the developer have an idea as to where the form tag is within the document.

After you've placed a form element inside the document, you should name it in the Properties Inspector. It's always a good idea to name all your form objects. Often when receiving data, the data will equal whatever form object it came from. For example, if the end user filled out a text field that asked for his name and the text field didn't have a name, the information, when returned, would look like this: `textfield1=Persons Name`. Now you could probably figure out that it's the end user's name, but not all answers will be so obvious. If you name the form object, it will return more helpful information. If you named the text field "name," the data returned would look like this: `name=Persons Name`, which is more helpful.

If you send information to a table in a database, you might want to name the form object the same name as the column of the table into which the data will be entered. Additionally, you should avoid spacing and special characters in your naming conventions.

Working with Text Fields

Text fields in forms allow the end user to type in information. The end user can enter in any combination of alphanumeric content. As the developer, you have several options when creating text fields.

Text Fields

You can add content other than form objects into the document. For example, before you insert a text field, you may want a label in the document to let the end user know what information the proceeding text field is looking for.

To insert a text field, be sure to have the Forms tab selected in the Insert panel. Here, you can click the Insert Text Field button, but first be sure to have a blinking cursor in your document showing where you want the text field to appear, which should be somewhere with the red, dashed lines. You can also choose Insert, Form Objects, Text Field. This will place a text field inside the red, dashed lines, as shown in Figure 6.3. If you get an alert message asking you to add a form tag, as displayed in Figure 6.4, this means your blinking cursor was outside the form delimiter. If you already have a form delimiter, choose No, replace your blinking cursor, and insert the text field again.

> **TIP**
>
> The warning dialog box pictured in Figure 6.4 offers the option to not show this message again. I recommend not checking this, because this is a helpful warning message. Often, you're not going to want a new form tag, and if Dreamweaver is about to create one, it's best if you know first.

After inserting the text field, and with it selected, notice the different options available for the text field in the Properties Inspector, as shown in Figure 6.5.

The first thing you should do is type in a name for this form object in the Properties Inspector. You should name it so that it corresponds to the information you're looking for. Also, notice there are Character Width and Max Characters options. The Character Width option is the size in which the text field will appear. If you type in a value of 25, the physical size of the text field will be able to display 25 characters. Do not get this confused with how many characters can be typed in or accepted by the field. The end user could still paste a resume, or even worse—a virus, into the text field even though the size is only 25. The text would simply scroll to the side, so only 25 characters can be visible at a time. Often, designers set a character size so that the form can accommodate a design.

If you want to limit how many characters the text field will accept, you must enter a value for Max Characters. This determines how many characters the end users can type. When limiting the characters, keep in mind the information you are looking for from the end users. If you want them to type in their favorite color, a Max Character value can be somewhere around 20; how many color names do you know that are larger than 20 characters? However, if you're looking for someone's name, you may want to leave a little more space.

Maybe the end users will include their first, middle, and last names, and maybe even Jr., II, or PhD. Perhaps a value around 60 is more appropriate. Whatever the case may be, you should limit the characters to some value to avoid unneeded, or even unwanted, information.

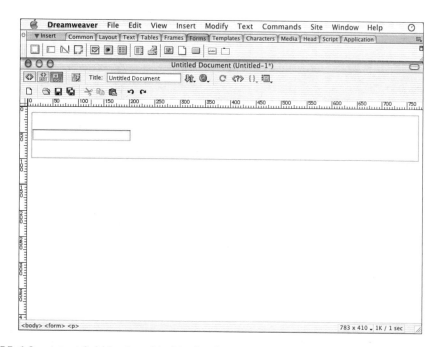

FIGURE 6.3   A text field is placed inside the document that appears between the form delimiter or dashed lines.

FIGURE 6.4   Dreamweaver warns you by asking you to insert a new form tag if you try to place form object outside the form delimiter.

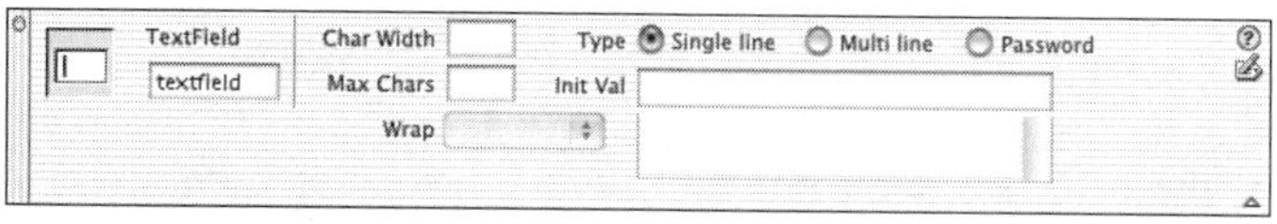

FIGURE 6.5   In the Properties Inspector, notice the options for the text field.

By default, text fields are blank. However, you can type in an initial value. If the information you wanted the end user to enter was a name, you might want the initial value to be something like "Please type your name." Then when the form is loaded, that text will already be in the text field, as shown in Figure 6.6. In many cases, developers do not like having an initial value in a text field, especially if they want to validate the form to make sure all form objects have been filled out or completed by the end user. If values are already inside the form objects, it's very difficult to check such a thing.

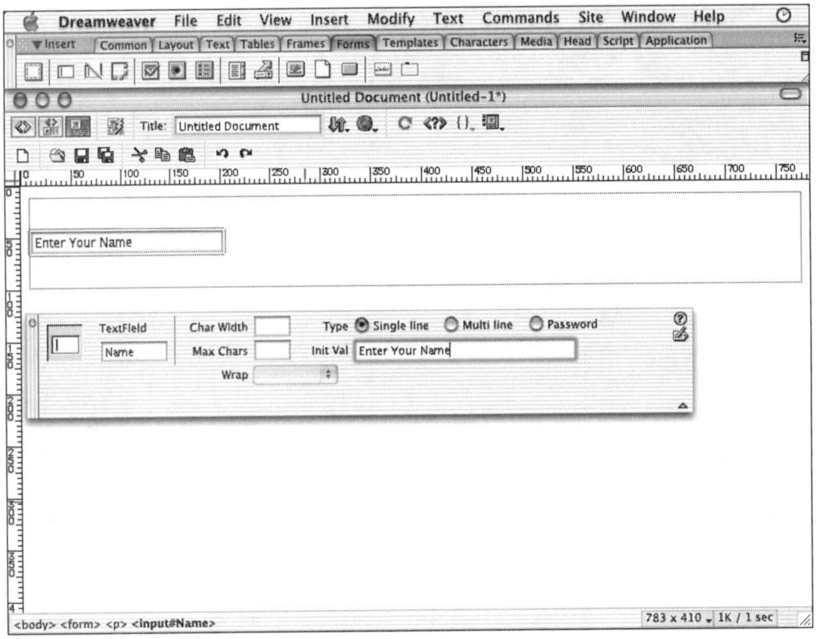

FIGURE 6.6   This text field has an initial value that appears inside the text field.

Password Text Boxes   A password text box is slightly different from a traditional text field. In a typical text field, the information typed by the end user is what is displayed in the text field onscreen. This is called echoing. In some situations, you may prefer the information not to be echoed—in the case of a password, for example. To do this, select the Password option in the Properties Inspector. With that option selected, when the end user types in the text field, the text appears as an asterisk (*) in Windows and a (•) bullet on Macintosh.

Only single-line text fields can have the Password option applied to them. It's also important to note that this option in no way encrypts the data. It's just a precaution from prying eyes when you're typing onscreen. After the data is sent, the Web administrator, or whoever looks at the data, will see whatever is typed into a password field as normal text.

Multiline Text Fields   Multiline text fields are an extension of the single-line text field. They pretty much behave the same way; they just offer an area for a user to enter more detailed information. Many form objects use the <input> tag, whereas a multiline text field uses a <textarea> tag. You can get a multiline text field into your document in a couple of ways. The first way is to highlight a single-line text field and in the Properties Inspector, choose the Multi-line option. When you do that, you'll notice that some options change in the Properties Inspector: the text field gets larger by three lines and scrollbars appear. The second way to add a multiline text field is to insert it from the beginning. Under the Forms tab of the Insert panel, click the Insert Text Area button or choose Insert, Form Objects, Text Area.

As you insert a text area or a multiline text field, notice the two options in the Properties Inspector. The Max Characters option has been replaced with a Number of Lines option, and the Wrap drop-down menu is no longer grayed out.

In the Number of Lines text field, enter a value for how many lines you want the text area to have. Three is the default, but you can add as many as necessary.

The next option is Wrap, and the selected option is default. This option changes the way text behaves in the multiline text field. When the end user is typing into the text field and types as far right as possible, instead of the cursor automatically advancing down to the next line, the box will scroll horizontally. For the text to move down to the next line, the end user has to press Return (Mac) or Enter (Windows) on the keyboard. To get the effect you desire, choose one of these four options:

- **Default**   This option will not insert the Wrap attribute in the <textarea> tag. Therefore, the way this text will behave in the text field is determined by the end user's browser preferences.

- **Off**   If you choose Off, the text will not wrap within the multiline text field.

- **Virtual**   This option will wrap the text on the computer screen. However, when the data is submitted, the information will be submitted as a single-line string.

- **Physical**   Choose this option if you want the data to wrap when submitted as well as having it wrap in the browser.

Working with Check Boxes and Radio Buttons

Often when working with forms, the developer is looking for specific information from the end user. Instead of creating a series of text fields for users to answer questions using their own words, you can offer various choices. This works out best for both parties: It's faster and easier for the end user to answer the questions, and the developer gets specific information. You can offer these choices in a couple of ways, but let's first look at check boxes and radio buttons.

Inserting Check Boxes   Check boxes are the ideal solution if you're looking for an answer to a specific question. With check boxes you can offer a variety of options for the end user to choose from.

To insert a check box, click the Insert Check Box button for the Insert panel under the Forms tab. You can also choose Insert, Form Objects, Check Box. After inserting the check box, be sure to give it a name in the Properties Inspector. If you don't give it a name, Dreamweaver will provide a generic name, such as "check box," which isn't going to mean much. You're also going to want to fill out the Checked Value option. Whatever you type in the Checked Value option is what the check box will equal when the data is passed to another page, database, or server.

A common situation for using a check box is when you have a question in a form that could have more than one answer. Notice in Figure 6.7 that there is a series of options for the end user to choose from.

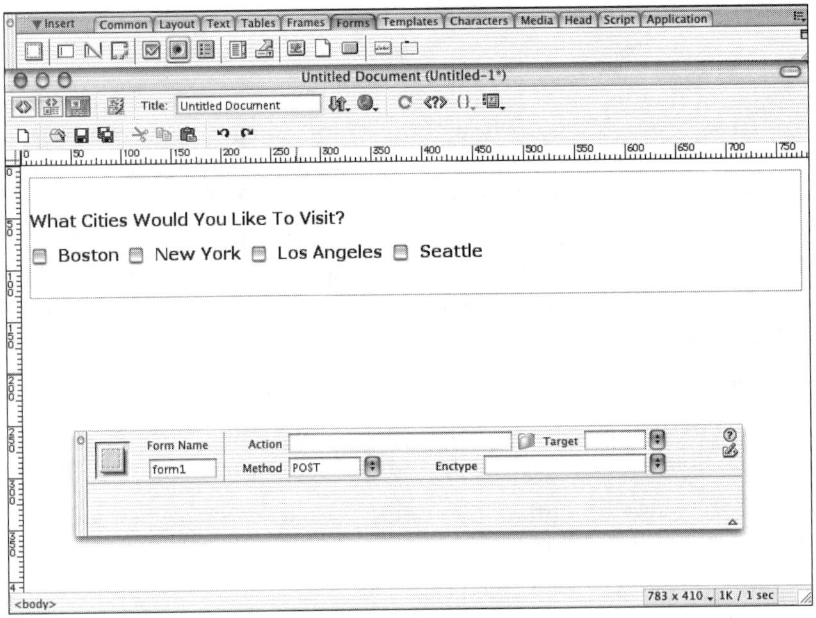

FIGURE 6.7   Check boxes offer the end user the option of selecting more than one answer.

Inserting Radio Buttons   Radio buttons behave much like their check box cousins, with a few exceptions. The biggest exception is that with radio buttons, only one of the options can be selected. When radio buttons are inserted into an HTML document, they should be inserted as part of a group.

You can insert a radio button by clicking the Insert Radio Button button in the Insert panel under the Forms tab. You can also choose Insert, Form Objects, Radio Button. When several radio buttons are inserted into a document and all are options for possible answers to the same question, they must be named the same to make them part of a radio button group. If they are not named the same, they are considered answers to different questions, and more than one can be selected at a time. This makes for a confusing situation for the end user and the person who will be receiving the data. The checked value is what distinguishes the radio buttons from one another.

TIP

If you need to insert radio buttons and name them all, it's a good idea to name one and copy the name. Then, paste the name into the remaining buttons. This will save time and potential human error, such as typos.

By default, none of the radio buttons will be selected, unless you choose the Initial State option. Often, companies automatically have Yes selected to a question like, "Would you like to be on our mailing list?" How nice of them!

A new, easier way to insert radio buttons is to insert them by groups. Again, this will save time and potential errors. The key here is that you must want the radio buttons to appear vertically in the document. If you want them to appear horizontally, you must do it the long way, as explained previously. To insert a radio button group, click the Insert Radio Group button from the Forms portion of the Insert panel. You could also choose Insert, Form Objects, Radio Group. Either way, this launches a dialog box as pictured in Figure 6.8.

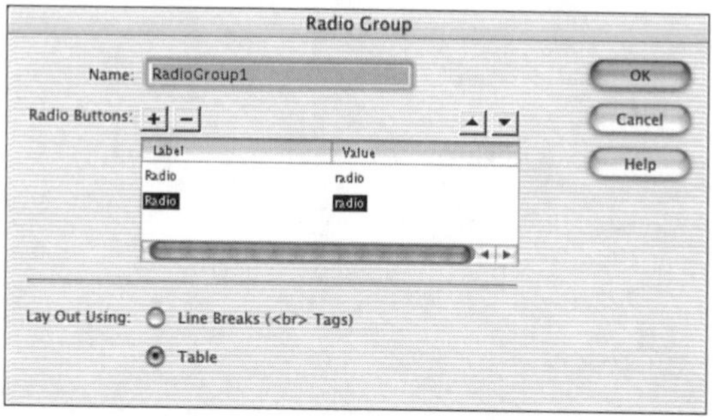

FIGURE 6.8 The Insert Radio Group dialog box offers an easy way to add a series of radio buttons to your Web page.

In this dialog box, you add a name for the radio group as well as the values for each of the different buttons.

Inserting a Radio Group

If you're interested in learning how to use the Insert Radio Group option, follow these steps:

1. Create a new document and save it as Radio_try.html.

2. Insert a form tag by clicking the Insert Form button on the Insert panel. Notice the red, dashed line form delimiter.

3. Place a blinking cursor between the dashed lines. Type in the question: **How many cylinders does your car have?**

4. Next click the Insert Radio Group button in the Insert panel under the Forms tab. This will launch the Radio Group dialog box.

5. For the Name option type **Engine**. Avoid spacing and special characters.

6. By default, two values will appear, labeled Radio, and their default value is also radio. Click to highlight the text to change it. You can change the value the same way.

7. For the first option, type in **4 cylinders** and for the value type in **4**. Avoid using spaces in your naming conventions.

8. For the second option, type in **6 cylinders** and **6** for the value.

9. Click the plus (+) sign to add another label and value. Type in **8 cylinders** for the label and **8** for the value.

10. Finally, choose whether you want the radio buttons to be separated by <br> tags or whether you want them to appear in a table. A table will offer more predictable results. Choose OK.

11. Notice as shown in Figure 6.9, the document now contains three radio buttons with labels appearing to the right of them.

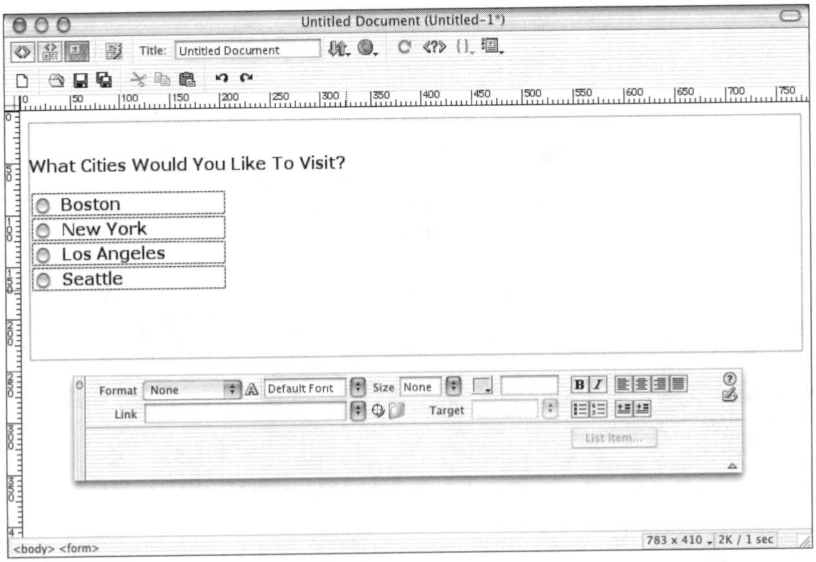

FIGURE 6.9   After using the Insert Radio Group option, the buttons appear clearly named and labeled in the document.

Working with Lists and Menus

Lists and menus provide another way to offer options to a question for an end user. The advantage in using a list or a menu is that there can be many options that will take up less space than radio buttons or check boxes.

Inserting a Drop-Down Menu   A drop-down menu behaves much like a menu system in an operating system, so they're very familiar to Web surfers and ultimately are very user friendly. The menu will generally open and drop downward, unless the menu is too close to the bottom, and then it will pop upward. Drop-down menus allow the end user to select one of the options.

To insert a drop-down menu, you can click the Insert List/Menu button in the Insert panel under the Forms tab of the Insert panel. You can also choose Insert, Form Objects, List/Menu. After the list/menu has been inserted into the document, highlight it. With it highlighted, notice that options are available in the Properties Inspector, as shown in Figure 6.10.

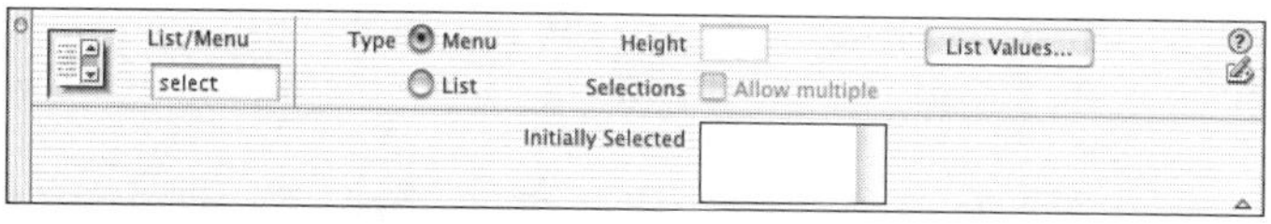

FIGURE 6.10   The Properties Inspector offers options to modify the list/menu.

In the Properties Inspector, be sure to name the list/menu; avoid spacing in your naming convention. For the type, choose Menu. To populate the menu with data, you must click the List Values button. This launches the List Values dialog box. Here you can type in labels and values. Labels are what will show up physically inside the menu. The values, however, are what will be passed to whatever application the form is sending data to.

Here you can type in a label and tab over to the value field to enter a value. Most of the time the information will be the same, or the value will be an abbreviated version of the label. Just be sure to avoid spacing in your label-naming conventions. You can continue to tab over to add additional labels and values. You can also click the plus sign to add more items. If you decide you no longer want an item and you want to delete it, simply select it and click the minus (–) sign.

You can even sort from top to bottom how the options will appear. Use the up and down arrows to rearrange the order of the options. When you are happy with the contents, choose OK. If you need to edit it, click the List Values button in the Properties Inspector to relaunch the List Values dialog box.

Finally, the list will not work in the Dreamweaver authoring environment. You must test the page in a browser by pressing F12 on your keyboard or by choosing File, Preview in Browser, Internet Explorer. Notice in Figure 6.11 that the drop-down menu works just as you anticipated it would.

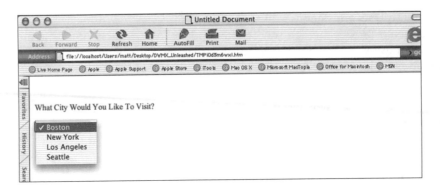

FIGURE 6.11   The drop-down menu in the browser offers all the options you listed in the List Values dialog box.

You can highlight one of the options in the drop-down menu to be selected initially in the Properties Inspector. Removing an initially selected value sometimes can be a trick. In the initially selected value scroll box located in the Properties Inspector, scroll all the way down to the bottom and click in the small white area. This will deselect any options.

> **TIP**
>
> Visit the companion Web site, located at http://www.dreamweavermxunleashed.com to see a QuickTime movie explaining how to create a drop-down menu.

Inserting Scrolling Lists

If radio buttons are cousins to drop-down menus, then check boxes are cousins to scrolling lists. Scrolling lists allow the end user to select multiple items. Developers can also control the height of a list, unlike drop-down menus.

You insert a scrolling list the same way you insert a drop-down menu. Choose the Insert List/Menu button from the Forms tab of the Insert panel.

You can add values to the scrolling list the same way you add values to the drop-down menu. Click the List Values button in the Properties Inspector to launch the List Values dialog box. After listing the values and exiting the List Values dialog box, you need to set up some options in the Properties Inspector.

You should be sure to check the Selections Allow Multiple option. If you're not going to allow the end user to select more than one item, you shouldn't be using the List option; create a drop-down menu instead. I say this because people expect to be able to select more than one item when using a list.

Next you have to determine how high you want the scrolling list. I recommend a value of least 4 because the scrollbar needs an up and a down arrow, plus a draggable box. To condense this in something less than four line heights looks bizarre. Refer to Figure 6.12 to see a comparison of lists set to different heights.

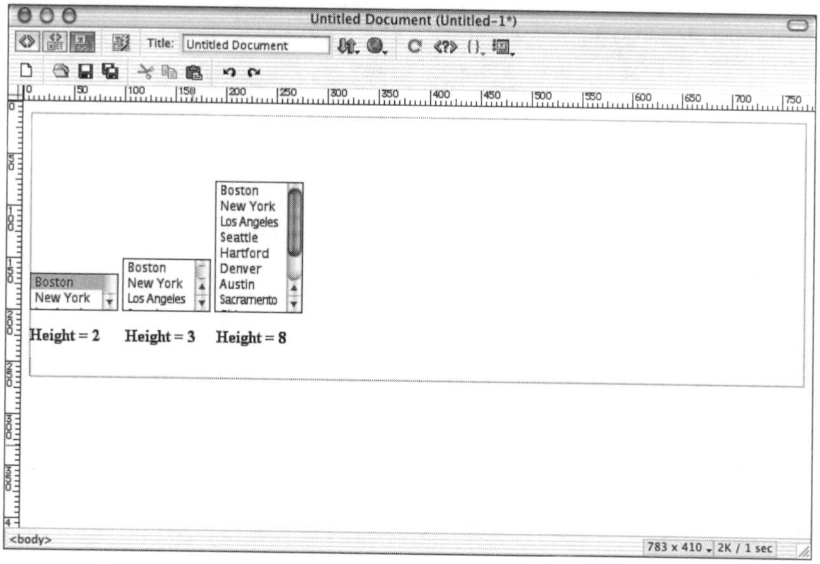

FIGURE 6.12   Notice the differences between scroll lists set to different height values.

When the list is in the Web browser, a user can select more than one item in one of two ways. The Shift key selects a range of values. For example, if you select the top option, hold down the Shift key, and then scroll down toward the bottom to select the last option, everything between the two options will be selected as well.

However, if the end user holds down the Command key (Mac) or the Control key (Windows) when selecting the options, only the options clicked will be selected.

One final note on this topic: the widths of both the drop-down menu and the scroll list are determined by the widest value in the form object.

Submit Buttons
After reviewing the major form objects, you may be wondering how you get this data from a Web browser to somewhere else. The first thing you need to do is add a Submit button. A Submit button sends the form data to the form action.

Inserting a Submit Button   You can insert a button by pressing the Insert Button button from the Insert panel under the Forms tab. You can also choose Insert, Form Objects, Button. After the button has been placed in the document, notice that there are several options in the Properties Inspector, as shown in Figure 6.13. The first is to name the form object and the second is to label it. The label is the text that will appear on the button; for example, if your form was a credit application, you may want the text "Apply Now" on the button, instead of Submit. To do this, simply type **Apply Now** in the label and the button will appear that way in the document, as shown in Figure 6.14.

FIGURE 6.13   Several options are available for the button form object.

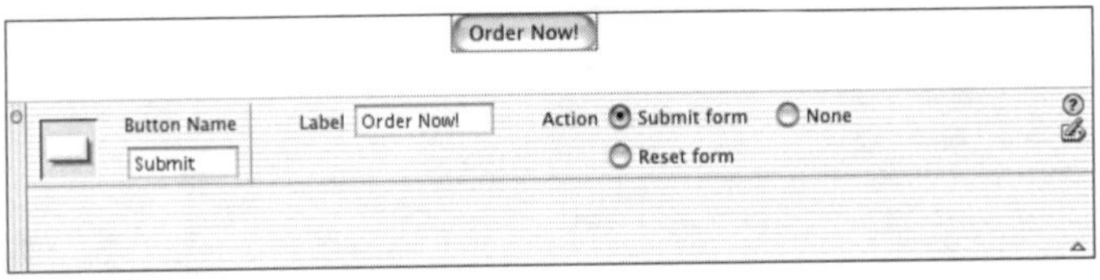

FIGURE 6.14   You can have whatever text you want on the button; simply type it into the Label option in the Properties Inspector.

You must also choose one of three action types for the button:

- **Submit Form**   This is the default action for the button. This action triggers the action located in the <form> tag. You can see the form's action by selecting the form, and the form's attributes, such as the action, will appear in the Properties Inspector.

- **Reset Form**   Use this option if you want a button that will set the form back to its initial state when loaded. Any information that the end user filled out will be cleared.

- **None**   Use this option to change the functionality of the button. The button is often referred to as a command button, which can be used to call JavaScript functions. If you do not add additional scripts to this button, it will not do anything.

Working with Form Actions

Form actions are used to collect all the information the end user enters into the form and process the form data after the Submit button is clicked. There are a variety of ways to process the data, and these are some of the most common methods:

- Write the form data to a database.

- Use the data to search a database.

- Send the information to an email account.

- Perform calculations based on the data input by the end user.

For these methods to be executed, you must couple the HTML form with an action. Actions are typically URLs pointing to some type of script. The URL can point to

- A server-side application page that uses a middleware scripting language such as ASP, JSP, ColdFusion, or PHP. These pages process the form data and commonly use the data to update or search table information in a database and return results back to the HTML page in the browser.

- A common gateway interface (CGI) script written in Java or Perl. A CGI script is also a server-side script that performs a particular action and returns the results of the action back to the client.

- An email address, which gathers the form data and sends it to a specified email account. When the process is complete, the form page reloads.

We'll be looking at the last two items toward the end of this chapter. If you're interested in learning more about the option of using a middleware (ASP, JSP, PHP, and so on) refer to Parts 4, 5, and 6 of this book.

There is also an option for enctype, which can specify a MIME media type.

Form Methods

There are also three options for the method in which you can present the form data to the server. The three options are default, GET, and POST. If you choose default, the method will be set to GET.

With the GET method, the information is sent to the URL specified in the action; however when using GET, the data must be limited to 255 characters. The data is not secure either. The information gathered from the form is attached to the URL string. Therefore, if the form contained private information, such as a credit card number, it would be visible in the location bar of the browser.

GET is commonly used when passing information from page to page in a Web application. Although GET has a downside, as mentioned previously, it is the most supported format. The majority of Web browsers use GET as the default method.

If you're looking for something more secure and don't want character limitations, you should use POST. POST is commonly used when sending data out of the browser without having to pass values inside the form to other pages within the site. The method you end up using will greatly depend on the type of page you're creating and what type of scripting language you're using with the form.

Testing a Form Locally

Here's a trick to test your form locally, to make sure everything is named properly and you achieved your desired results. Let me stress that this is for testing purposes only—you'd never want to post this to the Web.

To follow this exercise, visit the companion Web site located at http://www.
dreamweavermxunleashed.com. Navigate to the Chapter 6 section and download the file
form_test.html. After you download the file, open it inside of Dreamweaver; notice that it
is a completed form, as shown in Figure 6.15. Each of the form elements are named and
labeled properly.

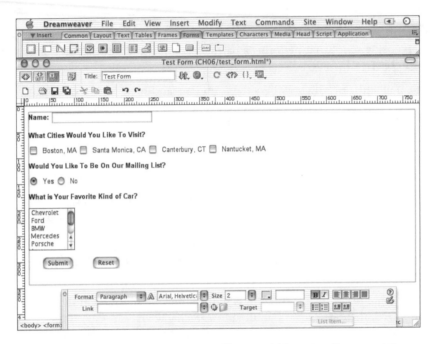

FIGURE 6.15   This file is a completed form; you'll now add functionality to test the page.

Testing a Form Locally

Follow these steps to learn how to test a form locally. Make sure you place the test_form.html
inside your local root folder of the site you have defined.

1. With the form_test.html file open, highlight the form tag in the Tag Inspector to select the
    form.

2. In the Properties Inspector, in the action text field, click the Folder icon to search for a file.
    This launches the Select File dialog box. In the dialog box, find the test_form.html file and
    click Choose (Mac) or Select (Windows). The actions will have the file call itself.

3. For the method, choose GET. When you choose GET, the form data will appear in the loca-
    tion bar of the browser.

4. Test this page in Internet Explorer. This technique does not work in Netscape. Choose File,
    Preview in Browser, Internet Explorer. This launches the browser.

5. In the browser, fill out the form and click Submit. After clicking submit, you'll see the
    results of the form in the location bar attached to the URL string, as shown in Figure 6.16.

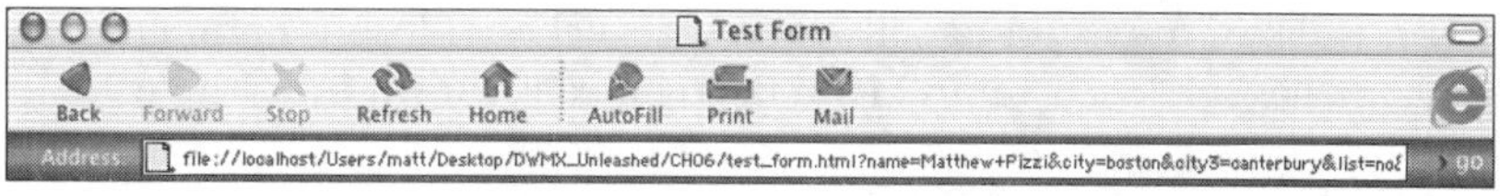

FIGURE 6.16   The results of the form appear in the location bar of the browser.

Additional Form Objects

Dreamweaver has additional form objects that are not used as much, but they add functionality not only to your form but to your HTML documents.

Graphical Buttons

Designers often wish they had more control over the appearance of a form. One thing that can be controlled is the appearance of the Submit and Reset buttons. To do this, you can easily add graphics in place of the buttons.

The easiest way is not to use the Insert Image File option from the Form section of the Insert panel. The best way is to insert an image through the Common tab of the Insert panel. Open the form_test.html file and delete the Submit button. Place a blinking cursor wherever you want the image button to appear and Choose Insert, Image; then search for the image of your choice. When you find the image and insert it into the document, highlight it, and in the Properties Inspector you'll notice a link choice. In the Link option, type in `javascript:document.test.submit();`. If you're adding this to a different form, be sure to change the part of the script "test" to the name of the form you're working on.

Test this page in a Web browser. Notice that the graphic you inserted acts as the Submit button (see Figure 6.17).

If you want to change the Reset button, use this script:
`javascript:document.form1.reset();`.

Label and Fieldset

A label provides an easy way to structurally associate the text label for a field with the field. A fieldset is a container tag for a logical group of form elements.

File Field

The file field isn't used all that often, but it enables end users to navigate their hard drives for a file and attach it to the form, much like an attachment in an email. The File field is a text field with a Browse button as shown in Figure 6.18.

Create Navigation with a Jump Menu

With a jump menu, you can create an easy, compact navigation option for the end user. A jump menu behaves like a drop-down menu; however, when an option is selected the page will "jump" to a specified hyperlink. To insert a jump menu, place a blinking cursor in the location where you'd like the menu to appear. Click the Insert Jump Menu button under the Forms tab of the Insert panel. You can also choose Insert, Form Objects, Jump Menu. This launches the Insert Jump Menu dialog box as shown in Figure 6.19.

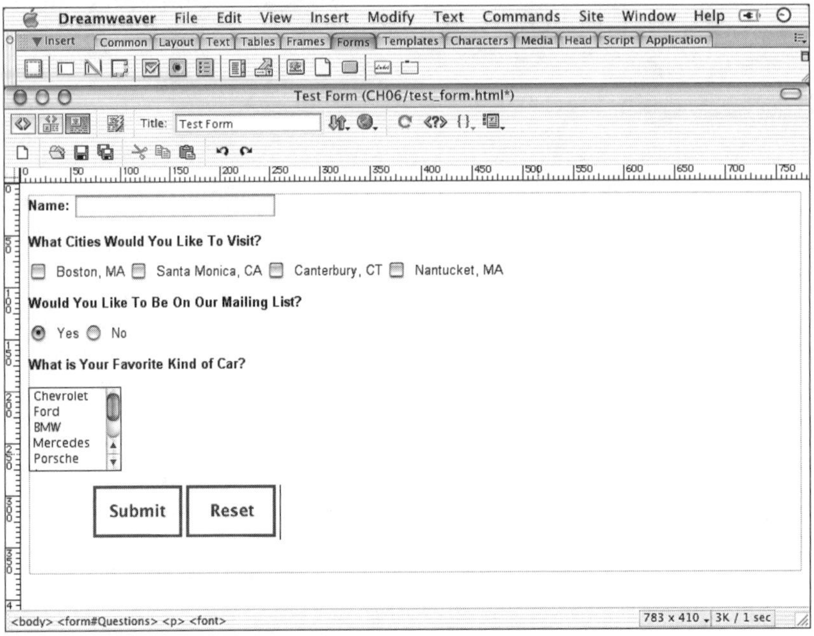

FIGURE 6.17   The form has a graphic for the Submit and Reset buttons.

FIGURE 6.18   The File field allows the end user to attach a file to a form.

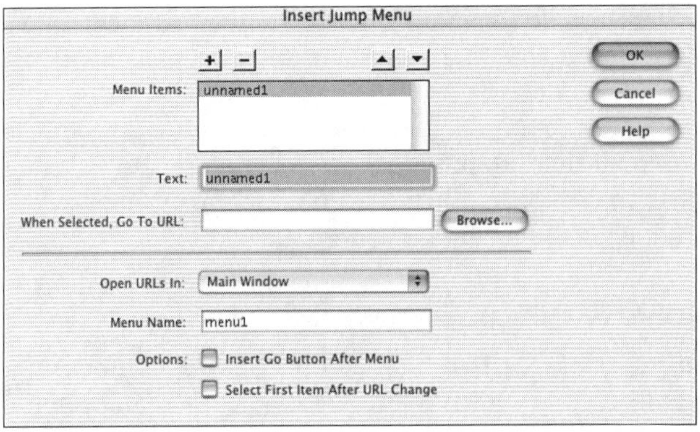

FIGURE 6.19   The Insert Jump Menu dialog box offers options to link different menu items to different pages.

You can add items by clicking the plus sign and adding the label of the menu item in the Text option. Type in the URL you'd like that menu item to link to. You can either browse for a local file, or you could type in an absolute URL.

The second portion of the dialog box offers options for where you want the link to open. You can target a frame in a frameset, in a new window, or in the existing window.

You can insert a Go button, which allows the end user to click the Go button to choose the first choice.

The final option is to have the menu reset after a link has been selected.

You can modify a jump menu a couple of ways. If you simply need to change some of the menu items, you can highlight the jump menu and in the Properties Inspector click the List Values button to open the List Values dialog box.

The second way is to highlight the jump menu and open the Behaviors panel. If the Behaviors panel is not open, choose Window, Behaviors. In the Behaviors panel, double-click the Jump Menu behavior to launch the original Jump Menu dialog box.

Hidden Field

The hidden field is a common way to store information on the page that the end user may not necessarily have to see. It's commonly used in conjunction with CGI scripts. In the last section of this chapter, we'll be creating a form that contains hidden fields to add functionality to our form.

Real World Forms, Building Forms That Work

Now that we know how all the different form elements work, we'll put together a form that actually uses a CGI script and we'll make our form visually pleasing.

The first thing we need to look at is how we can incorporate a form into a structured table. The trick is to make sure the table is placed between the red dashed form delimiter. If you try to place a form tag within the table, you'll only be able to place a form within one cell. A form cannot span across multiple cells, that's why you need to place the entire table between the form tags, this way you can place different form elements in different cells, yet they'll all be apart of the same form.

For the final exercise in this chapter, you may want to download the supporting files from the companion Web site located at http://www.dreamweavermxunleashed.com.

Formatting a Form with a Table

In this exercise you'll create a form that you'll design using a table.

1. Create a new document by choosing File, New. This launches the New Document dialog box. Choose a basic HTML page and click OK.

2. In the new document choose Modify, Page Properties. Set the background color to a gray or black color. Choose OK to exit the Page Properties dialog box.

3. When you're back inside the document, click the Insert Image button in the Insert panel under the Common tab. Navigate to the top_banner.gif file you downloaded from the Web site. Select that file and choose OK to place the graphic in your document. Finally, with the image selected, click the Align Center button in the Properties Inspector to center the image in the document, as shown in Figure 6.20.

4. Next, with a blinking cursor after the banner graphic, press Shift+Return (Mac) or Shift+Enter (Windows) to enter a line break. If you're having trouble getting a blinking cursor in the right location, select the graphic and then press the right arrow key on your keyboard. Then choose Insert, Form Object, Form. This places the form delimiter into your document.

5. Place a blinking cursor between the red, dashed lines and choose Insert, Table. This launches the Insert Table dialog box.

6. In the Insert Table dialog box, type in the following values: 2 columns, 5 rows, 450 pixels for the width, 0 pixels for spacing, 0 pixels for padding, and 0 for a border. Choose OK. Notice in Figure 6.21 that a table has been inserted into your page. If it's not centered automatically, highlight the table and choose Center from the Align drop-down menu in the Properties Inspector.

7. Type questions on the left side of the table. Align the text to the right.

8. Add form objects on the right side of the table. Align the form objects to the left.

9. Name all your form objects accordingly; avoid spacing and special characters in your naming conventions.

10. When the table is completely filled with objects and questions, place a blinking cursor outside the table on the right and press Return or Enter. Underneath the table insert a Submit and Reset button.

11. Save the form as form_design.html. You'll use the form later to add a CGI script, so the form will actually work.

When the table is complete, the form looks well designed, as shown in Figure 6.22. You can also test the form to see how it will appear in the real world.

The next step is to add functionality to this form by sending it to an email account. You're going to do this in two ways. The first way is to send it through using an email client, and the second is by sending it using a CGI script.

Sending Form Data Through Email

Sending a form through email is by far the easiest way. Depending on your site's needs, it may be sufficient as well. To send a form through an email client, follow these steps:

1. Open the form_design.html document you worked with in the previous exercise.

2. With the form open, make sure the Properties Inspector is visible; if not, choose Window, Properties Inspector.

3. In the Tag Inspector, located at the bottom-right corner of the document window, click the form tag to select the form.

4. In the Properties Inspector, for the action, type in `mailto:yourname@yourdomanin.com`. Of course substitute your email address after the `mailto:`.

5. For the method, be sure to select POST. That's it!

6. Test the page in a browser, fill out the form, and press Submit. Check your email!

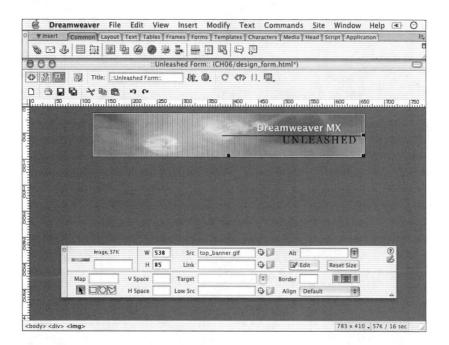

FIGURE 6.20   The graphic is centered in the document.

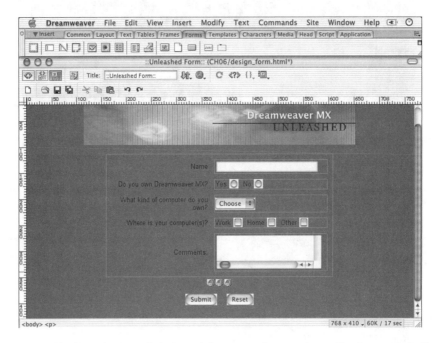

FIGURE 6.21   A table has been inserted into your document.

FIGURE 6.22   The form looks well designed, in comparison to the earlier forms we built.

Sending a Form with a CGI Script

Although the previous method is acceptable, you may want something a bit more professional. A more standard way of submitting forms like the one you built is with a CGI script.

A Note About CGI

CGIs are scripts that get executed on the server side. In the next exercise you'll be using a CGI script, which lives in the CGI-BIN of this book's companion Web site. CGI scripts are typically written in PERL or Java and most hosting companies offer free CGI script in the hosting plan's CGI bin. You can learn more about server-side scripts and how they work in Part IV of this book.

Sending a Form with CGI

In this exercise, you'll be using a CGI script on this book's companion Web site. There is nothing to download; all you need to do is source the CGI script that is located on the Unleashed Web server. This exercise is for testing only and should not be used in a real production environment.

1. Open the form_design.html page. Toward the right of the table, still inside the form tag, insert three hidden fields as shown in Figure 6.23.

2. The CGI script is looking for three variables, and you're going to give those variables values by using these hidden form fields.

3. Highlight the first hidden field, and in the Properties Inspector name it _MAILTO. _MAILTO is the variable the CGI script is looking for, which is going to provide the email address to send the form value to. For the value, enter your email address; for example, yourname@yourdomain.com.

4. Highlight the second hidden field and name it **_SUBJECT**. This is another variable, which is going to add whatever value you enter in the subject line of the email. In the value text field, enter whatever you want to show up in the subject line.

5. Select the third hidden field and name it **_THANKS**. This variable is going to send an HTML page to the browser after the form has been processed. I have created a document that is already on the server, called thanks.html. So, in the value field type in **thanks.html**. You could have a different document, but I'm not going to give you access to my server...heh, so you'll have to use my page.

6. Next, highlight the <form> tag in the Tag Inspector to select the form. In the Actions field of the Properties Inspector, you have to source the location of the script. In this case type this source: http://www.dreamweavermxunleashed.com/cgi-bin/tmail/tmail.cgi.

7. When you're done, preview this in a browser. As long as you have a connection to the Internet, fill it out and submit it. After submitting, the thanks page will appear, as shown in Figure 6.24. Check your email; the form will be there.

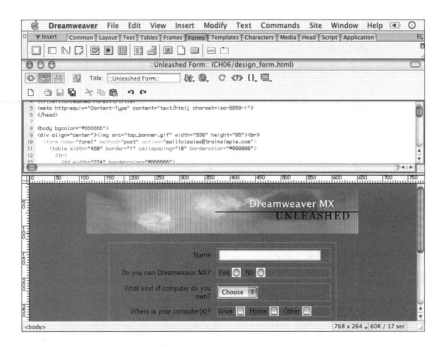

FIGURE 6.23   There are three hidden form fields inserted into the document.

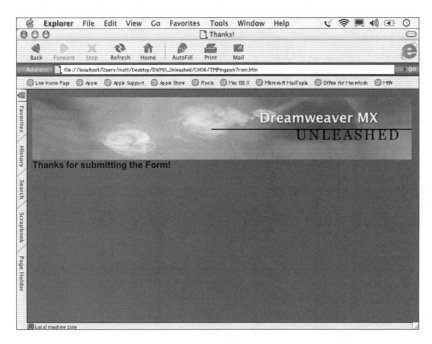

FIGURE 6.24   After you submit the form, the thanks page will appear.

Setting Focus in a Form

In the Dreamweaver classes that I teach, students often ask how they can get a blinking cursor to appear automatically in the form. You have to use JavaScript, but the process is a simple one. Suppose you wanted a blinking cursor to appear in the first text field of the form_design.html. The important thing is to know the name of the text field and to know the name of the form. Highlight each of them to get their names in the Properties Inspector. To set the focus, follow these steps:

1. You need to write a JavaScript that looks like this: `window.document.formname.fieldname.focus()`. In the next step, you'll do just that. You'll place the script in the proper location within the HTML and swap the form name and field name attributes with the actual names found within this form.

2. Click in the code and design view to view both the code source and the design, as shown in Figure 6.25. In the body tag, after the background attribute, type in the JavaScript after an onload command. When all is said and done the <body> tag should look like this:

```
<body bgcolor="#666666" onload="window.document.questions.name.focus()">
```

3. Preview your page in a Web browser and notice that a blinking cursor is in the first text field.

You can download a completed version of this file located on the companion Web site, `http://www.dreamweavermxunleashed.com`.

Summary

This chapter is the beginning of a higher level of Web development. Creating forms to interact with an end user really starts to show the strengths of the Web and offers endless possibilities.

As you get deeper into this book, you'll start having your form interact with middleware, which pushes the envelope for more personal engaging experiences for Web users.

Framesets

by Matthew Pizzi

Framesets offer yet another design option for the Web designer. Frames can give a developer flexible options in terms of structuring a navigation system. The advantages of frames are that they can offer a faster, easier Web experience for the end user.

Understanding Frames

Frames are essentially several documents contained inside one container document, typically called a parent frame. Refer to Figure 7.1 to see an example of four different HTML documents. At first glance, it may appear as if only three documents are in the browser, but remember that an HTML document holds the three together, thus making it four separate documents.

In addition to framesets streamlining the development process, they also streamline the Web experience for the end user. Many advantages exist, both for the developer and the end user, in creating a Web site that uses several HTML documents to present content.

> **TIP**
>
> Refer to the companion Web site located at http://www.dreamweavermxunleashed.com to see a QuickTime movie demonstrating the power and convenience of a frameset.

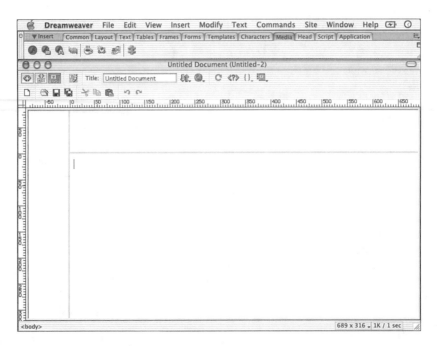

FIGURE 7.1   This document is cut into three sections. Each section is a separate, independent HTML document being held together by another HTML document that you can't see, called the parent frame.

The Advantages

The advantages of setting up a Web site that uses framesets can be profound. All elements that are constant throughout the Web experience do not have to be reloaded every time a link is clicked. It's typical to see an arrangement with a navigation structure on the left side, a logo with a banner ad on the top, and a main area where new pages will be loaded in. Figure 7.2 illustrates a real-world Web site that uses such a system.

By having the new content appear in the larger area, the site can appear more complete. Accessing new documents and swapping them out of the same location saves download time and offers an easier navigation experience for the Web user. Web sites seem very organized when frames are being used.

The Disadvantages

Along with all the advantages frames can provide, they also offer some disadvantages and challenges for a Web designer. The most important of these challenges is search engine placement. Most search engines will view the HTML text of a document to find any keywords associated with ones searched. The problem with this is that the parent document is where the search program checks for the HTML text because it's the document closest to the browser. The other frames or HTML documents are essentially placed on top of the parent, therefore being disguised from spiders and other search applications. Of course, there are some things you can do to help expose content within these documents, which you'll learn later in this chapter.

FIGURE 7.2 The *Titanic* movie's Web site, located at `http://titanicmovie.com/past/tour_index.html`, uses a frame structure with a navigation system on the left and a logo and banners on top.

Another disadvantage is bookmarks. When the end user is navigating through the Web site, the main portion of the document is being swapped out every time a link is clicked, until finally the end user finds the desired content. Then the end user decides to bookmark it or add it to the favorites by accessing the menu. Unfortunately, the page the user was looking at isn't bookmarked; instead, the parent frame is bookmarked because that's the closest frame to the browser. Remember, the frames are essentially inside the parent frame; think of the parent frame as a compartmentalized tray, and each compartment of the tray is a frame. Because the frame is in a compartment, the content is not exposed as a normal HTML document usually would be to a browser.

If the end users are savvy Web surfers, they may know that you can contextual-click the document to bookmark it. However, when they return to the link by using that bookmark or favorite, the surrounding frames will not accompany that document. This can be a disadvantage because users are not returning to your site for further exploration, but to a page within your site with no navigation to other portions of your Web site. So as a developer, you're potentially missing out on return business.

The last disadvantage is printing, for the same reasons as bookmarking pages. If the end user chooses File, Print, the parent frame is printed, which contains nothing but some HTML code.

Be Prepared

Finally, it's important to understand the difference between a frameset and a frame. A frameset doesn't contain any content. A frameset, generally, is considered the parent frame, and this frame has HTML tags that hold the position of the other frames or HTML documents in the Web browser. Framesets in some ways resemble tables because they are constructed of columns and rows. The HTML for a parent frame looks something like the following:

```
<frameset rows= "25%, *">
  <frame src="top.html">
  <frame src="bottom.html">
</frameset>
```

The frameset tag would be between the <body> tags.

This code represents a frameset, which contains two rows: one on top monopolizing 25% of the browser and one on the bottom that is a relative size. The bottom size changes, depending on the size of the browser window, whereas the top remains constant at 25%. Refer to Figure 7.3 to see what this page will look like in a Web browser.

There is also the columns attribute, which inserts an HTML document vertically. An example of a parent HTML document with vertical and horizontal frames could look like this:

```
<frameset cols ="50, 375" rows= "25%, *">
```

Relative options are also available for frame columns, which you will learn about when you get deeper into frames in this chapter.

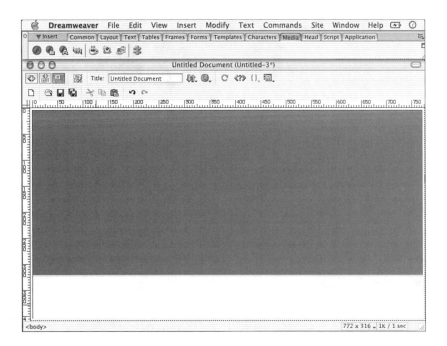

FIGURE 7.3 This page is divided to contain two rows, a top and a bottom row. Remember that a third document holds these together.

Creating Framesets and Frames

Dreamweaver offers several ways to create framesets. The different options that Dreamweaver offers you may be better suited to use in different situations. You'll have to review each of these techniques and decide which one is better suited for you and your current project. You may become partial to one way over the other and find yourself using that specific technique more often than the rest, which is also fine.

Creating a New Frameset Document

The easiest way is to create a set from the predefined offerings in the New Document dialog box. Create a new document by choosing File, New. This launches the New Document dialog box. In the dialog box choose the frameset category, as shown in Figure 7.4.

In the framesets column, choose the layout you prefer. On the right side you'll get a preview of what the frameset will look like as well as a description. When you're happy with your choice, click the Create button. This creates a new document in the appropriately divided frameset.

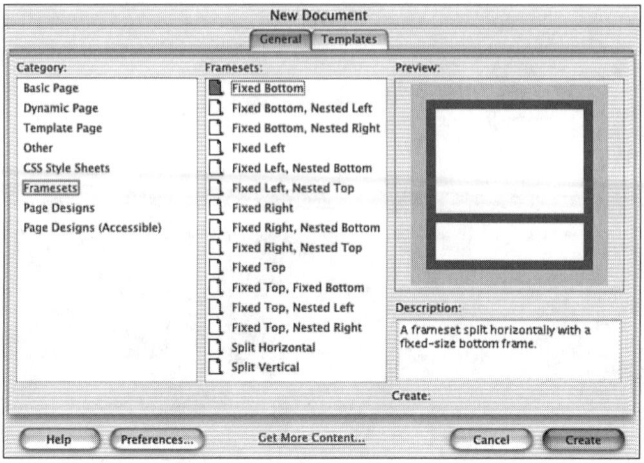

FIGURE 7.4   The New Document dialog box offers several options for creating new documents based on framesets.

Create a New Frameset with Menus and the Mouse

If you already have a document open and then decide you want to work with framesets, you can always add one after the fact. The first thing you need to do is choose Modify, Frameset, Split Right (you also have options for left, up, or down) as shown in Figure 7.5. This divides the page visually to represent the direction you asked Dreamweaver to split the page; in this case, it splits the page in two, as shown in Figure 7.6.

Creating Additional Frames

To create additional frames, make sure your frame borders are visible by choosing View, Visual Aids, Frame Borders. You can then click any of the frame borders that surround the document and hold down the Option (Mac) key or Alt (Windows) key while dragging. I'm going to click and drag down from the top of the document. This creates another split, dividing the document into additional separate frames as pictured in Figure 7.7.

Using the menu and the mouse will offer you the freedom to make framesets after you've already inserted a document. However, this is my least favorite way to create a frameset; I find that this way creates more problems later as I develop, yet that is my personal experience. You may like this way just fine.

Create a Frameset with the Insert Panel

Again, if you already have a document open, you can insert a frameset after the fact. Under the Frames tab of the Insert Panel, there's a series of predefined framesets you can create, as shown in Figure 7.8.

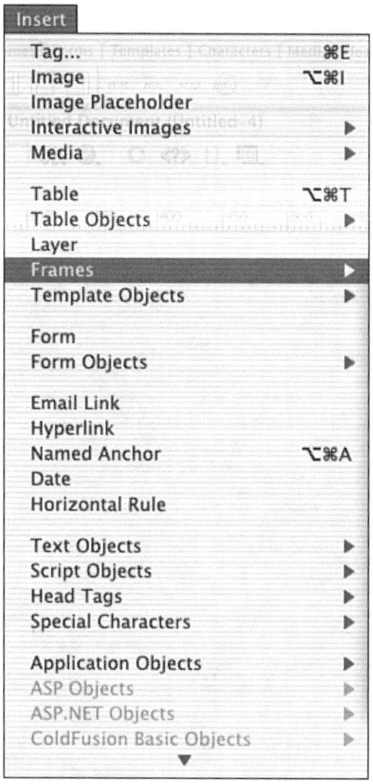

FIGURE 7.5 Choose Modify, Frameset, Split Frame (right, left, up, or down) to create a frameset in a new basic HTML document.

You can click any one of the frameset styles and the page will automatically divide into the appropriate frames. The small icons on the panel represent how the page will be split. The icons that split the page into several documents that are not parallel will create what's called a *nested frameset*.

By nesting a frameset, you can divide the page visually again by adding additional frames in a new frameset inside an existing frameset. Here's an example of what the code looks like for a nested frameset:

```
<frameset rows="80,*,80">
    <frame src="red.html">
 <frameset cols="379,379">
    <frame src="blue.html">
    <frame src="green.html">
  </frameset>
 <frame src="yellow.html">
</frameset>
```

Code like the preceding example gives you a result similar to what is pictured in Figure 7.9.

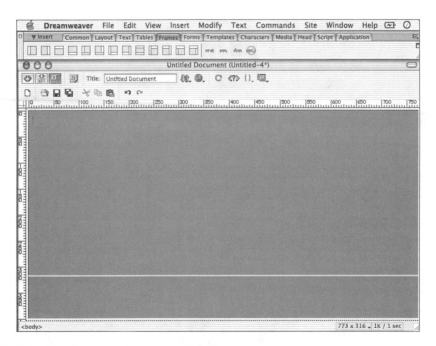

FIGURE 7.6   The document has been split in two.

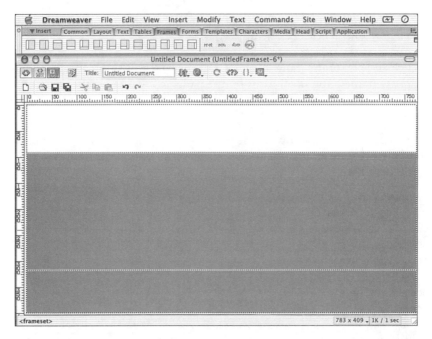

FIGURE 7.7   The document is divided even further with the addition of another row.

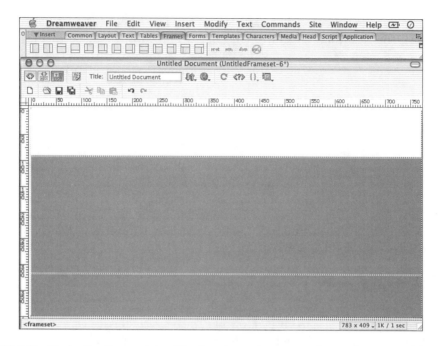

FIGURE 7.8 Under the Frames tab of the Insert panel, you can choose from several frameset styles.

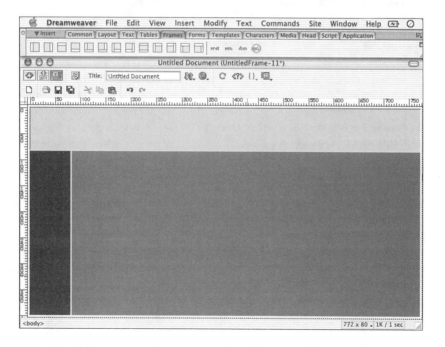

FIGURE 7.9 This figure represents a common layout for nested frames.

A common nested frameset is the Top and Nested Left Frames option, available from the Insert panel. The great thing about the frame object in the Insert panel is that with a single click of the mouse, you can insert a frameset that otherwise would take several key strokes and a mouse click to achieve using the techniques mentioned earlier.

These are the three ways you can create framesets in Dreamweaver. If you have a good plan, the fastest and easiest way to do it is from the New Document dialog box. If you have to create the frameset in a document that's already been opened, your next best bet is to use the Insert panel.

One thing I stress when using framesets is that you should be sure you have a plan. Having a good idea as to how you want your site structured will not only ensure a successful site, but it will make working with frames a lot easier. I notice that many of my students in a Dreamweaver class will overwrite certain documents when working with framesets, and many of these problems can be avoided by setting up and saving your frameset properly from the beginning.

Saving Framesets

After you set up the document, and you have as many frames as you would like present in the frameset, it's a good idea to save your work. The best way to save your document is to use the Save All Frames option under the File menu.

Using Save All Frames

This exercise will help you understand how frames should be saved and help prevent any problems in the future. It's very important to have a site defined in Dreamweaver when following these steps.

1. Create a new document, and in the New Document dialog box, be sure to choose frameset under the category side of the dialog box. Choose Fixed Left Nested Top for the frameset style. Click OK. This brings you back to the document, and it will be divided to reflect your frameset choice.

2. After setting a frameset in a way you like, choose File, Save All. This opens the Save All Frames dialog box.

3. It's important to note that a border surrounds the entire document, as shown in Figure 7.10. This border represents which HTML document in the frameset you're about to save. In this case, because the border is surrounding the entire document, you're about to save the parent frame. Name the document parent.html, unless you intend to have the frameset load when someone first visits the site; if that's the case, name it index.html. Click Save.

4. After you click Save, the Save As dialog box remains visible; however, the border now surrounds the main or larger portion of the frameset, as shown in Figure 7.11. Name this frame **main.html** and click Save.

5. After you click Save, the Save As dialog box is still active; however, this time the left frame has a border surrounding it. Save this file as left.html and click the Save button. It's a good

idea to gives these frames a logical name based on their position in the document. It will make targeting links to them a lot easier.

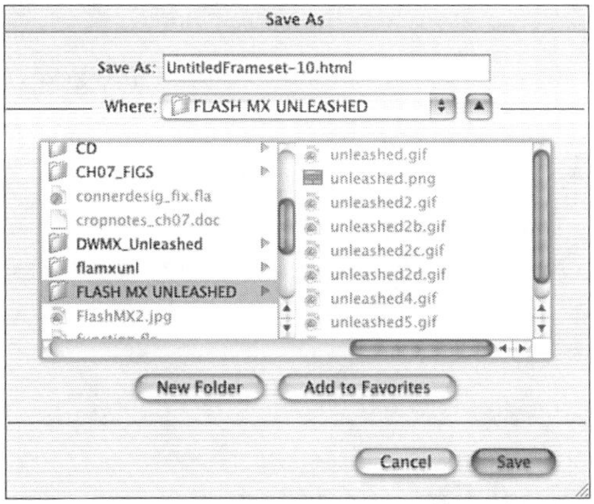

FIGURE 7.10   The Save As dialog box is active with a border surrounding the entire document. This means the parent frame is about to be saved.

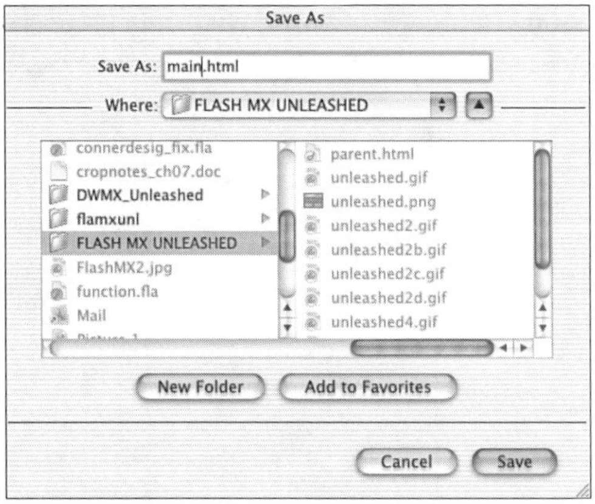

FIGURE 7.11   After you save the parent frame, notice the border that surrounds the larger frame, indicating which document is about to be saved.

6. The top frame is the one with the border around it. Call this top.html in the Save As dialog box and click Save.

TIP

Visit http://www.dreamweavermxunleashed.com, the companion Web site, to a view a QuickTime movie on how to save framesets.

In my experience, this is the best way to save a frameset. The goal of a frameset is to have different pages load into one main region, leaving other regions constant with a navigation system. Typically, and especially in the case of this exercise, the large portion of the frame will be the area that changes when links are clicked.

When working with framesets, it's a good idea to design and add content to the frame pages with the entire frameset open. That way, you can align and arrange content from the different frames. I strongly recommend that you do not design the pages that will be linked and loaded into the frameset with the frameset open. Design these pages independently in new, blank documents. Often in my classes, students accidentally overwrite the original files by designing new pages in the frameset. It's best to create the external files in their own documents and test the frameset frequently by linking and loading the external files through a browser.

Linking and targeting frames are covered later in this chapter.

Modifying and Resizing Frames

It's easy to resize and modify the appearance of a frameset. The first thing you need is precise control over selecting each frame, and the best way to do that is with the Frames panel. You can open the Frames panel by choosing Window, Others, Frame. This launches the Frame panel as shown in Figure 7.12. Notice that the Frames panel provides you with a small representation of what the divided document looks like.

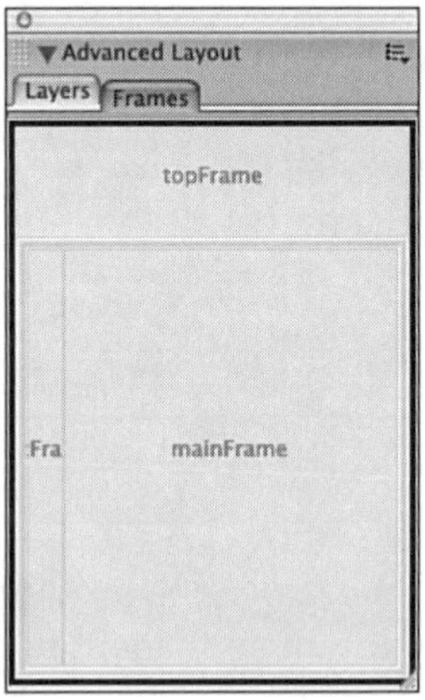

FIGURE 7.12   The Frames panel offers an easy way to select a particular frame.

When the Frames panel is open, you can click any one of the quadrants to select the particular frame. In the Frames panel, if you click in the frame you want to select, you get a highlight border around the corresponding frame in the document.

Titling the Frameset

If you want to title a document, and you want that title to appear in the title bar of the browser window, you must title the parent frame. Selecting the parent frame can sometimes be a little tough. Here's what I recommend: in the Frames panel, click in the top-left corner of the frames, just underneath the panel's tab. That will select the parent frame. If you're having trouble selecting that way, you can always click in any one of the frames, and in the Tag Inspector docked at the bottom-left corner of the document window, click the <frameset> tag closest to the edge of the document window. When that tag is bold, as displayed in Figure 7.13, you'll have the parent frame selected. Then at that point, if you title the document and preview it in the browser, your title will appear in the title bar of the browser window, as shown in Figure 7.14.

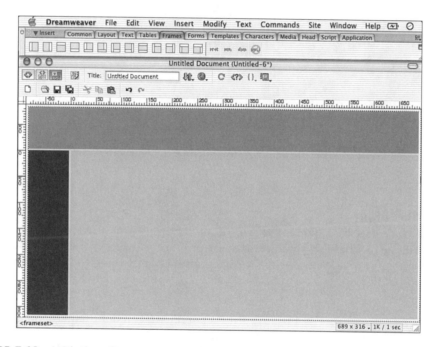

FIGURE 7.13   With the <frameset> tag closest to the border of the document window highlighted, the parent frame is selected.

You may want to title all your documents. As I mentioned earlier, it is possible for end users to add a particular frame to their favorites by contextual-clicking. If they return to a favorite that they bookmarked, the entire frameset will not be loaded, just the single document. When that document loads by itself, you may want it to have a title. You can select each of the frames by using the Frames panel. With each of the separate documents selected, you can title them differently in the toolbar.

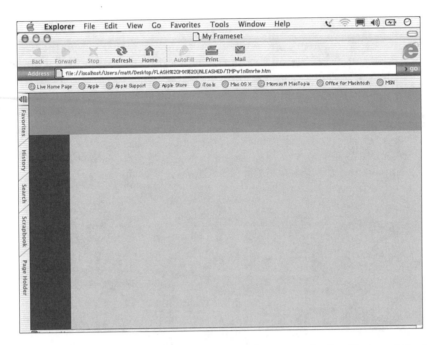

FIGURE 7.14   After you title the parent frame, the title appears in the title bar of the browser window.

Resizing Frames

When sizing frames, it's important to keep in mind how they are sized to begin with. Often, frames either have an absolute pixel size or they have a relative size. For example, if you had a frameset that consisted of a top and bottom frame, you could set the top frame to equal a specified pixel size. The bottom frame size would be relative to the size of the browser window.

All this talk about absolute and relative sizes is important. You must understand how this works if you plan to adjust the sizes of your frames.

The easiest way to change the size of a frame is to mouse over the border until your cursor changes to a two-way arrow; then click and drag. The only problem with resizing frames like this is that they're automatically converted into absolute sizes.

To avoid setting frames to absolute sizes by accident, you can resize them by using the Properties Inspector. Let's work with the frameset you saved earlier in this chapter. With that frameset open, you can highlight the entire frameset. Select the frameset by using the Frames panel, and click in the corner of the frame border inside the Frames panel. With the entire frameset selected, notice that sizing options are available through the Properties Inspector, as shown in Figure 7.15.

As Figure 7.15 shows, the Properties Inspector offers a small representation of the frames you have selected on the right side of the Inspector. In the case of Figure 7.15, you'll notice that the top frame in the representation is the one that is highlighted, so the information being displayed in the remaining areas of the Properties Inspector is referring to the top frame.

When you set a size for the frame, notice in the Properties Inspector that there is an area for Value and Units. The Units option offers a drop-down menu with three options: Pixels, Percentage, and Relative. Depending on the circumstances, your site design determines which one of these options you should choose.

FIGURE 7.15   When the parent frame is selected, options for resizing the frames appear in the Properties Inspector.

As you can see from Figure 7.15, I added a navigation system to the top portion of the frame. Because there is content in the frame that should always be visible, set the appropriate Value to a pixel size Unit. It's an advantage to set it to a pixel size to maintain the integrity of the navigational design; buttons and other elements will never shift. Setting a frame to a pixel size is also referred to as an absolute size.

If you click the bottom frame, in the small frameset representation in the Properties Inspector, your options change to resize the bottom frame, as shown in Figure 7.16.

You have the same sizing options for setting a Value to whatever Unit you specify. In the situation with the bottom frame, it's generally a good idea to set it to Relative. This simply means it will size relative to the browser window and the top frame. If the browser window is too small, the bottom frame will resize; however, the top frame will not. It's a bit different than percentage. With a percentage value, the frame will always want to be the percent size that you specify of the browser window.

Resizing a Nested Frame

Resizing a nested frame basically entails the same steps; however, you must select the nested frameset. Again, the easiest way to select the nested frameset is to use the Frames panel. Using this panel, click the frame border toward the center of the panel, as shown in Figure 7.17. When the frameset is selected, the Properties Inspector offers the same options in the Properties Inspector shown in Figure 7.18.

Here you have options for sizing the columns. The typical way to size a frameset designed like this is to set the column on the left to an absolute pixel size and set the column on the right to a relative size.

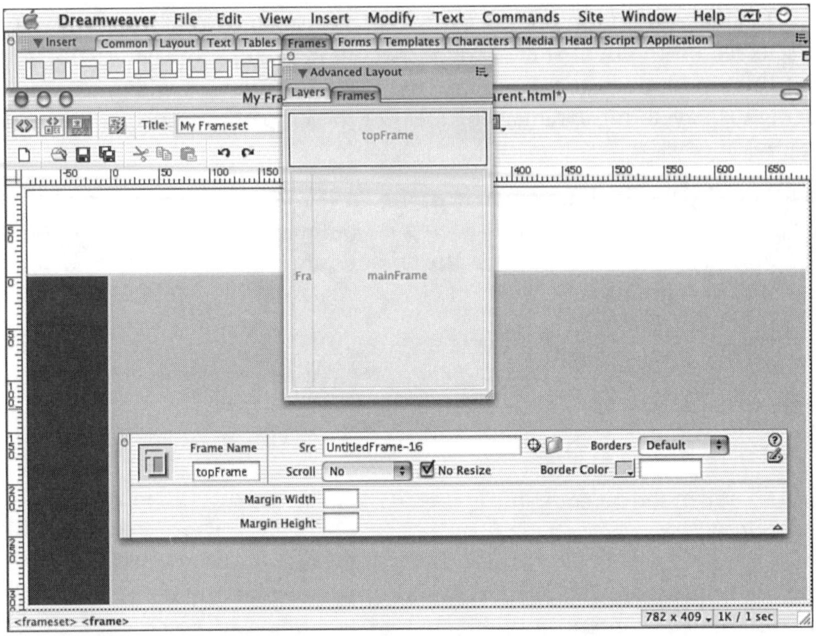

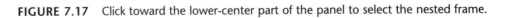

FIGURE 7.16   The Properties Inspector provides feedback based on which frame is high-lighted.

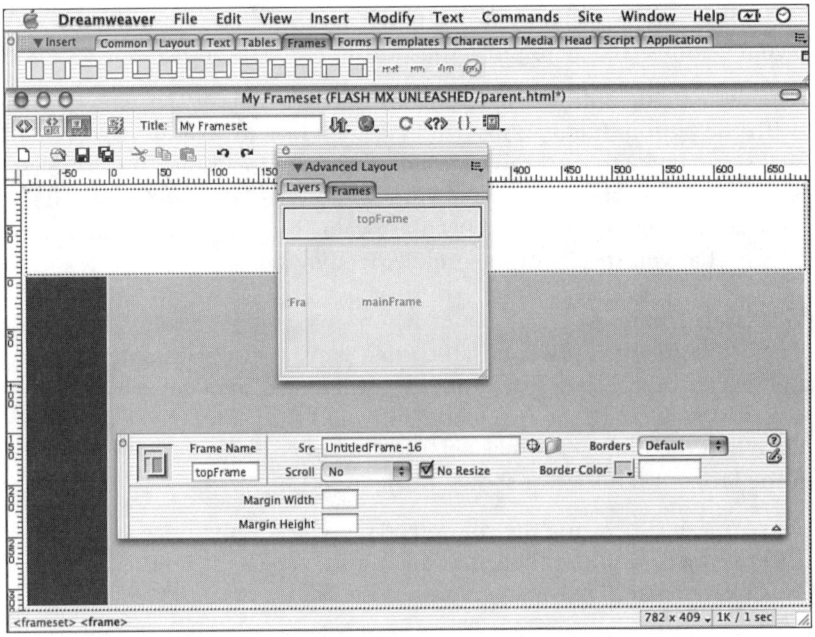

FIGURE 7.17   Click toward the lower-center part of the panel to select the nested frame.

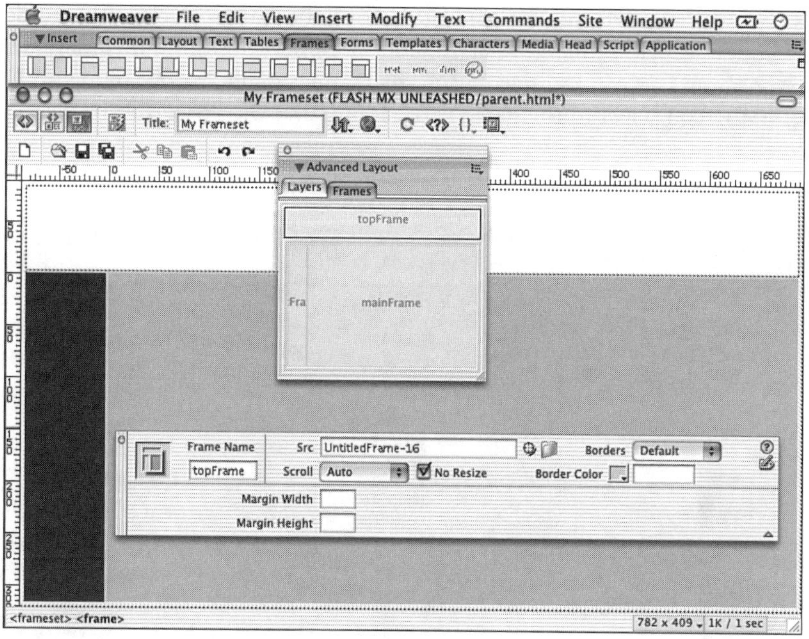

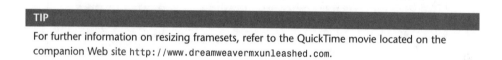

FIGURE 7.18   The nested frameset is selected.

> **TIP**
>
> For further information on resizing framesets, refer to the QuickTime movie located on the companion Web site http://www.dreamweavermxunleashed.com.

Deleting a Frame

After initially setting up the frameset, you may decide that you no longer need or want a particular frame. Deleting it is simple. Make sure that frame borders are visible; if they're not, choose View, Visual Aids, Frame Borders. Click and drag the frame border of the unwanted frame off the page. Voilà, the frame is deleted!

Adjusting Frame Attributes

An easy way to change the appearance of a frameset is to change the border size and color. You can easily change the size of the borders by entering a value in the Border Width field in the Properties Inspector when you have the frame selected. If you don't want borders, enter a value of 0. You can also choose No from the Border drop-down menu. If you choose Yes, you must enter a value greater than 0 for borders to appear in the browser. The final choice in the drop-down menu is Default. If you choose Default, the appearance of the border will be determined by the end user's browser.

There are also options for changing attributes of specific frames, such as the borders, border color, margin width, margin height, and more. To select an individual frame, click in whichever frame you want to select using the Frames panel. Notice in Figure 7.19 that whichever frame you select in the panel is the frame that the Properties Inspector provides options for.

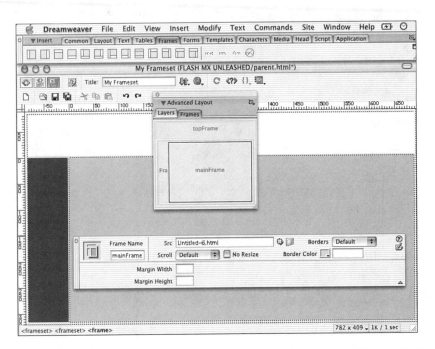

FIGURE 7.19   When you click in a frame in the Frames panel, options for that particular frame become available in the Properties Inspector.

Name

You can name each frame; however, do not confuse this with the filename or title of the document. This name simply helps identify the area of the frameset. This is extremely useful when linking documents to the frameset. It is also helpful when applying behaviors to links inside the frameset. It also allows JavaScript functions to be applied to specific frames, targeting them by frame name.

Avoid using spaces and special characters in your naming conventions. Also, never name a frame _blank, _top, _parent, _self. These are default target names that add functionality to linking frames and documents. For more information on this topic, refer to the linking portion of this chapter called "Targeting Frames."

Scroll

This option enables you to set the scrollbar for each frame. Often, designers like to have control over this option. A great deal of content might be in a particular frame, for example, and depending on the end user's screen size, you may want scrollbars to appear. This gives users the choice of using the scrollbar to reveal hidden content. Other times, a designer may not want scrollbars at all and opt for them to never show up. You can set that preference in the Properties Inspector using the following choices:

- **Yes**   This option creates scrollbars around the frame at all times. Unless you have a great deal of content in a frame, it's best visually not to choose this.

- **No**   This choice keeps scrollbars from ever appearing around the frame. Often, designers use this option to meet the needs of a specific design. Scrollbars can be a distraction to a particular layout or color scheme. If you can be sure that your content will remain visible on various monitors, use this option. If for any reason the content overflows the frame on a particular screen size, the end user has no way of viewing the hidden content.

- **Auto**   This choice offers the best of both worlds. Scrollbars appear only if necessary. Use this choice if the content in the frame yields unpredictable size results in a variety of browsers.

- **Default**   Whether the scrollbars appear is determined by the end user's browser.

Borders and Border Color

You can set the border size and color of the individual frame, regardless of the entire frameset's settings. This behaves much like borders for tables and table cells. However, if you're dealing with a nested frameset, there is a good chance the options you set here will affect the appearance of other frames within the document, because you're changing the <frameset> tag when changing settings in the Properties Inspector. If you have a frameset inside another, by changing the attributes of one tag, you can bet you're changing anything nested inside of it.

Frame Resize

If you are using borders, keep in mind that the default behavior inside the browser is having the capability to click and drag these frames to different sizes. As a developer, that's probably not what you had in mind.

If you set an absolute pixel value to one of the frames, the No Resize option is automatically checked. This eliminates the default resize behavior, so the end user will not be able to alter your design.

Margin Width and Height

Every HTML document has an offset, which means a small margin, only a few pixels wide, surrounds the entire document. With frames, it is common for a designer to want content from one frame to appear flush to the content of another frame. This is not possible with the default "cushion" around documents. To work around this, simply type in zeros for the Margin Height and Width text field options.

You can also get rid of the "cushion" in the Page Properties dialog box by choosing Modify, Page Properties.

Targeting Frames

Targeting frames is very important; this is what makes the frameset work. Creating hyperlinks in framesets entails one more step than a traditional link. You need to target which frame you want the linked page to load into. When you hyperlink a document, you highlight the text or graphic that you want the end user to click, and then type in a relative path to a local page or an absolute URL to link to an external site.

If that's all you did when linking in a frameset, without targeting, the page would load in the same frame as the hyperlinked item. For example, if there was a navigation system on the left side of the document, and I wanted a page to load into the main area, if I created a hyperlink without a target, you wouldn't get the results you were hoping for.

In the Target drop-down menu, you'll see the name of each frame within the frameset. The name refers to whatever you named the frame in the Properties Inspector. You'll also notice there are four default options as well.

- **_blank**   This target launches a new browser window when the hyperlink is clicked.

- **_parent**   This option opens the link in the parent frame of the frame the hyperlink is on. If, for example, you're inside a frame that is part of a nested frameset, it might not load in the top-level parent frame. Instead, it might load in the parent frame of the nested frame—yielding undesired results. If you're not dealing with a nested frameset, this option behaves like _top.

- **_self**   This target opens the linked document in the frame in which it was called. This behaves much like not targeting the document at all.

- **_top**   This option wipes out the frameset and loads into the browser like a normal document.

By targeting documents and links properly, you should be able to create a successful frameset that offers an easier navigation system for the end user. After lining and targeting documents properly, you should get your desired results.

Changing Page Properties

Often in my Dreamweaver classes, students ask if a background color option is available in the Properties Inspector. Don't be confused. Remember framesets are constructed of several HTML documents and you can change the background color and other document attributes through the Page Properties dialog box. You can access the Page Properties dialog box by choosing Modify, Page Properties. Command+J (Mac) or Ctrl+J (Windows) are the keyboard shortcuts.

Saving, Closing, and Opening a Frame

I decided to include this section based on common questions students ask in my Dreamweaver classes. As you work in your frameset, if you find you're working on only one frame, you can choose File, Save Frame. If you're modifying all or some of the frames, you can choose File, Save All.

I do not recommend the technique I'm about to discuss; it's too easy to make a mistake and overwrite files. However, this is a book about Dreamweaver and not about some careless mistakes I made in the past, so if you're careful, you should be okay, but when you do overwrite a file—it's not my fault.

Matt's Unapproved Technique for Creating a New Document

So you have a frameset designed and each frame looks great. Now it's time to start adding new pages. The pages you want to load into the frameset have to match, so it'll be easier to design a new HTML document with the frameset open. In fact, you start dismantling one of the frames and begin designing right on top of it. When you're satisfied, you need to save it, so here's how it is done.

After designing the frame in place, and after you're happy with it, you do not want to overwrite the original file because you still need it to show up when the page first loads. Therefore, choose Files, Save Frame As to launch the Save As dialog box. Here, type in the filename and choose Save. Here's the important part; if you still want the original frame to load in the location you created the new file, when closing the document, you'll get an alert message. It's asking you if you want to save the parent frame. The reason for that is because if you look at your document, one of the original frames has been replaced with the new one that you designed. So that you can see the new document in the place where you want it to load, the parent source HTML has been changed. It used to look like this:

```
<frameset rows="80,*" cols="*">
<frame src="top.html" name="topFrame" scrolling="NO">
    <frameset rows="*" cols="192,400*">
    <frame src="left.html" name="left">
    <frame src="main.html" name="mainFrame">
    </frameset>
</frameset>
```

But the frame src has been modified for the mainframe, so the code now looks like this:

```
<frameset rows="80,*" cols="*">
<frame src="top.html" name="topFrame" scrolling="NO">
    <frameset rows="*" cols="192,400*">
    <frame src="left.html" name="left">
    <frame src="page1.html" name="mainFrame">
    </frameset>
</frameset>
```

> **WARNING**
>
> The HTML in the parent frame may not reflect this before saving. The altered source appears in the HTML document only after it has been saved.

If you do not want to change the original document in the frame in which you designed a new page, choose No in the alert message.

Closing and Opening a Frameset

Closing a frameset is just like closing any other document. If you forget to save any changes made to a document, Dreamweaver warns you with an alert dialog box. However, how do you open your frameset so it appears in the same way? If you want to open the entire frameset, open the parent frame, or the parent HTML document. This opens all dependent files.

> **WARNING**
>
> If you saved a frameset but haven't added any content to it, after opening the parent frame, it may appear as if it isn't opening all the documents. This is because Dreamweaver turns off frame borders and you have to turn them back on by choosing View, Visual Aids, Frame Borders.

If you plan on previewing a frameset in a browser, you must save the frameset first. If you don't, Dreamweaver alerts you to save the frameset. If you check the Don't Warn Me Again box, Dreamweaver will automatically save the frameset when you test it.

No Frames Content

Older versions of Netscape and Internet Explorer do not support frames. If anyone out there uses an old 2.0 or 3.0 browser (I'm assuming few and far between), the user will not be able to see your site. However there is a tag inserted into frameset documents called <noframes>. This tag can act as an alternate for any browser that can't interpret framesets.

To create <noframes> content, choose Modify, Frameset, Edit No Fra[...] changes the document to reflect what's inside the <noframes> tag. If t[...] the document may look like a normal blank document. Design this page[...] would want your viewers to see the site if the browser wasn't frameset cap[...] you're done, choose Modify, Frameset, Edit No Frames Content to return to t[...]

iFrames

iFrames, which is short for inline frames, are part of the HTML 4.0 specification. Wha[...] interesting and useful about an iFrame is that you do not need to build an entire frames[...] What makes iFrames so useful is their capability to display scrollbars automatically. Therefore, you can have a region within your document that isn't obviously a frame and have a great deal of information or text that is scrollable.

For end users to see an iFrame, they must be using Internet Explorer 4 or later or Netscape 6 or later. Unfortunately, there is no easy way to create an iFrame within Dreamweaver; you must do it by hand. You may notice that in the code view, an iFrame button (also known as the floating frame button) in the Insert panel under the Frame tab becomes active. This will simply insert the <iframe></iframes> tags into the code for you.

The <iframe> tag has several attributes that you need to address. The most important is the source. The source specifies which HTML document you want to use in the floating frame. Next you have to specify the name of the frame as well the position. The final tag should look something like this:

```
<iframe src = "/foldername/filename.html" name="frameName"
style ="position:absolute; width:100px; height:150px; top:120px;
left:300px;></iframe>
```

It's important to note that in the Dreamweaver authoring environment, iFrames appear as layers. However, after you test it in a browser, it appears as an iFrame.

Summary

Framesets offer designers yet another option for laying out and structuring their sites. Personally, I thought framesets would be even more popular that they are. When designing with framesets, you have to keep in mind your target audience. Will their experience at your site suffer because of framesets' drawbacks? Will frames enhance their experience for ease of use and navigation? These are the questions you must ask yourself when planning out your site.

mes Content. This
his is the first time,
in a way that you
ble. When
he frameset.

r's
et.

CHAPTER **8**

Dreamweaver Templates

By Matt Pizzi

Templates will not only increase your productivity, but they also promote consistency throughout the design of your site. Templates are especially useful for sites that use a similar page design on the majority of their pages. Additionally they can be beneficial if there are contributing content developers who may not necessarily be in tune with page design. They can add their content only to regions that you, or the designer of the template, specify as areas that can be edited.

Templates are not recommended for those who often have many major changes to make across a variety of page designs. Templates are optimal when it is only certain regions that need changing or updating.

Any page that is created based on a template has a link associated with it. For example, if the original template was modified and saved, all pages that use that template would be automatically updated to reflect the new changes. This is one of the real strengths of templates.

Templates or Framesets?

Why do I have this topic? When I teach my Dreamweaver class, there is always at least one student who asks this question. Based on that experience, I am assuming that some of you reading this book right now might be scratching your head asking this very question.

The answer is simple. They have nothing to do with one another. You will not be making a decision between the two. In fact, you can use both. Remember that framesets are a set of separate documents held together by one parent document. Templates are documents that other pages will be based on. Who's to say that pages that load into your mainframe won't be based on a template? Therefore, there is no decision to be made between frame-sets, templates, or even tables for that matter. They all can be used together or independently of one another.

More About Templates

At the most basic level, templates have two states associated with them—locked and editable. By default, everything in the document is locked. When you create a template, it's up to you to define which area will be editable. These areas are generally the space in which you want content producers to add content. This will ultimately preserve the integrity of the design. This chapter discusses some of the ways you can create and apply templates. You'll also learn about some of the new features in Dreamweaver MX you can use when creating and working with templates. Templates in Dreamweaver are sometimes referred to as Dream Templates.

Creating a Template

Remember when you're creating a template that it's a blueprint for all other documents that are based on it. It's also a good idea, when creating a template, to use placeholders for regions that are editable. What I mean by that is if you have a cell in which you know you want the content provider to have the ability to insert a graphic, place an image place-holder in that cell. It's important to see how the HTML table is going to behave with a physical image in the cell and how that image placed in the cell will interact with the other components in the document. That way, when it comes time to insert the new image in the document based on the template, you're simply replacing a dummy image; there will be no surprises of columns or rows shifting. You don't want to be in the position of having to tweak the template to accommodate a graphic.

Some things you should keep in mind when creating templates are the following:

- **Include redundant meta information**   By including keywords and descrip-tions in your templates, you can save a lot of time from not having to type them over and over again. All the information in the <head> tag is included in the template.

- **Insert all necessary Styles and Behaviors in the template**   Because the <head> tag is essentially locked by the template, it's a good idea to include scripts. Often JavaScript, which behaviors are based on, will include the code between the <head> tags, and then the scripts are called from an object within the body. So you need to make sure that the code used by the behaviors is already present within the template.

- **Use Placeholders**   It's good to get in the habit of using placeholders so you can see how the document will be shaped. There is nothing worse than adding content and seeing that the design isn't successful because the area you designated for content wasn't sized properly.

Finally, you should know that your template is automatically saved within your local root folder in a folder called Templates. Dreamweaver saves the template with a DWT extension, which stands for Dreamweaver Template. It's important to leave the template within this folder. You don't want to be confusing the links in a template by moving to another location. The point of the template is to have several documents based on it, and if links are not working properly in the template, all the pages that are based on it will share the same fate.

You can create a template from a brand-new document or you can convert an existing design into a template.

Creating a Template from an Existing HTML Page

First, you're going to learn how you can create a template from an existing HTML page. To do that, follow these steps:

1. Open a page already designed, as shown in Figure 8.1.

2. With the page open, be sure to have access to the template objects. You can find them in the Insert panel under the Templates tab, as shown in Figure 8.2.

3. Click the Make Template button on the far-left corner of the Insert panel.

4. This launches the Save As Template dialog box shown in Figure 8.3. In this dialog box, choose what site you would like to save this template under, and name the template. When you're happy, click Save.

The document will automatically be saved in the site specified in a folder named Templates. When you open the Assets panel, notice under the template category, the template you just saved appears in the panel.

If you continue to add content to the page, it's a good idea when linking to use the browse or point-to-file icon in the Properties Inspector. The reason is that Dreamweaver moves the template file into a new folder. By creating the links through the Properties Inspector, you're guaranteed that Dreamweaver knows how to resource the links when it moves the file.

Creating a Template from a New Document

This is just another alternative for creating templates. If you know from the beginning what you want the template to look like, you can design in a document that is already saved as a template. There are several ways to accomplish this. To create a template from a blank document, follow these steps:

1. Create a new document by choosing File, New. This launches the New Document dialog box.

2. In the New Document dialog box, under the Category section, choose Template page. From the Template page section, choose HTML Template. You can also choose HTML Template from the Basic Page category.

3. Choose Create. This opens a new untitled document; however, notice the title bar reads <<Template>> indicating that it is, in fact, a template.

FIGURE 8.1   Notice the document has already been designed.

FIGURE 8.2   Under the Templates tab of the Insert panel resides several options for templates.

FIGURE 8.3   The Save As Template dialog box offers options for naming the template file as well as the site in which you want to save it.

The preceding steps show one of the ways to create a new template from scratch. As I mentioned earlier, Dreamweaver MX offers many ways to do that same thing. Here are the steps to another way of creating a template from a blank document:

1. Inside a blank document, access the Insert panel. In the Insert panel, click the Templates tab.

2. Under the Templates tab, click the Make Template button. This will effectively change the document into a template page.

Finally, with the Assets panel open, you can create a new template right from this panel. Click the template portion of the Assets panel and toward the bottom, you can click the New Template button. This changes the current document into a template.

Now that you have a new template file, you can start laying out your design.

Creating Editable Regions

By default, all areas of the template are locked and uneditable, which means the point of the template is pretty much rendered useless. If a content provider can't get in there and add content, what's the point? So in this section, you'll discover the different ways you can go about creating editable regions.

When an editable region has been defined, it is indicated in a new document based on the template as a small blue tab highlight, as shown in Figure 8.4. You can either create a new editable region, which is defining an area with no content as editable, or you can mark a region as editable, which makes the existing content editable.

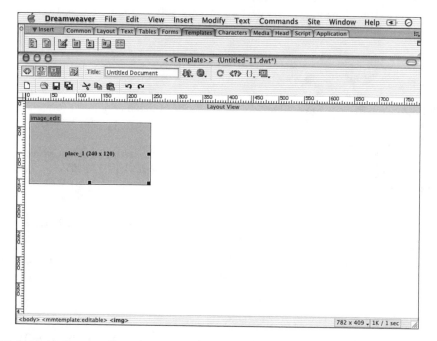

FIGURE 8.4 Notice that the editable regions are highlighted with a small blue tab indicating the name of the editable region.

You can place all kinds of different media into an editable region. Whether it's text, images, SWF files, or even Java applets, as long as it is content you would otherwise normally fit into a Web page, you can insert it into the editable region.

You cannot make any changes to a document's noneditable regions. If you decide that changes must be made outside the editable regions, you can either change the template, or you can break the link between the current document and the template page. You'll look at these options in just a moment; for now, let's look at how you can define different areas as editable. To make a region editable, follow these steps:

1. Make sure a defined template is open in the template-editing window. The easiest way to do this is to open the Assets panel, make sure the template category is selected, and double-click the template of your choice.

2. Select the content or place an insertion point in the area you want to define as editable.

3. In the Insert panel under the Templates tab, click the Editable Region button, as shown in Figure 8.5. This launches a small dialog box.

4. In the New Editable Region dialog box, type in what you want to name the region. When you're happy, choose OK. This brings you back to the document; notice the small blue tab with the region name appearing just above the region.

5. Now that this region has been defined as editable, save the template by choosing File, Save. You may get an alert message asking you to update pages; for now, choose Don't Update. You'll look at this feature in a page or two.

FIGURE 8.5 You make an area editable by clicking the Editable Region button located in the Insert panel under the Templates tab.

It's that easy to create an editable region in a Dreamweaver template. Next you need to know how you can apply a template to an open document. After you do that, you'll be able to test out the editable region.

Applying a Template or Creating a New Document Based on a Template

After creating your template, you probably want to use it to create pages. In the next couple of steps, you'll see how you can apply a template to a page.

1. Under the File menu, choose New Document. This launches the New Document dialog box. Create a basic HTML page.

2. Inside the New Document dialog box, open the Assets panel by choosing Window, Assets. In the Assets panel, click the Templates category. Notice that the template you've created is available.

3. Highlight the template in the Assets panel and click and drag it into the document. The document now carries the characteristics of the template. You could also have chosen Modify, Template, Apply Template to Page, or you could highlight the template in the Assets panel and click the Apply button in the bottom-left corner of the panel.

4. Also notice that you cannot select anything other than the regions you marked as editable.

This demonstrates the power of templates. Only the regions specified have room for additional content or modification. This document could be sent to a copy editor or a content provider, who could make modifications and add content only in those areas.

Creating an Editable Tag Attribute

As you saw in the previous example, templates can promote a nice consistent look throughout your Web site. With the addition of editable regions, you can even add or edit content to distinguish from page to page. However, generally the editable regions cater only to content. Designwise, all the pages will look identical. A new feature in Dreamweaver MX is the capability to edit certain tag attributes. For example, you could make certain attributes of the <body> tag editable by a content provider, such as the bgcolor attribute. This way, you can offer a consistent look without being boring. Moreover, you offer slightly more control to the developer just adding content to a template page.

You can specify what tag you want to be editable; furthermore, you can set what attributes of that tag you want to edit. You must be inside the Template Editing mode, so double-click the template found within your Assets panel. The way that the editable attribute works is that a parameter is set in the HTML code for whatever tag attribute is defined as editable. When individuals author a page based on the template, they have the option of altering that parameter through the Modify menu. We'll look at altering attributes right after you see how to define an editable attribute.

To create an editable tag attribute, follow these steps:

1. Inside the template, highlight an item you want to make editable. If you want the <body> tag to be editable, select the body tag in the Tag Inspector located in the bottom-left corner of the document window. For this exercise, I'm going to do just that. Select the <body> tag.

2. Then choose Modify, Templates, Make Attribute Editable. This opens the Editable Tag Attributes dialog box, as shown in Figure 8.6.

3. Notice in the Attribute drop-down menu, no information is provided. So you have to add the attribute you want to change. Click the Add button. This launches another small dialog box, as shown in Figure 8.7, that asks you to type the attribute. In this case, type in **bgcolor**.

4. The next thing you want to fill out is the label. Label it something that makes sense; in this case, because you're changing the background color, you should type something like **color** here.

5. In the Type drop-down menu, there are a couple of choices. There are four data types that will be accepted here: text, Boolean (true or false), color, and URL. In this case, because you want the bgcolor attribute to be editable, the color option is the best choice.

6. Next is an area to specify a default value. Enter in a value here if you want it to appear different from what the template-based document already carries for a value. In this case, leave it blank.

7. Choose OK. You've just defined an editable tag attribute.

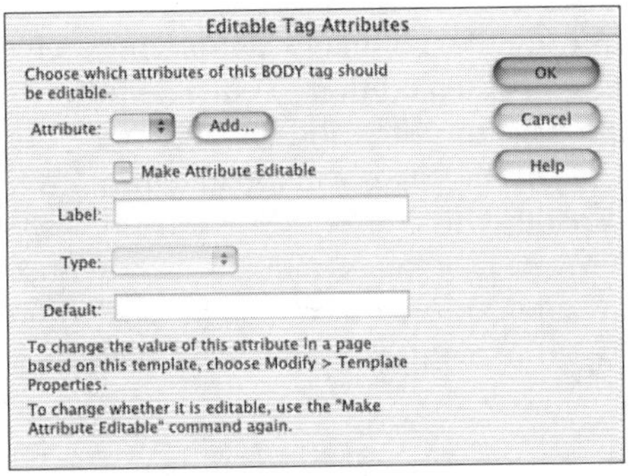

FIGURE 8.6   The Editable Tag Attributes dialog box offers several options for modifying the selected tag.

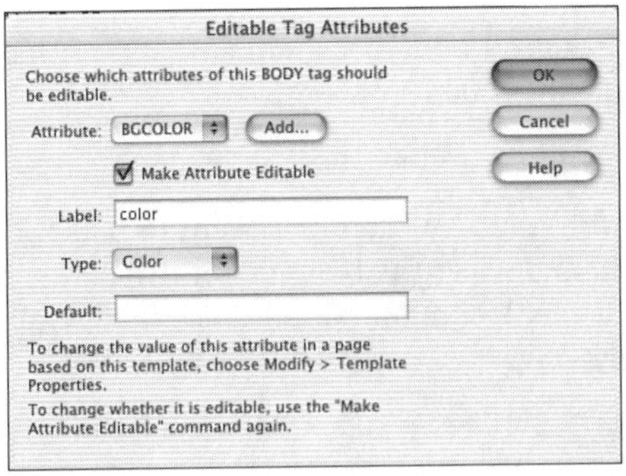

FIGURE 8.7   Type in the attribute for the selected tag that you want to make editable.

Now that your template has an editable tag attribute, how do you edit that attribute? The way that you edit a tag attribute is just as intuitive as it is to create one.

Create a new document and attach the template in the Assets panel in which you applied the editable tag attribute. To modify the background color, choose Modify, Template Properties. This launches the Template Properties dialog box shown in Figure 8.8.

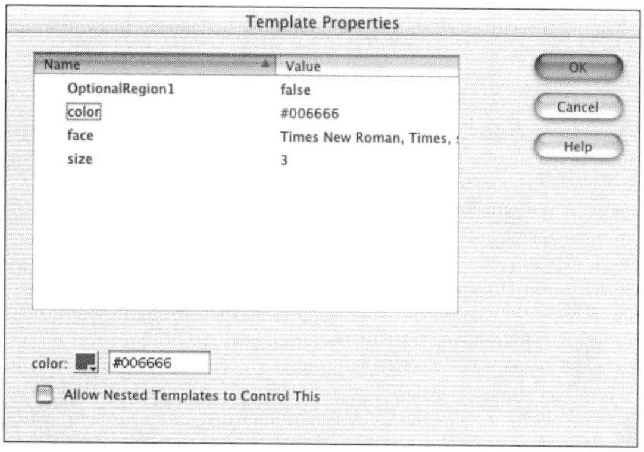

FIGURE 8.8   The Template Properties dialog box lists all the editable attributes of the tags you specified in that particular template.

Here you'll see each label of all the tags that you've made editable. This is why it's important to label each editable tag something that makes sense. Highlight the color attribute and notice that down toward the bottom, there is an inkwell where you can pick a color from the Web-safe color palette, or you can type the hexadecimal value into the text field.

Pick a color and choose OK. The background color of the template-based document you're working with now has the background color that you specified in the Template Properties dialog box.

You can do this for any tag you like. If you'd like the content provider to be able to pick font faces and colors, make that attribute editable. The more attributes you make editable, the more personality each page can have while still maintaining a high level of consistency.

Removing Tag Attributes

If you no longer want certain tag attributes to be editable, open the Assets panel, and in the Templates section, double-click the template for which you want to remove the editable tag attribute functionality.

Choose Modify, Templates, Make Attribute Editable. This opens the Edit Tag Attributes dialog box. In the Editable Attribute drop-down menu, select the attribute you'd like to modify. Deselect the Make Attribute Editable check box. When you're done, choose OK. The specified attribute is no longer editable on template-based pages.

Repeating Table

Another brand-new edition to Dreamweaver MX is the capability to create templates with repeat regions and tables that repeat. This can be extremely useful when additional content needs to be added. For example, an individual adding content to the template-based page might need one more row in the table they're inserting data into. If this is a normal table, the person is out of luck. The table has parameters established by the template master document to contain x number of rows and x number of columns. However, all that changes with this new enhancement to Dreamweaver's templates.

When developing the templates, if you're not certain how many items need to be listed to the table, create a repeating table. That way, if one template-based page needs more rows than the other, the person entering data into the template-based page will have the option of adding as many rows as necessary to do the job.

Adding a repeating table is simple. Make sure you're inside the editing environment of the template, and also make sure to have the Insert panel visible with the Templates tab active. To insert a repeating table, follow these steps:

1. Place a blinking cursor in the document where you'd like the table to appear.

2. In the Insert panel, click the Repeating Table button. You can also choose Insert, Template Objects, New Repeating Table. This opens the Insert Repeating Table dialog box as shown in Figure 8.9.

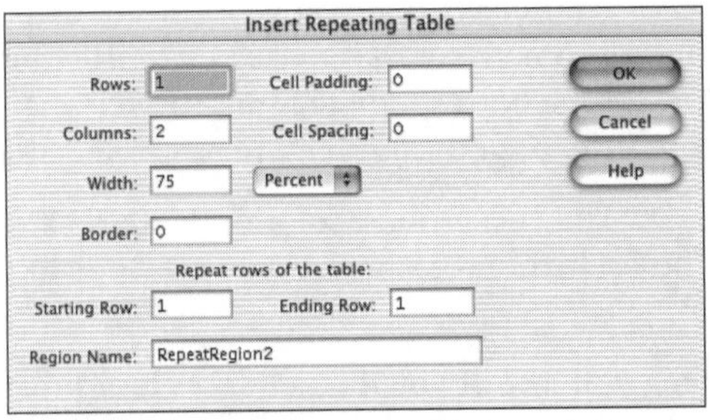

FIGURE 8.9   The Insert Repeating Table dialog box looks much like the Insert Table dialog box. Here you can specify what the table will look like.

3. Enter **2** for Columns, **1** for Rows. Make the table as wide as you'd like with as much space for cell spacing and cell padding as you like. I'm going to type in 0 for a border, and the Starting and Ending row will both be set to 1. Finally, name the repeating region **data**. When you're happy with the settings, choose OK. A repeating table is inserted into your document.

Insert Repeating Table Dialog Box Options

- **Rows**   This option specifies how many rows you'd like your table to have.

- **Columns**   This option determines how many columns the table will have.

- **Cell Padding**   Enter a pixel value to create an interior cushion for the cell, spacing the interior cell edge from the cell content.

- **Cell Spacing**   This option determines the space between cells in the table.

- **Width**   Enter a value, either pixel or percentage, based on how wide you want the table to appear in the browser.

- **Border**   This specifies the pixel width of the table border. Type in **0** if you don't want a border.

- **Repeat Rows of the Table**   These options specify what rows are to be included in the editable repeating section of the table.

- **Starting Row**   Enter a number to specify the row number where you want the repeating to begin.

- **Ending Row**   Enter a number to specify the row number where you want the repeating to end.

- **Region Name**   Enter in a name for the repeating region.

Back inside the document, notice that a blue tab is above the template, specifying that it's a repeating region.

Now you can create a new page based on this template and put the repeating table to use. Create a new basic HTML page and attach the template you've been working with. Notice in the template-based document that there are arrows and plus and minus signs above the template, as displayed in Figure 8.10. These controls allow you to add, rearrange, and even delete rows in the table.

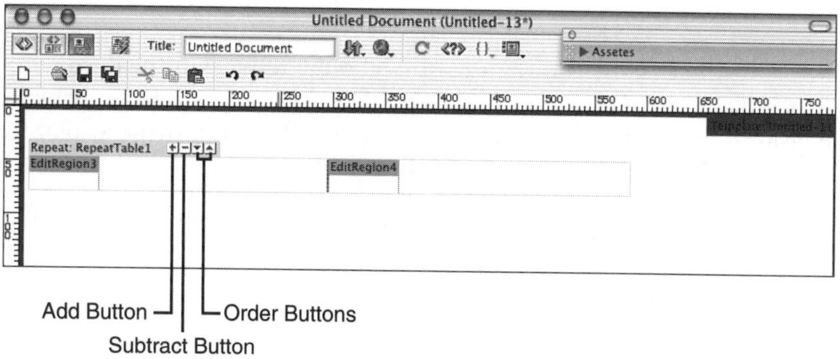

FIGURE 8.10   In the table, there are buttons to add, delete, and order the different rows that will repeat in the template-based document.

Enter in data in the first row; now that you need another, click the plus sign and a new row is added to the table. You can add as many rows as necessary. You can even sort the data by using the up and down arrows. Finally, if you added too many rows and need to remove some, click the button with the minus sign.

Repeating Regions

Most of the time in Web development if you need an area to repeat, it will most likely be a table. However, there is always the exception to the rule. You may have a situation where you need to add several photographs. The Repeat Region is designed for such a situation. It behaves much like a repeating table; however, it doesn't have to be a table.

If you want to change something other than the source of a graphic, you'll have to insert an editable region into the repeated region. I talked about creating editable regions earlier in this chapter.

To create a repeating region, follow these steps:

1. Open the template you want to add the repeating region to.

2. Place a blinking cursor in the area where you want to place the repeat region or select the object that you want to repeat. In this exercise, you're going to insert an image placeholder by choosing Insert, Image Placeholder. This will open the Image Placeholder dialog box as shown in Figure 8.11.

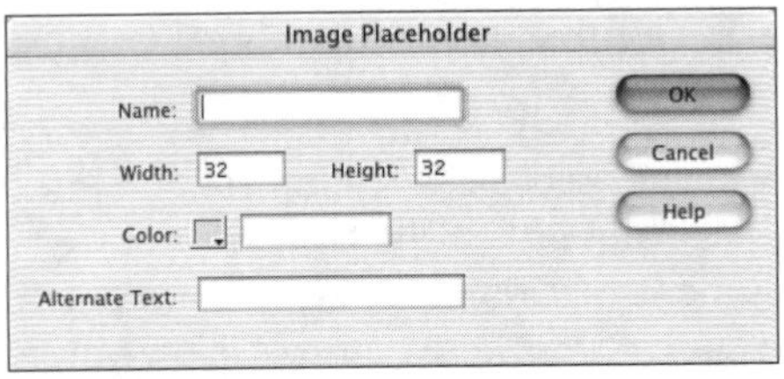

FIGURE 8.11   Enter in the dimension values in the dialog box where you want the placeholder to appear.

3. Enter in the dimensions you want the placeholder to have in the document. Images that eventually swap out with the placeholder do not need to have these same dimensions. You can also name the placeholder as well as provide a color for it. When you're happy with the settings, choose OK.

4. Notice the placeholder appears in the template with a tab above it, indicating that it is a repeating region.

5. Save the template by choosing File, Save.

Next, you have to create a new document and attach the template to see how the repeating region will behave in a template-based document. Create a new basic HTML page. After the page is open, attach the template by opening the Assets panel and clicking the Apply button. Notice in the document that you get the buttons as you do with a repeating table. You can add additional editable items by clicking the plus button; you can remove items by clicking the minus button; and you can also rearrange their order by using the up and down arrow buttons.

The purpose of a repeating region is to give a bit more flexibility to the individual adding content to the template-based document. It also offers several advantages to the creators of the templates. You do not need to know specifics about the content being added to template-based documents. The amount of products or images is no longer a concern for a template creator.

Optional Regions

An optional region is more or less a region that can be shown or hidden. This functionality can be determined either by the template author or the template user.

You can create an optional region in two ways: you can create it in the code view or you can create it in the Optional Region dialog box. The code you insert is a comment within the <head> portion of the HTML.

```
<!-- TemplateParam name="Name Something" type="Boolean" value ="false" -->
```

Code is also inserted into the area where you want the optional region to be placed. It looks something like this:

```
<!-- TemplateBeginIf cond="Name Something" -- >
<p><Content you wish to show or hide></p>
<!-- TemplateEndIf -- >
```

Of course, you would substitute "Name Something" with a name that makes more sense for the region, and you would actually have HTML that would add content to the document between the <p> paragraph tags.

Of course, this is Dreamweaver's WYSIWYG HTML editor, so you may just want to set it up through the dialog box. There is generally less room for error that way. To insert an optional region in a template, follow these steps:

1. Open a template by double-clicking it in the Assets panel.

2. In the document, select the item you want to make an optional region.

3. With the item selected, choose Modify, Template Objects, Optional Region. You also can click the Optional Region button in the Insert panel under the Templates tab or contextual-click the object and in the context menu, choose Optional Region. This will open the New Optional Region dialog box, as shown in Figure 8.12.

8

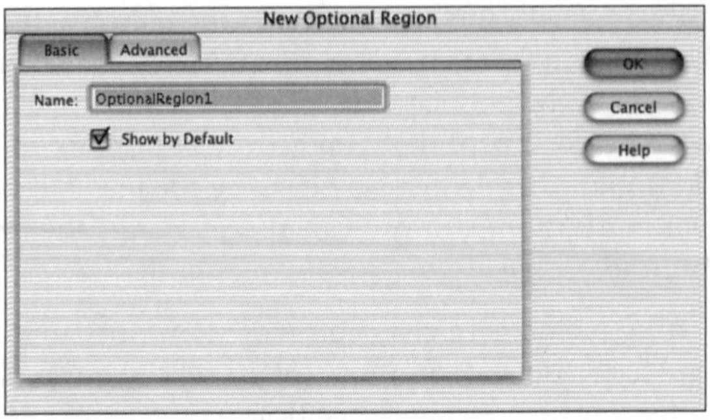

FIGURE 8.12   The New Optional Region dialog box offers the options of creating statements to either hide or display the selected region.

4. With the Basic tab selected, type in a name for the optional region. It's important to name this region something that will make sense to you later on. You will have to refer to this region by this name in a template-based document.

5. If you want the region to appear, leave the Show by Default option selected; if not, uncheck that option. The user of the template will have the option of changing this value by selecting Modify, Template Properties. In the Template Properties dialog box, the user has the option of hiding or showing the optional area, as shown in Figure 8.13.

6. When you're happy with the settings, choose OK.

There is also an Advanced tab in the Optional Region dialog box. The reason is so you can write your own expressions to add functionality and options to the optional region. The template expression language is a small subset of JavaScript and uses JavaScript syntax and precedence rules.

Nested Templates

A nested template is a template whose editable regions and designs are based on another template. Nested templates are handy when designing pages with only slight variations between them. To create a nested template, you must first save a document as a template and then create a document based on that template. With the new template-based document, save it as a template, thus creating a nested template. Editable regions in the base template are then passed through to the nested template and remain editable when pages are created based on a nested template.

Nested templates are new to Dreamweaver MX and should be used only if you're dealing with very similar pages with only subtle differences between them. In the previous sections of this chapter, you looked at how you could broaden the customization features of templates, and nested templates offer more control only to the template author.

However, when using nested templates, you offer the template user some of the same functionality as the template author, although the user is able to manipulate only editable regions.

Updating Template-Based Pages

One of the most impressive and powerful features of templates is the link that a template-based template shares with the template stored in the Assets panel.

Anytime that you make a change to the template page and save it, all templates that are created based on that template are automatically updated. You can even manually update pages by choosing Modify, Templates, Update. This can save a tremendous amount of time.

To update pages based on templates, follow these steps:

1. Open the template by double-clicking it in the Assets panel.

2. Make any changes in the template that you want to update. When you're done, choose File, Save. This automatically updates all template-based documents.

3. You can perform an update manually and receive feedback about the documents that have been updated by choosing Modify, Template, Update Pages. This opens the Update Pages dialog box shown in Figure 8.13.

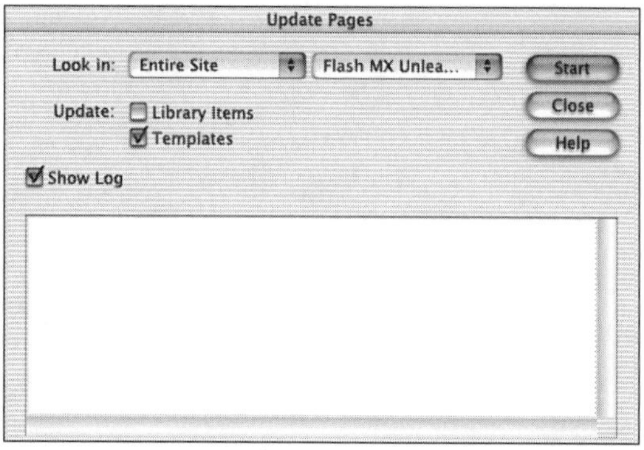

FIGURE 8.13   This dialog box offers options for updating pages both with library items and templates.

4. Choose Site from the drop-down menu labeled Look In. In the next drop-down menu, choose the site in which you want to update the documents. Make sure the Show Log option is checked. When you click the Start button, the bottom portion of the dialog box offers information about the documents that have been updated.

Detach from Template Command

You may run into a situation where you created a new document and applied a template to it. In this document, you don't want it to be updated when the template is changed. This is possible if you break the link between the template-based page and the template. You can accomplish this by using the Detach from Template command. Choose Modify, Template, Detach from Template to remove the template from the page. This effectively breaks the link between the current document and the template.

Summary

Templates can be a key factor if you're trying to promote consistency in your Web site, especially among a team of designers. They offer control for the author of the template to designate only certain areas and attributes that can be edited by other individuals.

They can also be a great way to save development and correction time. If something needs to be changed, you can change it in one location, the template, and essentially all other documents created with that template are updated automatically.

Assets and the Library

By Matt Pizzi

Dreamweaver MX offers a remarkable way of organizing a site's assets. An asset is an item that enhances or adds functionality to a Web design. Items such as images, Shockwave, QuickTime, Flash, JavaScript, and even colors or links are all considered assets. By storing these items in one central location, you're offered the benefit of quick access to any one of these items. No more shuffling around searching for the same content in the local root folder.

Furthermore, the Assets panel offers a Favorites section. Many times, Web sites have thousands of assets, and chances are you're not going to need access to all those assets on a regular basis, so Macromedia created an option within the Assets panel called Favorites. Within the Favorites you can store more commonly used assets, such as the graphics of a company logo, colors that you've been using throughout the site, or even commonly used hyperlinks that you use often on different pages. You'll notice in Figure 9.1 that the Assets panel is divided into several categories.

Working with the Assets Panel

For your Assets panel to work, you must have a local root folder already defined. The Assets panel more or less behaves like an index of all your site's content; however, for some of the assets to appear in the panel, that particular asset must be inserted into a document within your site. Some categories are an exception. Cloaked files will appear in your Assets panel as long as they are an asset that is compliant with the Assets panel. Cloaked files will remain hidden only from a server or host. To open your Assets panel, choose Window, Assets, or use the keyboard shortcut of F11.

FIGURE 9.1   The Assets panel offers several categories on the left side of the panel.

The beauty of the Assets panel is that it manages so many types of media and content. The options include the following:

- **Images**   Any image that is stored within your defined site, such as a JPEG, a GIF, or a PNG file, will automatically be added to the images assets list. Images do not have to be placed into the document first as in some of the other categories.

- **Colors**   This category contains all the colors used throughout your site, including background colors, link colors, and text colors.

- **URLs**   This houses all the external links used throughout your site, which include absolute addresses such as http, https, ftp, and even other URLs used by JavaScript, email, and local file links.

- **Flash**   This section stores all your SWF files. Any SWF file found within your defined site will appear here; however SWT and FLA files will not appear in the Assets panel; only the exported SWF is compliant with the panel. To learn more about Flash and Dreamweaver, refer to Chapter 14, "Inserting Flash and Shockwave," and Appendix C, "Integration with Flash MX."

- **Shockwave Movies**   Any Shockwave movie, typically generated from Director, that is found within your local root folder or defined site will be available in this section. To learn more about Shockwave and Dreamweaver, refer to Chapter 14.

- **MPEG Movies**   This section stores QuickTime and MPEG movies found within your local root folder. See Chapter 13, "Adding Video and Audio" for more information about working with video inside Dreamweaver.

- **Scripts**   This section can store scripts found within your defined site. Only separate script documents appear in the Assets panel. Scripts written within pages are not stored here; however, if you do write and use many of your own scripts, you may want to consider saving them as separate documents to take advantage of the Assets panel.

- **Templates**   Templates can add a great deal of consistency and organization within a site design. You can access all your site templates here within the Assets panel. Templates are covered in great detail in the previous chapter, Chapter 8, "Dreamweaver Templates."

- **Library**   In the Library section of the Assets panel, you can create, access, and manage a site's Library items. Library items are similar to Templates in terms of their functionality; however they're more focused on single items, in contrast to page designs. Refer to the end of this chapter for more information on library items.

How the Assets Panel Works

The Assets panel is divided into separate sections. The section on the left is for selecting a category. The lower-middle portion of the panel is a list of all the assets within the site for the particular category. The top portion offers a preview of the selected asset in the list.

When working with the Assets panel, be sure to have the site cache enabled. You can enable the site cache by choose Site, Edit Sites. This launches the Edit Site dialog box. Highlight the site you want to edit and click the Edit button. When you click the Edit button, the Site Definition dialog box appears. Be sure to have the Advanced tab selected and that you're in the Local Info category. In the middle of the box, click the Enable Site Cache check box, as shown in Figure 9.2.

If you add a link or color to a document in your Web site, you must save that document before the color and link will appear in the Assets panel.

Refreshing the Assets Panel

At some point in the development of your Web site, you'll find that you need to refresh the Assets panel so that the content is being displayed correctly. The Assets panel automatically updates every time you restart the application, but if you're in the middle of a project, that's not realistic. That's why there's a Refresh button, located in the bottom portion of the panel as shown in Figure 9.3.

Okay, you're probably wondering why you would need to update or refresh the Assets panel. Here are the most common reasons:

- If you exported a graphic from Fireworks or Photoshop into the local root folder while Dreamweaver was running, you would need to refresh to make that content viewable in the Assets panel.

- If you use the Site window/panel to remove an asset by deleting it, you would need to refresh the Assets panel for the panel to represent that change.

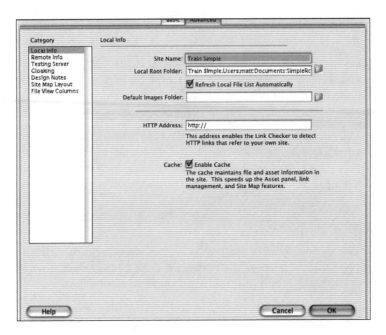

FIGURE 9.2   You can enable the site cache in the Site Definition dialog box. This ensures that your assets will appear in the Assets panel.

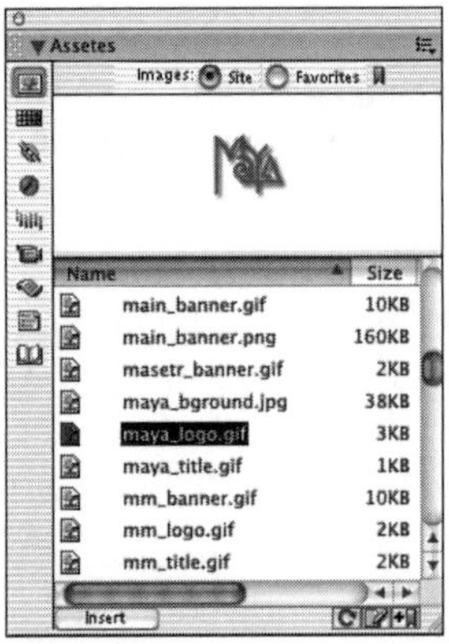

FIGURE 9.3   The Assets panel has a Refresh button to ensure that the most up-to-date content is being viewed.

- If you deleted an image or asset outside of Dreamweaver, such as in Windows Explorer, you would not only have to refresh the Assets panel for it to reflect the change, but you will have to refresh the entire site cache. To refresh the entire site cache, you can access the submenu located in the top-right corner of the Assets panel and choose Re-create Site List, as shown in Figure 9.4, or you can hold down the Command (Mac) or Ctrl (Windows) key while clicking the Refresh button. Finally, you can contextual-click in the Assets panel and access the Re-create Site List option from the contextual menu.

- If you've deleted some files that contain the only or last instance of a color or link asset, you should refresh the Assets panel to see that those particular assets have been removed.

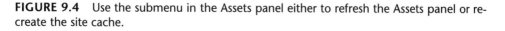

Refresh Site List
Recreate Site List

Edit
Insert

Add to Favorites

Copy to Site   ▶
Locate in Site

Help

Group Assets with   ▶
Rename Panel Group...
Maximize Panel Group
Close Panel Group

FIGURE 9.4   Use the submenu in the Assets panel either to refresh the Assets panel or re-create the site cache.

Inserting Assets

You can insert assets into your documents in a couple of ways. What you want to insert will determine which method you should use. To insert an asset, place a blinking cursor somewhere within the document. If you want precise placement, be sure to have a blinking cursor within a table or layer. Then move over to the Assets panel and highlight the asset you'd like to insert and click the Insert Asset button located toward the bottom of the panel, as shown in Figure 9.5. This places the selected asset in the position of your blinking cursor.

The easiest way is to simply drag and drop. To follow along with these steps, you should have a table set up within your document, and you should be working within a defined site. Within that defined site should be some graphical files to work with. To drag and drop an Asset, follow these steps:

1. Make sure your Assets panel is open. To open the Assets panel, choose Window, Assets or press F11.

2. In this situation, I want to place a graphic in the top cell of the document that I'm working with, as pictured in Figure 9.6. So it's important that the images category is the active category.

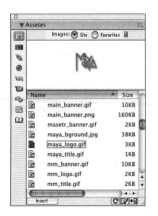

FIGURE 9.5   Click the Insert Asset button located at the bottom of the Assets panel to place an asset into your document.

3. You can browse through the images, looking at the previews the Assets panel offers. When you find one that you're happy with, select it, as shown in Figure 9.7.

4. Click and drag the graphic to the desired location—in this case, the top cell in my table. When the mouse is over the area where you want the graphic to appear, let go of the mouse, and the image will be placed properly inside the cell, as shown in Figure 9.8.

Another way, as I mentioned earlier, is to use the Insert button on the Assets panel. This technique is important, especially when applying links to images or colors to text. To apply links to an existing graphic, follow these steps:

1. Select the graphic within the document you want to apply the link to.

2. With that graphic selected in the Assets panel, be sure to have the link category selected.

3. After browsing through the different link assets, highlight the link you want to use.

4. With the image selected on the document and the link highlighted in the Assets panel, click the Apply button toward the bottom of the panel. The link text field of the Properties Inspector now shows the link you applied to the graphic, as shown in Figure 9.9.

Customizing the Assets Panel

The Assets panel was incorporated into Dreamweaver to enhance workflow. Macromedia knew that for workflow to be enhanced, it was important to allow people to customize features to better suit their work habits. The Assets panel is no exception.

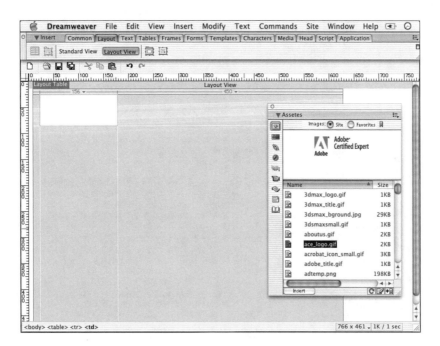

FIGURE 9.6 Notice that there is no content in the cell toward the top of the page. I'm going to insert an asset from the Assets panel into that location.

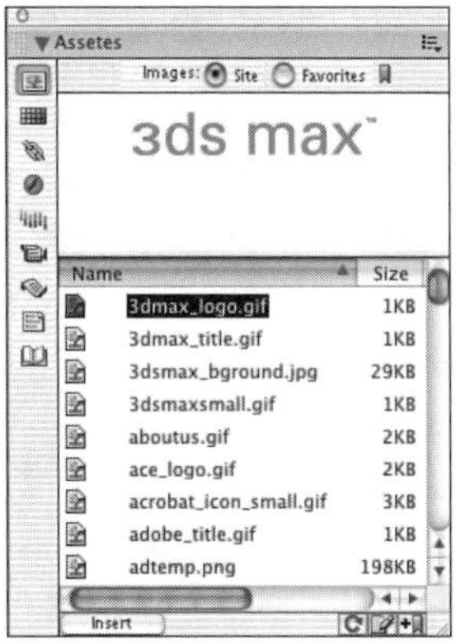

FIGURE 9.7 After browsing through the different images in the Assets panel, I clicked the one I wanted to select.

The first thing you can do is create a list of Favorites. This list can save you a tremendous amount of time shuffling through thousands of images, links, or whatever the asset may be. A section in this chapter titled "Adding Assets to Your Favorites" covers the process in greater detail.

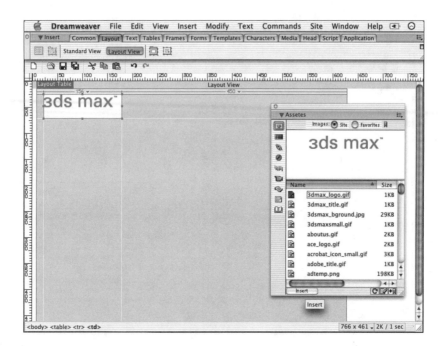

FIGURE 9.8   After dragging and dropping the asset on top of the cell, you'll notice the image automatically appears in the appropriate location.

Another option you have for customizing your experience with the Assets panel is changing the listing order of the assets. The default listing order is alphabetical, from A to Z for the name or value of the asset. If you click the name title header in the Assets panel, you flip the order from Ascending (A to Z) to Descending (Z to A). On the header of the column, an arrow either points down to indicate Ascending order or points up to indicate Descending order, as shown in Figure 9.10.

You can click any one of the headers to sort the list by that particular category. For example, if you wanted to sort by the smallest to largest file size, you would click in the size header.

You can further customize the appearance of the Assets panel by resizing the columns. To do this, hold your cursor directly over the dividing lines. When your cursor changes into a two-way arrow, click and drag the dividers in whichever direction you want to resize the columns. By resizing the columns, you can see additional content, such as the type and possibly the full path, as shown in Figure 9.11.

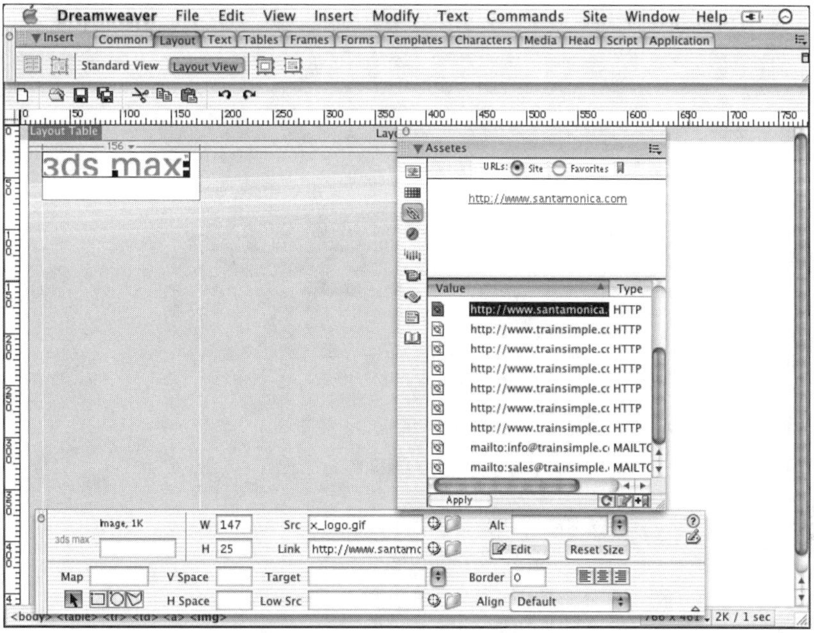

FIGURE 9.9   The Properties Inspector's link text field reflects the link assets you applied to the image.

Managing Your Assets

Now that you've been working with assets a bit, let's look at how you can manage them in your own sites and how you can share them with other sites. Often, you'll be working in a site and wishing you could have access to another site's assets. This is not an unreasonable request—it will just take a few steps of preparation. To copy assets from one site to another, follow these steps:

1. Select the assets you want to copy in the Assets panel. To select multiple assets, you can either hold down the Command (Mac) key or Ctrl (Windows) key while clicking the assets of your choice, or hold down the Shift key to select a range of items.

2. Contextual-click in the selected area, or you can access the submenu in the top-right corner of the panel. In the menu, choose Copy to Site, as shown in Figure 9.12.

3. When you choose the Copy to Site command, a submenu appears, as shown in Figure 9.12, offering all the possible sites you can copy the assets into. Choose the site that you want the selected assets to be available in. These files will then be copied into the site's corresponding folders. If the site does not contain the same folders for the files to be copied into, the folder will automatically be created to accommodate the assets.

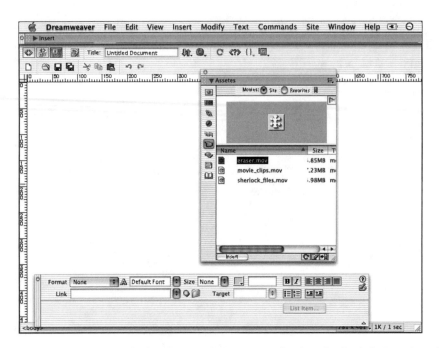

FIGURE 9.10   The arrow on the header is pointing up, indicating the list is being viewed in descending order.

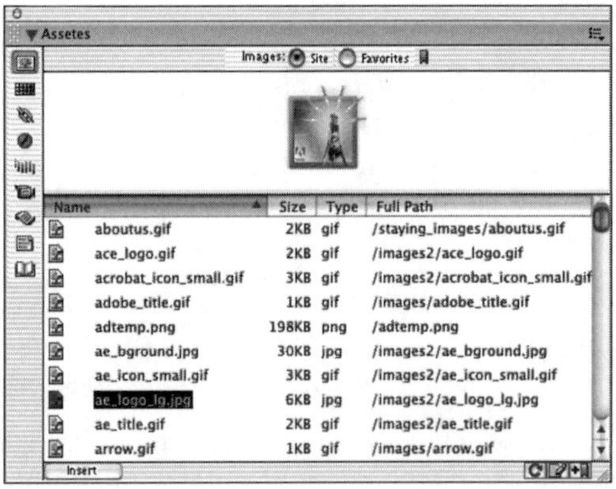

FIGURE 9.11   When resizing the columns in the Assets panel, you're able to view more information about the assets, such as the type and the path to where the asset is located.

Copying assets to other sites is that simple. Open the site that you copied the assets into to make sure that they appear in that site's Assets panel; keep in mind you may have to refresh the panel.

FIGURE 9.12   With assets highlighted, you can copy them to other sites by choosing the Copy to Site command in the context or submenus.

Another concern you may have when working with Assets is where the actual files are located. As you know, you can always see the path on the far right side of the Assets panel. However, a great feature is associated with the Assets panel, called Locate in Site. When you choose the Locate in Site command, Dreamweaver opens the Site window/panel and highlights the location of the selected files in the Assets panel. As Figure 9.13 illustrates, I have two images selected in the Assets panel as I contextual-click and choose the Locate in Site command from the contextual menu. Next, as Figure 9.14 shows, the Site window/panel appears with the selected files in the Assets panel highlighted within the site files, offering the location of the files within the site.

FIGURE 9.13   By contextual clicking in the highlighted asset, I have the option to choose the Locate in Site command.

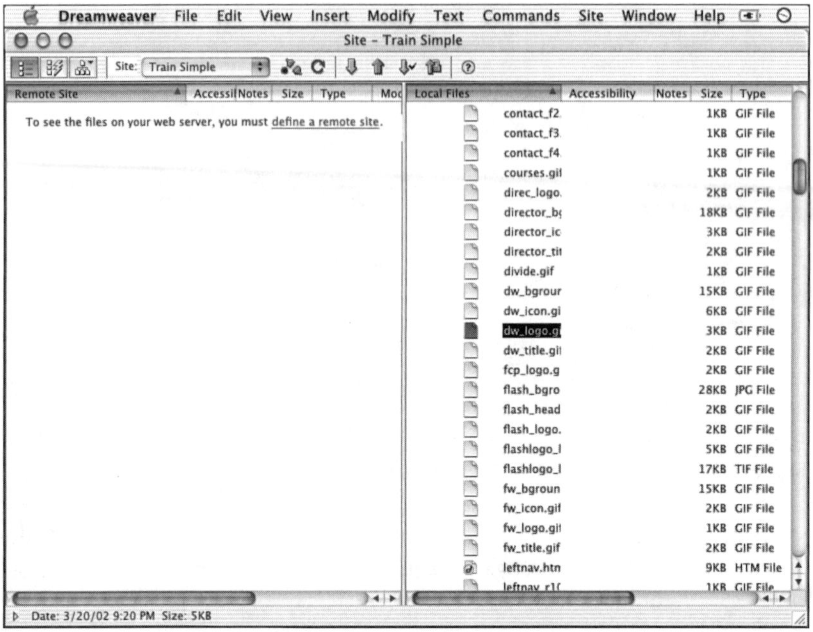

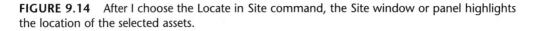

FIGURE 9.14   After I choose the Locate in Site command, the Site window or panel highlights the location of the selected assets.

Editing Assets

After using an asset, you may want to edit some of its properties. For example, if you needed to update a graphic, you can change or edit that image, and anytime that graphic is used within your Web site, it would automatically be updated as well. The reason is that if you inserted the graphic using the same asset, all instances of the image within your site are all sourced to the same file. To edit an image asset, do one of the following:

- Highlight the image in the Assets panel and click the Edit button at the bottom of the panel. This automatically launches the default editor for that file format. For more about default editors, refer to Chapter 15, "Integration with Complementing Programs."

- The second technique is a bit quicker. Double-click the asset icon, and that automatically launches the default editor for that file type.

However, this is not the case for unsourced assets, such as links and colors. These assets are not linked to anything; therefore, when you edit them, they'll only be updated in the Assets panel for future use. If you want colors and links to be updated like images are, you'll need to work with a library item, discussed later in this chapter.

To edit assets such as color and links, they must be contained within the Favorites section of the panel. When you click the Favorites radio button, your favorite colors and links will be revealed. Again, to add something to your Favorites list, refer to that section of this chapter. When you have the color you want selected, click the Edit button and the color swatch appears below the color name, as shown in Figure 9.15. If you decide you no longer want a different color with the swatch open, press Esc to make the swatch disappear without choosing a color.

To edit a link, do the same; highlight the link and click the Edit button at the bottom-right corner of the panel. This opens the Edit URL dialog box, as displayed in Figure 9.16, and you can specify a new URL.

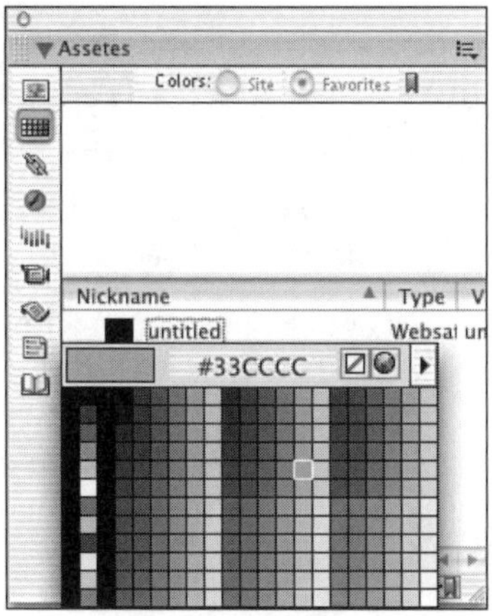

FIGURE 9.15   The color swatch appears inside the Assets panel when you're editing a color. The color has to be located under the Favorites portion of the panel.

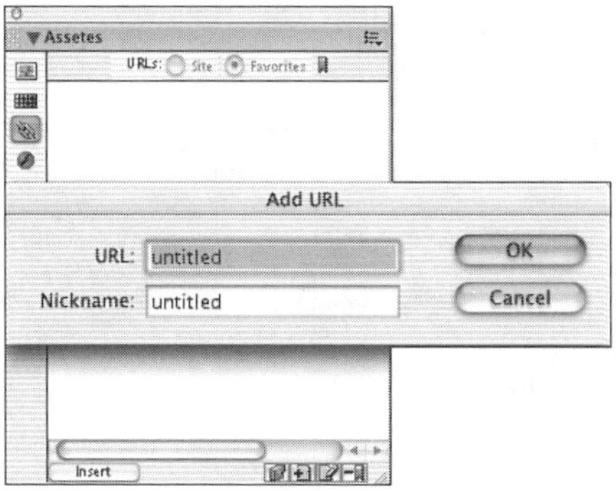

FIGURE 9.16   When you edit a link, the Edit URL dialog box is launched.

Adding Assets to Your Favorites

By adding assets to your Favorites, you can greatly increase productivity. When you're dealing with the Assets panel for an entire Web site, the content often can become unwieldy. Many times, while navigating through the Assets panel, you're looking for a specific file that you use frequently. Instead of having to search for these files again and again, you can store them in a Favorites list, which offers more direct access.

There are several ways to add assets to a Favorites list. You can use any one of the following techniques:

- Highlight the asset or assets you want to add to the Favorites and in the submenu of the Assets panel in the top-right corner, choose Add to Favorites, as shown in Figure 9.17.

- Select the asset or assets that you would like to add to the Favorites and contextual click in the Assets panel. In the contextual menu, choose Add to Favorites.

- You can also select the assets you want to add to the Favorites and click the Add to Favorites button, located at the bottom of the panel.

- Finally, you can highlight an asset already placed within a document, contextual-click the item, and choose Add to Favorites within the contextual menu, as shown in Figure 9.18. You can add assets only in the document that belongs to one of the specified groups within the Assets panel. If you try to add text, the Add to Color Favorites dialog box will appear if the text does not have a link. Otherwise, Add to URL Favorites dialog box will appear.

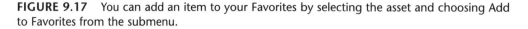

FIGURE 9.17   You can add an item to your Favorites by selecting the asset and choosing Add to Favorites from the submenu.

FIGURE 9.18 You can also add an item to the Favorites by contextual-clicking an instance within the document.

Remove Favorites

You can easily remove a favorite by following these steps:

1. Be sure to have the Favorites radio button selected in the Assets panel.

2. Select or highlight the asset you want to remove.

3. Click the Remove from Favorites button, located at the bottom of the panel. Or you can contextual-click and choose Remove from Favorites in the contextual menu. Finally, with the asset selected, you can also press the Delete key on your keyboard.

> **NOTE**
>
> When deleting favorites, you're not actually deleting the file in any way; rather, you are just removing it from the Favorites list.

Creating Folders to Organize Your Favorites

Another way to manage your favorite assets is to organize them into separate folders. This affords you the opportunity to organize by attributes other than the categories specified by the Assets panel. For example, in your images category, you can create several folders for the different types of images. You could create a folder called Products, which would contain different product images within your site. You could also set up a folder called Navigation, and this folder would contain all the graphics used in your site's navigation structure. The possibilities are endless, yet it does offer another way for the Assets panel to increase your productivity for a more efficient workflow.

To create a new folder for Favorites, follow these steps:

1. Make sure the Assets panel is open and you have the Favorites radio button selected. You can only add Asset Folders to the Favorites category.

2. Click the New Favorites Folder button located at the bottom-right corner of the panel. You can also create a new folder by contextual-clicking the assets and choosing the New Favorite Folder command from the contextual menu.

3. Name the folder and drag any asset that you want categorized into that folder, as shown in Figure 9.19.

FIGURE 9.19   You can easily organize your favorite assets by creating folders.

Creating New URL and Color Assets

You can create new color and URL assets right within the Assets panel. To create new assets for either of these categories, it's very important to be inside your Favorites section.

To create a new color, click the New Color button located toward the bottom of the panel. You can also access that option by choosing New Color from the submenu located in the top-right corner of the panel. When you choose the new color command, a swatch displays in which you can choose a color, as shown in Figure 9.20. Finally, after choosing a color, you can highlight it in the Assets panel and give it a nickname.

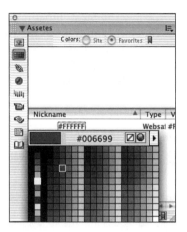

FIGURE 9.20   You can easily create a new color asset from within the Assets panel.

Creating a new link is just as easy. Select the URL category and be sure to view the Favorites section. Toward the bottom of the panel, click the New URL button, which launches the Add URL dialog box. Here you can define the nickname and the URL you want the asset to link to.

Working with Library Items

As convenient as assets are, sometimes you need something a little more powerful. To remain consistent within your Web site design, it often helps to have elements link back to one central or master element. This is exactly what library items offer. Library items can go far beyond simple graphics; in fact, a library item can be a navigation bar or even a JavaScript-based drop-down menu complete with hyperlinks. The great thing about a library item is that it not only will increase productivity by eliminating repetitive tasks, but it also greatly reduces the chance for human error. Suppose, for example, at the bottom of each page within your Web site you placed a footer that noted the copyright date. What if the copyright changes and you have this footer placed on 50 or more documents? That could turn out to be a monumental task for any designer; however, if the footer was saved and used throughout the site as a library item, the designer could update only the item in the library, and the footer on all the 50 or more pages would automatically update. The library inside of Dreamweaver offers some wonderful benefits and can play a crucial role in increasing your productivity.

> **NOTE**
>
> A library item can be any object that is inserted within the <body> tags of the HTML document. These objects can contain behaviors and JavaScript code.

The key about the library, and probably the most difficult part of the library equation, is having prior knowledge of what elements you want to use in the library. This will make or break your library efforts. Having a plan as to how your site will be structured is key, not only in Web development as a whole, but also in how you set up elements within Dreamweaver to take full advantage of its features.

Creating a Library Item

Before any updating can happen with a library item, you must first define something to be in the library. This is a pretty easy task. Remember, anything that can be placed within the <body> tag can be added to the library.

> **CAUTION**
>
> If you place text that has been styled by CSS into the library, you have to include the style sheet in the library as well.

To add an item to the library, follow these steps:

1. Highlight the object in the document that you want to add to the library.

2. Be sure to have the Assets panel open by choosing Window, Assets, and then select the library category. Click the New Library button located at the bottom of the Library panel, as shown in Figure 9.21.

3. A new library item appears in the library. Name the item by typing in the high-lighted text of the icon. Now the item is a library item.

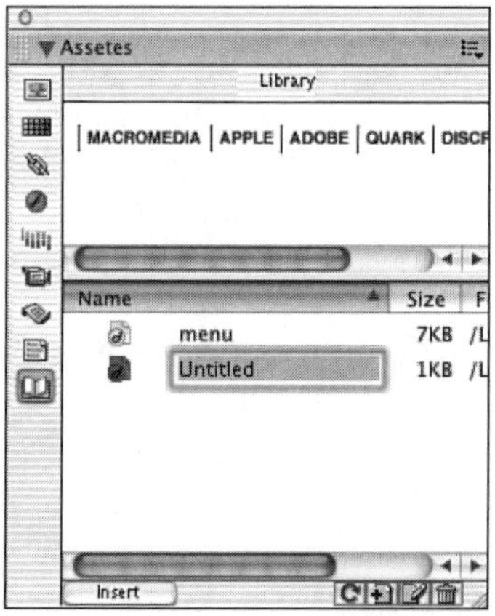

FIGURE 9.21   You can easily create a new library item by clicking the New Library button.

You can also create a library item by highlighting the content you want to add to the library in the document and choosing Modify, Library, Add Item to Library.

Finally, you can also drag the item from the document into the library section of the Assets panel. This creates an untitled library item. To title it, highlight the library item in the Assets panel and in the submenu, located in the top-right corner of the panel, choose Rename. This highlights the icon and allows you to type. Press Return (Mac) or Enter (Windows) to apply the new title.

Inserting a Library Item into a Document

One of the great things libraries can do is promote consistency through your Web site. Every site has core elements, such as a navigation system. It makes perfect sense to make these core elements library items, to enhance design consistency and improve productivity when you're updating these elements. One of the easiest things about library items is how you insert them into pages. This technique resembles many of the techniques discussed earlier when adding Assets to pages. In fact, that's why the library is part of the Assets panel.

After you've set up a site and you've set up some library items, to insert any one of those library items follow, these steps:

1. Place a blinking cursor in the area in which you want to insert the library item. This can be in a layer, a table cell, or just in the document.

2. In the Assets panel, under the library category, highlight the library item you want to insert.

3. Click the Insert button toward the bottom of the Assets panel and the library item will be placed in the document in the same location as the blinking cursor.

You can also drag the library item out of the Assets panel and drop it into the desired location of the document.

After you have the library item inserted into the document, when you select the item, you'll get a speckled mesh pattern around the object. Also note that the Properties Inspector indicates that it is in fact a library item, as shown in Figure 9.22.

FIGURE 9.22   When the library item is selected in the document, the Properties Inspector indicates that it is in fact a library item, and a meshed selection appears around the object.

Editing Library Items and Updating the Site

The great thing about editing a library item is that all occurrences of that library item throughout the Web site will also be updated. There's several ways to edit a library item. With a library instance in the document selected, click the Open button in the Properties

Inspector. You can also double-click the library item in the Assets panel. This will launch a new document window. This window is not a publishable document for the Web; rather, it acts as the editing environment for the library item. The title bar specifies that it's the library editing mode by labeling it <<Library>> instead of a document name, and the background color is gray, as shown in Figure 9.23.

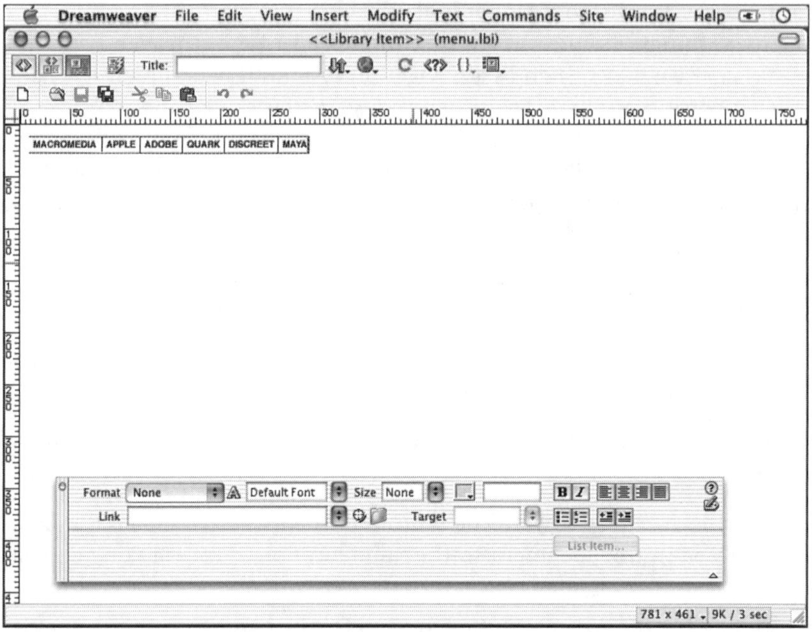

FIGURE 9.23   The title bar of the document indicates that you're in the library editing window, not in a traditional document window.

To finish the edit, follow these steps:

1. Inside the editing window, make any changes necessary. Launch an external editor such as Fireworks or Photoshop, if necessary. To learn more about working with other applications, refer to Chapter 15.

2. Make any text changes normally through the Properties Inspector or the Text menu.

3. When you're happy with your changes, choose File, Save. This opens the Update Library Items dialog box shown in Figure 9.24.

4. If you want all the files listed in the dialog box to be updated, click the Update button; otherwise, you will have to go into the individual files and detach the library instances from the actual library item. The next section covers detaching library items.

5. After you click the Update button, Dreamweaver shows you a log of all the updated areas inside the Update Library Items dialog box.

6. Close the library editing document and return to the site. Open any page containing the library item and notice that any library occurrence has been updated.

Detaching Library Items

In the previous exercise, you were able to edit your library item and update all instances of that library item with a click of a button. There may be situations in which you may not want to update all instances. Dreamweaver offers a workaround—you can detach the link that the instance has from its library counterpart.

You can go about detaching an item from the library in a couple of ways. The first is to highlight the occurrence in your document that you want to detach. In the Properties Inspector, click the Detach button, as shown in Figure 9.24.

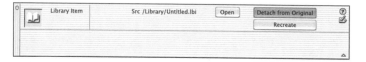

FIGURE 9.24   The Properties Inspector offers an option to detach the item from the library.

After you click the button, the link between the instance and the library item is broken. If you want to update this instance, you'll have to do it by hand. It can no longer be done automatically. If you want to reconnect the item to the library item, you must delete it from your document and re-insert it through the library in the Assets panel.

You can also detach content by Crtl+Clicking (Mac) or right-clicking (Windows) the instance and choosing the Detach from Original command in the contextual menu.

Finally, if you know that you want to use the library item, but you don't want the link to be preserved from the new occurrence to the library item, hold down the Command (Mac) key or Ctrl (Windows) key while dragging the library item out of the library.

Deleting Library Items

You may find that you no longer want or need a particular element to be part of the library. You can easily remove items from the library without affecting library instances.

To delete a library item, highlight it within the library portion of the Assets panel and click the Trash Can button toward the bottom-right corner of the panel. By deleting it from the library, you are not deleting all instances of the library item. All the instances remain in the document. However, if you want to edit or manipulate any one of the instances, you will still have to choose the Detach from Original command. By deleting the library item, the automatic update feature is gone.

Re-create

This option may seem a bit odd, but here's what it offers. If the instance of the library in a document looks at all altered or is missing, click the Re-create button and Dreamweaver will access and refresh the instance to equal the appearance of the library information.

Moving Libraries

If you find that you would like to use a library item in another site, Dreamweaver offers you that capability. If it's just one or two items in the library that you want to copy to another site, highlight the item(s) and Command+Click (Mac) or right-click (Windows) and choose Copy to Site in the contextual menu. After you select Copy to Site, a submenu appears with all the defined sites on your hard drive; then select the site of your choice.

> **NOTE**
>
> After the library item has been moved to another site, no relationship exists between the library items from one site to another.

Summary

Assets and library items are mostly workflow enhancements. However, as this chapter illustrates, you can see that the impact they can have on organization and productivity is profound. Dreamweaver is the standard Web development tool, and these two features are some of the reasons why Dreamweaver is elegant. These features are superior to any other rendition found in competing programs such as GoLive and (cough, cough) dare I say it...FrontPage.

To fully take advantage of Dreamweaver, and to take your Web development skills to the next level, you have to make good use of both of these features.

Cascading Style Sheets

By Kynn Bartlett

The cascading style sheets (CSS) language is a way to describe the appearance of Web pages by assigning styles to specific HTML tags and portions of the page. These styles allow a designer greater range of presentational effects than can be achieved by using only HTML styles. Dreamweaver MX makes it easy to edit and apply style sheets to new or existing Web documents.

If you're already familiar with CSS, you can skip over the following introduction and go directly to "Designing with CSS" to use Dreamweaver MX to build Web pages using styles.

A Brief Introduction to Styles

The font face of a line of text, the colored border around a sidebar, the underline of a link—these are all examples of styles in action. A style is simply the way in which markup, such as HTML content, is displayed to the user.

All browsers have built-in style rules for displaying HTML; for example, they display the <h1> tag as bold, extra-large text and the <p> tag as normal text with a blank line after it. These built-in style rules can be extended or changed by using CSS.

A style sheet is simply a collection of additional style rules that are added to the browser's rules, changing the way in which the browser displays the Web page. Most style sheets are separate files, commonly with the file extension CSS; by saving styles in a CSS file, you can attach the style sheet to any number of HTML pages. This makes it easy to control the presentation of the entire site from a single file or several files in combination.

The word "cascading" refers to the key concept of the cascade. The cascade is the method used to combine style rules from a variety of sources—not only the browser's styles and those of the Web designer, but also the user's preferred styles. In general, the more specific the style, the higher weight it is given in the cascade. A rule that applies to some paragraphs is more specific than one that applies to all paragraphs, and a rule set by the user is more specific (to that user) than one set by the browser.

The CSS language was originally defined by the World Wide Web Consortium's CSS Level One recommendation (December 1996) and was updated in May 1998 by the CSS Level Two recommendation. The CSS Level Two recommendation can be downloaded from `http://www.w3.org/TR/REC-CSS2` in a variety of formats, although it's rather dry reading.

CSS Styles and HTML Styles

CSS properties can create the same types of presentation effects as HTML tags and attributes, such as the `<font>` tag or the various attributes on the `<body>` tag.

But CSS styles go beyond the capabilities of HTML alone, enabling you to create effects such as links that change color when the mouse is moved or borders around any HTML elements. Beyond simple text effects, CSS styles can also be used to lay out the whole page, entirely avoiding the use of HTML tables for layout.

This allows HTML to be used for its primary purpose of conveying the structure of the Web page content, and the style sheet defines the presentation. This separation is quite helpful to Web users who have disabilities, especially visual impairments, because the page content can be accessed directly, yet still allow designers to create visually impressive Web pages. Thus, CSS offers the best of both worlds for the creative designer as well as the user with special needs.

The Syntax of CSS

CSS are created as ordinary text files, as HTML files are, but unlike HTML they don't use a system of tags and attributes. The CSS language instead uses a syntax of its own. Listing 10.1 is an example of a rather ordinary style sheet which sets several rules. Don't worry if you can't understand it yet; you'll be learning to understand CSS rules soon, and Dreamweaver MX automates the process of writing style rules for you.

LISTING 10.1   A Typical CSS Consists of Multiple CSS Rules

```
body {
        font-family: Arial, sans-serif;
}
h1, h2, h3, h4, h5, h6 {
        font-family: Verdana, sans-serif;
        color: teal;
}
```

LISTING 10.1 Continued

```
p {
        padding-left: 3em;
}
.person {
        padding-left: 0em;
        font-size: large;
        font-weight: bold;
        color: maroon;
}
.job {
        font-weight: bold;
```

This style sheet consists of five style rules. Locate the pairs of braces (curly brackets) to differentiate each style; each set of braces represents one rule. The style rule begins with a selector, which indicates what parts of the Web page should be styled by this rule. Then, within the braces are one or more declarations, consisting of a CSS property name, a colon, the value of that property, and a semicolon.

These properties determine how the style differs from the default values. For example, the font-family value specifies a certain font face that should be used by the browser instead of its default font (which is usually Times New Roman). Each CSS property can be assigned a certain set of values; for example, font-family can be assigned names of fonts, whereas padding-left can accept measurements. Dreamweaver MX makes it easy to assign values by providing pull-down menus with the appropriate values and units for each property.

> **NOTE**
>
> When setting measurements and font sizes, you can use several types of units. The most common are pixels and percentages, which work just like pixel and percentage values in HTML. Ems are based on the size of the current font, as set by the style sheet or the user's browser preferences; if the font is 12-point Arial, a measurement of 2 ems equals 2 times 12 points, or 24 points. Inches and centimeters can also be used as units of measure.
>
> Units that are based on a fixed physical size, such as pixels, points, inches, or centimeters, are absolute units. These are most useful if you know the exact dimensions of the output device with a fair degree of certainty. Percentages and ems are relative units, which—if used properly—adjust to the user's desired preferences, which is useful for users with disabilities. In general, relative units are more accessible, but absolute units are easier for designers to work with. If accessibility is a concern, use relative units even if it means slightly less control over the final output.

10

Link, Class, and Span

To use CSS styles with HTML files, several tags and attributes are used that aren't commonly seen outside of their roles in CSS.

The `<link>` tag is found only in the `<head>` section; it specifies a style sheet that is attached to the HTML file. Without using `<link>`, an external style sheet can't be associated with the Web page; `<link>` tells the browser to load those styles and apply them.

The `class` attribute is used to define custom styles in HTML; by setting a `class` attribute on any HTML tag, you make it part of a group of tags that can be selected by a style rule.

The `<span>` tag is used to designate a smaller part of an HTML element as being part of a class; it functions like a `<strong>` or `<em>` inline element, but with no specific styles attached to it.

Examples of these tags and attributes are shown in the HTML page in Listing 10.2. You won't need to memorize the syntax for these tags and attributes, because Dreamweaver MX creates them for you. However, you should be familiar with their function, in case you wonder why Dreamweaver MX is inserting all these strange things into your Web page!

LISTING 10.2   This HTML File Uses the *class* Attribute to Set Styles

```
<!DOCTYPE HTML PUBLIC "-//W3C//DTD HTML 4.01 Transitional//EN">
<html>
<head>
<title>Idyll Mountain Internet Employees</title>
<meta http-equiv="Content-Type" content="text/html; charset=iso-8859-1">
<link href="idyllmtn.css" rel="stylesheet" type="text/css">
</head>
<body>
<h2>Let's meet the Idyll Mountain team:</h2>
<p class="person">Liz Bartlett</p>
<p>As <span class="job">Chief Operations Officer</span>, Liz runs the
  business aspects of the company, and is also the primary designer
  for the majority of Idyll Mountain client sites.</p>
<p class="person">Kynn Bartlett</p>
<p>Although rarely seen around the office,
  <span class="job">Chief Technologist</span>
  Kynn Bartlett does system administration as well as trailblazing new
  technologies and leading our accessibility efforts.</p>
<p class="person">Maria Moreno</p>
<p>Our <span class="job">Graphic Designer</span> Maria is responsible
  for the visual design of most of our Web sites, and also for entries
  in the <a href="http://www.dogshow.com/">Virtual Dog Show</a>.</p>
<p class="person">David Waller and Laura Bishop</p>
<p><span class="job">Site Maintenance Specialists</span> David and Laura
  maintain and develop client Web sites according to the
  <acronym title="World Wide Web Consortium" lang="en">W3C</acronym>'s
  <acronym title="HyperText Markup Language" lang="en">HTML</acronym>
```

LISTING 10.2   Continued

```
and <acronym title="Cascading Style Sheets" lang="en">CSS</acronym>
specifications.</p>
</body>
</html>
```

You should be able to spot the `class="person"` and `class="job"` attributes in this HTML file; these refer to the style rules from Listing 10.1. Apart from these classes, the HTML file doesn't contain any presentational markup; `<font>` tags and their ilk are conspicuously absent. If you load the Web page in a Web browser, however, you'll see styles applied to the HTML thanks to the `<link>` tag referencing the style sheet. The end result of combining the HTML with the CSS is shown in Figure 10.1.

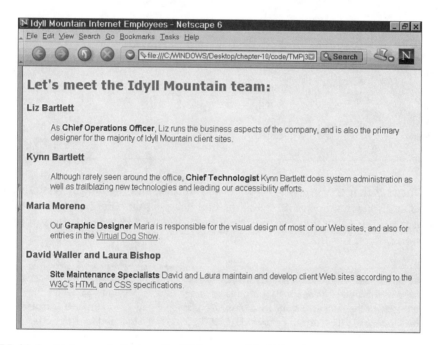

FIGURE 10.1   Netscape 6 displays the Web page with CSS styles.

Support for CSS Styles

Although CSS has been around since 1996, it's only recently that there has been widespread support for styles in the browsers. Early attempts at CSS implementation, notably Internet Explorer 3 and Netscape 4, were well-meaning but unfortunately contained serious bugs. Most Web developers wisely avoided using CSS until browsers would correctly interpret their designs.

The short listing of browser versions in Table 10.1 gives a rough idea as to the adoption of CSS by the browsers. This is just a representative sample of the most common browsers and doesn't include many of the other browsers out there, such as OmniWeb, Konqueror, or iCab.

TABLE 10.1   Browser Support for CSS

Browser and Version	CSS Implementation
Internet Explorer 3	Poor
Internet Explorer 4	Fair
Internet Explorer 5 (Windows)	Good
Internet Explorer 5 (Macintosh)	Great
Internet Explorer 6	Good-Great
Lynx	None
Netscape 3	None
Netscape 4	Fair
Netscape 6	Great
Netscape 7	Great
Mozilla 1	Great
Opera 3	Fair
Opera 4	Good
Opera 5	Good-Great
Opera 6	Great
WebTV	Fair

The good news is that CSS support continues to improve, and the newest versions are quite good at displaying most CSS styles. The bad news is that older browsers are still out there, and that means that you need to be sure to test your CSS-based designs in as many older versions as you can find.

> **NOTE**
>
> Several newer browsers have a special compatibility mode for HTML and CSS, where they adhere more closely to the published standards. Mozilla, Netscape 6 and 7, and Internet Explorer 6 turn on this mode when they encounter a valid DOCTYPE for HTML Strict and for a few other DOCTYPE declarations; other pages are done in a "quirky" mode for backward-compatibility with older browsers. For more information, see the following URLs:
>
> - `http://www.mozilla.org/docs/web-developer/quirks/`
> - `http://msdn.microsoft.com/library/default.asp?url=/ library/ en-us/dnie60/html/cssenhancements.asp`

A recommended basic test suite includes Netscape 4, Netscape 6 (or Netscape 7, or Mozilla), Internet Explorer, Opera, and Lynx. A good CSS design may not look the same on every browser—especially Lynx—but should be functional on all browsers and platforms. You can download these browsers from the following locations, if they're not already installed on your computer:

- Netscape for Windows or Macintosh: `http://www.netscape.com/`

- Mozilla for Windows or Macintosh: `http://www.mozilla.org/`

- Internet Explorer for Windows: `http://www.microsoft.com/windows/ie/`

- Internet Explorer for Macintosh: `http://www.microsoft.com/mac/`

- Opera for Windows or Macintosh: `http://www.opera.com/`

- Lynx for Windows or Macintosh: `http://lynx.browser.org/`

Designing with CSS

Dreamweaver MX makes it easy to design a Web page using CSS styles. The primary way to access CSS design features is through the CSS Styles panel. You can toggle this panel off and on with Shift+F11.

Creating a CSS-based design may require you to think differently about how you assemble a Web page. To start designing, create an HTML page, but don't assign it any specific HTML styles such as colors or alignment—you'll set those with CSS styles. Use HTML tags such as `<h1>` or `<strong>`, which give meaning to the text they surround, but avoid those which grant only appearance changes such as `<font>`.

After you've got your content in your HTML page, you can start adding CSS styles. The creation process has four steps:

1. Create a style sheet file.

2. Define the styles you want to use.

3. Apply the styles to the HTML page.

4. Test the styles in a variety of Web browsers.

Dreamweaver MX makes it easy to step through this process, automating your choices and doing the work of writing the CSS language for you.

Create a Style Sheet

To create a new style sheet in Dreamweaver MX, start by defining a style. Go to the CSS Styles panel in the Design window, and click the Add Style button—it looks like a plus (+) symbol next to a document. This opens the dialog window shown in Figure 10.2.

FIGURE 10.2   Creating a new style sheet in Dreamweaver MX.

You have three options for the type of style to create: a custom style, a redefined HTML tag, or a CSS selector. Custom styles, despite the name, are easiest to use; redefined HTML tags and CSS selectors are covered later in this chapter. By default, Dreamweaver MX names the first custom style .unnamed1, as you can see in Figure 10.2.

All custom styles have a single-word name, which identifies that style. Custom styles begin with a period, and if you don't add it in, Dreamweaver MX will remind you. In your HTML markup, the `class` attribute will be set to this style name to identify it, minus the leading period. A custom style can also be thought of as a class style, or a CSS style with a `class` selector.

> **TIP**
>
> You can name a class style anything you like; it's basically just an arbitrary word used to group these items. A descriptive name is good, especially one that describes the function instead of presentation details. For example, `class="detail"` makes more sense than `class="bluetext"`. Why? Well, you may want to change your styles later, and what if the details are no longer in blue? You should also avoid using style names that are the same as HTML tags or attributes, simply to avoid confusion.

In the sample style sheet in Listing 10.1, I created a class called `.person` by entering that class name in the New CSS Style dialog box.

The other option when creating a new style is to choose the file in which the style is defined. There are initially two options: defining the style in a new style sheet or defining it within the HTML document. The option This Document Only creates an embedded style sheet, which is covered later in this chapter. To make a new style sheet, select New Style Sheet and click the OK button. You will be prompted for a style sheet filename and location.

Your CSS file should be named .css because that's the commonly used extension for style sheets. Technically it doesn't need to follow this naming convention, but there's no good reason to go against the grain here.

Define Your Styles

After you've given a filename to your style sheet, you'll be presented with a window to set the options on your style. As shown in Figure 10.3, there are eight sets of options, and by default, you start on the Type option. You can set any number of text options at this point; in the example, I've chosen to make the text bold and change the color to teal.

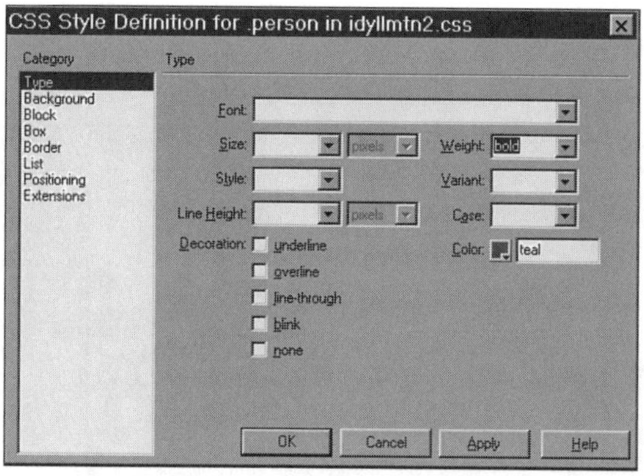

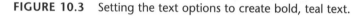

FIGURE 10.3   Setting the text options to create bold, teal text.

After you've set the options you desire, click the Apply button. Later in this chapter, I'll cover each option and explain what effect it has on your styles. When that's done, you've created your first style!

You can create more styles by selecting New CSS Style again; you won't need to create a new style sheet, because you can store them all in the same style sheet file.

Apply Your Styles

Dreamweaver MX gives you a number of ways to apply CSS styles to your Web page. The simplest is to use the CSS Styles window. Make sure the window is open by pressing Shift+F11, and check that the Apply Styles option is selected.

Then, in your HTML file, choose the text that you want to receive the style. Highlight the section with the mouse, and then click the symbol to the left of the style name. This symbol looks like a short piece of chain next to a stylized S, and it's the symbol for applying a style. The text you selected will change to your new style.

You can remove the style by highlighting text and clicking the button next to No CSS Style; this symbol is a red line through the stylized S.

10

> **TIP**
>
> To apply a style to an entire paragraph, click anywhere within the paragraph, and then click the Apply Style button. This will apply the style to the whole paragraph at once.

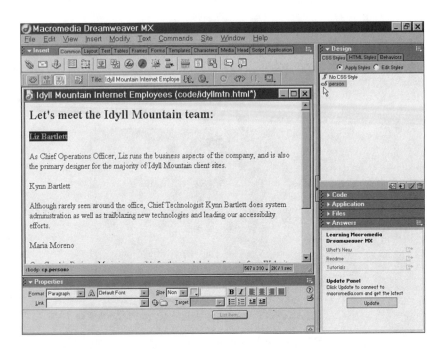

FIGURE 10.4   Highlight text and then apply a style using the CSS Design panel.

You can also use the Properties window to apply a CSS style. The Properties window operates in two modes—HTML properties and CSS properties. To switch to CSS style, you'll need to click the toggle button, which looks like the letter A. You'll then be able to select a style from the pull-down menu, as shown in Figure 10.5.

Three other ways exist to set the style of HTML text. You can select a style from the CSS Styles option on the Text menu; you can highlight the text and right-click (or Ctrl+click) and apply it via the context menu; or you can edit the HTML directly in code view and add an appropriate `class` attribute.

Test Your Designs

After you've applied your styles, you'll want to test how they look in a browser. Dreamweaver MX's design view will show you the effects of some styles, but not all of them; to get a real test of your new styles, you need to test in several browsers. Remember that not all browsers treat CSS the same way, so you will need to test in a variety to make sure your designs look decent and can be used reliably.

Use the Preview in Browser option from the File menu—or the equivalent toolbar button, which looks like a globe—to display your HTML page and style sheet in a browser. The screenshot in Figure 10.6 shows how the browser interprets the CSS file and applies it to the Web page.

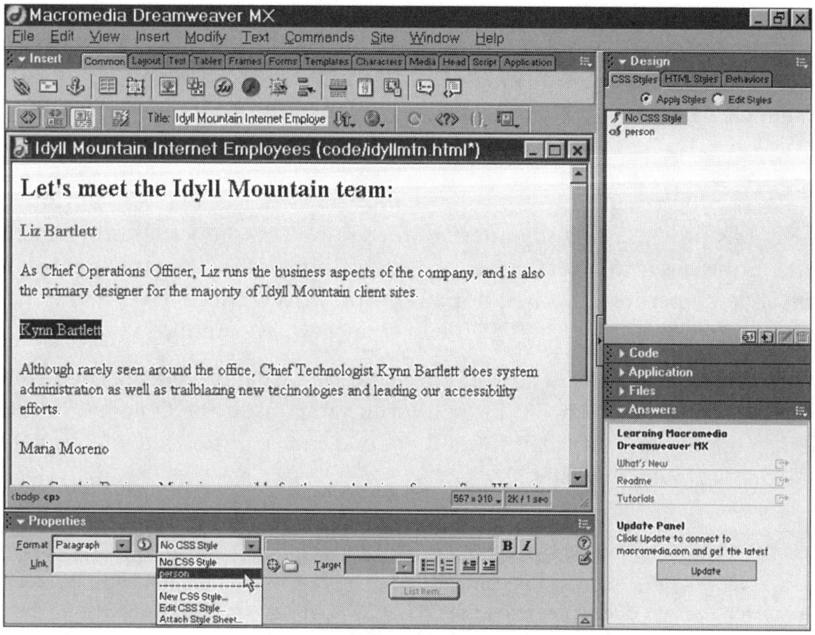

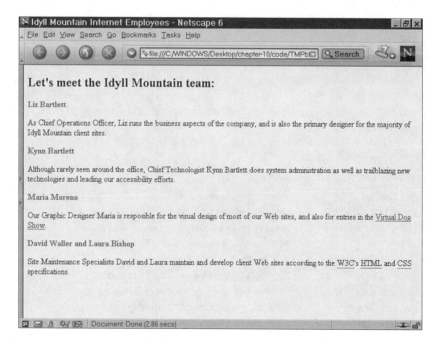

FIGURE 10.5   Styles can be applied using the Properties window, after toggling to CSS mode.

FIGURE 10.6   Our styles have been successfully applied to the HTML file, as shown by Netscape 6.

If your styles work on the first try, congratulations! In most cases, you may need to do some editing and changing based on the results of testing in a variety of browsers. Don't worry, that's common; it's an unfortunate fact of life for CSS designers that browser testing is an essential chore.

Style Properties

Dreamweaver MX provides a handy interface for setting CSS properties on your styles, dividing the properties into several menus of related options. These menus can set all the most useful style properties, although not all CSS properties are covered; additional CSS properties can be set by editing the CSS file in code view, as described later in this chapter.

The rest of this section describes each option menu in turn and the associated style properties. To learn more about each CSS property, you can consult the O'Reilly CSS Reference accessible through the Answers menu. Another good source of CSS knowledge is Teach Yourself CSS in 24 Hours, published by Sams.

> **NOTE**
>
> Dreamweaver MX does not give the name of CSS properties in the option menus; for example, it has a box for Size and doesn't mention the CSS property name `font-size` anywhere. This makes Dreamweaver MX somewhat easy to use, but it can make it difficult to look up CSS properties in other references. For this reason, style options in this chapter will be followed by the name of the CSS property in parentheses.

Text Options

The text options control the appearance of the selected text. Many of these options are very similar to the `<font>` tag in HTML, although CSS styles offer you greater control than allowed in HTML styles. The complete list of text options, and the effects produced by each, are shown in Table 10.2.

TABLE 10.2   CSS Text Properties

Option (CSS Name)	Effect
Font (`font-family`)	Sets the font face choice(s) and default font family.
Size (`font-size`)	Sets the size of the text to absolute or relative sizes.
Weight (`font-weight`)	Sets the text to bold, light, bolder, lighter, or a numeric value (100 is lightest, 500 is normal, and 900 is darkest).
Style (`font-style`)	Sets the font to italic or oblique.
Variant (`font-variant`)	Sets the text to small capital letters instead of lowercase letters.
Line Height (`line-height`)	Sets the line spacing; a value of 2 ems equals double-spaced text.
Case (`text-transforms`)	Changes the case of the text using CSS.
Decoration (`text-decoration`)	Adds special effects to the text such as underlines, overlines, strikethroughs, or blinking text.
Color (`color`)	Sets the (foreground) color of the text.

One concept unique to CSS that does not appear in HTML is that of generic font families. When you specify a `font-family` value, you are actually listing several fonts. If the user's computer doesn't have the first font, the browser will pick subsequent fonts from the list until it finds a match. Your final `font-family` value should be a generic font that is similar to the specific fonts you're attempting to use.

The generic fonts are `sans-serif`, `serif`, `monospace`, `fantasy`, and `cursive`. Each browser has a default value for each generic family, and it will use that if no other font from your list is found. For example, if you set a `font-family` value of `Georgia, serif` and the user's computer doesn't have the Georgia font installed, the browser will display the generic serif font (which, for most browsers, is Times New Roman).

Background Options

In HTML, you can set the background for the whole page or for individual table cells. With CSS styles, you can set a background for any part of the page and a background image as well. The background options are summarized in Table 10.3.

TABLE 10.3 CSS Background Properties

Option (CSS Name)	Effect
Background Color (`background-color`)	Sets the background color.
Background Image (`background-image`)	Selects a background image, which (by default) is tiled.
Repeat (`background-repeat`)	Determines if the background image tiles (`repeat`), repeats horizontally (`repeat-x`), repeats vertically (`repeat-y`), or doesn't tile at all (`no-repeat`).
Attachment (`background-attachment`)	Determines if the background image scrolls when the page scrolls, or remains fixed.
Horizontal (`background-position`)	Determines the initial placement of the background image; can be `left`, `middle`, or `right`, a measurement, or a percentage.
Vertical (`background-position`)	Determines the initial placement of the background image; can be `top`, `middle`, or `bottom`, a measurement, or a percentage.

The Repeat, Attachment, Horizontal Position, and Vertical Position options apply only if there's a chosen background image. Background images may not load if the user has image loading turned off, so you'll want to choose a background color that is similar to your background image, if possible.

TIP

When you set the text color, it's a good idea to also set the background color and make sure that there is good contrast between the foreground and background. This will help users with visual impairments read your page more easily. Also, if you set the text color alone and not the background, you could cause problems for your users who set their browsers to different default colors. For example, setting the text to black but not the background to white will make your words invisible to users with white-on-black default settings, a common combination for people with low vision.

Block Options

The block options are CSS properties that affect the display of a block of text. These options are shown in Table 10.4.

TABLE 10.4   CSS Block Properties

Option (CSS Name)	Effect
Word Spacing (`word-spacing`)	Increases or (for negative values) decreases the spacing between words.
Letter Spacing (`letter-spacing`)	Increases or (for negative values) decreases the spacing between letters.
Vertical Alignment (`vertical-align`)	Determines the vertical placement relative to the text baseline.
Text Align (`text-align`)	Determines the horizontal alignment; `justify` aligns the text on both right and left.
Text Indent (`text-indent`)	Indents the first line of the text by a given measurement or percentage.
Whitespace (`white-space`)	Determines whether whitespace will be ignored (`normal`, the default), treated as preformatted text (`pre`), or displayed without line wrapping (`nowrap`).
Display (`display`)	Sets a block so that it's not displayed (`none`) or is displayed as another type of markup element.

The display property can be used to make an element invisible; this can be useful for text you want to show to users who aren't using a CSS-enabled browser, because the display property will be ignored along with all other CSS. Just don't use it to show a message such as "Upgrade your browser, loser!" because that's plain rude.

> **TIP**
>
> You might assume that you can use the Text Align option to center tables and other block elements; unfortunately, that's an incorrect—but natural—assumption. The CSS `text-align` property aligns only inline content such as text; if you need to center a block element such as a `<table>`, set the margins of the left and right sides to the value `auto`. Margin is one of the box options.

Box Options

CSS browsers display all HTML elements as a series of nested boxes. The box options control the characteristics of those boxes, as shown in Table 10.5.

TABLE 10.5   CSS Box Properties

Option (CSS Name)	Effect
Width (width)	Sets the width of the display box to a measurement or a percentage.
Height (height)	Sets the height of the display box to a measurement or percentage.
Float (float)	Makes the box float to the right or left, and subsequent content flows around it on the other side.
Clear (clear)	Stops content from flowing around boxes that float on the right or left.
Padding (padding)	Sets the padding of the box to a measurement or percentage; can be set separately on each side.
Margin (margin)	Sets the margin of the box to a measurement or percentage; can be set separately on each side.

An HTML element's CSS display box is like an onion; it is composed of a number of layers wrapped around each other. The outer layer is the margin; the margin is transparent, and the value of the margin specifies the minimum distance that box must be from another nearby box. Vertical margins will *collapse*, which means that only the largest value will be used between two boxes. This makes sense; it's like if Lois said "everyone has to stay three meters away from me" and Clark declared "everyone has to stay one meter away from me." They will obviously use the larger limit of three meters, instead of adding them together and staying four meters from each other.

Within the margin is the border layer, which is set by the border options (covered in the next section). Within the border is the padding; the padding isn't transparent, but is set to the same background color (or image) as the element itself. The innermost part of the display box is the element content itself. The width and height properties set the content width, not the total of the content, the padding, the border, and the margin, or some combination thereof.

Border Options

The border options enable you to draw lines around CSS display boxes. Each box can have one border, but you can style each side of that box differently if you want. The border options are shown in Table 10.6.

TABLE 10.6   CSS Border Properties

Option (CSS Name)	Effect
Style (border-style)	Sets the type of line used to draw the border; can be set separately on each side.
Width (border-width)	Sets the width of the line used to draw the border as a measurement or percentage; can be set separately on each side.
Color (border-color)	Sets the color of the line used to draw the border; can be set separately on each side.

10

The lines drawing a border can be set to give a three-dimensional effect by the use of outset or inset or by using different colors on the top and left borders.

List Options

The list options shown on Table 10.7 affect only lists created with the HTML <ul> or <ol> tags, and they apply only to the <li> elements within those lists. These properties enable you to change the appearance of the marker before each list item, which is a bullet for unordered lists (<ul>) or a counter for ordered lists (<ol>).

TABLE 10.7   CSS List Properties

Option (CSS Name)	Effect
Type (list-style-type)	Determines the type of marker used before each item in the list; can be bullets (disc, circle, square) or counters (decimal, lower-roman, upper-roman, lower-alpha, upper-alpha).
Bullet Image (list-style-image)	Selects an image file (GIF, JPEG, or sometimes PNG) that replaces the list marker.
Position (list-style-position)	Determines whether the list marker is placed inside or outside of the margin of the list item.

Unfortunately, the CSS language does not have a way to specify the starting value for a list counter; for example, there's no way to start counting at six using CSS rules.

Positioning Options

The positioning options enable you to precisely lay out the Web page using CSS properties instead of HTML tables—in theory, at least. In practice, the CSS positioning properties tend to be irregularly supported, and it takes a lot of work and testing to make Web pages that work correctly in most browsers. In most cases, it's easier to simply use <table> markup for layout. The options for positioning CSS are shown in Table 10.8.

TABLE 10.8   CSS Positioning Properties

Option (CSS Name)	Effect
Type (position)	Chooses the positioning scheme used to place the box.
Width (width)	Sets the width of the display box to a measurement or a percentage.
Height (height)	Sets the height of the display box to a measurement or percentage.
Visibility (visibility)	Determines if the box is shown; if not shown, the space for the box is still reserved in the layout.
Z-Index (z-index)	Determines the stacking order for boxes placed over each other; higher-numbered boxes are at the top of the stack.

TABLE 10.8   Continued

Option (CSS Name)	Effect
Overflow (`overflow`)	Determines what should be done if the space required to display all the content exceeds the dimensions set by the height and width; excess content can flow out of the box (`visible`), be clipped (`hidden`), or be accessed via scrollbars (`scroll`).
Placement (`left`, `right`, `top`, `bottom`)	Places the box as an offset from its content box, as determined by the chosen positioning scheme.
Clip (`clip`)	Sets a mask within the box that hides displayed content outside of the clipping box.

To use CSS positioning, first you must decide on the positioning scheme to be used: `static`, `relative`, `absolute`, or `fixed`. The scheme determines the context box for the positioned element, and its final position is located relative to that context box.

Static positioning is simply the normal way pages are laid out without CSS positioning; it's the default value. Relative positioning calculates the static position and then applies offsets relative to that position. Absolute positions are calculated based on the location within the browser window or within any parent element that's been positioned. Fixed positioning is like absolute positioning, except that the fixed content never scrolls when the page scrolls; it remains fixed in position.

Offsets move the positioned box relative to its context box, with positive offsets moving toward the center of the box and negative toward the outside. These offsets are determined by the values given to the `top`, `right`, `bottom`, and `left` properties.

Extensions and Filters

The extensions and filters options constitute a catch-all category; it's where Dreamweaver MX places miscellaneous CSS properties. These properties are shown in Table 10.9.

TABLE 10.9   CSS Extensions and Filters

Option (CSS Name)	Effect
Page Break Before (`page-break-before`)	Tells the printer to start on a new page before printing this element.
Page Break After (`page-break-after`)	Tells the printer to start on a new page after printing this element.
Cursor (`cursor`)	Change the pointer when the mouse is over this element.
Filter (`filter`)	Apply a special effect filter; nonstandard CSS.

The filters are poorly supported—and because they're not part of the CSS specifications, that's to be expected. You shouldn't rely on them, although the majority of browsers will simply ignore those properties.

10

Shorthand Properties in CSS

If you open up the Preferences dialogue box in Dreamweaver MX and look at the CSS preferences, you'll find they deal exclusively with something called *shorthand properties*, as shown in Figure 10.7.

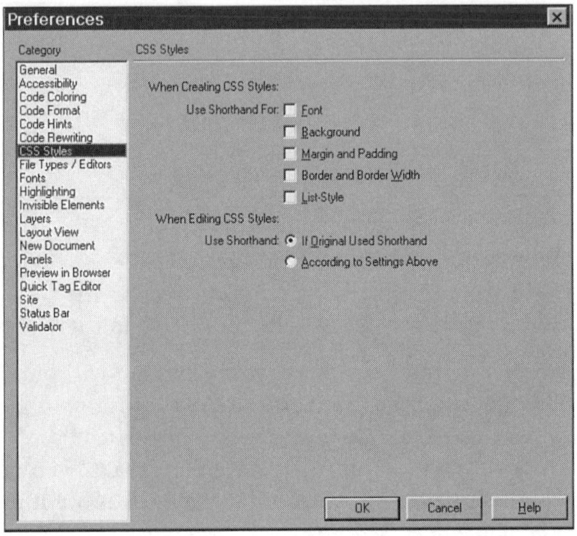

FIGURE 10.7   CSS preferences in Dreamweaver MX control the use of shorthand properties.

A shorthand property is a simple way of writing several properties at once. For example, consider the following rules:

```
background-color: blue;
background-image: url("mybg.gif");
background-repeat: repeat-y;
background-position: top left;
```

Those rules can be written more compactly using the `background` shortcut property:

```
background: blue url("mybg.gif") repeat-y top left;
```

The CSS Preferences panel is allowing you to choose whether Dreamweaver MX will write certain properties using this shorthand notation or will write out every rule. The list of shorthand properties is shown in Table 10.10.

TABLE 10.10   CSS Shorthand Properties

Shorthand Property	Properties Set
font	font-style, font-variant, font-weight, font-size, line-height, font-family
background	background-color, background-image, background-repeat, background-attachment, background-position
margin	margin-top, margin-right, margin-bottom, margin-left
padding	padding-top, padding-right, padding-bottom, padding-left
border	border-style, border-width, border-color
list-style	list-style-type, list-style-image, list-style-position

If you set Dreamweaver to use shorthand properties, keep in mind that setting a shorthand property has two effects: it sets all associated properties to their default values, and then it sets the listed values. So if you use the shorthand property font with a value of 8px Verdana, remember that you've also just set the font-weight to normal (the default value for that property).

Dreamweaver MX writes the properties for you most of the time, so there's no great value in turning on the shorthand properties in CSS preferences.

CSS Validation

Dreamweaver MX enables you to check your HTML code for validity and conformance to accessibility standards, but unfortunately, it does not provide the same capability for style sheets.

Instead, you can use the W3C's CSS validator, which runs via the Web, to check your CSS for code mistakes or omissions. You can verify your style sheet by going to http://jigsaw.w3.org/css-validator/. Sample output from the CSS validator is shown in Figure 10.8.

Working with CSS Styles

Now that you have a basic understanding of CSS properties, you're ready to create more extensive style sheets that take advantage of the power of CSS. Dreamweaver MX is your helpful assistant in developing, editing, and deploying CSS styles.

Editing Styles

After you've defined a style, you'll eventually want to go back and edit it. To do this, open the CSS Styles panel with Shift+F11 or select it from the Window menu. The CSS Styles panel has two settings: Apply Styles and Edit Styles. Select the Edit Styles setting and the display changes to list each of your styles and allows you to edit each one, as shown in Figure 10.9. If you choose a style and click the Edit Style Sheet button—which looks like a pencil writing on lined paper—you'll find yourself in the familiar CSS options menus, and you can change the style properties.

10

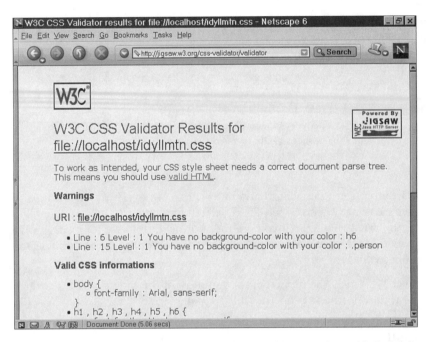

FIGURE 10.8   The W3C's CSS validator can spot code problems and provide helpful warnings.

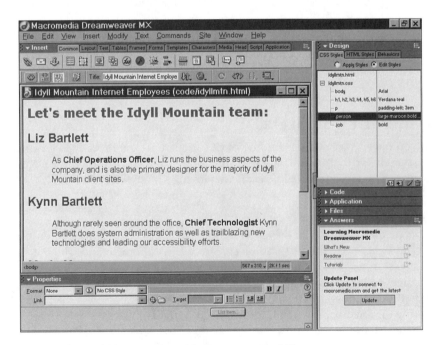

FIGURE 10.9   Editing CSS properties with Dreamweaver MX.

If you like a style and want to reuse it in your style sheet, select Duplicate from the CSS Styles menu. This will let you create a new style with the same definitions as the old one; you can then further edit the new style if you want.

You can also delete styles that you're no longer going to use; click the Trash Can icon or choose Delete from the CSS Styles menu.

Redefining HTML Tags

As you've previously learned, you can use custom class styles to apply CSS properties to selected text. Dreamweaver MX also helps you redefine the appearance of any HTML tag—for example, you can add a text indent to all paragraph <p> tags, or you can make all <h1> elements use a specific font style.

To redefine an HTML tag, choose the option Redefine HTML Tag when creating a new CSS style. You can choose the name of the tag from the pull-down menu, or you can type it, without angle brackets, into the field provided. Then set the property options as you normally would.

> **TIP**
>
> The style sheet in Listing 10.1 has a rule that affects the h1, h2, h3, h4, h5, and h6 tags—these are redefined HTML tags, but the rule uses a combined selector, which is described later in the section "Using CSS Selectors." You could create the same effect by creating six different rules, redefining the h1, h2, h3, h4, h5, and h6 tags separately.

Changing the Entire Page

Redefining the <body> tag has the effect of changing the entire page; this is how you'd set a background for the whole page or set the font for the text. Just as the HTML attributes text, link, vlink, alink, and bgcolor affect the whole page, so does a body style extended to all tags within the body. This is a process called *inheritance*, and it's part of the cascade from which the CSS language gets its name. Subsequent styles that are more specific—such as an h1 style—can change the inherited style properties.

An example of the effect of body rules can be seen in Figure 10.10. The body rule was edited and the text property Style was set to italic. This has the effect of setting the whole page in italic.

Using CSS Selectors

There are additional selectors you can use in your CSS style sheets besides class styles and redefined HTML tags. To create a style based on a CSS selector, you choose the CSS Selector option when creating a new CSS style, and then type in the CSS selector you want to use.

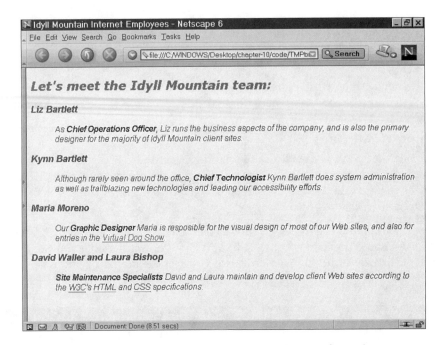

FIGURE 10.10   Changing the text style for the body tag changes the entire page.

The different categories of CSS selectors are listed in Table 10.11, along with an example and the example's purpose. The attribute, child, and adjacent sibling selectors are implemented in only a few of the newest browsers, so you may want to avoid using those in most cases.

TABLE 10.11   A Selection of CSS Selectors

Selector Type	Example	Function
Simple	li	Selects all list item tags
Class	span.person	Selects all <span> tags with class="person"
ID	#main	Selects the one tag with id="main"
Universal	*	Selects all tags
Combined	h1, h2, h3, .header	Selects the h1, h2, and h3 tags, and all tags with class="header"
Descendant	.footer p	Selects all paragraph tags that are the descendant of a tag with class="footer"
Pseudo-Class	a:hover	Selects all anchor tags that are in the "hover" state
Pseudo-Element	p:first-line	Selects the first line of text of paragraph tags
Attribute	td[axis="expense"]	Selects all table data cells with the attribute axis="expense"

TABLE 10.11   Continued

Selector Type	Example	Function
Child	`ol.outline > li`	Selects all list item tags that are the direct children of an ordered list tag with `class="outline"`
Adjacent Sibling	`h1 + h2`	Selects all h2 heading tags that immediately follow an h1 tag

Combined and descendant selectors are among the most commonly used CSS selectors. A combined selector is a group of other selectors separated by commas. The style applies to any elements that match any of the comma-separated selectors. A descendant selector is composed of two or more selectors with spaces between them. The CSS style is applied to any elements that match the final selector and that are contained by elements matching the previous selectors.

Pseudoclasses are selectors that are dependent on the user's actions and the state of the browser. A pseudoclass is written as an HTML tag name followed by a colon and then the name of the pseudoclass. These are most commonly used with link styles, and Dreamweaver MX provides four link-related selectors as pull-down options when creating CSS selector styles.

The `a:link` selector lets you set a style on unvisited HTML links, and the `a:visited` sets the style for visited links. These are the equivalents of the HTML link and vlink attributes on `<body>`, although you can change more than the color using HTML. The `a:active` selector sets the active link style when the link has been clicked but the new page hasn't yet loaded, and the `a:hover` selector determines the style when the mouse pointer is over the link. A pseudoclass selector can be combined with other selectors, so if you want to set all the links within a navigation bar to a certain style, define a class nav on the bar, and create a style with the CSS selector `.nav a:link`. This will apply the style to all `<a>` links that are descendants of something in the nav class.

Attaching a Style Sheet

A primary advantage of using CSS styles—instead of HTML styles—is that you can write a style sheet once and have it apply to a number of Web pages on the same site. Similarly, you can apply multiple style sheets to the same Web page, creating a composite page style based on several style sheets.

To attach a style sheet to a Web page, select the Attach Style Sheet option from the CSS Styles menu; you can also click the Attach Style Sheet icon, which looks like a few links of a chain touching a style sheet document. You can attach multiple style sheets in this way, or attach a style sheet that was originally created for another Web page. To remove the style sheet, select it in the CSS Styles panel in Edit Styles mode, and click the Trash Can.

10

Embedded Style Sheets

An attached style sheet is very useful for those styles that you want to apply to other pages on your same site. But if you have styles that you're going to use only on one page, you may want to incorporate the style directly into the HTML code for that page alone. This is known as creating an embedded style sheet. An embedded style sheet is stored in the <head> section of the page and is enclosed by a <style> tag.

To create an embedded style sheet, select the option This Document Only when creating a new CSS style. This creates the new style within your HTML document instead of an external file. An example of such an embedded style sheet is shown in Figure 10.11.

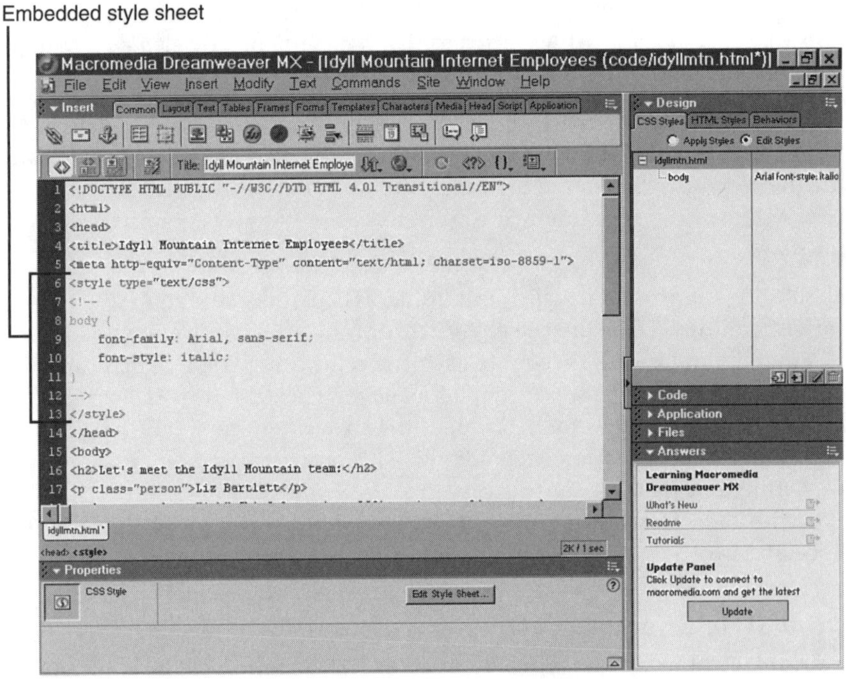

FIGURE 10.11   An embedded style sheet appears in the head of the HTML page, in code view.

If you need to extract an embedded style sheet and make it a linked style sheet instead, you can use the Export Style Sheet option from the CSS menu.

Converting CSS to HTML

As noted before, not all browsers understand CSS well. If you have to deal with older browsers often, you may want to create an alternative version of your page, which uses

HTML <font> tags and other older markup instead of CSS styles. Dreamweaver MX makes this a simple and painless process.

To do this, open your HTML file (with attached style sheets) in Dreamweaver MX and then choose Convert from the Edit menu. The option to convert to 3.0 Browser Compatible will create and open a new version of your HTML file, with styles converted to presentational markup, as shown in Listing 10.3. Save this new file with a different name, such as idyllmtn_oldbrowsers.html.

LISTING 10.3   The Styles Have Been Converted to HTML Tags and Included in the HTML Source Code

```
<html>
<head>
<title>Idyll Mountain Internet Employees</title>
<meta http-equiv="Content-Type" content="text/html; charset=iso-8859-1">
</head>
<body>
<h2><font color="teal" face="Verdana, sans-serif">Let's meet the Idyll
  Mountain team:</font></h2>
<p><b><font color="maroon" size="4"
  face="Arial, sans-serif">Liz Bartlett</font></b></p>
<p><font face="Arial, sans-serif">As <b>Chief Operations Officer</b>,
  Liz runs the business aspects of the company, and is also the primary
  designer for the majority of Idyll Mountain client sites.</font></p>
<p><b><font color="maroon" size="4"
  face="Arial, sans-serif">Kynn Bartlett</font></b></p>
<p><font face="Arial, sans-serif">Although rarely seen around the office,
  <b>Chief Technologist</b> Kynn Bartlett does system administration
  as well as trailblazing new technologies and leading our accessibility
  efforts.</font></p>
<p><b><font color="maroon" size="4"
  face="Arial, sans-serif">Maria Moreno</font></b></p>
<p><font face="Arial, sans-serif">Our <b>Graphic Designer</b> Maria
  is responsible for the visual design of most of our Web sites, and
  also for entries in the <a href="http://www.dogshow.com/">Virtual
  Dog Show</a>.</font></p>
<p><b><font color="maroon" size="4" face="Arial, sans-serif">David Waller
  and Laura Bishop</font></b></p>
<p><font face="Arial, sans-serif"><b>Site Maintenance Specialists</b>
  David and Laura maintain and develop client Web sites according to
  the <acronym title="World Wide Web Consortium" lang="en">W3C</acronym>'s
  <acronym title="HyperText Markup Language" lang="en">HTML</acronym>
  and <acronym title="Cascading Style Sheets" lang="en">CSS</acronym>
```

10

LISTING 10.3   Continued

```
    specifications.</font></p>
</body>
</html>
```

Keep in mind that in the conversion process, some of your styles will be lost in the translation. For example, there's no HTML tag that sets padding, so the new version of this
Web page doesn't have the padding found in the original.

Editing CSS in Code View

Dreamweaver MX provides handy option menus for setting a wide variety of CSS styles,
but these menus don't cover everything you can do with style sheets. To get the most out
of your CSS styles—or to edit someone else's style sheet—you will eventually need to work
with CSS in code view.

In code view, you're working directly with the CSS language, writing the selector, the
braces, and the declarations instead of letting Dreamweaver MX do it for you. The code
view for CSS is shown in Figure 10.12.

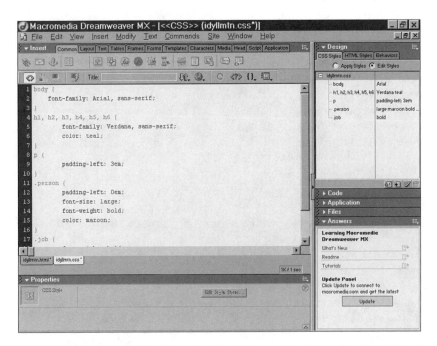

FIGURE 10.12   Editing a style sheet in code view lets you directly manipulate CSS rules.

To enter code view, you need to open a style sheet via the Open option on the File menu or create a blank style sheet with the New option from the File menu. Then you'll see the raw CSS codes displayed for you, ready to be edited. Save the file via the Save option on the File menu when you're done with it!

Starting with Dreamweaver MX Style Sheets

To make it easier to use CSS styles, Dreamweaver MX comes with a selection of standard style sheets that can be used as the basis of your own style sheets. Using these style sheets is easy; simply choose New from the File menu and select from the available style sheets. The style sheet you pick will open in code view in Dreamweaver MX, and you can edit and save your modified style sheet.

The list of Dreamweaver MX style sheets is shown in Table 10.12. Most of these style sheets also define class styles that you can use in your designs along with any custom class styles you create.

TABLE 10.12   Dreamweaver MX Style Sheets

Style Sheet Name	Effects
Basic: Arial	Sets the text (body, th, and td) to Arial font; defines no class styles.
Basic: Times	Sets the text (body, th, and td) to Times New Roman font; defines no class styles.
Basic: Verdana	Sets the text (body, th, and td) to Verdana font; defines no class styles.
Colors: Blue	Selects a blue color scheme; defines no class styles.
Colors: Blue/Gray/Purple	Selects a blue, gray, and purple color scheme; defines no class styles.
Colors: Blue/White/Yellow	Selects a blue, white, and yellow color scheme; defines no class styles.
Colors: Red	Selects a red-on-black color scheme; defines no class styles.
Colors: Tan/Brown	Selects a tan and brown color scheme; defines no class styles.
Colors: Yellow/Brown	Selects a yellow and brown color scheme; defines no class styles.
Forms: Accessible	Sets the text (body, th, td, and form controls) to Arial font, using relative units.
Forms: Arial	Sets the text (body, th, td, and form controls) to Arial font, using absolute units.
Forms: Times	Sets the text (body, th, td, and form controls) to Times New Roman font, using absolute units.
Forms: Verdana	Sets the text (body, th, td, and form controls) to Verdana font, using absolute units.
Full Design: Accessible	Defines a complete page style in Arial font set using relative units; colors are blue, green, and gray.

10

TABLE 10.12   Continued

Style Sheet Name	Effects
Full Design: Arial, Blue/Green/Gray	Defines a complete page style in Arial font set using absolute units.
Full Design: Georgia, Red/Yellow	Defines a complete page style in Georgia font set using absolute units.
Full Design: Verdana, Yellow/Green	Defines a complete page style in Verdana font set using absolute units.
Link Effects	Creates special effects around links.
Text: Accessible	Sets the text (body, th, and td) to Times New Roman font, using relative units.
Text: Arial	Sets the text (body, th, and td) to Arial font, using absolute units.
Text: Times	Sets the text (body, th, and td) to Times New Roman font, using absolute units.
Text: Verdana	Sets the text (body, th, and td) to Verdana font, using absolute units.

The style sheets identified as Accessible are created with relative units and thus are made to conform to the user's font requirements instead of overriding them with absolute font sizes.

The complete list of class styles defined in Dreamweaver MX style sheets is shown in Table 10.13, as well as the style sheet in which they're available. These classes correspond to the most common types of Web design tasks you'll encounter when using CSS.

TABLE 10.13   Predefined Class Styles in Dreamweaver MX Style Sheets

Class Style	Style Sheet	Purpose
.small	Forms, Text	Small text size
.medium	Text	Medium text size
.big	Forms, Text	Large text size
.xbig	Text	Extra-large text size
.bodystyle	Forms, Text	The main text content's style
.expanded	Text	Text with spaced-out letters
.justified	Text	Justified text
.box1	Forms, Full, Text	A box with a 3D border
.box2	Forms, Text	A box with a solid border
.title	Full	The title of the page
.subtitle	Full	The subtitle of the page
.header	Full	The large text at the top of the page
.nav	Full	The navigation bar's style
.navLink	Full	Each item of the navigation bar
.sidebar	Full	A sidebar's style

TABLE 10.13   Continued

Class Style	Style Sheet	Purpose
`.sidebarHeader`	Full,	The header of the sidebar
`.sidebarFooter`	Full	The footer of the sidebar
`.footer`	Full, Text	The page footer's style
`.legal`	Full	Legal notices (the fine print)
`.promo`	Full	Promotional text
`.titlebar`	Full	The title bar
`.dingbat`	Full	Dingbats
`a.hidden`	Link Effects	Invisible links
`a.nav`	Link Effects	Navigation links
`a.menu`	Link Effects	Menu links
`a.box`	Link Effects	Links with borders
`input.big`	Full	A wide input field
`input.small`	Full	A narrow input field

You can attach multiple style sheets to any HTML document, which means you may want to create several style sheets and combine them. To make a quick and easy design, you could create and save style sheets based on the Text: Times and the Color: Red sheets. You can see how this looks in Figure 10.13; it took less than a minute to create these styles.

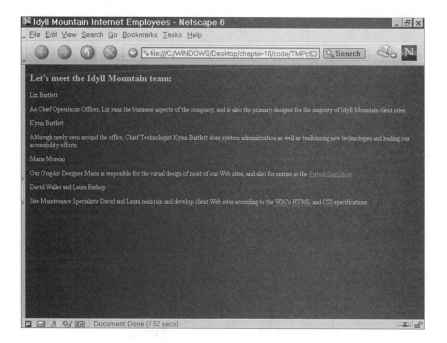

FIGURE 10.13   Using the Dreamweaver MX style sheet Text: Times and Color: Red as a base lets you start quickly.

Alternatively, a Full Design style sheet can be used as the basis for a more complex design. Figure 10.14 shows what a difference the style sheet can make on the appearance of a page.

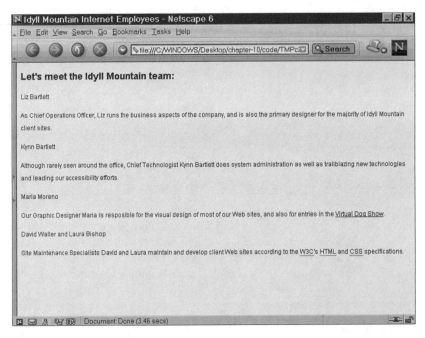

FIGURE 10.14   Choosing a different starting style sheet, such as Full Design: Georgia, produces a different effect with the same HTML.

Writing Advanced CSS

To use specialized CSS properties—which aren't covered in the CSS styles options in Dreamweaver MX—you'll need to add them manually. Many of these properties are rather obscure and not often needed; for example, the `cue-after` property defines a sound to be played by an audio browser. The complete list of CSS properties is available via the Answers menu in the O'Reilly CSS Reference.

Importance, Order, and the Cascade

As mentioned earlier in this chapter, the C in CSS stands for "cascading," and is a reference to the cascade. The cascade is the method for combining several styles, which may have conflicting notions as to the value of a CSS property. For example, three rules might specify the color of the text, and all three might conceivably be applicable. The cascade allows the browser to determine the "winner" for those parts of the styles which conflict; if there is no conflict, the styles can be combined and applied.

The general principle in the cascade is that the most specific style wins. Thus, if you have one style about body and another about h1, the h1 is going to be more specific, so the headline will follow the second style in the case of a conflict. A class style is considered more specific than a redefined HTML element, and an ID selector—one of the types of CSS selectors—is more specific than a class selector.

If two conflicting styles are equally specific—such as two rules about h1—the next rule is that the style declared later in the style sheet—the "newer" style—takes precedence. In our hypothetical case, both h1 styles would be applied to all first-level headings, and if there were conflicting styles—one setting the color blue and another setting it red—the second style would prevail for that property.

For this reason, order can be crucial for creating and perfecting CSS style sheets. Dreamweaver MX doesn't automatically move styles around for you, but in code view you can cut and paste styles to put them in the preferred order.

The cascade order can also be changed by the use of a special keyword, called !important. That's an exclamation point before the word important. Although this may appear to mean "not important" in the eyes of most programmers, in the CSS language it means "very important." The !important keyword placed after a property declaration jumps that declaration to the very front of the priority order. If there's a conflict, any style with !important after it will beat any style without it.

In Listing 10.4, you can see an example of a style sheet that was created to illustrate the cascade in action, and see how you can change that order by using !important.

LISTING 10.4   The Cascade Will Be Used to Determine the Effects of These Conflicting Styles

```
p {
        color: white ! important;
}
p {
        color: violet;
}
p {
        background-color: blue;
}
p {
        background-color: black;
}
.person {
        background-color: red; color: green;
}
```

10

In evaluating this style sheet, the browser gives highest priority to any !important styles. The first p style would ordinarily be superceded by the second p style on the issue of text color, but the first style has the magic keyword !important—so the color of the text is white.

The third p style loses out to the later-defined fourth p style for the background-color property, so the background color is black. For HTML tags which are set class="person", the .person style is more specific than the p tags, so the background-color will be red—except that the first p style is !important, so the text color will be white.

Figure 10.15 is a screenshot showing how the browsers use this logic to get the results described.

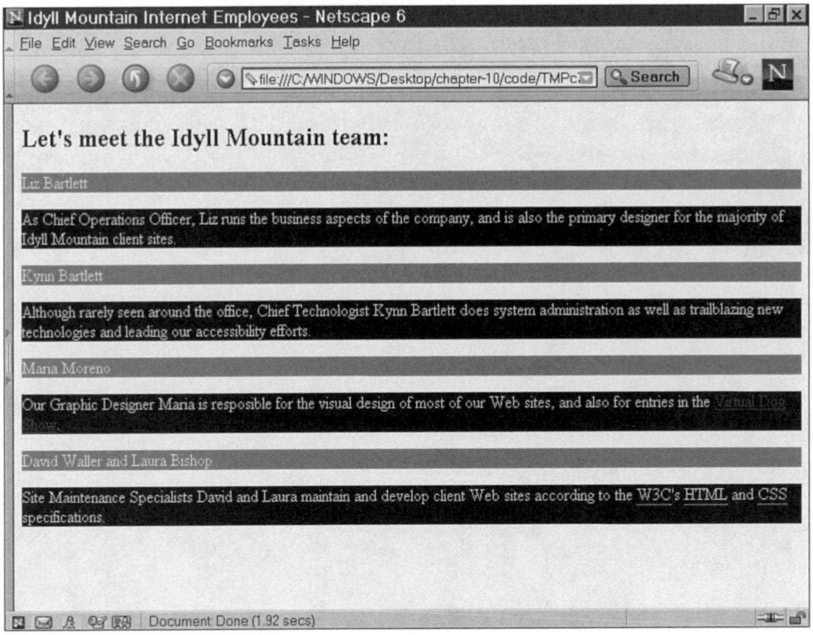

FIGURE 10.15   The cascade order was used to determine the colors of the text and background.

CSS Comments

Nearly every computer language invented allows for the developer to insert comments, and CSS is no exception. A comment is embedded in the code and ignored by the browsers, but is available to the designer to read and edit. To create a comment in a style sheet, simply add a slash and an asterisk (/*) at the start of the comment, and end it with an asterisk and a slash (*/). Everything between the markers will be ignored by the browser.

Comments are most often used to provide internal documentation so that other designers who may use your style sheet can understand it. They're also useful for avoiding those head-scratching moments when you ask yourself, "What was I thinking?" You can also use comments to prevent certain rules or properties from being applied, without deleting them entirely; this is useful for testing purposes.

As shown in Listing 10.5, comments can also be used for copyright and author information. In this listing, each class style is described; you don't have to do this, but it's good practice.

LISTING 10.5 Comments Make This Style Sheet Easier to Read and Understand

```
/*idyllmtn.css
   Style Sheet for the Idyll Mountain Internet staff page

   Copyright (c) 2002 by Kynn Bartlett <kynn@cssin24hours.com>
*/

body {
    /*Default font for the page*/
    font-family: Arial, sans-serif;
}

h1, h2, h3, h4, h5, h6 {
    /*Make the headers more distinct*/
    font-family: Verdana, sans-serif;
    color: teal;
}
p {
    /*This will add padding to all paragraphs...*/
    padding-left: 3em;
}
.person {
    /*...except for those where class="person"*/
    padding-left: 0em;
    font-size: large;
    font-weight: bold;
    color: maroon;
}
.job {
    /*Make the job title stand out*/
    font-weight: bold;
}
```

10

Inline Style Attributes

You can attach a style sheet to an HTML document with the <link> tag, or you can embed it within the <style> element. A third way to apply styles to HTML is by using inline style elements. An inline style element enables you to apply a style directly to a section of HTML without specifying it in the style sheet; this can be useful for quickly adding a style that appears in only one place on your site.

As shown in Listing 10.6, you simply set the attribute style to the declaration portion of a style rule. There's no need for a selector, because the selection is the content of the tag with the style attribute.

LISTING 10.6   A Snippet of HTML Code That Uses an Inline Style Attribute

```
...
<p>Although <span style="color: red; font-weight: bold;">
  rarely seen around the office</span>,
  <span class="job">Chief Technologist</span>
  Kynn Bartlett does system administration as well as trailblazing new
  technologies and leading our accessibility efforts.</p>
...
```

Inline styles are much less useful than attached or embedded styles, and for that reason, Dreamweaver MX doesn't support them. To add an inline style in Dreamweaver MX, you need to edit the source code and add the attribute. You might need to use inline styles if you want to apply a specific style only once, but in general, it is easier to create a class style and store it in an attached or embedded style sheet.

Media-Specific Styles

The CSS specification enables you to designate style sheets that are used only by specific media types, which are broad categories of output devices. The default media type is screen, which assumes that your browser will be displaying the Web page on a monitor. The complete list of CSS media types is shown in Table 10.14.

TABLE 10.14   Media Types Defined by CSS

Media Type	Description
aural	Pages read out loud by synthesized voice; for example, screenreaders for the blind.
braille	Content represented by raised dot characters on Braille terminals for blind users.
emboss	Pages printed out as raised dots in Braille, on thick paper.
handheld	Content displayed on a limited-size handheld screen.
print	Pages printed out on paper.
projection	Content displayed as slides or transparencies projected on a large screen.
screen	Pages displayed on a color monitor.

TABLE 10.14 Continued

Media Type	Description
tty	Content printed on teletype devices or other media with limited display capabilities, which print characters only of a fixed size and type.
tv	Pages displayed on a television screen, possibly taking advantage of sound capabilities but with limited interaction.

To create a style sheet for a specific media type, such as print, simply create a new style sheet based on your original, and change the style rules that don't apply to the new output device. For example, many printers are black and white, so color might not be as useful. In Listing 10.7, the print.css style sheet has replaced color properties with other style effects.

LISTING 10.7   /*print.css

```
Print Style Sheet for the Idyll Mountain Internet staff page

Copyright (c) 2002 by Kynn Bartlett <kynn@cssin24hours.com>
*/

body {
    font-family: Arial, sans-serif;
    font-size: 12pt;
    /*An absolute font size has been set*/
}

h1, h2, h3, h4, h5, h6 {
    font-family: Verdana, sans-serif;
    text-decoration: underline;
    /*Headers are underlined, and are not teal*/
}
p {
    padding-left: 3em;
}
.person {
    padding-left: 0em;
    font-size: large;
    font-weight: bold;
    border: 2px solid black;
    /*Names are in boxes, and are not maroon*/
}
.job {
    font-weight: bold;
}
```

10

To attach both this style sheet and the normal style sheet to the same HTML file—but have them apply to different media types—save them as different names and attach each to the HTML document. Then open the HTML document in code view and change the `<link>` tag. Add the media attribute to each `<link>`, as shown in Listing 10.8.

LISTING 10.8   The Head of an HTML File That Attaches Two Style Sheets—One for Screen and One for Print

```
...
<head>
<title>Idyll Mountain Internet Employees</title>
<meta http-equiv="Content-Type" content="text/html; charset=iso-8859-1">
<link href="idyllmtn.css" rel="stylesheet" type="text/css"
      media="screen">
<link href="print.css" rel="stylesheet" type="text/css"
      media="print">
</head>
...
```

When you load this Web page in your browser, one style will be displayed on the screen, and a second will appear on your hard copy when you click Print.

Design Time Style Sheets

Dreamweaver MX enables you to specify style sheets that are displayed only while you are editing and that aren't included in the Web page when it's saved or previewed. These are called design time style sheets, and are accessed through the CSS menu.

You create a design time style sheet the same way you create any other style sheet; however, because this is intended only for your eyes and no one else's, you don't need to worry about making it look pretty. The purpose is to make certain things stand out while you're editing, as shown by the styles in Listing 10.9.

LISTING 10.9   This Style Sheet Highlights Acronyms, Abbreviations, Headers, and Two Class Styles

```
/*while-editing.css*/

abbr, acronym { background-color: silver; }
.person {
        background-color: #FFCCFF;
}
.job {
        background-color: #66FF66;
}
```

LISTING 10.9 Continued

```
h1, h2, h3, h4, h5, h6 {
        border: thin dotted teal;
}
```

After you've saved your style sheet, you can apply it to your editing environment by choosing Design Time Style Sheet from the CSS menu. Add the style sheet by clicking the plus sign and browsing to find it. Dreamweaver MX will now display the HTML page using the styles you've defined in your design time style sheet, as shown in Figure 10.16.

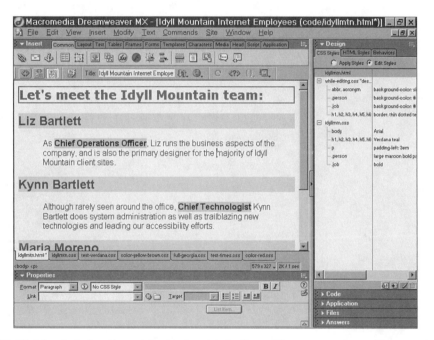

FIGURE 10.16 A design time style sheet assists in the editing process by making certain tags stand out.

Remember that these styles will not be shown in your browser, even when you preview the page; they are used by Dreamweaver MX only while you're in design view. Design time style sheets effectively enable you to extend Dreamweaver MX's display capabilities to highlight whatever you like while editing!

Summary

CSS, if used correctly, can greatly extend your ability to create attractive Web designs. Current browsers have good support for CSS standards, in a definite improvement over the older versions. CSS is also of benefit to users with disabilities who may find presentational HTML hard to display.

Dreamweaver MX lets you define and edit styles through a menu interface, making it easy to apply styles to text, create boxes, or even lay out a page. You can create a custom class style, redefine the appearance of an HTML tag, or employ CSS selectors for more precise definition. Dreamweaver MX's code view for CSS lets you utilize the full power of CSS in your designs.

CHAPTER **11**

Layers in Dreamweaver

By Matt Pizzi

Introduction to Layers

As you've worked with tables, you may have noticed that sometimes it's hit or miss to get content placed where you want it or need it. After working with merging and splitting cells, adding transparent GIF spacers, and experimenting with the horizontal and vertical spacing, you may be thinking that there's got to be a better way. This is where layers comes in.

When you think of layers, if the first thing that comes to mind is Adobe Photoshop and digital imagining—stop. Although a stacking order is associated with layers, they're better known for alternative design options. Layers in the world of Web design means freedom from messy table workarounds and total control of content layout. The W3C included absolute positioning in the cascading style sheets (CSS) specification, offering precise placement of DHTML's layers.

For layers to be visible in a browser, it must be a 4.0 or later version of Netscape and Internet Explorer. Typically the tag used to generate a layer is the <div> or <span> tags. These tags were chosen because they're rarely used by the HTML 3.2 specification. However, Netscape 4.0 is not compliant with the CSS standards with regard to layers and cannot read layers within these standard tags. Netscape 4.0 uses the <layer> and <ilayer> tags to generate layers. The <layer> tag refers to absolute positioning, whereas the <ilayer> tag refers to relative positioning. If compatibility with Netscape Navigator 4 is of no concern to you, the <div> or <span> tags will be fine. It's important to note that in Dreamweaver MX, you no longer have the capability to create Netscape 4-compliant layers in the WYSIWYG authoring environment;

you'll have to hand code it. If the end user is viewing a site with a Web browser that is not compatible with layers, the result will be detrimental to the design of the site. Content will be missing and items will appear misaligned. Be aware of your target audience when using layers in your site.

Layers also offer a third dimension, much like their names suggest. This dimension is called the z-index, ripped from geometric practices based on x, y, and z coordinates. The higher a layer's z-index value, the closer it appears to the front of the screen. The lower the z-index value, the further away it will seem, resulting in an item closer to the background.

Layers or Tables?

The age-old question—well, it's been only a few years because layers haven't been around too long—but still a question that can baffle many designers. Again, the answer depends on who your audience is: will they have current browsers or will they have older ones? The other thing you should consider is whether your design requires layers. If it doesn't, at least you'll have peace of mind knowing that if you use tables, your site is compatible with the majority of browsers.

If your site is geared toward people who are typically cutting edge, and you would expect them to have new browsers, layers can be a viable option. Furthermore, layers allow you to experiment a bit and create a more radical design. What's great is that Dreamweaver is extremely user friendly when it comes to layers and offers you the capability to design in a WYSWIG environment without touching the code. That is, if you don't want to touch the code.

Creating Layers

To start using layers effectively, you must know the basics of inserting layers and manipulating them inside of Dreamweaver. There are a couple of ways to insert layers into a document. The first is the more casual way, which is reviewed in this section. The second way offers precise placement and control, using the CSS Styles panel, which is covered in a later section of this chapter.

Before you start drawing and inserting layers, I'd like to mention that you have the option of adding as many layers as you need into your document. However, with a high number of layers, it can sometimes take a browser a while to render them all. Additionally, many layers may drain the system resources of your computer as you develop inside of Dreamweaver.

Overlapping Layers

You can even draw layers on top of existing content within the document as well as draw them on top of one another. If you are overlapping layers, you're locked into using layers; there is no way to convert the layered content into tables. Furthermore, if the end user is viewing the page with a browser that doesn't fully comprehend or support the layer tag information, the design can yield unpredictable results.

Drawing Layers

One of the easiest ways to create a layer is to draw one. To draw a layer, make sure the Insert panel is visible. In the Insert panel, be sure to have the Layout tab highlighted. Under the Layout tab, it's important to have the Standard View selected. This offers two options on the far-left side of the panel, as shown in Figure 11.1. These options are for inserting a Table and for inserting a Layer.

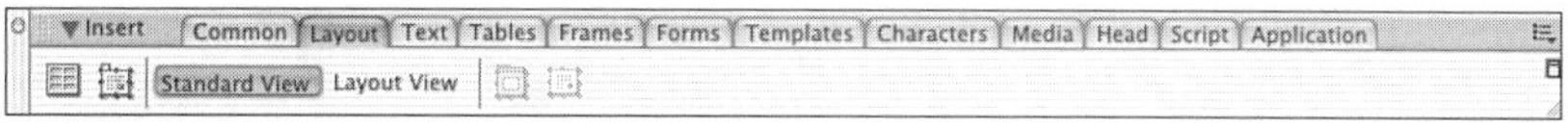

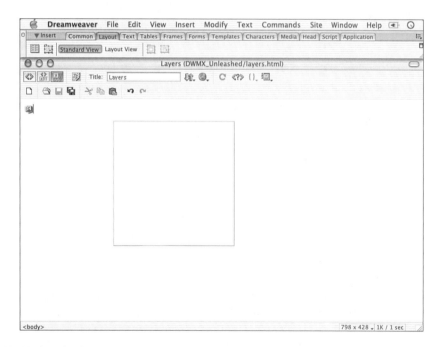

FIGURE 11.1   Two options are available under the Layout tab of the Insert panel for inserting either a table or a layer.

Click the Draw Layer button and notice that your cursor changes to a crosshair. This crosshair indicates that you can draw out a layer. Simply click and drag out a layer, much like you're drawing a square in a graphics program. When you're happy with the size, stop dragging; notice that a layer is now in the document, as shown in Figure 11.2.

FIGURE 11.2   The layer is placed in the document where you drew it.

When the layer is not selected, it has a beveled gray border as shown in Figure 11.2. You can select the layer by clicking the handle of the layer in the top-left corner, or you can click the small layer icon that appears in the top-left corner of the document, as shown in Figure 11.2. If the small layer icon is not visible, choose View, Visual Aids, Invisible Elements. If it's still not visible, you have to adjust the invisible elements to be shown in the Preferences dialog box, accessible by choosing Edit, Preferences.

Finally you can open the Layers panel by choosing Window, Others, Layers. This opens the Layers panel as shown in Figure 11.3. Here you can click the layer name to select the layer. Notice when the layer is selected, a bounding box appears around the layer with resize handles (also shown in Figure 11.3).

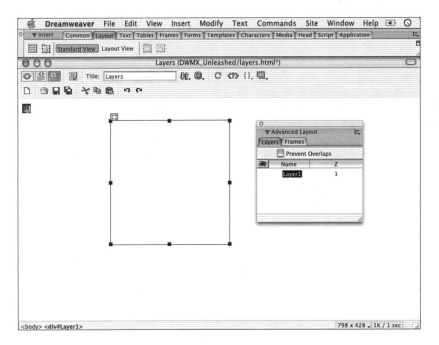

FIGURE 11.3   When the layer is selected, resize handles surround the layer like a bounding box.

Inserting Layers

You can also insert layers, which automatically places a layer in your document at a default size. To do this choose Insert, Layer. You can change the default dimensions of a layer by choosing Edit, Preferences. This launches the Preferences dialog box. Click in the Layers category, and there you have the option of changing the default size, as pictured in Figure 11.4.

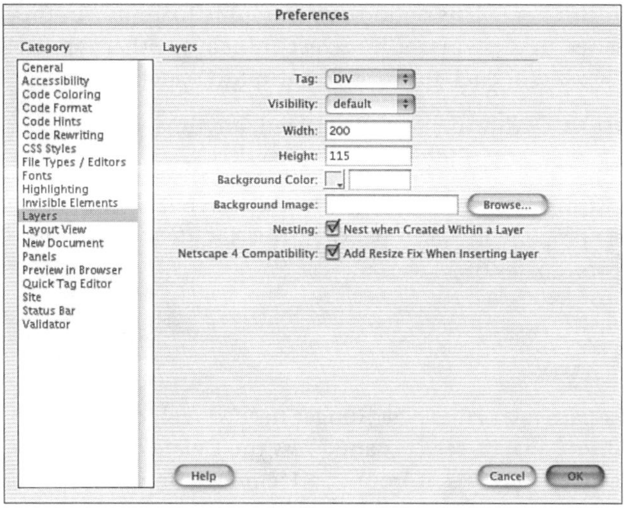

FIGURE 11.4   In the Preferences dialog box, you have the option of changing the default size of an inserted layer.

Setting Defaults of Layers

Quite a few options exist for the default setting of an inserted layer, as Figure 11.4 suggests. Here's a breakdown of what the different preferences offer. These options are located in the Properties Inspector:

- **Tag**   This option sets Dreamweaver to use either the `<div>` or `<span>` tags when inserting layers. The `<div>` tag is the most common and it's selected by default; however, you can opt to use the `<span>` tag. If you want the page to be compatible with Netscape Navigator 4.0, you can't create layers in Dreamweaver in the WYSIWYG environment. You must hand code the layers using the `<layer>` or `<ilayer>` tags.

- **Visibility**   This option determines the initial state of the layer. The options are Default (determined by the end user's browser), Inherit (takes on parent's setting in a nested layer), Visible, or Hidden. This option affects both inserted and drawn layers.

- **Width**   This option sets the default width of an inserted layer. The measurement unit is set to pixels. The default is 200.

- **Height**   This option sets the default height size of an inserted layer. This value is based on pixels and the default value is 115.

- **Background Color**   This option sets a background color for an inserted or drawn layer. You can select from any one of the 216 Web-safe colors using the swatch that pops up from the inkwell.

- **Background Image**   This option sets a graphic to appear in the background of either an inserted or drawn layer. To select an image, either type in a path to where the image is located or click the Browse button to search for one.

- **Nesting Option**   With this option selected, anytime you insert or a draw a layer, it will be nested or placed inside another.

- **Netscape 4 Compatibility**   This adds code to your HTML document to help position the layers properly in Netscape Navigator 4. Often, Netscape 4.0 will lose the positioning coordinates of a layer.

Deleting a Layer

If you decide that a particular layer is no longer needed, you can easily delete inside of Dreamweaver. To delete a layer, select it and press the Delete or Backspace key on your keyboard. This effectively removes it from the document. You can also contextual click next to the layers, as shown in Figure 11.5, and choose Remove Tag <div> from the contextual menu. This technique is best used when only one layer is present in the document and you are using the <div> tag to create layers.

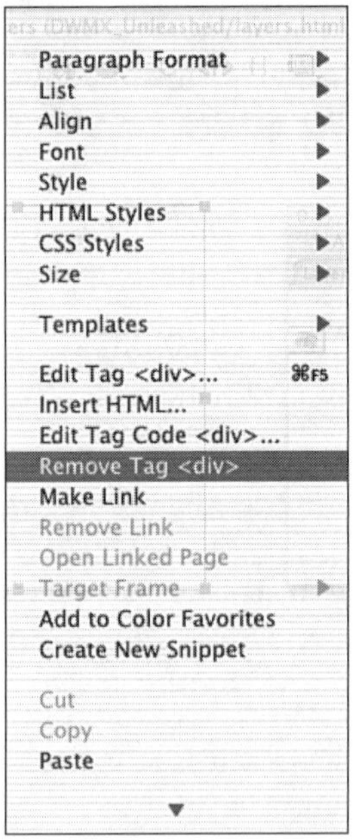

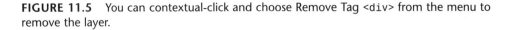

FIGURE 11.5   You can contextual-click and choose Remove Tag <div> from the menu to remove the layer.

Embedding a Layer with Style Sheets

By inserting a layer with the previous techniques, you're really positioning by eye, at least at this point. However, what I consider to be one of the great strengths of layers is the precise placement they offer. By using the CSS Styles panel inside of Dreamweaver, you do in fact have the capability to precisely place the layers anywhere within the document.

Although this way may seem a bit more technical and less visual, it offers some other advantages in addition to precise placement. By inserting a layer with the CSS styles, you can attach the layer to an external style sheet so that the layer appears in the same place on every page. Of course, you also have the advantage of being able to control the text's size and font family through the CSS style.

Cascading style sheets are covered in great detail in Chapter 10, "Cascading Style Sheets." Refer to this chapter if a concept appears vague, for I'm going to discuss only layer placement with CSS in this chapter.

Creating a Layer with Style Sheets

Follow these steps to learn how to insert a layer in a precise location by using CSS.

1. Make sure the CSS Styles panel is visible. If it is not, choose Window, CSS Styles to open the CSS Styles panel.

2. In the CSS Styles panel, click the New Style button located in the bottom-right corner of the panel. This opens the New CSS Style dialog box as shown in Figure 11.6.

3. In the New CSS Style dialog box, choose Make Custom Style (class) from the Type category. Type in a name for the style. Also, choose Define in This Document Only. Click OK. This launches the Style Definition dialog box.

4. In the Style Definition dialog box, choose the Positioning category. This changes the options that are presented on the right side, as displayed in Figure 11.7.

5. In the top category, choose settings for the Type, Z-Index, Visibility, and Overflow. For Type choose Absolute, and for Visibility choose Visible from the drop-down menu. You're probably familiar with absolute and relative sizing; however, Static may be a bit confusing. Refer to the note at the end of this exercise for an explanation as to what the Static option offers. Set Overflow and Z-Index to Auto, and finally, type in a value for width and height to determine the size of the layer. Choose Pixels in the drop-down menu for the units.

6. In the next section, Placement, enter values for the Left, Top, Right, and Bottom positions. The default increment is pixels; however, you can change the units in the drop-down menu located to the right of the text field.

7. Finally, leave the Clip portion of the dialog box set to the defaults. You'll look at clip options later in this chapter. When you're happy with your settings, choose OK. Refer to Figure 11.8 to see my settings.

8. This brings you back to the document. Notice the style in the CSS Styles panel. Click the style once to apply it so it will appear in your document as shown in Figure 11.9.

Remember that layers are part of the CSS Style specification. This can yield great benefits. By adding a layer to your style sheet, especially external ones, you have the flexibility of adding specific text with a specific style to any or all documents.

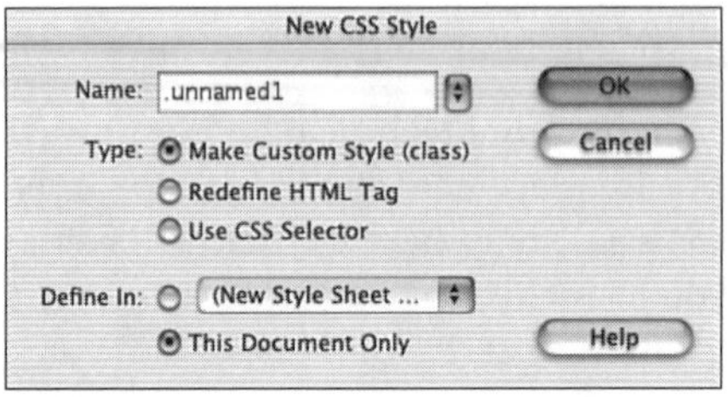

FIGURE 11.6   The New CSS Styles dialog box offers options for creating a new CSS style.

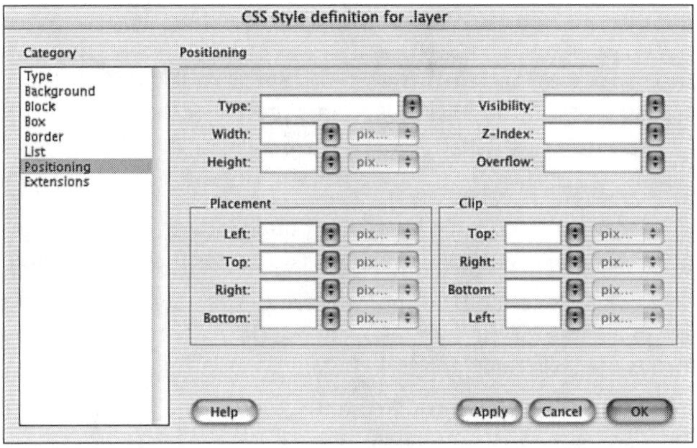

FIGURE 11.7   The category you select on the left determines which options are available in the body of the dialog box.

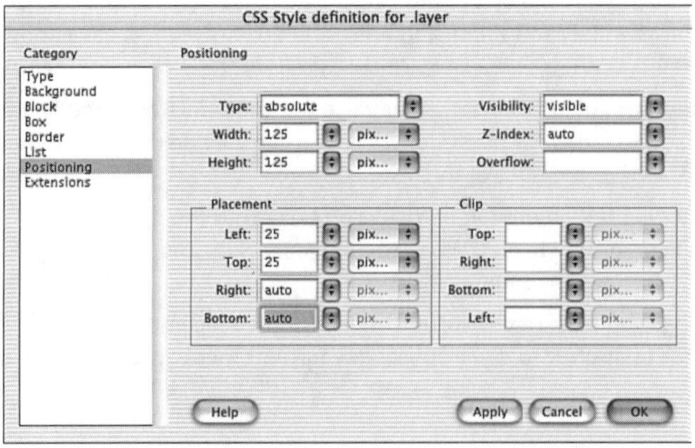

FIGURE 11.8   These are the settings I used to create my layer in the CSS Styles.

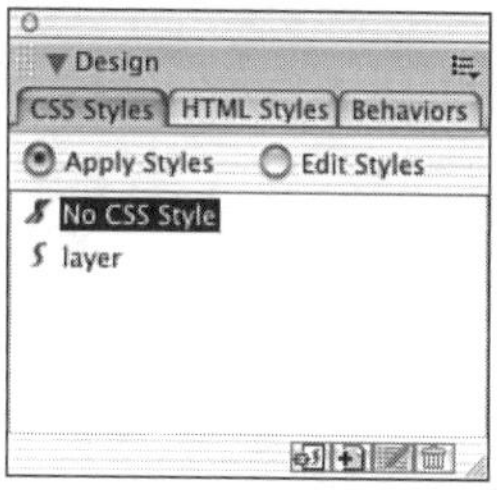

FIGURE 11.9   After I click the style in the CSS Styles panel, the layer is placed in the exact coordinates that I specified in the Style Definition dialog box.

> **NOTE**
>
> The Static option for sizing ignores the Left and Top attributes. By choosing this option you forfeit precise control over the placement. Preview your document in a browser to see the results.

Absolute and Relative Positioning

Absolute sizing uses pixel values based on the top-left corner of an HTML document, whereas relative positioning is based on the size of the browser window at any given time. It can be a bit tricky to gauge how relative positioning will appear in a browser. However, it can be useful if you want the content to reposition itself in case a change occurs with the browser's window size.

Inserting Content into Layers

Inserting a variety of different content into layers is simple. The easiest way is to place a blinking cursor inside the layer. Then choose an object to insert from any one of the tabs in the Insert panel. You can insert anything from an image to a table and from Flash content to a QuickTime movie.

You can also insert content simply by dragging something over from the Assets panel. If you have anything stored on the Clipboard, you also have the option of pasting content into that layer.

Sizing, Positioning, and Modifying Layers with the Properties Inspector

After inserting content into a layer, you might need to resize it. For example, in Figure 11.10, you'll notice that I inserted an image into the layer; however, the layer is much larger than the graphic. With the layer selected, you can grab the bottom-right corner handle by clicking and dragging it all the way into the graphic. When you drag into the graphic and attempt to make the layer smaller than the content, the layer automatically resizes to the smallest possible size, not leaving an excess space around the graphic.

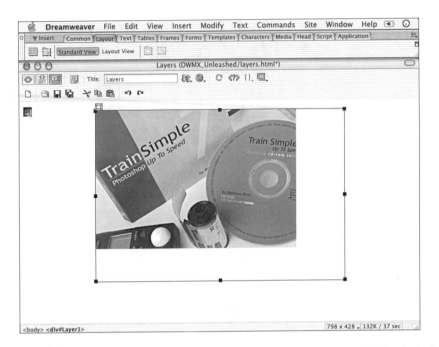

FIGURE 11.10   In this figure, the layer is much larger than the content inside it. Grab the handles on the side to resize the layer.

To precisely resize the layer, you should use the Properties Inspector. With the layer selected, as shown in Figure 11.11, the Properties Inspector offers a host of options.

FIGURE 11.11   The Properties Inspector offers a series of options for manipulating the selected layer.

If you have the dimensions of the image (if you don't, select it and the Properties Inspector provides you with the width and height information), you can size the layer to equal those dimensions. With the layer selected in the Properties Inspector, you can enter in a value for the width and height of the layer. Enter the values of the width and height from the image, and the layer will size perfectly around the graphic.

TIP
You can also resize the layer pixel-by-pixel by holding down the Command (Mac) key or Ctrl (Windows) key and simultaneously pressing an arrow in the direction that you want to increase or decrease the size of the layer.

Sizing Multiple Layers

Dreamweaver enables you to change the dimensions of more than one layer at a time. To select multiple layers, you can use a couple of options. The first is to hold down the Shift key on the keyboard as you click each of the layers in the document. Second, you can highlight the top layer in the Layers panel, and then hold down the Shift key and click the bottom layer in the panel; all the layers in between will be selected, as shown in Figure 11.12.

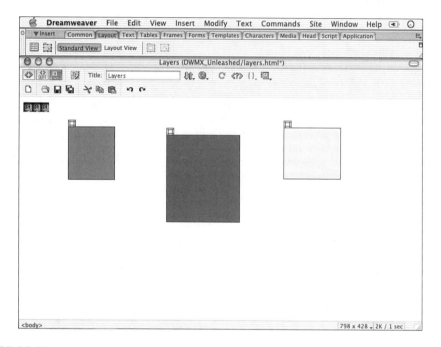

FIGURE 11.12   You can easily select multiple layers by holding down the Shift key while selecting layers in the Layers panel.

After selecting more than one layer, you can resize them all through the Properties Inspector by entering values for the width and height. You also have the option of choosing Modify, Align, Make Same Height or Make Same Width. When you choose this option, the layers will size to the width and height of the first drawn layer, unless you've deleted it, in which case it will use the largest layer to size the rest of the layers.

Positioning Layers

There are many options for positioning layers outside of the CSS Style option we looked at earlier. The most obvious way is to click and drag the handle in the top-left corner of the layer. This enables you to place the layer anywhere you want, positioning it by eye. You can also select the layer and move it pixel-by-pixel with the arrow keys on the keyboard. However, if you want to be absolutely precise, you can set the layer's Left and Top coordinates through the Properties Inspector.

Positioning Layers Through the Properties Inspector

If you want to position a layer using the Properties Inspector, you can position the layer by adding values in the L and T options. The value you enter here represents a number relative to the document's top-left corner and the layer's top-left corner. For example, if you entered 0 in both spaces, the layer's top-left corner would be flush with the document's top-left corner. Add or subtract the number of pixels you want to move the layer toward or away from the top-left corner. If you type in negative values, the layer will be cropped by the document and some or all of the content will not be visible in a browser window.

Nesting Layers

You can easily place a layer inside another by nesting. The easiest way to nest a layer is to turn nesting on in the Preferences dialog box. You can access the Preferences dialog box by choosing Edit, Preferences. In the layers portion of the dialog box, be sure to select the Nesting option. With this option selected, if you draw a layer inside another, you're guaranteed that the layer will be nested inside the layer you're drawing into.

A nested layer is much like a nested table. The nested layer moves with the parent layer and it can inherit the parent's visibility attribute.

Nested layers sometimes yield unpredictable results in different Web browsers and will almost certainly choke many versions of Netscape.

Changing Attributes of a Layer

When a layer is selected, several options become available for that layer through the Properties Inspector, as shown in Figure 11.13.

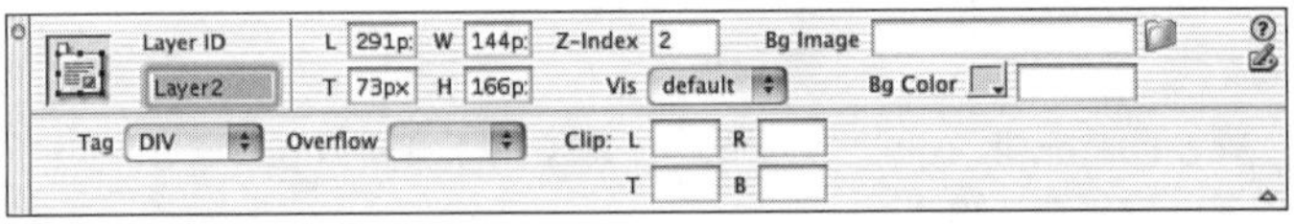

FIGURE 11.13   The Properties Inspector offers several options for altering the appearance or properties of a layer.

With all these options available, it may be confusing as to what they can offer in terms of altering the layer. Here's a small breakdown:

- **Layer ID**   Use this option to name the layer. Whatever you name your layer, that name can be used for communication with JavaScript or other behaviors. If you change the Layer ID in the Properties Inspector, it updates the Layers panel and vice versa. When naming layers, avoid spacing and special characters.

- **L and T**   Use these options to set the vertical and horizontal measurement for the location of the layer's top-left corner, relative to the top-left corner of the document.

- **W and H**   Type in a value for the dimensions of your layer size in width and height.

- **Z-Index**   This option determines how close or how far away a layer appears to the screen. The highest number is the topmost layer and the lowest number is the bottommost layer. You can set the z-index by typing a value into this text field or by using the Layers panel.

- **Vis**   The initial value for this is Default. Many browsers interpret this as visible; however, you might want to choose Visible from the drop-down menu, just to play it safe. You can also choose Hidden, which will make the layer invisible. The hidden choice is commonly used in conjunction with some behaviors. Refer to Chapter 19, "Behaviors," for more information on using layers with behaviors. Another option is available, called Inherit. This option is used for child layers nested inside parent layers. The nested layer will take on the same attributes as the parent. I discuss nested frames in greater detail later in this chapter.

- **BG Image**   This option is much like a table. You can set an image to appear behind the layer. If the image is smaller than the layer, it will repeat itself to create a tiled effect.

- **BG Color**   Like tables, you can use this option to set a background color for a layer.

- **Tag**   This option enables you to choose what HTML tag to use to create the layer. Internet Explorer 4 and later, as well as Netscape 6, can interpret the <div> and <span> tags for creating layers. Netscape 4 understands only <layer> and <ilayer> tags, which are no longer options in Dreamweaver MX. If you are designing specifically for Netscape 4.x, you'll have to hand code the tags.

- **Overflow and Clip**   These options are discussed in detail next.

Overflow

As you know, you can set an absolute size for a layer in the Properties Inspector. However, if you size the layer smaller than the content that is inside the layer, the overflow attribute will control how that content appears. There are four supported overflow attributes:

- **Visible**   This is the default setting. Visible will ignore the parameters you set for the width and height of the layer and automatically resize the layer to display all its contents.

- **Hidden**   This option crops the content that appears outside the specified dimensions so that it's not visible.

- **Scroll**   This makes horizontal and vertical scrollbars appear, regardless of the need for them.

- **Auto**   This option makes the horizontal and vertical scrollbars appear only if they are needed.

The Overflow attribute is supported by Internet Explorer 4.0 and later, as well as Netscape 6. It's also important to note that the Overflow option will not appear in the Dreamweaver MX authoring environment. You'll have to preview the page in a browser version just mentioned to see the results. Refer to Figure 11.14 to get an idea as to what the overflow attribute will look like when published.

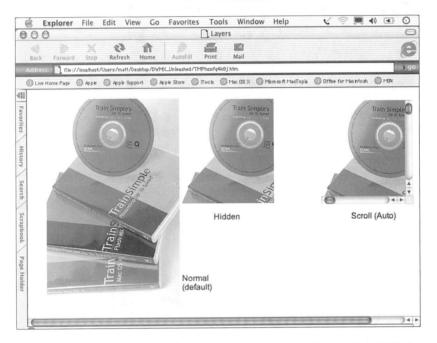

FIGURE 11.14   Notice the differences between the overflow attributes. The attributes are visible only in the Web browser.

Clipping

The Clipping option for layers is much like cropping an image in an image-editing program. However, the layer doesn't physically remove the excess image information; rather, the layer behaves like a mask, hiding the specified content.

In the Properties Inspector, you enter in values for the Left, Top, Right, and Bottom. All these value are measured from the layer's top-left corner. The values can be set to any unit accepted by the CSS standards, which include pixels (default), inches, centimeters, millimeters, ems, or picas.

Normally you'd type in a value for each of the options; however, you can use the word *auto*. Auto will set the Left and Top coordinates to 0,0, whereas auto in the Right and Bottom attributes will leave them virtually unchanged.

Use the Clipping Attribute

In this exercise you're going to crop the appearance of an image using the clipping attribute in the layer's Properties Inspector. Often it can be tricky as to what values you should enter in the Left, Top, Right, and Bottom attributes; however, you can use a temporary layer to help with finding those values. To precisely clip a layer, follow these steps:

1. Draw or insert a new layer. After the layer is placed within the document, insert an image into that layer.

2. Next you're going to draw a layer inside the existing layer. If you do not have nesting turned on in your preferences, hold down the Command (Mac) key or Ctrl (Windows) key while drawing the layer to turn nesting on temporarily. Draw the layer in the location in which you want to clip the image.

3. Shift the layer around for precise placement. After having the layer positioned properly, write down the dimensions in the Properties Inspector for the Left, Top, Width, and Height.

4. After you've jotted down the measurement values, delete the layer.

5. Next, highlight the layer in which the image resides. In the clip values in the Properties Inspector, enter the same values that you copied from the temporary layer. Enter the Width and Height values you copied into the Right and Bottom options, respectively.

6. As Figure 11.15 shows, the layer has masked out the portion of the image that was outside the original temporary layer.

FIGURE 11.15   The image in the layer has been masked to display only the area that was inside the original temporary layer.

Modifying Layer Properties with the Layers Panel

The Layers panel can also offer great assistance when modifying and managing layers. Although not as many options are available through this panel as through the Properties Inspector, you might find it instrumental in selecting layers, adjusting their visibility, or even changing the stacking order of the z-index. Notice in Figure 11.16 that the Layers panel has several icons.

- **Eye Closed**   This icon represents a hidden layer.

- **Eye Open**   The open eye means that the visible attribute has been turned on.

- **No Icon**   This means the Vis attribute in the Properties Inspector has been set to default.

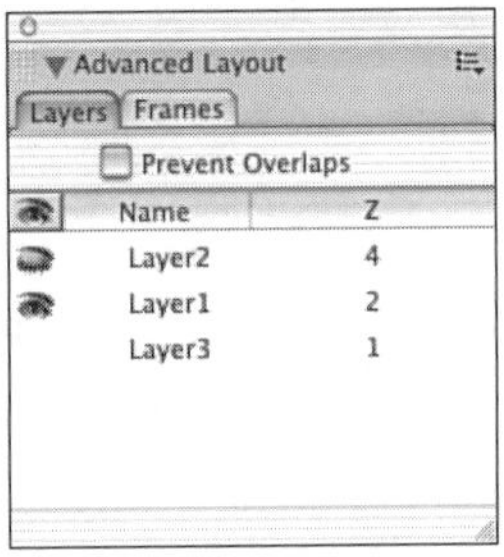

FIGURE 11.16   The Layers panel has several icons, representing different attributes that have been set through the Properties Inspector.

You also have the option of changing the layer's name. To change the name, double-click the text of the name to see a blinking cursor appear. Use the blinking cursor to delete or type anything that you want.

You can also use the Layers panel to change the z-index or stacking order of layers. You can control the stacking order by clicking and dragging a layer either above or below other layers, as shown in Figure 11.17.

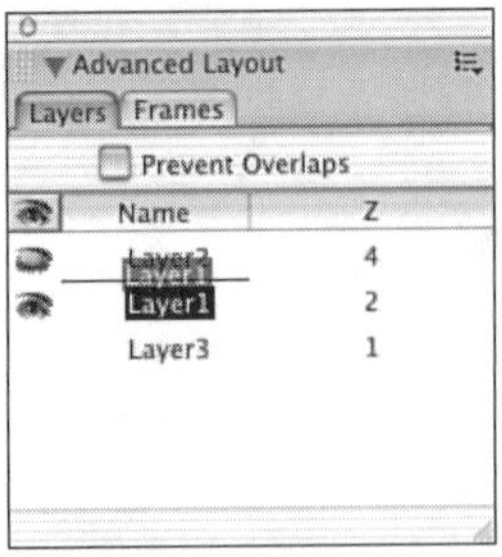

FIGURE 11.17   You can change the stacking order of layers, much like you would in any other graphics application; click and drag the layer either above or below other layers in the panel.

Nesting with the Layers Panel

A common task that can be performed through the Layers panel is nesting and unnesting layers.

Creating Nested Layers with the Layers Panel

To create a parent-child nested layer relationship by using the Frames panel, follow these steps:

1. Make sure the Layers panel is visible. If it's not, choose Window, Others, Layers to open the panel.

2. Draw two layers that are not nested in the document.

3. Notice that there are two layers now inside the Layers panel. To nest these layers, simply hold down the Command (Mac) key or Ctrl (Windows) key while dragging the layer you want to be nested on top of the other layer. After the layer is on top, release the mouse and notice that the layer disappears; however, an arrow (Mac) or plus sign (Windows) appears to the left of the layer name, as shown in Figure 11.18.

4. To reveal the nested or child layer, click the arrow or plus sign, as shown in Figure 11.19.

5. To undo the nested layer, drag the child or nested layer above or below the current layer.

As previously mentioned, nested layers can yield unpredictable results, especially in different browsers. It's important to keep that in mind when designing with layers.

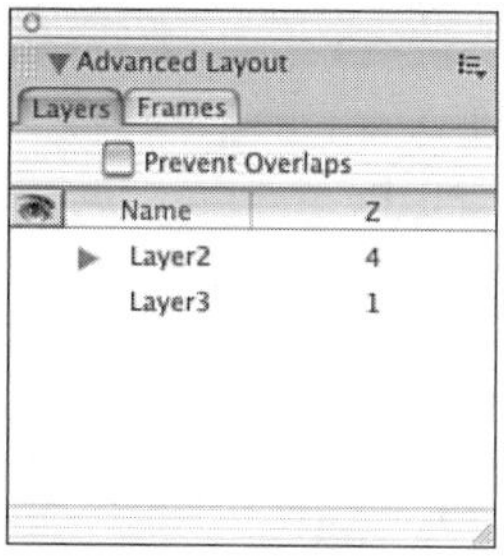

FIGURE 11.18   When a layer is nested, it is indented underneath the parent layer and an arrow appears at the left side of its name.

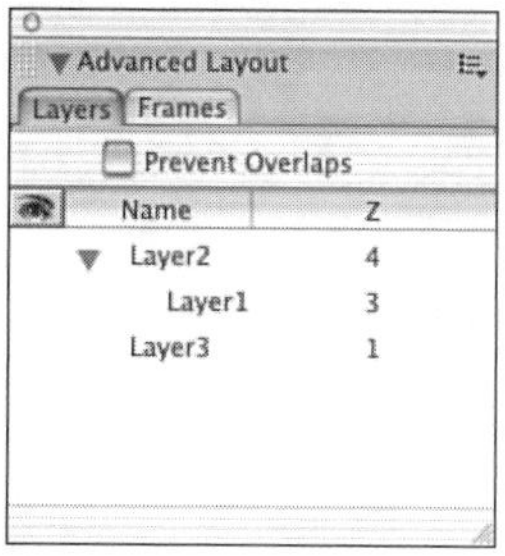

FIGURE 11.19   To reveal the nested layer in the Layers panel, click the arrow to twirl it down.

Designing a Page with Layers

Being able to design pages with layers lends more flexibility to the developer. However, layers still are viewable only by the latest versions of Web browsers, and unless you really know your specific audience, it may be safer to create a layout with tables. An option is to have two versions of your site as well: one that embraces the latest standards and another that caters to mass acceptance and compatibility. Whichever you decide, it's a snap creating two versions of a design in Dreamweaver MX.

Aids to Help Lay Out Layers

When designing pages with layers, a few things inside Dreamweaver can help you place layers precisely. The first thing you might consider doing is turning on the visibility of the rulers.

Rulers

You can easily make the rulers visible by choosing View, Rulers, Show. A couple of options exist within the Rulers submenu to help your layout become a successful one. If you need to change the ruler's increments, those options are available there.

If you need to change the 0,0 origin point of the rulers, click and drag from the top-right corner. You'll begin to drag a large crosshair, as shown in Figure 11.20. Place the center of the crosshair where your desired 0,0 mark would be for the x,y coordinate. To return to the original origin point, choose View, Rulers, Reset Origin.

Grid

Unfortunately, the rulers do not offer the standard guides you can drag out from the top or left side of the document. However, Dreamweaver does offer the grid, which can be a handy companion to the rulers. You can view the grid by choosing View, Grid, Show Grid. Now depending on your project, the default settings for the grid may not be beneficial; however, there are several options for modifying the grid. To modify the grid choose View, Grid, Grid Settings, which launches the Grid Settings dialog box as shown in Figure 11.20.

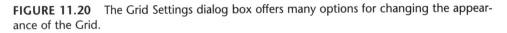

FIGURE 11.20   The Grid Settings dialog box offers many options for changing the appearance of the Grid.

You can change the following options:

- **Color**   You can change the color of the grid, especially if the default or currently selected color competes too much with the foreground.

- **Show Grid**   Check this box to have the grid appear in the document; leave unchecked for it to remain invisible.

- **Snap to Grid**   With this option enabled, the layers will snap to the grid lines.

- **Spacing**   The value entered into this box determines the space between grid points or the size of the grid squares. Use the drop-down menu to the right of it to determine what unit of measure to use.

- **Display**   You can have the grid appear as solid or dotted lines.

Using the grid and the ruler can greatly enhance the layout of your layers. Refer to Figure 11.21 to see the document with the rulers and grid visible.

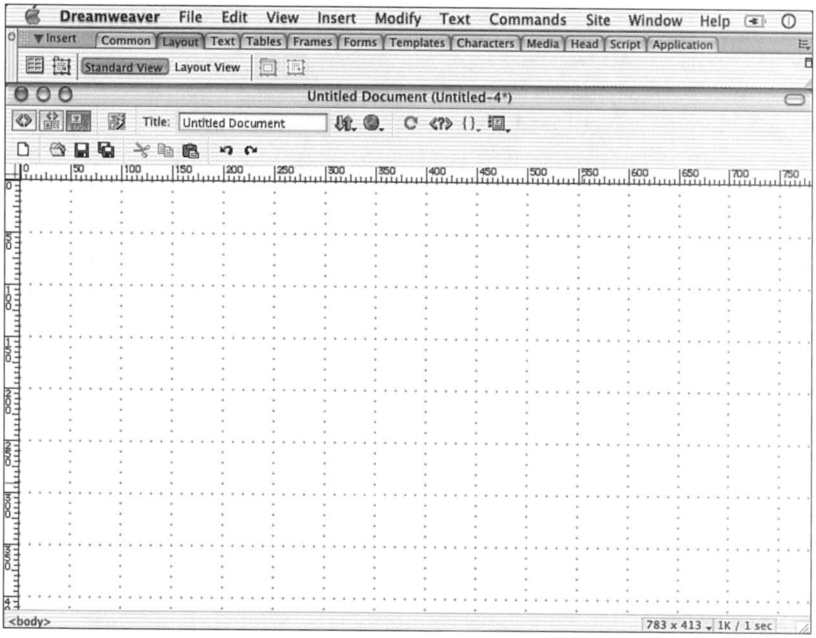

FIGURE 11.21   The document has both the rulers and the grid visible. Having these aids visible can greatly increase the accuracy of layer placement.

Prevent Overlaps

If your intention is to be able to make this document compatible with many of the Web browsers, at some point you will have to convert the layers into a table. You cannot convert layers that overlap one another into a table. To avoid potential future problems, you may want to check off the Prevent Overlaps option in the Layers panel, as pictured in Figure 11.22, or you can choose Modify, Arrange, Prevent Layer Overlaps.

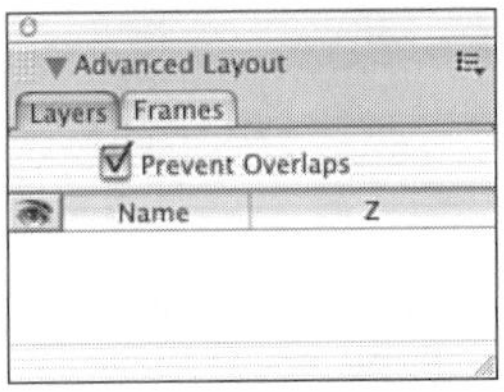

FIGURE 11.22   Choose the Prevent Overlaps option in the Layers panel if you intend to convert the layers to a table.

Converting Layers to Tables

By adding content such as images and text into many layers, I was able to come up with a nice design, as pictured in Figure 11.23.

When I was designing the page, I made sure that the Prevent Overlaps option was selected in the Layers panel so that none of the layers would overlap. I now want to make a version of this page that will be compatible with the majority of Web browsers. The first thing I'm going to do is save a new copy of this document by choosing File, Save As. In the Save As dialog box, I'm going to save this document inside my local root folder as index_table.html.

After saving a new version of this document, I'm going to choose Modify, Convert, Layers to Table. This opens the Convert Layers to Table dialog box, as shown in Figure 11.24.

You can see several options in this dialog box; here's what they mean:

- **Most Accurate**   This option generates a table as complex as necessary so that it ensures the most accurate placement of your content when the switch has been made from layers to tables. By default, this option is selected.

- **Smallest**   This option collapses any empty cells smaller than a pixel size that you specify. By merging empty cells, it ultimately creates a cleaner, simpler table. Unfortunately, it generates a less-accurate table, which may outweigh the advantages of a cleaner, faster-loading table. I recommend choosing Most Accurate and merging the cells by hand to clean up the table.

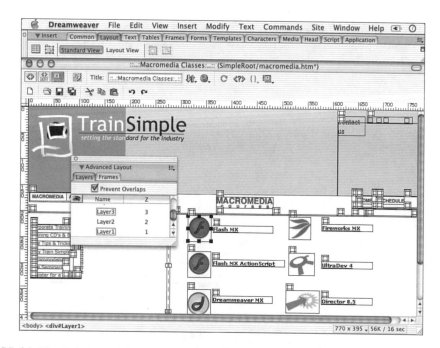

FIGURE 11.23   I designed the entire page by laying content out into different layers.

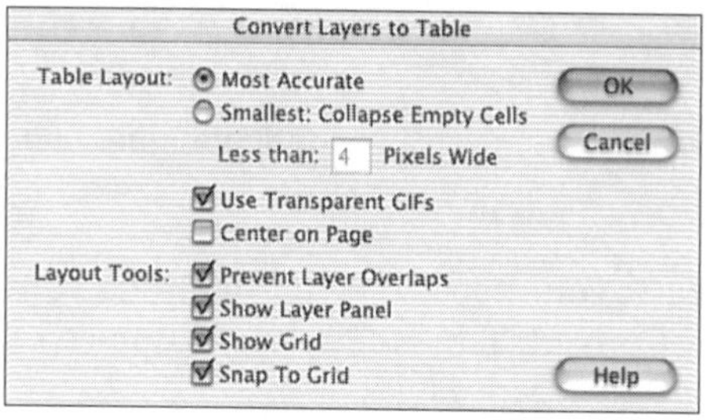

FIGURE 11.24   The Convert Layers to Table dialog box has a host of features to assist in the transition.

- **Use Transparent GIFs**   When this option is selected, Dreamweaver places transparent GIFs in all the empty cells in the table. This prevents browsers from collapsing the empty cells.

- **Center on Page**   This option centers the table on the page by using the `<div>` tag with the align attribute. Without choosing this, the table is placed in the default location of the top-left corner of the browser window.

- **Layout Tools**   These options will display or not display the visual tools. Each of these tools were reviewed earlier in this chapter.

When you're happy with the settings, choose OK. This converts the layers into tables, as shown in Figure 11.25. Preview the page in a Web browser to ensure that the results are satisfactory.

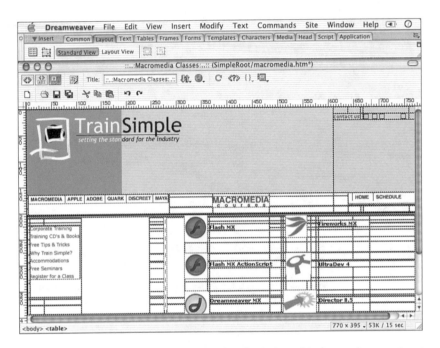

FIGURE 11.25   The document, which was previously designed in layers, is now structured in tables.

If the results aren't quite what you expected, you can always convert the table back to layers by choosing Modify, Convert, Table to Layers. This opens the Convert Tables to Layers dialog box as pictured in Figure 11.26.

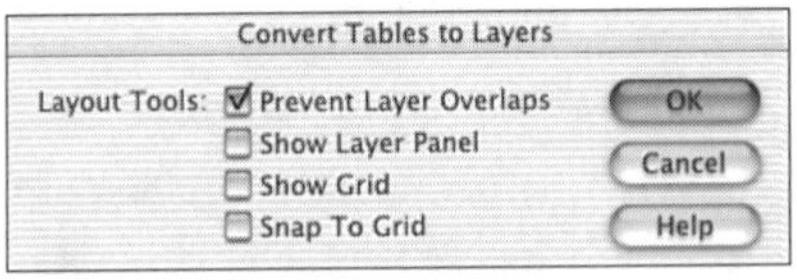

FIGURE 11.26   The Convert Tables to Layers dialog box offers some basic options for the conversion.

Check off the element you want to take effect and choose OK. Now that the layout is in layers again, you can make tweaks and adjustments and then convert the layout back to tables. You may find yourself doing this a couple of times.

Now you have two versions of the same layout: one for current browsers and one for older browsers. Finally, you can use a behavior to check to see what browser the end user is using to view your site. You'll learn more about how to use this behavior in Chapter 19.

Summary

Layers offer a great way to design pages, especially with the inclusion of the CSS standards. They can provide great flexibility; however, with everything on the Web, they'll require a bit of sacrifice if you want to use them. You have to decide if the benefits outweigh the negatives for the project you are working on.

Layers can also provide a tremendous amount of interactivity. You'll learn how you can use layers to add richer media to your sites in Chapter 12, "DHTML," and Chapter 19, "Behaviors."

PART III

Adding Interactivity

IN THIS PART

DHTML

by Matt Pizzi

In this chapter, you'll learn what you can do with Dynamic HTML (DHTML). In the previous two chapters, you dabbled a bit in the area of DHTML with layers and cascading style sheets (CSS). Each of these components are part of the DHTML specification. DHTML is a broad topic, and one that cannot be fully covered in this chapter. So this chapter focuses on what Dreamweaver MX can do with DHTML.

We develop in an interesting time, and aside from the potential it has for creating a richer, more interactive experience for the end user, DHTML often takes a backseat in the interactivity department. DHTML is great for precise placement of layers, and it alleviates many types of problems when dealing with CSS; however, when you're attempting to engage the viewer into the site, there are better solutions. Macromedia would have you think so, as well, with Flash.

In terms of providing rich content over the Web, I'd have to agree with Macromedia. The Flash Player has more penetration into the market than any other plug-in style application. However, understanding what Dreamweaver can produce with DHTM, might be enough for your audience in the way of interactive content.

I want to list some of the key features of DHTML. There are often better solutions for these features in this list, but I want you to be aware of the potential that DHTML might have in your Web projects.

1. **CSS**   Cascading style sheets, at this point in Web development, are probably the most important element of DHTML. As described in Chapter 10, "Cascading Style Sheets," CSS is better used for controlling and positioning text and blocks of text.

2. **Absolute Positioning**   With DHTML you can place any Web compliant object into the document with single-pixel accuracy.

3. **Dynamic Content**   When using DHTML, content can be added or removed from the HTML page during runtime.

4. **Downloadable Fonts**   This feature enables Web designers to embed specific fonts to control the appearance of type on any given Web browser.

5. **Data Binding**   Bind information in a table or form that automatically updates data with information on the server side without having to reload the entire page.

Something you should be aware of when considering using DHTML is that not all the functionality it offers is cross-browser friendly. Also, the implementation of DHTML in Dreamweaver isn't exactly WYSIWYG. Again, Macromedia's vision of improving the Web is not through DHTML standards, but with their technologies, such as Flash and Shockwave. If you've developed in Flash, and especially now with the promise of the Communication Server and topics like Flash remoting, it's hard to argue with their vision. So now that we've looked at CSS styles in Chapter 10, and worked with layers in Chapter 11, let's look at what Dreamweaver will allow us to do with DHTML in Dreamweaver's WYSIWYG design view environment.

Animation with the Timeline

You have the capability when using DHTML to animate layers. This can go far beyond a simple layer moving from one side of the document to another; in fact, you can create entire Web presentations using layers. You can even incorporate Dreamweaver's JavaScript behaviors into the timeline. This can be a nice alternative to other technologies that might require a plug-in. Before getting any deeper into this chapter, be sure to have a strong understanding of layers and how they work. If you're not completely clear about how layers work, refer to Chapter 11, "Layers."

Requirements to Keep in Mind

As mentioned earlier, animating with timelines may be a nice alternative to other technologies that would require a plug-in or ActiveX control. You should be aware of some guidelines when considering the use of animated layers.

- Animated layers require Internet Explorer 4.0 or later and Netscape 6.0 or later. Netscape 4.x could be used; however, that version of Netscape uses its own propriety tags to generate layers—the `<layer>` and `<ilayer>` tags. If you code these tags, the layers will not appear in any version of Internet Explorer or Netscape 6.0.

- If you want to animate any object in your HTML document, it must first be inserted into a layer. Dreamweaver will not allow you to add any other object to the timeline, other than a layer or an image. If you try, you will get an alert message warning you, as displayed in Figure 12.1.

- When selecting a frame rate, keep in mind that this will be considered a "desired frame rate," which means that the animation will play at the specified frame rate or as close to that specified frame rate as possible, depending on the power of the end user's machine.

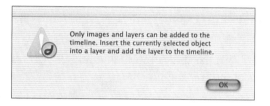

Only images and layers can be added to the timeline. Insert the currently selected object into a layer and add the layer to the timeline.

OK

FIGURE 12.1   If you try to insert an item other than a layer or an image into the timeline, Dreamweaver will warn you that it can't be done.

How the Timeline Works

When animating layers with the timeline in Dreamweaver, you might want to look at the code being generated. You'll notice that Dreamweaver writes about 60 lines of code to perform a simple animation. However, if you've never used an animation program before like Flash or Director, the timeline and how the timeline works may be confusing to you. Refer to Figure 12.2 to see the timeline and its different components.

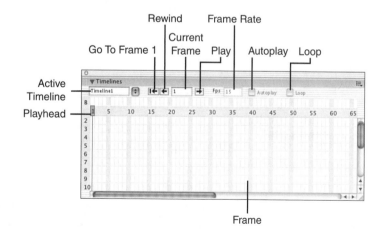

FIGURE 12.2   The timeline is constructed of several components, which will add functionality to your animations.

Elements of the Timeline

To access the Timeline panel, choose Window, Others, Timeline.

- **Options Bar** The top portion of the timeline offers a series of options to control the timeline. The timeline drop-down menu lets you activate a particular timeline. You can control the animation by stepping through the timeline with the left and right arrows with a corresponding text box to the current frame. There is also a button that will move the playhead back to frame 1. You can also set the frame rate for the animation, turn on looping, and set an option for Autoplay. Looping plays the animation from the beginning after it reaches the end.

- **Behavior Channel** This channel indicates what frames have behaviors associated with them.

- **Frame Numbers** This bar indicates frame numbers. This can be handy when adding or moving content on the timeline.

- **Frames** These are the actual containers of the animated information. They are much like a cell in a traditional animation or a frame in a filmstrip.

- **Playhead** This bar allows you to move through the animation and displays the current frame's information in the document.

- **Layers** These numbers correspond to a layer within the timeline.

Frames and Keyframes

When discussing animation, I often like to refer to the old-fashion flipbook concept. Remember those old books, where if you flipped through the pages quickly you would see the content within those pages animate? Essentially, that's what's happening in Dreamweaver. The timeline allows you to assemble a virtual flipbook.

The timeline is constructed of a series of frames. To view the frames, you can scrub (drag) the playhead back and forth over the populated frames. To see what a populated frame looks like, refer to Figure 12.3.

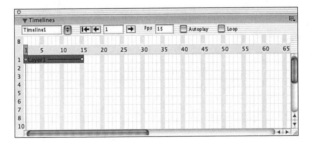

FIGURE 12.3 The frames that appear in the timeline that are of a different color than a traditional frame contain content; therefore, they are referred to as populated frames.

In Figure 12.3, the first and last frames in the populated frames in the timeline appear as circles. These circles are known as keyframes. A keyframe is a frame that represents a major change within the animation. The frames between the two keyframes are known as in between frames. The great thing when animating in Dreamweaver is that Dreamweaver does most of the work. In the instance shown in Figure 12.2, there are only two keyframes, so in theory, the layer should show up in the location of the first frame and in a different location on the last keyframe. However, in this case, the layer moves across the document to reach its new destination on the second keyframe. The reason for this is that Dreamweaver is *tweening* the animation. Tweening means that all the frames between the first frame and the second frame are all drawn for you, creating the effect of motion.

This is how animation works in a traditional studio. The lead animator would draw the first frame of an animation and the last frame. Typically, these need to be the most detailed because they stay on the screen just a bit longer than the rest of the frames. Then a team of "in-betweeners" comes in and paints all the in-between frames to complete the animation.

Frame Rate

The frame rate determines how many frames per second the viewer will see. The higher the frame rate, the more realistic the animation will appear. To give you a frame of reference, film plays at 24 frames per second (fps) and digital video plays at 29.97 or 30fps.

The default frame rate in Dreamweaver is 15. Even though video and film play at 30fps and 24fps, respectively, film and video don't have bandwidth restrictions like Web pages do, and the manner in which film and video are viewed is more standardized. When animating for the Web, your animation is at the mercy of the end user's machine. The processor speed, the speed of the Internet connection, how much RAM is available, and the quality of the video card all play crucial roles in the appearance of an animation. So if you're developing on the latest and fastest computer, you're not getting an accurate representation as to how this animation will look to the world. That's why it is especially important to test your page on several types of computers. If it chokes on a fairly standard computer, you may want to reconsider the frame rate of the animation, as well as the content you're trying to animate. Large graphical files are more difficult to process than text.

So the moral of the story is, you can specify a frame rate, but ultimately, the speed of the animation is determined by the strength of the computer playing it.

Adding Layers to the Timeline

Dreamweaver offers several ways to add layers to the timeline. You can use either a series of keyboard shortcuts: Command+Option+Shift+T (Mac) or Ctrl+Alt+Shift+T (Windows), or you can use the command listed under the menu: Modify, Timeline, Add Object to Timeline, or finally, you can just drag the layer into the Timeline panel.

If you insert an object into the timeline by choosing Modify, Timelines, Add Object to Timeline, it will automatically set the object's time to 15 frames, and it will always start the object's time at frame 1. However, if you drag the layer into the timeline, you have a bit more flexibility as to where and what frame it starts on the timeline.

The first time you insert a layer into a timeline, Dreamweaver will pop up an alert message explaining the limitations of the timeline, as shown in Figure 12.4. If you don't want to see this dialog box, choose Don't Show Again.

FIGURE 12.4   The alert message explains the limitations of animating a layer in the timeline.

Creating an Animation with the Timeline

In this exercise, you'll create animation by adding a layer to the timeline and modifying the way the animation appears.

1. Draw a layer anywhere in the document.

2. Place a blinking cursor in the document, and insert an image by choosing Insert, Image. Search your hard drive for an image and select it. Notice that the image now appears in the layer.

3. Next, select the layer. It's very important to have the layer selected and not the image. You can animate only layers. Refer to Figure 12.5 to see an example of a selected image; it has only three handles. However, when you select a layer, eight resize handles appear as shown in Figure 12.6.

4. With the layer selected, choose Modify, Timeline, Add Object to Timeline. The timeline is now populated with two keyframes on frames 1 and 15. This animation lasts for 15 frames and is playing at 15fps, so it will last one second. The span of 15 frames is often referred to as the animation bar.

5. You now want to create some animation. Highlight frame 15 by clicking it. Then drag the layer to the other side of the document. You'll notice a line drawn from the starting point to the ending in the document when you release the mouse from dragging the layer, as displayed in Figure 12.7.

6. In the timeline, check the AutoPlay option as well as the Loop option. This way, the animation plays automatically, and when the animation is complete, it will start playing again from the beginning.

7. Preview the document in a browser by choosing File, Preview in Browser, Internet Explorer, or by pressing F12 on your keyboard. Notice that the animation is playing in the browser.

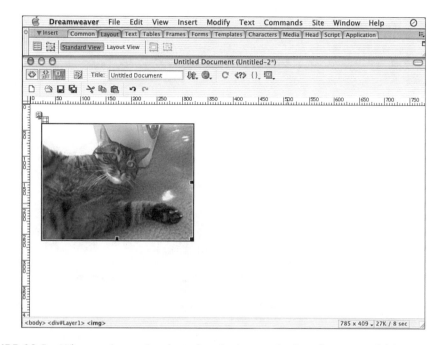

FIGURE 12.5   When an image is selected, only three resize handles are available.

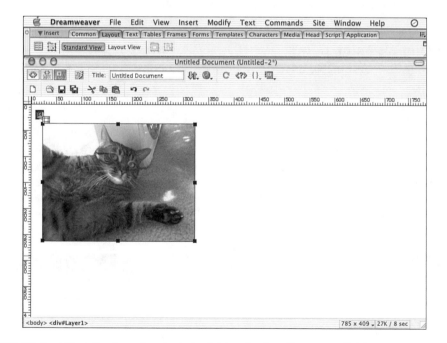

FIGURE 12.6   When the layer is selected, eight resize handles are available.

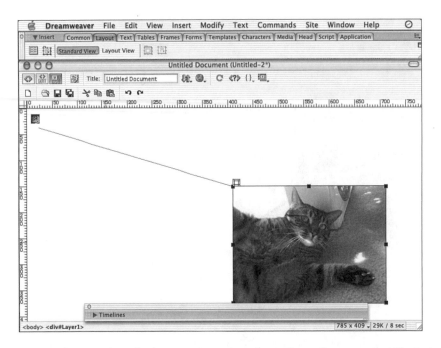

FIGURE 12.7   After you drag the layer to a new location, a line will appear that illustrates the direction and course of animation the layer will take.

Modifying an Animation

After you create your initial animation, you can easily modify its appearance. You can accomplish this in several ways.

Increase the Duration of the Animation

You may decide you want your animation to play more slowly. Perhaps you think it zips across the screen rather quickly. If this is the case, people usually would want to lower the frame rate. Remember, though, the lower the frame rate, the less natural the animation will look. What you need to do to slow the animation down is give the timeline more frames to play. So instead of leaving the default animation length to 15 frames, increase it to 30 frames. You can do this by highlighting the last keyframe and dragging to frame 30, as shown in Figure 12.8.

CAUTION

Unlike Flash, DHTML will never drop frames. Often, with slower computers, if it can't keep up with the frame rate of the animation, Flash will just dismiss or drop some frames to keep up. DHTML plays every frame. If the frame rate is too high, the animation will just play slowly in comparison to the desired effect.

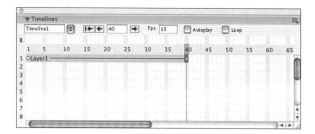

FIGURE 12.8   You can easily extend the animation by dragging the last keyframe to any frame further than the default of 15.

Changing the Starting Point

You can easily change the starting point of the animation in a way similar to extending it. Highlight the first keyframe and drag it to the desired start location. By doing this when you preview the animation in a browser, the layer will stay paused in the same location for a moment before it starts animating. You can also preview the animation within the Dreamweaver authoring environment by clicking and holding down the right arrow or play button on the timeline.

> **CAUTION**
>
> If you test the animation and the entire image doesn't animate, it could mean one of two things. Your graphic is too large for a computer to process an animation, or the computer viewing the animation is not powerful enough. When using layers for animation, it is important to keep in mind the audience that will be viewing this.

Adding Keyframes

Keyframes play a crucial role in animation; in fact, they represent most of the changes happening in the animation. That's why it can become very handy to know how you can insert your own keyframes. If you want to suddenly change the direction of the animated layer, that is easily done by simply adding a keyframe.

There are a couple of ways you can add keyframes. To add keyframes to the timeline, follow these steps:

1. In the Timeline panel, highlight the animation bar you want to add keyframes to.

2. With the animation bar selected, move the playhead to the frame location in which you want to add the keyframe.

3. You can add the keyframe in one of two ways: Choose Modify, Timeline, Add Keyframe, or Ctrl+Click (Mac) or right-click (Windows) on the frame in which you want to add the keyframe, and in the contextual menu choose Add Keyframe. Notice in Figure 12.9 that a keyframe has been added to the timeline.

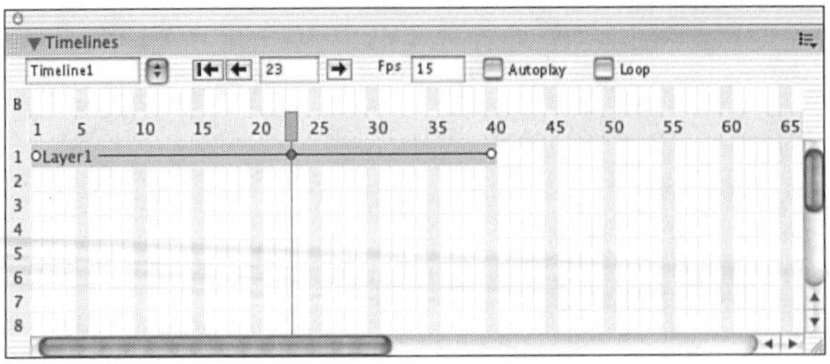

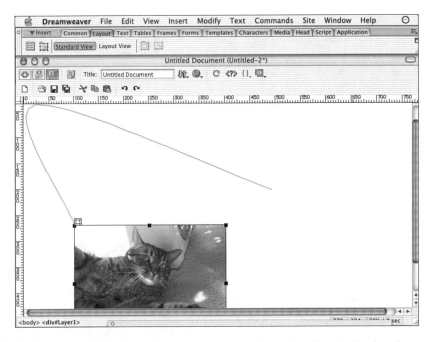

FIGURE 12.9   The timeline now has an additional keyframe.

You can then select the layer in the document and reposition it, changing the direction of the animation as shown in Figure 12.10.

FIGURE 12.10   After placing a keyframe, you can alter the animation further by changing the layers position on that keyframe.

Removing Timeline Components

Having flexibility is important when creating animations, and sometimes you might like to have the flexibility to remove certain elements from the timeline. You can do this just as easy as adding elements.

You can remove the entire timeline by choosing Modify, Timeline, Remove Timeline. This effectively deletes your entire animation.

You can remove objects from the timeline in a similar way. The most convenient way is to contextual click the timeline to gain access to all the remove options, as shown in Figure 12.11.

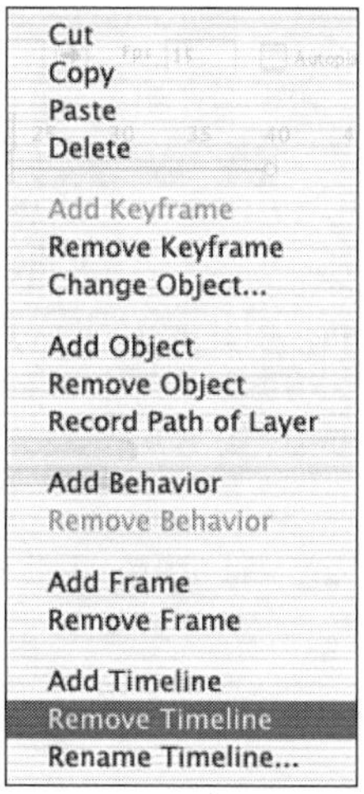

```
Cut
Copy
Paste
Delete

Add Keyframe
Remove Keyframe
Change Object...

Add Object
Remove Object
Record Path of Layer

Add Behavior
Remove Behavior

Add Frame
Remove Frame

Add Timeline
Remove Timeline
Rename Timeline...
```

FIGURE 12.11   Notice that the context menu offers all the options to remove timeline components.

The contextual menu offers the capability to remove keyframes as well as frames, objects, behaviors, and the timeline. You can also copy, cut, and paste timelines between documents.

Recording the Path of a Layer

From the previous two sections, you might have seen that to make a complex animation requires a lot of practice and a lot of keyframes. Adding keyframes and moving the layer in the desired location on that keyframe offers a more complicated, natural movement. However, a feature in Dreamweaver can cut out a lot of the work for you. It's a command called Record Path of Layer, and the command does pretty much that.

When you choose Record Path of Layer, Dreamweaver follows the path in which you drag the layer around in the document. It's very useful, and accurate. The slower you drag, the more keyframe points it sets, offering slower motion in that area. As you drag faster, generally fewer keyframe points are set, offering a quicker style of animation. This is a nice shortcut to get an animation to appear the way that you want without having to mess around with setting keyframes and moving and adjusting the layer on each of those keyframes.

To record the path of the layer that you are dragging in the document, follow these steps:

1. Create a new document. In the new document, either insert or draw a layer.

2. Place a blinking cursor in the layer so you can place an image inside of it. Choose Insert, Image and find an image on your hard drive you'd like to animate.

3. Be sure to have the Timeline panel open by choosing Window, Others, Timeline.

4. Next, choose Modify, Timeline, Record Path of Layer.

5. Now start dragging the layer around the document in a way that you want it to animate. Notice that Dreamweaver draws a path in the document to give you an idea of the route the animation will take, as shown in Figure 12.12.

6. When you're happy with the path, stop dragging. Notice in the timeline that all the keyframes have been placed, as displayed in Figure 12.13. Also, take notice of how the keyframes are placed. If you dragged slower in some areas, there will be a tighter cluster of keyframes in the timeline to represent that.

7. Check Autoplay and preview the animation in a browser, or hold down the Play button in the timeline to see how the animation looks in action.

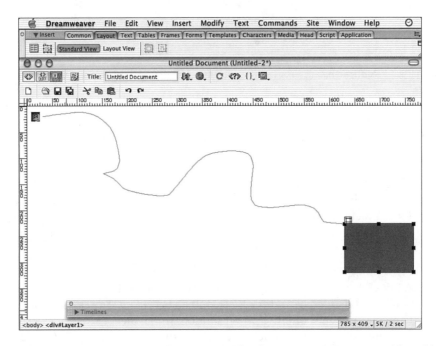

FIGURE 12.12   As you drag, the path appears in the document, giving you an idea of how the animation will look.

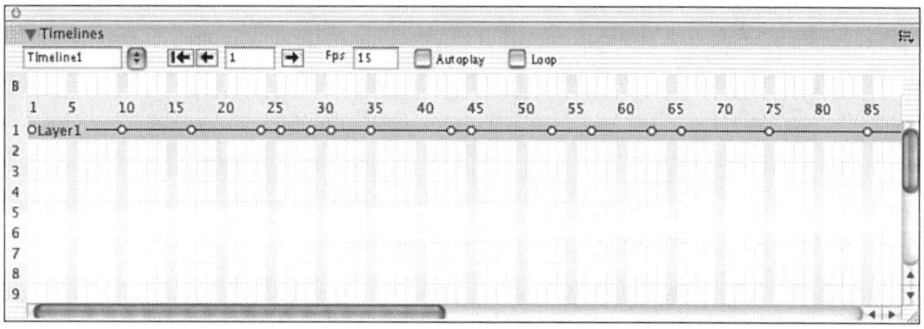

FIGURE 12.13   All the keyframes in the timeline have been placed to create the animation to mimic the movement of your dragging the layer around.

Triggering Behaviors from the Timeline

Dreamweaver offers the capability to have the timeline trigger behaviors. This can be useful if you need the timeline's playhead to move to a certain area of the timeline. Perhaps you would like an alert message to pop up at the end of an animation. Whatever the case, the process is quite simple in Dreamweaver MX. To learn more about behaviors, refer to Chapter 19, "Behaviors."

To have an alert message pop up at the end of the animation, follow these steps:

1. Create an animation with a layer.

2. Move the playhead to the last frame and select the last frame.

3. Choose Modify, Timeline, Add Behavior. You can also contextual click and choose Add Behavior from the contextual menu, or you can double-click the frame in the behavior track. This will open an alert telling you how to add the behavior and opens the Behaviors panel as shown on Figure 12.14.

FIGURE 12.14   The alert message tells you to click the plus sign to add a behavior.

4. In the Behaviors panel, click the plus sign and choose Popup Message. This opens a dialog box where you can type in a message as shown in Figure 12.15.

5. Type **The animation is now complete** into the message window. Choose OK to exit this dialog box.

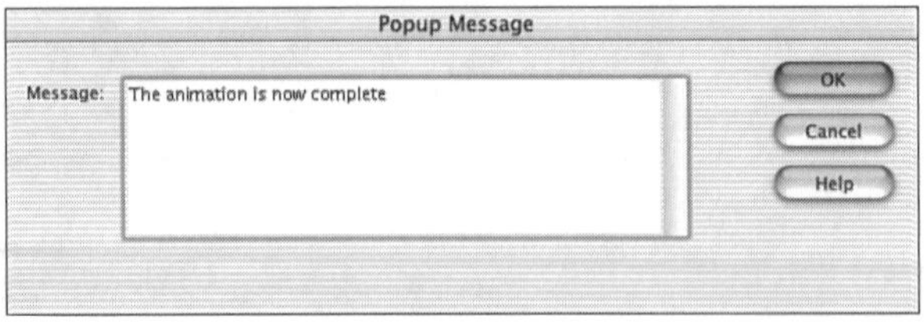

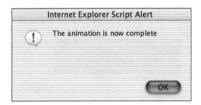

FIGURE 12.15 You can type in a message that you want to appear in the Alert dialog box.

6. In the Behaviors panel, the event should be set to the frame number to which you applied the behavior. Be sure to have Autoplay checked in the timeline and Loop turned off.

7. Preview the animation in the browser. As Figure 12.16 shows, when the animation is over, the alert message pops up with the message you typed in the dialog box earlier.

FIGURE 12.16 The alert message appears when the animation is over.

Controlling the Timeline with Behaviors

Trigger events from the timeline are one thing, but you can also control the timeline with behaviors by means of something else, like text or graphics. Maybe you would like to give end users the freedom to play and stop the animation at their leisure. This isn't a bad idea, either; sometimes animations in Web pages can become distracting or annoying to end users, which ultimately makes them leave your site. However, if you offer them the option of controlling the animation, they may be more likely to stay.

Download the play and stop graphics from the companion Web site located at http://www.dreamweavermxunleashed.com to follow these steps in controlling the timeline.

Before we walk through step-by-step, there are a few things that must be in place first. First, you need an animation. In this animation, make sure that Autoplay is not selected and Loop is. You want the end user to determine when to play and stop the animation. To do that, follow these steps:

1. Draw a layer somewhere in the document that won't interfere with the animation. Place a blinking cursor inside the layer to insert the images you either created or

downloaded from the companion Web site. Choose Insert, Image if you downloaded the graphics, and choose play.gif from your hard drive. Repeat the process to insert stop.gif.

2. Highlight the Play button and open the Behaviors panel. You can open the Behaviors panel by choosing Window, Behaviors. Click the plus sign to add a behavior, and in the menu choose Timeline, Play Timeline. This will open a dialog box, as shown in Figure 12.17, asking what timeline to play. Choose the timeline; in this case, you probably have only one, so choose Timeline1.

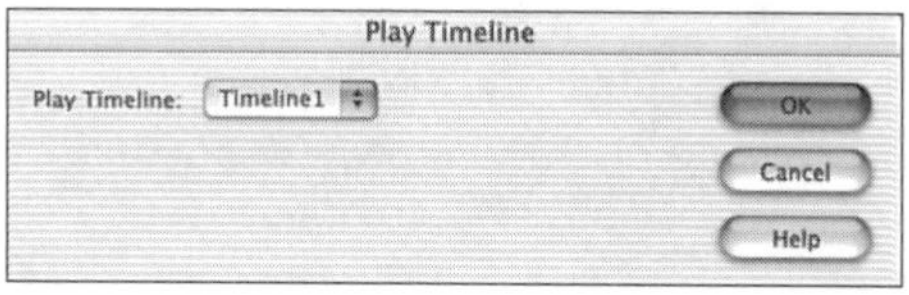

FIGURE 12.17   Choose which timeline you want to play from the drop-down menu.

3. Repeat step 2 for the Stop button and choose Stop Timeline for the behavior. The dialog box offers the option of choosing a specific timeline or All Timelines. In this case you have only one timeline, so choosing All Timelines is fine.

4. Preview the animation in a Web browser. The animation does not play until you press the Play button, and the animation does not stop until you press the Stop button.

Use the Behaviors panel in conjunction with the timeline and create a powerful combination. You can add user interaction with the Web site by using the DHTML features that Dreamweaver provides. It's not nearly at the level of Flash or Shockwave applications, but on the positive side, end users do not need a plug-in or an ActiveX control to view this content. They simply need Internet Explorer 4.x or Netscape 6.

Creating a Slide Show by Changing the Image's Source

Another powerful use for the timeline is the option of creating a slide show. Remember the only object you can add to a timeline other that a layer is an image. However if you want the image to animate, it has to be placed within a layer; only layers can animate in DHTML. However, if you add an image to the timeline, although you may not be able to animate it, you will be able to change the image's source over time.

You can follow these steps exactly if you download the gato_images folder from the companion Web site located at http://www.dreamweavermxunleashed.com.

To create a slide show, follow these steps:

1. Open a new document. Draw a layer in the center of the document. The layer is simply for placement of the graphics and has nothing to do with the animation.

2. Place a blinking cursor in the document and insert an image. I'm working with the Gato images, so I'll insert the gato_close_up.jpg image.

3. Next, with the image selected, choose Modify, Timeline, Add Object to Timeline. You'll get an alert message explaining that you can change only the source of the image as shown in Figure 12.18.

FIGURE 12.18   An alert message warns that you can change only the image source.

4. Drag the last keyframe out to frame 60.

5. Next, select the animation bar (all the frames) and place the playhead over frame 10. With the playhead positioned properly, choose Modify, Timeline, Add Keyframe. This places a keyframe on frame 10.

6. With the playhead still positioned over frame 10, highlight the graphic. In the Properties Inspector, the SRC text field indicates the source of the image. Click the folder icon next to it and search for gato_in_actopn.jpg in the Select Image Source dialog box as shown in Figure 12.19. Click OK. Notice the image is different on frame 10; however if you move (scrub) the playhead back to frame 1, the original image is still present.

7. Repeat steps 5 and 6, adding keyframes every 10 frames and switching the image's source.

8. Next, make sure Autoplay is not checked, but looping is. Add the Play and Stop images like you did in steps 1 and 2 of the previous exercise. Also, add the Play Timeline and Stop Timeline to each image.

9. Preview the slide show in a Web browser. Click the Play button to see the animation and the Stop button to Stop it.

> **NOTE**
>
> You can download a complete working copy of this exercise from this book's companion Web site located at `http://www.dreamweavermxunleashed.com`.

Summary

DHTML and the timeline offer the traditional Web developer the opportunity to create engaging, interactive Web sites. As previously mentioned, the capabilities are nowhere near what Flash and Shockwave content is, but it does provide a solution that doesn't require a plug-in or ActiveX control.

As with all rich media, make sure your project requires such interactivity with the end user. DHTML is simply a tool, like any other, to communicate your message with a viewer. If that gets confused with "Hey, look at my logo flying around, because it's cool, but doesn't really serve a purpose," then you failed as a Web developer.

The timeline can be a powerful addition to your Web site designs when used properly and effectively.

12

CHAPTER **13**

Adding Video and Audio

by Matthew Pizzi

In this chapter, you'll learn how you can add multimedia elements such as audio and video to your Web sites. Incorporating such media into your site can offer an interesting way to communicate with your audience. Your message and audience determines which type of format you should deliver it in and how long the presentation should be.

Media Players

To view video on the Web, you must have a media player. Furthermore, you must have the appropriate media player that the media file is suppose to be viewed with, in most cases. Many sites offer the same media content in three formats: Windows Media Player, Real, and QuickTime.

The world of media players is constantly changing. Even as I'm writing this chapter, Apple has announced QuickTime 6 and Real has announced a new player initiative that will allow its One Player to natively play all file formats intended for the other media players. Following is a breakdown of the strengths and weaknesses of the three players (as of this writing). However, first I'd like to point out the differences between a progressive download video and streaming video. The technologies are as similar as they are different, and it's important to understand them both.

Streaming Video

The best way to explain streaming video is to equate it with a telephone conversation or watching a TV show. When you're talking to someone over the phone, you hear that person's voice. Whenever the person is done speaking, everything that individual said, in terms of data, is gone. The instant you hear the person on the other end is the instant that information is no longer available, and if you missed something, the person will have to repeat it.

Streaming video is the same, in the sense that the instant that you see the video is the same instant that the data displaying that video is removed from your system without a trace. In the player, the data is replaced by new video data, much like watching TV.

Each media format has its own streaming server software to deliver the video feed. Often, the quality of the video is small and pixilated in comparison to the progressive download counterparts. However, a lot of this is changing with new standards of MPEG-4 compression supported by Apple's new QuickTime 6 and Real's new media player. As of this writing, Microsoft's Media Player will support its own propriety software to compete with MP4.

With all the advancements, the bottom line is that you still need broadband to view video files on the Web. Although this may seem like an issue now, within a year or two, a dial-up modem will be as antiquated as an Apple II Plus or Commodore 64. When broadband is available to the masses, and technologies such as MPEG-4 gain momentum, digital video will revolutionize the way we get content from the Web.

As for right now, video does still carry some hefty file sizes, therefore requiring a lot of download bandwidth by the end user.

Progressive Download

A progressive download file actually downloads digital information to your computer in the form of a file that can be saved after the video has been cached to your machine. A progressive download does just that. It downloads to your computer, playing off your hard drive locally, which benefits from better throughput than what you can get over the Internet. The result is cleaner, bigger, crisper, higher-quality video.

The downside is that it can take longer to view the video because you have to wait for it to download to your machine. However, with a fast Internet connection, you may not notice the difference because when enough of the video has downloaded, the video will start playing using the playing time as download time for the rest of the video. Apple's QuickTime is the best exploiting this technology and offers the highest video quality when content is offered this way.

QuickTime

Apple Computer was ahead of its time back in the early 1990s when it introduced an application called QuickTime. QuickTime was the first application that enabled you to play digital video on a computer. Today QuickTime sets the standard in multimedia playback. As you can see in Figure 13.1, the QuickTime Player offers a clean, brushed-aluminum interface for viewing downloaded movies and a simple play/pause progress bar embedded into a browser, as shown in Figure 13.2.

FIGURE 13.1   The QuickTime Player has an easy-to-use interface with core video controls in an accessible, viewable area.

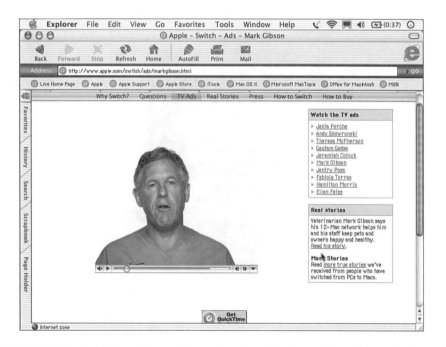

FIGURE 13.2   The QuickTime Player offers a simple navigation without distracting from the content after it is embedded into a document.

Often, people confuse QuickTime with the QuickTime Video format. The QuickTime Player is almost a separate operating system dedicated to viewing all sorts of different content including QuickTime Video, Flash 5 and earlier, AVI, QTVR, MP3, MPEG-4, and much more.

QuickTime 6 offers streaming capabilities as well as progressive download options. It's important to understand that the author and content provider of the video determines which format to deliver it in. If you want to offer QuickTime streaming video, you must have Apple QuickTime Streaming Software, which is available for Mac OS X Server, Linux, Solaris, and Windows NT/2000. For more information on Streaming Server, visit `http://www.apple.com/quicktime/servers`.

QuickTime enjoys roughly 30% of the market for rich media and is the top choice for graphics professionals. QuickTime offers the highest-quality video playback, and now with the support of MPEG-4, MPEG-4 streaming content will be sure to catch the eye of quality-conscious developers. QuickTime 6 Player is available for Mac OS and Windows.

Windows Media

Windows Media is now a very viable platform with about 50% of the market. Of course its biggest advantage over its competitors is the automatic inclusion of it in the Windows Operating System (see Figure 13.3).

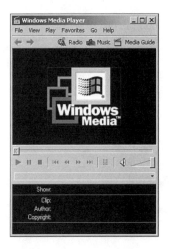

FIGURE 13.3   The Windows Media Player interface offers controls to Play, Stop, Rewind, and Fast Forward through media content.

However, I will say after watching video streams in other formats and comparing them to Windows Media, the quality is pretty impressive. Just like QuickTime and Real, you must have a streaming server configured to run Windows Media Streaming video. For more information on streaming servers, visit `http://www.microsoft/windows/windowsmedia`. Windows Media Player 9 does not support MPEG-4 video, but does offer a comparable proprietary architecture for video on the Web.

In addition to playing streaming video, it can also handle other formats such as ASF, ASX, MPG, QT, AIF, MOV, and AU. For more information about the player, visit `http://www.microsoft.com/.windows/mediaplayer`.

RealMedia

RealNetworks was the first to offer a streaming server and is the grandfather of streaming video. As of this writing, it has the market share to prove it with more than 55% of viewers using the RealPlayer. The RealOne Player eliminates the need for a Web browser when you're looking for streaming content on the Web.

Real also offers the RealPlayer in more platforms than any other media player. The RealPlayer is available for Windows, Macintosh, Unix, Linux, and OS/2.

RealOne has the capability to view video, images, Flash, audio files such as MP3 and AIFF. The RealOne player is a free download, but Real does offer a subscription-based plan to view certain content from CNN, ABCNEWS, E!, and FoxSports, to name a few.

Adding Video to Your Pages

Most Internet users will have at least one of the media players installed on their systems, if not all three. Typically, depending on which site you visit, you will determine which media player is best suited for your needs.

Embedding Video Clips

If you're looking to provide video content without the expenses of streaming server software, embedding digital video into a Web page might be the best solution. The QuickStart feature of Apple's QuickTime is a nice way for the viewers to quickly gain access to viewing the movie without having to wait for the entire clip to download.

Typically, video clips are delivered in one of the following common formats:

- **MPEG (MPG, MPEG, MPE)**   The MPEG format was standardized by the Motion Picture Expert Group. Generally, Windows machines will play MPEG content with Windows Media Player and the Mac will play it with QuickTime.

- **QuickTime (MOV)**   QuickTime movies can contain an assortment of different technologies that require playback in the QuickTime player. However, it's not uncommon to have Windows Media Player try to hijack and play the movie itself in Windows.

- **QuickTime Video (MOV)**   A QuickTime video can contain video and audio and can be played back by all three media players.

- **Video for Windows (AVI)**   This is the format originally created by Microsoft, which is now unsupported by the company; it can also be played back in all three media players, much like QuickTime video.

Codecs

Although movie clips come in many formats, it's important to understand that for the video to be viewable, the proper codecs must be installed in the media player. The word codec comes from combining the words Encoder and Decoder. A codec is used when compressing video and is required by the player to decompress during playback. Many codecs are already installed in Windows and QuickTime, so it's generally not a problem. If you need a codec, you can usually find it somewhere on the Web. Sorenson and Cinepak are common codecs to use when compressing digital video.

Linking Video

The file formats mentioned previously: MPEG, QuickTime, and AVI, are good choices for linking video content into a page. As I mentioned earlier, many of the players offer some kind of fast-start scenario where the movie starts playing after a certain amount of data has been downloaded, allowing it the rest of the playing time to download the rest of the content. Linking video into an HTML document is easy. Just follow these steps:

1. Select an image, text, or any other element in your document that you want to act as the trigger to launch the movie.

2. In the Properties Inspector, next to the Link text field, click the Browse for File icon (folder).

3. In the Select File dialog box, search for the movie you want to link. Choose OK (Mac) or Select (Windows).

4. The link text field is automatically filed in with the appropriate path to the video, as displayed in Figure 13.4.

5. Preview the document in a browser by pressing F12. A window opens with your media player containing the video you selected, as shown in Figure 13.5.

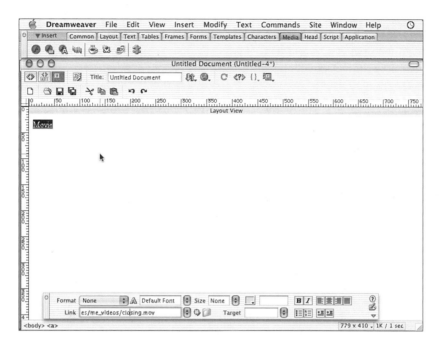

FIGURE 13.4   The path to the video clip is automatically placed within the Properties Inspector.

FIGURE 13.5   After you press the link, the file and media format will launch the appropriate media player, if it is installed in your system.

Embedding Video with the <Embed> Tag

When you embed video into an HTML document, you as the developer have slightly more control over how the video will appear in the browser. When you insert video into an HTML document, you use the <embed> tag. To embed a movie clip, follow these steps:

1. In the Insert panel, click the Media tab and then click the Insert Plug-in button. This launches a Select File dialog box.

2. Select a file you want to insert into the document. After you've found the file, click OK (Mac) or Select (Windows).

> **NOTE**
>
> You can also drag any media files from the Assets panel, which will already contain the source information.

3. This places a plug-in movie holder into the document displayed at 32×32 pixels as shown in Figure 13.6.

4. In the Properties Inspector, you must specify the dimensions of the movie in the H and W text fields. Or you can size the plug-in by dragging the handles to size it manually.

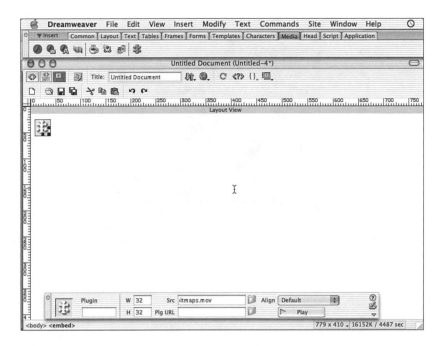

FIGURE 13.6   The Properties panel shows the icon that appears in the document, and it gives you options to manipulate the plug-in.

To preview how the video will appear in the Web page, press the Play button in the Properties Inspector with the movie selected. The movie plays inside the HTML document, as shown in Figure 13.7.

FIGURE 13.7   When you press the Play button, the plug-in movie starts playing inside the Dreamweaver document.

Notice that there are options for adding parameters to the embedded plug-in. You can find a list of compatible parameters for both QuickTime and RealMedia G2 found at `http://www.apple.com` and `http://www.realnetworks.com`, respectively.

Playing Video Clips on the Web

The type of video you're trying to view on the Web will determine what the player looks like. QuickTime is the most integrated with the Web page. As you can see in Figure 13.8, the QuickTime player, after it is embedded into the document, has a controller with a couple of options.

The controls of the QuickTime Player are fairly straightforward; however, there are some additional options. Holding down the Shift key while pressing down on the speaker will allow you to gain extra volume, as shown in Figure 13.9. If you have QuickTime Pro, a $30 upgrade from Apple, you have the capability to save certain QuickTime content from the drop-down menu on the right as well as some editing capabilities.

FIGURE 13.8   The QuickTime player offers a progress bar as well as controls for playing and pausing the video and controlling the audio.

FIGURE 13.9   Holding down the Shift key while pressing down on the volume level enables you to turn up the volume above and beyond what's normal.

Adding Audio to a Web Page

The best audio for the Web is MP3 because of its small file size and high quality. You can use several audio formats, which include file types such as WAV, AIF, RA, RAM, and RMF, to name a few.

Linking to Audio Files

The easiest way to add sound to your Web pages is to link to it. Select whatever text, image, or object you'd like to use to activate the audio, and when the end user clicks it, it automatically launches the associated media player to handle that file. If the QuickTime player needs to be launched, a new browser window opens holding the QuickTime player, much like when linking to video files. To link to an audio file, follow these steps:

1. Select text, image, or any object that you want to trigger the audio file.

2. In the Properties Inspector in the link text field, enter the path of the audio file you want to play. You can also browse for the file by clicking the folder icon to the right of the text field.

3. You have no control over where or how the media player will appear when linking audio; however, if you embed it, as described in the next section, you'll see how you can control the appearance a bit more.

Embedding Audio Files

When you embed audio into your Web site, you are offering a more integrated approach than linking audio. When it's embedded, it's actually part of the Web page. You also have more control over the audio in terms of volume, visible controls, and starting and ending points. To add sound, you must use the plug-in object in Dreamweaver; unfortunately there is no sound or audio category in the Assets panel. To insert audio, follow these steps:

1. Place a blinking cursor in the area of the page where you want to insert the audio.

2. Under the Media tab of the Insert panel, click the Insert Plug-in button, or choose Insert, Media Plug-in. This opens a Select Files dialog box.

3. In the Select Files dialog box, choose the file you want to play in the document. Choose OK (Mac) or Select (Windows).

4. A default plug-in placeholder is inserted into the document.

5. You can resize the plug-in by grabbing the resize handles and dragging, or you can enter in values for the H and W fields in the Properties Inspector.

Embed Attributes

To have the audio playing in the background, you can add a "hidden" attribute to the <embed> tag. This will make the audio have a more integrated feeling because it will be seamless without the visibility of a media player.

You can use a variety of attributes to control the appearance or visibility of a media player. In the Properties Inspector, click the Parameters button to launch the Parameters dialog box. Here are the most popular attributes or parameters:

```
Parameter - hidden, value = true
Parameter - autostart, value = true
Parameter - loop, value = true
```

Summary

Adding rich media such as video and audio can offer a great way to add more depth to your site. The great thing about both these mediums is that they can remain optional for the end user. Although both options require plug-ins by the end users, they often add to your existing site's content.

With people and Web surfers demanding more from their Web experiences, offering digital video and audio on your site may be just enough to have them return to your site time and time again.

When you offer such content, let the end user know how large the file size is when linking to such media. This will allow them to determine whether the content is worth the wait to view. You may also want to offer the content in more than one format so that it's compatible with many different media players.

Inserting Flash and Shockwave

by Matt Pizzi

Some of the most interesting Web sites use Flash technology. Even if the entire site is constructed in Flash, it ultimately needs to be embedded into an HTML document to be viewed on the Web.

Many Web sites that offer games and some online learning often use the Shockwave player. These two technologies from Macromedia are among the most widely distributed and widely used platforms for delivering rich media over the Web.

These applications offer designers and developers total freedom from restrictive HTML standards and provide a great alternative to static Web page development. Often, people visit a site strictly on a "wow" factor for the Flash content. If the designer uses Flash effectively, appropriately, and creates a useable site with Flash interactivity, it can bring more traffic to your site. The payoff in using Flash is that you reach more people, and chances are people will stay at your site longer and explore it.

In this chapter you'll discover how you can embed Flash and Shockwave movies into your HTML documents. Even if you're not developing a complete Flash site, you still may want to add some Flash components to enhance your HTML design. Macromedia claims that about 95% of the people on the Web can view Flash content. The Flash Player is one of the widely distributed pieces of software; it comes bundled with all the major Web browser and operating systems. The only concern with using Flash should be file size. Flash creates small file sizes in comparison to what you have for a presentation for that file size; however, a lot of animation and sound may make the file a bit too large for your average dial-up Internet user. That's why using a combination of

HTML and Flash content can offer a middle ground when determining whether your site will be based on Flash or HTML.

Creating Flash Buttons in Dreamweaver MX

Dreamweaver offers you the capability to author Flash content, without even using Flash. This provides a nice alternative for those who want to use Flash in some areas of their site, but don't want to make the investment and commitment to learning Flash.

First let's look at how you can create a Flash button within Dreamweaver. If you're an experienced Flash developer, this feature may be a little weak for you because it is a bit limited in the sense that you're using canned or premade Flash graphics that don't offer much in the way of editability. However, if you're not an experienced Flash developer, this may be right up your alley. You don't need to know any Flash, nor do you even need to own it.

The Insert Flash Button command can be found on the Insert Panel under the Media tab, as shown in Figure 14.1.

FIGURE 14.1   The Insert Panel offers options for inserting Flash content under the Media tab.

You can also access the command by choosing Insert, Interactive Images, Flash Button. However, before you apply this command, be sure to save your document first. After your document is saved, follow these steps to insert a Flash button:

1. Place a blinking cursor in the document where you want the Flash button to be inserted. If you don't save the document, you will get an alert message informing you that it must be saved before inserting a button, as shown in Figure 14.2.

FIGURE 14.2   You must save the document before inserting a Flash button.

2. In the Insert panel click the Insert Flash Button option to launch the Insert Flash button dialog box pictured in Figure 14.3.

3. In the top portion of the dialog box, labeled Style, you get a preview of how the button will look and behave after it is placed inside the document.

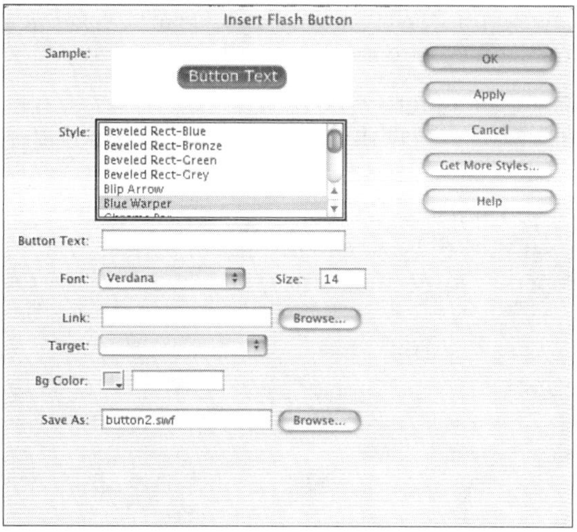

FIGURE 14.3   The Insert Flash Button dialog box has a series of options and a variety of Flash–styled buttons to choose from.

4. In the Style selection box, you can choose from a variety of different style. Click one to select it and a see a preview in the Style box above it.

5. In the Text field, type in the text you want to appear on the button.

6. You can also choose a font and a font size. The font size is in points. Click the Preview button to see what the font and font size will look like when placed on the button. After you click the Preview button, the Flash button will be placed in the HTML document; however, the Insert Flash Button dialog box is still open. So, after viewing the button, if you want to change something, you can do it right inside the dialog box.

7. The Link option enables you to hyperlink the button to a local file by clicking the Browse button, or you can link it to an external Web site by providing the absolute URL. If you don't enter a link here, you can always add one later in the Properties Inspector.

8. If you're working with framesets, you can choose a frame in the target drop-down menu, or you can choose _blank to open the link in a new window. Again, you can always fill this information out later in the Properties Inspector after you return to the document.

9. You can also choose background color. By default, the background color is white; however, you may want the background color of the button to match the background color of the document. You can either use the inkwell, or you can type in a hexadecimal value.

10. Finally, you can name the SWF file that Dreamweaver is going to create for you. You can type in a name and browse for the location in which you want it saved.

11. Click Apply to again get a preview of what the button is going to look like, and if you're happy, click Save to save this Flash file and return to the document.

When you return to the document, you'll notice you have a Flash element inserted into the document. If you want to see how the button will behave, you need to play the Flash movie through the Properties Inspector. Notice the Play button in the Properties Inspector, as shown in Figure 14.4.

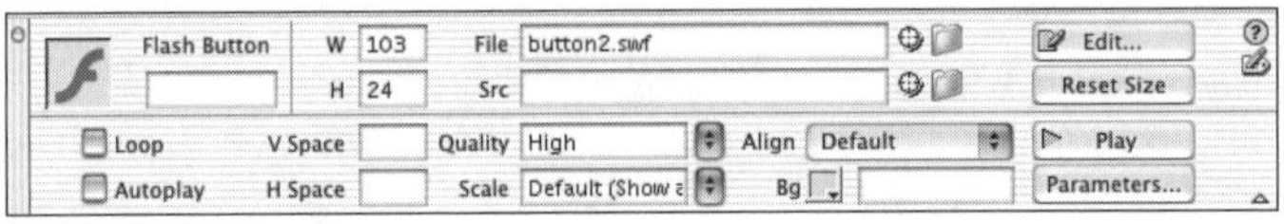

FIGURE 14.4   The Properties Inspector offers options to Play and Stop the Flash animation. You can preview Flash in the Dreamweaver authoring environment. Dreamweaver has a built-in Flash player.

If you couldn't find a style that you were really happy with, you can always download additional files off the Macromedia Exchange. The best way to get to the Exchange is to click the Get More Styles button, which automatically connects to Macromedia's site.

Creating Flash Text in Dreamweaver MX

Like the option of adding buttons, you also have the option of adding Flash text. Dreamweaver will make an SWF file based on text you type into the dialog box. What's really nice about Flash text is that it's vector based, so all the lines in the type appear super smooth.

The Insert Flash Text command also can create buttons of sorts. You have an option of creating rollover text, so when the end user mouses over the text, it will change to a rollover state that you specify. You can do all this without knowing Flash, or even owning a copy of it.

To create Flash text, follow these steps:

1. Create a new basic HTML document. Make sure you save it, because you can add Flash text only to a saved document.

2. Place a blinking cursor in the area where you want to insert the Flash text.

3. Click the Insert Flash Text button from the Insert panel under the Media tab, or choose Insert, Interactive Media, Flash Text. This launches the Insert Flash Text dialog box as displayed in Figure 14.5.

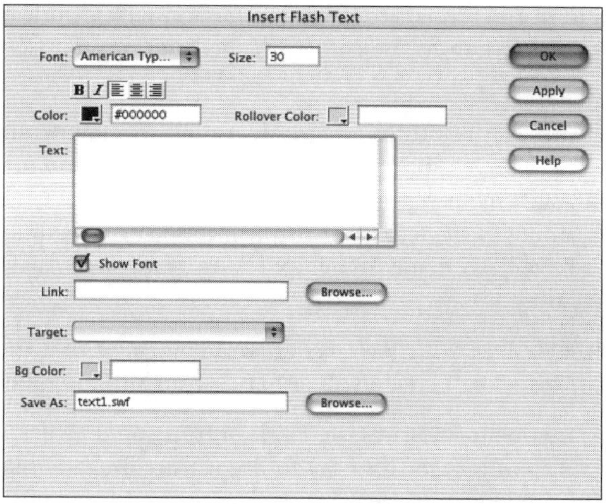

FIGURE 14.5 The Insert Flash Text dialog box offers options for typeface, color, and size. There is also an option to create a rollover version of the text.

4. In the first section of the dialog box, you see font options for the Flash text. You can choose a typeface, the size of the text, the color, and other attributes such as alignment and bold or italic styling.

5. If you want the text to behave like a rollover button, choose a different rollover color by clicking the inkwell to access the swatches, or type in a hexadecimal value.

6. In the text scroll box, type in the text that you want to appear as Flash text in your Dreamweaver document.

7. If you want to hyperlink the text to another document or Web site, add the link in this text field. If you decide not to add a link, you can always add one later through the Properties Inspector.

8. You can target a frame or _blank to open a new browser window in the target dropdown menu.

9. You may want to set the background color to the same background color that you are inserting this file into.

10. Finally, you can name the file and browse to save it in a certain location.

11. To preview the Flash text, press the Apply button. You have the opportunity to make any changes before clicking the OK button.

After you're back inside the document, you'll notice the Flash text is placed where you had the insertion point when choosing the Insert Flash Text command. If you added a rollover state and want to preview it, you can accomplish this right within Dreamweaver.

Highlight the text and in the Properties Inspector push the Play button. When you mouse over the text, you'll see it switch to the color you specified in the Insert Flash Text dialog box.

A quick note about using Flash buttons and Flash text—I would encourage you to use these features if they help serve a purpose. However, if you have no other Flash content in your document, don't start by using one of these options. It doesn't make sense to require the end user to have a plug-in or ActiveX control simply to view some text or a button that otherwise could have been made in a graphics program such as Fireworks or Photoshop and saved as an image.

If you're already using Flash in your Web design and you think that the Flash buttons or Flash text that Dreamweaver can create will enhance your site, then go for it.

Second, I discourage anyone from using the Flash buttons on a professional site. I say this not to downplay or take away from this easy-to-use feature, but the majority of professional Web developers use Dreamweaver and the majority of these buttons are fairly recognizable as stock Dreamweaver Flash creations.

Inserting Flash Files

For the most part, inserting Flash movies into Dreamweaver is almost as easy as inserting an image. Flash files, of course, have some parameters that can be set by Dreamweaver.

You can insert a Flash file by clicking the Flash button under the Common tab of the Insert panel. You can also choose Insert, Media, Flash. This will prompt a search for file dialog box where you search for the Flash file. If the Flash file is already saved within your local root folder, you can open the Assets panel by choosing Window, Assets. In the Assets panel, select the Flash category and drag the Flash file into the document.

When the Flash move is inside the Dreamweaver document, note all the options available in the Properties Inspector, as pictured in Figure 14.6.

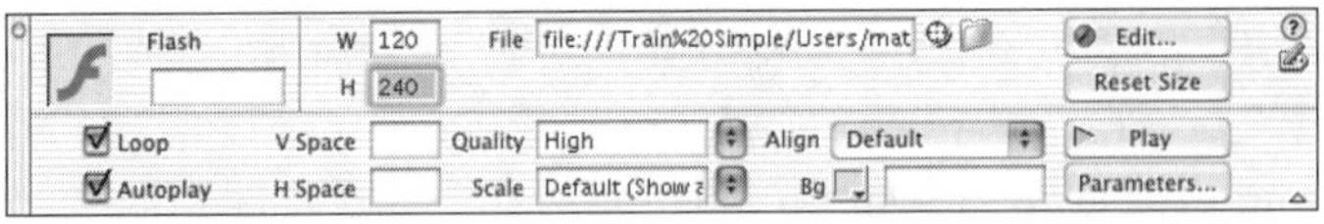

FIGURE 14.6   There are several options for the Flash file in the Properties Inspector.

The Properties Inspector offers the option to play the movie to get a preview of what the Flash content will look like when it is inserted into the document.

Also, an option is available for specifying the width and height. If these numbers appear bold, they are not the native size set by the author in Flash. Click on the H and the W to set it to its original size.

Aside from all the traditional attributes of alignment, the Properties Inspector offers some additional attributes you can set for your Flash movies. Here's an overview of these options:

- **Loop**   By default, Loop is checked, which will play the animation from the beginning after it reaches the end.

- **AutoPlay**   This option plays the Flash movie as soon as possible.

- **Quality**   This drop-down menu offers four options: High, Low, AutoLow, and AutoHigh. High quality turns antialiasing on to smooth the lines in the animation. Low turns off antialiasing, offering a more jagged look, but the animation will play more smoothly, especially on older machines. AutoHigh, plays in the high quality of antialiasied lines until the performance of the system deteriorates. AutoLow is the opposite of AutoHigh. It will begin the animation in low quality, and switch to high quality when the system performance is adequate.

- **Scale**   This option determines how the movie will fit into the dimensions specified by the width and height options. There are three choices in the drop-down menu. ShowAll: this option plays the entire movie in the specified dimensions, but will maintain the aspect ratio of the document's original dimensions established in Flash. ExactFit: this option scales the Flash movie to fit the exact dimensions specified by the width and height options in the Properties with total disregard for the Flash movie original aspect ratio. NoBorder: This option fits the movie to the dimensions specified in the Properties Inspector while maintaining the movie original aspect ratio. Some of the movie can be cropped when using this setting.

When scaling a Flash movie, make sure you do it in a way that isn't detrimental to the appearance of the movie. If all the content within the Flash movie is vector-based Flash artwork, you have a lot more freedom to scale in Dreamweaver. However, if bitmap graphics are within the Flash movie, scaling, it could distort the appearance of some graphics. It's a good idea to export the final Flash movie in the dimensions you want it to appear on the Web. When that file is brought into Dreamweaver, the developer should respect those sizes and try not to alter them, if possible.

Additional Flash Parameters

You can add additional attributes to the Flash file by clicking the Parameters button. This launches the Parameters dialog box as shown in Figure 14.7.

Two parameters you can add are `salign` and `swliveconnect`. Each of these attributes enables you to control the appearance of the Flash file when using other attributes in the Properties Inspector.

You can use the `salign` attribute to determine how the Flash movie will position itself to the surrounding frame when the `Scale` attribute is set to ShowAll. You can also control

14

how the movie gets cropped, by specifying the alignment with Top, Left, Right, and Bottom values.

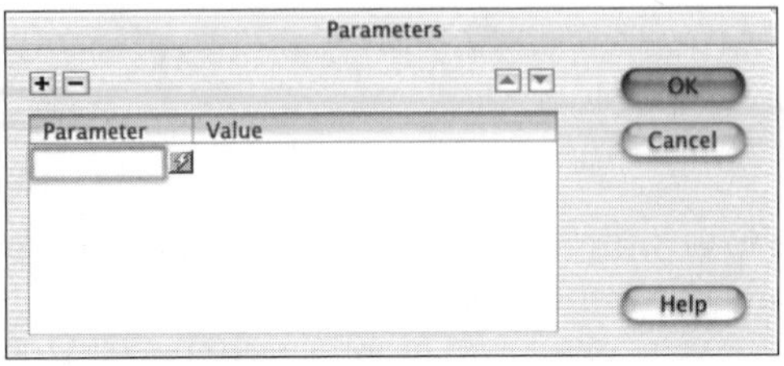

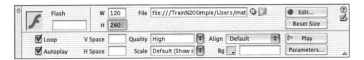

FIGURE 14.7   The Parameters dialog box offers an area to place additional attributes to a Flash file.

The `swliveconnect` attribute is used when your Flash movie is communicating to JavaScript through an FSCommand.

RoundTrip Flash Editing

In the next chapter, you'll discover how you can edit images without ever leaving Dreamweaver. You can modify an image, and as soon as the image is saved in the image-editing program, it's automatically updated in Dreamweaver. If you've used a previous version of Dreamweaver, this feature may be familiar to you.

With Dreamweaver MX, you can edit Flash content much in the same way. After importing a Flash movie, you might decide some adjustments need to be made. With the Flash movie selected in your Dreamweaver document, notice the Edit button in the Properties Inspector as shown in Figure 14.8.

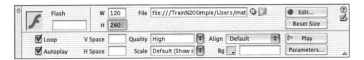

FIGURE 14.8   The Properties Inspector has an Edit button when the Flash movie is selected.

When you click the Edit button, Flash automatically launches. You can then make your changes in Flash and re-export a new SWF file. That new SWF file is automatically sourced in Dreamweaver so there's nothing to re-import. To use the RoundTrip Flash Editing feature in Dreamweaver, follow these steps:

1. Visit the companion Web site located at `http://www.dreamweavermxunleashed.com` and download the flash_move.zip file. This file contains an SWF file.

2. Import the Flash file by clicking the Flash button on the Insert panel under the Common tab.

3. After placing the Flash movie, highlight it, and in the Properties Inspector, click the Edit button. This automatically launches Flash, as shown in Figure 14.9.

FIGURE 14.9   Flash automatically launches when you click the Edit button in the Properties Inspector.

4. You might see a dialog box, as shown in Figure 14.10, asking you to find the source of the movie. To edit the SWF file, the FLA file must be opened in Flash. Search your hard drive for the folder and click OK to open the movie in Flash.

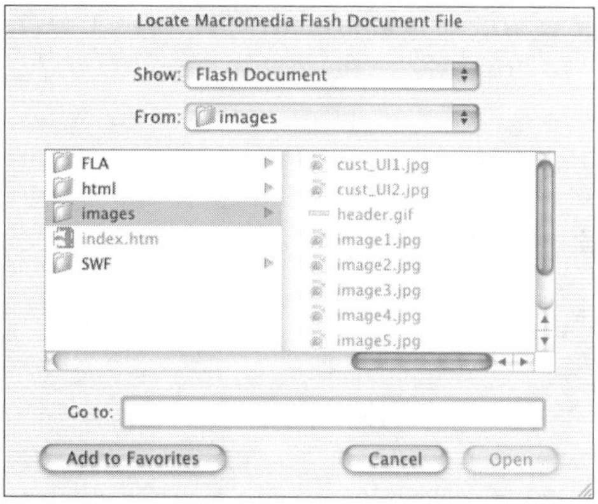

FIGURE 14.10   A dialog box appears, asking you to find the original FLA file associated with the Flash movie.

5. You now have full access to Flash, with the opportunity to make any changes necessary in your document. When you're happy with your changes, click the Done button located in the top-left corner of the document window as shown in Figure 14.11.

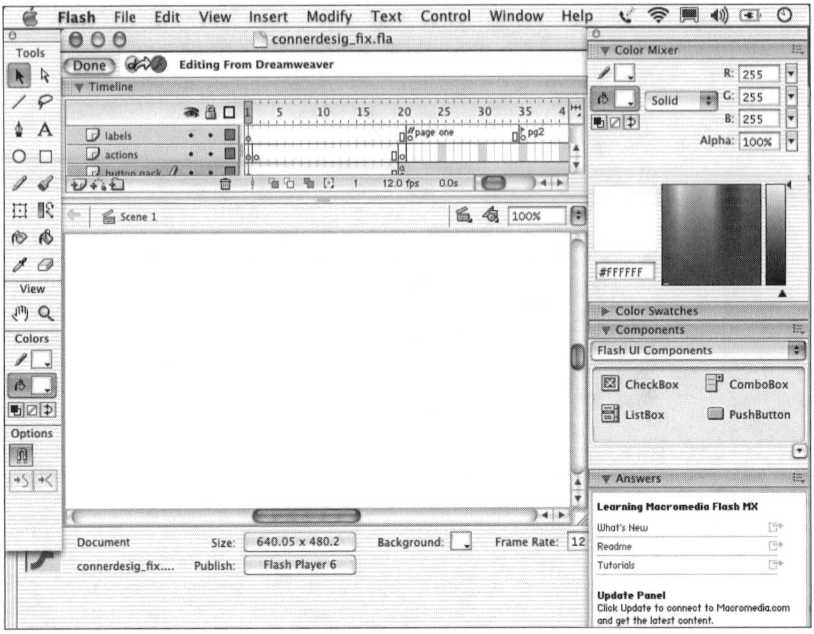

FIGURE 14.11　The Done button is located in the top-left corner of the document.

6. After you've pressed Done, Flash exports a new SWF file. Next, you exit Flash and return to Dreamweaver with a new updated file. Press the Play button in the Properties Inspector to preview the new Flash movie.

The new RoundTrip Flash Editing feature in Dreamweaver MX can save a lot of time for developers. It also offers you the opportunity to experiment with your Flash movies and enables you to make editing decisions based on what is currently in your HTML document.

NOTE

You can watch a QuickTime movie that further illustrates the power of the Flash RoundTrip Editing feature in Dreamweaver MX at this book's companion Web site: http://www.dreamweavermxunleashed.com.

Inserting Shockwave into a Dreamweaver Document

Inserting Shockwave content into Dreamweaver is just as painless as its Flash counterpart. Director is used often on the Web to create games and other engaging experiences, yet it seems as if not as many people author with Director. If this is the case for you, I posted a file you can use to get familiar with inserting Shockwave content. Navigate to this companion Web site located at http://www.dreamweavermxunleashed.com. A Director Shockwave file called wackamole.zip is available for download. This is a small game authored in Director and exported as a Shockwave file for use on the Web.

Many times in the classes that I teach at Train Simple, people ask me what the differences are between a Flash and a Shockwave file and which is better to author content in. This can be a tricky question to answer, but everyone's opinion is different. Over the past couple of years, Macromedia has closed the gap between Flash and Director; in fact, I would say the advantage for Web authoring lies with Flash because of its wider acceptance, its standard scripting language, Communication Server, and its integration with middleware.

However, a good Director developer can probably pull off any project, and the same for the Flash developer. So it ultimately comes down to personal preference. Typically, Flash performs better on the Web and Director is better for game and CD-ROM development.

To insert a Shockwave file into Dreamweaver, follow these steps:

1. Create a new basic HTML page and save it within the defined site in which you are working. Make sure to download the wackamole.zip file off the http://www.dreamweavermxunleashed.com Web site.

2. With the Insert panel open, under the Media tab, click the Shockwave button or Choose Insert, Media, Shockwave. This opens the Select File dialog box.

3. In the dialog box, search for the wackamole.dcr file that you unzipped from the downloaded file. Click Choose (Mac) or Select (Windows).

4. Notice that the Shockwave file has been inserted into the document, as shown in Figure 14.12. The content you see in Dreamweaver is a placeholder icon. However you'll notice that the width and height of the icon is 32×32 pixels.

5. Resize the Shockwave movie. The Properties set in Director for the width and height are 625×300. Plug those numbers into the width and height, respectively.

6. If you want to see what the movie will look like, push the Play button in the Properties Inspector. Notice in Figure 14.13 that you get a preview of the move right within Dreamweaver. You must have the Shockwave Player installed on your system.

> **NOTE**
>
> If you have more than one Flash or Shockwave movie in your document and you'd like to preview them all at the same time, choose View, Plug-ins, Play All or Stop All.

7. If you need to pass additional parameters to the Shockwave player, you can do it by clicking the Parameters button in the Properties Inspector.

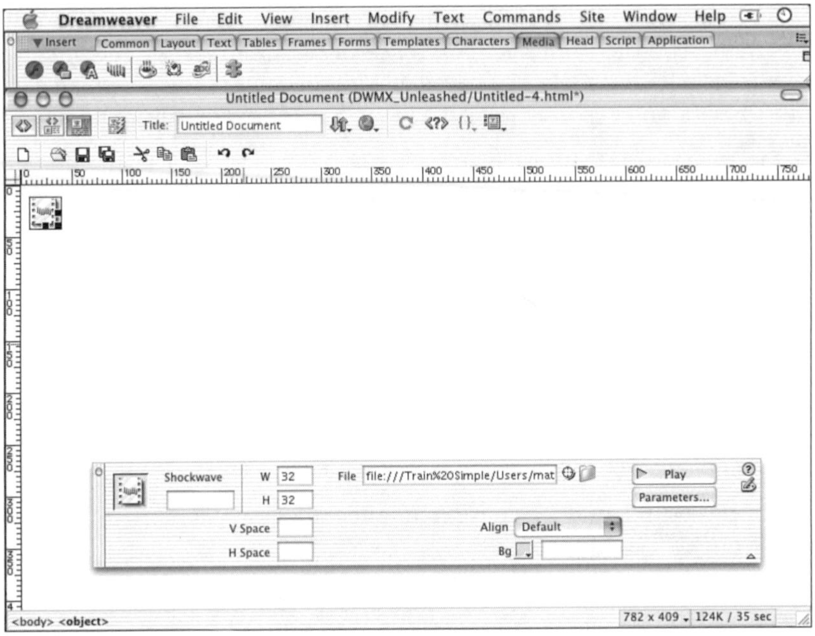

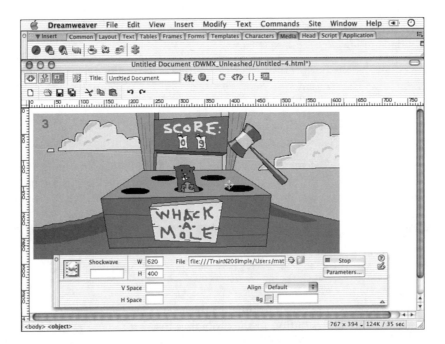

FIGURE 14.12   The Shockwave file has been inserted into the HTML document.

FIGURE 14.13   Notice that the Shockwave movie plays right inside of Dreamweaver. To stop playing the movie, press the Stop button in the Properties Inspector.

Inserting Flash and Shockwave content is simple with Dreamweaver. Typically, more code is required to include an application such as Flash or Shockwave, so it is a big timesaver just being able to source one of these files much like you would an image.

Controlling Shockwave and Flash Movies with Behaviors

Dreamweaver has built-in behaviors that enable you to control a Flash or a Director movie. You can create buttons that communicate directly with these files. To demonstrate this, I've set up a file that contains four pictures. What you're going to do in Dreamweaver is import four image files that look like buttons, each labeled picture1 through picture4.

After you insert the Flash movie into Dreamweaver, you can import each of the button graphics. You can then apply the behaviors to each of the button graphics, telling the Flash file to move to a specific frame that corresponds with the picture number.

To follow along in this exercise, visit the companion Web site located at `http://www.dreamweavermxunleashed.com` to download the file called slide_show.zip. Unzip the file, and you'll see a FLA file along with four GIF files.

14

Controlling a Flash with Behaviors

In this exercise, you'll control how a Flash movie plays.

1. Create a new basic HTML document. Choose File, Save As and save it as slide.html.

2. Under the Media tab of the Insert panel, click the Flash button to insert a Flash movie. Search for the slide_show.swf file you downloaded from the site.

3. After the file is placed within the document, name the movie in the Properties Inspector. Name it **Show**.

4. In the Properties Inspector, be sure to uncheck Autoplay and Loop.

5. Next, insert the four images named pic1, pic2, pic3, and pic4.

6. Make sure you highlight the image named Picture 4 in the document. You'll apply the behavior to this button first.

7. Open the Behaviors panel by choosing Window, Behaviors.

8. Click the plus (+) button to add a behavior, and in this case, choose the Control Flash or Shockwave behavior to open the dialog box.

9. In the drop-down list, you'll see all the Flash or Shockwave movies in your document. Because you have only one, all you should see is Show, the Flash movie you named and inserted earlier.

10. When the end user clicks this button, you want the movie to advance to the fourth frame. So highlight the Go To option and in the text field type in **4**.

11. Choose OK. After you return to the document, look in the Behaviors panel. Make sure the event is set to onClick. If that event is not available in the drop-down menu, choose Show Events For toward the bottom of the list. Be sure that 4.0 and Later Browsers is showing.

12. Repeat steps 10 and 11 until all four buttons have behaviors.

13. Back inside the document, choose File, Preview in Browser, Internet Explorer. Notice the slide show is being controlled by the buttons you've created in Dreamweaver.

In most real-world situations, you'll probably have the navigation system right within Flash or Director. However, if you want to create disjointed controls, this is one solution.

Summary

Flash and Shockwave can add a lot of depth to your Web sites. When used properly, they can be an effective communication tool and offer compelling reasons for customers and people to revisit your site and get the word out that the site is engaging and offers a good experience.

Because these popular technologies are produced by Macromedia, the integration between them and Dreamweaver are second to none and offer several features to enhance your workflow and productivity.

Integration with Complementing Programs

By Matt Pizzi

This chapter is about applications that add functionality to Dreamweaver. Most notably is Fireworks MX. The tight integration between these two products makes for an efficient Web design studio. We'll also look at other applications such as Adobe Photoshop/ImageReady.

Macromedia has included some features that simplify the process of making changes to images. When developing for the Web, especially for a client, changes always have to be made. It can get brutally time-consuming to open your image-editing application, tweak the graphic, and re-export the image. After exporting, you would then have to re-import it into Dreamweaver. Fortunately, that's not the case—you can do all this without ever having to re-import anything into Dreamweaver; in fact, it's much like not having to leave Dreamweaver at all.

To take advantage of these integration features, it's important to have Fireworks MX installed on your system. This chapter also covers how to integrate Dreamweaver with Photoshop, so make sure you have at least version 5.5 of Photoshop installed on your system to complete the Photoshop exercises.

Specifying External Editors

In the Preferences dialog box, you can specify which external application you want to handle your image editing. To access the Preferences dialog box, choose Edit, Preferences. In the Preferences dialog box be sure to select the File Types/Editors category, as displayed in Figure 15.1. Here you can specify which application you would like to use to modify existing content within Dreamweaver. First, take a look at graphical file formats. You can set up which applications you're going to use to edit GIF, JPG, and PNG files. Remember that to select a particular application, you must have it installed on

Preferences

Category — File Types / Editors

General
Accessibility
Code Coloring
Code Format
Code Hints
Code Rewriting
CSS Styles
File Types / Editors
Fonts
Highlighting
Invisible Elements
Layers
Layout View
New Document
Panels
Preview in Browser
Quick Tag Editor
Site
Status Bar
Validator

Open in Code View: .js .asa .css .cs .config .inc .txt .as

☑ Enable BBEdit Integration

External Code Editor: [ ] Browse...

Reload Modified Files: Prompt

Save on Launch: Prompt

[+] [−]   [+] [−]   Make Primary

Extensions   Editors
.png   Fireworks MX (Primary)
.gif   Adobe Photoshop 7.0
.jpg .jpe .jpeg
.fla

Help   Cancel   OK

your system.

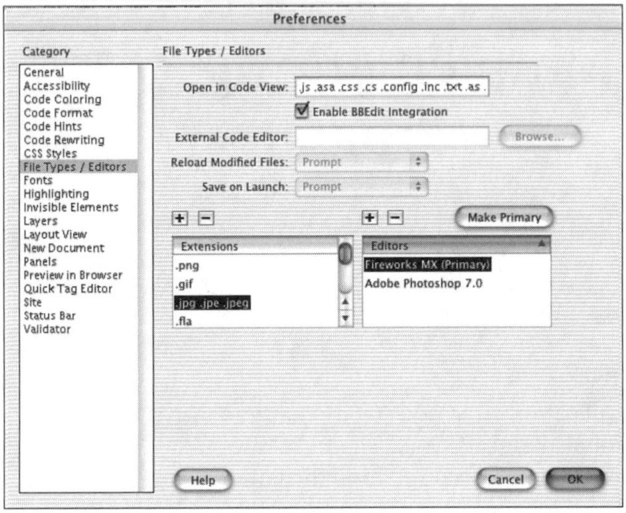

FIGURE 15.1   In the Preferences dialog box, under the File Types/Editors category, you can specify which application you want to use to edit a particular file format.

You also have the option of making an application primary; this is the application used by default to edit the selected graphic of the selected file format. However, if you contextual click the graphic inside of Dreamweaver, you'll have the option of selecting any other application you add to the list. To add an application to the list, follow these steps:

1. Open the Preferences dialog box by choosing Edit, Preferences.

2. In the Preferences dialog box choose the File Types/Editors category.

3. In the File Extension scroll box, choose the file extension you want to pick an editor for.

4. To the right, click the plus sign just above the Editor option box to launch the Select External Editor dialog box as pictured in Figure 15.2. In this dialog box, navigate to an application on your hard drive that you want to add to your list of editors.

5. When you find an appropriate editor, choose Open. Notice in Figure 15.3 the new editor has been added to the list.

6. If you prefer to use the application you just selected as the default, highlight it in the option box and click the Make Primary button. Notice to the right of the

application name, it reads (primary). This will act as the default editor when you ask Dreamweaver to edit that particular file type.

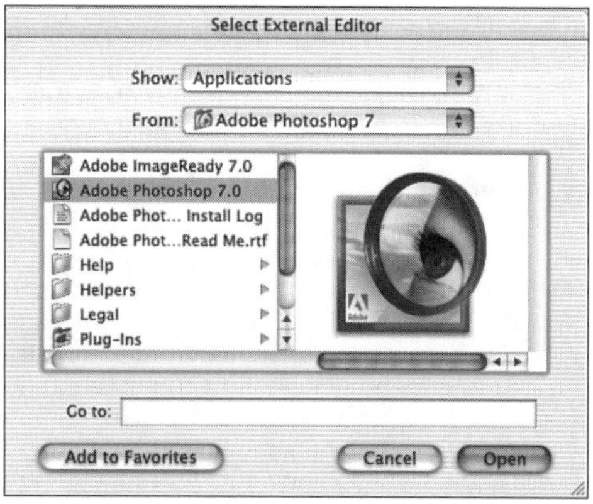

FIGURE 15.2   Choose an application you want to use to edit the highlighted extension.

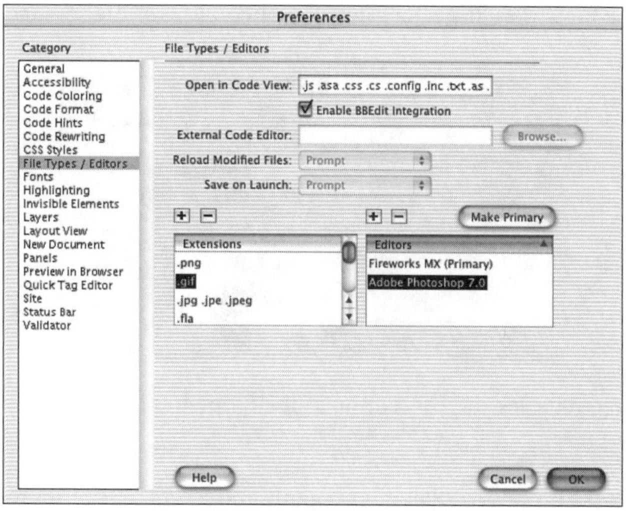

FIGURE 15.3   After you open the application through the Select External Editor dialog box, it is added to the list.

Editing Images in Dreamweaver with Fireworks

The great thing about the external editors is that you never have to close Dreamweaver, nor do you have to re-import content. Editing or modifying images after placing them inside of Dreamweaver is a snap. This feature was named RoundTrip Editing by the folks at

Macromedia. For this feature to work, you must have an image-editing application. To edit images, follow these steps:

1. Create a new document and save it as image_edit.html. Be sure to save it in a defined site that you are working with.

2. Insert an image by choosing Insert, Image. Search for a graphical file on your hard drive and select it.

3. With the image selected, notice the Edit button in the Properties Inspector, as shown in Figure 15.4.

4. Because Fireworks MX is my primary graphics editor for both JPG, and GIF files, when I click the Edit button it automatically launches Fireworks MX, as shown in Figure 15.5.

FIGURE 15.4   The Properties Inspector offers the option to edit the selected image.

FIGURE 15.5   After you click the Edit button in the Properties Inspector, the primary external editor launches.

5. When Fireworks is open, a dialog box opens and asks you the source of the graphic, as shown in Figure 15.6. You can select Yes to use the graphic that is Dreamweaver, or from the drop-down menu, you can choose other graphics to use as the source. I recommend that if you have a copy of the PNG native Fireworks file, use that. It avoids a double-compressed graphic. You can normally get away with compressing an image twice, but anything more than that will result in a serious degradation of quality. In this case, I don't have the native Fireworks file, so I'm going to choose Yes. I do however, want to make sure that I'm going to be happy with the changes I make, because I don't want to have to recompress this graphic for a third time.

6. After choosing Yes, your image is ready for editing inside of Fireworks. Make any and all changes inside the Fireworks editing environment; you have full access to Firework's tools.

7. When you're happy with changes, click the Update button. This exits Fireworks and brings you back into Dreamweaver with the new, updated image.

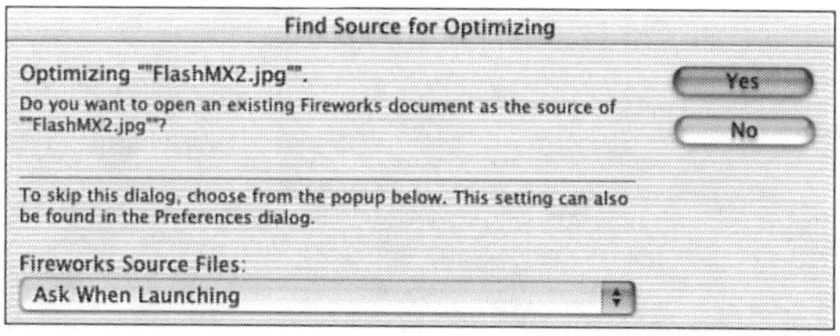

FIGURE 15.6   A dialog box appears as Fireworks launches, asking you to determine the source of the image you want to edit.

Optimizing an Image in Dreamweaver with Fireworks

You may run into a situation when a graphic's file size is just too large. Instead of deleting the image in Dreamweaver and then opening it in Fireworks to optimize and export it, and then finally re-importing it into Dreamweaver, you can use one simple command. Under the Command menu, you can optimize an image with Fireworks. To use this command successfully, follow these steps:

1. Be sure to have a document open with a graphic placed inside of it. Also, make sure you save the document before applying this command.

2. Highlight the graphic in the document. Choose Commands, Optimize Image in Fireworks. Much like the previous example, this automatically launches Fireworks.

3. When Fireworks opens, a dialog box similar to the one in the previous exercise asks you the source of the image. Choose Yes to accept the defaults. This launches the Optimize window.

4. In this dialog box are three tabs. You can manipulate the graphic in any way through this dialog box. After you're happy with the settings, click the Update button.

5. After clicking the Update button, you exit Fireworks and return to Dreamweaver. Notice that the image has automatically been updated.

The Optimize Window in Fireworks

I wanted to explore some of the options you have available to you in the Optimize dialog box. This dialog box is identical to the Export Preview dialog box that you access through the File menu in Fireworks. However, if you're not too familiar with Fireworks, this will at least give you the opportunity to understand how to optimize graphics. Optimizing graphics is a very important topic, especially when you're trying to create a fast-loading site.

The Options Tab

I won't be revealing every option in this dialog box, but I will note the most significant features. The first tab to be highlighted is the Options tab, as shown in Figure 15.7.

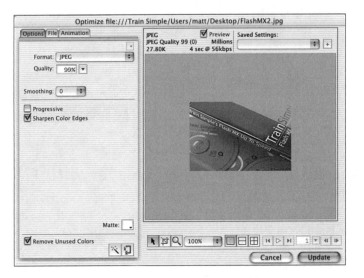

FIGURE 15.7   The Optimize dialog box by default has the Options tab selected.

This is the portion of the dialog box where you try to get the file size down to the smallest file size while maintaining quality by specifying which compression algorithm to use. Here's a breakdown of the available options:

- **GIF/Animated GIF**   This allows you to save the document as a GIF or Animated GIF. GIFs are best used for graphics with fewer colors and for color without any tonal range. When saving GIFs, you save a color look-up table with it. The lower the number of colors stored in the palette, the smaller the file size. You can also apply a loss, which will remove pixels from the image to reduce the file size. Finally, when you optimize an image as a GIF, you can add transparency by removing a specified color from the image.

- **JPEG**   This file format is best for saving images with many colors or for colors with tonal range. Typically, photographs fit this description. Notice there is a quality slider. JPEG compression works by removing pixels from the graphic, which ultimately reduces the file size. The lower the quality percentage you set in the slider, the more pixels it will remove, providing a smaller file size. There is no standard quality setting. Each image is different. You have to find the balance for the graphic you're working with at that particular moment in time. I recommend experimenting with several quality settings.

There is also an option for smoothing, which will blur the pixels a bit. This can be beneficial if you have to really squeeze the file size down and take the image to the edge where some artifacting is visible. If you do see compression artifacting, sometimes a small amount of smoothing can help camouflage the image quality deterioration.

- **PNG 8/24/32**   PNG files are most closely related to the GIF file format and work in much the same way. You can preserve and create transparency; however, with PNG 24 and PNG 32, more colors are available to you. The PNG file format was—and I guess still is—supposed to wipe out the GIF file format, but the complications between the browser wars left the PNG file format fighting for compatibility. Depending on your target audience, PNGs may or may not be a good choice for you.

The File Tab

The File tab offers some basic options for the file in general, such as dimensions as shown in Figure 15.8.

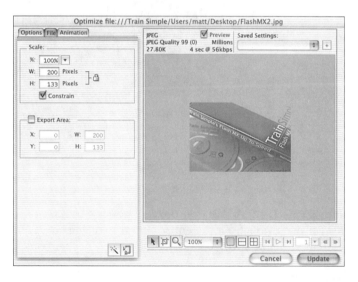

FIGURE 15.8   The File tab offers different options for changing the dimensions of the image.

- **Scale**   Here you can change the scale of the image, either based on a percentage or you can enter actual pixel values for the width and height. When entering pixel values, you may want to check the Constrain check box; just be sure to preserve the proportions of the image.

- **Export Area**   This area is more or less a place to specify how you want the image cropped. If you check the Export Area check box, you will get a bounding box around the image. You can drag any one of the handles and the corresponding x, y, w, and h values will automatically update.

The Animation Tab

The Animation tab is used when trying to update a GIF animation. You cannot create an animation from this portion of the dialog box; rather, it offers options for updating animated GIFs. As Figure 15.9 would suggest, you can modify the position of frames and the duration of frames, you can control the looping attribute of the animation, and you can even remove frames.

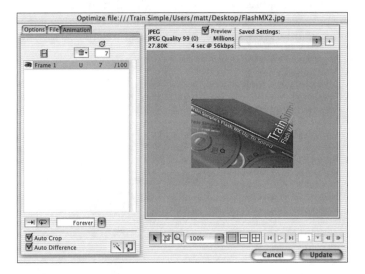

FIGURE 15.9   The animation portion of the Optimize dialog box offers options for updating a GIF animation.

Additional Options in the Optimize Dialog Box

Some options are available throughout the entire Optimize dialog box. Some of these features can be extremely helpful, which is why I want to point them out. Refer to Figure 15.10 to see each of the components.

- **Export Wizard**   If you're new to optimizing graphics and need a helping hand, here it is. This option is good if you're not quite sure what the different options are or if you're new to image optimization.

- **Optimize to Size Wizard**   Even if you're a pro at optimizing graphics, you'll find this quick and convenient. When you click this button, a small dialog box opens, and in this dialog box you can enter the desired file size. Fireworks then reduces the image down to meet the file-size requirement. If the image quality is too poor, you'll have to accept a higher file size for that image.

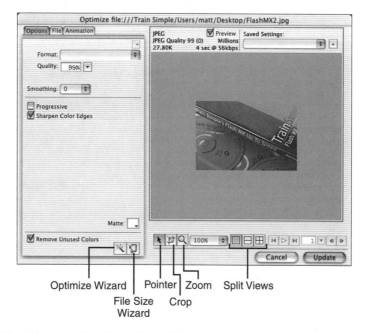

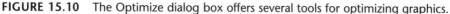

Optimize Wizard   Pointer Zoom Split Views

File Size   Crop
Wizard

FIGURE 15.10   The Optimize dialog box offers several tools for optimizing graphics.

- **Pointer Tool**   The pointer tool is the black arrow, which simply allows you to select the image. If you cannot see the entire image in the dialog box, when you click with the pointer tool, it automatically turns into the hand tool.

- **Crop Tool**   If you need to crop the image, you can use this tool. Simply position the bounding box around the image to determine how you want it cropped.

- **Zoom Tool**   This tool enables you to zoom into the image by placing your cursor over it and clicking. You can zoom out of the image by holding down the Option (Mac) key or Alt (Windows) key while clicking with the Zoom tool. You can also use the drop-down menu to choose the level of magnification.

- **Preview Window Controls**   Here you can determine how many preview windows you'd like to have open when optimizing the graphic. This can be beneficial because you can apply different optimization settings to the different quadrants in the window. Notice in Figure 15.11 you can have up to four windows.

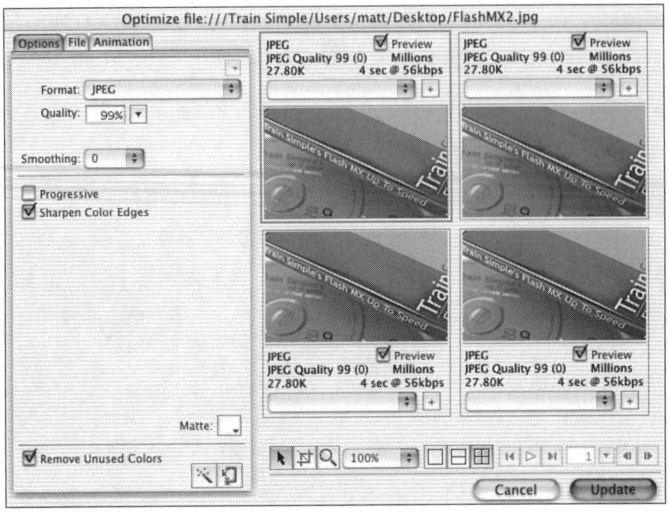

FIGURE 15.11   The Optimize dialog box has four windows open to preview different compression settings.

Inserting Fireworks's HTML Command

When you create a rollover button, an image map, a drop-down menu, or even an entire Web page with JavaScript functionality, you must import not only the image produced in Fireworks, but also the code that Fireworks produced. This is easy enough to do in Dreamweaver MX.

Creating a Button in Fireworks

The first thing you need to do is create a rollover button inside Fireworks. Then you need to import that button into Dreamweaver. I will briefly review how to make a button in Fireworks; however, if you need to learn Fireworks MX, several books are available on the topic. To create a button in Fireworks, follow these steps:

1. Create a new document by choosing File, New. This launches the New Document dialog box. Specify the dimension you would like for this image. There is no need to be too picky, you can fix any size problems later. Click OK to open the new document.

2. In the new document choose the Rectangle tool. In the Tools panel also choose a fill color and a stroke color. Draw a box on the document as shown in Figure 15.12.

3. The shape you just drew is probably smaller than the dimensions of the document. You want the document and the box to be the same size. To do this choose Modify, Canvas, Trim Canvas. The rectangle and the document are now the same size.

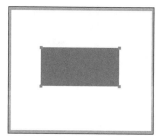

FIGURE 15.12 Draw a rectangle on the document. Notice that the rectangle's dimensions are smaller than the document's.

4. With the rectangle selected, press F8 on your keyboard to bring up the Convert to Symbol dialog box. Here type in the name and choose Button for Type.

5. This automatically draws a slice around the rectangle. Double-click the slice to enter the button symbol editing mode.

6. Click the Over tab to edit the Over state of the button. Click the Copy Up Graphic button toward the bottom-right corner of the dialog box, as shown in Figure 15.13. This will carry over any attributes, including the graphic as a whole, from the Up state.

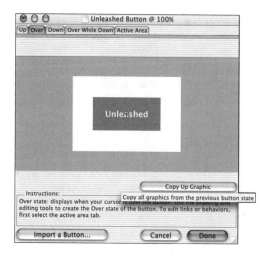

FIGURE 15.13 You can copy the previous state of the button by pressing, in this case, the Copy Up Graphic button.

7. After you click the button, the Up state is copied to the Over state. Notice that all the tools are still available to you. Highlight the square and in the Tools panel

change the fill color. This is the color the button will change to when the end user hovers over the button.

8. Click the Down tab. In the Down state click the Copy Over Graphic button. The Down state now has the same attributes as the Over state. Select the square and change the color or make some other physical change. This is how the button will appear when the end user clicks it.

9. Repeat step 8 for the Over While Down state. Over While Down occurs when the end user clicks the button and, without releasing the mouse button, mouses away from the button and then, still holding the mouse button down, mouses back over the button. Yes, it's as practical as it sounds.

10. Finally, click the Active Area tab. This is the same concept as a hot spot in an image map. This defines what area activates the button. For the best results, make sure the active area covers the entire graphic. Click Done when you're finished making all changes.

11. Click the Preview tab at the top of the document to see how your button will behave in a browser.

Now that you have a button made, you're ready to export it out of Fireworks. For a rollover graphic to work, JavaScript is written so the button's behaviors will work properly in a Web browser. Our main goal is to take this button we've created in Fireworks and import it into Dreamweaver. When we export this button, it's very important to export an HTML file along with it. To export this button choose File, Export. This opens a dialog box. In the Save As drop-down menu, be sure to select HTML and Images. You may want to save this file in the local root folder of the site you're working on in Dreamweaver. Next, check off the Put Images in a Sub Folder option and browse to find an image folder inside the local root folder of the site you are working with in Dreamweaver. After all that is set, click Save.

Inserting Fireworks HTML

Now that you have created a button in Fireworks, you're ready to bring it into Dreamweaver. The process is quite simple. Follow these steps:

1. Place a blinking cursor anywhere in the document to act as the insertion point.

2. In the Insert panel under the Common tab, click the Fireworks HTML button to open the Insert Fireworks HTML dialog box. All you have to do here is browse for the HTML file generated by Fireworks.

3. Click the Browse button and the Select File dialog box will appear. Navigate to the location of the HTML document you exported from Fireworks. When you find it, click OK to return to the Insert Fireworks HTML dialog box.

4. Click OK in the Insert Fireworks HTML dialog box. The button now appears inside your Dreamweaver document. Preview this document in a browser to make sure the rollover works.

Inserting Fireworks HTML is that simple. Unfortunately, the process is a bit more complex if you're a Photoshop user. We'll take a look at that toward the end of this chapter. Depending on your comfort level with code, it may be worth it to explore Fireworks as your Web imaging authoring tool.

Creating a Web Photo Album

Dreamweaver and Fireworks integration goes beyond inserting Fireworks HTML and updating graphics on-the-fly. Dreamweaver can actually control Fireworks, and that's what we're going to look at by using the Create Photo Album command. This feature is very powerful and can automate many tasks if you need to post large quantities of images on the Web. Furthermore, you don't even need to know HTML—less so than working with Dreamweaver alone—to make the most out of this feature.

The Create Web Photo Album command works with a folder of images that can open any of the following formats: GIF, JPEG, TIFF, PSD, PICT, BMP, and PNG. The images can be resized for thumbnails anywhere from 36×36 pixels to 200×200 pixels. If you would like to follow along for this exercise, navigate to the companion Web site located at `http://www.dreamweavermxunleashed.com`. Here you can download the zipped folder called gato_images. This folder contains several images of my cat, Gato. We're going to create a Web photo album of him.

15

Creating a Web Photo Album

Follow these steps to create your own Web photo album. This exercise illustrates the power of communication between Dreamweaver MX and Fireworks MX.

1. Create a new basic HTML page. In the new document choose Commands, Create Web Photo Album. This launches the Create Web Photo Album dialog box as shown in Figure 15.14.

2. In this dialog box you should give the album a title. In this case, because we're using pictures of my cat, enter the title **Matt's Fat Cat**.

3. The next text field is looking for subheading information. Again, because we're using pictures of Gato, type in **Gato Jobs Weighs 20lbs!**

4. For other info, type **Gato is now 2 years old.** All this heading content will appear on the top of the page.

5. Next select the folder you want this command to use to create this Web photo album. Click the Browse button and select the gato_images folder that you've downloaded from the companion Web site.

6. In the next line you need to decide where the thumbnail images that Fireworks is going to create should be saved. Choose a folder located within the local root folder of the site you're currently working with.

7. Determine the size in which you want the thumbnail images to appear. Choose 36×36 and leave the option to show the filenames checked.

8. Next, type in a value for how many columns you want Dreamweaver to create when laying out the thumbnail graphics. In this case, type in **4**.

9. Choose a thumbnail format. For this exercise, choose JPEG-Better Quality.

10. You also have to choose the quality for the actual image in the photo album. Again, choose JPEG-Better Quality. (I don't like to sacrifice quality when it comes to my cat.) You can also leave the scale at 100%.

11. Leave Create Navigation for Each Photo as well. It makes it easier to navigate through the different images in the album.

12. Choose OK. Fireworks will launch, and you'll see a batch dialog box as shown in Figure 15.15.

After the process is complete, you'll have an entire layout of pictures in a Web photo album, as shown in Figure 15.16. Preview this page in a browser; you can click any one of the thumbnail graphics and you'll get linked to a page with a larger version of the image, as shown in Figure 15.17. Also notice in Figure 15.17 that a navigation bar is located in the top-left corner.

FIGURE 15.14   The Create Web Photo Album is packed with several options to get your images organized in an easy-to-navigate page.

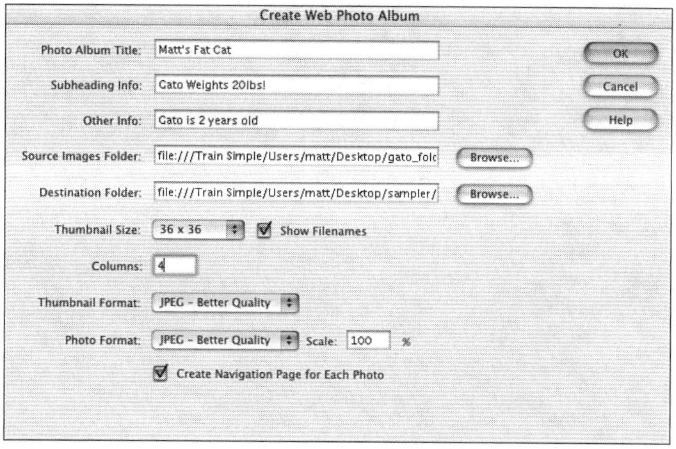

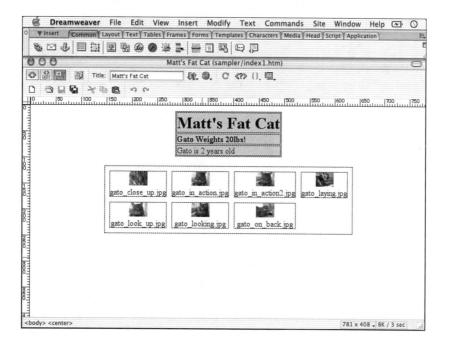

FIGURE 15.15   The Batch Process dialog box indicates how long the process might take.

FIGURE 15.16   After the album is created, you'll see all the thumbnails of the images in the folder you specified.

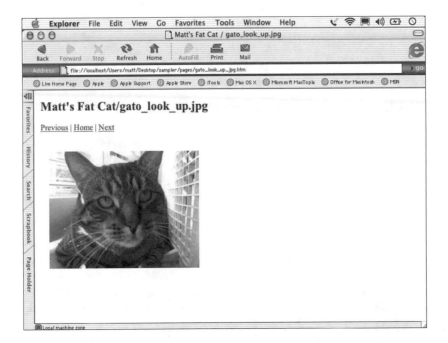

FIGURE 15.17   After clicking a thumbnail, you're brought to a detail page. You can also navigate through the images in the detail page format.

Using Photoshop with Dreamweaver MX

This is an especially important topic to cover because the majority of creative professionals use Photoshop and ImageReady to create Web graphics. If you are a Photoshop user, you will miss out on some of the perks that Fireworks offers; however, it is still possible to create content in either Photoshop or ImageReady and get it into Dreamweaver. The first topic we'll look at is using Photoshop as an external editor.

Using Photoshop As the External Editor

Make sure you select Photoshop as an external editor in the Preferences mentioned earlier in this chapter. Then you can select the graphic within the document and Ctrl+Click (Mac) or right-click (Windows) and select Edit With, Adobe Photoshop in the contextual menu. This automatically launches Photoshop. When the image is inside Photoshop, make all necessary changes to the image. After you're happy, choose File, Save. Close Photoshop and return to Dreamweaver. You'll notice that the image has been automatically updated.

Using Photoshop as an external editor isn't much of an inconvenience; however, when it comes to importing JavaScript-based content or Image Maps created in Photoshop into Dreamweaver, that's where it's not quite as seamless.

Importing Content Created in ImageReady

If you use Photoshop to create content for the Web, but use Dreamweaver to lay out your content, you can get your Photoshop material into Dreamweaver. The process is a bit more tedious. When creating your material in Photoshop, try to keep in mind that you want it to end up in Dreamweaver.

Create the content as usual, whether it is a button, an image map, or even an entire site. When exporting, be sure to export both an HTML document as well as the images. Save the images somewhere within your local root folder. Save the HTML document there as well. Try to save it in the same locations as you would if you were working in Dreamweaver.

After the files have been exported, open the HTML document that Photoshop or ImageReady has generated for you. Copy all the contents of the HTML document that pertain to the Photoshop content you want to get into Dreamweaver. If you have nothing in your Dreamweaver document, it's easy. Highlight all the HTML in the Photoshop-generated document and copy it. Then back in Dreamweaver, switch to the code view and delete all the code and paste the Photoshop HTML. After you return to the design view, your Photoshop content will appear in the document.

However, if you want only to add a button you've created in Photoshop to a cell in a table inside of Dreamweaver, it gets a bit tricky, especially if you don't know HTML. To do this, put a blinking cursor in the cell you want to add the content to. This places a blinking cursor in the appropriate location of the HTML code. Open the HTML document that Photoshop has generated in Text Edit (Mac) or Notepad (Windows) and copy only the necessary HTML and JavaScript. Avoid copying tags like `<html>`, `<head>`, and `<body>`. After you've copied the code, paste it into the appropriate locations. You may have to copy and paste different sections of the code, making this a several-step process.

Summary

You can see the power and workflow advantages of using Dreamweaver with other applications. Macromedia has done an outstanding job of integrating Fireworks with Dreamweaver and they're so efficient when used together.

I'm a long-time Photoshop user. In fact, I often refer to Photoshop as the best desktop software application. So not taking anything away from Photoshop, the marriage between Dreamweaver and Fireworks has even the most diehard fan of Photoshop looking at the possibility of using Fireworks. If you also develop in Flash, you'll appreciate the logic Fireworks uses when creating symbols, especially button symbols. The process is simple.

If you own Studio MX, you should be taking advantage of Dreamweaver's tight integration with its sister product, Fireworks MX.

PART IV

Introduction to Web Applications

IN THIS PART

CHAPTER **16**

Introduction to Web Applications

By Thomas Myer
Principal, Triple Dog Dare Media

What is a Web application? That's the question I'll try to answer in this chapter. Anyone who has spent any amount of time with Web applications might tell you that Web applications consist of many pieces; they can be implemented in Java, ASP, PHP, Perl/CGI, and they might be based on database tables, XML files, or other data sources. If you search on "Web application" at any search engine, you're likely to uncover hundreds (if not thousands) of white papers, case studies, and marketing hoopla over how great they are.

Before we get into all that, though, I'd prefer to step back a little and take in the overall picture. Although Web applications seem like a very complex topic, they're actually very simple conceptually.

A Web application is a Web site that contains dynamic pages instead of static ones. Dynamic pages contain instructions, sometimes by themselves, sometimes mixed in with HTML code and content, that get processed and executed by a Web server. In other words, an individual page's final content is not determined until a visitor views that page.

An example of a dynamic page is a news feed that gets updated regularly. Instead of writing news headlines to a static HTML page, the news items are updated in a database, and instructions on the dynamic page extract the database information and display it for the viewer.

Another example of a dynamic page is a search results page. Anytime a user enters a search term into a search engine and clicks Find or Search, a Web application, working in the background, searches through a list of files or database records and then returns results that match the entered search term.

For the most part, Web applications are usually built to handle lots of data moving through a system, such as content published on a site, information captured from visitors, or personalization systems that display content according to a visitor's preferences.

Although Web applications can do a variety of tasks in a variety of contexts, they're all very much the same under the covers. Learn to build one, and you can probably figure out how to build others.

From an architectural standpoint, Web applications usually have three components, or layers:

- A presentation layer, or what you know as the user interface. This layer includes all HTML code, Flash components, and images.

- A business logic layer (also known as middleware), which contains processing instructions in such languages as JSP, PHP, or ASP.

- A data layer, which might contain database tables or flat files (such as XML) that are processed by the middleware and displayed on the user interface.

This three-layer approach is known as a "three-tier architecture." Delivering a Web application in these three tiers allows parallel development—the visual designers can lay down their design frameworks and page flows without impacting how the database design unfolds, and the middleware/business logic developers can create their code without having to worry about design issues.

At some point, obviously, the three elements have to come together (the integration phase), but if everyone has followed the technical specifications, things shouldn't be too bad.

> **NOTE**
>
> You didn't think you could develop a complex application without a specification, right? A good specification includes use cases, an application workflow (detailing how the pages interact with each other), and a database diagram.

Many site owners find it very convenient to use Web applications in place of static pages. After they have a Web application installed, they can update content in a database and have those changes appear on their site. They can also separate the look and feel (design) of their site from their content, which makes it easier for them to update their sites without having to undergo painstaking manual changes. Furthermore, they can back up all their content using an automated database tool that can be set to run at a convenient time, like 2 a.m.

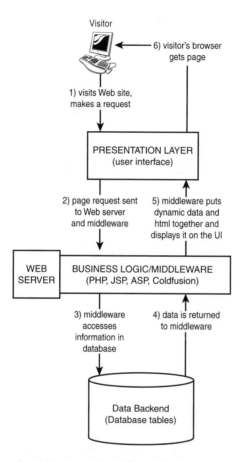

FIGURE 16.1   Three-tiered architecture of a Web application.

Some of these concepts might be foreign to a design-centric view of the Web. After all, many Web applications remove the designer from having to make further updates to a site after it's live. This has been viewed as both a curse and a blessing—a curse because it has seriously impacted designer's revenues (the owner of a Web application doesn't have to hire a designer to update site pages); a blessing because designers want to *design*, not update, content.

Dreamweaver MX comes with added support to create, test, and deploy Web applications. Before we get much further along, though, I want to define some terms that you'll hear throughout this section of the book and cover options you have for middleware and databases.

Terminology

As with any other field of human endeavor, Web applications come with a lexicon of jargon. The rest of this chapter is devoted to explaining some of this jargon, as well as putting it into the context of the three-tiered architecture—particularly the middleware and data layer portions.

Server-Side Scripting

If you've done any JavaScript coding, you understand client-side scripting. Client-side scripting is handled by a visitor's Web browser and can be different depending on the browser they're using. You know that, in some cases, you have to put in certain checks to make sure your code will work in Internet Explorer and Netscape Navigator.

Server-side scripting happens on the server. When a visitor requests a dynamic page from a Web server, the server processes the page. If it finds any special processing instructions (such as including a certain file, checking for a certain variable, or querying a database) the server completes its processing and then displays the results back to the visitor's browser.

In addition to being handled by the server, server-side scripting languages generally have more features and capabilities. For example, with a server-side scripting language such as JSP or PHP, you can extract files from and write files to the server's file system, run more sophisticated encryption programs (for e-commerce security), and complete other tasks. These tasks can be fulfilled on a high-end server machine instead of being handled by the end user.

Databases

A database is a collection of information stored in logical containers called tables. Each table normally contains related information, such as personal statistics, product data, or inventory.

When you peek inside a table, you'll see that it is made up of the following:

- **Rows**   A row is a complete data record, such as a company's complete shipping address or a person's vital statistics.

- **Fields**   A field is a particular piece of information in a data record, such as a first name, a title, or a phone number.

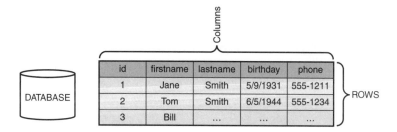

FIGURE 16.2   Database fields and rows.

For example, a database table for your customers might have the following fields:

- customerid

- firstname

- lastname

- address

- city

- state

- zip

- phone

- email

- notes

Together, the fields of a database table make up its schema, or structure.

Why Databases Are Better Than Flat Files

What's the point of having database tables? Why not just have flat text files that contain long lines (rows) each divided by commas into fields:

```
1,Tom,Smith,123 Main St.,Anytown,TX,12345,512-555-1212,tom@smith.com,
➥New customer.
```

This approach might work, but imagine what would happen each time a user added information to the file. The Web application would have to open the file, go down to the end of the file, and add a line. If more than one person at a time wanted to add information to the file, most everyone would have to wait in line. Multiply this problem if a user needed to update a line of information or delete a line.

Databases were invented to help solve these problems. Modern database systems offer fast data retrieval, easily managed information, and features such as data locking to prevent users from walking all over each other.

Data Types

But just having a list of fields isn't enough. You have to tell the database what data type can be contained by these fields. Data types define what kind of data is acceptable to that field and can include the following:

- Autocreated ID numbers, used to uniquely identify a record

- Characters, such as letters, numbers, and special characters

- Integers, or whole numbers

- Floating numbers, or numbers with decimals

- Binary information, such as images and spreadsheets

- Date and time stamps, to record when something happened or when something is due

- Options, such as on/off, yes/no and so on

Data Lengths

Knowing what fields are in a database table and the data types that are allowed in those fields still isn't enough. A database table also needs to know how much data to allow in each field. You can define different kinds of data lengths, but here are some suggested data lengths:

- **Names (character data)**   64 characters is usually sufficient.

- **IDs (integer data)**   10 characters.

- **Passwords (character data)**   10–16 characters.

- **Addresses (character data)**   128 characters.

- **Dates (date stamps)**   6–12 characters.

TIP

Each database has different options for length on each data type. Be sure to read the user documentation that comes with your database software.

Adding Information to a Table

There are a variety of ways to add information to a database from a Web application, but the most widely used is an HTML form.

When a user enters information into an HTML form and clicks the Submit button, each element in the form (fields, lists, and check boxes, for instance) is converted to a variable that matches the name given to that element in the HTML code.

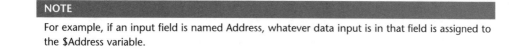

NOTE

For example, if an input field is named Address, whatever data input is in that field is assigned to the $Address variable.

These variables are then processed by the middleware, which connects to the database and inserts the information from the form using SQL (Standard Query Language). The information is inserted into the database, one row at a time.

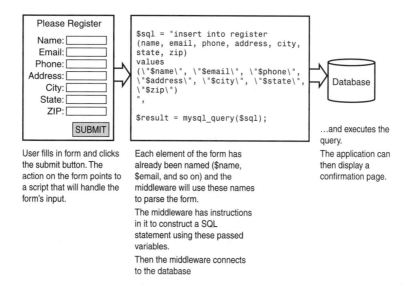

FIGURE 16.3   The process of inserting information into a database from a Web form.

Therefore, to continue with the example, your first customer data record might look like this:

- customerid: 1
- firstname: Tom
- lastname: Smith
- address: 123 Main Street
- city: Anytown
- state: TX
- zip: 12345
- phone: 512-555-5555

- email: tsmith@foo.org

- notes: First time using the Web site.

Because we are using a customerid to uniquely identify this customer, another Tom Smith—even one that lives on the same street in the same town—would never be confused for this Tom Smith. This kind of ID is called a primary key, which becomes important when we start talking about relational databases (more on this later).

Queries

A query is used to insert, update, delete, and extract data from a database. Queries can be very specific, such as extracting all rows in which TX is in the state field (using the preceding example), or they can extract (or delete) all records in a table.

Database Management Systems and Relational Systems

A database isn't just a table, though—it can be a number of tables in the same database. To continue the preceding example, you might have other tables in your database besides a customer database. You might also have a table that holds product information (if you have an e-commerce site, for example). All these tables reside in a database management system, or DBMS. Popular DBMS packages include Microsoft Access, MySQL, and Oracle.

A relational database is a series of database tables that relate to each other. Although this may not seem very important, think about what happens when you start adding tables to your database. To pursue the example, you add a product table to your database and store information in that table about each of your products.

Now comes the tough part: you need a table to store information about each sale you make on the site. In the old-fashioned way of doing things, you'd have to build a table (let's call it Sales) and use it to record every single piece of information about the customer and every single piece of information about the product they bought. Not only is this a terrible waste of space, but it can create havoc every time you change information (such as a customer's address or product description), you'd have to keep track of all the places you need to make changes, every time you have to make changes. Not very pretty.

Using a relational database is much easier. If you wanted to track which customers purchased which products on your site, you would need only a simple table that tracked two numbers: a customerid and a productid.

The customerid would tell you which customer made the purchase, and the productid would tell you what product was purchased. Each ID would point back to a unique ID in the customer and product tables. This simple notation keeps you from having to repeat (and keep track of) information such as telephone numbers and addresses.

Connecting to a Database

From the Web application's standpoint, it has to connect to a database before it can do any extracting, adding, updating, or deleting of information. To connect to a database, it must know the following information:

- Where the database server resides
- The username and password to get into the database server
- The name of the database to open

In some cases, as with Microsoft ODBC data sources, you can set up a Data Source Name (see the following section) that can simplify the connection process. With PHP, JSP, and other languages, you can create connection objects that handle connecting to a database for you.

Structured Query Language

Structured Query Language, or SQL (pronounced "sequel") was designed as a data operations language in a relational environment. Each SQL command, or statement, can do any of a number of operations, including the following:

- Select rows from a table (or tables).
- Add a row to a table.
- Update a row in a table.
- Delete a row from a table.
- Create or delete a table.

Chapter 27, "SQL Primer," covers SQL syntax in more detail, but for right now, I'd like to cover the basics of selecting rows from a table.

Starting with Select

The easiest way to learn SQL is to start with a simple SELECT statement. Let's continue with the customer table example. If you recall, the table had the following fields, or schema:

- customerid
- firstname
- lastname
- address
- city

- state

- zip

- phone

- email

- notes

If you want to see all the records in the database, you would use this command:

```
select * from customer
```

For most Web applications, though, doing a SELECT * on a database table could lead to trouble, as this means the visitor must patiently wait for the entire database to load in the browser. Even with a fast connection and heavy-duty server, this operation could take some time—especially if the site gets a lot of visitors.

To filter some of the records that get extracted, you can modify your SELECT statement in various ways. The first is to replace the * with actual field names in the first clause of the statement.

```
select customerid,city,state from customer
```

The previous SELECT statement would retrieve only three fields from each record in the database table.

If you want to further filter what gets retrieved from the database, you can add a where clause to the end of the SELECT statement. A where clause defines a condition that must be met. Only those records that match the condition in the where clause get extracted:

```
select customerid,city,state from customer where state = 'tx'
```

The previous SELECT statement would retrieve only three fields from each record in the table, but only if the state field had "tx" in it. Effectively, this operation restricts the recordset, or records returned, to those customers in Texas.

You can make your where clauses fairly complex, stringing them together with ands and ors:

```
select customerid,city,state
from customer where state = 'tx'
and email like '%.org'
```

The previous example not only shows that two conditions have to be met, but it also introduces the like operator and the wildcard (%). In the first case, both conditions have to be met for a record to be returned—that is, the customer must have a Texas address and an email address that ends in ".org." Using or instead of and would have extracted records that matched either condition.

In the second case, the like operator allows you to pull out records for which you have only partial information. For example, you may know only part of an email address, or just the first few letters of a person's name or street address. Using the = operator would have returned no records because = is expecting to match exactly what you tell it to match.

The wildcard symbol (%) instructs the database to match any number of characters, or any length. In the preceding example, the SQL statement matched any number of characters and ".org" in the email field of the customer table. In this case, ".org" would come at the end because the wildcard symbol fills in the front part of the field. To match a specific set of letters at the front of a field and then anything else at the end, use this notation:

```
select customerid,firstname,lastname,email
from customer
where email like 'tom@%'
```

The previous example would have extracted all records for customers with 'tom' in their email address. This means that your recordset would have included customers with emails such as tom@abc.com, tom@xyz.com, tom@tom.com, and so on.

SQL statements are not case sensitive, nor are they whitespace sensitive. This fact allows us to write SQL statements without regard for line breaks. In fact, the preceding SQL statement could have been written like this:

```
SELECT customerid,city,state FROM customer
WHERE email
LIKE 'tom@%'
```

For more information on SQL, refer to Chapter 27. It includes further detail on select statements,

Data Source Name

When you are trying to access an ODBC (Open DataBase Connectivity) data source, such as a Microsoft SQL Server database or Excel spreadsheet, you can significantly speed up operations by setting up a Data Source Name (DSN).

A Data Source Name (DSN) is a logical name that refers to not only the data source, but also the drive it sits on. On Windows machines, you use the Control panel to access a tool to create a DSN. Creating a DSN can simplify the commands you give to connect to that database.

Middleware Options

As I said earlier, middleware is software that handles most, if not all, business logic in a Web application. Over the past 10 years, as the Web has matured, dozens of different middleware options have appeared.

Most middleware options have a lot in common. For example, most of them interact with relational databases; they can process complex requests from Web browsers and can write files to and read files from a file system. So which option is the best for you? Most are pretty much the same, so choosing an option isn't just a case of features. Web developers soon discover that the most important criteria for selecting an option is its flexibility. Will this option allow them to easily access a database? Build objects to keep redundant code to a minimum? It's a lot like buying a pair of jeans: you want to go with what looks good and fits right.

The following sections describe some of the more popular options.

PHP

PHP has taken the Web by storm. More servers run more PHP pages than any other language. PHP is a lightweight, easy-to-learn, and quickly deployed open-source scripting language with a number of convenient features. The language's lineage is Perl and C, so many developers familiar with those languages will find making the switch (as I did) very easy. Every day, more and more modules are added by a growing community of open-source developers.

PHP works very well with many database solutions, but it is almost always mentioned in the same breath as the mySQL database system. PHP can run on Windows, Unix, and Mac servers; it supports IIS, Apache, and other Web servers.

As for functionality, PHP supports object-oriented programming, nesting of modules, and custom functions. It has a rich set of built-in tools that let you access XML files, mail servers, database archives, Java APIs and objects, the server's file system, and a lot more.

PHP commands (or directives) are embedded into HTML pages between special tags (<? ?>). These directives are handed off to the PHP engine by the Web server, which then processes the directive and hands output back to the Web server for display in the Web browser. For example, the following code snippet will print "Hello there!":

```
<html>
<title>My first PHP</title>
<body>
<h1>My first PHP</h1>
<?
echo "Hello there!";
?>
</body>
</html>
```

PHP pages are usually created as templates that hold HTML and directives for displaying dynamic content. In this way, PHP (and other middleware options) can save you a lot of time in developing and deploying a site.

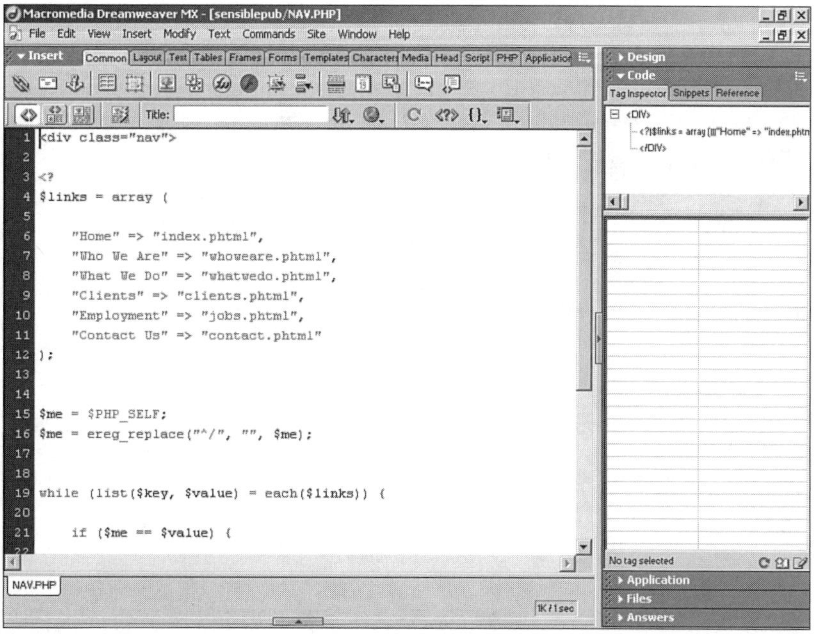

FIGURE 16.4   PHP code in Dreamweaver MX.

For more information on PHP, refer to Chapter 24, "PHP and MySQL."

ColdFusion MX

Macromedia ColdFusion MX is described as a rapid server-scripting language for creating Web applications. It uses a language called ColdFusion Markup Language (CFML) to interact with databases and dynamically create pages.

CFML tags are embedded directly into HTML, and each command has a start tag and an end tag, which look like this:

```
<cfmytag> </cfmytag>
```

Each ColdFusion application is a set of pages with CFML commands in them. Developers can use the built-in functions, create their own, or integrate COM, C++, or Java components into their code.

ColdFusion supports both JDBC and ODBC data sources.

ColdFusion MX is an integrated development environment (IDE) that can be run as part of a suite with Dreamweaver. The ColdFusion IDE allows developers to develop, test, and deploy ColdFusion applications.

ASP

ASP, or Active Server Pages, is a Microsoft-developed Web-scripting language. Like many other middleware options, ASP allows you to embed special instructions in HTML pages that can do a variety of tasks, such as connect to a database, perform looping instructions, and conditionally test for certain values.

ASP runs natively on Microsoft's IIS Web server. Although ASP is normally written in VBScript (a derivative of Visual Basic), it also supports JavaScript, ActiveX Data Objects (ADOs), and even PerlScript.

ASP directives are placed between special tags in HTML, which look like this:

```
<HTML>
<TITLE>My First ASP</TITLE>
<BODY>
<h1>My First ASP</h1>
<% Response.Write("Isn't ASP cool?") %>
</BODY>
</HTML>
```

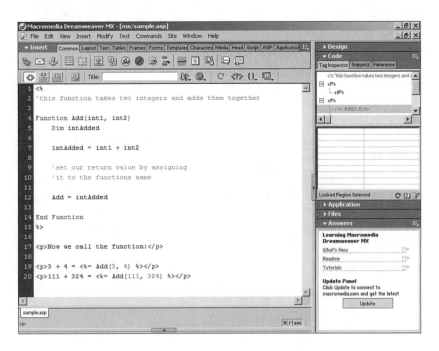

FIGURE 16.5   ASP code in Dreamweaver MX.

For more information on ASP, refer to Chapter 22, "ASP and ASP.NET."

ASP.NET

ASP.NET, or ASP+, is Microsoft's next generation of the ASP line. ASP.NET supports compiled code written in C++, C#, Perl, and Visual Basic and allows separation of code from HTML formatting (called "code behind method"). Because the language can be compiled, it can run faster than its interpreted predecessor, ASP.

Although ASP.NET isn't compatible with ASP, the two can run side-by-side on the same server.

For more information on ASP.NET, refer to Chapter 22.

JSP

Java Server Pages, or JSP, is an extremely popular and robust middleware option. JSP brings together the power and portability of Java with the native UI-rendering capabilities of an HTML browser.

JSP can run under the control of a servlet (the most popular is Tomcat) or it can integrate with Java Beans, which are bits of compiled code that can do various functions (such as access a database or return search results).

JSP is a full development language with robust object-oriented features and extended capabilities that make it the right choice for building extensive, complicated applications.

Like many other middleware options mentioned here, JSP tags are embedded directly into HTML, and look like this:

```
<html>
<title>My First JSP</title>
<body>
<h1>My First JSP</h1>
<% out.println("JSP is cool!"); %>
</body>
</html>
```

For more information on JSP, refer to Chapter 23, "JSP."

Database Options

Not too long ago, databases were the realm of specialized geeks. If a database was too slow, that was okay because it sat on a mainframe and processed inventory and payroll checks.

Now, databases are everywhere, and they're hooked into seemingly every single Web application. Today's databases need to be fast, reliable, and scalable. If a database goes down (or slows down), a company's revenues might disappear because their only sales channel might be an online catalog with shopping cart.

As with middleware, dozens of databases are available, but I'll discuss only the most widely used here. Each has its own strengths and drawbacks. Some are free, and some cost hundreds of thousands of dollars to license.

Informix

Informix (or DB2) is an IBM relational database solution. Although it isn't known much beyond mainframe and enterprise server environments, it is number 2 (right behind Oracle) in market share in the database space.

DB2 runs on IBM's servers, AIX (IBM's version of the Unix operating system), Windows NT, 2000, and XP servers, and Linux.

IBM boasts that DB2 is the first Web-ready, multimedia-capable database solution on the market, and that it is a great solution for starting small and scaling up to larger operations.

The DB2 database packages include support for SQL queries, XML, Java APIs, OLAP, and sophisticated application development tools. The Windows versions integrate well with ASP. The Linux and Unix versions integrate with PHP, JSP, Perl, and Python.

DB2 supports OLTP (online transaction processing), which means that it is built to handle (and process) thousands of simultaneous transactions.

SQL Server

SQL Server is Microsoft's relational database management system. The system's roots are in small, department-centric database applications, but as the Web's demand for robust database tools has matured, so has Microsoft's offering.

SQL Server, as its name implies, is a SQL-based relational database with support for XML. It integrates natively with Microsoft's ASP scripting language.

SQL Server supports OLTP (online transaction processing), which is essential in a modern Web environment.

Oracle

The undisputed 800-pound gorilla of the database market is Oracle. No wonder that it was the original relational database management system vendor.

Oracle systems have a reputation as being the Rolls-Royces of the industry—and yes, that means the price tag comes with it, too. Oracle databases are extremely robust (some customers report that they've never lost data in years of operations) with extensive capabilities for data storage, retrieval, archiving, reporting, exporting, and a lot more besides.

Oracle supports OLTP, row-level locking of data (very handy if you have lots of users updating information in your database), data partitioning (for performance and security), support for XML and Java objects, and it runs natively both on Windows and Unix implementations.

Oracle is the surefire pick if you need the Sherman tank approach to data handling. However, for the scant of pocketbook, an Oracle solution may be too much.

Sybase

Sybase is best known as a financial markets and business intelligence relational database vendor. Its systems offer support for SQL, ODBC and JDBC connections, Java objects, XML, and applications that focus on business intelligence.

Sybase has its pulse on a very sticky problem. To understand your customers, you have to understand what they're doing—what they buy from you, where they go on your site, what they are asking for. However, after you turn on the great data collection machine, it doesn't take any time at all to collect gigabytes of data on all manner of things.

How do you penetrate that pile of data and extract something that will drive profits? How can you keep your systems running fast when they get clogged with all this vital data?

Sybase's tools offer answers to these questions, with slick extraction, mining, and reporting tools. On top of all that, Sybase is the most affordable of all the proprietary vendors.

MySQL

MySQL is usually mentioned in the same breath as PHP. The two play together really well. MySQL is an open-source (and free) relational database system, and its popularity on the database side matches PHP's on the middleware side.

MySQL allows for blazing fast selection of data, and comparable performance for data inserts and updates. The native command-line interface supports Linux, Windows, and Mac OS X environments. If you don't like the thought of messing around with a command-line interface, don't despair; many PHP-based interfaces are available to make life simpler.

> **NOTE**
>
> Don't let "open source" scare you away. Many open-source technologies, including MySQL, offer extremely versatile and robust features, all for free. Support comes from a worldwide group of users and developers, most of whom are all too happy to help out.

Current versions of MySQL don't support certain widely available features of other relational database systems. For example, you can't build subqueries with MySQL. This may not seem like a big deal, but the day will come when you'll want to run more complex queries. I've also found that its OLTP capabilities aren't quite there yet—I've seen cases in which one user logs in, and, after entering some data, gets somebody else's data. This is rare, and there are ways to code around these crossed wires to keep them from happening, but it is annoying.

Word on the street is that these (and other) issues are being worked on, both by the cadre of core developers at MySQL and the open-source community at large.

Despite some of its shortcomings, MySQL is easy to use, simple to deploy, and can handle copious amounts of data (and transactions) before showing wear and tear.

Access and FileMaker Pro

Microsoft Access is a SQL-based database tool that was originally designed for desktop users. It has a wide array of tools that allow users to easily create tables, forms for data entry, queries, and reports. In the past, I've accessed Access databases through a Web application and have never been impressed by its performance.

FileMaker Pro originally was a Macintosh-only database system that has since expanded into the Windows world. It has a nice set of visual design tools that allow users to easily create data entry forms and other necessary widgets. However, FileMaker Pro is not a scalable solution beyond a small group of users—it just doesn't have enough oomph to handle a large volume of data being accessed by thousands of users.

Summary

Understanding what a Web application is, and how different it is from a static Web site, is only the first step. Making decisions about middleware and databases all comes down to one thing: what tools are easily available?

If your company has Oracle installed and there are plenty of JSP developers available to build and support your Web application, then that's likely the way you'll go. However, if you are running a small company and cost is an issue, PHP/MySQL (or some other open-source combination) might be more prudent.

Chapter 17, will take the concepts that I've covered here and get down to the nitty-gritty of setting up a Web server and database, and preparing for database connectivity.

Web Application Preparation

by Thomas Myer
Principal, Triple Dog Dare Media

Introduction

Now that you understand the basic structure behind a Web application, it's time to set one up. If you have a lot of experience with Web design, you know that running a development Web server is crucial to success. Having a development Web server running on your own machine means that you can test your designs before posting them to a live environment.

If your design experience has been limited, you may never have had to set up your own Web server. Don't worry, it's not that scary.

A Web application requires two major components to run properly:

- A Web server

- An application server

The Web server responds to all requests that are made of it by visitors using Web browsers. The application server handles all dynamic requests and connects to a data source. You can think of the application server as middleware plus database.

First, I'll walk you through setting up a Web server; then you'll go through the process of setting up an application server.

Setting Up the Web Server

This section covers the two most popular Web servers out there: Microsoft's Internet Information Server (IIS) and the Apache Foundation's Apache Web Server.

> **NOTE**
>
> I will also discuss Personal Web Server (PWS) in the IIS section.

Each section includes information on getting the software, as well as installing and configuring it. I also provide easy tests for you to check that the Web server is up and running properly.

Although Web servers can be fairly complex, with many toggles, functions, and configuration options, for our purposes, all we want to do is get them set up and communicating with an application server. This means, realistically, that you'll choose most of the default options when you run through the installs.

> **NOTE**
>
> When you visit some Web server software distribution sites, you'll notice a lot of instructions for the different versions and platforms. You may even get a choice between compilable and executable software. If you are installing a Web server on a Windows-based machine, you'll want to choose an executable package (either EXE, ZIP, or MSI).

> **Which Server Should I Install?**
>
> One Web server is much like another, so which one should you install? It depends on the kind of middleware and database you plan to use.
>
> If you are planning to use ASP (or ASP.NET) along with SQL Server, install Internet Information Server (IIS) or Personal Web Server (PWS). These technologies were all developed by the same company (Microsoft) and generally speaking, are complementary.
>
> If you are planning to develop in a ColdFusion environment, use the built-in Web server that ships with ColdFusion.
>
> If you are going to be using JSP or PHP along with MySQL or Oracle, install Apache.

Internet Information Services/Personal Web Server

The Internet Information Services (IIS) server is Microsoft's Web server. Personal Web Server (PWS) is a lightweight Web server that is easy to install and can be used for testing applications under development.

Before you get started installing these Web servers, check your computer's hard drive because these Web servers sometimes come preinstalled on Windows machines. If you have an \inetpub directory in your C: or D: drives, you don't have to follow these directions.

Which version should you install? It depends on the version of Microsoft Windows your machine is running:

- Windows 95, Windows 98, and Windows NT Workstation users should install PWS.

- Windows NT Server, Windows 2000, and Windows XP users should install IIS.

Installing PWS

You can get PWS from the Windows 98 CD-ROM or from the Microsoft site.

If you have a Windows 98 CD-ROM, follow these instructions:

1. Insert your Windows 98 CD-ROM into your CD-ROM drive.

2. Click Start, and then click Run.

3. In the Open box, type the following path to the Setup.exe file, where *m* is the letter of your CD-ROM drive:

```
m:\add-ons\pws\setup.exe
```

4. Click OK.

5. Follow the instructions in the Setup Wizard.

> **NOTE**
>
> Be sure to accept C:\Inetpub\wwwroot as the Web server's document root.

If you don't have the Windows 98 CD-ROM, you can go to http://www.microsoft.com and do a search on PWS10a.exe, which is the downloadable code package for PWS. After you download it to your desktop, double-click the file's icon and follow the Setup Wizard's instructions.

Installing IIS

To install IIS on Windows 2000 or Windows XP, follow these instructions:

1. In Windows 2000, choose Start, Settings, Control Panel, Add/Remove Programs.

2. In Windows XP, choose Start, Control Panel, Add/Remove Programs.

3. Choose Add/Remove Windows Components.

4. Select the IIS box and follow the installation instructions.

> **NOTE**
>
> If you have Windows NT Server, IIS should already be installed. Check for a C:\Inetpub or
> D:\Inetpub directory. If it exists, IIS has been installed.

Confirming Proper Web Server Setup

After you've installed either PWS or IIS, create a simple HTML file in Dreamweaver MX.
Type the following HTML code into Dreamweaver:

```
<p>My first Web page.
```

Save the file as index.html and save it to the \Inetpub\wwwroot directory on either the C:
or D: drive.

Then, point your Web browser to `http://localhost/index.html`. If you see your test page,
the Web server was installed properly.

Apache

Setting up Apache on a Windows machine is very simple. To get a copy of Apache, go to
`http://www.apache.org` and choose the latest stable package. At the time of this writing,
the stable packages are 2.0.40 (in the 2.0 branch) and 1.3.26 (for the 1.0 branch).

> **NOTE**
>
> Be sure to download the executable version of Apache, not the compilable version.

Either Apache version is a robust, secure application. After you've found the proper
package, follow these instructions:

1. Download the package to your desktop.

2. Double-click the executable file. This starts the installation wizard.

3. Read and accept the terms in the license agreement by clicking Next.

4. On the next screen, enter the following information and click Next:

   - Your machine's network domain (that is, `www.yourdomain.com`)

   - Your machine's server name (that is, `tom.yourdomain.com`)

   - The administrator's e-mail address (that is, `tom@yourdomain.com`)

5. Select Typical installation and click Next.

6. Set a home directory for the Web server. Be sure to accept the default setting
   (C:\Program Files\Apache Group). Click Next.

7. Click Install to begin the installation.

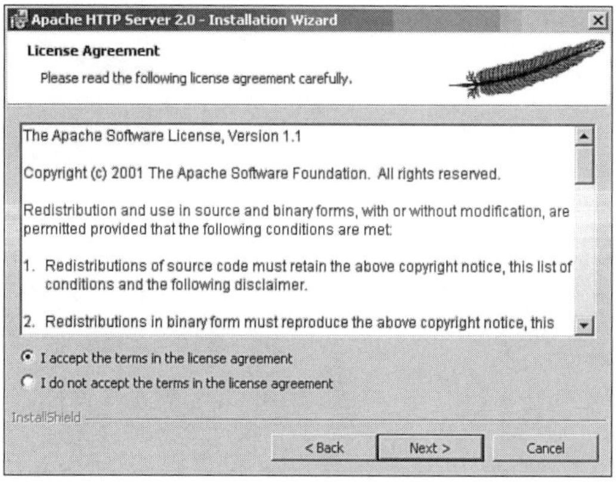

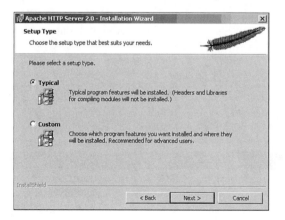

FIGURE 17.1 Accept the terms of the Apache License Agreement.

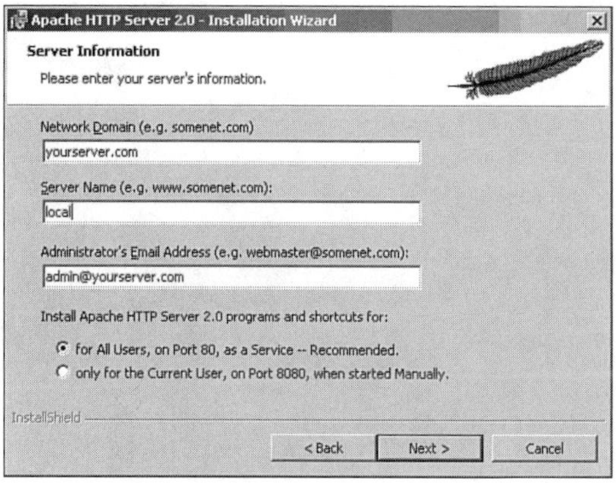

FIGURE 17.2 Enter your server's vital statistics.

FIGURE 17.3 Select Typical installation.

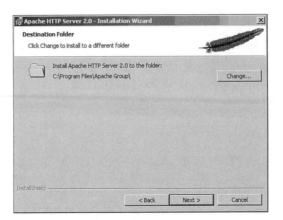

FIGURE 17.4   Accept the default setting for Apache's home.

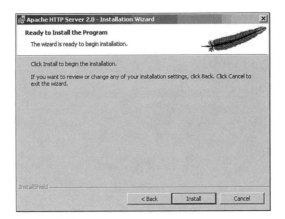

FIGURE 17.5   Click Install to complete the process.

As soon as you click Install, the Apache installer begins copying files. Various screens will flash open and closed during this process. When the installation process is complete, Apache will display a confirmation page.

Confirming Proper Web Server Setup

You can test to make sure Apache was installed properly by pointing your browser at `http://localhost`. You should see an Apache placeholder page in the language corresponding to your browser language preference.

TIP

Do you want to see the Apache placeholder page in Spanish? Go to `http://localhost/index.html.es`. How about in German? Go to `http://localhost/index.html.de`.

Apache Docroot

The default docroot for Apache 1.x Web servers is

`C:\Program Files\Apache Group\Apache\htdocs.`

The default docroot directory for Apache 2.x Web servers is

`C:\Program Files\Apache Group\Apache2\htdocs.`

Any files you put in the docroot directory (and in any of its subdirectories) can be viewed by visitors to your server.

Working with Apache

On Windows 2000 and Windows XP, Apache runs as a Windows service, which means that it starts up automatically when you turn on your machine and can continue running when you log off.

If you click the Start button and go to Apache HTTP Server, Control Apache Server, you'll see the different commands for controlling the server. You can

- Start the Apache Web Server.

- Stop the Apache Web Server.

- Restart a stopped Apache Web Server.

- Monitor Apache Servers (this controls error and access logging on your server).

In upcoming pages, as you install a database and middleware, you will learn how to alter Apache's configuration files. These alterations are necessary for the Web server to properly execute JSP, PHP, or other middleware code.

Setting Up the Application Server

The application server consists of the middleware and database. Regardless of the options you use in both cases, both components of the application server need to be able to talk to each other and to the Web server.

What this means is that you must have a Web server up and running first before you install any middleware or database software. It also means that after you get any middleware and database components working, you'll need to configure your Web server software to recognize and talk to these components.

The following sections walk you through these installation and configuration procedures.

PHP/MySQL

PHP and MySQL are usually installed at the same time. The following information should get you up and running on Apache or IIS.

Installing PHP on Apache 1.3.x or 2.0.x

To install PHP and get it working with Apache, follow these instructions after you've installed Apache:

1. Go to http://www.php.net and download the latest stable Windows binaries. This is usually packaged as a ZIP archive.

2. After the ZIP archive downloads, create a \php directory right off your hard drive's root (that is, D:\php or C:\php).

> **WARNING**
>
> It's important that your PHP directory not have spaces in its name; otherwise, Apache and other Web servers might crash.

3. Extract the contents of the ZIP archive to this \php directory.

4. Open the \php directory and rename the php.ini-recommended file to php.ini.

5. Open the php.ini file in a text editor and find the extension_dir variable in the file. Change this line so that the variable is set to C:\php. The line should look like this when you're done:

```
extension_dir = c:\php
```

> **NOTE**
>
> In some cases, you'll have to use forward slashes (/) instead of backslashes (\) when editing configuration files; sometimes it's the other way around. Sometimes you put quotes around the values set for variables, and sometimes not. Confusing, isn't it? Just be sure to follow these directions to the letter.

6. Save your changes to the php.ini file and copy it to your %WINDOWS% directory. On NT/2000/XP machines, this directory is C:\winnt. On 95/98/ME machines, this directory is C:\windows.

7. Copy the \php\php4dts.dll file to either the \windows\system or \winnt\system32 directory on your machine.

8. Now it's time to configure Apache to work with PHP. Open the \program files\apache group\apache2\conf\httpd.conf file in a text editor and make the following changes:

   - Search for LoadModule and then add the following line at the end of the LoadModule section:

   ```
   LoadModule php4_module c:/php/sapi/php4apache.dll
   ```

- Search for AddType and then add the following line at the end of the AddType section:

```
AddType application/x-httpd-php .php .phtml
```

- Search for ScriptAlias and then add the following two lines at the end of the ScriptAlias section:

```
ScriptAlias /php/ "c:/php"
Action application/x-httpd-php "/php/php.exe "
```

9. Save your changes to the httpd.conf file.

10. Stop the Apache Web Server by clicking Start, Apache HTTP Server, Control Apache, Stop.

11. Restart the Apache Web Server by clicking Start, Apache HTTP Server, Control Apache, Restart.

12. You can test your Apache Web Server setup by creating a test file called index.php. Insert the following line of code into the file:

```
<p>My first php: <? echo "hello world!"; ?>
```

13. Save the file to the htdocs directory of Apache and point your browser to http://localhost/index.php. If you see the "hello world!" message, PHP and Apache are talking to each other.

Installing PHP on IIS

To install PHP on an NT/2000/XP Server running IIS 4 or later, you have two options for setup: using the CGI binary (php.exe) or the ISAPI module.

> **ISAPI or CGI?**
>
> When given the choice, choose ISAPI over CGI. It's faster, more reliable, and more secure. However, I've included directions for CGI setup in case your version of Windows or IIS doesn't support ISAPI access.

In either case, you'll need to do the following:

1. Go to http://www.php.net and download the latest stable Windows binaries.

2. After the ZIP archive downloads, create a \php directory right off your hard drive's root (that is, D:\php or C:\php).

> **WARNING**
>
> It's important that your PHP directory not have spaces in its name; otherwise, Apache and other Web servers might crash.

3. Extract the contents of the ZIP archive to this \php directory.

4. Start the Microsoft Management Console (under Control Panel, Administrative Tools) and right-click the Web Server node.

5. Select Properties.

To use the CGI binary:

1. Click the Configuration button under Home Directory, Virtual Directory, or Directory, and then enter the App Mappings tab.

2. Click Add, and in the Executable box, enter `C:\php\php.exe`.

3. In the Extension box, type the file name extensions you want associated with PHP scripts (.php and .phtml are two good ones). You'll have to enter them in one at a time.

4. Stop IIS completely (NET STOP iisadmin).

5. Restart IIS (NET START w3svc).

To use the ISAPI module:

1. Click the Configuration button under Home Directory. Add a new entry to the Application Mappings.

2. Enter `C:\php\php4isapi.dll` as the Executable.

3. Supply .php and .phtml as Extensions.

4. Leave Method exclusions blank.

5. Check the Script engine check box.

6. Stop IIS completely (NET STOP iisadmin).

7. Restart IIS (NET START w3svc).

You can test the PHP installation by creating a simple PHP file, saving it to the \inetpub\wwwroot directory, and then pointing your browser at that file.

Installing MySQL

MySQL is available as free software from `http://www.mysql.com`. Follow these instructions to install and configure MySQL with PHP.

1. Go to `http://www.mysql.com/downloads` and download the latest stable release for Windows. It is a ZIP archive between 12MB and 15MB in size, so it will take some time to download.

2. After the ZIP archive downloads, extract the files to a temporary directory on your desktop.

3. Double-click the setup.exe file.

4. Click Next to accept the legal disclaimers and terms of usage.

5. Accept C:\mysql as the default directory for MySQL and click Next.

6. Select Typical installation and click Next.

7. Click Finish.

8. After the installation completes, create a my.ini file in Notepad (or other text editor) and populate it with the following data:

   ```
   [mysqld]
   basedir=c:/mysql
   datadir=c:/mysql/data
   ```

9. Save this my.ini file in either C:\windows or C:\winnt, depending on your Windows version.

10. Click the Start button and then click Run. Type `Command` and click OK. This opens a C:\prompt window.

11. Type the following commands into the window:

    ```
    cd \mysql\bin
    mysqld -standalone
    ```

    The first command changes the directory to the mysql binaries directory, and the second command starts the mysql server in standalone mode.

12. Using the Start button, create a second C:\prompt window. Change directories to the \mysql\bin directory and type:

    ```
    mysql
    ```

13. This command starts MySql in interactive mode. You should see the following on your screen:

    ```
    Welcome to the MySQL monitor. Commands end with ; or \g.
    Your MySQL connection id is 1 to server version: 3.23.52-max-debug
    ```

17

```
Type 'help;' or '\h' for help. Type '\c' to clear the buffer.

mysql>
```

Testing MySQL

Now you can issue commands directly to MySQL. PHP should also be able to communicate with MySQL. To test this, create a test table in MySQL:

1. Switch to the built-in test database by typing the following command:

   ```
   use test
   ```

2. Create a simple two-field database called mytest by typing the following lines, one line at a time into MySQL:

   ```
   create table mytest (
   name varchar(32),
   birthday date
   );
   ```

3. Add a few records to this new database, one at a time:

   ```
   insert into mytest (name,birthday)
   values
   ("tom", "1971-06-05");

   insert into mytest (name,birthday)
   values
   ("john", "1944-01-05");
   ```

4. Create the following simple PHP file and save it to your Web server's docroot:

   ```
   <html>
   <title>test php</title>
   <body>
   <?
   //first, connect to db
   if (!($mylink = mysql_connect( "localhost", "root", "")))
   {
       print "<h3>could not connect to database</h3>\n";
       exit;
   }
   mysql_select_db( "test");

   //now issue the sql query
   ```

```
$sql = "select * from mytest";
$result = mysql_query($sql);

while (list($name, $birthday) = mysql_fetch_array($result)) {
    echo "$name's birthday is <b>$birthday</b>.<br>";
}
?>
</body>
</html>
```

5. Point your browser to this file. If you see a list of names and birthdays, PHP was able to connect to the MySQL Server. You're in business.

SQL Server

Although Microsoft's SQL Server isn't a free, open-source tool, you can get a 120-day trial download at http://www.microsoft.com/sql/evaluation/trial.

Before you can install and run the software, make sure that you're logged in to your system as an administrator. Then see if you meet some basic system requirements:

- Microsoft Windows 2000 Server with Service Pack 1 (SP1) or later
- Microsoft Windows NT Server 4.0 with Service Pack 5 (SP5)
- Microsoft Windows XP Professional
- Microsoft Windows XP Home Edition
- Microsoft Windows 2000 Professional

After you sign up for the 120-day trial, download the package and follow these instructions:

1. Double-click the executable package.

2. Select SQL Server 2000 Components.

3. Select Install Database Server. This starts the SQL Server Installation Wizard. At the Welcome screen, click Next.

4. In the Computer Name dialog box, you can leave Local Computer as the default option for your system. Click Next.

> **NOTE**
>
> If you are installing SQL Server on a remote computer, click Remote Computer and type a computer name; you also can click Browse to locate a remote computer.

5. In the Installation Selection dialog box, click Create a New Instance of SQL Server, or install Client Tools, and then click Next.

6. Click through the software licensing and user information confirmation screens.

7. Click Server and Client Tools in the Installation Definition dialog box and then click Next.

8. In the Instance Name dialog box, choose the Default instance and then click Next.

9. Choose Typical as the setup type, and then click Next.

10. In the Service Accounts dialog box, accept the default settings, enter your domain password, and then click Next.

11. In the Authentication Mode dialog box, accept the default setting and click Next.

12. Click Next to start copying files.

13. After the installation is complete, select the computer restart option and click Finish.

The application binaries for SQL Server are located at \Program Files\Microsoft SQL Server\Mssql\Binn. You can start SQL Server by double-clicking the database server.

You can also access SQL Server by clicking Start, Microsoft SQL Server.

ColdFusion

ColdFusion MX is available on the Macromedia Studio MX CD-ROM. TO install ColdFusion, follow these steps:

1. Place the Studio MX CD-ROM into the CD-ROM drive.

2. On the splash screen, click ColdFusion MX Developer Edition. ColdFusion MX prepares the installer.

3. Click Next on the Welcome screen.

4. Accept the terms and then click Next.

5. Enter your name, company name (if applicable), and the ColdFusion MX serial number. Then click Next.

6. Select Complete Installation and click Next.

7. Select a Web server from the list and click Next.

> **WARNING**
>
> Macromedia strongly recommends that you use the standalone Web server that comes with ColdFusion MX.

8. Accept the default Webroot folder location and click Next.

9. Select a password for the ColdFusion Administrator and click Next.

10. Click Install to start copying files.

11. After the installation process ends, click Finish and restart your system when prompted.

After it's installed, ColdFusion MX runs as a service. You can stop, start, or configure this service by clicking the Start button and then selecting Settings, Control Panel, Administrative Tools, Services. You can then select Macromedia ColdFusion MX Application Server from the list to access commands.

You can start the ColdFusion Administrator by choosing Start, Macromedia ColdFusion MX, Administrator. The Administrator is a browser-based tool that lets you access all server features and configuration settings.

Tomcat

Tomcat is a JSP/Servlet engine used to serve up JSP pages. It is available as part of the Apache Jakarta project. This project includes various implementations of Tomcat that follow the different Servlet and JSP specifications.

Before you can download Tomcat, though, you need to have a Java Development Kit (JDK). You can find a JDK by going to Sun's `http://java.sun.com/j2se` page and downloading a version 1.2 (or later) release.

Install the JDK according to the instructions included with the release. Be sure to install the JDK in a \JDK folder in your C:\ or D:\ drive root.

Finally, open a shell window (using Start, Run) and set a JAVA_HOME variable pointing to the directory in which you installed the JDK:

```
set JAVA_HOME=\jdk
```

After you've set up the JDK, you can download Tomcat 3.3.1 (this release follows the JSP 1.1 and Servlet 2.0 specifications), found on the downloads page at `http://jakarta.apache.org/downloads/binindex.html`.

> **WARNING**
>
> Be sure to pull down a Release build of Tomcat 3.3.1. Release builds are the most stable code packages.

Next, follow these instructions:

1. Download the ZIP file containing the Tomcat binaries for Windows.

2. Create a \tomcat directory off your C:\ or D:\ drive root.

3. Extract the contents of the ZIP to this \tomcat directory. This should create a subdirectory named jakarta-tomcat-3.3.1.

17

4. Open a shell window by clicking the Start button and choosing Run; then type **command** and press the Enter key.

5. Change directories to the subdirectory created in step 3.

6. In the shell window, type the following command:

```
set TOMCAT_HOME=tomcat\jakarta-tomcat-3.3.1
```

7. You can browse Tomcat services by visiting http://localhost:8080.

Getting Tomcat and Apache to Cooperate

After you have Tomcat installed, you will need to get Apache and Tomcat working together. To do this, you must make some changes in Apache's httpd.conf file. Include the following text to the end of that file, save it, and restart Apache:

```
# This loads the jserv module--used by Tomcat as an apache adapter
LoadModule jserv_module libexec/mod_jserv.so

<IfModule mod_jserv.c>
# once the module loads, set up jserv parameters
ApJServManual on
ApJServSecretKey DISABLED
ApJServMountCopy on
ApJServLogLevel notice

# sets the base communication protocol
ApJServDefaultProtocol ajpv12

# here are the default locations of host and port
ApJServDefaultHost localhost
ApJServDefaultPort 8007

# the following redirects all Web server paths that
# start with /jsp to Tomcat
ApJServMount /jsp /root

# You can also listen on a specific host and port:
# ApJServMount /examples ajpv12://hostname:port/root
</IfModule>
```

Database Connectivity

Database connectivity varies depending on the middleware you are using and the type of database you're trying to access.

For example, if you are using PHP/mySQL, you can generally place a command in your PHP files to access or point to a MySQL server and let it go at that. Database connectivity is fast, simple, and repeatable.

In PHP, database connectivity might look like this:

```
if (!($mylink = mysql_connect( "localhost", "root", "")))
{
    print "<h3>could not connect to database</h3>\n";
    exit;
}
mysql_select_db( "test");
```

The first part is an if clause that tests to see if the mysql_connect command can actually reach the database server. If it can't, PHP will exit gracefully with a message. Otherwise, PHP executes the mysql_select_db command, which, as the name of the command implies, selects a database for access.

In PHP, putting this command in a header.php file and then including this file on all other pages means that every part of your application has instant database access.

The same can be said for JSP and ASP implementations. Each of these languages has similar approaches to connecting to a data source.

However, if you are trying to access an ODBC data source, such as a SQL Server database, an Excel spreadsheet, or a Microsoft Access database, you need to set up a Data Source Name (DSN) on your Windows machine.

A DSN can allow faster access to a data source, and depending on the type of DSN you set up—User, System, or File—you can benefit from security settings.

Setting Up a DSN

The following example shows you how to set up a DSN that points to a Microsoft Access database. The example then shows you how to create a simple ASP file that queries this database.

Step 1: Set Up a Test Database

The first step is setting up a simple Microsoft Access database. Open Microsoft Access and create a table. This table should have two fields:

- name
- birthday

Populate this table with some names and birthdays of your friends or relatives—it doesn't matter what the table holds, we're just using it to make sure we can see the database.

Name the table mytable. When you're done, save the database as dsntest.mdb.

17

Step 2: Create the DSN

Now that you've created the database, you're ready to set up a DSN that points to the database. Follow these instructions to set up a DSN:

1. Click the Start Button and go to the Control Panel.

2. Click Administrative Tools and then select Data Sources (ODBC).

3. Click the System DSN tab.

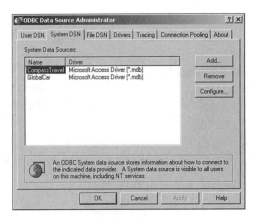

FIGURE 17.6   The System DSN tab of Data Sources.

4. Click Add.

5. Select the Microsoft Access database drive and click Finish.

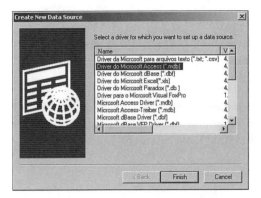

FIGURE 17.7   Select Microsoft Access from the list of available drivers.

6. Provide your new DSN with a name. Generally speaking, it's a good idea to give your DSN a name that is descriptive. Call your new DSN testaccessdb.

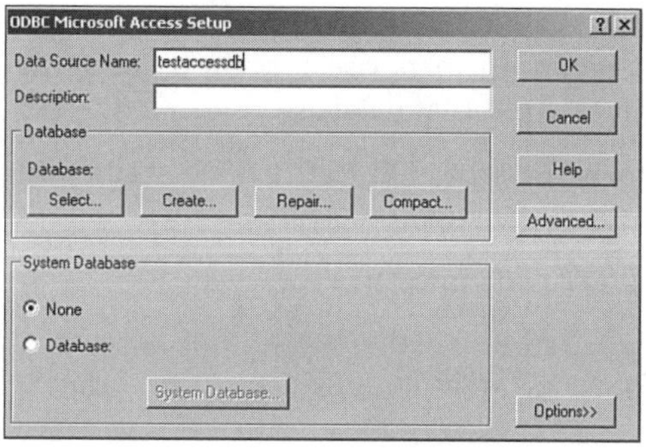

FIGURE 17.8   Choose a name for your DSN.

7. Under Database, click Select and browse to find the dsntest.mdb database file. Click OK when you're finished.

8. Click Advanced to set a username and password for the dsntest.mdb database. Set both of these to **test** for this example. Click OK when you're finished.

9. Click OK to close the ODBC Microsoft Access DSN Setup.

10. You should now see testaccessdb listed as a Microsoft Access Driver on the System DSN list. Click OK to close the ODBC System Administrator dialog box.

Step 3: Create the ASP File

Now that you have a database and a DSN pointing at it, you can create the ASP file to access the database through a Web browser. To create the ASP file, follow these steps:

1. Open Dreamweaver MX.

2. Create a new file and open the code view. Then type the following ASP code:

```
<%
dsn = "testaccessdb"
dbuser = "test"
dbpass = "test"

Set Conn = Server.CreateObject("ADODB.Connection")
Set rs = Server.CreateObject("ADODB.RecordSet")
Conn.Open dsn, dbuser, dbpass
```

First you set up some variables. The dsn variable holds the name of the DSN you set up in step 2. The dbuser and dbpass variables hold the username and password you set up.

After that, the code sets up a connection object and a recordset object. The first handles the connection to the database, and the second will handle any and all information we request from that database.

Finally, the code opens a connection to the DSN by accepting parameters for the DSN, the username, and the password.

3. Enter the following ASP code into Dreamweaver:

```
sql="select * from mytable"
Response.Write "<B>SQL STATEMENT: </B>" & sql & "<HR>"
RS.Open sql, Conn
%>
```

After you've set up the connection, build a sql variable to hold your SQL statement. Then pass this SQL statement to the recordset object you've created.

4. Enter the following ASP code into Dreamweaver:

```
<table border=1>
<tr valign=bottom>
<%
For i = 0 to RS.Fields.Count - 1
%>
<td><b><% = RS(i).Name %></b></td>
<% Next %>
</tr>
```

This code pulls out the names of the fields in your database (name and birthday, in this case) and places them in table cells. The For loop captures all the field names efficiently, so this code works whether you have 1 field or 500—or make lots of changes to your database table.

5. Enter the following ASP code into Dreamweaver:

```
<%
Do While Not RS.EOF
%>

<tr valign=top>
<% For i = 0 to RS.Fields.Count - 1 %>
<td><% = RS(i) %></td>
<% Next %>
</tr>
```

This code presents a While loop that continues until the end of the recordset retrieved by the SQL query. It pulls out, using a For loop, each row in your database (in this case, the individual names and birthdays you stored in the database table).

6. Enter the following ASP code into Dreamweaver:

```
<%
RS.MoveNext
Loop
RS.Close
Conn.Close
%>
</table>
```

This code tells ASP to continue looping through the recordset object until all information gathered by the SQL query has been displayed. Then the ASP code closes the recordset and connection objects, saving memory.

> **NOTE**
>
> You'll notice from this ASP example that some languages are a lot more verbose than others. For example, to do the preceding in PHP would have required about one-third the amount of code. Does this mean that PHP is inherently better than ASP? No, not necessarily, although some language purists might use this kind of comparison to state their case for a favorite development language. You have to remember that a language is no better or worse than any other. The only way a language should be judged is if you can learn it quickly and if it allows you to do the things you need to do.

7. Save the file as test.asp and place it in your Web server's docroot folder.

8. You can test this file by pointing your browser at the file. The file should display the contents of your dsntest.mdb table.

Summary

This chapter has covered a lot of ground. We've discussed setting up Web servers, middleware software, and database backends—including DSNs for fast retrieval of ODBC data.

Although these subjects might seem very daunting at first, you can be sure that a little bit of experience setting up Web servers, databases, and middleware will give you lots of insight into the nuts and bolts of how Web applications work.

## CHAPTER 18

Dreamweaver MX for Application Development

by Matthew Pizzi

In the previous chapters, you learned how you can use Dreamweaver MX to create Web applications, and you looked at the possibility of managing dynamic data. The chapters also laid some groundwork for setting a Web server that is prepared to serve these application pages containing server-side scripts.

To build a successful application, as you can probably tell from the previous two chapters, certain parameters must be set up and defined. After having a working application server, you must also have an established connection between the pages you create in Dreamweaver and the database you want to send and retrieve data from.

The middleware you want to use determines how you open communication with the database. Dreamweaver MX supports a variety of connections from a standard DSN (Data Source Name) to other more advanced connections, such as OLE DB.

After you've established which connection you'll be using, you'll then have the capability to query the different tables in the database through Structured Query Language (SQL), which is covered in greater detail in Chapter 27, "SQL Primer." These queries in Dreamweaver are often called *recordsets*.

Create a Connection with a Data Source Name

To send or retrieve data from a data source, you must open a connection with that data source through Dreamweaver. The first type of connection you'll be connecting to is called a Data Source Name, or DSN. Data sources come in different formats, such as graphics files. A database created by Access is a different type of file than a database created by Oracle or FileMaker Pro. To offer a variety of applications to access different data sources, the Open Database Connectivity standard was developed. Open Database Connectivity, commonly referred to as ODBC, is a universal language that all databases speak. With the appropriate drivers installed for the particular database, the application has the capability to read and write information to and from the database.

Windows systems already have the appropriate drivers installed for Access, SQL Server, dBase, Oracle, FoxPro, Excel, and Paradox. If you're developing with a Macintosh, you will normally connect to the ODBC driver that resides on the testing server.

One of the great things about ODBC is that it simplifies the process of moving the database from the testing server to the actual application/Web server. Just as a domain name is an alias for an IP address—for example, www.trainsimple.com is an alias for 206.234.12.23—the DSN is an alias or nickname for the actual location of the data source.

A negative to using a DSN is that they're generally less efficient than other standards when connecting to data sources. However, they are probably more than adequate for low-to-moderate production servers. If you're developing a more robust application, you may want to consider some of the other methods discussed later in this chapter. If you plan to develop a Web application with ASP.NET or PHP, they will not support DSNs and you must use an alternative connection standard.

DSNs, however, are great to use—especially in the development phase of the application. On a Windows machine, DSNs are managed though the ODBC Data Source Administrator. Remotely, DSNs are managed and configured by the systems administrator.

To configure a DSN on a Windows 2000 or a Windows XP system, follow these steps:

1. From the Start menu choose Control Panel. This opens the Control Panel folder.

2. Inside the Control Panel folder, double-click the Administrative Tools folder to open it.

3. Inside the Administrative Tools folder, double-click the Data Sources (ODBC) icon. This launches the ODBC Data Source Administrator dialog box as shown in Figure 18.1.

4. In the ODBC Data Source Administrator, click the System tab. The System tab lists all DSNs previously configured on your system.

5. Click the Add button under the System DSN tab to open the New Data Source dialog box, as shown in Figure 18.2.

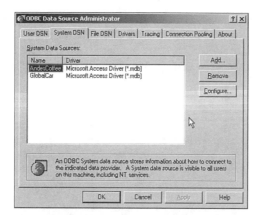

FIGURE 18.1   The ODBC Data Source Administrator dialog box offers options for managing and configuring data sources.

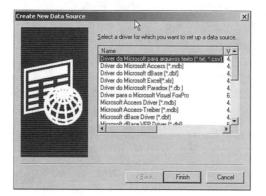

FIGURE 18.2   The New Data Source dialog box provides the options for choosing the appropriate driver for the database that the data source will point to.

6. In the New Data Source dialog box, choose from the list of drivers that match the database that you are working with. If the driver for your database is not found in this dialog box, visit the manufacturer's Web site to download the appropriate driver.

When you find the driver, select it and click the Finish button to exit the New Data Source dialog box and launch the ODBC Setup dialog box, as shown in Figure 18.3.

7. Specify a name for the data source. Avoid spacing and special characters in your naming conventions.

8. Provide the appropriate path of the data source; each database has slightly different requirements:

For an Access database, click the Select button to open a dialog box that enables you to search your hard drive for the database. It's very important that the database is

18

located in the hard drive directory. When you find the database in the hard drive, it will automatically appear on the left side. All databases found within that directory will appear; choose the one you want the data source to use and click Select. If you need to provide a username and password to access the database, click the Advanced tab to provide that information.

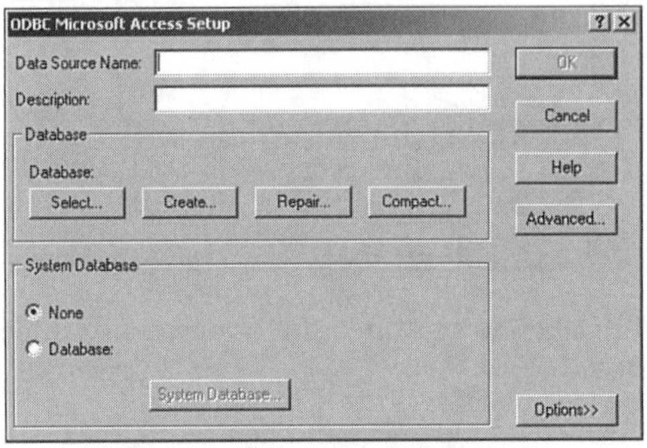

FIGURE 18.3   In the ODBC setup dialog box, you have the option to provide a name and description for the data source.

For an Excel spreadsheet, the process is the same; however, you must select the appropriate Excel workbook. Select options to limit the numbers of rows and columns accessed.

With SQL Server, select the name from the server drop-down list. If your computer is acting as the server, choose Local and click Finish.

For a MySQL database, enter the MySQL hostname or IP address and the entire path to the MySQL database. You can also enter a username and password in the same screen, if necessary. The MySQL ODBC driver also offers a host of features that you can enable or disable.

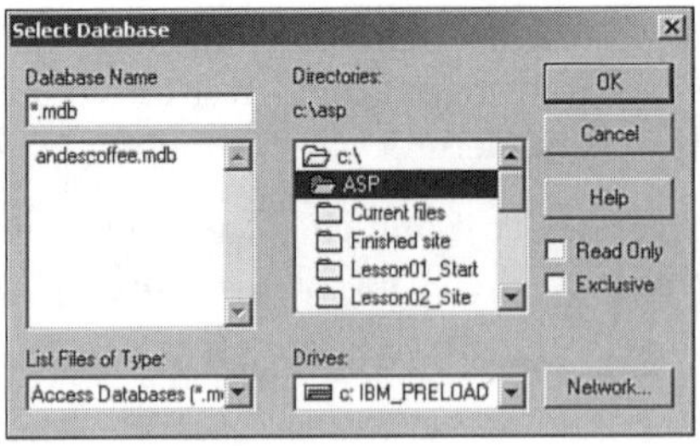

FIGURE 18.4   In the Select Database dialog box, select the database you want to use for the data source.

9. When you've finished the ODBC setup, you can click OK in the remaining dialog box to exit the setup.

After you've set up a DSN, you're ready to connect with it through Dreamweaver. After you've established a connection with your DSN through ODBC, you can start the Web application development process.

Connections for ASP

We'll first review how to establish a connection with an ODBC DSN in Dreamweaver MX for ASP. When teaching Web application development, I often tell my students that ASP is one of the most convenient middlewares to develop with if you're developing on the Windows platform. Although the procedures are similar for the different server models that you may choose to use, it is beneficial to look at them step-by-step because the variations between the server models warrants that we do so.

To establish a connection with the DSN, follow these steps:

1. Be sure to have the Application panel open. If the Database tab is not visible, choose Window, Databases. This will open the Applications panel as shown in Figure 18.5.

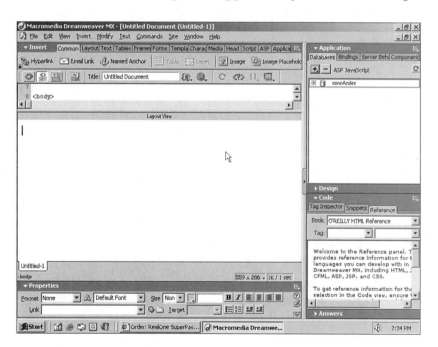

FIGURE 18.5   The Database panel enables you to configure the connection between Dreamweaver and the DSN.

2. In the Database panel, click the Add button (+) to access the drop-down menu. In the drop-down menu, choose Data Source Name (DSN) to launch the Data Source Name dialog box as shown in Figure 18.6.

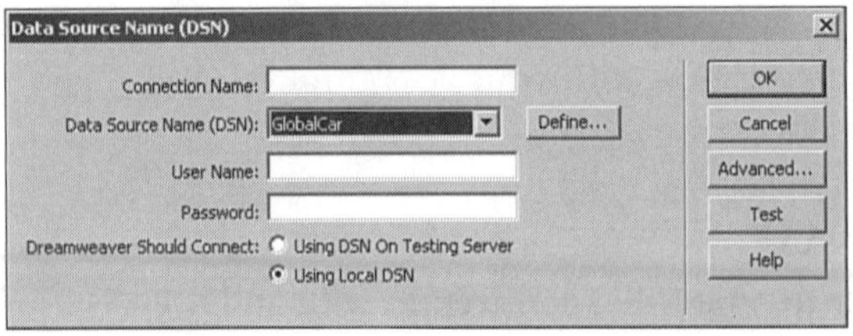

FIGURE 18.6   The Data Source Name dialog box offers the option to configure the data source connection.

3. The first option is to determine whether you're using the DSN on the testing server or on your local machine. If you're using the DSN on the testing server, choose the Dreamweaver Should Connect Using DSN On Testing Server option; otherwise, you should choose Using Local DSN. If you're developing on a Macintosh, you will have to use the DSN on the testing server.

4. Enter a name for the connection. It's good to add the prefix conn and avoid spacing in your naming conventions. For example, a name could look something like this: connGlobal. The reason for this is that it will stand out in the code, making it easier to debug.

5. If you're defining a local DSN, choose the name or option from the Data Source Name (DSN) drop-down menu.

   If you're defining a DSN on the remote server, enter the name of the DSN.

6. If required, enter a username and password into the appropriate fields.

7. Some databases allow you to limit the number of database items available in a single connection. To limit the available tables, click the Advanced button. Here you can enter the desired Schema or Catalog.

8. To make sure your connection is established properly, click the Test button. This launches an alert message specifying that the connection was made successfully. If the connection was not made successfully, double-check the naming convention of the DSN and be sure that the database file wasn't moved to a different directory.

9. After you've made a successful connection, click the OK button. Notice that the new connection is available through the Connections dialog box.

10. Click the Done button to exit the Connections dialog box.

As you can see, establishing communication between the DSN and Dreamweaver is pretty straightforward; however, it is a crucial component of authoring Web applications. As I mentioned earlier, the process can vary slightly, depending on which type of middleware you plan to use. Therefore, in the next sections, we'll review the same process for ColdFusion and JSP.

Connections for ColdFusion

The ColdFusion Administrator integrates with the ODBC Data Source Administrator to use the DSNs already configured on the system that you are working with. You also have the option of creating new DSNs right within the ColdFusion Administrator.

After establishing a new DSN in either the ODBC Data Source Administrator, as reviewed earlier, or through the ColdFusion Administrator, follow these steps to create a connection between Dreamweaver MX and the DSN:

1. Open the Database panel by choosing Window, Database. In the Database panel, click the Modify Data Source button, as shown in Figure 18.7.

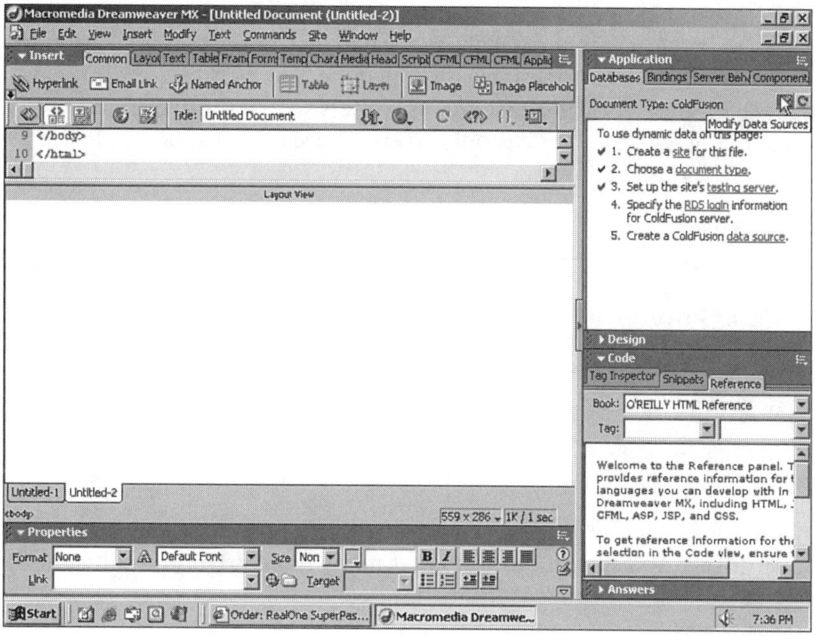

FIGURE 18.7   Choose Modify Data Source from the Database panel to open the ColdFusion Administration page.

2. After you choose Modify Data Source, the ColdFusion Administration page will open.

3. On the ColdFusion Administrator home page, choose ODBC from the Data Sources category.

4. On the ODBC data sources page, choose the appropriate driver for the database you are using from the drop-down menu. Click the Add button when finished.

5. Enter the name of the DSN in the data source field. Enter the path to the database in the Database File field, or click the Browse button to search for the database on the hard drive. If required, enter a username and password.

6. When you're happy with your settings, click the Create button. ColdFusion will create and verify the DSN, making it a visible option in the ODBC Data Source page.

As you can see, the process for setting up a DSN connection for ColdFusion varies slightly from its ASP counterpart; however, the process is just as easy, but ultimately a bit more reliable.

Connections for JSP

As you might assume, JSP uses the JDBC (Java Database Connectivity), in contrast to ODBC. Therefore, the process for establishing a connection between Dreamweaver and the Data Source is a bit different. Dreamweaver MX offers six JDBC drivers, plus an additional option for installing additional or custom drivers. The six drivers included with Dreamweaver MX are the following:

- MySQL Driver

- Sun JDBC-ODBC Driver

- Oracle Thin Driver

- I-net Driver for SQL Server

- IBM DB 2 App Driver

- IBM DB 2 Net Driver

The list that follows provides examples of what the syntax might look like for the three most popular drivers. You should be aware that many more drivers for different databases are available at Sun Microsystem's Web site, located at
`http://java.sun.com/products/jdbc/drivers`.

Sun JDBC-ODBC Bridge

- **Supports**   Any ODBC-compliant driver.

- **Driver Field Parameters**   sun.jdbc.odbc.JdbcOdbcDriver.

- **URL Field Parameters**   jdbc:odbc:DSN_Name (substitute the DSN_Name with actual name of DSN).

Oracle Thin JDBC Driver

- **Supports**   Oracle databases.

- **Driver Field Parameters**   oracle.jdbc.driver.OrcaleDriver.

- **URL Field Parameters**   jdbc:oracle:thin:@server_name:database_port:SID
  (replace @server_name with actual server and switch the database_port with actual
  port number).

I-net JDBC Driver

- **Supports**   SQL Server databases.

- **Driver Field Parameters**   com.inet.tds.TdsDriver.

- **URL Field Parameters**   jdbc:inetdae:server_name:database_port?database=
  database_name (replace server_name with actual server name, replace database_port
  with actual port number, and replace the last data_base name with the actual name
  of the database).

When downloading additional drivers, be aware of the robustness of the different types of
drivers. There are Type 1 drivers, which are the earliest implementations of the standard
and the least robust. The types of drivers work their way up to Type 4; Type 4 drivers are
native Java applications and are the most robust. Whenever possible, try to download
Type 4 drivers.

To establish a connection in Dreamweaver MX with JSP, follow these steps:

1. Make sure the Database panel is visible. Choose Window, Database to open the
   panel.

2. Click the Add (+) button to access the drop-down menu. In the drop-down menu,
   select the driver of your choice to launch a dialog box. In Figure 18.8, for example,
   the Oracle Thin JDBC driver has been chosen.

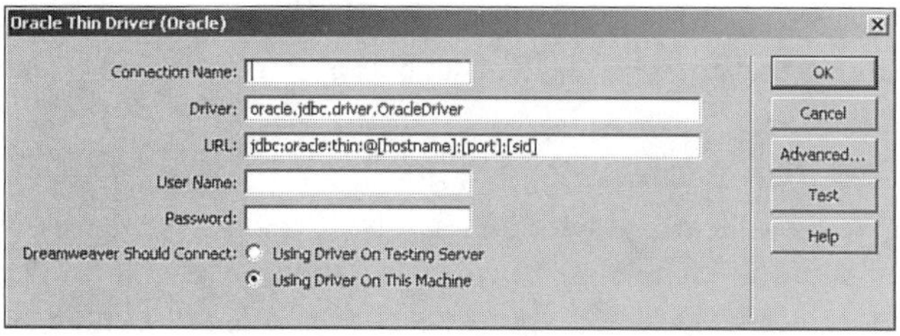

FIGURE 18.8   Each JSP driver offers options in brackets indicating data you need to specify.

3. If you're creating a connection on a testing server, choose Using Driver on Test Server Options; otherwise choose the Using Driver on This Machine.

4. If you're creating a custom connection, be sure to enter the driver name in the driver field, as specified by the manufacturer of the driver.

5. Give the connection a name. Remember, it's good to use the conn prefix for the name and avoid spacing in your naming conventions.

6. If you're using one of the standard drivers, replace the information in the brackets with the proper information about your hostname and database name.

7. If required, enter a username and password into their respective fields.

8. If you want to limit the available tables, click the Advanced button. Here, if the database supports it, you can specify the desired Schema or Catalog.

9. With all those settings in place click the Test button to make sure the connection was made successfully.

10. After the connection has been verified, click the OK button to return to the Connections dialog box.

11. In the Connections dialog box, notice that the new JSP connection you just established is available. Click Done to exit the Connections dialog box.

We will review connections settings for the other two server models that Dreamweaver offers development with ASP.NET and PHP. However, it's important to note that ASP.NET does not support DSNs, and PHP's server model in Dreamweaver MX offers support only for MySQL connections through its own ODBC drivers.

Custom Connection Strings

As you can see, it's quite simple to set up a DSN connection. As mentioned earlier, however, it's not the most robust option. With Dreamweaver MX, you have two choices for creating custom strings: a DSN-less connection and an OLE DB connection.

A connection string contains the name of the driver, the path to the data source, and any additional information that may be needed, such as a username and password.

DSN-less Connection with ASP

When developing Web applications with DSNs, one of the big hassles can be getting the system administrator of the Web server to configure the DSN if you don't have access to that area of the server. If you can't get your DSN configured, your application is then crippled and useless.

Often, developers like to bypass such ordeals by creating a DSN-less connection. With a DSN-less connection, there is no need for such actions to be taken by system administrators.

A DSN-less connection uses the same drivers as its DSN counterpart; however, the DSN-less connection does not rely on a defined Data Source Name.

The syntax for configuring a DSN-less varies a bit from database to database, but all have the same five essential parts:

- **Driver**   The proper name for the driver can be found at the manufacturer's Web site or locally in your machine's ODBC Administrator.

- **Path to Data Source**   Depending on the database that you are using, you normally will specify the entire path to the database. This is called the DBQ. However, some databases provide an exception, such as SQL Server and Oracle. The parameter for these databases appears in two parts: an area for both the server name and the database name.

- **User Name**   If a username is required by the data source, you must provide it in the string. This part is often abbreviated in the connections string as UID.

- **Password**   If a password is required by the data source, you must provide it in the string. This part is often abbreviated in the connections string as PWD.

- **Provider**   This is an optional entry, but it refers to the mechanics of the ODBC driver application. The provider for ODBC will always be MSDASQL. Because these two elements go hand in hand, if it is omitted, the connection string will still work.

If you had an Access database called trainsimple.mdb, and you wanted to make a DSN-less connection through a custom string, the string would look like the following:

```
Provider=MSDASQL; Driver={Microsoft Access Driver (*.mdb)} ;
DBQ=c:\training\data\trainsimple.mdb; UID=matthewp; PWD=vangogh2;
```

You can easily swap out the driver if you were using a SQL Server database.

To create a DSN-less connection in Dreamweaver, follow these steps:

1. Be sure the Database panel is open by choosing Window, Database.

2. Click the Add (+) button and choose Custom String from the drop-down menu. This launches the Custom String dialog box, as shown in Figure 18.9.

3. Enter a name for the connection. Remember, it's good practice to add the conn prefix so that it's easier to find the connection in the code when debugging.

4. Type in the connection string as reviewed previously in the Connection String field.

18

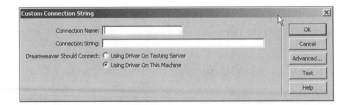

FIGURE 18.9   The Custom String dialog box offers options for creating a custom connection string.

5. If you're creating a connection for a testing server, choose that option; otherwise, choose Using Driver on This Machine.

6. If your database permits it, you can limit the available tables. To do this, click the Advanced button. Here you can enter the desired Schema or Catalog.

7. To make sure your connection was set up properly, click the Test button. This should return an Alert Message saying that the connection was made successfully.

8. Click OK to exit the Custom Connection String dialog box. Notice that the connection is now available in the Database panel.

Connections for ASP.NET with OLE DB

As you discovered in the previous section, a DSN-less connection does not require an actual Data Source Name. However, DSN-less connections do rely on the actual ODBC drivers. ODBC itself is a translator that relies on OLE DB to make the connection. A more efficient way to communicate with the database is directly through the OLE DB.

An OLE DB connection looks similar to a custom connection string. The exception is that only the Provider parameter, and not the Driver parameter, is included. Here's what a OLE DB connection string would look like, based on a Microsoft Access database called train-simple.mdb:

```
Provider=Microsoft.Jet.OLE DB 4.0;
Data Source= c:\training\data\trainsimple.mdb;
```

ASP.NET requires you to use an OLE DB connection, and Dreamweaver MX makes the process simple.

To create an OLE DB connection for ASP.NET in Dreamweaver MX, follow these steps:

1. Make sure the Database panel is open by choosing Window, Database.

2. Click the Add (+) button and choose OLE DB for the type of connection from the drop-down menu. The OLE DB Connection dialog box appears, as shown in Figure 18.10.

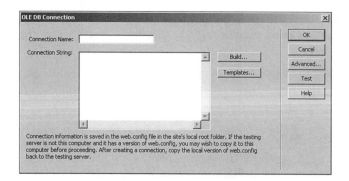

FIGURE 18.10   The OLE DB dialog box offers a large area for you to type in a custom connection string.

3. Provide a name for the connection. Remember to use the prefix conn so that it's easier to identify the connection in the code when debugging. Avoid spaces in your naming conventions.

4. Type a complete connection string into the Connection String text field. If you want to avoid typing in the connection string, manually click the Build button (Windows only). This launches the dialog box shown in Figure 18.11 and completes each of the tabs with the required information.

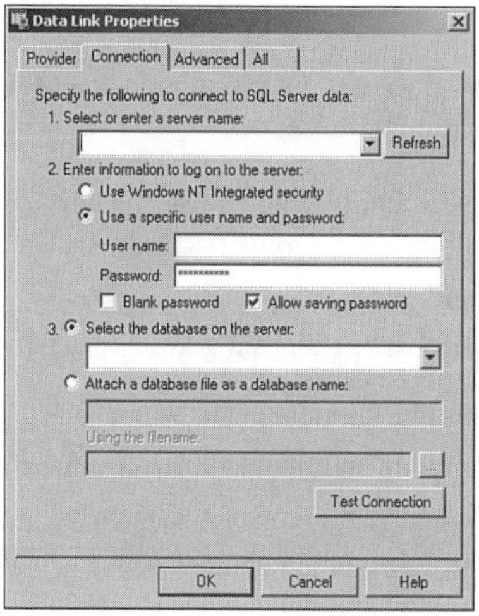

FIGURE 18.11   The Data Link dialog box offers an easier way to create complicated connection strings.

5. To make sure the connection was properly configured, click the Test button. Dreamweaver will open an alert message informing you whether the connection was a success or not.

6. When you're done, click OK to exit the OLE DB Connection dialog box. When you return to the Database panel, notice that the new connection is available.

Connections for PHP

Dreamweaver MX's PHP server model supports only MySQL connections. To create a connection with MySQL in Dreamweaver, follow these steps:

1. Make sure the Database panel is open by choosing Window, Database.

2. Click the Add (+) button and choose MySQL Connection from the options in the drop-down menu. This opens the MySQL Connection dialog box, as shown in Figure 18.12.

FIGURE 18.12 Complete the requested information in the MySQL Connection dialog box to establish a connection with the database.

3. Name the new connection. Remember to use the conn prefix in your naming convention for easier debugging; avoid spacing in your naming conventions, as well.

4. Enter in the IP address or domain name of your MySQL server. If you're running the server locally on your machine, there's a good chance the domain will be localhost.

5. Specify the database username in the username text field.

6. Specify the database password in the password text field.

7. Type the name of the database into the Database field or click the Select button and choose from a list of options.

8. To make sure the connection was properly configured, click the Test button. Dreamweaver will open an alert dialog box indicating whether the connection was made successfully.

9. Click OK to exit the MySQL Connection dialog box. Notice the connection ID now available in the database panel.

Summary

As you can see, Dreamweaver MX offers several options for different types of databases. The server model you're using for your application development determines which of these connections is best suited for your particular project.

Remember that if you need specific drivers for a database that you're using, visit the manufacturer's Web site and the necessary information should be available for you to obtain the proper software.

18

PART V

Behaviors and Middleware

IN THIS PART

CHAPTER 19

Behaviors

by Matthew Pizzi

In many cases, you may want to add functionality to your Web page. Often, Web developers will use the famous pop-out window or even make layers appear and disappear. What's great about these behaviors is that Dreamweaver writes all the JavaScript to make these behaviors happen. This can be a tremendous help to those not wanting to learn JavaScript and a time-saver for those who do know it.

What's important to know about behaviors is that they're canned JavaScript snippets of code. They do what they do—nothing more and nothing less. If you know JavaScript, you can modify and tweak to your heart's content; however, if you don't know JavaScript, this may be a source of frustration for you.

For the most part, the behaviors available to you are practical for real-world applications. You might find that you want to accomplish something that isn't offered by the behaviors and will be forced to write the JavaScript yourself. If you find that there is quite a bit you want to accomplish and there is no way to do it through the Behaviors panel, learning JavaScript may be a worthwhile investment.

Before you jump to any conclusions about the value of behaviors, let's take a look in detail at what they really have to offer. To open the Behaviors panel, choose Window, Behaviors.

Something you should know about behaviors is they have to be applied to a specified <tag>. Whether it's the <body> or <a> anchor tag, it must be attached to some form of an HTML tag. Which tag you should attach the behavior to depends on what your desired effect is, in terms of how the behavior is triggered.

As shown in Figure 19.1, you also have to specify a target browser when applying a behavior. Your best bet, in terms of options and compatibility, is to choose 4.0 or Later Browsers. This offers a broader range of events to activate the JavaScript, or behavior. If you choose 3.0 Browsers, the results between different browsers and different operating systems are unpredictable.

By choosing 4.0 and Later Browsers, you ensure compatibility with the majority of the Web audience. However, the behaviors are still a bit finicky when you're trying to achieve complete cross-browser and cross-platform compatibility.

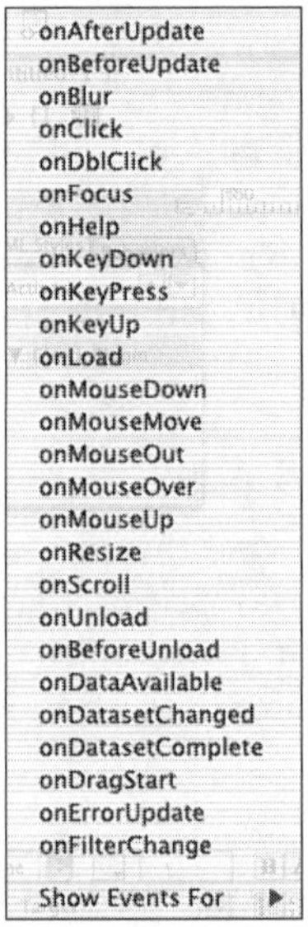

FIGURE 19.1   Notice all the different events when 4.0 or Later Browser is selected in the Event drop-down menu of the Behaviors panel.

If you refer to Figure 19.2, you'll note all the different behaviors available to you. You can even build your own or download additional behaviors from the Macromedia Exchange. As I mentioned earlier, if there's something specific you want to perform and you don't want to invest the time in learning JavaScript, you may have some luck on the Exchange, located at `http://www.macromedia.com/dreamweaver/exchange`.

You'll notice that some of the behaviors are grayed out and not available. The reason for that is you don't have the proper content, either on the document or selected, as you click the plus sign button to see the behaviors. Some behaviors can be attached, or applied, only to specific tags.

FIGURE 19.2   Different behaviors that ship with Dreamweaver MX can add functionality to your Web pages.

Attaching Behaviors

Applying a behavior is quite simple. Although some vary a bit, the general rule is to follow these steps:

1. Select either an object or a tag inside the Dreamweaver document. If you want to apply the behavior to the entire page, make sure you select the <body> tag. If you want to apply the behavior to text, you must make the text a hyperlink. The easiest way to do that is to place a pound (#) sign in the Link text field of the Properties Inspector.

2. Open the Behaviors panel by choosing Window, Behaviors. In Figure 19.3, the Behaviors panel has the selected tag that you're applying the behavior to in the top of the panel.

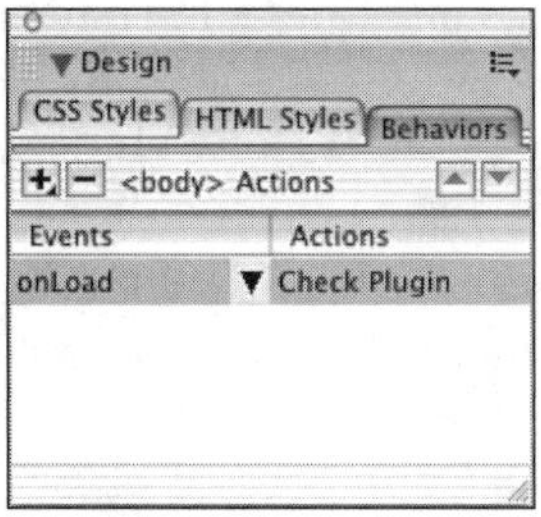

FIGURE 19.3   The tag that is selected in the document that you are applying the behavior to appears in the top of the panel.

3. Click the Add Behavior (+) button and choose from the list the behavior you want to apply. Typically, this launches a dialog box.

4. Enter the parameters in the dialog box and choose OK. This applies the action to the selected object.

5. After you apply a behavior, you can choose what event you want to trigger the behavior. Click the down arrow after the event to get a list of different events.

That's the general way to apply a behavior. However, the parameters from one behavior to another can vary dramatically. In this chapter, we'll deconstruct the different parameters for each behavior and I'll give a practical example why you might use some of these behaviors.

Open Browser Window

This is one of the most practical behaviors, and it's the one students in my Dreamweaver classes seem to like the most. To create a pop-out window, much like the annoying ads that pop up when you're on the Web, you must have an HTML document to open in the new window that's going to pop-up. In this example, the pop-up window will pop open when the page first loads.

To create a pop-up window, follow these steps:

1. Make sure you're working in a defined site. Create a new basic HTML document.

2. In the new document, add any content that you want to appear in the pop-up window. Title the document in the Title text field of the document.

3. Save this document by choosing File, Save As. Save this as pop_out.html. Take note of the document's visible dimensions.

4. Create a new document. In this document add any content you want. After adding content (which is optional for this example) open the Behaviors panel by choosing Window, Behaviors.

5. Highlight the <body> tag in the Tag Inspector located in the bottom-left corner of the document.

6. With the <body> tag selected, click the Add Behavior (+) button in the Behaviors panel and choose Open Browser Window in the drop-down menu. This launches the Open Browser Window dialog box, as shown in Figure 19.4.

Typically the trick with popping up new browser windows is to make them look less like a browser window and more like a traditional window in an operating system. For example, look at this ad from Orbitz in Figure 19.5. It doesn't resemble a browser window very much.

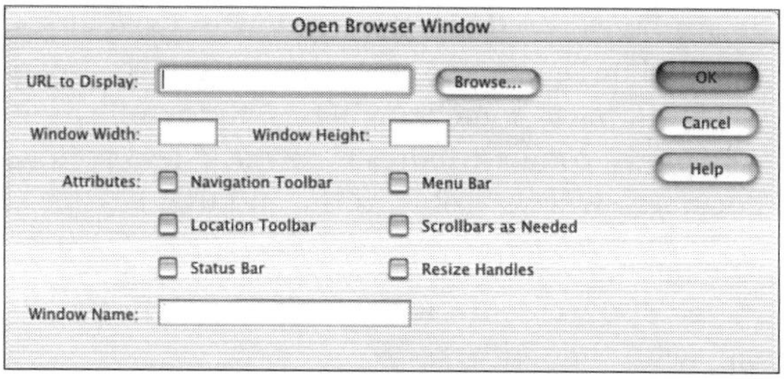

FIGURE 19.4   The Open Browser Window dialog box offers several parameter options for determining the appearance of the new browser window.

FIGURE 19.5   This pop-up window by Orbitz doesn't have many browser window attributes, such as location and navigation bars.

1. When setting the parameters, you must keep in mind how you want the window to appear. The first option is sourcing the HTML document you want to appear in the pop-up window. You can do that either by typing in the name and path of the page or clicking the Browse button and searching for it.

2. Next, you must specify the dimensions. As I said in step 3 of the previous exercise, when the sourced HTML document is open, you can get the dimensions from the bottom, as shown in Figure 19.6. Use these dimensions for the Window Width and Window Height text fields.

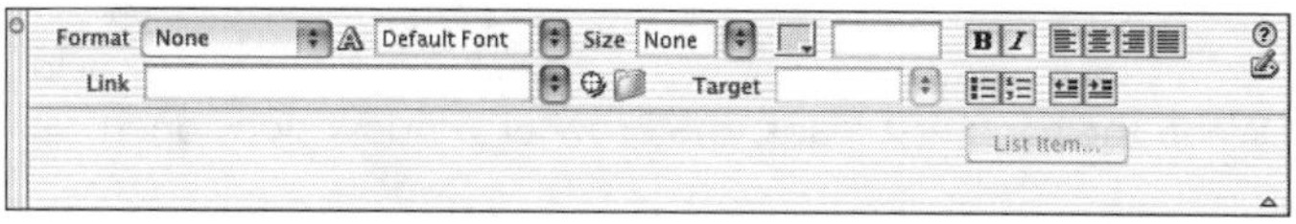

FIGURE 19.6   The dimensions are displayed at the bottom of the document window.

3. Check any of the attributes you'd like the window to have. If you want a look similar to the Orbitz ad in Figure 19.5, you wouldn't select any of these attributes. Typically, if you want to select some parameters, the Scrollbars as needed and resize handles are usually pretty good attributes to select. These options ensure that all the content in the document will be visible to the end user.

4. Finally, you must name the Window. Avoid spacing and special characters in your naming conventions. The JavaScript will use this name in the function. Choose OK when you're happy with the settings.

5. After you return to the document, check the Behaviors panel and make sure the event is set to onLoad. If onLoad is not available, make sure you're viewing events for at least 4.0 and later browsers. If it's still not available, make sure you had the <body> tag selected when you attached the behavior.

6. Preview the document in a browser. After the page loads, the browser window pops open, as shown in Figure 19.7.

7. Save this document as trigger.html.

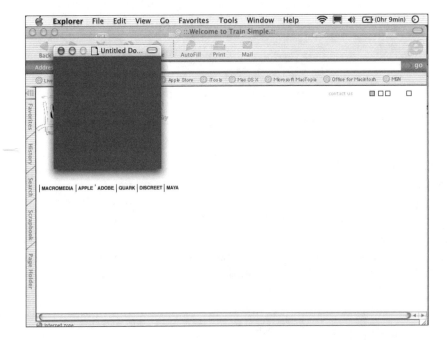

FIGURE 19.7   When the page first loads, the browser window pops open.

You can also highlight <a> anchor tags and have the behavior happen when someone clicks a link. This is just one example of how to use the Open Browser Window behavior.

Calling JavaScript

This behavior enables you to insert simple JavaScript or to call and communicate with JavaScript functions. Of course, this is no good if you don't know JavaScript, but it can be helpful if you pick some JavaScript code and you're sure where to place it within the HTML.

In the previous example, you created a pop-up window. A common element you find in most pop-up windows is a close button. To create one of these Close buttons, you must insert the JavaScript yourself because no behavior is built in to Dreamweaver to deal with this.

Creating a Close button is simple. Follow these steps to learn how to make your own Close button:

1. Open the pop_out.html document that you created in the previous example.

2. Create a Close button graphic in your favorite image-editing program, or visit the companion Web site at `http://www.dreamweavermxunleashed.com` and download close.gif.

3. In the pop_out.html document, place a blinking cursor where you want the Close button to appear. Choose Insert, Image and navigate your hard drive to find the Close button graphic. When you find it, choose OK.

4. With the graphic in the document, select it, and in the Behaviors panel click the Add Behavior (+) button. In the drop-down menu choose Call JavaScript. This opens the Call JavaScript dialog box as shown in Figure 19.8.

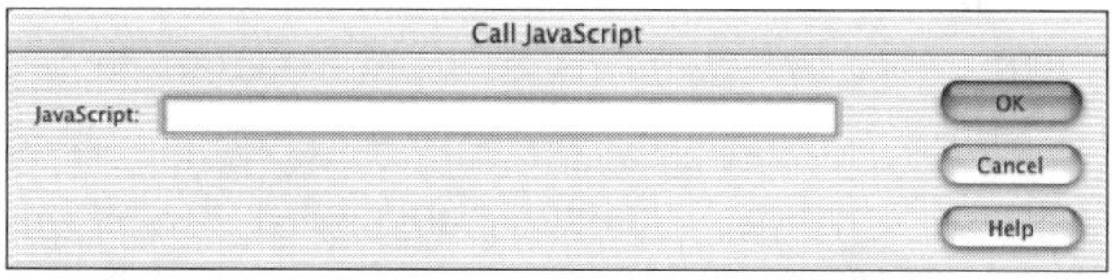

FIGURE 19.8   The Call JavaScript dialog box has a text field in which you can type JavaScript code.

5. In the text field, you need to type in the JavaScript that will close the window. The script is quite simple. In the text field, type **window.close ()**. After you type that script, choose OK.

6. Dreamweaver automatically places the JavaScript in the head portion for the HTML document and hyperlinks the selected button to call that script. Save the document by choosing File, Save.

7. Open trigger.html and preview it in the browser. When the page first loads, the pop-up window appears, this time with a Close button. Click the Close button and the pop-up window will close.

The call JavaScript behavior can be used for a variety of scripts, but this should give you a working example of why you might want to use this behavior in real-world development.

Change Property

This behavior allows you to dynamically change attributes of the following tags:

```
<layer> <div> <form> <textarea> <span> <img> <select>
```

You can also alter the `<input>` tags different types such as:

```
radio checkbox text and password
```

The properties that can be altered vary from tag to tag. You might have a variety of reasons why you would consider changing the properties of an object, and in this example, we'll go through the necessary steps to make that happen.

To apply the Change Property behavior, follow these steps:

1. Create a new document and save it. Save this document as change.html.

2. You need to add an element to the document to change and something to trigger that change. Let's change the background color of a layer. Choose Insert, Layer to place a layer within the document.

3. Select the layer and name it **box** in the Properties Inspector. When you're working with behaviors, it's very important to name all your objects.

4. Next, type the word **Change**. After typing the word, select it, and in the Properties Inspector type a pound (#) sign into the Link text field. This surrounds the text with an anchor tag. Remember, behaviors get attached to certain tags, and the anchor tag is one of them.

5. With the text selected, open the Behaviors panel. Click the Add Behavior (+) button and choose Change Property from the drop-down menu. This launches the Change Property dialog box as shown in Figure 19.9.

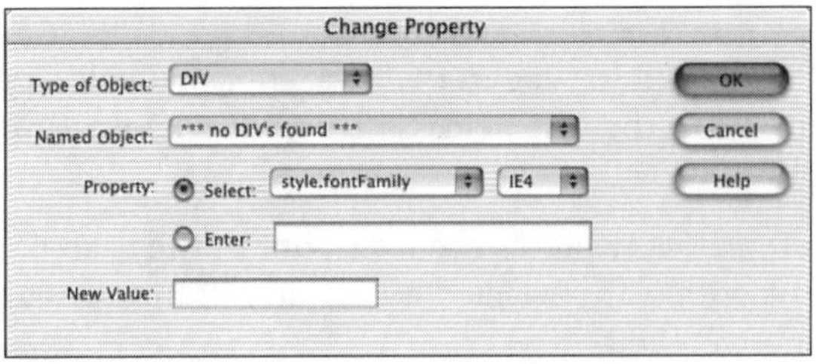

FIGURE 19.9   Choose an object for which you would like to change the property in this dialog box.

6. You'll notice the first option of the dialog box is a drop-down menu to choose the object you want to change. You're more or less selecting a tag in this drop-down menu. Because you want to change the background color of the layer, choose DIV in the drop-down menu.

7. The next option offers all the named <div> elements in your document. Select Box.

8. In the Property section, choose the Select radio button, and in the drop-down menu to the right of the radio buttons, choose style.backgroundColor.

9. In the next drop-down menu, choose the target browser. In this case, I'm going to choose Internet Explorer 4.

10. In the New Value text field, type in the hexadecimal value, such as #336699.

11. Choose OK, and preview the page in the browser. After you click Change Hyperlink, the layer's background color will change.

This is just one example showing how you can use the Change Property behavior. As you can see from different options in the drop-down menus, there's plenty this behavior can offer. If this behavior is a key component in your Web site, be sure to test it in a variety of browsers and operating systems.

Check Browser

Common practice in Web development is to make a variety of pages, intended for users using different browser versions. The Check Browser behavior allows you to check what the end user is using for a browser and redirect the user to the appropriate page.

As you can see in Figure 19.10, there are several options for redirecting the user to different pages.

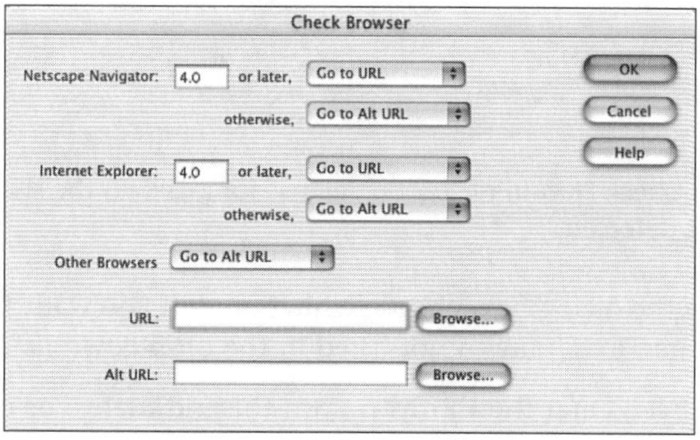

FIGURE 19.10   The Check Browser behavior is ideal for catering to a broader audience of browsers and platforms.

Toward the bottom of the dialog box, you can set two URLs—a default and an alternate. Above that, you can set the browser versions to check for both Netscape and Internet Explorer. Depending on which browser the end user has, you can either direct the user to the URL or Alt URL.

Normally, you would attach this behavior to the body tag, so choose onLoad and you'll be able to check to see what browser version the end user has.

This behavior is best used when checking for 4.0 browsers. If you need to check for a 3.0 browser, the behavior isn't compatible with Internet Explorer 3 on the Macintosh.

Check Plug-In

This behavior is similar to the Check Browser behavior. With this behavior, it's possible to check whether end users have the plug-in installed on their systems. If the plug-in is detected, you send the users to a specified page. If it's not found, you can direct them to an alternate page.

You can check for various plug-ins, such as QuickTime, Flash, Shockwave, LiveAudio, and Windows Media Player. Often, when using plug-ins to deliver content, developers create two versions of the same page—one that uses the plug-in and one that doesn't.

Although this behavior does not check for specific ActiveX controls, with the way that Dreamweaver writes code between the <embed> and <object> tags, in most cases it can still determine whether the end user has the appropriate application. As you can see in Figure 19.11, the dialog box is similar to that of the Check Browser dialog box.

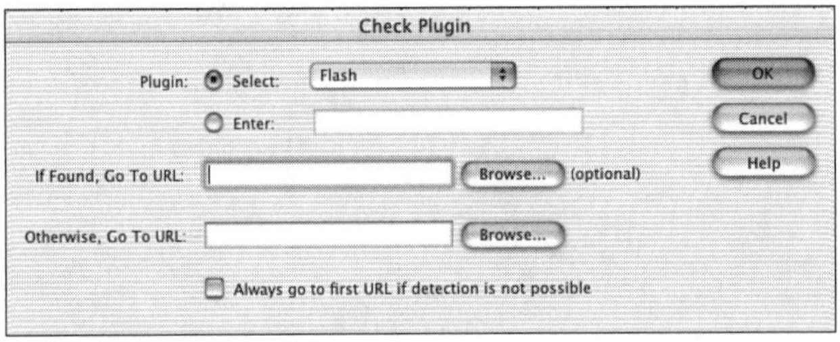

FIGURE 19.11   The Check Plug-In dialog box allows for a URL in the situation of the plug-in being detected or not detected.

In the top portion of the dialog box, choose which plug-in you want to detect. Use the Enter text field to search for a plug-in not listed in the drop-down list.

In the If Found text field, enter the URL you want the end user to be directed to. You can either type in a relative or absolute URL, or you can click the Browse button and search for a page within your local root folder.

In the Otherwise text field, do the same by entering in a URL; however, this page should be the page that does not require the plug-in for the end user to see and get information from.

Drag Layer

The Drag Layer behavior offers the capability to create high-impact interactivity with the end user. The downside is that it doesn't work well in a variety of browsers. However, if you believe that you cater to a tech-savvy group, the chances of them using a dated browser shouldn't be of much concern. The flip side is that if the people visiting your site are general users of the Internet, they probably don't care about the latest browsers and may be content using an older version of Internet Explorer or Netscape.

Again, it all comes down to your target audience. Develop with them in mind, and if you think that something like the Drag Layers behavior will enhance their experience, it probably will. There is no right or wrong answer; only you can determine if it's appropriate.

The Drag Layer behavior allows for the layer to be dragged in several ways. These are the types of effects you can have with the Drag Layer behavior:

- Drag the layer anywhere in the document.

- Restrict dragging to a particular direction based on the x,y coordinate you specify.

- Drag only a portion of the layer.

- Change the stacking order of the z-index.

- Specify a drop target and have the layer snap to that target if it is within a specified snapping pixel radius.

Setting up a Drag Layer behavior is pretty painless. However, some of the options may be a bit confusing, but if you walk through this exercise step-by-step, it will make more sense. Before moving on, it's important that you have a good understanding about how layers work. Refer to Chapter 11, "Layers in Dreamweaver," to learn more about them.

Creating a Draggable Layer

In this exercise, you're going to create a layer that you'll be able to drag all over the document. When the layer, as it's being dragged, reaches a certain point and you release the mouse, we'll make sure that the layer snaps into place.

1. Create a new basic HTML document. Choose File, Save As and save it as drag.html.

2. Next, choose Insert, Layer. This will place a layer in your document. After the layer has been inserted, select it in the Properties Inspector and name it **drag**.

3. Place a blinking cursor inside the layer and choose Insert, Image. Insert an image of your choice.

4. After you place an image in the layer, draw another layer on the opposite side of the document. Select this new layer and in the Properties Inspector, name it **target**.

5. Also, in the Properties Inspector, write down on a piece of paper the Left and Top coordinates. You'll use these values in a moment to specify the drop target.

6. The final step in creating the target layer is to set its z-index to a very high value. This way it will always appear on top. In the Z-Index option in the Properties Inspector, enter in a value of **1000**.

7. You're now ready to attach the Drag Layer behavior to the first layer, drag. With the drag layer selected, open the Behaviors panel and click the Add Behavior (+) button. Choose the Drag Layer behavior. This will open the Drag Layer dialog box, as shown in Figure 19.12.

8. In the first drop-down menu, choose the drag layer, because this is the layer you want the end user to be able to drag.

9. For Movement, choose Unconstrained. This will allow the end user to freely drag the layer all over the document. If you choose Constrained, you must specify the coordinates in which you want the layer to be constrained.

10. For the Drop Target option, enter in the Left and Top coordinates you took from the target layer.

11. There is also an option for Snap Within. The value you enter here represents pixels. The default is set to 50, which means if the layer that is being dragged is released within 50 pixels of the target layer, it will snap to the top and left coordinates you specified in step 9. If you leave this option empty, the snap feature will be disabled.

12. Click the Advanced tab. For the Drag Handle option, choose entire layer, which means the end user can drag this layer from any point.

13. Check the option to bring the layer to the front while dragging. However, after the end user releases the layer, you want it to appear behind the target layer. Earlier you specified a z-index of 1000 for the target layer, and the drag layer has a z-index of 1. In the drop-down menu, choose Restore Z-Index. This places the drag layer back to its original value of 1, which is less than 1000, so when the end user releases the mouse it will appear as if the layer went inside the target layer.

14. Choose OK. When you return to the document, preview it in a browser. Notice that you can drag the layer all over the document, and if you release it close enough to the target layer, it automatically snaps into place and disappears behind the target layer.

Practical applications for the Drag Layer behavior include things such as games, learning interactions, and interactivity with the end user.

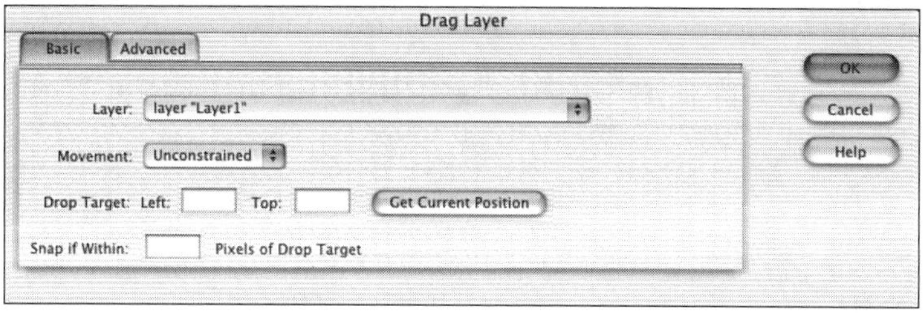

FIGURE 9.12   The Drag Layer dialog box offers a Basic tab and an Advanced tab.

Go to URL

The Go to URL behavior is essentially the same thing as creating hyperlinks. However, the Go to URL behavior offers a bit more flexibility.

A common task for the Go to URL behavior is to hyperlink two pages to open in two different frames in a frameset. Notice in Figure 9.13 that you not only have the option of specifying a link, but you also have the capability to target different frames.

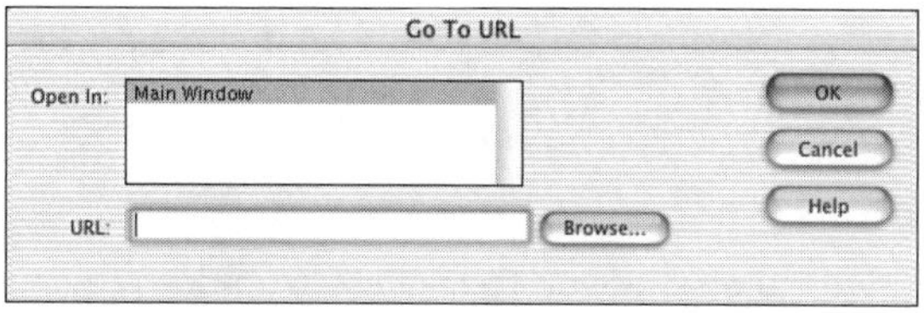

FIGURE 9.13   The Go to URL dialog box offers an option to create a link and target a frame for which that link should appear.

To target two frames with the same link, follow these steps:

1. Highlight the object that you want to apply the behavior to. If it's text, be sure to place a pound (#) sign in the Link text field of the Properties Inspector to surround the text with an anchor tag.

2. In the Behaviors panel, click the Add Behavior (+) button. In the drop-down menu choose Go to URL. This will launch the Go to URL dialog box.

3. Highlight which frame you'd like this linked page to open in.

4. Either type in a path or browse your hard drive for a file. An asterisk appears next to the frame this link will open in.

5. Choose OK to return to the document.

6. To apply another link to the same object, repeat steps 1 through 5.

Jump Menu

A jump menu offers a compact way to a navigation system to your site. It behaves much like a drop-down menu; however, when an option is selected, it opens a link based on the selection.

Many sites will use these jump menus to save space. If you have several link options available to your viewer, but have no way of including all that link information in the designated area, a jump menu could be a nice alternative. As you can see in Figure 19.14, the jump menu offers several link features. Refer to Chapter 6, "HTML Forms," to see how to set up a jump menu and to learn how to interact with them.

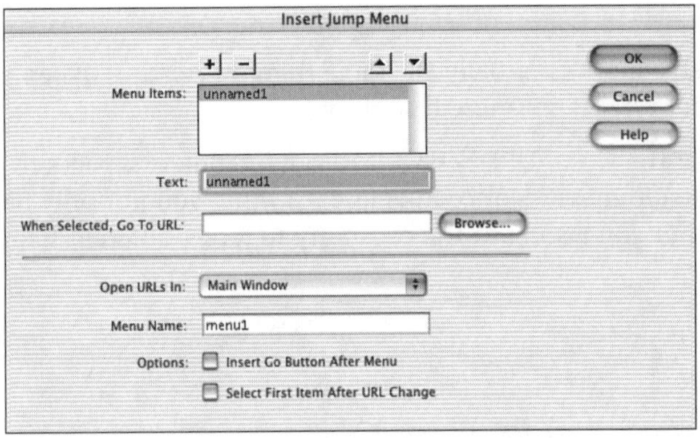

FIGURE 19.14   A jump menu enables you to create a drop-down menu, with each option linking to a different page or Web site.

Play Sound

The Play Sound behavior is designed to attach a sound to your document to play hidden in the background. The browser will generally use the Netscape LiveAudio plug-in or Microsoft's Windows Media Player.

To apply the Play Sound behavior, follow these steps.

1. Highlight whichever object you want to trigger the behavior in the document. Typically the sound will play in the background and will start playing on load. If this is the desired effect, highlight the <body> tag in the Tag Inspector.

2. In the Behaviors panel, click the Add Behavior (+) button and choose Play Sound from the drop-down menu. This opens the Play Sound dialog box, as pictured in Figure 19.15.

3. Press the Browse button and search for a file in one of the following file formats: WAV, MID, AU, and AIFF.

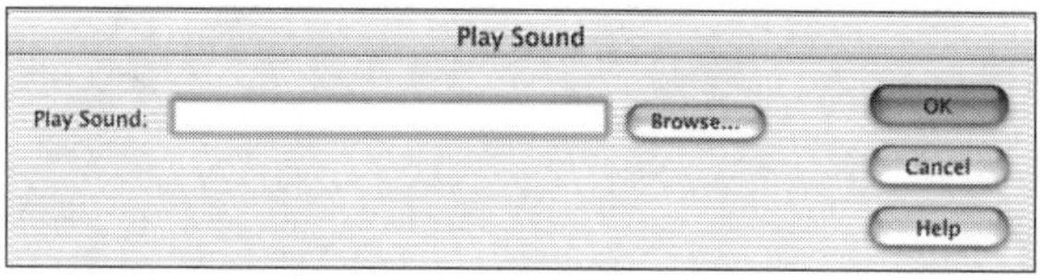

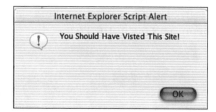

FIGURE 19.15 In the Play Sound dialog box, you can enter the location of the sound you want to play.

4. After you've found the file, click OK. You will return to the document.

5. Preview the document in a browser, and notice that after the page loads, the audio file starts playing in the background.

Dreamweaver uses the `<embed>` tag, and if you look in the code, you'll notice some attributes are also applied. You can change these attributes to better serve your desired effect. The attributes are `loop=false`, `autostart=false`, `mastersound`, `hidden=true`, `width=0`, `height=0`.

If you are a Mac user and you're using Internet Explorer, the sound may pop open in a new window for the QuickTime Player to play the sound. If you want to use this behavior, keep in mind that this will happen on occasion with the Mac.

Pop-Up Message

You can have an object within your document trigger an alert message window through the use of JavaScript. An alert message is a small dialog box that pops up in the middle of the screen, as shown in Figure 19.16.

FIGURE 19.16 An alert message is a small dialog box that appears in the middle of the screen after something triggers it to pop open.

To add the Pop-up Message behavior, follow these steps:

1. Highlight whatever object in the document you want to trigger the Pop-up Message behavior.

2. In the Behaviors panel, click the Add Behavior (+) button and from the drop-down menu choose Pop-up Message; this opens the Pop-up Message dialog box, as shown in Figure 19.17.

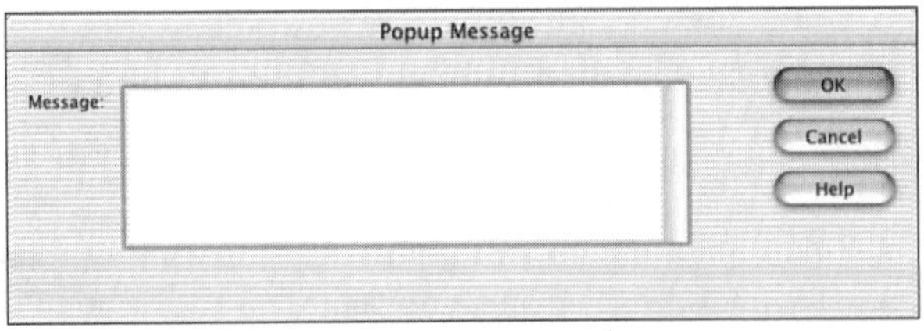

FIGURE 19.17 Type in whatever message you want to appear in the Pop-up Message window when it opens, based on the highlighted object you set as the trigger.

3. Type in any message. This is the message that will populate the alert window.

4. Click OK when you're done. You will return to the document. Preview this page in a browser and notice that after you click the trigger, the Pop-up window alerts you with the message you typed into the Pop-up Message dialog box.

Preload Images

Images that are dependent on other behaviors are often best if preloaded. For example, if you have a rollover graphic, you would want the over state image of the button to be loaded before the event actually took place. If it wasn't loaded, the up state would swap out with a graphic that wasn't there, causing a broken image link to appear.

However, if you preloaded the rollover image, the behavior would be deactivated until that image was present and loaded. Typically, you'll add the Preload Images behavior to the <body> tag. To attach the Preload Images behavior, follow these steps:

1. Select the <body> tag in the Tag Inspector.

2. In the Behaviors panel, click the Add Behavior (+) button. Choose Preload Images from the drop-down menu. This opens the Preload Images dialog box, as shown in Figure 19.18.

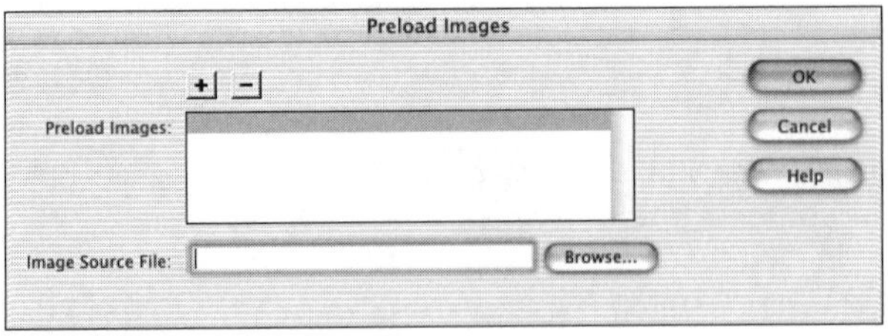

FIGURE 19.18 The Preload Images dialog box enables you to specify which image(s) you'd like to preload.

3. Click the Browse button to search for an image you'd like to preload.

4. Click the plus sign to add additional images to the behavior.

5. If you decide you'd like to remove one you've added, click the minus sign button.

6. When you're done, click OK.

Set Nav Bar Image

This behavior enables you to create a navigational system using a variety of states and buttons. The Set Nav Bar dialog box, as shown in Figure 19.19, is identical to the Set Nav Bar command found in the Insert panel and menu.

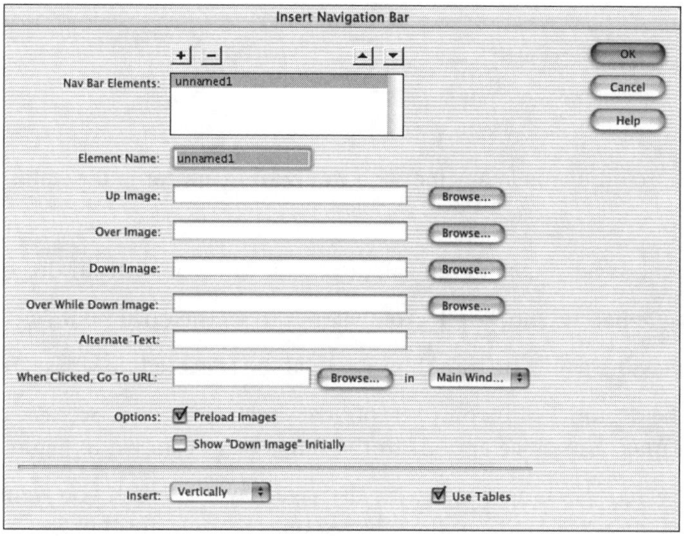

FIGURE 19.19   The Set Nav Bar dialog box has several options for creating multiple buttons with up to four states.

To learn more about the Nav Bar and how to use it, refer to Chapter 4, "Dreamweaver MX Essentials."

Set Text

The Set Text behavior has four subheadings. Each works in a very similar manner, but some of the options are more specific to what you're trying to set the text to. The four subheadings are

- Set Text of Frame
- Set Text of Layer

- Set Text of Status Bar

- Set Text of Text Field

In this example, you're going to set the text of the status bar. The status bar is located in the bottom-left corner of the browser window. To set the text of the status bar, follow these steps:

1. Highlight whatever object you want to trigger this behavior.

2. In the Behaviors panel, click the Add Behavior (+) button and choose Set Text, Set Text of Status Bar. This opens the Set Text of Status Bar dialog box, as shown in Figure 19.20.

FIGURE 19.20   You can type in any message you want to appear in the status bar of the browser window.

3. Type in a message; you can even call JavaScript functions within this dialog box.

4. When you're happy, choose OK. You will return to the document.

5. In the Behaviors panel, be sure this event will be triggered onMouseOver.

6. Preview the document in a browser; notice when you mouse over the object you selected earlier, a message appears in the status bar, as shown in Figure 19.21.

7. However, when you mouse away, the message stays visible. If you want it to disappear as you mouse away from the selected object, apply another Set Text to Status Bar behavior and leave the text field blank in the dialog box. After you choose OK, be sure the event in the Behaviors panel is set onMouseOut.

The other Set Text behaviors work in a similar way, but offer the option of setting the text to a frame, a layer, or even a text field.

NOTE

Refer to the companion Web site located at `http://www.dreamweavermxunleashed.com` to see some QuickTime movies further illustrating the features of the Set Text behavior.

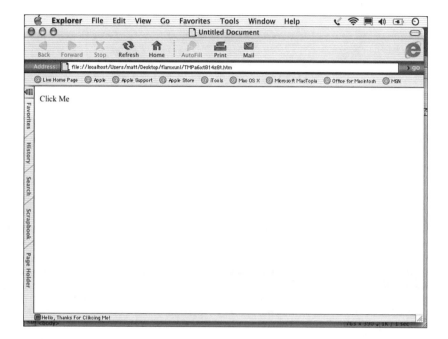

FIGURE 19.21 The status bar reveals the message you typed in step 3.

Show-Hide Layers

A great advantage of layers is that they're part of DHTML. With that, they have the capability to be hidden or visible. With JavaScript, or in Dreamweaver's case—behaviors, you can dynamically turn the visibility of a layer on or off.

To apply the Show-Hide layer behavior, follow these steps:

1. Select the object in your document that you want to trigger the behavior.

2. Make sure all the layers in your document are named. You can name each layer in the Properties Inspector.

3. In the Behaviors panel, click the Add Behavior (+) button. In the drop-down menu, choose Show-Hide Layers. This opens the Show-Hide Layers dialog box, as shown in Figure 19.22.

4. To reveal a hidden layer, highlight the name of the layer you want to show and click the Show button.

5. To hide a visible layer, highlight the name of the layer you want to hide and click the Hide button.

19

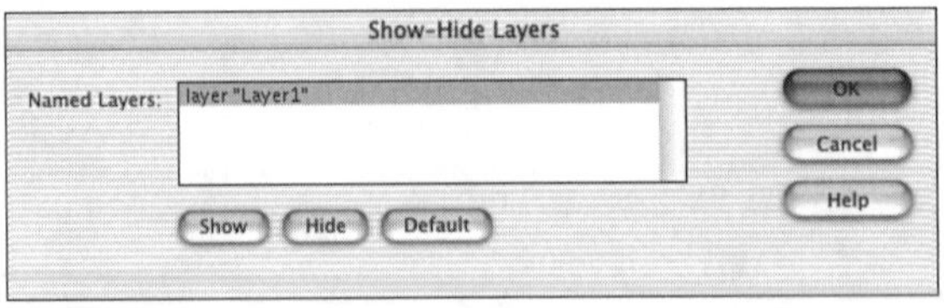

FIGURE 19.22   The Show-Hide layer dialog box offers the option of turning the visibility of the specified layers on or off.

6. To set a layer's default visibility value, click the Default button.

7. When you're happy with the setting, click OK to return to the document.

Using Show-Hide layers can add a great deal of functionality and interactivity to your pages.

> **NOTE**
>
> Refer to the companion Web site located at http://www.dreamweavermxunleashed.com to see some QuickTime movies further illustrating the power of the Show-Hide layers behavior.

Show Pop-Out Menu

A drop-down or pop-out menu is a popular way to create navigational systems within Web sites. The problem with them generally is getting them to work properly both in Netscape and Internet Explorer.

This commonly requires complex JavaScript code. However, a new feature in Dreamweaver MX offers the capability to create a drop-down menu with ease. It's called the Show Pop-Out Menu behavior, which is covered step-by-step in Chapter 1, "What's New in Dreamweaver MX."

Swap Image/Swap Image Restore

Disjointed rollovers are a popular trick in Web development. A disjointed rollover is when the end user mouses over one item and triggers something else within the document to change. It is much like a traditional rollover except that the rollover image is placed in a location other than the same location as the button.

In Figure 19.23, the Swap Image dialog box offers the option of highlighting any named image within your document and setting its image source to another file when you click the Browse button.

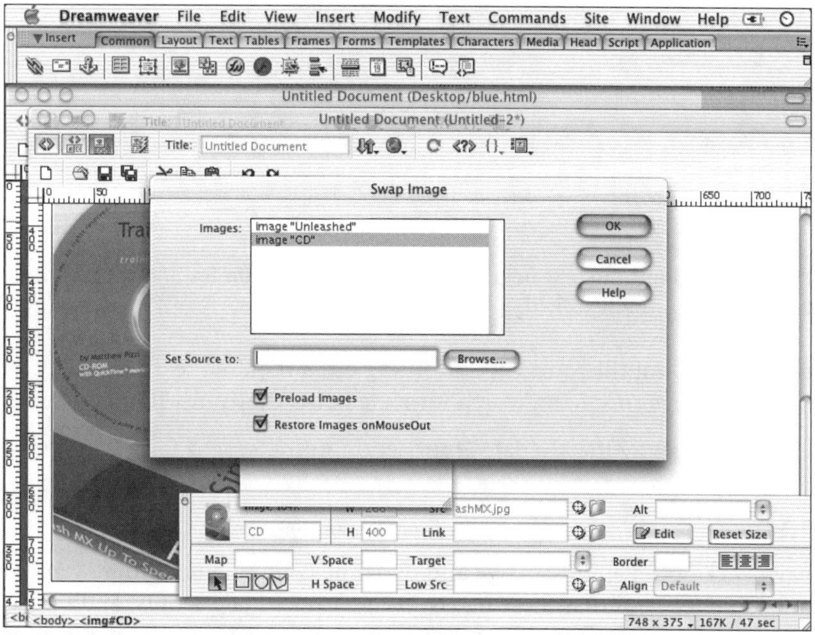

FIGURE 19.23   In the Swap-Image dialog box, you can set the source of the selected image.

WARNING

When using the Swap Image behavior, be sure to name all images in the Properties Inspector; this is the only way you'll be able to identify what image you're swapping out.

Validate Form

The Validate Form behavior enables you to require certain form elements to be filled out by the end user. You can specify that text fields must contain data.

Furthermore, you can specify what type of data you're looking for. You can ask for a numeric value, which would be appropriate for a ZIP Code or phone number text field. You can also ask for an email address, which will detect the @ sign in data entered into the field.

You can also require any data by checking off the Required check box in the Validate Form dialog box, as shown in Figure 19.24.

Unfortunately, you cannot require the end user to answer questions that use radio buttons, check boxes, drop-down menus, or select boxes.

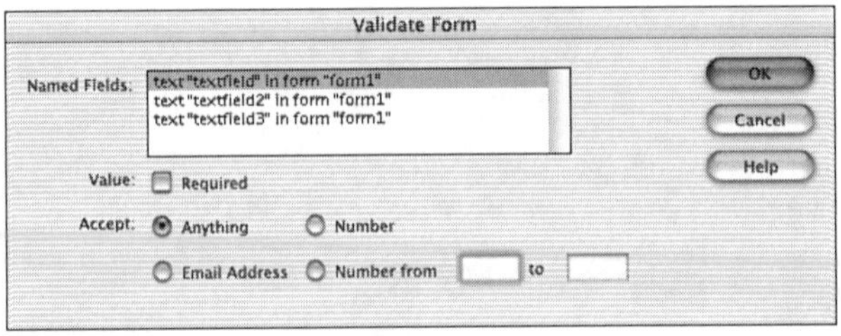

FIGURE 19.24   Highlight the text field you want to require data for and specify what type of data must be present in the text field.

If end users try to submit the form without filling out a required text field, they will receive an alert message specifying which form elements they must fill out.

You would normally apply the Validate Form action to the <form> tag.

Summary

Using behaviors can offer an interactive and dynamic component to your Web designs. It is important to understand that these behaviors are canned JavaScripts, and to get full compatibility, you must tweak the JavaScript code by hand. This sometimes can be a source of frustration for developers, but it's always a good idea to get a little JavaScript under your belt.

If you want to learn more about JavaScript and you're new to programming, I recommend picking up *The Book of JavaScript*, published by No Starch Press and written by me!

## CHAPTER 20

Extending Dreamweaver MX

By Zak Ruvalcaba

The beauty in Dreamweaver does not lie solely in the fact that you can build high-scale Web sites and applications; it also lies in its interface. Interface, you ask? Dreamweaver, unlike many applications on the market today that force you to purchase costly third-party extensions and work in the rigid menu-driven environment that they provide, allows for complete customization and control by you, the user. A relatively new concept in software development, Dreamweaver MX, along with its predecessors, was developed with user workflow and task achievement in mind, regardless of how you prefer to work.

Because Dreamweaver MX was built on a JavaScript/HTML foundation, all menus, dialog boxes, objects, and commands are completely customizable with just a little knowledge of JavaScript, HTML, and XML. This chapter focuses on extending Dreamweaver MX's IDE by allowing you to customize your workflow and produce the following:

- Custom objects
- Custom behaviors
- New menu items
- Your own public extensions

Working with Objects

Part of Macromedia's customization initiative are objects. Objects are HTML files that use JavaScript to insert a string of HTML code into the user's workspace. As you may have already noticed, Dreamweaver MX comes installed with a host of predeveloped objects, completely ready for you to take advantage of. Everything ranging from tables to frames, forms to head content, and scripts to characters, objects make adding code to your workspace as easy as clicking a button. That code can be anything from this:

```
©Copyright Zak Ruvalcaba, 2002
```

to this:

```
<font face="arial" size="3">&copy;Copyright Zak Ruvalcaba, 2002</font>
```

Anything that can be constructed using HTML can be customized through the use of an object.

Understanding Objects

As previously mentioned, Dreamweaver MX comes preinstalled with ready-to-use objects. Those objects, like most of Dreamweaver MX's configuration files, are located within the Configuration folder of the program directory. Within that folder you can navigate to and open the Objects folder. As shown in Figure 20.1, the Objects folder contains a list of subfolders corresponding to the specific tab within the Objects panel.

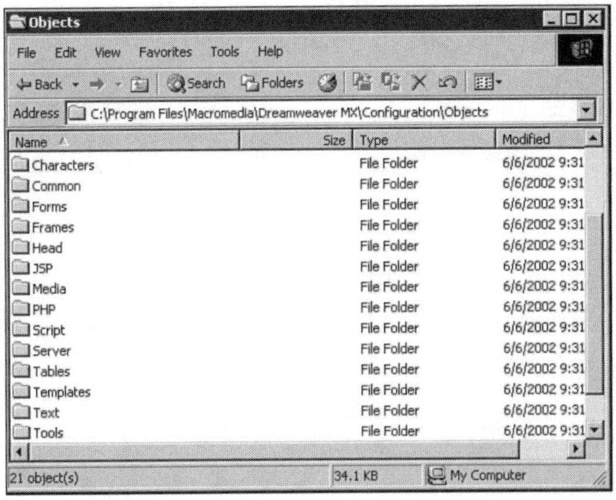

FIGURE 20.1   The Objects folder contains all the objects as they relate to the Objects panel.

As you add folders, more tabs are added to the Objects panel. Within the sections are three files that compose the structure of an object. They are:

- **The HTML file**   The HTML file is the front end for what the object will do. It contains all the code that the object will insert into the user's workspace.

- **The JavaScript file**   The JavaScript file contains all the client logic that the HTML page will use when the button is pressed from the Objects panel. It is optional to use the JavaScript file because the code could be contained within the <head> tag of the HTML file. A separate JavaScript file is always easier to maintain in the long run.

- **The Image file**   The Image file is a standard GIF image that you can customize and place within your Custom Objects folder. The GIF image is typically named the same as the HTML and JavaScript file and is what appears under the tab in the Objects panel. A default GIF image (generic.gif, located in the root of the Objects folder) is available for you to customize using your favorite image editor.

Figure 20.2 shows the Text folder along with the three files that correspond to each object.

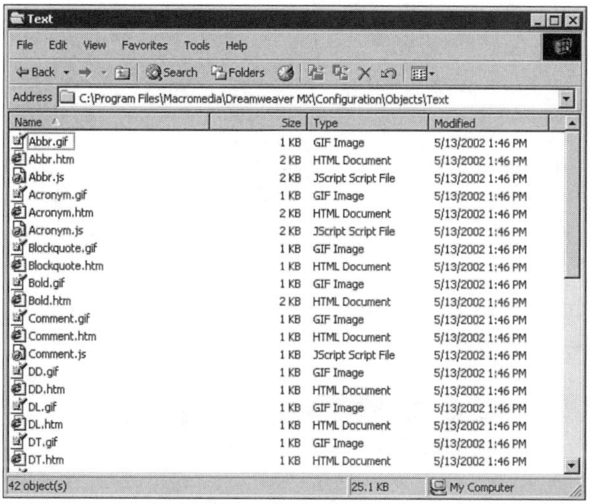

FIGURE 20.2   Opening the Text folder reveals the three files that belong to each object.

Dreamweaver MX objects range from fairly simple to complex. You can make it so that when users click the Object button, it inserts plain HTML text, or you can make it so that when users click the Object button, it prompts them with a dialog box allowing them to input data. Either way, objects streamline the way you interface with the IDE.

> **TIP**
>
> An integrated development environment (IDE) is a programming environment that has been created as an application program, typically consisting of a code editor, a debugger, and an interface builder.

Objects are composed of five key elements; they are

- **The Files**   Generally, objects consist of an HTML page, an image file, and an external .js file that contains all the client logic. It is completely possible to combine the HTML page with the .js file into one HTML page. This is the preferred method.

20

- **Location**   Objects reside in their corresponding folder within the Objects folder. Depending on which tab you want your object in, you simply move all the files to that folder.

- **Page Title**   The page title is the name of the object as it appears when your mouse rolls over the corresponding image.

- **objectTag() function**   The objectTag() function returns the value of what is to be inserted into the page.

- **User Interface**   The user interface (UI) resides within the <body> tag of the object and generally uses a <form> tag along with a textbox control to capture user input.

The Simple <sup> Tag Object

Now that you have a basic understanding of how objects are constructed, let's put that idea to work by creating a simple object that inserts the <sup> tag into your code.

If you've worked with special characters (the copyright symbol, for instance), you know that whenever they are inserted, they always end up looking like part of the text rather than superscripted to the top of the line. To alleviate that problem, a simple object could be created. Follow these steps:

1. Begin by making a copy of generic.gif (located in the root of the Objects folder) and place it into the Text folder. Rename the GIF sup.gif.

> **NOTE**
>
> The <sup> tag is a text-level formatting element and is the reason why it is placed into the Text folder.

2. Next create a new HTML document in Dreamweaver and write the following code:

```
<html>
<head>
<title>SUP</title>
<script language="JavaScript">
function objectTag() {
return "<sup></sup>";
}
</script>
</head>
<body>
</body>
</html>
```

3. Save the file into the Text folder, naming it sup.htm.

4. Navigate to the Text tab and select your new object. Figure 20.3 shows how in code view the object will insert the correct tags that you specified within the objectTag() function.

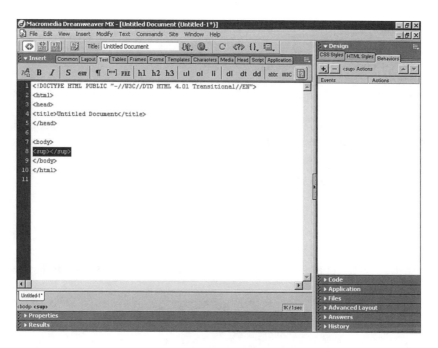

FIGURE 20.3   Selecting the new object will insert the appropriate tags.

NOTE

Restarting Dreamweaver MX forces the Object panel to reload all its objects. If you make any changes to any of the objects, you must restart Dreamweaver MX before the changes will take effect.

The Advanced <sup> Tag Object

After you've gotten past the excitement of creating your first object, you'll quickly find that the object does no more than insert a simple tag into the body of the document. Even if you wanted to place some text within that tag, it would still be necessary to switch to code view and type it in; by that time, the whole tag could have been written.

The power behind customized objects lies in the fact that they can receive user input. By simply modifying the body tag to contain some HTML code that defines the UI, this can be accomplished:

1. Open sup.htm and rewrite the <body> tag to contain the following code:

```
<body>
<form name="supForm">
<p>What text would you like to Superscript?</p>
<p><input type="text" size="3" name="supText"></p>
</form>
</body>
```

2. Next, modify the objectTag() function so that it concatenates the value of the text box to the opening and closing <sup> tags:

```
function objectTag() {
var supText = document.supForm.supText.value;
return '<sup>' + supText + '</sup>';
}
```

3. Save the file again, and close and then restart Dreamweaver MX.

4. Select the sup object again to produce a result similar to that shown in Figure 20.4.

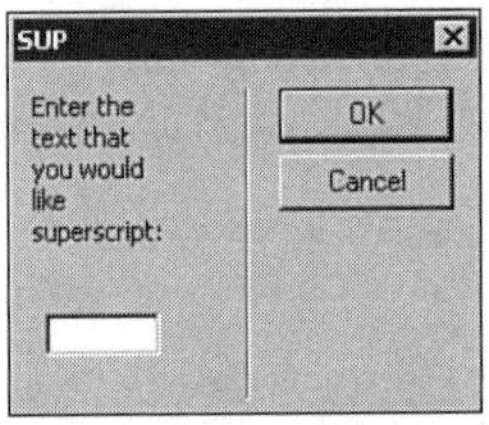

FIGURE 20.4   Selecting the new object launches a dialog box allowing you to enter custom text to superscript.

Working with Behaviors

In the previous chapter you became familiar with some of the prewritten JavaScript capabilities that Dreamweaver MX offers. You were able to manipulate your application to include client-side logic that was already developed for you. But what if you need to accomplish a task that isn't on the list of preinstalled behaviors? Would you be out of luck? The answer is no!

Because of Dreamweaver MX's customizable behaviors list, behaviors can be created and removed just as easily as they are added to your workspace. You know how to use behaviors and may even know a little about how they work, but understanding how to create custom behaviors lies first in understanding what a behavior is and what it is composed of.

A behavior is a chunk of code that gets inserted into your working environment when you select it from the Behaviors panel list. Instead of adding plain HTML code, a behavior generally inserts JavaScript code, complete with an event and a resulting action.

> **TIP**
>
> An event is what causes the action to happen. For instance, when you click a form's Submit button, you expect the results to be sent to a specific location. The event for the button press could be called an onClick event.

Behaviors are composed of API procedures and functions, which, in essence, allow you to insert exactly what you want into your workspace.

> **TIP**
>
> API stands for Application Programming Interface. They are the building blocks for programs, and they are what developers program against in almost all software development environments.

From your experience with behaviors thus far, you should surmise that behaviors do the following:

- Behaviors create two chunks of code—a function that performs the action you have created and a function call from the object that you have inserted.

- Behaviors generally allow you to edit them by double-clicking the Behaviors panel. You'll notice that when you double-click in the Behaviors panel, the original values that you inserted still appear.

- Behaviors should allow you to choose their event handler when making the function call.

Understanding Behaviors

Like most software applications, Dreamweaver MX has a standard procedure for how it handles plug-ins. In this case, Dreamweaver MX is handling much more than a simple plug-in; it's handling code that you write and customize for multiple people to use. Imagine the complexity. In this case, however, it's not all that complex if you can remember some basic elements that compose the location and structure of a typical Dreamweaver MX behavior:

- **The File**   For the most part, behaviors consist of an HTML page as the user interface and an external .js file that contains the code that is to be processed. It is completely possible to develop everything within one HTML page.

- **Location**   Behaviors reside in the Actions folder, which resides within the Dreamweaver MX directory. The full path usually reads: C:\Program Files\ Macromedia\Dreamweaver MX\Configuration\Behaviors\Actions. If you navigate within the directory, you will notice that the names of the files resemble the names of the behaviors within the behaviors list. Adding a folder in the directory creates a submenu within the behavior list. Figure 20.5 shows the comparison between the files in the directory and the behaviors within the behaviors list.

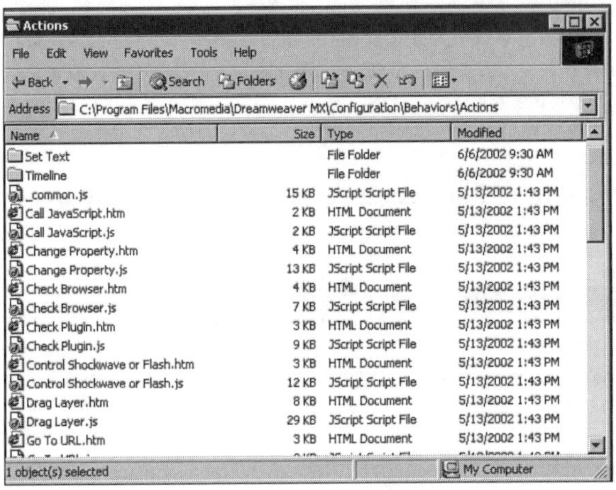

FIGURE 20.5   The Actions folder contains all the behaviors that are exposed within the behaviors list.

- **Page Title**   The page title is the name of the behavior as it appears in the behaviors list.

- **Defined Function**   The defined function is the code that will be inserted into your document.

- **BehaviorFunction() function**   The behaviorFunction() function is part of the Dreamweaver API and is required typically just below the defined function. The behaviorFunction() function simply returns the name of the defined function without the parentheses.

- **applyBehavior() function**   Also part of the Dreamweaver API, the applyBehavior() function returns the name of the function that is to be inserted into the workspace environment.

- **User Interface**   The user interface is what the person selecting the behavior will see when selecting the behavior from the list. Typically, when creating custom behaviors, you would want people to enter some sort of value that is in turn passed on to the defined function. The UI resides within the <body> tag of the HTML page.

The Simple Resizer Behavior

To understand how a behavior works is to illustrate how they are written. The key elements that make up a behavior have been introduced to you, now it's just a matter of putting them together.

Begin by navigating to the Dreamweaver MX Behaviors folder and create a new folder called Custom Behaviors, as shown in Figure 20.6. Remember, by creating a folder within the Actions folder, you are effectively creating a submenu to store other behaviors within the behavior list.

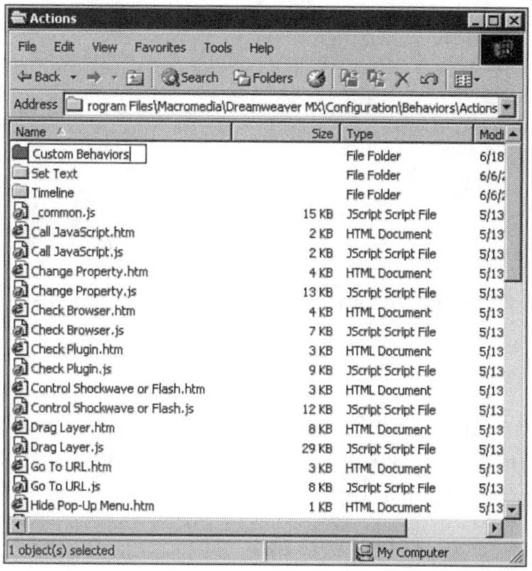

FIGURE 20.6   Create a new folder called Custom Behaviors within the Actions folder.

1. Open Dreamweaver MX and create a new HTML file. Immediately save it into the Custom Behaviors folder and call it window resizer. The result is shown in Figure 20.7.

> **NOTE**
>
> If you had Dreamweaver MX open while you created the folder, it will not appear in the behaviors list until you restart the application.

2. Change the code within the <title> tag to read window resizer. Remember, this is the name as it will appear within the behaviors list. The code should resemble the following:

```
<!DOCTYPE HTML PUBLIC "-//W3C//DTD HTML 4.01 Transitional//EN">
<html>
<head>
```

20

```
<title>Window Resizer</title>
</head>

<body>

</body>
</html>
```

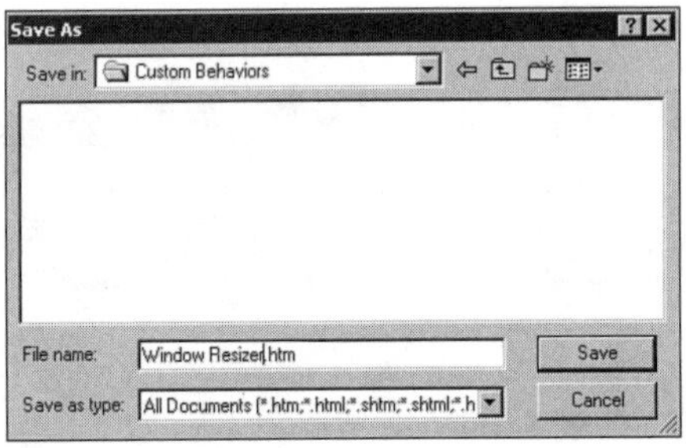

FIGURE 20.7 Save the HTML file within the new Custom Behaviors folder.

3. Add script blocks within the <head> tag.

4. Next, add the defined function for the window resizer. Name it resizeWindow. The riseTo method of the Window object will be used along with the width and height values that it accepts as parameters.

```
<!DOCTYPE HTML PUBLIC "-//W3C//DTD HTML 4.01 Transitional//EN">
<html>
<head>
<title>Window Resizer</title>
<script language="JavaScript>
function resizeWindow() {
window.resizeTo(200,200);
}
</script>
</head>

<body>

</body>
</html>
```

5. Now add the behaviorFunction() and the applyBehavior() functions, returning the name of the resizeWindow() function in both cases. Remember that the behaviorFunction() function does not return the "()" at the end of the function name.

```
<!DOCTYPE HTML PUBLIC "-//W3C//DTD HTML 4.01 Transitional//EN">
<html>
<head>
<title>Window Resizer</title>
<script language="JavaScript">
function resizeWindow() {
window.resizeTo(200,200);
}
function behaviorFunction() {
return "resizeWindow";
}
function applyBehavior() {
return "resizeWindow()";
}
</script>
</head>

<body></body>
</html>
```

6. Now that the logic of the behavior has been taken care of, you are ready to begin on the UI. In this case, you will create a simple dialog box that will display to users, letting them know what is happening.

TIP

OK and Cancel buttons are automatically inserted by Dreamweaver; you simply need to supply the content.

```
<!DOCTYPE HTML PUBLIC "-//W3C//DTD HTML 4.01 Transitional//EN">
<html>
<head>
<title>Window Resizer</title>
<script language="JavaScript">
function resizeWindow() {
window.resizeTo(200,200);
}
function behaviorFunction() {
```

```
return "resizeWindow";
}
function applyBehavior() {
return "resizeWindow()";


}
</script>
</head>

<body>
<table width="200"><tr><td>This behavior will resize the browser
➥window.</td></tr></table>
</body>
</html>
```

7. You've created your first behavior! Now save the file as sample.htm and close it. Open a new HTML file and add a link as you normally would. The result should look similar to Figure 20.8.

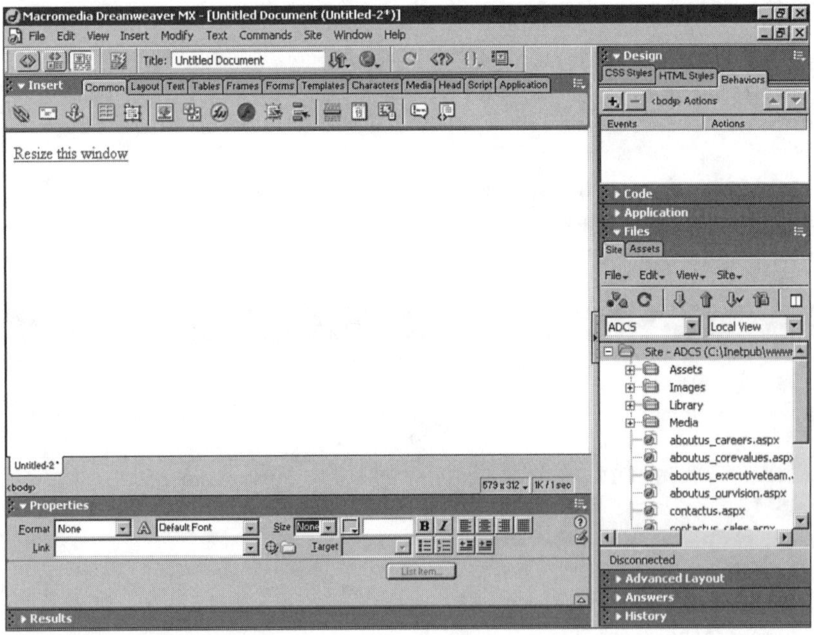

FIGURE 20.8 Create a new HTML file and insert a link.

8. Restart Dreamweaver MX so that your behavior's list will reload, and open up sample.htm again.

9. Highlight the new link and apply the Window Resizer behavior to it as shown in Figure 20.9.

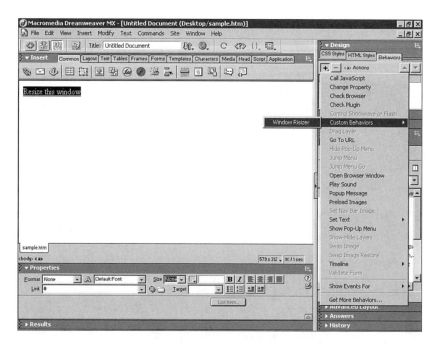

FIGURE 20.9   Apply the new Window Resizer behavior to your link.

10. After you have added your new behavior, examine the code by switching to code view. Figure 20.10 shows how the function was added to the <head> tag. An event handler was also added to your link that calls the function.

11. Save sample.htm again and try it in the browser.

The Advanced Resizer Behavior

Aside from the basics that we have covered so far, your behaviors can accept input from your users. Up until this point, the behavior did no more than resize the browser window to the values that you provided to it. But what if you wanted to change it so that the user could enter their own values to change the browser window size? This could be accomplished by following these steps:

1. First change the UI to accept input from a standard HTML text box:

```
<body>
<form name="resizeForm">
<table width="200">
<tr><td colspan="2">What do you want to resize the browser window
```

20

```
➡to:</td></tr>
<tr><td>Width:</td><td><input type="text" name="width" size="10"></td></tr>
<tr><td>Height:</td><td><input type="text" name="height" size="10"></td></tr>
</table>
</form>
</body>
```

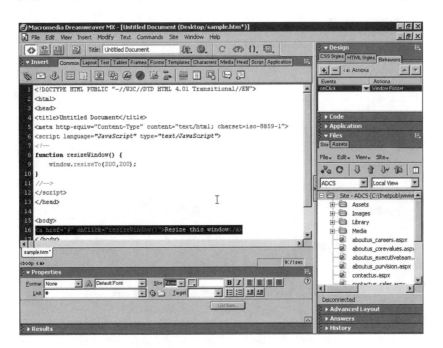

FIGURE 20.10   Dreamweaver MX adds the JavaScript code for you.

2. Second, change the applyBehavior() function to accept the two text field values and return a concatenated value for width and height:

```
function applyBehavior() {
var width = document.resizeForm.width.value;
var height = document.resizeForm.width.value;
return "resizeWindow(" + width + ", " + height + ")";
}
```

3. Now, modify the defined function so that it accepts the two values as parameters: width and height.

```
function resizeWindow(width, height) {
window.resizeTo(width, height);
}
```

4. Save the behavior and restart Dreamweaver MX. Reopen sample.htm and delete the behavior that it currently has and reapply it. Notice this time you are asked to type in the values for the resizer. Figure 20.11 shows the dialog box that will appear.

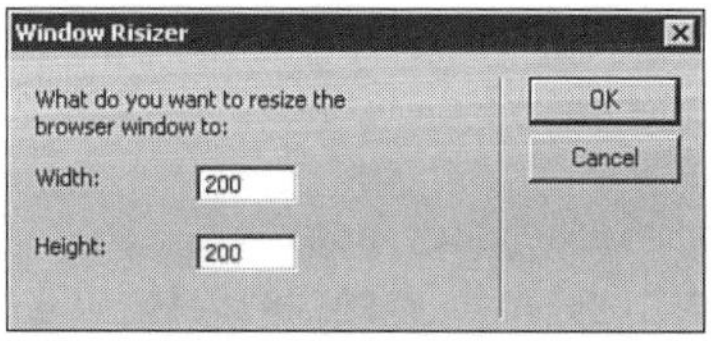

FIGURE 20.11   The UI that you created should appear, allowing you to input values for the resizer.

Advanced Behavior Functions

Aside from the basic elements that are required for the behavior to work, you can also include optional functions to enhance the usability of your behaviors. Listed below are a few of them:

- **initializeUI() function**   Adding this function to the head of your behavior causes the cursor to land inside of a text box that you specify. It also makes sure that the dialog box is selected when it is called from the panel list. You are free to do anything you want within this function, although the code below is typical for what you may see:

```
function initializeUI() {
document.resizeForm.width.focus();
document.resizeForm.width.select();
}
```

For usability purposes it is always a good idea to add this function, especially when working with form elements within a behavior file.

> **NOTE**
>
> You will also need to add the onLoad event to the body tag for the function to be called: <body onLoad="initializeUI()">.

- **canAcceptBehavior() function**   Aside from being able to gray out specific events that you do not want the user to be able to use, you can also use this function to specify which event should be used as the default. The following function can be added to your script to default the event to onMouseUp rather than onClick:

```
function canAcceptBehavior() {
return("onMouseUp");
}
```

20

- **inspectBehavior() function**   If you've been working with the newly created behavior, you will have noticed that when you double-click the behavior within the Behaviors panel, it doesn't remember the values that you entered. It forces you to reenter the values. The inspectBehavior() function can be added to solve this problem:

```
function inspectBehavior(resizeFunctionCall) {
var argArray = new Array;
argArray = extractArgs(resizeFunctionCall);
document.resizeForm.width.value = argArray[1];
document.resizeForm.height.value = argArray[2];
}
```

Just after the closing script tag, place a link to the shared string.js file. The string.js file contains functions that are needed for the behavior to function appropriately.

```
<script src="../../../Shared/MM/Scripts/CMN/string.js"></script>
```

- Notice how the values of the text boxes within the UI are placed into an array. This is how Dreamweaver MX stores the values that you have entered.

> **TIP**
>
> The Configuration/Shared folder contains helpful scripts that you can use when working with extensions. The string.js is one of those scripts that comes in handy when working with strings.

Working with .JS Files

If you look inside the Actions folder again, you will notice that your file is the only one without an accompanying .js file. This is done to separate the client logic from your UI, resulting in cleaner code that is easier to maintain. To create a new .js file for your new behavior, follow these steps:

1. Cut all the script content out of the head of your file, as shown in Fig 20.12. Be careful not to cut the link to the string.js file.

2. Create a new file by selecting New from the File menu.

3. Select Basic Page and JavaScript.

4. Paste your code in and delete the script tags.

5. Make sure to save the file in the same location as your HTM file.

6. In the HTM file, add the following line:

```
<script src="Window Resizer.js"></script>
```

7. Save the behaviors file and restart Dreamweaver MX.

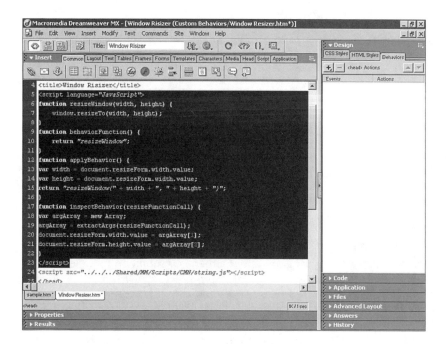

FIGURE 20.12   Cut out all the script content.

Customizing Dreamweaver MX Menus Using menus.xml

Another integral part of Dreamweaver MX are the menu items. You navigate them to open files, copy text, insert commands, and view help all through the core drop-down menus that Dreamweaver MX contains. Like most software applications, everything that you could possibly insert, view, edit, or interact with are available through these drop-down menus. Unlike most software applications, Dreamweaver MX enables you to customize the menu items or subitems to meet your needs.

Because all the menus are generated from one XML-based file, you as the user have complete control to add, remove, and change keyboard shortcuts as well as rearrange, rename, and remove menu items.

Menus.xml Tag Syntax

Before you begin making any changes to the menus.xml file, it might be helpful to see how it is structured. XML, like HTML, is tag based, which means that for every opening tag, there must be a closing tag, although some tags simply close themselves by adding the "/" at the end. If you open the menus.xml file, located in Macromedia\Dreamweaver MX\Configuration\Menus, you will notice that it is very much structured like an HTML page but contains slightly different syntax. The reason for this is that it is XML. XML

20

defines data, not how data should be structured, which is what HTML takes care of. By defining the data that menus should contain, Dreamweaver MX can, in turn, use the information to dynamically construct the menus whenever the application is loaded.

> **NOTE**
>
> Never open the menus.xml file in Dreamweaver MX; open it in a different text editor such as Notepad.

XML, unlike HTML, allows you to create your own tags, hence the reason for the custom tag syntax. Navigating the menus.xml file for the first time can be somewhat of a challenge. The following explanations should help to clear things up:

- **\<menubar>**   Provides information about a menu bar in the Dreamweaver MX menu structure.

- **\<menu>**   Provides information about a menu or submenu to appear in the Dreamweaver MX menu structure. This tag must reside within the \<menubar> tag.

- **\<menuitem>**   Defines a menu item for a Dreamweaver MX menu. The tag must reside within a menu tag.

- **\<separator>**   Indicates that a separator should be present in the menu. This tag must reside within a \<menu> tag.

- **\<shortcutlist>**   Specifies a shortcut list in the menus.xml file. This tag will contain one or more \<shortcut> tags.

- **\<shortcut>**   Specifies a keyboard shortcut in the menus.xml. This tag must be contained within a \<shortcutlist> tag.

With this knowledge, you should now be able to rearrange menu items.

Rearranging Menus and Menu Items

Editing the menus.xml file allows for great control over how your menus are structured. A lot of people, including myself, are used to working within environments that they are familiar with. When a new program comes out that deviates from the traditional File, Edit, View, structure, it becomes difficult to adapt. Fortunately with Dreamweaver MX, that can be changed. Modifying the menus.xml file enables you to move items within a menu or out of and into another menu, add or remove separators, and add menu bars and even move one menu into another menu.

> **NOTE**
>
> Before you make any modifications to the menus.xml file, you should make a copy of it as a backup.

To move a menu item, follow these steps:

1. Open the menus.xml file in Notepad.

2. Cut an entire menu item tag from the beginning to its closing tag, as shown in Figure 20.13.

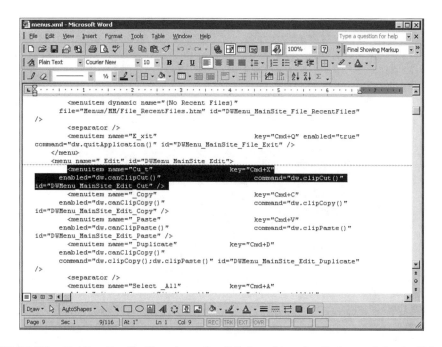

FIGURE 20.13   Cutting the "cut" and moving it below "copy" will change it in the IDE as well.

3. Paste the menu item tag into its new insertion point, making sure that it is still nested within a menu tag.

4. Restart Dreamweaver and check the menu that you pasted the menu tag into.

Changing the Name of a Menu or Menu Item

You can easily change the name of a menu or menu item by following these steps:

1. Open the menus.xml file in Notepad.

2. To change a menu item, simply change the name attribute.

3. Save and close the file and restart Dreamweaver MX.

20

Changing Keyboard Shortcuts Using the Keyboard Shortcuts Editor

Possibly the easiest way to change shortcuts is by using the shortcuts editor, available from the Edit menu. Selecting this command launches the Keyboard Shortcuts editor pictured in Figure 20.14.

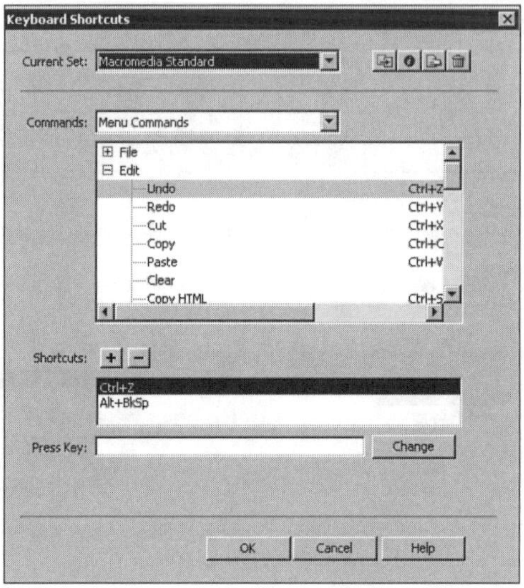

FIGURE 20.14   The easiest way to modify shortcuts is by launching the Keyboard Shortcuts editor from the Edit menu.

The Keyboard Shortcuts editor contains a few important features that are worth mentioning:

- **Current Set**   Indicates the keyboard shortcuts sets that Dreamweaver MX supports.

- **Commands**   The commands allow you to choose from a specific menu bar. Notice that depending on which window you are in, the menu bar changes. Commands enable you to navigate between all of these.

- **Shortcuts**   Indicates the shortcut that the command is currently set to.

- **Press Key**   Place your cursor in this field and click the keyboard combination to change the keyboard shortcut.

To change a keyboard shortcut using the editor, follow these steps:

1. Select the set from the Current Set selector. Default is Macromedia Standard.

2. Select the command set that you would like to change.

3. Select the shortcut from the shortcuts list.

4. Place your cursor inside the Press Key field and select the shortcut that you would like to change it to.

5. Select Change.

Sharing Extensions

After you've created your first distributable object or behavior, you may want to share it with the world. Sharing extensions is not all that uncommon, in fact Macromedia has a whole section of its Web site devoted to extension sharing: The Macromedia Exchange. This section focuses on preparing your extensions for submission to the Macromedia Exchange, including the following:

- **Documentation**   Documentation means creating a help file so everyone who is using your extension knows how it works.

- **Distribution**   Distribution means using the installer file to create an MXI file and bundling it into an extension using the Extension Manager.

- **Submission**   Submitting your extension to the Macromedia Exchange is the final step performed.

Documentation

A good extension is useful only if people know how to use it. You've probably noticed by now that when you select a preinstalled behavior that contains a dialog box, you're either given a textual explanation toward the bottom of the text box, explaining how the behavior works, or you're given a Help button. The Help button is used to allow the user of the behavior to access online help, providing more in-depth analysis of what the behavior can do and how it can be used. To create documentation for your extension, follow these steps:

1. Create a new HTML file in Dreamweaver MX and write some information about how your extension works, as shown in Figure 20.15. You may also include a screen capture if you think that is necessary.

2. Save the HTML file into a working folder within the Configuration\Shared folder. Copy any necessary images into that folder because they will be needed for the HTML page to work correctly. Figure 20.16 illustrates this point.

3. Open the Window Resizer.js file and create a new function called displayHelp(). This function is also part of the API. Notice that the code makes calls to other methods within the API, specifically getConfigurationPath() and browseDocument(). getConfigurationPath() dynamically maps a path to the users configuration folder. After the folder has been found, you append the path to the location where the file

20

should reside. Then, call the browseDocument() method, which opens the file that resides in that path.

```
function displayHelp() {
var theURL = dw.getConfigurationPath();
theURL += "/Shared/CustomBehaviors/sizerwindow.htm";
dw.browseDocument(theURL);
}
```

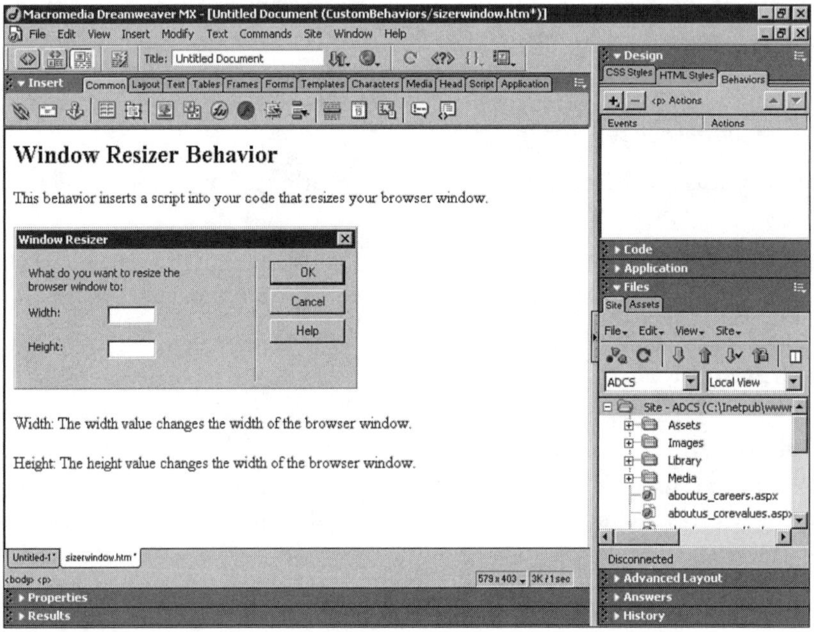

FIGURE 20.15   Create an HTML page describing your extension.

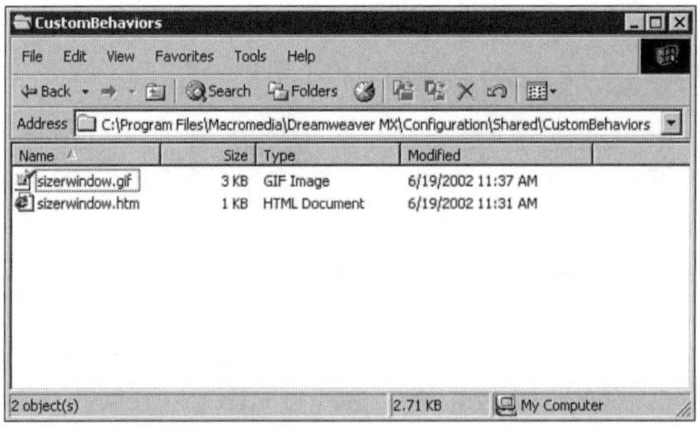

FIGURE 20.16   Save your HTML file and optional images into a custom folder that you create within the Configuration\Shared folder.

4. Save that file and restart Dreamweaver MX. This time, create a new HTML file with a link and insert the new behavior. If you click the Help button, it launches the HTML help file that you created, similar to Figure 20.17.

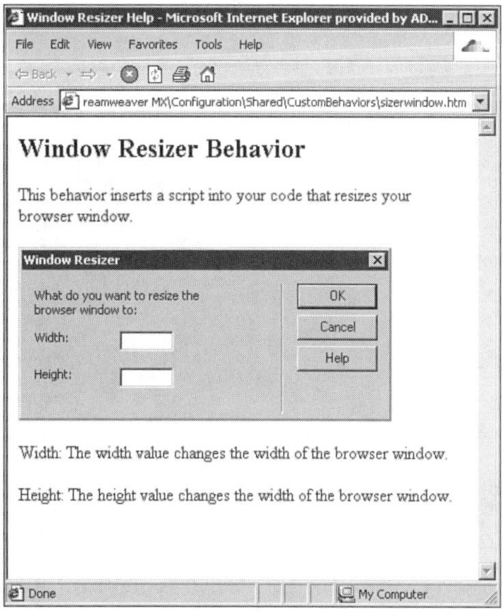

FIGURE 20.17   A browser window is launched complete with your help file.

> **NOTE**
>
> Complete guidelines for how extensions should be created are available from Macromedia's Web site at http://www.macromedia.com/exchange/dreamweaver. Click the Site Help topic Macromedia Approved Extensions.

Distribution

After you've completely documented how your behavior should work, you are ready to package it up for distribution. Using the Extension Manager shown in Figure 20.18, you can package your extension into a special installation file known as a Macromedia Extension Installation, or an MXI.

> **NOTE**
>
> You must have the latest release of Macromedia's Extension Manager to create extensions for the new MX releases. For Dreamweaver MX, you can download the newest release of the Extension Manager from http://dynamic.macromedia.com/bin/MM/exchange/main.jsp?product=dreamweaver.

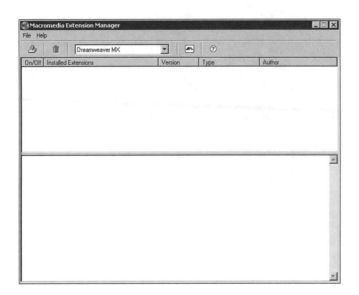

FIGURE 20.18   The Extension Manager enables you to package your extension into a special installation file also known as an MXI.

The process is easier than you may think and can be accomplished by following these simple steps:

1. Put all the necessary files (help files, HTML files, JS files, and GIF files) into a separate folder outside of the Configuration folder, as shown in Figure 20.19.

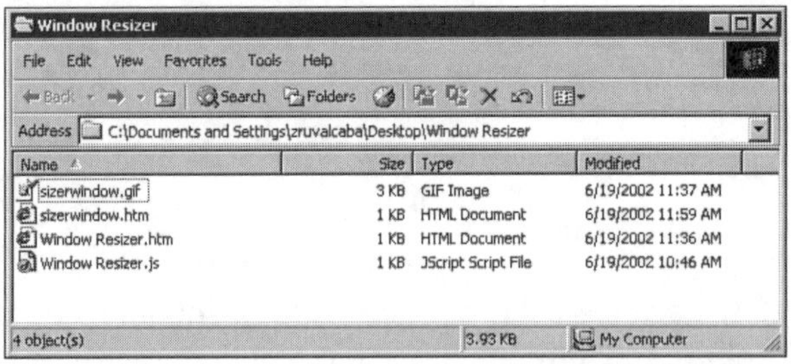

FIGURE 20.19   Place all your files into a separate folder outside of the Configuration folder.

2. Copy one of the sample.mxi files from the Extension Manager's sample directory into the directory that you created to store all your files and rename it WindowSizer.mxi. You can use this as a template for building your own installation file. The MXI file is basically an XML file that contains information, such as the

platform the extension requires, the author's name, the type of extension, and a brief description.

3. Fill in all the required information for name, version, type, product name, author name, description, and filenames. Note that the filenames require a location from where to grab the files and a destination to install the files. The finished code should look similar to Figure 20.20.

FIGURE 20.20   Modify the MXI file to include all relevant information.

4. From the Extension Manager, select File, Package Extension. Locate the MXI file and select OK. The MXP, or Macromedia Extension Package, will appear in the same directory as the MXI file.

To install the extension, follow these directions:

1. Open the Extension Manager.

2. Select File, Install Extension.

3. The package will be installed into the appropriate folders and the extension will appear within the Extension Manager, as shown in Figure 20.21.

20

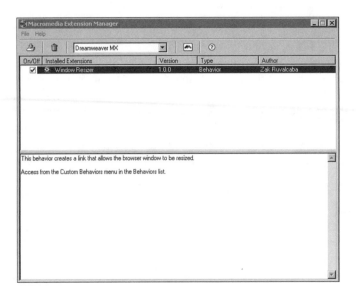

FIGURE 20.21   The extension will appear within the Extension Manager.

Submission

After you have completely documented, tested, and packaged your extension, you are ready to share it with the rest of the development community on the Macromedia Exchange. The process is relatively simple and can be completed in these steps:

1. Visit the Macromedia Dreamweaver exchange at `http://dynamic.macromedia.com/bin/MM/exchange/main.jsp?product=dreamweaver` shown in Figure 20.22.

2. Click Submit Extension.

3. Follow the checklist and submit your extension when you are ready.

FIGURE 20.22   The Macromedia Exchange.

Summary

As you've seen, customization in Dreamweaver is a revolutionary way of managing your workflow and customizing your development environment. Although you have only scratched the surface, you can begin to see the endless possibilities that are available to you by developing your own objects and behaviors. The Macromedia Exchange provides Dreamweaver MX with features that the software industry has never before seen: free software in the form of modular code. Dreamweaver MX opens the door to a whole new world of development—one that is not limited by design potential or development knowledge, but in your willingness to take the application as far as your workflow needs require.

20

## CHAPTER 21

Working with CGI and Java Applets

By Hugh Livingstone

We have extensively covered Dreamweaver MX's capability to help you design Web pages, and we are now starting to look at Web applications. Before we dive into the specifics of particular middleware and database options, let's look at two Web technologies that are available to everyone, whatever server you are running, and even if you have no server of your own at all.

Server-Side Programming

You should now prepare for a change of direction. After looking at Web page design, and as we get deeper into creating Web applications, we are going to look at the other side of the Web application coin—server-side programming.

Everything we have used Dreamweaver MX for so far has been working inside the user's browser. HTML for page design, Flash for multimedia effects, and JavaScript behaviors for greater interactivity are all client-side technologies designed to take advantage of modern browser capabilities.

The use of these client-side technologies is vital for the use of any Web site. However if you want your pages to interact with a database or give customized responses to each user, you have to look at server-side scripting. Only by running a program on the Web server itself can you connect up to a database, display a page counter or guest book, or serve different pages to different types of browsers and platforms. To do this, you need to send information from the user's browser, through the Web server, to a program that processes the information before sending it back via the server to the user's browser.

The Eternal Problem of the Web

Using client-side technologies is usually a little easier than writing code for the server (despite the enormous amount of help we can get from Dreamweaver), but you are generally sending your pages "into the great unknown." A request is made and the page is returned to the browser without us knowing anything about the computer type, browser software, or what additional plug-ins and other software is available to that user. This may be a very sophisticated page, such as a Flash movie that interacts with the user, but unless the browser has been sent all the information it needs, and it can understand that information, the page won't work.

A plain HTML page provides a stark illustration of this problem. The HTML in the page never changes and is the same for every user that requests that page. If the page includes tags such as <FRAME> or (whispering this very quietly) <blink> or <marquee>, some users will get the page displayed quite differently from what you intended, while other users will see the page correctly.

Dreamweaver produces clean HTML code that displays well in most of the browsers in use. But ultimately, there is little you can do to help users who have unusual, or unexpected, configurations. (The golden rule of Web design is that there is never a "wrong" browser, only "wrong" pages!)

> **NOTE**
>
> You can use a JavaScript behavior to redirect users to different pages, depending on their browser type, but this is not the best solution. This means that every correction and update must be done on at least two, possibly three, pages—a recipe for mistakes and inconsistency.

CGI to the Rescue

Imagine, though, if the page could contain different HTML tags, depending on the type of browser that requested it. To do this you would need to find out the browser type from the request and process the page on the server before it is sent to the user's browser.

Since the beginning of the World Wide Web, page designers have wanted to do this sort of thing, and to do so, they have turned to CGI, which stands for Common Gateway Interface. It is not a programming language, but a set of rules for how a Web server talks to a program running on it.

HTML forms control how information is sent from a browser to the Web server and which script or program will process it. CGI controls how that script works and how information is sent through the server back to the browser. In the CGI world, the server acts as a gateway between a program and the client.

CGI programs can be written in any programming language that the Web server understands, but many server scripts are written in the Perl language. We will look at Perl in a bit more detail later, but for now all you need to know about Perl is that it's very good at handling strings of text, and it also gets on well with Unix, the traditional operating system of Web servers. It is these two factors that have made Perl popular as the Web has developed.

Client-Side Versus Server-Side Programming

Having explored the power of JavaScript behaviors and Flash using Dreamweaver, you may be asking why you would want to use server-side programs (within which I include both CGI and application servers). Indeed, some tasks could be done either on the client or on the server. For example, validating a form to ensure that the user enters the correct data could be done using JavaScript or a server-side program.

The Advantages of Server-Side Programs

There are some tasks that can be done only on the server. You do not want and cannot give every person who uses your Web site direct access to your databases. Database requests are filtered through the Web server so users see only the data that you want them to see.

Server-side programming enables you to save bandwidth. By filtering records and requests at the server, you just send subsets of 10 or 20 records instead of thousands of records. Nor do you need to send enough HTML, JavaScript and Flash code to cover every operating system/browser combination—just what is required for the particular client that has requested the page.

Even tasks that can be done on both the client and the server—such as form validation—have advantages when done on the server.

Processing of programs on the server allows for platform independence—the CGI script sends plain HTML to the client, and you do not have to rely on features that will work only in, for example, Internet Explorer version 4 or demand that JavaScript is enabled in the browser. Remember that some users, particularly those within security-conscious organizations, such as banks or insurance companies, may have browser features such as JavaScript, Java, and ActiveX controls turned off.

Server-side programming allows a wider range of clients—particularly thin clients such as PDAs and embedded devices—to be supported by your Web site. You don't have to rely on any client-side processing.

> **NOTE**
>
> The enormous popularity of the Internet has led to an explosion of devices that can connect into it. Originally, you needed to have a computer to hook into the Internet. Now you can use mobile phones, PDAs such as Palm Pilots, and TV sets. Even household devices can be connected up— for remote control, remote servicing, or for your fridge to tell you when it has run out of milk (and order it itself!). These devices, which do not have much computing power themselves, are collectively known as *thin clients*. Thin clients are likely to have small, specialized operating systems and just enough power to carry out a limited number of tasks.

A major advantage of server-side processing that leads many organizations to adopt it is security. Because all the processing is done on the server, the client sees only the results of the process, not the processing itself. You do not have to expose your code as you do when using JavaScript. Information that hackers could find useful, such as field and table names or database paths, remain hidden.

For example, if you had to verify a password using JavaScript, the user could find out what password you were expecting by simply viewing the source code.

Advantages of Client-Side Programming

Server-side programming is extremely useful and the best solution in some situations. However, there are still many advantages to client-side programs. There are some things that can be done only on the client—especially when manipulating the user interface. It would be impractical to have to make a call to the server to simply stop or pause a video frame. Mouseover effects, animation, and interaction with the user can be done only using client-side solutions.

One of the problems of server-side programming is that you need to have permissions to configure and manipulate the Web server. By default, Web servers do not allow programs to run on them, unless they are specially configured to do so. If you do not have these permissions (for instance, if you are renting Web space from an ISP), you may need to look for client-side solutions to provide the functionality you want.

Client-side scripting also relieves the server of routine tasks that the browser is quite capable of doing. For instance, today's client-side image maps are much better than the early server-side image maps that made Web servers very slow.

> **NOTE**
>
> You should, if possible, use the browser to check forms. You can use the Validate Form behavior to do this. Of course, you may encounter browsers that have limited capabilities and do not support JavaScript, so you also use a server program to check the form from these browsers.

Most important, client-side scripting is much faster than server-side scripting—imagine the page having to make a new request to the server each time an image is rolled over on your page. Dynamic HTML and Flash both take advantage of this to give much richer user interfaces and almost instant response to user actions.

Beyond CGI

Basic CGI and Perl scripts have been used since the beginnings of the Web, but CGI is being superseded by application servers. Application servers, such as ASP, JSP, ColdFusion, and PHP (also known as middleware), have overcome some of the performance problems associated with CGI. They are also written in languages that are easier to understand for HTML developers (in the case of ColdFusion) or for Windows programmers (in the case of ASP). Almost anything you can do with CGI you can also do using an application server. Many Web servers have the application server built in, or the application server is easily installed, making the Web server simpler to administer than the early Unix machines.

You can think of application servers as CGI scripts with bells on. Most of the processes described here for CGI apply to application servers, and the principles are the same.

Finally, and important for us, Dreamweaver MX provides much better support for application servers than for CGI scripts.

But the strength of CGI is its ubiquity. Every Web server runs CGI, no matter how old it is. If you have investigated getting your Web site hosted, you'll know you usually have to pay a lot more to get ASP or ColdFusion from your ISP. Yet even free Web hosting gives you access to a few useful CGI scripts. Because CGI has been around so long, and runs on so many servers, you can usually find a CGI script to do almost anything you want and it will often be free.

How CGI Works

To really understand the power of CGI and how you can use it, we will look at the nitty-gritty of how CGI works when it is used on a Web server. Nothing is overly complicated about CGI; it simply extends the process that occurs when an ordinary Web page is requested by a user.

HTML Documents

As explained previously, the Web is a conversation between two computers. The computer trying to fetch a Web page is called the client. The client machine is running a Web browser—the software that requests and displays pages of HTML. When the client wants a Web page, it sends a URL to a server.

At the other end of the conversation is the Web server. This computer is running Web server software that enables it to respond to URL requests by retrieving a copy of the page from its own hard disk and sending it on to the client. Figure 21.1 illustrates this familiar process.

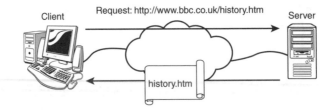

FIGURE 21.1   The Web server responds to a URL request from the client.

If you're using dynamic HTML or Flash to provide interactive Web pages, the process is the same as this, except that the page sent to the client contains additional JavaScript code or Flash movies.

CGI Pages

With static Web pages, a server does not process any data—it simply examines the request it receives from a client and sends the page. But when you use CGI programs, you get the server to do some work before sending a page to the client. If the URL indicates that a CGI program should be used, the Web server starts the CGI program, the CGI program generates the page content, and the server passes that content to the client, as shown in Figure 21.2.

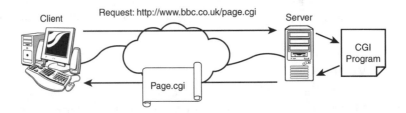

FIGURE 21.2   With CGI, the server processes the script before responding to the client.

Giving Information to the Server—CGI Environment Variables

You can see the URL in the browser's address bar or status bar, but when the client makes a request to a server, it gives the server more information than the page it wants. The client also sends the server additional information you cannot see, such as its own IP address (otherwise, where would the server send the page back to?) and the browser type. When the server responds to the client, it also sends information in addition to the requested page, such as its own name and IP address and the type of Web server software it is running.

This additional information is called CGI Environment Variables. A partial list of the useful ones is shown in Table 21.1. You need to refer to your own particular Web servers documentation to get a full list.

TABLE 21.1 Selected CGI Environment Variables

Variable	Description
CONTENT_LENGTH	The number of bytes that the script can expect to receive from the client if method POST is used.
CONTENT_TYPE	The content type of the information supplied in the body of a POST request.
HTTP_ACCEPT	Additional information given by the client. This is used to list the MIME formats that can be accepted by the user; for example, if the client browser can accept JPEG and GIF images, this variable will contain image/gif, image/jpeg.
HTTP_USER_AGENT	By looking at this variable, the browser used by the client can be determined. For example, if Internet Explorer version 5.5 is being used by the client, this variable will contain the value `Mozilla/4.0 (compatible; MSIE 5.5; Windows NT 5.0)`. The general format of this variable is software/version/operating system but is slightly different for each browser.
PATH_INFO	This is the trailing part of the URL after the script name but before the querystring (if any).
QUERY_STRING	The information that follows the question mark (?) in the URL that referenced the script.
REMOTE_ADDR	The IP address of the client.
REMOTE_USER	If the user had to log on to the server, this contains the username supplied by the client and authenticated by the server.
REQUEST_METHOD	The HTTP request method (GET or POST).
SCRIPT_NAME	The relative URL of the script program being executed.
SERVER_NAME	The servers hostname (or IP address).
SERVER_PORT	The TCP/IP port on which the request was received (usually 80).
SERVER_SOFTWARE	The name and version of the Web server software that is running.

Passing Your Own Information to the Server

You can call a CGI program from a Web page in two ways. The easiest way is to put the program's name in a hyperlink. The Web browser sends the URL to the server and the CGI program is run.

The other way to start the CGI program is to make it the action of an HTML form. The following form calls a program called formhandle.pl when the Submit button is clicked.

```
<form action="../cgi-bin/formhandle.pl" method="get">
Enter your name:<input name="username">
Enter your password:<input type="password" name="pword">
<input type="submit">
</form>
```

When you use a form, the values of each form object are automatically passed to the CGI program. If the form method is GET, you can see the name and value of each form object appended to the action of the form to make a single, long URL. After filling in the preceding form, the URL would look something like this:

```
http://www.server.com/cgibin/formhandle.pl?username=hugh&password=sherbertlemon
```

If the form method is POST, this information is sent to the server as one of the CGI environment variables, still as one long string of form object names and values, but you cannot see it in the URL. You should use POST for forms that pass confidential information or for forms that have lots of form objects in them and would make the URL too long for the server to handle (usually above 255 characters).

You can also pass parameters into a CGI program with a link. You need to construct the link URL as though it was a form using the GET method.

To construct such a link, start with the URL to the CGI program. At the end of the filename goes a question mark, then each parameter name, an equal sign, and its value. Each parameter name/value pair is separated by an ampersand.

Dreamweaver helps you to construct these links with the Parameters button. Start to make a hyperlink as you would normally—on the Properties palette, click the Link Folder button. This brings up the Select File dialog box, and you can choose the file to link to. Either choose the CGI script file or manually enter it. Then click the Parameters button. For each parameter you want to add, click the plus (+) button in the top-left corner, and then add the parameter name and its value. The Parameters dialog box is shown in Figure 21.3.

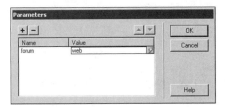

FIGURE 21.3   The Parameters dialog box helps you construct a parameterized URL.

When you are constructing these URLs, bear in mind that you are not allowed to have spaces or other special characters in the string. For these characters to be included, they must be replaced by the character's ASCII value as a hexadecimal number. If that sounds complicated—don't worry! Both JavaScript and PERL have a special function called escape to do this (and unescape to turn these values back to normal). If you are entering the strings manually, the following table lists the ASCII values of common characters.

TABLE 21.2   Common Characters and Their Hexadecimal ASCII Equivalent

Sign	Hexadecimal ASCII value	Description
	%20	Space
!	%21	Exclamation mark
"	%22	Double quote
#	%23	Pound or number sign
$	%24	Dollar sign
%	%25	Percent
&	%26	Ampersand
'	%27	Single quote/apostrophe
(	%28	Open parenthesis
)	%29	Close parenthesis
*	%2A	Asterisk
+	%2B	Plus sign
,	%2C	Comma
-	%2D	Dash/hyphen
.	%2E	Period
/	%2F	Slash
~	%7E	Tilde

The CGI Process Step-by-Step

To summarize, this is what happens to a request for a CGI script step-by-step. Some of these steps would be the same if the request was for a static HTML page; others are specific to the CGI process. This is the same process that happens with application servers:

1. A URL is constructed. It may be hardcoded into the page, typed into the browser address bar, or the result of a form submission. This URL refers to a CGI script file (often these have the extension PL or CGI) and may contain additional information.

2. Client makes a request to the server, using the constructed URL.

3. The URL is converted to an IP address (this step happens to all HTTP requests).

4. A connection is established with the server.

5. The server receives the request for the CGI file. The client waits for a response.

6. The server starts a new instance of the CGI script.

7. The CGI script generates a new page using the information it has received with the URL and CGI environment variables.

8. The page is sent back to the client as a server response.

9. The CGI script exits.

10. The connection between the client and server is dropped.

11. The client renders the page onscreen.

Using Prewritten CGI Scripts

Because CGI is such a long established technology, others have already done many of the things you are likely to use CGI for. Many Web sites let you download scripts for free and put them on your own Web server.

You may also find that your ISP will provide you with prewritten CGI scripts. In some cases, ISPs will not allow you to put your own scripts on their server for security reasons, but will allow you to use their own provided scripts at no charge. Figure 21.4 shows some of the scripts that my ISP makes available to me for use with my free Web space. The key to using any of these free scripts, whether provided by your ISP or others, is to read the instructions in the readme file carefully.

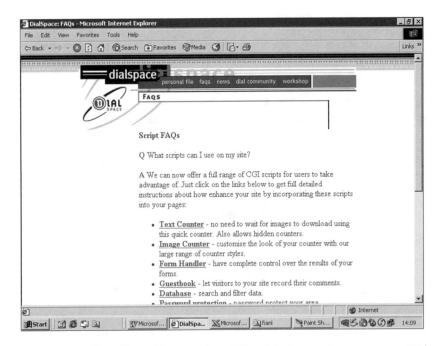

FIGURE 21.4   Most ISPs will provide some free CGI scripts for you to use on your Web space.

Perl

Most CGI scripts are written in Perl. Perl is a general purpose programming language, an acronym of Practical Extraction and Report Language. In the words of its creator, Larry Wall:

"The language is intended to be practical (easy to use, efficient, complete) rather than beautiful (tiny, elegant, minimal)."

Perl is often described as a "gaffer-tape" language because it is often used to tie different documents together or to try and get different systems talking to each other. Its main strength lies in its capability to easily manipulate large strings of text.

Perl is not a difficult language to learn, but to go into any detail here would be beyond the scope of this book. I recommend *Teach Yourself Perl in 24 Hours* by Clinton Pierce (Sams Publishing) if you want to learn Perl in any depth.

Much of Perl looks rather like JavaScript—so if you already know a bit of JavaScript, you would probably feel happy poking around with Perl programs. However, most of the time you will want to look at programs that have already been written, and you will only have to do simple modifications, which will usually be documented in a readme file.

Dreamweaver MX does not have any tools to help you write Perl, so you have to rely on the code view and your sharp eyes to spot any mistakes! You will need to configure Dreamweaver to read Perl files in code view. To do this, from the Edit menu choose Preferences, and then select the File Types/Editors category.

In the top text box (marked Open in Code View) add the .pl extension (see Figure 21.5).

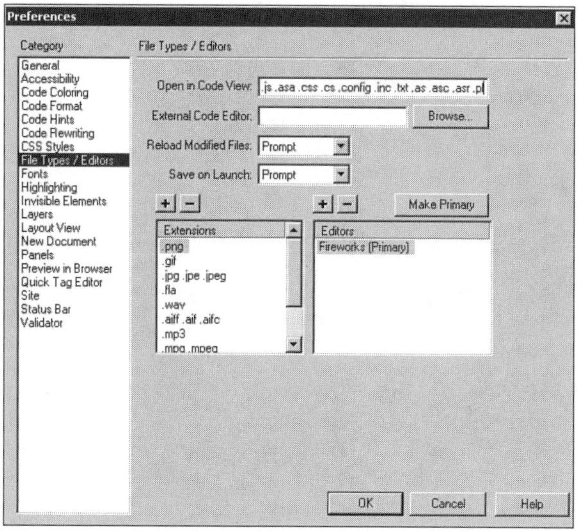

FIGURE 21.5   Using Dreamweaver preferences, you can configure the File Types so that Dreamweaver can open Perl files.

Perl programs are written in plain text, and each time they are run, a Perl interpreter reads the text and translates it into machine code. This is why Perl programs are called scripts. The first line of any Perl script needs to point to the Perl interpreter, and is usually `#!/usr/bin/perl`.

If you have a Unix machine, and the Perl interpreter is located in a different location, you will have to change this line. In Windows you can safely ignore this line—the Windows Perl interpreter does not read it.

Except for this line, all other lines in a Perl program finish with a semicolon (;). Leaving this out is usually the source of most errors in Perl.

Lines in the program that are just comments start with the symbol #. These lines will be ignored by the Perl interpreter but are very useful to understand what's going on in the program—you should include lots of them, and read comments put in by others.

Variables

If you are using downloaded Perl programs, generally all you have to do is change the values of variables. Variables in any programming language, Perl included, are holders for data values. These values can be changed as the program progresses, or they can have different values for different users, so the variable called name is equal to "Hugh" for me, but may be equal to "Sally" for someone else. Age could also be a variable, as could address, or item number.

A Scalar Variable in Perl holds letters, numbers, phrases—in fact, whatever you like. It begins with a dollar sign ($) and the name cannot have any spaces in it. It's a good idea to give your variables sensible, descriptive names—it makes a script easier to understand. If you want to give the variable a value, do something like this:

```
$age=34
$customer_no=567
$value=34.99
$name="Hugh"
$tip = "Don't eat stuff off the sidewalk"
```

Notice that groups of letters to form words and phrases are surrounded by quote marks—these are called strings.

Arrays

An array variable is a special kind of list variable. It holds many scalar variables in numbered slots or elements, starting at elements zero. Here is an example of an array variable.

```
$customer(0) = "Fred Smith"
$customer(1) = "Charles Fox"
$customer(2) = "Sally Jones"
```

## 21

Or you may see arrays defined like this

```
@customer("Fred Smith", "Charles Fox", "Sally Jones")
```

> **NOTE**
>
> The @ sign is used in this case to indicate the array variable. This automatically fills in the elements with values, starting at element zero.

Although this barely scratches the surface of Perl, it should be enough to let you read Perl programs that you have downloaded from the Web. However, to test out Perl programs you will need to have Perl installed on the same computer as your Web server.

Installing Perl

Perl is open-source software. This means it's free and maintained by volunteers. Bugs are usually found—and fixed—pretty quickly, and you can even view and modify the source code if you really want to.

Perl runs on almost any operating system, although it was originally developed for Unix and so retains a few peculiarities for that operating system (peculiar if you are used to Windows or Macs!). We will install Perl for either Windows or Mac. The current version of Perl is version 5, but the sub-versions change frequently. You should download the version marked as the latest "production" or "stable" version.

Installing Perl on Windows

First, check to see if you might already have Perl. Open up an MS-DOS window, and at the C:\ prompt type

```
C:\>perl -v
```

If Perl is already there, you will get the version number (if it is earlier than 5, you need a new version). If Perl does not exist and needs to be installed, DOS will reply `bad command or file name`.

The easiest way to get and install Perl is to download it from Active State. They have bundled Perl with an easy-to-use installation routine. Go to `http://www.activestate.com` and download the latest version.

After downloading it, double-click set-up.exe and follow the prompts. Perl will be installed and it will also configure both the computer and the Web server installed on the machine.

Installing Perl on the Mac

Again, first check to see if you already have Perl. Run File Find (Command+F) to look for MacPerl. If it is found, open it, and look at About Perl under the Apple menu. It should be at least version 5.2.0 Patchlevel 5.004. Otherwise, install a new version.

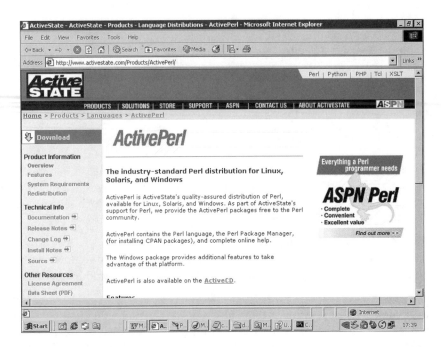

FIGURE 21.6   The Active State Web site—from here you can download Perl for Windows.

To install Perl, download it from

```
http://www.perl.com/CPAN/ports/mac/
```

Download the most recent macperl.appl.bin. If you are unsure which file to use, look in the Mac_Perl.info text file. Unstuff it and run the installation program.

To access the documentation properly, MacPerl comes with a utility called Shuck, located in the MacPerl folder. Add a file extension mapping for .pod files to the Shuck application.

Using a CGI Script

To show how easy it is to use prewritten CGI scripts, we will create a guest book. The CGI script we are using, called simply Guestbook, can be freely downloaded from Matt's Script Archive at the URL:

```
http://www.scriptarchive.com/
```

CGI Checklist

- Before using any script, you should check a few things and write down the answers for later use. If you are renting Web space, you may need to contact your ISP or read their FAQ. If the server is at your company, you may need to speak to the system administrator.

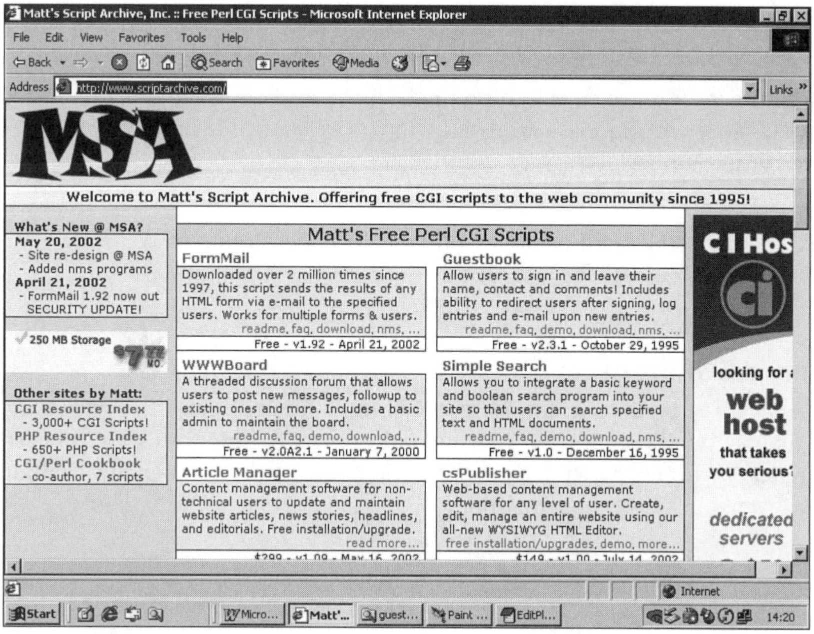

FIGURE 21.7   Matt's Script Archive is a great resource for common CGI scripts.

- First ensure that your Web server is working correctly—test it out on a static HTML page.

- Check the operating system and Web server type being used. For the examples, I am using Microsoft Internet Information Server and Windows 2000. CGI scripts should work with any Web server that has been configured to use CGI (and nearly all are) but check that this is the case, too.

- Find out the location of Perl on the Web server. The first line of every program looks something like this:

```
#!/usr/bin/perl
```

This line tells the script where the Perl interpreter is. You may need to change it to reflect your own server setup. If the Web server runs under Windows, you probably won't need to set this line (we do not in our setup).

- Find out the location of the Web servers log files to help you debug script that is not working. Some Web servers, such as IIS, will display CGI errors to you. Others may hide messages in a log file—and you can't fix a script unless you know what's wrong with it!

- Find out the extension to be used for CGI programs. Most Perl programs end .pl but some servers require them to end in .cgi (our setup uses .pl).

- Check the location of your CGI program directory. You usually have to place scripts in a directory with special permissions to run programs. It's usually called /cgi-bin and is at the top level of the server.

- Check the URL of the CGI directory. This is usually the URL of the server with the CGI directory added; for example, on your local development Web server, it may well be `http://localhost/cgi-bin/`.

Installing a CGI Program

Download the guest book program file guestbook.zip. You will need to unzip it using a program such as WinZip or Stuffit. After uncompressing the file, you should see the following files (if you have used a different guest book script, the filenames will differ but hopefully there will still be a readme file).

```
addguest.html
guestbook.html
guestlog.html
guestbook.pl
readme
```

The HTML files are static Web pages (addguest.html includes a form) associated with the script. This script is a Perl file called guestbook.pl.

Now open and print out the readme file to see what needs changing for your script. Open the guestbook.pl in code view. You need to change the following variables:

$guestbookurl needs modifying to give the full URL of the file guestbook.html.

$guestbookreal gives the path to the guest book file according to the file system on your computer. If you're using IIS, it is likely to be something like

c:/inetpub/wwwroot/yoursite/guestbook.html

$guestlog is the location of the guest book file, according to the file system on your computer—you will probably keep it in the same directory as guestbook.html.

$cgiurl is the URL to the guestbook.pl file.

If you are renting Web space, you may need to check these details with your ISP. See Figure 21.8 for a view of guestbook.pl open in Dreamweaver's code view. As you can see, I have set the variables for use on my local IIS server (localhost).

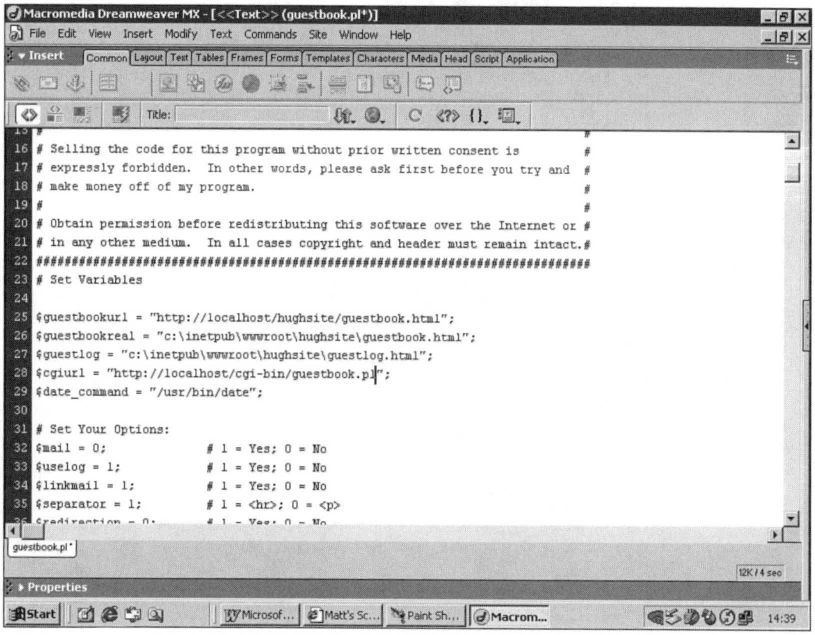

FIGURE 21.8 Guestbook.pl is open in Dreamweaver's code view, so you can make small changes to it for use on your own Web server.

The Readme file also tells you the permissions you need to set if your Web server is Unix. If you are using IIS, you don't need to do this.

You should open the HTML files in design view. The site users are going to see both guestbook.html and addguest.html, so you will probably want to personalize both files and make them part of the overall Web site design. In their raw state, they both are very plain and boring. You can do almost anything you like to them, except change the names of the form objects.

You will also need to change the action property of the form in addguest.html to point to the URL of guestbook.pl. As you can see in Figure 21.9, the action has been changed to reflect the URL on my own server, and I have applied my own template to the file. This page also has a link back to the guest book entries—you will need to amend the URL for that, too.

The file guestbook.html has a relative link to addguest.html—check it and amend if necessary. After you have completed these changes, transfer the file to your server, view addguest.html, and add a guest book comment.

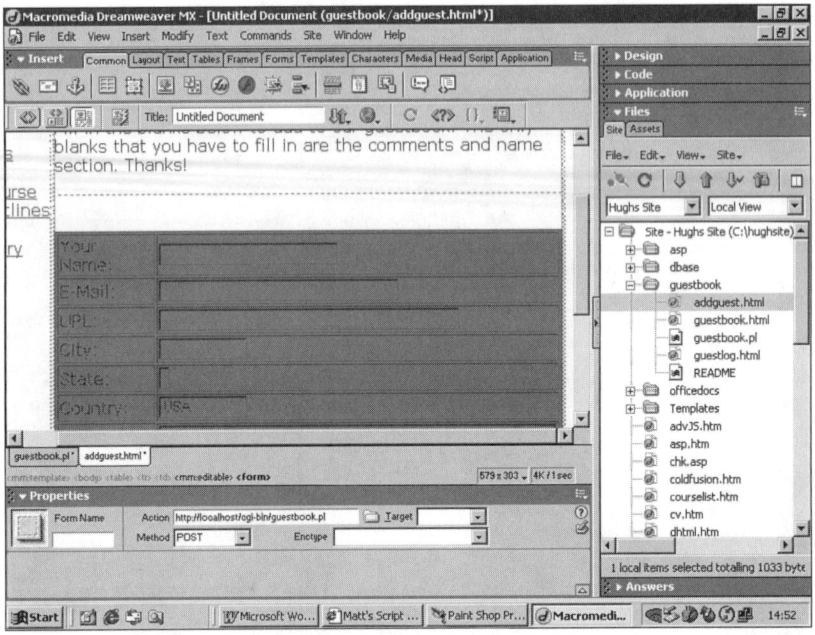

FIGURE 21.9   The Guestbook form page, addguest.html, is open in Dreamweaver's design view, and the action of the form is being changed.

Possible Problems

If you are using IIS as your Web server, the error messages will be displayed in the browser and will hopefully be quite explanatory. These are the two likely problems and their solution.

Perl Syntax Problems

If the error is a Perl syntax problem, this indicates you have edited guestbook.pl inadvertently. The best solution is to go back to the original file and change the variables again. Make sure it's only the variables that get changed—nothing else.

File Not Found

If you get this message after submitting addguest.html, you have probably not correctly defined the action of the form. Check this and try again.

Java

If you cannot or do not want to use CGI or an application server, you may want to use Java applets to provide some of the functions that you can get from CGI. Java applets can be used for page counters, chat rooms, searching and news tickers, and much more.

Java is a programming language with a unique property. The same program file can run on any type of machine. A program written in Java, unlike any other language, can run on Windows PCs, Macs, Unix machines, PDAs—even smart cards.

> **NOTE**
>
> At a 1998 Java conference, the delegates were all given a ring that ran a small Java program to remember their coffee preferences. The coffee machine also ran a Java program to read the preferences and served the appropriate black/white/sugar combinations to delegates (presumably coffee was a Java blend).

With traditional programs, after you have written the code, it gets compiled into an .exe file. This file contains all the machine-level code needed to run the program. This code is unique for the particular processing chip it was compiled for.

However, when you "compile" Java code, it does not produce machine-level code but something called bytecode in a file that has the extension .class. The processor does not read bytecode directly, but by a special software component called a Java Virtual Machine (JVM). JVMs exist for almost every computer platform and are usually installed as part of the operating system. Both Internet Explorer and Netscape Navigator browsers also contain a JVM.

The JVM contains a lot of the code needed for a Java program to interact with the operating system, so the bytecode file can be kept quite small. The capability to run on any machine and to keep code files small makes Java the perfect language for the Internet.

Small Java programs, called applets, can be written for use in Web pages. Your Web page can contain Java applets if you use the HTML <applet> tag. For security reasons, some things cannot be done with a Java applet. An applet cannot read or write files on the user's machine. It cannot start any other program on the user's machine or read many of the system properties. You will also notice that an applet window looks different from an operating system window, so that the user knows the window has come from your Web page.

The Java language itself is very strictly object oriented (see Chapter 20, "Extending Dreamweaver MX," for an introduction to objects) and is not a very easy language to learn if you have not done programming before. However, the community spirit of the Web comes the rescue again, because for most of the things you would want to use Java for, you can download an applet from the Web.

Because Java can run on any type of machine, it is used for both server-side and client-side programming. It can do some things within a client browser that are normally done server side, and if you cannot use CGI scripts, this is very useful. Dreamweaver MX gives you the capability to visually insert Java applets into your document.

Most Web designers will want to place a copy of the applet on their own server along with their HTML files, but it is also possible to use an applet that is kept on another server. You will use a remote applet for the first Java exercise—the creation of a chat room.

Using a Java Chat Room

Many companies offer chat room facilities. They are usually free, but in return, your chat pages will show an advert. One company offering chat rooms is ParaChat. It offers both free and paid-for chat rooms. The chat room works by running Java both on the company's own server, to store the responses by the chatters, and on your Web page, to display the chat conversations to your users. To use the free chat, go to `http://www.parachat.com` and follow the links to the free chat rooms. In this exercise, choose the HTML Chat option.

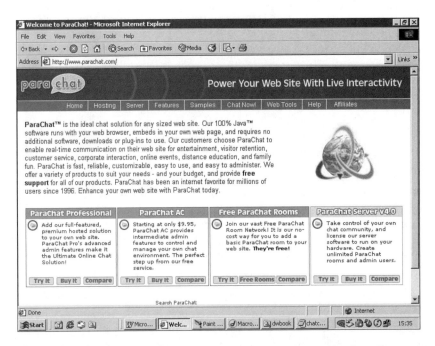

FIGURE 21.10   The ParaChat Web site gives you simple chat rooms for free. If you wanted a chat room with more powerful capabilities, you can also purchase one from them.

You need to fill in a form to register, and afterward, you will be sent an email with the HTML code you need to include in your Web page. You can paste this code into a page on your Web site using code view. This email also gives you a URL to a page that shows you the parameters required to customize your chat applet. If you switch to design view, you will just see a large gray rectangle with a coffee cup logo on it. You can resize the applet to fit within your design and you can also do some basic formatting by setting parameters as described in the next section.

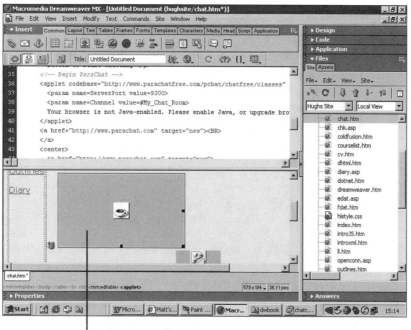

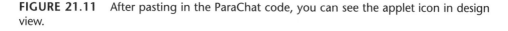

Applet icon

FIGURE 21.11   After pasting in the ParaChat code, you can see the applet icon in design view.

Setting Property Parameters

Most Java applets allow some degree of customization using parameters, and the ParaChat applet is no exception. The parameter names will be different for each applet, and you will need to refer to the applet's documentation to find the names to use and the options available.

To set parameters in Dreamweaver MX, click the applet itself. The Properties palette, as shown in Figure 21.12, will change to show the Java applet properties. Many of these properties have already been set with the HTML code you pasted in. Table 21.3 shows a list of the properties you can set using Dreamweaver.

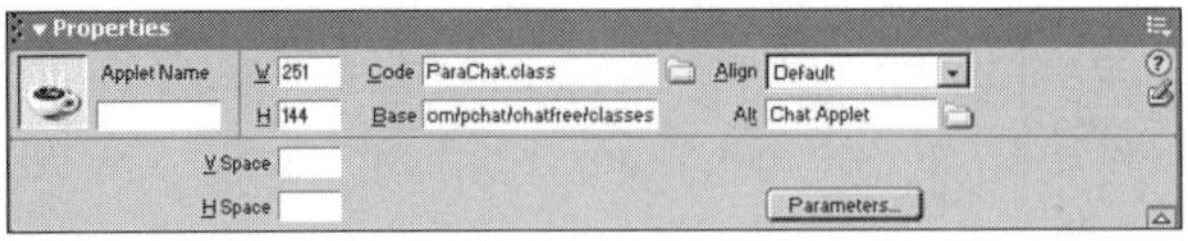

FIGURE 21.12   The Properties palette lets you set the applet properties.

TABLE 21.3   Java Applet Properties

Property	Description
Name	You need to fill this in only if you are going to use JavaScript behaviors on your applet. Most of the time it can be left blank.
W	The width of the applet in pixels as it will be displayed on the page. It can be changed by dragging with the mouse as well as by entering new values into this box.
H	The height of the applet in pixels as it will be displayed on the page. Both W and H are like the W and H properties of an image.
Code	Specifies the name of the file of the Java applet. It will have the extension .class. By clicking the icon, you can browse to this file.
Base	By default, the browser expects the code file to be in the same directory as the HTML file it is included in. If the .class file resides in another directory, or on another server, the URL to that location should be entered here. This can be a relative or an absolute URL. If Dreamweaver enters it for you after you browsed to the file, you should check it carefully to make sure that it matches the location on your remote server.
Align	This is how the applet is aligned on the page, relative to the rest of the text on the page. It acts just like the align attribute of images.
Alt	Alternative text or an image that displays if Java has been disabled. To choose an image click the folder button and browse to the image file.
V Space, H space	The white space around the applet, just like V Space and H Space with images.

Near the bottom of the Properties palette is a button marked Parameters. Clicking this opens up a small dialog box, as shown in Figure 21.13. You can see that some parameters have already been set and you can add your own after referring to the documentation. To add a parameter, click the plus (+) button and then fill in the parameter's name and its value.

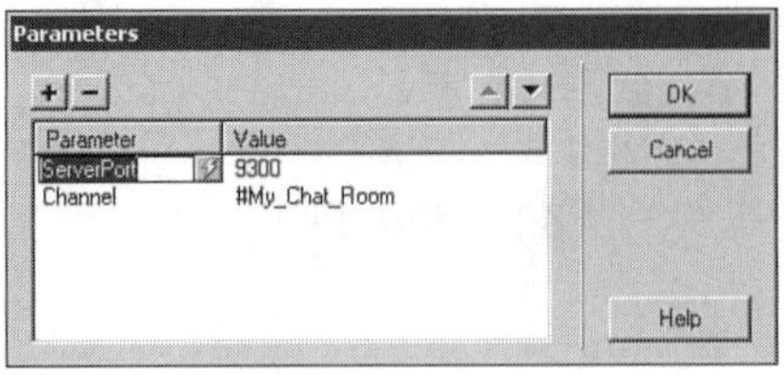

FIGURE 21.13   Add a parameter by clicking the plus (+) button in the Parameters dialog box.

If you now preview the page, you should be able to test out the chat applet.

> **NOTE**
>
> ParaChat is one of a number of free chat rooms available. Although they offer slightly different interfaces and functions, they all are inserted in your Web page the same way.
>
> Users that view Web pages from behind a firewall will probably have problems using chat applets. Firewalls are rarely configured to allow chat communications through.

Applets Versus CGI Scripts

For some functions, such as chat rooms and search engines, both Java applets or CGI scripts can be used. Remember that applets work on the client side, whereas CGI scripts run on the server. You may also want to consider the following:

- Java applets have an advantage in that you do not need to make any changes to the server. If you are not allowed to configure your server or use CGI, applets are your only option. It is usually easier to insert an applet in the page than it is to configure the server. If you are nervous about messing around with a Web server, you may prefer to use an applet.

- Applets will work only if the user has a Java-compatible browser (nearly all browsers in use today support Java) and they have Java enabled (it is enabled by default). Some corporations do not allow their browsers to run Java for security reasons. CGI scripts, because they do all the processing on the server, do not violate security restrictions.

- Applets generally have more limited functionality than CGI scripts do. For database access, for instance, you would almost certainly need to use CGI or an application server.

Project: Inserting a Search Engine into an HTML Document

There are many ways of providing a search engine with CGI or application servers, but if you can't use CGI, you can use a Java applet. Browsing through http://www.freewarejava.com, we found a search applet called sitesearch (http://www.lundin.info/search.asp). This applet seemed to work best and have the most options of the many applets listed, but the other applets all work on the same principles. Follow these steps:

1. Download the applet and print off the documentation for reference later.

2. After unzipping the downloaded file, copy the search.class file into the top level of your site folder (and remember to upload to your testing server and remote server).

3. You can copy the applet tag example that is given in the documentation or insert the applet using the Insert menu (Insert+Media+Applet) or the Media tab of the Insert bar in Dreamweaver.

4. If Dreamweaver inserts a directory name in the Base property, delete it. As a minimum, you need to set the firstpage parameter—this is the page that the applet will start searching from. It searches through the pages by following hyperlinks from this first page specified. See Figure 21.14 to see the applet in design view.

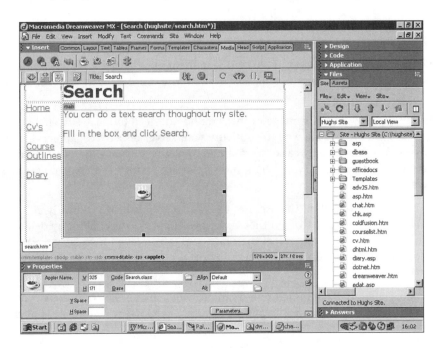

FIGURE 21.14   Click the Applet icon in Dreamweaver's design view. You can see the Applet properties, and yours should match those shown here.

There are many other options that can be set to make the applet match your page colors and to set the text displayed in the applet. See the documentation for details.

Summary

In this chapter, we moved away from the design of traditional HTML pages and looked at what we could do with server-side programming. You saw the differences between client-side programming, using JavaScript or Flash, and server-side programming using CGI or an application server. You also learned about the situations in which it is appropriate to use each technology.

By understanding the way that the common gateway interface (CGI) works, you can see how potentially powerful it can be. By learning to program the way the server responds to users, you can give different responses to different users, based on the type of browser they are using, the way they fill in forms on your Web site, and even depending on the time of day!

Different languages can be used to create CGI programs, but the most common is Perl. You looked at Perl quickly so that you would be able to understand the basics of a Perl program, even if you are unable to write a full program yourself. Many Web sites provide prewritten Perl programs for you to use. To show how this can be achieved very easily, you downloaded a prewritten Perl script for a guest book, modified it for your own server setup, and installed it on your Web site.

You also looked at Java, a programming language which straddles the divide between client-side and server-side programming. Java is a complicated language to learn, although potentially very powerful. However, you can use Java programs that others have written and make available for use—often for free.

You used a small, client-side Java program, called an applet, to provide a chat room on your Web site.

21

CHAPTER **22**

ASP and ASP.NET

By Zak Ruvalcaba

Introduction to ASP

In 1997, Microsoft introduced Active Server Pages (ASP) as a means of competing with then-popular CGI for creating dynamic and scalable Web applications. Because of its relative simplicity and learning curve, ASP has grown to be one of the top server-based scripting languages used by Web developers. Unlike CGI, which required complex object-oriented programming languages (PERL/C++) to be used, ASP used a simple subscript of Visual Basic known as VBScript. Because VBScript closely models the constructs of plain English, it was found to be easy to write and manipulate, giving it a definite advantage over Perl and C++. Another major advantage to using ASP was that it came prebundled with IIS. Web developers needed only to have a running Windows server environment with IIS and they were ready to begin creating ASP, in contrast to competitor products such as ColdFusion, which required ColdFusion Server to be installed before CFML could be run adequately.

The ASP Object Model

ASP is simple to write after you know its object model. Basically, ASP consists of five major objects that can be used to perform any task from handling user requests to delivering user responses. The five objects are

- The request object

- The response object

- The session object

- The application object

- The server object

The Request Object

Applications do not simply function as standalone programs, they require input from an external location. For every action to be taken on the application side, a request has to be made. The request object handles the request from the client-side application. The request object has specific methods that a developer can program against, such as

- **Cookies**   Cookies represents a collection of cookie values that will be sent to the system as a request. The following is an example:

```
<%
strTown = Request.Cookies("SavedLogin")("Town")
%>
```

  In this example, "SavedLogin" is the cookie name and "Town" is the value contained within the cookie.

- **Form**   Returns the value of a specified form object. The following is an example:

```
<%
myValue = Request.Form("TextBox1")
%>
```

The Response Object

With every request coming into the application, the response object accesses the response that is to be sent back to the client. It also makes available a series of methods that the developer can program against. Some of these methods are

- **Write**   Write does exactly what it says. It writes code or markup wherever you specify within the page. An example may resemble the following:

```
<%
Response.Write("Hello World")
%>
```

- **Redirect**   Redirect immediately sends the user to a new URL. An example may resemble the following:

```
<%
Response.Redirect("sample.asp")
%>
```

- **Cookies**   Cookies represents a collection of cookie values that will be sent back to the user in the response. The following is an example:

```
<%
Response.Cookies("SavedLogin")("Town") = Request.Form("City")
%>
```

In the preceding example, the value "Town" which is contained within the "SavedLogin" cookie is being set to the value of the form object "City".

- **Expires** Expires sets a flag on the cookie, letting the server know when this cookie will expire. The following is an example:

```
<%
Response.Cookies("SavedLogin").Expires = Date + 30
%>
```

In the preceding example, the cookie "SavedLogin" expires in 30 days.

The Session Object

The session object provides a place for variables and object references to be available for a single person during the life of the session. By default, sessions time out within 20 minutes. The session object makes available a series of methods that the developer can program against. Some of these methods are

- **Abandon** Clears all available sessions. An example may resemble the following:

```
<%
Session.Abandon
%>
```

- **Contents** Contents return the names and values that are contained within the session object.

- **Timeout** Timeout defines the timeout period for the particular object. Even though the default is 20 minutes, a different timeout can be specified at any time.

The Application Object

The application object provides a place for variables and object references to be stored and used by all files available within the application. The application object makes available a series of methods that the developer can program against.

The Server Object

The most obvious purpose for the server object is for the instantiation of objects. The server object also makes available a series of methods that the developer can use. Some of these methods are

- **CreateObject** CreateObject is used in the instantiation of new COM objects or Windows APIs. The following is an example:

```
<%
Set objMail = Server.CreateObject("CDONTS.NewMail")
%>
```

- **MapPath**   MapPath provides a developer with the opportunity to return the full physical path of a file. Typically, MapPath is used when you are pointing to a UDL file that resides in the project folder. When moving the application to a new machine, developers do not have to comb through all of their code to make the changes globally. The following is an example:

```
<%
myLocation = Server.MapPath("sample.asp")
%>
```

myLocation could return:

```
c:\InetPub\wwwroot\Project\sample.asp
```

- **Transfer**   Transfer stops execution of the page that the user is currently on and sends the user to a new URL. The following is an example:

```
<%
Server.Transfer("sample.asp")
%>
```

Other ASP Objects and Components

Aside from the five basic objects available in ASP, you are also able to use other objects to accomplish specialized tasks. For instance, if you wanted to read from and write to a text file, you could use the file system object. If you wanted to continuously rotate banner advertisements, you could implement the AdRotator component. ASP offers many other objects and components that can be quickly instantiated using the CreateObject method of the server object. The list of additional objects and components is as follows:

- **ActiveX Data Objects (ADO)**   ADO is an API from Microsoft that allows developers building Web applications access to databases. Typically, ADO program statements, combined with SQL statements, are written within an HTML file identified as an ASP page. The user sends a request and a response is sent back with the appropriate data from the database.

- **Collaboration Data Objects (CDO)**   CDO is an API from Microsoft that enables developers building Web applications to include messaging services within their applications. Using ASP with CDO, a developer could write code that sends email to clients and allows employees to schedule meetings, review appointments, schedule events, and so on.

- **File System Object**   The file system object is an API from Microsoft that allows developers building Web applications to access drives, folders, and directory information from the server. Using the file system object, a developer could allow users to create folders and write to and read from files within those folders.

- **Dictionary Object**   The dictionary object provides developers the opportunity to store names and values within a list similar to an array. Unlike an array however, a dictionary's values can be referenced by name rather than by index, as is the case with arrays.

- **ASPError Object**   The ASPError object provides a developer with a series of objects to use when debugging and catching errors within code.

Configuring the Web Store to Run ASP

Dreamweaver MX provides excellent integration for ASP, including drag-and-drop objects from the Objects panel, ASP objects from the Insert menu, recordsets from the Bindings panel, and many server behaviors to help you get started producing dynamic content. To configure the Web Store application to run under ASP, follow the three steps outlined next:

1. Define a new site for the Web Store application.

2. Choose a document type.

3. Configure the application testing server.

Define a New Site for the Web Store Application

One of the most important things you can do with any Web application, whether it is dynamic or static, is to define a new site for it. Creating a new site ensures link integrity, helps when performing global find and replaces and link changing, and provides the benefits of site reports. You can define a new site for the Web Store application by following the steps outlined next:

1. Start Dreamweaver MX and open the Application panel. Figure 22.1 shows the three steps to creating an application within Dreamweaver MX.

FIGURE 22.1   Creating a new site involves three steps: defining the location of the site, choosing a server technology, and picking a testing server.

2. From either the Database, Binding, or Server Behaviors panels, select Site from step one.

3. After you have selected the Site link, select the Advanced tab from the Site Definition window. Figure 22.2 shows the site definition information.

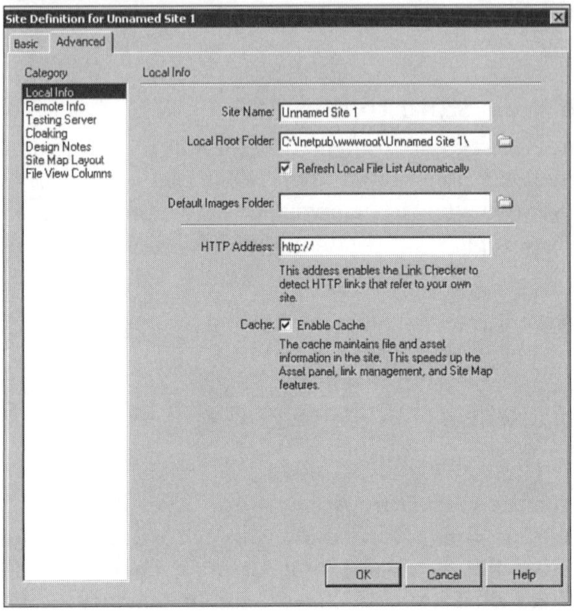

FIGURE 22.2   Use the Site Definition window to define properties for your Web application.

4. Enter Web Store for the Site Name.

5. Navigate to your local root folder where your application resides. If you have not already done so, create a Project folder somewhere on your computer called Web Store and another folder within that called Images. This folder will serve as the repository for all the files that will reside in your application.

6. Refresh File List Automatically should be checked.

7. Navigate to the Images folder within the Web Store folder.

8. Enable Site Cache should be checked.

9. Press OK.

Figure 22.3 shows how you should now have a check mark next to step one in any of the three tabs (Database, Bindings, Server Behaviors) within the Application panel.

FIGURE 22.3   After you have defined your site, a check mark will appear after the first step.

Choose a Document Type

The document type will serve as the object model for the type of application you want to create and run. To define a document type follow these steps:

1. Choose Document Type from step 2 in either the Database, Bindings, or Server Behaviors tab within the Application panel.

> **CAUTION**
>
> Sometimes step 2 may already be checked after you've defined your site. Dreamweaver MX does not know the model that you plan to use and will just default to the last one picked. You must still perform this step.

2. When the Document Type dialog box appears as shown in Figure 22.4, select ASP VBScript.

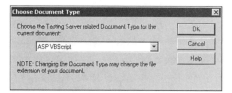

FIGURE 22.4   Choose the Document Type that you want to use in your application.

3. Select OK.

Configure the Application Testing Server

The final step in defining the Web Store application is setting up the testing server. Remember, in a Microsoft server environment, Web applications are run in the

C:\Inetpub\wwwroot directory. Before you can define the testing server, you must properly create the project folder within the C:\Inetpub\wwwroot directory. To do so, follow these steps:

1. Navigate to C:\Inetpub\wwwroot.

2. Create a new folder called "Web Store."

3. Inside of Web Store, create a new folder called Images.

CAUTION

Depending on which features you are using within your ASP environment, it may become necessary to create an application out of the project folder within IIS.

You are now ready to define the testing server:

1. Choose Testing Server from step 3 in either the Database, Bindings, or Server Behaviors tab within the Application panel.

2. The site definition for the Web Store window will appear.

3. Select ASP VBScript from the Server Model drop-down list.

4. Select Local/Network from the Access drop-down list.

5. Navigate to C:\Inetpub\wwwroot\Webstore as the testing server folder. Click Select.

6. Refresh File List Automatically should be checked.

7. http://localhost/webstore should be set as the URL prefix. Your settings should appear similar to Figure 22.5.

8. Click OK to set the site definition.

Using ASP with Dreamweaver MX

ASP integration begins with the Application panel. Most of the functionality that you will use, whether it is creating a database connection or working with recordsets, will spawn from the Application panel, most notably the Database, Bindings, and Server Behaviors tabs. The features that make up the ASP integration include the following:

- **The Database panel**   The Database panel provides you with a way of defining a database connection by inputting or constructing your own custom string or by using the Data Sources Administrator to create a Data Source Name (DSN).

- **The Data Bindings panel**   The Data Bindings panel enables you to work with recordsets, stored procedures, server variables, session variables, and application variables. You can also find more data sources from the Macromedia Exchange by selecting Get More Data Sources.

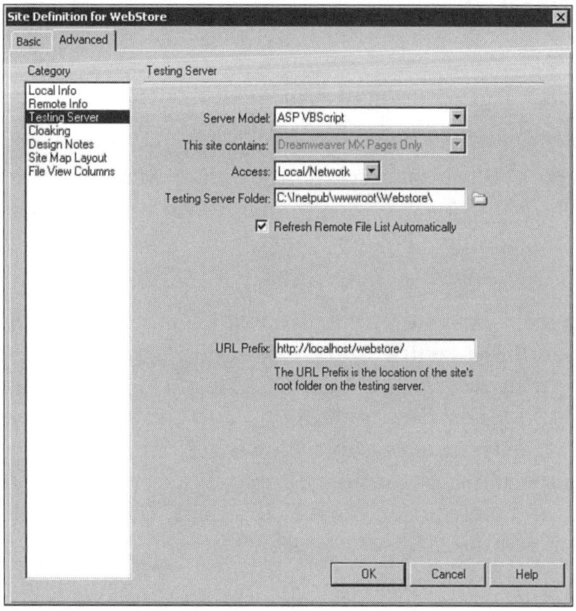

FIGURE 22.5   Configure the testing server for the Web Store application.

- **The Server Behaviors panel**   The Server Behaviors panel gives you the opportunity to work with Data Sources such as recordsets and stored procedures. It also affords you the ability to work with various data binding, paging, and authentication features.

- **ASP objects**   ASP objects are available either through the Insert menu or the Objects panel. With ASP objects, you have the ability to insert various predefined data handling, string manipulation, and conditional statement objects.

Introduction to ASP.NET

ASP.NET, part of Microsoft's new strategy for delivering software as a service, is the next generation environment for developing server-based, dynamic applications. Utilizing the .NET Framework, ASP.NET provides developers with a rich set of controls with which to build, deploy, and maintain applications and Web Services.

Introduction to .NET

.NET is Microsoft's new strategy for delivering software as a service. By reinventing the Application Services Provider (ASP) business model, Microsoft hopes to achieve independence from the long-standing boxware paradigm. The key features that make up .NET include the following:

- **.NET platform**   The .NET platform includes the .NET Framework and tools to build and operate the services, clients, and so on.

- **.NET products**   .NET products currently include MSN.NET, Office .NET, and Visual Studio .NET, which provide developers a rich environment for creating Web services utilizing such programming environments as C++, Visual Basic .NET, ASP.NET, C#, and so on.

- **.NET My Services**   An initiative formerly known as "Hailstorm," the .NET My Services are a set of user-centric XML Web services currently being provided by a whole host of partners, developers, and organizations hoping to build vertical market application for devices, applications, and the Internet. The collection of My Services currently extends to passport, messenger, contacts, email, calendar, profile, lists, wallet, location, document stores, application settings, favorite Web sites, devices owned, and preferences for receiving alerts. Figure 22.6 shows the MSN browser and some of the .NET My Services.

FIGURE 22.6   The MSN browser is one of the .NET products and includes ways of interacting with a myriad of Web services.

The .NET Framework

The .NET Framework is the environment for which .NET applications are built. The .NET Framework specifically is designed for Web Services and supports development across a larger spectrum. The three main parts of the .NET Framework are

- The Common Language Runtime (CLR)

- The Framework classes

- ASP.NET

Although the .NET Framework is just a small piece of the pie, it lays the foundation for .NET applications and Web Services. Remember, that the .NET Framework, although crucial in the .NET strategy, is only a small piece of the .NET platform and the .NET platform is just one-third of the .NET initiative.

> **TIP**
>
> Why is the .NET Framework relevant to Dreamweaver MX? If you are to build ASP.NET applications using Dreamweaver MX, you will first have to install the .NET Framework SDK. The .NET Framework SDK can be downloaded from Microsoft's Web site at www.microsoft.com.

The Common Language Runtime

One of the most important features within the .NET Framework is the Common Language Runtime (CLR). The CLR manages programming simplicity by exposing a unique compilation and execution flow.

In the past, ASP supported VBScript and JScript as languages that could be used to write the applications. The CLR currently supports about a dozen, with the possibility for many more. The reason this can be accomplished is simple—source code is compiled to Intermediate Language (IL) code, which in its simplest definition is just assembly code.

Figure 22.7 shows how source code is compiled to IL code and metadata is created using the metadata engine. The IL and metadata are linked, resulting in a DLL or assembly. When executed, the IL code and any class that the application may use are combined using the class loader. The Just-In-Time (JIT) compiler produces more code that is passed onto the runtime for execution.

The .NET Framework Class Library

The .NET languages are all about classes. Everything, right down to adding two numbers, implements a class in some form or fashion. The .NET Framework exposes a vast set of classes and namespaces appropriately named the Framework Class Library. These are contained within a set of namespaces called the Base Class Library that provides basic services for handling data, errors, garbage collection, strings, numbers, and more. In all, there are about 90 namespaces that contain about 3,400 classes.

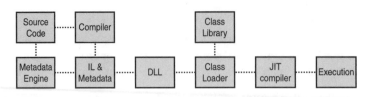

FIGURE 22.7   The CLR involves a complex series of operations before final execution.

Understanding Namespaces

As I mentioned, the Framework Class Library contains roughly 3,400 classes, all organized within a hierarchy of namespaces. If you think of the hierarchy as a tree of namespaces, System would be at the root, and all other namespaces would stem from that. For example, if you wanted to work with writing and reading text files, you would probably use the System.IO namespace. If you wanted to create a connection to an Access database, you would probably need the System.Data.OleDb namespace, and if you wanted to create a Web form utilizing Web controls, you would need to use the System.Web.UI.WebControls namespace. As you can see, namespaces are grouped through a hierarchy of namespaces, separated by dot syntax, and are relatively easy to use.

> **NOTE**
>
> Because there are so many namespaces, it is nearly impossible to remember which one contains the class that you need to expose. You can view a list of all the namespaces in the Framework Class Library by viewing the Reference Documentation for the .NET Framework.

Although for the most part you will have to Import most namespaces into your ASP.NET pages, some you will not. ASP.NET implicitly imports a group of namespaces known as the ASP.NET Base Classes. These include the following:

- **System**   Contains all the data types as well as classes that relate to working with numbers and time.

- **System.Collections**   Contains classes for working with collection types such as arrays.

- **System.Collections.Specialized**   Contains classes for working with specialized collections such as string collections.

- **System.Configuration**   Contains classes for working with the Web.Config file and other configuration settings.

- **System.Text**   Contains classes for creating and manipulating strings.

- **System.Text.RegularExpressions**   Contains classes for doing regular expression matches.

- **System.Web**   Contains the classes for working with the Web, including traditional request and response properties.

- **System.Web.Caching**   Contains the classes used for caching content with a page.

- **System.Web.Security**   Contains classes used for implementing authentication.

- **System.Web.SessionState**   Contains classes used to implement the state of a session.

- **System.Web.UI**   Contains classes used in the construction of ASP.NET pages.

- **System.Web.UI.HTMLControls**   Contains the classes for HTML controls.

- **System.Web.UI.WebControls**   Contains the classes for Web controls.

ASP.NET Page Structure

Before you can begin writing ASP.NET pages, it is important to discuss how the page is even constructed. Aside from containing code (server-side execution and dynamic content) and markup for structure, ASP.NET pages also contain seven distinct elements. These are

- Directives

- Code Declaration blocks

- ASP.NET controls

- Code Render blocks

- Server-side include directives

- Server-side comments

- Literal text and HTML tags

In the following sections, we will discuss the four most important ones.

Directives

Directives are used within an ASP.NET page to tell the compiler how it should compile the page. The most useful directives are Page and Import, but you can use any of the following as well: Control, Register, Assembly, and OutputCache. Directives are inserted at the top of an ASP.NET page and look like the following:

```
<%@Page attribute=value %>
```

ASP.NET Controls

ASP.NET controls provide a way for you to develop dynamic Web applications without having to embed clumsy and antiquated scripts. Because ASP.NET controls render the code that the user will actually see, ASP.NET controls can be considered the building blocks for the dynamic and interactive portions of your Web applications. ASP.NET controls take the form of

- **HTML Controls**   HTML controls are constructed by simply adding the runat="server" attribute within any ordinary HTML tag. HTML controls are discussed later in the chapter.

- **Web Controls**   With Web controls, Microsoft basically re-invented HTML. Web controls provide all the dynamic input and output for the ASP.NET page.

- **Custom Controls**   Although ASP.NET comes bundled with ready-to-use controls, at times you might want to create your own custom controls to interact with.

- **Validation Controls**   Validation controls are used in the validation of form objects.

- **Rich Controls**   Rich controls include the calendar control, XML control, and the ad rotator control.

- **Data Controls**   Data controls provide a means of interacting with data from a database. Data controls include the DataList, DataGrid, and Repeater.

- **Mobile Controls**   Mobile controls provide a means for creating rich Web applications for handheld devices.

Code Render Blocks

Code render blocks allow the user to define code when the page is rendered, not compiled. Code render blocks can be written similar to the following:

```
<%
Dim strText As String = "My Message"
Response.Write(strText)
%>
```

Literal Text and HTML Tags

The final and most important element that you can include in your page is plain old HTML. HTML lays the foundation for your ASP.NET page and is what ultimately controls the structure and design of the content within it.

Configuring the Web Store to Run ASP.NET

Dreamweaver MX provides excellent integration for ASP.NET, including a library of controls available from the Tag Chooser, drag-and-drop objects from the Objects panel, ASP.NET objects from the Insert menu, DataSets from the Bindings panel, and many server behaviors to help you get started producing dynamic content including the DataGrid, DataList, and Repeaters controls. To configure the Web Store application to run under ASP.NET, follow the three steps outlined next:

1. Define a new site for the Web Store application.

2. Choose a document type.

3. Configure the application testing server.

Define a New Site for the Web Store Application

One of the most important things you can do with any Web application, whether it is dynamic or static, is to define a new site for it. Creating a new site ensures link integrity, helps when performing global find and replaces and link changing, and provides the benefits of site reports. You can define a new site for the Web Store application by following the steps outlined next:

1. Start Dreamweaver MX and open the Application panel. Figure 22.8 shows the three steps to creating an application within Dreamweaver MX.

FIGURE 22.8   Creating a new site involves three steps: defining the location of the site, choosing a server technology, and picking a testing server.

2. From either the Database, Binding, or Server Behaviors panel, select Site from step one.

3. After you have selected the Site link, select the Advanced tab from the Site Definition window. Figure 22.9 shows the site definition information.

4. Enter **Web Store** for the Site Name.

5. Navigate to your local root folder where your application resides. If you have not already done so, create a Project folder somewhere on your computer called Web Store and another folder within that called Images. This folder will serve as the repository for all the files that will reside in your application.

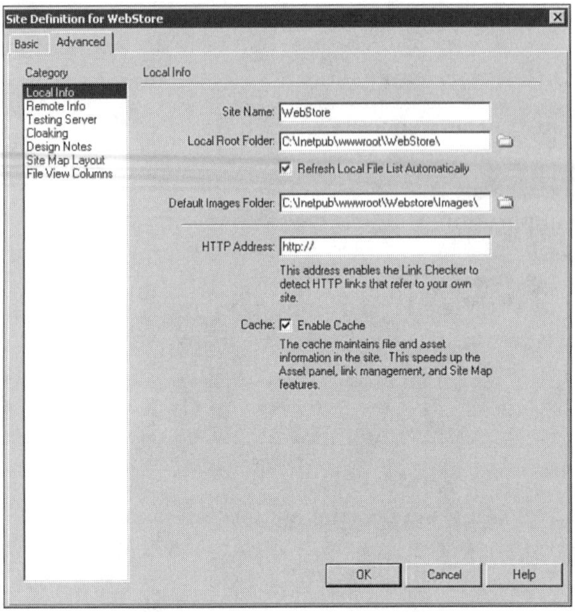

FIGURE 22.9   Use the Site Definition window to define properties for your Web application.

6. Refresh File List Automatically should be checked.

7. Navigate to the Images folder within the Web Store folder.

8. Enable Site Cache should be checked.

9. Press OK.

Figure 22.10 shows how you should now have a check mark next to step one in any of the three tabs (Database, Bindings, Server Behaviors) within the Application panel.

Choose a Document Type

The document type will serve as the object model for the type of application you want to create and run. To define a document type, follow these steps:

1. Choose Document Type from step 2 in either the Database, Bindings, or Server Behaviors tab within the Application panel.

> **CAUTION**
>
> Sometimes step 2 may already be checked after you've defined your site. Dreamweaver MX does not know the model that you plan to use and will default to the last one picked. You still need to perform this step.

FIGURE 22.10   After you have defined your site, a check mark will appear after the first step.

2. When the Document Type dialog box appears as shown in Figure 22.11, select ASP.NET VB.

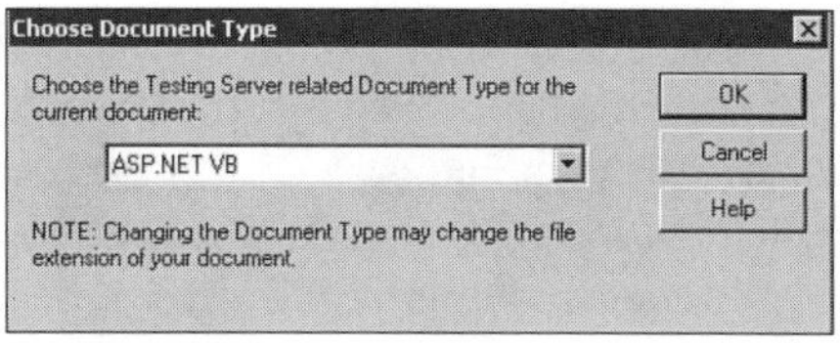

FIGURE 22.11   Select ASP.NET VB as the Document Type.

3. Select OK.

Configure the Application Testing Server

The final step to defining the Web Store application is setting up the testing server. Remember, in a Microsoft server environment, Web applications are run in the C:\Inetpub\wwwroot directory. Before you can define the testing server, you must properly create the project folder within the C:\Inetpub\wwwroot directory. To do so, follow these steps:

1. Navigate to C:\Inetpub\wwwroot.

2. Create a new folder called Web Store.

3. Inside of Web Store, create a new folder called Images.

You are now ready to define the testing server.

1. Choose Testing Server from step 3 in either the Database, Bindings, or Server Behaviors tab within the Application panel.

2. The site definition for Web Store window will appear.

3. Select ASP.NET VB from the Server Model drop-down list.

4. Select Local/Network from the Access drop-down list.

5. Navigate to C:\Inetpub\wwwroot\Webstore as the testing server folder. Click Select.

6. Refresh File List Automatically should be checked.

7. http://localhost/ should be set as the URL prefix.

8. Select OK.

There will also be a reminder that Dreamweaver MX will deploy what it calls "supporting files" to the bin directory. Select Deploy to bring up the Deploy Supporting Files to Testing Server dialog box. Remember, this is accomplished because of the CLR. The CLR compiles the source code and any metadata into IL code, which is then linked into a DLL or assembly within the bin directory. The file remains there until execution.

Using ASP.NET with Dreamweaver MX

Like ASP, ASP.NET integration begins with the Application panel. Most of the functionality that you will use—whether it's creating a database connection, working with DataSets, or displaying dynamic content within DataGrids or DataLists will spawn from the Application panel, most notably the Database, Bindings, and Server Behaviors tabs. The features that make up the ASP.NET integration include the following:

- **The Database panel**   The Database panel provides you with a way of defining a database connection to either a SQL Server database or a supported OLE DB type.

- **The Data Bindings panel**   The Data Bindings panel allows you to work with DataSets and Stored Procedures. You can also find more data sources from the Macromedia Exchange by selecting Get More Data Sources.

- **The Server Behaviors panel**   The Server Behaviors panel gives you the opportunity to work with Data Sources such as DataSets and Stored Procedures, Data Controls in DataGrids, DataLists, and Repeaters, and various other record-handling mechanisms.

- **The Components Panel**   The Components panel allows you to work with Web Services.

- **The Tag Chooser**   The Tag Chooser gives you access to controls such as Web controls, validation controls, Macromedia server controls, and ASP.NET specific style information and templates.

- **ASP.NET Objects**   ASP.NET objects are available either through the Insert menu or the Objects panel. You can insert various predefined ASP.NET objects including data handling objects, namespace objects, and various other controls.

- **The Web.Config File**   The Web.Config file is usually automatically created for you after you define a database connection. Residing in the root directory of your project folder, the Web.Config file contains crucial configuration information that the compiler relies on.

Beyond Dreamweaver MX

Dreamweaver MX is a powerful authoring environment that provides the developer with a feature-rich set of controls, objects, behaviors, and commands. As you progress in your Web application development, however, you may come to a point when Dreamweaver MX simply cannot do what you need it to accomplish. One example is the capability to read and write to text files or the capability to automatically generate emails. These are two fairly popular tasks Dreamweaver simply has no way of handling. In instances like these, you will need to go beyond Dreamweaver MX and into the world of coding.

Sending Email with ASP

Suppose for a moment that you wanted to send an email confirmation to your customers regarding an order that they had just placed. You could have an interface that looks similar to the one in Figure 22.12.

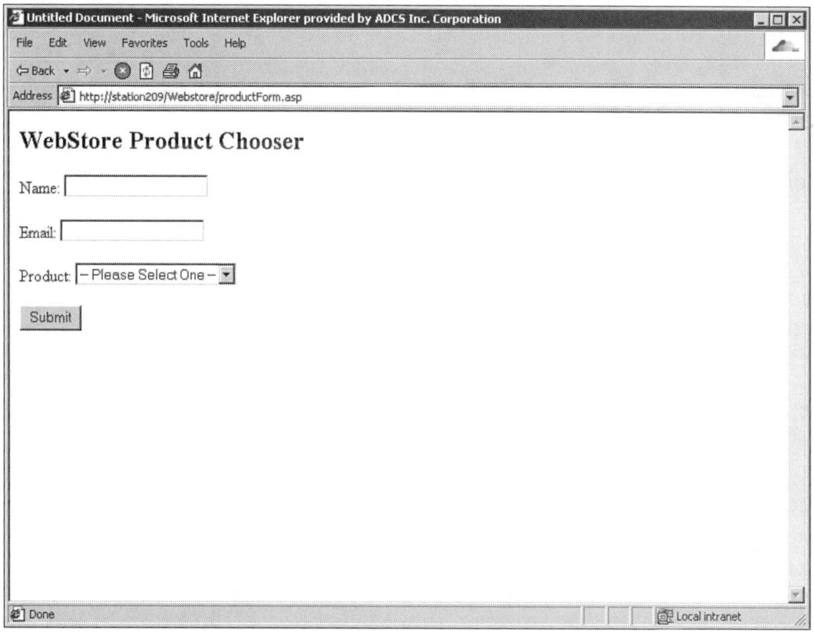

FIGURE 22.12   A simple interface that could generate an email to a customer.

The interface includes a simple text box for users to input their names and email addresses and a drop-down list that includes products that the user can choose from. All in all, the code could resemble the following:

```
<%@LANGUAGE="VBSCRIPT" CODEPAGE="1252"%>
<html>
<head>
<title>WebStore Product Chooser</title>
</head>
<body>
<h2>WebStore Product Chooser<h2>
<form name="form1" method="post" action="">
Name: <input name="name" type="text" id="name"><br><br>
Email: <input name="email" type="text" id="email"><br><br>
Product:
<select name="product" id="product">
<option selected>-- Please Select One --</option>
<option value="Shirt">Shirt - $12.99</option>
<option value="Pants">Pants - $34.99</option>
<option value="Shoes">Shoes - $79.99</option>
<option value="Hat">Hat - $12.00</option>
</select><br><br>
<input type="submit" name="Submit" value="Submit">
</form>
</body>
</html>
```

Obviously, if the user clicked Submit, it wouldn't do much, but if the code were to be modified slightly, it could be very much dynamic.

First, make the form post to itself by adding the name of the file to the action attribute: action="productForm.asp".

Second, add the following code just after the first line to generate the email:

```
<%
Dim strName, strEmail, strProduct, body, objMail
strName = Request.Form("name")
strEmail = Request.Form("email")
strProduct = Request.Form("product")
If (strName <> "") Then
Set objMail = Server.CreateObject("CDONTS.NewMail")
objMail.From = "sales@webstore.com"
objMail.To = strEmail
objMail.Subject = "Your order has been confirmed"
objMail.body = strName & " Your order has been confirmed for: " & strProduct
```

```
objMail.Send
Set objMail = Nothing
Response.Write("Thank you for ordering")
Else
%>
```

Don't forget <% End If %> as the very last line in the document. Stepping through the code, you can see that the If statement performs a check to see whether the strName variable is empty. If it is, it will show just the HTML code until the user submits the form for the first time. When the form is submitted, the variable then becomes populated and the send mail code gets called. The code instantiates a set of server objects known as collaboration data objects (CDO) and goes through the motions populating the From, To, Subject, and Body fields. The final step is performed with the email being sent and a Thank You message is presented to the user.

Sending Email with ASP.NET

You can tweak the preceding code slightly to generate the same results with ASP.NET. Rather than the HTML code looking like it did in the following example, it could look a bit more like the following:

```
<%@ Page Language="VB" ContentType="text/html"
ResponseEncoding="iso-8859-1" %>
<html>
<head>
<title>WebStore Product Chooser</title>
</head>
<body>
<h2>WebStore Product Chooser</h2>
<form action="productForm.aspx" method="post" name="form1" runat="server">
Name: <asp:textbox Columns="30" ID="name" runat="server"
TextMode="SingleLine" />
<br><br>
Email: <asp:textbox Columns="30" ID="email" runat="server"
TextMode="SingleLine" />
<br>
<br>
Product:
<asp:dropdownlist ID="product" runat="server">
<asp:listItem value="shirt" text="Shirt - $12.99"></asp:listItem>
<asp:listItem value="pants" text="Pants - $39.99"></asp:listItem>
<asp:listItem value="shoes" text="Shoes - $79.99"></asp:listItem>
<asp:listItem value="hat" text="Hat - $12.99"></asp:listItem>
</asp:dropdownlist>
```

```
<br><br>
<asp:button onClick="Button_Click" ID="btnSubmit" runat="server" Text="Submit" />
</form>

</body>
</html>
```

To generate the email, first you need to add the mail namespace. You can select the Import Namespace object from the Insert, ASP.NET Objects menu. Make sure you add it as the very first line of code:

```
<%@ Import Namespace="System.Web.Mail" %>
```

Next, add the subroutine that will handle the click event for the button control:

```
<script runat="server">
Sub Button_Click(s As Object, e As EventArgs)
Dim objMail = New MailMessage
objMail.From = "sales@webstore.com"
objMail.To = email.Text
objMail.Subject = "Your order has been confirmed"
objMail.Body = name.Text & " your order has been confirmed for: " &
product.selectedItem.Text
SmtpMail.SmtpServer = "localhost"
SmtpMail.Send(objMail)
End Sub
</script>
```

Figure 22.13 shows the email message that was sent to me from our example.

Notice that in this example, the code was placed into a subroutine with two parameters being passed in. "s As Object" treats the controls as objects going in and "e As EventArgs" handles the arguments that they raise. Also, notice that a new MailMessage was instantiated and its properties are set. The final step sends the email message.

One item to consider before actually testing your code is that you will receive an error if you do not configure IIS to allow relay access to the localhost. To do this, follow these steps:

1. Run IIS and right-click the default SMTP server.

2. Select the Access tab.

3. Select Relay.

4. Click to limit access to the "List Below," and then add your computer as 127.0.0.1.

5. Uncheck the Allow All Computers. The results should look similar to Figure 22.14.

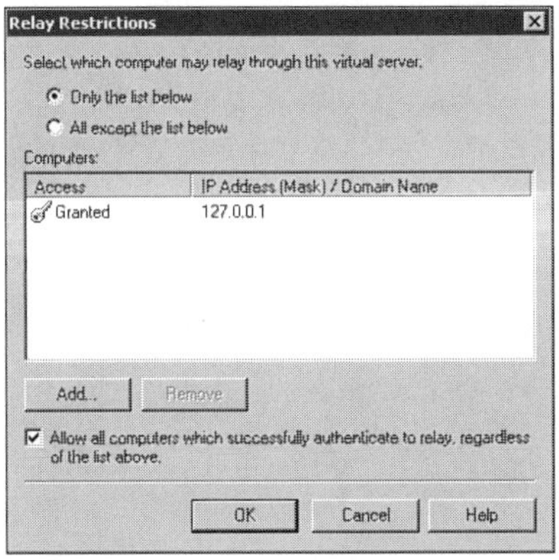

FIGURE 22.13   A new email from sales@webstore.com confirms that the code works.

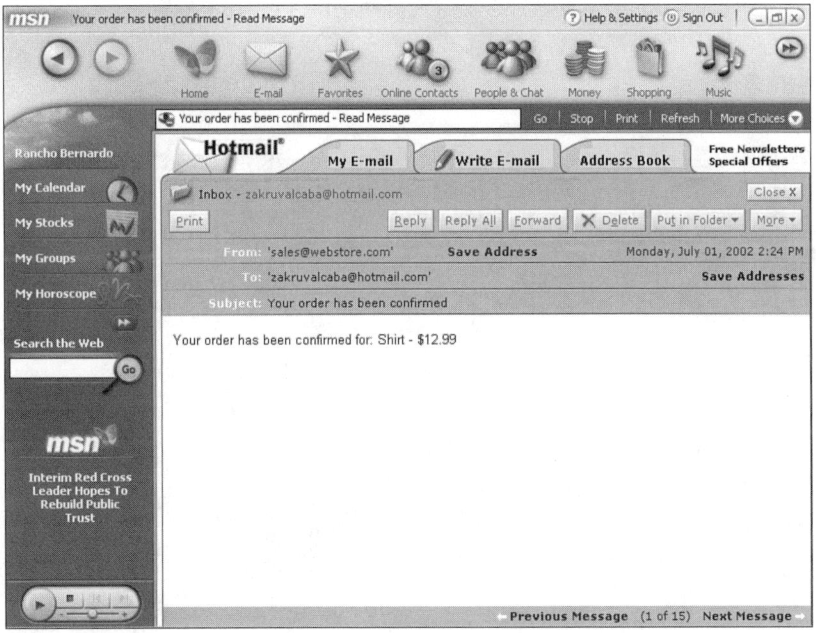

FIGURE 22.14   Configure IIS to allow the email to be sent through the localhost.

- Select OK and close IIS.
- Now test the product form.

Code Snippets

Code snippets are a good way of saving and reusing chunks of code that you have previously written. For instance, now that you have created the form mailer in both ASP and ASP.NET, you may want to save it so that when you want to accomplish a similar task in the future, you know it will be in a handy place. In the Snippets panel, you can create snippets, create snippet folders, move snippets to a specific folder, or share snippets with other members in your collaborative environment. To create a new snippet for the email code you created previously, follow the steps outlined next:

1. Create a new folder by selecting the New Folder icon in the Snippets panel. Call it ASP.NET.

2. Highlight the entire subroutine that you created.

3. Right-click and select Create New Snippet. Figure 22.15 shows the highlighted code with the menu.

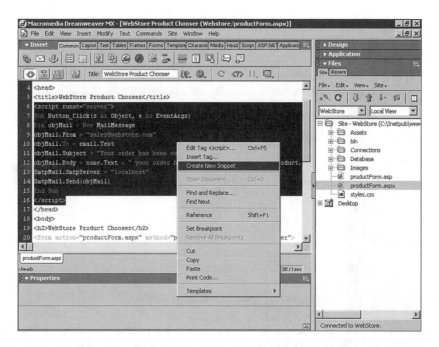

FIGURE 22.15   A new snippet can be created by highlighting the code and right-clicking.

4. Give your snippet a name and description as shown in Figure 22.16.

5. Select OK.

6. Your new snippet will appear in the Snippet panel.

FIGURE 22.16   The new snippet appears within the Snippet panel.

Summary

ASP emerged on the Web development stage with tremendous force. The capability to create dynamic Web applications with relative simplicity enthralled Web developers and programmers alike. Although ASP.NET is comparatively new, it already shows far more promise than its predecessor.

CHAPTER 23

JSP

By Thomas Myer
Principal, Triple Dog Dare Media

Introduction

JSP stands for Java Server Pages. It's a powerful, full-featured scripting language that enables you to use Java functions in a Web browser environment.

Combined, Java and the Web browser make a powerful team. Because Java is open source and largely platform independent, it's easy to extend it—the community is always adding more features to its core feature set. On the other side of the equation, the Web browser is a ubiquitous interface for rendering content that is globally available. You could say that it's a marriage of two strong feature sets: Java functionality and the native interface capabilities of the Web browser.

Technically speaking, JSP can be combined with HTML code inside HTML files. Anytime a user requests a JSP page, the JSP code is processed by a servlet. This servlet can hand more complex tasks off to one or more JavaBeans that communicate with data sources, or it may handle the connection by itself.

Because Java is such a powerful and expressive language, JSP was designed with the beginner in mind. Although advanced Java developers can use the full feature set of the Java language, beginners can use JSP actions to accomplish a lot of functionality with basic commands.

Dreamweaver MX includes support for a Tag Chooser, which makes it even easier to use these JSP actions and other tags.

The Tag Chooser is a tool that enables you to easily add tags from different scripting languages. This chapter introduces you to using the Tag Chooser to insert JSP tags into your documents. After that, you'll learn about hand coding your own JSP tags, JavaBeans, servlets, and debugging your code.

JSP in Dreamweaver MX

Dreamweaver MX supports hand coding of JSP in your files, but it also has some handy tools that can make you more productive.

- The Tag Chooser helps you insert well-formed JSP tags into your documents. The Tag Chooser displays different parameters required by the JSP tag, so you can be sure to enter them properly.

- Includes allow you to place repeatable HTML snippets into separate pages that you can then include from other pages in an application.

- You can save JSP code into Code Snippets that you can use in your application. Code Snippets are saved in a kind of library—to use a snippet, just select it and insert it into your code.

Tag Chooser

You can access the Tag Chooser by clicking the Tag Chooser button on the toolbar or by right-clicking inside your Dreamweaver document and choosing Insert Tag from the pop-up menu (see Figure 23.1).

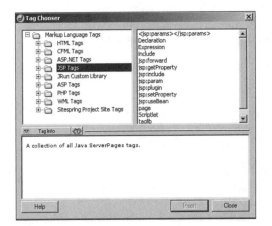

FIGURE 23.1   The Tag Chooser can help you insert well-formed JSP tags into your HTML documents.

To use the JSP tags, click the JSP Tags folder. This folder is organized in the following manner:

- Directives, which lists the three in-page directives (page, include, and taglib) available in JSP.

- Scripting elements include declarations (for defining methods and variables), expressions (for generating output), and scriptlets (free-form JSP).

- Standard actions, which include everything you need to work with JavaBeans and perform page forwarding and other tasks.

To insert one of these elements into your HTML code, double-click it, fill in the required parameters as provided by the Tag Chooser, click OK, and then click Insert (see Figure 23.2).

For more information on each of these items, refer to the "Hand Coding JSP Tags" section later in this chapter.

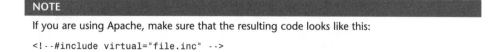

FIGURE 23.2   Creating a `<jsp:forward>` action with the Tag Chooser.

Includes

Server-side includes enable you to place repeated chunks of HTML and JSP into their own files. You can then reference those files using a server-side include from another file. Although you will notice a small hit on performance, it's usually negligible compared to the time and effort spent making the same updates to dozens and dozens of pages.

To insert an include in Dreamweaver MX, follow these steps:

1. Choose Insert, Script Objects, Server-Side Include.

2. Browse the file folder structure and select the file you want to include.

NOTE

If you are using Apache, make sure that the resulting code looks like this:

```
<!--#include virtual="file.inc" -->
```

And not like this:

```
<!--#include file="file.inc" -->
```

Do just the opposite on IIS.

TIP

Some Web servers are configured to scan for server-side includes automatically, and others check only for files with a special extension, such as .shtml or .inc. If Tomcat is configured properly on your system, you shouldn't have any problems.

Refer to the "Hand Coding JSP Tags" section to learn about the `<jsp:include>` tag and the `<%@ include %>` directive.

Saving Code Snippets

Dreamweaver MX enables you to save any content, HTML markup, or JSP code as Code Snippets that you store in the Snippets library.

To save a piece of JSP code as a snippet, follow these steps:

1. Highlight the JSP code you want to save as a Snippet.

2. Click the Snippets tab under Code in the right pane.

3. Click the Create New Folder icon.

4. Name the new folder **JSP Snippets**.

5. Double-click the folder to open it.

6. Click the Create New Snippet icon.

7. In the Snippet dialog box, give your snippet a name that's descriptive of the code.

8. Optionally, provide a description of the code.

9. Choose Insert Block (this works for most JSP code blocks) instead of Wrap Selection.

NOTE

Wrap Selection is used to wrap code before and after any selection you've highlighted with the mouse. It's a handy way to wrap <b> and </b> tags around a word you've highlighted, but it isn't very useful when you're inserting JSP code.

---

10. Choose Code as the Preview Type.

11. Click OK to close the dialog box.

To use a Code Snippet, click where you want the snippet to go and then double-click it from the list of snippets. Dreamweaver MX inserts the snippet into your document.

Beyond Dreamweaver

Although Dreamweaver includes support for JSP tags, you can do a lot more with JSP when you start hand coding tags. The following sections cover creating JSP tags, handling form data, working with cookies, creating beans, and debugging your code.

Hand Coding JSP Tags

The following section introduces you to scriptlets, declarations, expressions, and directives. This section will provide plenty of information to get you started.

> **NOTE**
>
> I'll discuss JSP actions in the JavaBeans section. Although not all actions relate to JavaBeans, it's easier to explain them then.

Scriptlets

A scriptlet is any block of JSP code between <% opening and %> closing delimiters. Because JSP code is processed by a Web server, only the results of the JSP code are displayed, not the code itself.

To generate output, use the `out.print()` or `out.println()` methods, like this:

```
<html>
<head>
<title>Welcome</title>
<body>
<h1>My First JSP</h1>
<%
out.print("This is my first JSP page.");
%>
```

> **TIP**
>
> The `out.print()` method doesn't put any line breaks into your HTML. If you need to generate a lot of HTML and you don't want it all in one big line when you view source, use the `out.println()` method instead.

Scriptlets aren't limited to generating output. You can also use them to declare values for different variables. In the following example, a series of scriptlets are used to format an HTML table:

```
<%
    String vertAlignHdr = "bottom";
    String vertAlignReg = "top";
    int colSpan = 2;
    int tblBorder = 1;
%>
<table border="<% out.print(tblBorder); %>">
<tr valign="<% out.print(vertAlignHdr); %>">
<th>Header 1</th>
<th>Header 2</th>
</tr>
<tr valign="<% out.print(vertAlignReg); %>">
<td colspan="<% out.print(colSpan); %>">content</td>
</tr>
</table>
```

Scriptlets are suitable for small amounts of code—when you start adding a lot of complexity, it becomes harder to debug. It also means that you're mixing your presentation layer (or GUI) with your business logic layer, which can mean extra work and heartache. At a certain level, working with JavaBeans is a much better way to go.

Testing, Looping, and Switching

In Java, you can use if, while, for, and switch statements to test a condition or loop through a series of values.

You can use the if statement to check whether a condition is true or false and to run code, depending on which way the condition tests.

In the following example, the if statement tests to see if one number is higher than another: If it tests true, the code prints one message; if not, it prints another.

```
int number = 10;
int anothernumber = 5;

if (number > anothernumber) {
    out.println(number + "is higher than " + anothernumber + ".<br>");
}
else {
    out.prinln(number + "is lower than " + anothernumber + ".<br>");
}
```

You can use the for loop to execute a block of code a specific number of times. It's a handy tool for doing a lot of work.

The for loop starts out with a number that initializes the loop, an iterator that either increases or decreases the count, and sandwiched in between them, a test to control how many loops are made. Whenever the test returns true, the code block inside the for loop is executed.

In the following example, the for loop prints out the numbers 0 through 9 followed by the HTML <br> tag.

```
int counter;
for (counter = 0; counter < 10; counter++) {
    out.println(counter + "<br>");
}
```

A while loop is like a for loop, except it tests for a condition and continues to loop until the first time the condition is false.

You can rewrite the preceding for loop example as a while loop:

```
int counter = 0;
while (counter < 10) {
    out.println(counter + "<br>");
}
```

A while loop is typically used to iterate over the entire set of records retrieved from a database table.

When an if statement gets too complex, you can usually use a switch statement to simplify the code's structure.

A switch statement allows you to execute a section of code depending on the value of an expression that you specify. These expressions are matched by case values.

In the following example, different blocks of code are executed depending on the incoming severity of a problem (as defined by the severity test):

```
switch (severity) {
    case 1:
    out.println("show stopper<br>");
    break;

    case 2:
    out.println("serious problem<br>");
    break;

    case 3:
    out.println("minor problem<br>");
    break;

    case 4:
    out.prinln("inconvenience<br>");
    break;

}
```

The break statement at the end of each case value prevents the switch statement from testing all remaining case values.

Declarations

A declaration is a scripting element that enables you to declare variables and methods you'll use on a JSP page. You have to define all methods and variables before you can use them. Declarations begin with a <%! delimiter and end with a %> delimiter.

> **NOTE**
>
> Although you can declare variables inside a scriptlet (as seen in the previous section), the preferred method is to use a declaration.

In the following example, I declare the values of various variables:

```
<%!
    String name = "Tom";
    int age = 31;
    String birthday = "June 5";
%>
```

After these variables have been assigned values, I can refer to them elsewhere in my JSP page:

```
<p>Hello, my name is <% out.print(name); %>.
<p>I'm <% out.print(age); %> and my birthday is <% out.print(birthday); %>.
```

Expressions

Simply put, an expression is a scripting element that allows you to generate output on a JSP page. Although a lot of what you can do with expressions can be done with scriptlets, expressions don't require as much coding. Instead of beginning an expression with a <% delimiter, you'd use a <%= delimiter. The = part is shorthand for out.print() or out.println().

In the following example, I set a variable inside a declaration and then use an expression to generate output:

```
<%!
String mySite = "World of JSP";
%>
<h1>Welcome to the <%= mySite %>!</h1>
```

Directives

Directives provide information about a JSP page to the software that's processing the page. In JSP, there are three directives:

- Page, which enables you to specify configuration information about the page.

- Taglib, which enables you to define a tag library and a prefix that can be used to reference the custom tags.

- Include, which enables you to include a file inside a JSP file.

A directive must be contained between a `<%@` opening delimiter and a `%>` closing delimiter.

Here's an example of an include directive:

```
<%@ include file="/jsp/footer.html" %>
```

> **NOTE**
>
> Any JSP commands in an included file will not be processed by the Web server. To reuse Java code, start using JavaBeans (see the section on JavaBeans a little later in this chapter).

Here's an example of a taglib directive:

```
<%@ taglib uri="http://www.mysite.com/tags/xyz" prefix="xyz">
```

Here's an example of a page directive:

```
<%@ page autoFlush="true" contentType="text/plain" %>
```

> **NOTE**
>
> Because the page directive has so many complex parameters, it's probably a good idea to use Macromedia MX's built-in Tag Chooser to help you build the tag.

Handling Form Data

One of the most common tasks you'll undertake in JSP programming is handling form data. Whenever a user logs in to a site, answers a survey, or handles more complex tasks such as entering information into a database, you'll need to process that form data and do something with it.

To handle data from a form, you must first create a form. The action property of the `<form>` tag must point to a JSP page that will process the form. Each of the form elements (text fields, check boxes, and so on) has a name assigned to it, and the JSP processing page can refer to those elements by name.

In the following example, a simple form is created to gather a person's name and age:

```
<html>
<title>Form</title>
<body>
<form action="/scripts/processform.jsp" method="post">
Enter your name: <input type="text" name="name"><br>
Enter your age: <input type="text" name="age"><br>
<input type="submit" name="Submit">
</form>
</body>
</html>
```

Save the file as **form.html** and place it in your Web server's docroot.

Now that you have a form, create the processform.jsp page:

1. Add the necessary information to the page for context:

   ```
   <html>
   <title>Thank you for filling out the form</title>
   <body>
   <p>Thank you for filling out the form.
   ```

2. Next, use the getParameter() method of the request object to gather information on each form element.

   ```
   You said your name is: <% request.getParameter("name") %>.<br>
   You said your age is: <% request.getParameter("age") %>.<br>
   </body>
   </html>
   ```

3. Save the file as processform.jsp in your Web server's docroot and view the form.html page. After you fill in the form and click Submit, the JSP page should process the form and display the results.

Cookies

Web servers run on the HTTP protocol, which is stateless—in other words, a Web server doesn't know who you are, nor can it distinguish one visitor from another. It just handles requests and serves up pages and other files.

Although this makes for an easy-to-implement communication protocol, it also means that it becomes harder to provide customized content for visitors, to gather and remember their preferences (such as background color, font size, and other information), and to allow convenient bypass of a login screen ("remember me").

Each cookie in JSP can be created with the cookie object. You can use this object to create keys and values for any cookie. For example, suppose that you want to store a message on a visitor's computer and then display it back to her when she returns.

The next sections cover creating and reading cookies.

Creating a Cookie

1. The first step in creating a cookie is to initialize the Cookie object:

   ```
   <%
       Cookie msgCookie = new Cookie("message", "JSP is cool!");
   ```

2. Next, specify when the cookie will expire, in seconds:

   ```
       msgCookie.setMaxAge(3600);
   ```

3. Next, specify which of your JSP pages can access this cookie:

   ```
       msgCookie.setPath("/jsp");
   ```

> **NOTE**
>
> For added security, specify your Web site domain (that is, www.yourdomain.com) with the setDomain() method: msgCookie.setDomain(www.yourdomain.com). This keeps unauthorized JSP pages from other sites from accessing the cookies you create.

4. Now send the cookie to the visitor's computer using the `response.addCookie()` method:

   ```
       response.addCookie(msgCookie);
   %>
   ```

5. Add whatever HTML to this page you think is appropriate, and save the file with a .jsp extension to a folder in your Web server's docroot.

The next time a visitor hits this .jsp page, a cookie containing a brief message will be saved to the visitor's system.

Are Cookies Secure and Ethical?

Although some people may not like the idea that a file is being written to their systems, cookies are stored as text files, not executable code. There have been no cases of viruses ever being spread using cookies.

Think about a Web world in which there were no cookies—you'd have to log in to your favorite sites each time, and those sites would have to resort to other methods to track what your interests and preferences are.

Also note that you can create any number of cookies to store visitor information, but most Web browsers limit a domain to storing 20 cookies on a visitor's computer at any one time.

Reading a Cookie

To read values stored on a computer as cookies, you can use the `request.getCookies()` method. Because you'll possibly be retrieving multiple values, store this information into an array and use a for loop to iterate over the array.

The for loop also allows the JSP page to test for the existence of cookies—if no cookies exist, or if the visitor doesn't allow cookies to be written to his or her system, the for loop will exit gracefully without causing an error.

1. First, set up the array that will hold the results of your cookie request:

```
<%
Cookie[] cookiesfromVisitor = request.getCookies();
```

2. Next, iterate over the elements of the array using a for loop and the length attribute:

```
for (int x = 0; x < cookiesfromVisitor.length; x++) {
```

3. Print out the names and values that are retrieved:

```
    out.print(cookiesfromVisitor[x].getName() + " contains the value ");
    out.print(cookiesfromVisitor[x].getValue() + "<br>");
}
%>
```

4. Save the file with a .jsp extension to your server's docroot.

JavaBeans

A JavaBean is a class file that stores Java code (for more on classes and objects, read the sidebar). Although you can do the same things with a JSP file as you would with a JavaBean, putting too much business logic inside your JSP pages is a bad idea.

For one thing, if you repeat code segments throughout your application, it becomes harder to debug and update your application. It's also harder to share your application with other developers that need to do the same or similar things.

JavaBeans solve both of these problems. JavaBean code is centralized, so any changes to a JavaBean ripples throughout your application. Other developers can also use your JavaBeans to extend their work—this is particularly useful whether developers create generic beans (which perform basic functions like data access) or highly specialized beans (which perform unique or problematic tasks).

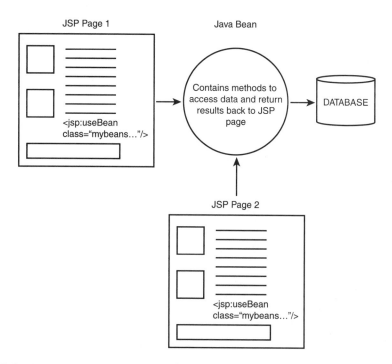

FIGURE 23.3   JavaBeans in a JSP architecture.

Classes and Objects in Java

Java is an object-oriented language, which means that any program written in Java is structured around objects—self-contained, reusable packets of procedures and data. Although object-oriented programming comes complete with a whole slew of specialized jargon, I'll provide a concrete metaphor to make it easier to understand.

Let's start with a familiar object in the real world—a car. A car is an object with certain properties. It has two or four doors, it has an engine of a certain size, a readout for current speed, a top speed, and a gas tank that holds so much gas.

A car is much more than a collection of properties, however. A car can also do things. It can turn left and right, accelerate, decelerate, and play music (if it has a radio). A sophisticated car may also have subcomponents that have their own unique mechanisms—I'm thinking here of chairs and mirrors that adjust to a driver's saved settings.

If a car were an object in the Java world, the properties (number of doors and so on) would be called fields. Fields in Java can store different types of information, such as text strings, integers, and references to other objects.

What an object can do would be called a method. A method can be generic or highly specialized, but each is task-oriented. Our car might have a method called accelerate() and another called turnLeft().

A car, however, doesn't pop into being all by itself, and neither does an object. An object needs a template, called a class file, to help define it. In fact, to a class file, an object is merely an instance of the class. A single class can create many different objects, just as a car factory can create many different cars.

The nice thing about objects is their extensibility. To put it into the terms of our ongoing metaphor, after you understand how to drive one kind of car (a sleek sports car) you can probably figure out how to drive another kind of car (a truck).

Why? Because all you have to know to get going are the properties and the methods. Think about it: Turning left with one car is the same as with another. Just turn the wheel counterclockwise. The car handles everything else, which means you don't have to know what's going on inside the guts of the machine.

Similarly, objects allow programmers to use methods (sometimes with passed-in arguments, or information the method needs to do its work) without having to understand all the details. The programmer uses an object's method, the method does its work behind the scenes, and out comes a result.

Creating a JavaBean

You can create a JavaBean in Dreamweaver MX or a text editor. JavaBeans are usually stored in the \classes directory of your Tomcat installation. The following instructions take you through each step of the process of creating your first JavaBean, which we'll call Name—we'll use it to set and get people's names.

1. In Dreamweaver MX or a text editor, declare your class and initiate the class's name variable by typing the following text in a new file:

```
public class Name {
    private String name;
```

> **NOTE**
>
> Classes can be public (accessible by any class or object), protected (accessible only by its own class or subclasses belonging to the class), or private (accessible only by its own class). Most classes are public.

2. Now create some methods. The first method will be the object's constructor. Constructors always have the same name as the object, and they're usually used to instantiate variables and do other housekeeping when the Bean is built (or constructed). In the following example, the constructor sets the value of the string name to "Tom":

```
public Name() {
    name = "Tom";
}
```

NOTE

Java is case sensitive, so that means that the name of the constructor method must match the name of the object. That means that the name(), NAME(), Name(), and NaME() methods are all considered different.

3. The second method, getName(), is known as the getter method. It enables you to get the value of the variable name from the object:

```
public String getName() {
    return name;
}
```

4. The third method, setName(), is known as the setter method. It enables you to set a different value for the name variable:

```
public void setName(String newName){
    name = newName;
}
```

NOTE

The void keyword indicates a method that does not return a value.

5. The fourth method will print out a series of asterisks:

```
public string asterisks (int num) {
    String output = "";
    for (int x = 0; x < num; x++) {
    output = output + "*";
    return output;
}
```

6. Make sure that you put in the curly brace that closes off the opening brace that started the class:

```
}
```

7. Finally, save your file as Name.java. In Java, you must name your source file the same as the name of the Bean. The same case-sensitive rules apply here as they did with the constructor.

23

Compiling a JavaBean

Now that you've created a Bean, you have to compile it. Compiling Java source code turns it into bytecode, which is executed by the Java interpreter. This bytecode is said to be obfuscated, because no one can open it up and see how your code works. This makes it more secure as well as faster.

1. Open a DOS prompt window and change directories to where you installed the Java Development Kit.

2. On the command line, type **javac** followed by the name of the .java file you want to compile. For example:

```
javac Name.java
```

3. If the Java compiler didn't run into any problems, the command prompt will reappear. When you list the directory contents, you'll notice a new file with the same name as your .java file, but with a .class extension:

```
Name.class
```

4. Copy the newly created .class file to the \classes directory under your Tomcat installation.

Java Compile Errors

There are two types of errors you'll get when you compile Java source code: compiler errors and source code errors.

Compiler errors occur because your operating system can't find the Java compiler. Make sure that you're in the right directory and try again. If problems persist, you may have to reinstall Java.

Source code errors result from errors that the compiler finds in your source code. In this case, the compiler will display the type of error it found and on what line. In this case, open the .java file, make your changes, and try again.

Using a Java Bean from a JSP Page

Now that you've compiled a JavaBean, you're ready to use it from a JSP page. JSP provides the <jsp:useBean> for setting up a Bean. After you initialize the Bean using <jsp:useBean>, you can access that Bean's properties and methods.

To set up a JavaBean, follow these instructions:

1. In your JSP page, type the <jsp:useBean> tag. This tag has various properties that make it work: the class (which points to where the Bean resides), an id (to identify the instance within your JSP pages), and a scope (see the sidebar).

```
<jsp:useBean class="beans.Name" id="Name1" scope="session" />
```

2. To find out what value is set for this JavaBean's name property, you need to use the
   <jsp:getProperty> tag.

   ```
   <jsp:getProperty name="Name1" property="name" />
   ```

   > **NOTE**
   >
   > This tag must have a counterpart method inside the JavaBean. For the name property, the
   > method must be named getName—in other words, the name of the method must be the same
   > as the property, but the first letter is capitalized. The entire name is prefixed by get.

3. To change the value of this Bean's name property, you need to use the
   <jsp:setProperty> tag.

   ```
   <jsp:setProperty name="Name1" property="name" value="Tony" />
   ```

   > **NOTE**
   >
   > This tag must have a counterpart method inside the JavaBean. For the name property, the
   > method must be named setName—in other words, the name of the method must be the same
   > as the property, but the first letter is capitalized. The entire name is prefixed by set. Additionally,
   > the setName method must be of type public void.

4. To see the change in the value assigned to the name variable, use the
   <jsp:getProperty> tag again:

   ```
   <jsp:getProperty name="Name1" property="name" />
   ```

5. Now access the JavaBean's asterisks() method. Because this method returns a value,
   you can use an expression. In the following example, you're asking the asterisks()
   method to print out 10 asterisks (*) in a row:

   ```
   <%= Name1.asterisks(10) %>
   ```

6. Save the file with a .jsp extension to a folder in your Web server's docroot.

7. Point your browser at the JSP file and view the results.

> **Understanding Java Bean Scope**
>
> A JavaBean can exist for just one request or for as long as the application is online. The time it
> has to "live" is called scope. When you instantiate a JavaBean using the <jsp:useBean> tag, you
> don't have to set a scope—the default scope is set to page.

The scopes are defined next:

request   The JavaBean is available for only one request by a client.

page   The JavaBean is available only from the page that instantiated it (therefore, it can handle many requests).

session   The JavaBean is available to a single client for as long as that session continues.

application   The JavaBean is available to all clients for as long as the application is available.

OTHER ACTIONS

Although you'll be using the `<jsp:useBean>`, `<jsp:getProperty>`, and `<jsp:setProperty>` actions frequently, other actions have nothing to do with beans and include:

<jsp:forward>   Enables you to forward visitors to another page.

```
<jsp:forward page="index2.jsp" />
```

<jsp:include   Enables you to include the contents of another file inside another file.

```
<jsp:include page="footer.html" flush="true" />
```

<jsp:param>   Enables you to add further name-value pairs to another action tag. For example, if you wanted to forward visitors to another page and then tell them, after they got to their destination, where they came from, you could add a sentFrom parameter to the `<jsp:forward>` tag:

```
<jsp:forward page="index2.jsp">
<jsp:param name="sentFrom" value="index.jsp" />
</jsp:forward>
```

NOTE

When you use a `<jsp:param>` tag, note the use of opening (`<jsp:...>`) and closing (`</jsp:...>`) action tags around it.

If you wanted to look up the sentFrom parameter on the destination page, use the `getParameter()` method of the request object, as you would with a form element:

```
<%= request.getParameter("sentFrom") %>
```

Be aware that when you use the `<jsp:forward>` tag, the server stops processing that page as soon as it hits that action tag.

Debugging JSP Code

You'll hardly ever create perfect code, even when you become an experienced JSP coder, so it's inevitable that you'll be presented with an error message when you run your code.

Sometimes the error is simple (dividing by zero) and sometimes its more complex (using the wrong data type when attempting to cast an object).

Sometimes the error messages are useful, sometimes they're not. JSP provides error (or exception) handling routines that make it easier for you to understand the problem—and fix it.

Whenever an error occurs, an object is created that stores information about the error. This information is usually pasted onto the screen in place of the JSP page that's supposed to run:

```
Error:500
Location: /examples/math.jsp
Internal Servlet Error:
    org.apache.myserver.myserverException: / by zero
    at org.apache.myserver.runtime.JspServelt$JspServletWrapper…
```

The easiest way to keep this raw data dump from happening is to use a try...catch block. Use the try statement to encapsulate the block of code, and the catch block to handle any exceptions:

```
<html>
<title>Some Simple Math</title>
<body>
<h2>Some Simple Math</h2>
<%
    int quantity = 0;
    int cost = 100;

try {
    int costperquantity = cost / quantity;
    out.print("Cost per quantity is " + costperquantity);
}
catch(ArithmeticException e) {
    out.print("Error occurred: did you divide by zero?<br>");
}
```

If you have a code block that may cause multiple errors, you can continue to add catch blocks that handle each exception type. These catch blocks can accurately pinpoint the problems encountered in any block of code and are a lot more useful than a giant screen full of error messages.

23

Another way to handle exception handling is to set a page directive that specifies an error-handling page and then do the error/exception handling there.

1. The first step is to add a page directive that sets the errorPage property. This directive must be at the top of a .jsp page:

```
<%@ page errorPage="error.jsp" %>
<html>
<title>Welcome</title>
<body>
Let's do some math:
<%
int bad = 100/0;
%>
</body>
</html>
```

2. Save the file as badmath.jsp to your Web server's docroot.

3. Next, create the error.jsp page. Make sure that the page starts off with a page directive that specifies the page as an error page:

```
<%@ page isErrorPage="true" %>
<html>
<title>An error has occurred</title>
<body>
<h1>An error has occurred</h1>
```

4. You can leave the file simple, with a message that says "An error has occurred," but you will more than likely need more detail than that. To get that detail, use the getMessage() method of the exception object:

```
Here's the error message:<br><br>
<% exception.getMessage() %>
</body>
</html>
```

5. Save the error.jsp page to the Web server docroot, then browse the badmath.jsp page. The browser should display the following error message:

```
Here's the error message:

/ by zero
```

Summary

This chapter has only scratched the surface of JSP, a powerful and versatile scripting language. If you want to learn more about JSP coding, JavaBeans, and servlets, read *Teach Yourself JavaServer Pages in 21 Days* (ISBN: 0-672-32449-0), a forthcoming title by Steve Holzner, available from Sams Publishing.

CHAPTER **24**

PHP and MySQL

By Thomas Myer
Principal, Triple Dog Dare Media

PHP has taken the Web by storm. It's a lightweight language with powerful, built-in features that allow developers to create complex sites fast. PHP is usually mentioned in the same breath with MySQL, a popular open-source software. The two technologies work well together, hence their popularity.

In this chapter, I'll cover PHP basics, such as variables, arrays, and control structures, and then touch on more advanced topics, such as functions and working with MySQL. Then I'll cover the use of Dreamweaver MX to make your coding more productive.

Basic PHP

PHP stands for Personal Home Page. It was first developed in the early 1990s as a quick, lightweight scripting language for building dynamic Web pages. The inventors of the lan–guage originally modeled PHP on Perl and C, so programmers familiar with these languages will have absolutely no problem with PHP.

In this section of the chapter, I'll discuss basic syntax, variables, arrays, expressions and operators, and control structures. By the end of this section, you'll have the basics down, and that will give you enough background for the sections that follow, which discuss creating custom functions and working with MySQL.

Basic Syntax

All PHP code is placed between <? and ?> tags directly in HTML markup. The PHP parser ignores everything outside of these PHP tags and processes whatever is inside them. Here's a basic, simple PHP command inserted inside HTML:

```
<p>Hello, my name is <? echo $name ?>.
```

Whatever value has been assigned to the variable $name appears after "Hello, my name is" when the page is rendered for the visitor.

As in other scripting languages, if all you're doing with a block of code is generating output, you can use an expression. An expression is a shortcut; basically, it means that you can use the <?= symbol instead of typing echo to generate output. Like this:

```
<p>Hello, my name is <?= $name ?>.
```

PHP doesn't care about whitespace or line endings within the <? and ?> blocks, so you can create code blocks, or scriptlets, that look like this:

```
<?
if ($expression) {
    echo "$expression must be true!";
} else {
    echo "$expression must not be true!";
}
?>
```

Each line must have an instruction separation; in most cases, this means putting a semi-colon at the end of a command. However, a closing brace (}) or end of block (?>) also serves the same purpose. The following statements all have proper instruction separations:

```
<?= $name; ?>
<? echo $name ?>
<? if ($test) { echo $one } else { echo $two } ?>
```

You can add comments to your code in various ways. Comments are ignored by the PHP parser, but they make it much easier for you to understand your code—especially if you don't come back to it for several months.

You can use Perl-style hashes (#)—anything after the # is a comment:

```
<?
echo $name; #this is a comment
?>
```

You can also use C and C++ style one-line comments (//):

```
<?
echo $name; //this is a comment
?>
```

If you have a lot of comments, you can embed them between multiline comments using /* and */, as in C and C++:

```
<?
/*
the following piece of code
generates output from the variable $name
*/
echo $name;
?>
```

> **WARNING**
>
> If you are using the C/C++ multiline comments, don't nest them, because this can cause problems. For example, don't do this:
>
> ```
> /*
> some comments /* this will cause problems */
> */
> ```

Variables

Variables are the simplest data container in PHP. They are known as scalars and are one dimensional. PHP is not strongly typed, so a variable can hold any kind of value you want and can even switch between types. For example, the same variable can start out holding a person's name (characters), and then numbers, a Boolean value, or a date.

Variable names are case sensitive and always start with a dollar sign ($) followed by a letter or underscore, followed by any number of other letters, underscores, and numbers. Variable names that start with a number are not valid.

Here are some examples of variables:

```
$variable; //valid
$Variable; //valid, different from the one above
$VaRIAble; //also valid, also different from both above
$_variable; //also valid
$4variable; //not valid
$!variable; //not valid
```

You can assign a value to a variable when you create it, but you don't have to. Use the = operator to assign a value to a variable:

```
$variable = "some random text";
$Variable = 1234; //treated as numbers
$VaRIAble = "1234"; //treated as text, at least for now
```

You can copy the contents of one variable to another, like this:

```
$cowsays = "moo";
$newcowsays = $cowsays;
```

Now both variables have a value of "moo." Assigning a value to a variable is known as using an expression. I'll cover expressions in more depth in a later section.

Arrays

Variables are very useful data containers. However, they're one-dimensional. What happens when you want to store a number of related items in the same container, like a shopping list?

You could certainly try to put all items from a shopping list into a variable, but it would look like this:

```
$shoppinglist = "eggs cheese bread soup jelly";
```

What now? How can you break this value apart and do something useful with it? You can, but not easily. The smarter approach is to use an array.

PHP provides two types of arrays: simple arrays and associative arrays.

Simple Arrays

The simple array (or list) is just a list of scalars. You can build a simple array using the array() function. To continue the shopping list example:

```
$grocerylist = array("eggs", "cheese", "bread", "soup", "jelly");
```

Elements in simple arrays are indexed by number. The first element is numbered 0, the second element is numbered 1, and so on. To access elements in an array, you use bracket notation, placing the index value within brackets, like this:

```
$grocerylist[0]; //eggs
$grocerylist[5]; //jelly
```

If you wanted to, you could use the = expression to build an array one line at a time:

```
$grocerylist[0] = "eggs";
$grocerylist[1] = "cheese";
```

You can overwrite an existing element by reassigning the value it previously had:

```
$grocerylist[0] = "chicken"; //no more eggs!
```

Associative Arrays

The second type of array is known as an associative array. Whereas a simple array is indexed by number, the associate array is indexed by keys. Therefore, an associative array describes a relationship between keys and their values.

For example, if you were running a dog owner's club, you could use an associative array to describe relationships between people and the dog they own:

```
$kennelclub = array(
    "Tom" => "Kafka",
    "Jane" => "Snuggles",
    "Mitch" => "Fido"
);
```

Each key-value pair is separated by an arrow (=>) and represents the relationship. To access an element's value, all you'd have to do is use bracket notation with the name of the key inside the brackets:

```
$tomsdog = $kennelclub["Tom"]; //$tomsdog now holds "Kafka"
$tomsdog = $kennelclub[Tom]; //same thing
```

PHP allows you to create multidimensional associative arrays. For example, for your $kennelclub array, you may want to list more information than just the dog's name. Simply use another array() for each value in a key-value pair:

```
$kennelclub = array(
    "Tom" => array("name" => "Kafka", "age" => "5"),
    "Jane" => array("name" => "Snuggles", "age" => "10"),
    "Mitch" => array("name" => "Fido", "age" => "3")
);
```

Although getting the value of an element is trickier (you have to be more specific), you'd use the same bracket notation:

```
$kafka_age = $kennelclub[Tom][age];
```

> **NOTE**
>
> Earlier I stated that associative arrays use keys as indexes. Don't be misled by this statement—an associative array could certainly use numbers as keys (an ID, for example). The difference is that the index for an element in a simple array is assigned programmatically. For example, if you reverse the order of elements in an array, element 6 (the last element) would become element 0 (the first element). That's not true with associative arrays.

Array Functions in PHP

PHP has many built-in functions that help you work with arrays.

array_pop   Enables you to remove the last element from an array and place it in a variable:

```
$grocerylist = array("eggs", "cheese", "bread", "soup", "jelly");
$last = array_pop($grocerylist);
//$grocerylist is now: eggs, cheese, bread, soup
```

array_push   Enables you to add an element to the end of an array:

```
$grocerylist = array("eggs", "cheese", "bread", "soup");
array_push($grocerylist, "tomatoes");
//$grocerylist is now: eggs, cheese, bread, soup, tomatoes
```

array_reverse   Enables you to reverse the order of elements in an array:

```
$grocerylist = array("eggs", "cheese", "bread", "soup", "tomatoes");
$reverselist = array_reverse($grocerylist);
//$grocerylist is now: tomatoes, soup, bread, cheese, eggs
```

count   Returns the number of elements in an array:

```
$grocerylist = array("eggs", "cheese", "bread", "soup", "tomatoes");
$numberofelements = count($grocerylist);
//$count should be 5
```

sort   Enables you to place the elements of an array in alphabetical order:

```
$grocerylist = array("eggs", "cheese", "bread", "soup", "tomatoes");
sort($grocerylist);
//$grocerylist is now: bread, cheese, eggs, soup, tomatoes
```

For a complete list of array functions, be sure to visit http://www.php.net, the home page for the PHP community. The site includes complete online documentation.

Expressions and Operators

Expressions and operators form the basic building blocks of PHP. With expressions and operators, you can perform tasks on data stored in variables and arrays, and much more.

The basic expression is called an assignment, which you've already seen. To recap, you can assign a value to a variable using the = operator:

```
$variable = 1;
```

Other assignment operators are available, the most common being the .= operator. This operator enables you to add (or concatenate) a value to the end of an existing value. It's a handy operator when you're running out of room in a line or want to programmatically add more information to the end of a value:

```
$name = "John";
$name .= " Smith";
//$name is now "John Smith"
```

Another good operator to know is the . operator, which allows you to piece together different strings to produce a value:

```
$a = 123;
$b = $a . " Main Street";
//$b is now: "123 Main Street"
```

The . operator is typically used to construct HTML markup strings that contain PHP variables and other code:

```
echo "<a href=\"my.php?id=" . $id . "\">" . $linktext . "</a>";
```

Other extremely common expressions involve comparisons. These expressions evaluate either to 0 (false) or 1 (true). You can use the following comparison expressions:

- > (greater than)
- >= (greater than or equal to)
- == (equal to)
- != (not equal to)
- < (less than)
- <= (less than or equal to)

These comparisons are usually used in if statements, so I'll cover them in more detail in the next section, "Control Structures."

The most common operators involve simple arithmetic:

```
$first = 1;
$second = 2;
$sum = $first + $second; //1 plus 2
$difference = $first - $second; //1 minus 2
$product = $first * $second; // 1 times 2
$quotient = $first / $second; // 1 divided by 2
$modulus = $first % $second // the remainder of 1 divided by 2
```

You can also increment and decrement a variable using the ++ and -- operators. Depending on whether you put the increment/decrement operators before or after the variable gives you a different returned value:

```
$first = 1;
echo $first++; //returns value of $first, then increments it by 1 (should be 1)
echo $first; //now it's 2
echo ++$first; //increments value by 1, then returns value of $first (should be 3)
echo $first; //still 3
echo $first--; //returns value of $first, then decrements it by 1 (should be 3)
echo $first; //should be 2
--$first; //decrements value by 1, then returns value of $first (now it's 1)
echo $first; // back to 1
```

Control Structures

One of the most common tasks you'll perform in your code is making decisions based on some condition. In PHP and other languages, you use a control structure (also called a branching statement or loop) to determine what code to run.

if

The most common control structure is the if statement. The if statement allows conditional execution of code based on an initial test of a condition. The if statement is usually a comparison. If the comparison evaluates to true, the block of code within the if statement is executed. Otherwise, the statement evaluates to false and the code is not executed.

For example, you might run a block of code if a returned variable has a certain value (say the value 3). In PHP, this example would look like the following:

```
if ($value == 3) {
    echo "value is $value!";
    //execute block of code
}
```

By itself, this is a useful test because it keeps code from executing if $value is not 3. However, what if you want to execute another block of code if $value is not set to 3? In PHP, you can add an else statement to the end of the if statement to define what happens if the initial comparison evaluates to false.

```
if ($value == 3) {
    echo "value is $value!";
    //execute block of code
} else {
    echo "value is something else, unfortunately";
}
```

Now you know when $value is set to 3 and when it isn't. If you wanted even more detail than that, you can add elseif statements before the else. In this case, each elseif statement represents a specific test and the else statement becomes the default answer if no other statement before it evaluates to true.

For example, we can add an elseif statement that checks to see if $value is less than 3:

```php
if ($value == 3) {
    echo "value is $value!";
    //execute block of code
} elseif ($value < 3) {
    echo "value is less than 3";
} else {
    echo "value is greater than 3, apparently";
}
```

You can continue adding elseif statements for each value you want to test, but at some point, it becomes easier to use a switch statement instead.

switch

A switch statement consists of a series of cases that are evaluated line by line against a variable being tested. Switch statements are fast, easy to read, and a good alternative to an if statement with a lot of branching.

For example, you might have an instance in which you are testing to see what item from a drop-down list was selected. The drop-down list has three selections from a dinner menu: steak, salad, and soup.

An if statement for testing what selection was made would look like this:

```php
if ($selection == "steak") {
    echo "Steak was selected.";
} elseif ($selection == "salad") {
    echo "Is a salad really all you want?";
} else {
    echo "You ordered soup.";
}
```

Here's that same functionality done with a switch statement. The break statements are used to "break out" of the switch statement—in other words, to stop evaluation of the $selection variable.

```php
switch ($selection) {
    case steak:
    echo "Steak was selected.";
    break;
```

24

```
        case salad:
        echo "Is a salad really all you want?";
        break;

        case soup:
        echo "You ordered soup.";
        break;
}
```

for

The for loop allows you to loop over a block of code and perform repetitious work. The for loop uses a value (usually an integer) to initialize itself; a second variable to test whether it should continue looping; and finally, an increment or decrement to adjust the value.

For example, the following for loop prints out the numbers 1 through 10:

```
for ($x = 1; $x <= 10; $x++) {
    echo "$x<br>";
}
```

foreach

The foreach loop is similar to the for loop, but it allows you to iterate over an array. You use the name of the array and then name a substitute variable used by the foreach to iterate over each element of the array:

```
foreach ($grocerylist as $item) {
    echo "current item is $item<br>";
}
```

A variant of this syntax is used to iterate over an associative array:

```
foreach ($kennelclub as $key => $value) {
   echo "$key is the owner of $value<br>";
}
```

while

The while loop is similar to the for loop, except it has only one test. If the test evaluates to true, the block of code is executed and the test is evaluated again.

For example, the following block of code is executed until the value of $variable is 10 or greater:

```
$variable = 1;
while ($variable <= 10) {
    echo "value is still less than or equal to 10!<br>";
```

```
    $variable++;
}
```

while loops are extremely useful for reading in the entire contents of a file (the loop continues to execute code until the last line of the file is reached) or a recordset returned by a query.

Advanced PHP

Although PHP is considered a scripting language, it has quite a number of advanced features. There isn't room enough in this chapter to cover every one of those features, so I'll only discuss creating custom functions and working with MySQL.

Functions

PHP has hundreds (if not thousands) of built-in functions, some of which you've already been introduced to. A function is merely encapsulated code, a repeatable process that you can call on to perform a task.

For example, the built-in function called count() returns a count of the number of elements in an array. There's no need for you to figure this out manually or to reinvent the wheel. If you need to know how many items are in the array $foo, use count($foo) to get back the number of elements.

As useful as all the built-in functions are, PHP wouldn't be complete unless it allowed you to create your own custom functions.

To create a function, you (naturally) use the function statement. An example of a very simple function is one that says hello:

```
function sayhello() {
    echo "Hello!";
}
```

To say hello, you would call that function from your code:

```
<? sayhello() ?>
```

Let's create a more complicated function that does some easy math and then call that function from the code.

The function you're creating will add two numbers that you pass to it, and that means that the function has to know that you are passing *arguments* to it. You can tell a function to expect arguments by listing those arguments right after the name, in parentheses:

```
function addtwo ($first, $second) {
}
```

24

Now that you have a function and it knows to expect some arguments as input, you can fill in the body of the function. In this case, you create an expression that adds the two arguments, and then you return that value:

```
function addtwo ($first, $second) {
    $sum = $first + $second;
    return $sum;
}
```

To use this function, you would call it from your PHP code, passing the arguments in, like so:

```
<p>2 + 4 equals: <b><?= addtwo(2,4) ?>
```

The answer should be 6. (Did you catch the use of <?= to generate output from the function?)

Obviously, functions can be much more complex than this, but even understanding them at this level is a monumental step forward as a PHP programmer. For example, once you understand functions, you can start working with object-oriented PHP, because all an object really is, is a bunch of functions called methods.

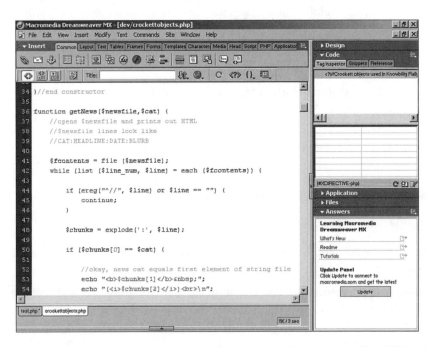

FIGURE 24.1   Understanding PHP functions allows you to start understanding PHP objects.

Working with MySQL

PHP has a good number of built-in functions that make working with MySQL fast and easy. The following section describes some of the ones you'll use on a constant basis—and some more advanced ones, such as creating databases and dropping tables.

Connecting to MySQL

Before you can send SQL statements to a MySQL database, you'll need to actually connect to the database server. You can use the mysql_connect function to do this:

```
$link = mysql_connect($server, $user, $password) or die ("Couldn't connect!");
```

In this case, mysql_connect is expecting three arguments: the name of the database server (localhost if it's on your own machine), the username, and the password.

The die function provides feedback that the connection couldn't be made (this could be because the username or password are wrong or because the server is unavailable).

Selecting a Database

After you've successfully connected to the database, you can select a database to work from with the mysql_select_db function:

```
mysql_select_db("news");
```

> **NOTE**
>
> Remember that selecting a database isn't the same thing as selecting a table. Tables reside in a database, but before you can query or update those tables, you need to use the proper database.

Creating a Database

Creating a database enables you to set aside a space in which you can create a group of related tables. This is useful if you need to create a development sandbox for your own experimentation or keep tables for different projects separate from each other.

Although you can create a database from the MySQL interface, it's just as easy to create a database from PHP using the mysql_create_db function:

```
mysql_create_db("mytestdb") or die ("Could not create database!");
```

> **NOTE**
>
> You must connect to MySQL as an administrator for mysql_create_db to work. Make sure that your mysql_connect statement is passing the proper administrative username and password.

24

Querying a Database Table

You can send queries to MySQL using the mysql_query function. In most cases, you'll want to store your SQL query in a variable and then execute the mysql_query function on that variable:

```
$sql = "select * from info";
$result = mysql_query($sql);
```

Looking at a Recordset

After you send a query to a database, you'll need to look at those results. The easiest way is to use a while loop to iterate over the results. Inside the while loop, you'll use the mysql_fetch_array function to output each row of the recordset:

```
$sql = "select * from info";
$result = mysql_query($sql);

//the list function gives a variable name to each
//field extracted from the database table
while (list($id, $title, $body) = mysql_fetch_array($result)) {
    echo "$id:<br>";
    echo "$title<br>";
    echo "$body<hr>";
}
```

Inserting Records

Insert commands take the following form:

```
insert into tablename (column1, column2, column3)
values (value1, value2, value3)
```

To insert a record in a table, send an insert command using the mysql_query function:

```
$sql = "
insert into info
(title, body)
values ("A title", "A body")
";

$result = mysql_query($sql);
```

Updating Records

Update commands take the following form:

```
update tablename
set column=value
where column=value
```

Although update commands seem more complex than insert commands, they really aren't. What you are saying is, "For all records in a table, update the value of a column only if that record has a certain value in a given column."

For example, if you had a table that consisted of names, departments, and phone numbers, you may want to update the table by changing all the department names (it seems that someone at HQ has decided to change the name of Marketing to Corporate Communications). Doing this by hand would be very tedious and time-consuming.

It's much faster and easier to use an update command:

```
update employeelisting
set department = 'Corporate Communications'
where department = 'Marketing'
```

To send this command to MySQL from PHP, embed it into a variable and pass the variable to mysql_query:

```
$sql = "
update employeelisting
set department = 'Corporate Communications'
where department = 'Marketing'
";

$result = mysql_query($sql);
```

Deleting Records

The delete command has the following form:

```
delete from table
where column = value
```

In essence, you're asking MySQL to delete from a table those rows that match the where clause.

For example, if you wanted to delete all employee records for everyone in the Facilities group, you'd use:

```
delete from employeelisting
where department = 'Facilities'
```

> **WARNING**
>
> If you don't use a where clause on a delete command, MySQL will quietly and lethally delete all records in the database table. You've been warned.

To send this command to MySQL from PHP, simply embed it into a variable and pass the variable to mysql_query:

```
$sql = "
delete from employeelisting
where department = 'Facilities'
";


$result = mysql_query($sql);
```

Checking Inserts, Updates, and Deletions

If the SQL statement you are sending to MySQL is inserting a new row, updating an existing row, or deleting one or more rows, you can check that the SQL code actually executed with the mysql_affected_rows function.

If the function returns 0, the action failed (that is, no rows in the table were affected). Otherwise, the number returned by this function indicates how many rows were affected.

```
$sql = "delete from info where id = 3";
$result = mysql_query($sql);

$affected = mysql_affected_rows($result);

if ($affected == 0) {
    echo "<b>warning: no deletion occurred!</b><br>";
} else {
    echo "deletion successful<br>";
}
```

Creating a Table

You can create tables in MySQL, but the easiest way to create them is from PHP. As with querying a database table, you compose your table creation script as a variable value and pass that variable to the mysql_query function.

Table creation syntax is very straightforward in MySQL:

```
create table nameoftable (
    column1 columntype attributes,
    column2 columntype attributes,
    primary key (column_name)
)
```

For example, the following table can contain information about an employee:

```
create table employees (
    employeeID integer not null auto_increment,
    firstname varchar(32) not null,
    lastname varchar(32) not null,
    email varchar(64) not null,
    birthdate date null,
    hiredate date not null
    primary key (employeeID)
)
```

In this case, the employeeID serves as the primary key for the table. It is an integer and set to auto_increment. That means that each time you add a record to the table, the employeeID is automatically incremented and generated for you.

The firstname, lastname, and email are all varchars, which means that they contain text characters (numbers, letters, and special characters) that are not padded with space at the end—in other words, varchar fields are variable length.

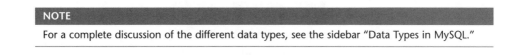

NOTE

For a complete discussion of the different data types, see the sidebar "Data Types in MySQL."

Also take notice that all three of these fields (firstname, lastname, and email) are all set to not null, which means they have to be filled in. If they aren't filled in, MySQL will reject the insert or update operation.

To insert this create table command into MySQL from PHP, embed the entire command into a variable and pass the variable to mysql_query:

```
$sql = "
create table employees (
    employeeID integer not null auto_increment,
    firstname varchar(32) not null,
    lastname varchar(32) not null,
    email varchar(64) not null,
    birthdate date null,
    hiredate date not null
    primary key (employeeID)
)";

$result = mysql_query($sql);
```

Altering a Table

Sometimes you need to alter an existing table's structure. MySQL enables you to change various parts of a table.

To change a table's name, use the following form:

```
alter table tablename rename new_tablename
```

To change the employees table to the staff table, use the following:

```
alter table employees rename staff
```

To add or drop a field, use the add column and drop column clauses of the alter command:

```
alter table staff add column phone varchar(16) not null
alter table staff drop column birthdate
```

The best way to change a column definition is to use the change clause of the alter command:

```
alter table staff change phone phone varchar(20) null
```

Notice that you have to state the name of the column twice: once to state that it's the one you want to change and again as part of the change definition.

To send an alter table command to MySQL from PHP, embed the entire command into a variable and pass the variable to mysql_query:

```
$sql = "alter table staff drop column birthdate";
$result = mysql_query($sql);
```

Dropping a Table

Sometimes you have to drop a table—in other words, delete the entire structure along with all its data.

To drop a table, use the drop table command:

```
drop table staff
```

It's as simple as that.

To send a drop table command to MySQL from PHP, embed the entire command into a variable and pass the variable to mysql_query:

```
$sql = "drop table staff";
$result = mysql_query($sql);
```

WARNING

The drop table command deletes the entire table—structure and data. You've been warned.

Data Types in MySQL

MySQL comes with a range of column types. Each is different from the others.

char   The char column type accepts text strings and has a maximum length of 255 characters. This is a fixed-length type, which means that MySQL will insert as many spaces as it needs to fill the field to its maximum value. For example, a char(16) column that receives a text string 10 characters long will be padded with 6 blank spaces. The spaces are removed from the string when data is extracted from this type of field.

varchar   The varchar column type accepts text strings and has a maximum length of 255 characters. This is a variable-length type, which means no padding. MySQL keeps track of how long each individual field is. Most of your text string fields will be varchar.

tinytext   The tinytext column type is the first of the binary text character types (or BLOBs). It is variable-length and can contain 255 characters. All 255 characters can be indexed.

text   The text column type is similar to tinytext, except that it can hold 65,535 characters. The first 255 characters can be indexed.

mediumtext   The mediumtext column type is similar to text and tinytext, but it can hold 16,777,215 characters. The first 255 characters can be indexed.

longtext   The longtext column type is similar to text, tinytext, and mediumtext, but it can hold 4,294,967,295 characters. The first 255 characters can be indexed.

enum   You can use the enum column type to restrict data entry to a certain set. It's normally used when you want yes/no or true/false responses:

```
answer enum ('yes', 'no') default 'no'
```

integer   The integer column type can hold whole numbers. Integers can be unsigned or signed. Unsigned integers can be in the range of 0 and 4,294,967,295. Signed integers can be in the range of –2,147,483,648 to 2,147,483,648. In most cases, you'll be using unsigned integers.

tinyint   The tinyint column type can store small whole numbers. As with the integer data type, tinyints can be unsigned or signed. Unsigned tinyints can be in the range of 0 to 255. Signed tinyints can be in the range of –128 to 127.

mediumint   The mediumint column type can store small integers between –8,338,608 and 8,338,607 (signed) or 0 and 16,777,215 (unsigned).

bigint   The bigint column type can store integers between –9,223,372,036,854,775,808 to 9,223,372,036,854,775,807 (signed) or 0 to 18,446,744,073,709 (unsigned).

float   The float column type can store a floating-point number that must be signed. Acceptable values are –3.402823466E+38 to –1.175494351E-38, 0, and 1.175494351E+38 to 3.402823466E+38.

double   This is a double-precision floating point column type. It must be signed.

datetime   This data type is for a combination of date and time values. MySQL displays the DATETIME value as YYYY-MM-DD HH:MM:SS format. However, you can set the values using either strings or numeric values.

timestamp   The TIMESTAMP data type range is between 1970-01-01 00:00:00 to 2037-12-31:23:59:59.

year   This can be formatted in either the default 4-digit format or a 2-digit format. The acceptable values are 1901-2155 and 0000. If you want to use the two-digit format, the acceptable values for the years 1970-2069 are 70-69.

> **NOTE**
>
> For a complete list of MySQL functions, be sure to visit `http://www.php.net`, the home page for the PHP community. The site includes complete online documentation.

Working with Dreamweaver MX for PHP Development

Dreamweaver MX has two capabilities that make working with PHP more productive:

- Tag Chooser
- Code Snippets

The Tag Chooser

Dreamweaver MX's Tag Chooser can help you insert well-formed PHP tags in your documents.

You can access the Tag Chooser by clicking the Tag Chooser button on the toolbar or by right-clicking inside your Dreamweaver document and choosing Insert Tag from the pop-up menu.

When the Tag Chooser is open, double-click the PHP folder. You have two choices: expressions and scriptlets.

If you select expression, the Tag Chooser inserts the following PHP code into your document:

```
<?php echo ?>
```

If you select scriptlet, the Tag Chooser inserts the following PHP code into your document:

```
<?php ?>
```

You can then insert your code in between the start and end tags.

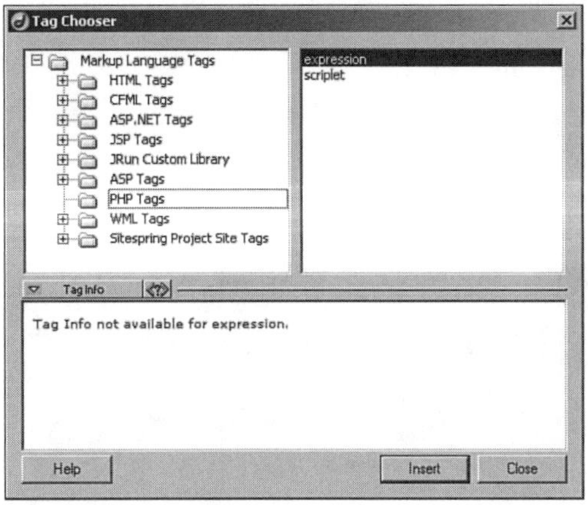

FIGURE 24.2   Using the Tag Chooser to select a PHP expression.

Saving Code Snippets

Dreamweaver MX allows you to save any content, HTML markup, or PHP code as code snippets that you store in the Snippets library.

To save a piece of PHP code as a snippet, follow these directions:

1. Highlight the PHP code you want to save as a snippet.

2. Click the Snippets tab under Code in the right pane.

3. Click the Create New Folder icon.

4. Name the new folder PHP Snippets.

5. Double-click the folder to open it.

6. Click the Create New Snippet icon.

7. In the Snippet dialog box, give your snippet a name that's descriptive of the code.

8. Optionally, provide a description of the code.

9. Choose Insert Block (this works for most PHP code blocks) instead of Wrap Selection.

> **NOTE**
>
> Wrap Selection is used to wrap code before and after any selection you've highlighted with the mouse. It's a handy way to wrap <b> and </b> tags around a word you've highlighted, but it isn't very useful when you're inserting PHP code.

10. Choose Code as the Preview Type.

11. Click OK to close the dialog box.

To use a code snippet, click where you want the Snippet to go and then double-click it from the list of snippets. Dreamweaver MX inserts the snippet into your document.

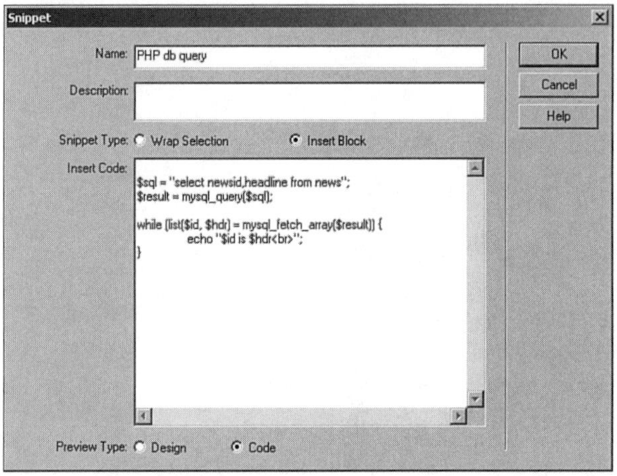

FIGURE 24.3   Use the Code Snippet feature to save frequently used PHP code.

Summary

Together, PHP and MySQL provide most of the functionality you need to start creating powerful and versatile dynamic Web applications.

CHAPTER **25**

Looking Ahead

by Zak Ruvalcaba

Forging Ahead

Although Dreamweaver MX cannot fully integrate every conceivable technology and language within its framework, it can better prepare itself and its users for emerging technologies. This section helps you understand those technologies that are on the verge of being used by the global Web development community and what Dreamweaver is doing to integrate those technologies within its development environment.

XHTML

You have probably heard of the term XHTML but might not be sure what it is. This section's purpose is to clear up any questions or rumors regarding the subject. In fact, the popular rumor is that XHTML is this revolutionary new language that will streamline the way developers create Web pages. Although there is truth to that statement, it isn't entirely correct. Yes, XHTML is aimed at streamlining the way developers create Web pages, but it is not a new technology. As you will see, XHTML has its roots in HTML and XML and is quite simple to pick up within the scope of this short section.

As just mentioned, XHTML has its roots in HTML and XML. Makes sense, right? Combine the eXtensible Markup Language with the Hypertext Markup Language and you're bound to get the eXtensible Hypertext Markup Language or

XHTML. But what makes XHTML so extensible if its roots lie in HTML? As you may know, over the years HTML has turned into a mishmash of "bad" code. This isn't by any means the fault of the language. After all, when HTML was first conceived, it was meant to be written correctly and well formed. Over the years, as browsers began to fight for superiority, browser manufacturers began correcting users code by adding misplaced or forgotten tags, combining invalidly nested tags, and even removing tags when they didn't have to be there. Try the following line of code in your favorite browser:

```
<html>
<head>
<title>Bad HTML Example</title>
<body>
<h1>Some more bad HTML
</body>
```

Still works, right? Even though the closing </html>, </h1>, and </head> tags are all missing. Although this seems more of a flaw of the browser, you can partially thank the browser manufacturers for fixing the problems that we as developers were bound to make. Could you imagine if you were writing hundreds of lines of HTML and you got an error every fifth line as the browser was parsing the document? Who would ever want to write HTML? The problem now becomes the evolution of micro Internet devices in PDAs and cell phones. Because the browsers in these devices have to be small enough to compensate for the amount of memory they contain, browsers can't afford to check and correct errors for you any longer. In comes XHTML. Because XHTML combines the power and robustness of HTML with the rules and well-formed attributes of XML, it's the perfect language not only for well-formed hand-held Web sites, but large scale corporate ones as well.

XHTML is the new generation of HTML. If you haven't noticed, the HTML specification stopped at 4.01. It's been there for a couple of years now. The World Wide Web Consortium (W3C) recommends its newest XHTML 1.1 standard when creating Web sites and as you will soon learn, Dreamweaver MX has complete support for it. XHTML is written similarly to HTML, with some minor differences in the way that it's written. The most important differences are the following:

- **XHTML elements must be properly nested**   In the past, developers could accidentally write tags that were improperly nested. For instance, the following code would italicize and bold the text "Hello World":

  ```
  <b><i>Hello world</b></i>
  ```

  As you can see, this line of code contains an improperly nested bold tag. The correct way of writing this using XHTML standards would read:

  ```
  <b><i>Hello world</i></b>
  ```

- **Tag names must be in lowercase**   Why does it matter if tags are lowercase versus uppercase? XML is case sensitive. For this reason, the XHTML specification states that all XHTML tags and attributes should be written in lowercase. Remember, in XHTML the `<BR>` and `<br>` tags are considered different tags.

- **All XHTML elements must be closed**   Although this seems like an obvious point, think again. Although most elements in HTML contain closing tags, empty elements exist that do not contain closing tags. For example, consider the following code:

```
<form name="form1" method="post" action="someform.asp">
<input type="text" name="fname"><br>
<input type="text" name="lname"><br>
<input type="submit" value="Submit">
</form>
```

Although this seems correct in HTML, it is completely wrong in XHTML. Notice that the `<input>` and `<br>` tags don't have closing tags associated with them. In HTML they don't. In XHTML, even empty elements must have the closing tag, or "/". The correct way of writing the preceding code is the following:

```
<form name="form1" method="post" action="someform.asp">
<input type="text" name="fname" /><br />
<input type="text" name="lname" /><br />
<input type="submit" value="Submit" />
</form>
```

This is now correct because even the empty elements within the code have closing tags associated with them.

- **Attribute values must be quoted**   In the past, you could write a tag and its attributes and completely ignore the fact that attribute values were missing their quotes. For example, the following code would be fine in HTML:

```
<img src=Images/myimage.gif width=400 height=400>
```

The following line would have to be rewritten for XHMTL. The result would encapsulate the attribute values within quotes like this:

```
<img src="Images/myimage.gif" width="400" height="400" />
```

- **Attribute minimization is forbidden**   With HTML there were certain tags—form tags, for instance—that could contain minimized attributes. In HTML you could create a read-only text box and a checked check box by writing the following code:

```
<input type="text" name="fname" readonly>
<input type="checkbox" name="cbox1" checked>
```

The correct rewrite within XHTML would be as follows:

```
<input type="text" name="fname" readonly="readonly" />
<input type="checkbox" name="cbox1" checked="checked" />
```

- **The id attribute replaces the name attribute**   In HTML 4.01, the name attribute was used to give reference to HTML tags such as input, img, div, span, map, and so on. In XHTML, the name attribute is deprecated. The id attribute should be used instead.

- **The XHTML DTD defines mandatory elements**   Although this topic can cover an entire chapter, it is important to point out that all XHTML documents must contain the DOCTYPE declaration. The reason for the DOCTYPE is simple:

  - Document Type Declaration, or DTD, specifies the syntax of a Web page in SGML.

  - DTD is used by SGML applications such as HTML to specify rules about how a page is written; XHTML is specified in an SGML document type definition or DTD.

  - An XHTML DTD describes in precise, computer-readable language the allowed syntax and grammar of XHTML markup.

  - There are three types of DTDs—Strict, Transitional, and Frameset. They can be written similar to the following:

    ```
    <!DOCTYPE html PUBLIC
    ➥"-//W3C//DTD XHTML 1.0 Strict//EN"
    [ic:cc]http://www.w3.org/TR/xhtml1/DTD/xhtml1-strict.dtd>
    <!DOCTYPE html PUBLIC
    ➥"-//W3C//DTD XHTML 1.0 Transitional//EN"
    ➥http://www.w3.org/TR/xhtml1/DTD/xhtml1-strict.dtd>
    <!DOCTYPE html PUBLIC
    ➥"-//W3C//DTD XHTML 1.0 Frameset//EN"
    ➥http://www.w3.org/TR/xhtml1/DTD/xhtml1- frameset.dtd>
    ```

NOTE

The DTD is not related to XHTML is any way and therefore does not need to be written in lower-case and does not require a closing tag.

- **CSS is used instead of block-level formatting options** For years, developers got away with formatting text quickly with the use of the font tag, cellpadding and cellspacing attributes with tables, left margin and top margin attributes in the body, and so on. Now with XHTML, developers are forced to use CSS whenever formatting needs to be accomplished.

As you can see, XHTML should be quite familiar to you if you know HTML. It's a simple matter of remembering rules that should be habit by now if you wrote HTML pages the correct way from the start. If you don't care, that's okay too, because Dreamweaver alleviates the heartache by including a check box that instantly turns on the "well-formed" code-writing features within Dreamweaver MX. This check box can be turned on by selecting it whenever you create a new document. Figure 25.1 shows where that check box is located.

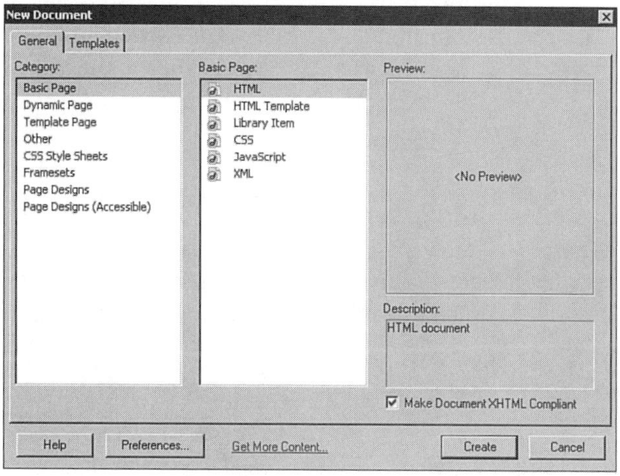

FIGURE 25.1 Turn on XHTML compatibility within Dreamweaver MX.

XML

HTML, as you know, is short for Hypertext Markup Language. The "Markup" refers to the library of tags that describes how data should be laid out within a page. The browser then parses the information out of those tags and presents it to the user in a friendly and legible fashion. What HTML doesn't do is give any information about what the data means, called metadata. Without metadata, search engines and other data-filtering techniques have to rely on keyword searches or even content searches to retrieve information for the user. Even so, they can miss entirely, returning paint chips rather than potato chips.

XML is about metadata and the fact that different people have different needs for how they categorize and organize that data. Like HTML, XML is a set of tags and declarations. Rather than being concerned with how the data is structured and subsequently parsed by the browser, XML provides information on what the data means and how it relates to other data.

In the near term, it provides an immediate opportunity for intranet database-driven site development. As is the case within large organizations, many departments may use the same database in different ways. Accounting needs payable and receivable information. Sales wants to monitor information by salesperson to figure out commission structures. Marketing wants data organized by product and industry segment to figure out future release strategies. Using XML, you will be able to customize the presentation of the queried data in a fashion most useful to the person making the query.

Like HTML, XML's purpose is to describe the content of a document. Unlike HTML, XML does not describe how that content should be displayed. Instead, it describes what that content is. Using XML, the Web author can mark up the contents of a document, describing that content in terms of its relevance as data. For example, the following HTML element:

```
<P>Star Wars Episode I: The Phantom Menace</P>
```

describes the contents within the tags as a paragraph. This is fine if all we are concerned with is displaying the words "Star Wars Episode I: The Phantom Menace" within a Web page. But what if we want to access those words as data? Using XML, we can mark up the words "Star Wars Episode I: The Phantom Menace" in a way that better reflects their significance as data:

```
<film>Star Wars Episode I: The Phantom Menace</film>
```

XML does not limit you to a set library of tags. When marking up documents in XML, you can choose the tag name that best describes the contents of the element. For instance, in the preceding example, you may need to differentiate between the VHS version and the DVD version. This can be achieved by using an attribute to describe the type. XML allows you to place attributes on elements. Using an attribute, you could describe "Star Wars Episode I: The Phantom Menace" as a film and then specify whether that film is the DVD version or the VHS version:

```
<film version="DVD">Star Wars Episode I: The Phantom Menace</film>
```

The following document describes the contents of a personal video library:

```
<H1>The Library of Zak Ruvalcaba</H1>
<TABLE>
<TR>
<TD>Star Wars Episode I: The Phantom Menace</TD>
<TD>Star Wars Episode I: The Phantom Menace</TD>
```

```
<TD>The Return of the Jedi</TD>
</TR>
</TABLE>
```

This document provides us with information, but that information is not too clear. Does Zak own two copies of the DVD version? Does he own a DVD version and a VHS version? The code below may be better suited for the preceding example:

```
<library>
<owner>Zak Ruvalcaba</owner>
<films>
<film version="DVD">Star Wars Episode I: The Phantom Menace</film>
<film version="VHS">Star Wars Episode I: The Phantom Menace</film>
<film version="VHS">The Return of the Jedi</film>
</films>
</library>
```

Because XML is concerned with how data should be defined, it does not make a good presentational language. If you created an XML document from the preceding example and tried to view it in the browser, you would get little more than a simple collapsible menu showing you the items within the tags. Despite this, XML plays a crucial role in Web development and will continue to do so now and in the future. For now, know that technologies that we use today include remnants of XML, including XHTML, Web Services, WML, and so on. If you are interested in creating XML files within Dreamweaver MX, you can select the XML document by selecting New from the File menu, as shown in Figure 25.2.

25

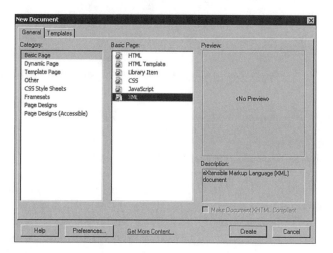

FIGURE 25.2   Select the XML file from the New File menu.

XML Web Services

Looking back over the past few years, it's hard to imagine networked computers without the Web. The Web allows for networked communication with hundreds of services provided by hundreds of companies and organizations. From a user standpoint, if you can type, you can access these services. From an application service provider (ASP) standpoint, if you can set up a Web site, communication is opened up to other services. The problem doesn't lie in the access of those services but in the communication between the users and the services. The Web Service movement aims to solve this problem by facilitating the communication between users and services and even services between services.

By "services," I don't mean the typical online shopping or auction service, such as Amazon.com or eBay. Services can range from something as simple as a service that checks the weather or validates a credit card to something as complex as an airline flight reservation service that automatically deducts money from a centralized account that you specify, updates a global calendar that you maintain, and even reserves a hotel and rental car based on the destination that you desire. Seem far off?

Web Services are new types of Web applications. They are self-contained, modular programs that can be published, found, and called via the Web. They perform functions, which can range from something as simple as validating a credit card to updating hotel reservations. After a Web Service is deployed, users, applications, and other Web Services can invoke those functions within the Web Service. Still seem like it's too good to be true? Think again. Web Services are currently being used in Microsoft's My Services and Passport initiatives. The Passport authentication service is a self-contained Web Service that exposes an authentication scheme allowing other developers and applications to validate a user's credentials from one location. What this means is that if every developer used the Passport authentication service, it would eliminate the need for ever having to program your own login page.

So what makes up a Web Service? The basic framework within a Web Service lies within its platform:

- **XML**   XML is the meta language used to write specialized languages to articulate interactions between clients and services.

- **HTTP**   HTTP drives how we access information on the Web.

- **SOAP**   The Simple Object Access Protocol, or SOAP, is a protocol specification that defines a uniform way of passing XML data between networks. SOAP stems from the fact that no matter how great current middleware services (CORBA, DCOM, and the like) are, they still need some sort of wrapper. Think of SOAP in terms of HTTP. With HTTP, a user requests a page usually by typing in the HTTP address, and a response is returned in the form of a Web site. The protocol that the Web site was delivered with was HTTP. SOAP, on the other hand, is the protocol used to define how objects are accessed and transferred across networks, typically packaged up using XML within a SOAP envelope "wrapper." A user or service makes a SOAP request and a response is returned, just as is the case with HTTP.

- **UDDI**   The Universal Description, Discovery, and Integration Service, or UDDI, provides a mechanism for clients to dynamically find other Web Services. Using a UDDI interface, applications can locate and use other Web Services. You can think of UDDI as a DNS for business applications.

- **WSDL**   The Web Services Definition Language, or WSDL, provides a way for Web Service providers to describe how and what their Web Services do, where they reside, and how to invoke them.

Now that you have some familiarity with Web Services, what they do, and what they are composed of, let's build a Web Service that performs a simple calculation of two numbers. You can begin creating your Web Service by following these steps:

1. Open a document in Dreamweaver MX and switch to code view.

2. Immediately save your file as sample.asmx. ASMX is the extension given to Web Services.

3. Add the code that follows. The code should include the Web Service directive, the Web.Services namespace import, and the Service1 class that defines the Calculate function. Notice the function is distinguished as a Web method by the special <WebMethod()> tag. The function accepts two parameters (X and Y) as integers and performs a simple addition on them.

```
<%@ Webservice class="Service1" %>
Imports System.Web.Services
Public Class Service1
   Inherits System.Web.Services.WebService
   <WebMethod()> Public Function Calculate(x As Integer, y As Integer)
     Calculate = x + y
   End Function
End Class
```

4. With the Web Service now created, you can launch the browser to test its functionality. Navigate to the folder where your Web Service is located and find the ASMX file. The service screen shows you a list of all available Web methods. Figure 25.3 shows that we just have the Calculate function. Obviously you never wrote code that resembles what you are seeing. This screen is a service of the .NET SDK and is available with its installation for use in testing Web Services.

5. Selecting Calculate redirects you to a new screen that will allow you to input the X and Y values that the function will accept and perform the calculation on. Click the Invoke button, as shown in Figure 25.4.

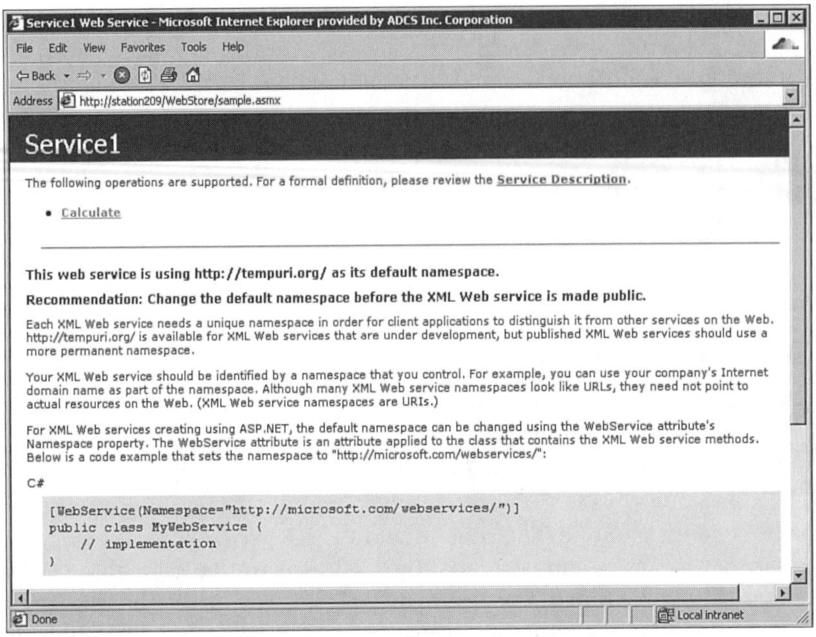

FIGURE 25.3   The service contains just one method, Calculate.

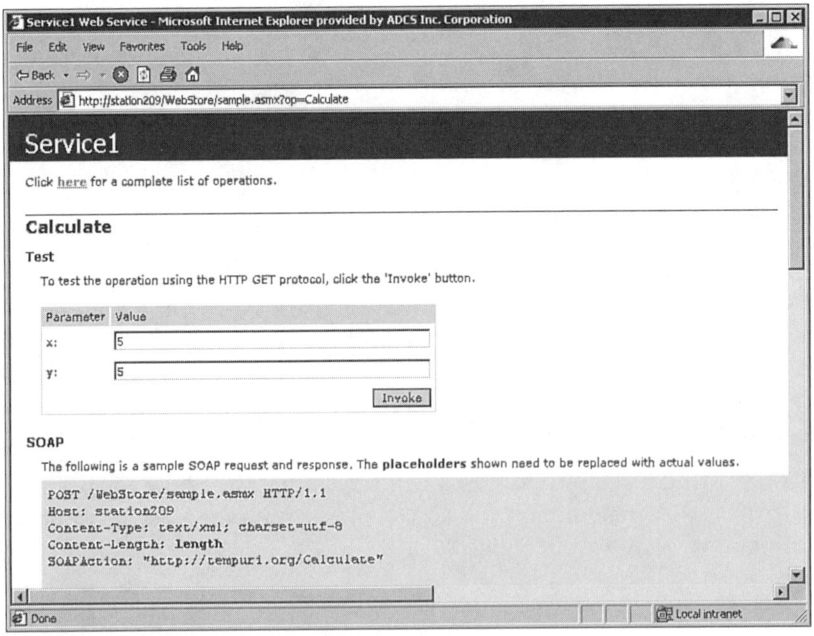

FIGURE 25.4   Click the Invoke button to invoke the function.

6. The result of the calculation is shown in XML format similar to that of Figure 25.5.

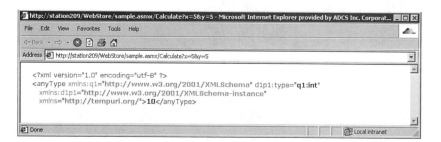

FIGURE 25.5   The result of the calculation is shown in XML format.

7. Obviously this does no one any good if it's not applicable in a programmed environment. You can generate a proxy class that you will be able to program against within your ASP.NET pages. This allows for customization of Web controls that invoke and return values for the Web Service. Begin the process of generating the proxy class by opening the Command window. Select Start, Run, and type **cmd**. The Command window will open.

8. Switch to the folder that the ASMX file is located in by using the CD command. Type the following code to generate the VB code that contains the necessary code to eventually generate the proxy class:

```
wsdl /l:vb http://localhost/WebStore/sample.asmx?WSDL /n:AppSettings
```

The result is shown in Figure 25.6.

9. Now generate the new proxy class by typing in the following code:

```
vbc /out:Service1.dll /t:library
/r:system.Web.dll,system.dll,system.xml.dll,system.Web.services.dll,system.
➥data.dll
Service1.vb
```

The result is shown in Figure 25.7.

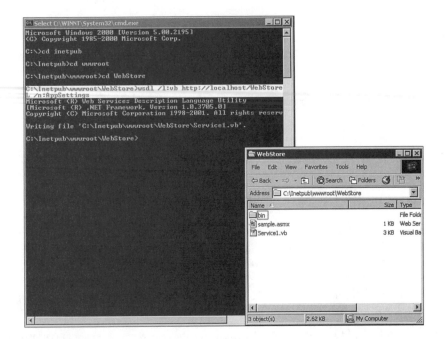

FIGURE 25.6   Generate the new VB file.

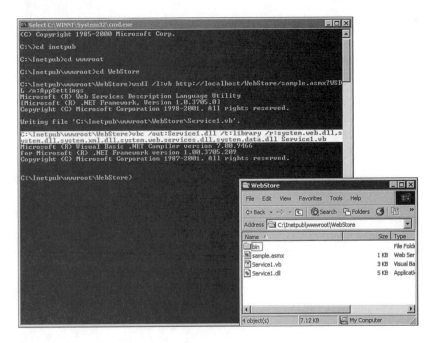

FIGURE 25.7   Generate the new proxy class.

10. Notice that each time you run the code, the new file is created within the folder that contains the original ASMX file.

11. Now open Dreamweaver MX and create a new ASP.NET page. Make sure that the proxy class (Service1.dll) is located within the Bin directory of the project you are working with.

12. Switch to the Components tab and select the "+" icon.

13. Select Add Using Proxy Classes as shown in Figure 25.8.

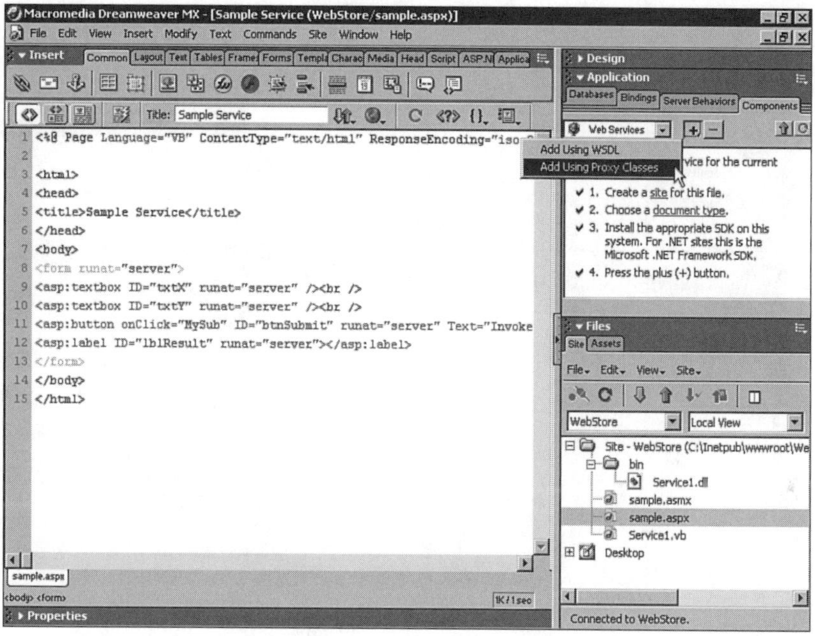

FIGURE 25.8   Add the new proxy class.

14. Browse to the location of the proxy class as shown in Figure 25.9. Make sure that the .NET DLL Reader is selected.

15. Select OK. The Web Service is shown within the Components panel. You can view the Calculate function by expanding the service.

16. Add two new textbox controls, one button control, and a label control as shown in Figure 25.10.

FIGURE 25.9   Find the class file.

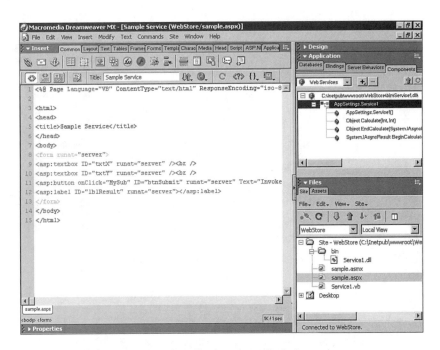

FIGURE 25.10   Add new controls to handle the user calculation values.

17. Now create a new script tag within the `<title>` tag. Drag the service in followed by the Calculate function. Code similar to Figure 25.11 should be created for you.

18. Next add the subroutine, the text value parameters, the code to set the label, and an onClick event to the button, as shown in Figure 25.12.

19. Save your work as sample.aspx and test it in the browser. The result is shown in Figure 25.13.

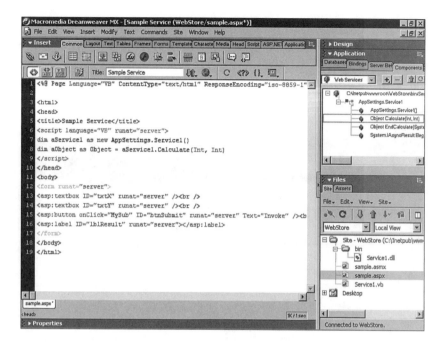

FIGURE 25.11   Drag the object and method into the Code window.

How simple was that? Imagine how complex this can get. You could create Web Services to handle all sorts of functions. In fact, hundreds of Web Services are available already that allow you to create searches, check weather, stocks, and so on.

WML

To better understand the Wireless Markup Language, you first should understand the protocol that it sits on. Founded by the WAP Forum in 1997 by Ericsson, Motorola, Nokia, and Unwired Planet, WAP, or the Wireless Application Protocol, was developed to show-case Internet-based content on wireless devices. The WAP protocol is the leading standard for information services on wireless devices such as digital mobile phones. Although it is based on Internet standards (HTML, XML, and TCP/IP), it consists mainly of the WML language specification, a WMLScript specification, and a Wireless Telephony Application Interface (WTAI) specification. To fit into a small wireless terminal, WAP uses a Micro Browser, a small piece of software that makes minimal demands on hardware, memory, and CPU.

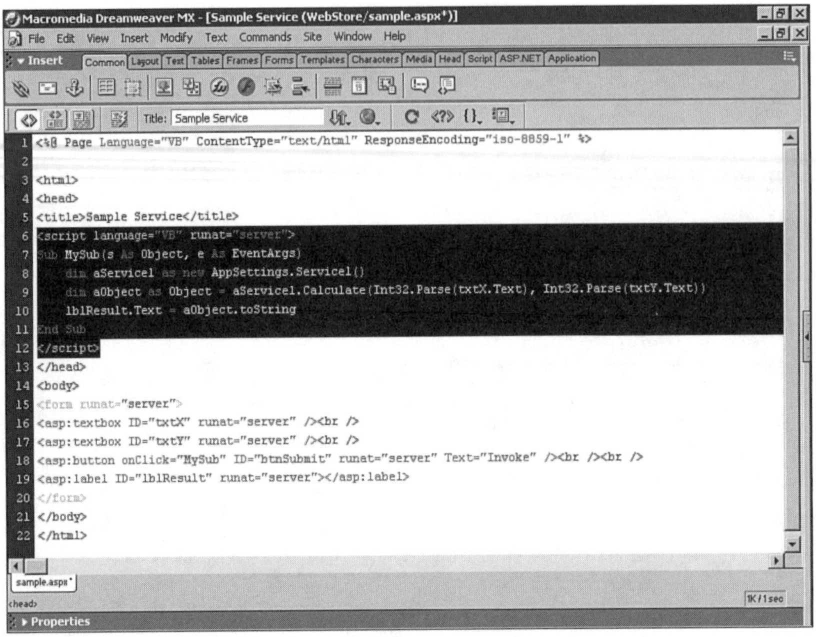

FIGURE 25.12   Add the appropriate code to complete the subroutine.

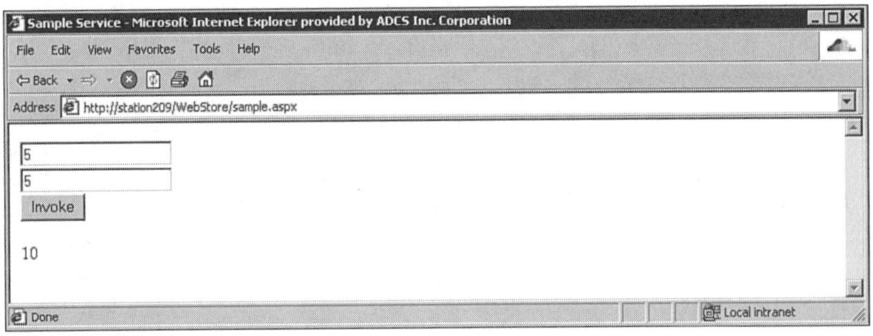

FIGURE 25.13   Test the ASPX file within the browser. Set values and invoke the method passing in the parameters to return a result.

Micro browsers display information written in a restricted markup language called WML. WML stands for Wireless Markup Language. It is a markup language similar to SGML, but because it is based on XML, it has much stricter syntax. Because WML is an XML application, all tags are case sensitive and must be properly closed. WML pages are called decks and are constructed as a set of cards related to each other with links. When a WML page is accessed from a mobile phone, all the cards in the page are downloaded from the WAP server. The following is a simple example of a WML page:

```
<?xml version="1.0"?>
<!DOCTYPE wml PUBLIC "-//WAPFORUM//DTD WML 1.1//EN"
"http://www.wapforum.org/DTD/wml_1.1.xml">

<wml>
<card id="example1" title="Example 1">
<p>Example 1</p>
</card>

<card id="example2" title="Example 2">
<p>Example 2</p>
</card>
</wml>
```

As you can see from the example, the WML document is an XML document. The DOCTYPE is defined to be WML, and the DTD is accessed at www.wapforum.org/DTD/wml_1.1.xml. The document content is inside the <wml> and </wml> tags. Each card in the document is inside <card> and </card> tags, and actual paragraphs are inside <p> and </p> tags. Each card element has an id and a title.

Although a full reference on WML is beyond the scope of this book, it is important to note that WML contains important formatting elements that are worth mentioning because of their relevance within Dreamweaver MX. They are:

Tag	Purpose
Deck/Card Elements	
<access>	Defines information about the access of a deck
<card>	Defines a card in a deck
<head>	Contains information about the document
<meta>	Defines meta information about the document
<template>	Defines a template for all the cards in a deck
<wml>	Defines a WML deck
<!-->	Defines a comment
Text Elements	
 	Defines a line break
<p>	Defines a paragraph
<table>	Defines a table
<td>	Defines a table cell
<tr>	Defines a table row

Tag	Purpose
Text Formatting Tags	
`<b>`	Defines bold text
`<big>`	Defines big text
`<em>`	Defines emphasized text
`<i>`	Defines italic text
`<small>`	Defines small text
`<strong>`	Defines strong text
`<u>`	Defines underlined text
Anchor Elements	
`<a>`	Defines an anchor
`<anchor>`	Defines an anchor
Image Elements	
`<img>`	Defines an image
Event Elements	
`<do>`	Performs a task when the user clicks a link
`<onevent>`	Contains code to be executed when an event occurs
`<postfield>`	Contains information to be sent to the server
Task Elements	
`<go>`	Represents the action of switching to a new card
`<noop>`	Says that nothing should be done
`<prev>`	Returns to the previous card
`<refresh>`	Refreshes a specified card
Input Elements	
`<fieldset>`	Used to group together elements in a card
`<input>`	Defines an input field
`<optgroup>`	Defines an option group in a selectable list
`<option>`	Defines an option in a selectable list
`<select>`	Defines a selectable list
Variable Elements	
`<setvar>`	Sets a variable
`<timer>`	Defines a card timer

You can access WML-specific tags by first creating a WML page. Select New from the File menu and choose Other from the category. Select WML page from the subcategory as shown in Figure 25.14.

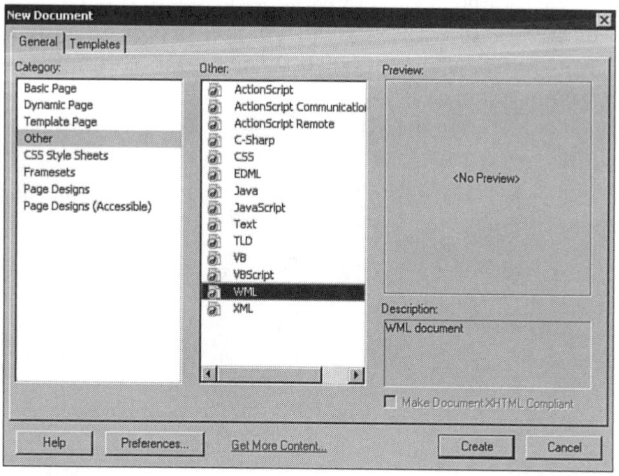

FIGURE 25.14 Create a new WML page.

With the page created, you are now able to insert WML-specific tags by selecting them from the Tag Chooser as shown in Figure 25.15.

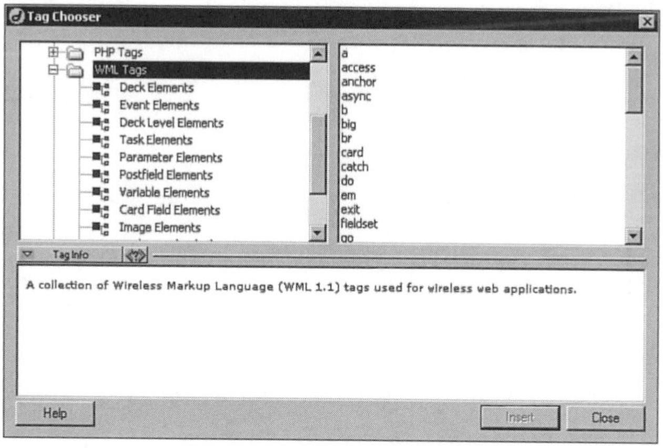

FIGURE 25.15 Insert WML-specific tags from the Tag Chooser.

Summary

As you can see, Dreamweaver MX's support is unprecedented when it comes to technologies and languages that are still on the forefront of the Web development industry. Although some of these technologies aren't as new as they may seem, they are still very much in development and are undergoing constant specification changes. The most exciting by far is that of Web Services. As the industry changes to accommodate the new paradigm of application development and sharing, so will the need for a development platform that can grow to meet the needs of those who are developing the solutions. Dreamweaver MX's support for Web Services along with its support for XML and XML-based technologies and its XHTML compliance make it the development tool to meet the needs of the solution developers.

PART VI

Database-Driven Pages

IN THIS PART

CHAPTER **26**

Database Primer

by Zak Ruvalcaba

As you begin to build dynamic Web applications using Dreamweaver MX, it will become increasingly obvious that you need to store data and allow its access through your application. Whether you are building a small, company-wide intranet store with access limited to employees or a feature-rich Internet Web store that millions will visit, you will need some system for storing all the order, customer, cost, and product information. You may not want to stop there; you might want to include some way of tracking how many of a certain item you have left in your inventory. You might need to determine how many items are selling during a particular week of the month; if that is the case, you will need some way of determining sales transactions. Like a filing cabinet that stores files and, subsequently, data within those files, you will need some system of storing all your data for easy access and quick retrieval.

In 1970, E. F. Codd, an employee with IBM, proposed his idea for what would become the first relational database design model. His model, which proposed new methods for storing and retrieving data in large applications, far surpassed any idea or system that was in place at that time. His idea of "relational" stemmed from the fact that data and relationships between them were organized in "relations," or what we know today as tables. Even though Codd's terminology of what we know today as tables, columns, and rows was different, the premise behind the relational model has always remained consistent. Although the model has undergone revisions and changes over the past 30-plus years, the idea of storing and retrieving information in large applications has not changed, solidifying the need for the relational database model.

What Is a Database?

The best way to think of a database is in terms of a filing cabinet. In the previous paragraphs, I mentioned that a database can be thought of like a filing cabinet. The filing cabinet contains drawers, the drawers contain folders, and the folders contain documents that have information on them. A database is similar in concept. A database contains drawers, otherwise known as tables; those tables contain folders, or columns, which in turn contain rows of information pertaining to the particular column that they are in.

For a moment, let's take the preceding Web store example and break it down to see exactly what kind of information we would need and just how we could break it up to make it manageable.

- **Customers** We would need some way of keeping track of all our registered customers, along with shipping addresses, billing addresses, credit card information, and so forth.

- **Inventory** If we are to keep track of how many of a certain item we have sold as well as quantities in stock, we would need some way of keeping track of our inventory.

- **Product Information** Some way of differentiating between all our products is necessary, including sizes, colors, prices, and other characteristics that relate to a specific item.

- **Transactions** We would need to include a history of all transactions and a way of knowing which customers are ordering what so that we can recommend products to people dynamically in the future.

Traditionally, we could take all these elements and create a Word document or perhaps a spreadsheet within Excel and physically write on these documents whenever someone ordered something. We could take these documents and store them into folders alphabetically and even store all the folders within one central filing cabinet. Although this is a traditional example of how business can work, it very closely resembles how the modern database operates in relation to our traditional model. The filing cabinet, the drawers, folders, and even the documents within them all represent the basic parts of a modern database structure:

- Database Management System

- Database

- Tables

- Columns
- Rows

The Database Management System (DBMS)

The Database Management System (DBMS) represents the framework from which you design, store, and manage all the databases that you create. Figure 26.1 shows the SQL Server Enterprise Manager. The Enterprise Manager is a centralized location for managing and interacting with all your databases.

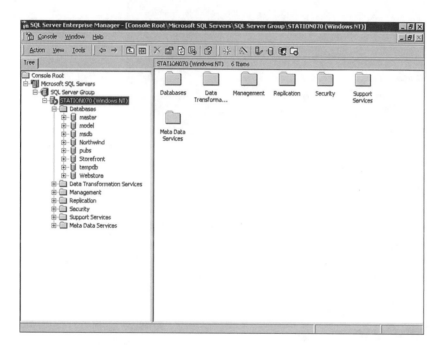

FIGURE 26.1   SQL Server Enterprise Manager is the typical Database Management System (DBMS).

Although smaller databases such as Access do not have what is traditionally known as a DBMS, Access does provide you with a way of interacting with and managing a single database file. Figure 26.2 shows how you can open a database through Access.

If you look at the Web store example again, you can begin to imagine how the DBMS looks much like the filing cabinet discussed earlier. Unlike a filing cabinet, however, which typically contains two to four drawers, a DBMS can manage hundreds, possibly thousands of databases—all of which are immediately at your fingertips.

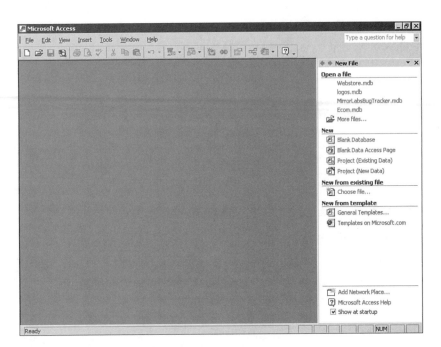

FIGURE 26.2   Access does not provide a typical DBMS, but it does allow for access to any single database file.

> **NOTE**
>
> Many databases other than SQL Server and Access are available. So many, in fact, that we cannot begin to cover them in the scope of this book. For the sake of simplicity, Access and SQL Server are discussed here whenever possible.

The Database

Inside your DBMS are individual databases containing yet even more data related to a specific project. Although for most projects you would never need more than one database, you may in the future realize that your project has grown far beyond the scope of a single database—that because of security or maintenance reasons, you require more. Figure 26.3 shows SQL Server Enterprise Manager with a list of the various databases that are housed within its framework.

Tables

After a database has been created, just as it has been for the Web store, you might want to begin storing information that is relevant to a specific part of the Web store. As mentioned earlier, tables are very similar to file folders within a file cabinet's drawers. It would be a mistake to store all the information about inventory, product information, customers, and even transactions within one file folder; instead, you'll break these out, just as we did at the beginning of the chapter, and create different file folders or tables to store all the information.

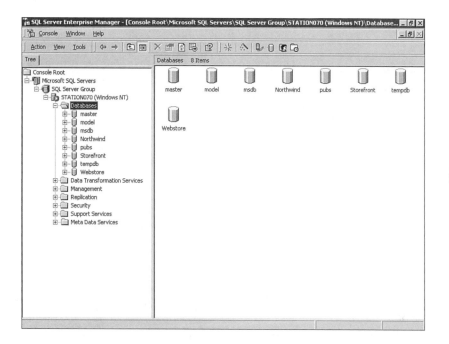

FIGURE 26.3   SQL Server Enterprise Manager and a list of the databases that it contains.

Figure 26.4 shows the Web store database within the Enterprise Manager of SQL Server. By selecting and expanding the Web store database from the view in the left column, you can begin to see all the tables that can reside within the Web store.

Notice that there are more tables than just the four outlined in the beginning of the chapter. If you think in terms of space and redundancy, you will see exactly why you need to include more than just the four main tables. As far as the customers table is concerned, you could have a customer that has multiple credit cards on file—hence the need for a separate credit card table. You could have a product that is available in numerous colors or, depending on what you sell, different formats and perhaps even sizes and makes.

TIP

The process of organizing data in an effort to avoid redundancy within tables is known as normalization and is discussed in depth toward the end of this chapter.

26

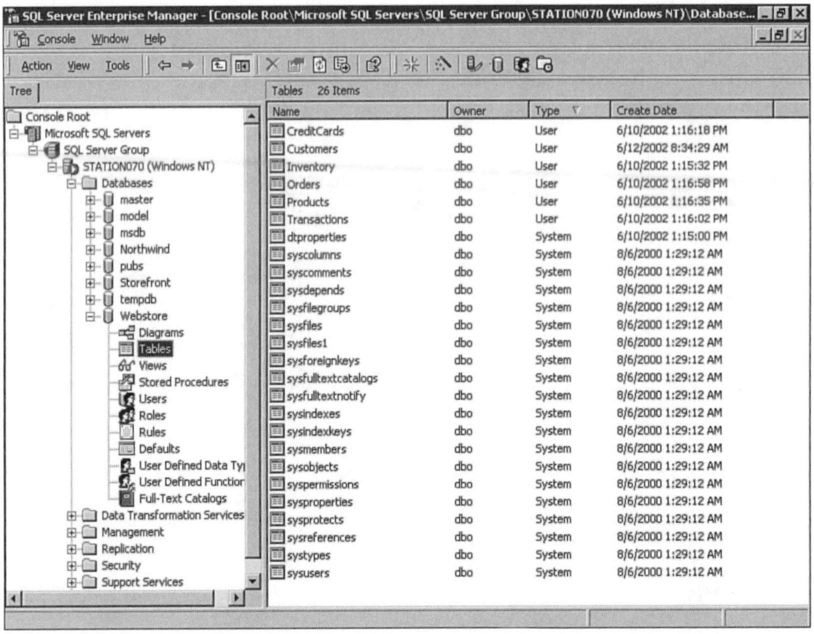

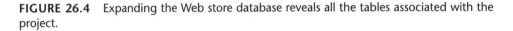

FIGURE 26.4   Expanding the Web store database reveals all the tables associated with the project.

Before you begin any project, you will typically sketch all this out in an effort to reduce data duplication within your tables. Again, how you branch out your information and create tables depends on how big in scope your project is.

Columns

After you outline all your tables, the next step is to decide on what information will be included within those tables. For instance, you may want to include first name, last name, phone number, address, city, state, ZIP code, and so on for all your customers within the customers table. You may also need to include product names, descriptions, and some sort of unique identification within your products table. You may even want to combine certain aspects of certain tables and place them into the orders table, in which you would end up with information from the customers table as well as the orders table to come up with a final requisition.

Theoretically, columns represent bits of information or more detailed descriptions of the table that they are contained in. Just as you have a customers table, all customers must have names and physical addresses. Just as you have a products table, all products must have names and descriptions. Figure 26.5 shows what the customers table may look like after columns have been outlined.

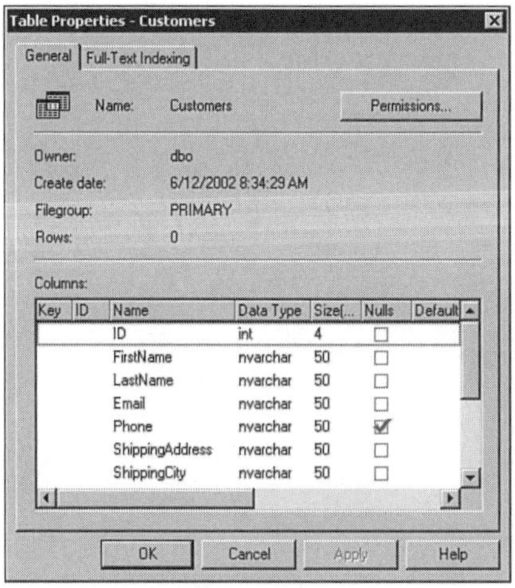

FIGURE 26.5   The customers table displays all the columns that are associated with it.

Rows

Think back to the example that I mentioned earlier regarding the documents within the folders and the folders within the drawers that are contained within the filing cabinet. Rows represent the actual data within those documents. Similar to the columns within the tables, rows represent the actual data within the columns. Suppose that this is a real Web store—after people begin registering and purchasing items, the rows would expand and fill up with information as shown in Figure 26.6.

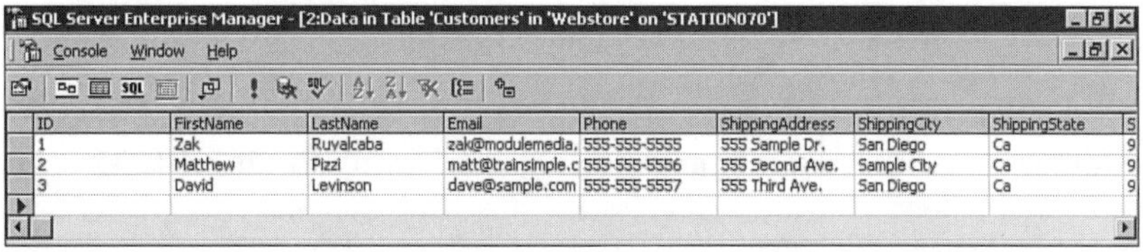

FIGURE 26.6   The customers table with multiple rows of information.

Beyond the Basics

Now that we have gotten the basic structure of a database out of the way, let's begin thinking about what really drives the database. Aside from the data within the tables, other characteristics and functions within the database can improve performance, reduce network traffic, increase security, lower development time, and dramatically decrease maintenance efforts. Some of these functions and characteristics are listed next:

- Stored Procedures

- Triggers

- Views

- Security

- Relationship Management

- Keys

- Normalization

Stored Procedures

Stored procedures are a way of actually storing code that you use to work with your database on the database itself. They are a way of modularizing repetitive code so that you never have to write the same line of code within your applications more than once. You simply create a stored procedure within your database and call it through your application, passing in parameters as necessary. In return, the stored procedure executes complex tasks and can return a recordset of information back to the application that is calling it.

> **TIP**
>
> When a user makes a request for information from the database, information is returned with a recordset. A recordset is a cluster of information bundled within an object that the developer can then dynamically iterate through to retrieve the data sent back by the database.

Triggers

Triggers, which are similar to stored procedures, can be set up to run with your database data. Triggers are predefined events that run automatically whenever a specified action (preferably Insert, Delete, or Update) is performed on a physical file. Although it may sound a bit confusing as to what triggers actually are and what they can do, think of triggers as a way of enforcing business rules that you may have described within your database. They enforce stability and integrity within your tables.

> **TIP**
>
> Referential integrity refers to the process of setting up tables with rules so that data cannot alter any of your tables without first abiding by those rules.

For example, in the Web store database, you could set up another table for customers to place a listing of all their phone numbers.

> **NOTE**
>
> For the sake of demonstration, the customers table is set up to accept only one phone number; ideally, you would want a customer to store phone numbers associated with day and evening. Both numbers would be stored in a separate table along with a third table to determine the type of phone number it is. All three of the tables would be connected through a relationship.

If the customer ended a relationship with the Web store, you could have useless phone number information that would not be associated with any customer. Triggers would make sure that if a customer ended a relationship with the Web store, not only their information within the customers table is deleted, but also the relationship with the phone numbers table.

Views

Views are awkward to think about at first because their name is deceiving. A view isn't actually what it implies; rather, it is a virtual table whose contents are defined by a query. Much like a real table with rows and columns, views exist as a stored set of data values. Rows and columns of data come from the tables that are referenced and are produced dynamically when the view is called.

For example, you could have multiple databases set up throughout your company—one for sales, one for marketing, and possibly one for operations. You could use a view to combine similar data within all those databases to produce a virtual table with sales numbers, marketing reports, and even information from operations.

Security

Security is always important to any facet of engineering, not just database development. Ensuring that your database is secure and accessible only by certain individuals or departments is crucial. Many database management systems provide a means for setting security options for users and groups of users. Figure 26.7 illustrates how you could modify permissions for specific users with SQL Server. Access, on the other hand, enables you to modify security settings by right-clicking the database file, selecting Properties, and choosing the Security tab, as shown in Figure 26.8.

Relationship Management

When you create new tables in your database, an important aspect to consider is that of relationships. We have already touched on what relationships are and how they relate to your tables. For example, you could create a separate table for credit cards and assign that table a relationship with the customers table. The reason for doing this is simple. It allows you to store more than one credit card for a particular customer. Suppose a user wanted to store more than one credit card or even phone number. You would end up duplicating the same information numerous times for one particular customer. This is inefficient and unnecessary. Instead, create a separate table for credit cards and assign each row within that column a unique identifier, usually an automatically generated number. The relationship would exist between the unique identifier within the customer table (CustomerID) and that identifier within the credit cards table. Figure 26.9 displays a relationship between the customers table and the credit cards table.

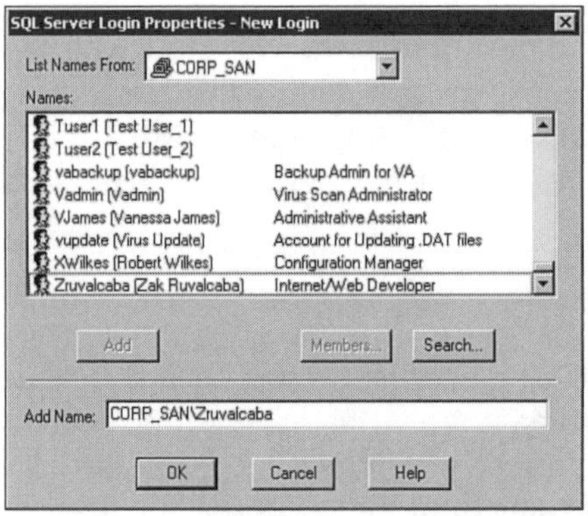

FIGURE 26.7   Adding users and permissions using the SQL Server Enterprise Manager.

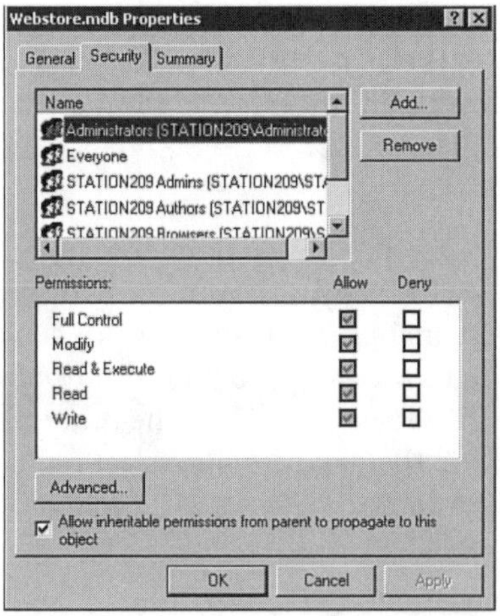

FIGURE 26.8   Adding users and permissions to an Access database file.

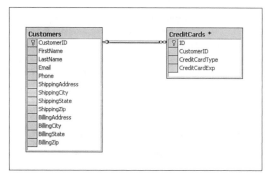

FIGURE 26.9   Relationships are added to avoid data duplication within tables.

Three types of relationships exist between database tables:

- One-to-one
- One-to-many
- Many-to-many

One-to-One Relationships
A one-to-one relationship means that for each record that exists in one table, only one other related record can exist in another table. One-to-one relationships are rarely used, and when they are, it is usually because of a limitation with the database that requires data to be stored separately—usually because of its size.

One-to-Many Relationships
A one-to-many relationship is by far the most common of relationship types. A one-to-many relationship means that for each record in one table, multiple records can be associated with it that exist in a second table. These records are usually related based on a unique number. In the customers/credit cards example earlier in this chapter, a one-to-many relationship created a relationship between one customer and the many possible credit card numbers that could be stored in a second (credit cards) table.

Many-to-Many Relationships
A many-to-many relationship exists when many records in one table are related to many records in a second table. Many-to-many relationships are difficult to illustrate in a typical relational database model and are not often used in practice.

Keys
Many of the records in your database will contain information that is very similar in nature. You may have a thousand customers in your customers table, and a hundred of

those customers may be from San Diego. If you extracted all those records from the database, how would you be able to differentiate between all the records? Obviously you could differentiate by name, but what if you had three records in the database with the names John Smith from San Diego? A way to differentiate is through the use of unique keys.

Think about why uniqueness is so important. If you had more than one record in the database that was the same, what would be the sense in storing multiple copies? It would be a waste of space. Also, if you tried to update or delete a record from a database that matched a second record, the database would not be able to match the record that you were trying to work with and may end up either deleting the wrong record, throwing an error, or corrupting the data within your tables. Records can be identified through the use of three different keys:

- Candidate keys
- Primary keys
- Foreign keys

Candidate Keys

A candidate key is a set of columns that are unique across the board. Take the following example:

ZipCode	Area
92069	San Marcos
92115	San Diego
92105	San Diego
92128	San Diego

In this example, the ZipCode column could be considered a candidate key because the values never repeat. Although the Area names do repeat, together with the ZipCode value, they become unique and can make up a candidate key. Because the Area column contains repetitive information, it cannot be considered for a candidate key and could never be unique.

Primary Keys

Whereas candidate keys can be made up of several columns, a primary key is usually made up of a single column that designates a row in the table as unique. For the most part, primary keys can exist even though they have no relationship to the data that is being stored. Database developers will often create primary keys with an automatically generated number, guaranteeing that the row will always increment by one and remain completely unique from the previous record. Primary keys are the most useful when referenced from a second table through the use of foreign keys. The table that follows illustrates a simple table within a database that may contain ZIP codes. Because the primary key is different, the records remain completely unique.

ZipPK	ZipCode
1	92069
2	92115
3	92105
4	92128

> **NOTE**
>
> Because no ZIP code will ever be added more than once, you could make the ZIP code the primary key.

Foreign Keys

A foreign key is a column that contains values that are found in the primary key of another table. A foreign key may be null and almost always is not unique. Consider the following example:

ZipPK	ZipCode
1	92069
2	92115
3	92105
4	92128

AreaPK	AreaName	AreaFK
1	San Diego	3
2	San Diego	2
3	Tijuana	-
4	San Marcos	1
5	San Marcos	1
6	San Diego	4
7	San Diego	4

The AreaFK column in the second table is a foreign key to the ZipPK primary key in the first table. Notice that the ZipPK values are unique and not null, but the ClrFK values may be null and often repeat. A null foreign key means that that row does not participate in the relationship. In a one-to-many relationship, the primary key has the "one" value, and the foreign key has the "many" values.

Normalization

As discussed earlier in the chapter, normalization is the process of organizing data in an effort to avoid duplication. Often this process involves separating data into discrete related tables. Advantages to normalization usually include space, performance, and easier maintenance.

Typically, normalization involves the process of identifying all the data objects that should be in your database, all their relationships, and defining the tables required and the columns within each table. Consider how the Web store database would look if we did not normalize the data into separate tables:

Customer	Order	Price
Zak	Shirt	$12
Patty	Shirt	$12
Zak	Pants	$35
Makenzie	Shoes	$75
Jessica	Blouse	$20
Judy	Shoes	$75
Jessica	Blouse	$20

If the preceding table was used specifically to keep track of the price of items and you wanted to delete a price, you would end up deleting a customer, as well. Instead, you could separate the customers into their own table and the products along with their price into a second table. If a specific customer orders a product, the product and its price are placed into a third table (orders) along with the corresponding customer data.

There are roughly five normal forms that define how data is laid out within a database.

The First Normal Form

The first normal form basically states that all rows in a table must contain different data. No duplicate rows are permitted. It also states that all entries within a specific column must be of the same type—for instance, a column named Customer must contain only names of customers.

The Second Normal Form

The second normal form states that no field can be inherited from another field. For example, if you store the full name of a customer in the customers table, you could not create a second field to store only the last name of a customer, because the data would be redundant.

The Third Normal Form

The third normal form states that duplicate information is not allowed in the database. This is the model that you achieved in the foreign key example. Instead of storing the credit cards of a customer within the customers table, you separate it out into a second table, allowing for multiple credit cards to be entered.

Domain/Key Normal Form

A domain/key normal form states that a key uniquely identifies each row in a table. By enforcing key restrictions, the database will be freed of modification irregularities. Domain/key normal form is the normalization form that most database developers try to achieve.

Designing the Web Store Database

Now that you have become familiar with the inner workings of a database and how to actually create tables, columns, and rows, lets actually walk through the creation of the Web store database using Microsoft Access.

> **NOTE**
>
> Access is the database that was chosen for the Web store because it is easy to acquire and its interface is relatively easy to learn.

Before you begin designing any database, take a few points into consideration:

- What kind of data do I want to store?

- Who will be accessing my data?

- What kinds of people will be able to change items in the database?

- What changes or additions will I need to make in the future?

The kind of data that you will be storing in the database is the most important question that you can ask yourself. Will you be storing textual information with like names, address, products, and prices, or will you be storing large binary objects such as sound files and images directly in the database. Answering this question can help you pick the appropriate database that will suit your needs. In this case, because you are simply storing names, addresses, products, and prices, you can get by just fine with Access. If you need to include images in your work, you can simply create a reference to the location on the server where the image is located.

26

How you plan to access the data in the database is also an important consideration. Will you have people selecting and viewing records and possibly updating and deleting records, or will you be building a large database full of financial records? If the first is correct, Access will suit your needs.

> **CAUTION**
>
> Bear in mind, however, if you were creating a real database for a Web store, you might think twice about choosing Access to store credit card information. Although Access will suit your needs, it may not offer the same level of security that its big brother server replacement, SQL Server would.

After all these questions have been answered, it is safe to assume that you are ready to begin architecting your database. Begin by opening a new instance of Access and creating a new database. Assuming you are using Microsoft Access 2000 or later, follow these steps:

1. From the File menu, select New.

2. When the docked menu on the right appears, select New Database.

3. You will be prompted to give your database a name and location to save it. For now, save it in the root of C:\Inetpub\wwwroot. This will eventually be where you create the Web store application. Click Create. Figure 26.10 shows the screen that you will see along with the proper file saving location.

4. Figure 26.11 shows the empty database window with the Tables page selected.

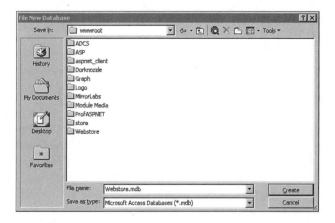

FIGURE 26.10   Save your database to the root of C:\Inetpub\wwwroot.

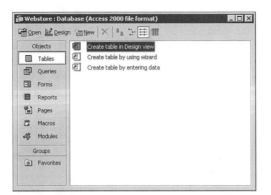

FIGURE 26.11 An empty database appears, allowing you direct access to begin creating tables.

You are now ready to begin creating all the tables that will be used in the Web store. We have already outlined the main tables that we will use; they are as follows:

- Customers

- CreditCards

- Inventory

- Orders

- Products

- Transactions

The Customers Table

The customers table will be reserved for all the "clients" accessing and purchasing items from our Web store. The customers table will include such data as name, addresses, email addresses, usernames and passwords, and possibly, phone numbers.

You can begin creating the customers table by selecting Create Table in design view. Figure 26.12 shows the design view that you will be seeing after it has been selected.

Notice that when the design view is open, you can begin entering all the columns (Fields) that will be used within your table. You are also able to input a data type that corresponds with the "type" of information those fields will contain. Data types are also useful for conserving space and for performing calculations and mathematical computations that you could not ordinarily do if a field was of a different type other than number. All the data types are listed next:

- **Text**   Text data type is the most commonly used data type and can contain up to 255 characters and/or numbers.

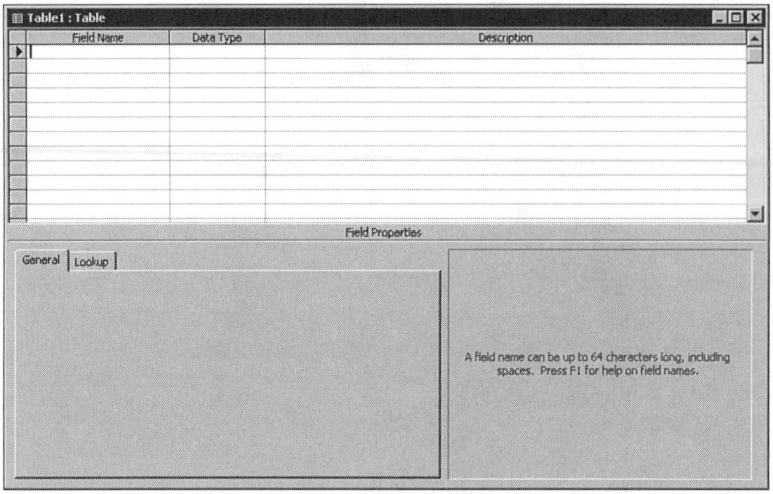

FIGURE 26.12   The design view allows you to begin creating columns for your table.

- **Memo**   Similar to the text data type, the memo data type supports up to 65,535 characters.

- **Number**   Use the number data type when you expect to perform calculations—for example, if you need to calculate the total of six items that a user may have selected within the products table.

- **Currency**   Similar to the number data type, currency should be used when money is involved. You should use the currency data type when defining your cost column within the products table.

- **AutoNumber**   AutoNumber is generally reserved for columns whose value you want to increment. Generally, autonumber is reserved for the field that contains the primary key. This ensures that all data within that column are unique.

- **Date/Time**   The date/time data type is most useful when you want to sort items in your fields chronologically.

- **Yes/No**   The yes/no data type is useful when either something is selected or it is not. It returns either a true or a false value and generally simulates a checkmark effect.

- **OLE Object**   When you plan on embedding or linking objects from another source, you can use the OLE object data type.

- **Hyperlink**   When you want the field to jump to a Web address, use the hyperlink data type.

- **Lookup Wizard**   The Lookup Wizard creates a field that is generally limited to a list of prespecified values.

NOTE

If you are working with SQL Server, you have many more options to choose from and some of the same ones available in Access, but you will notice that some of the data types that you would think have the same name are actually referenced differently.

You can begin adding your columns to the table by writing the values into the fields and then assigning them a valid data type. The customers table should be created with the following information:

Field Name	Data Type
CustomerID	AutoNumber
FirstName	Text
LastName	Text
Username	Text
Password	Text
Email	Text
PhoneNumber	Number
BillingAddress	Text
BillingCity	Text
BillingState	Text
BillingZip	Text
ShippingAddress	Text
ShippingCity	Text
ShippingState	Text
ShippingZip	Text

Figure 26.13 shows what the completed table should resemble.

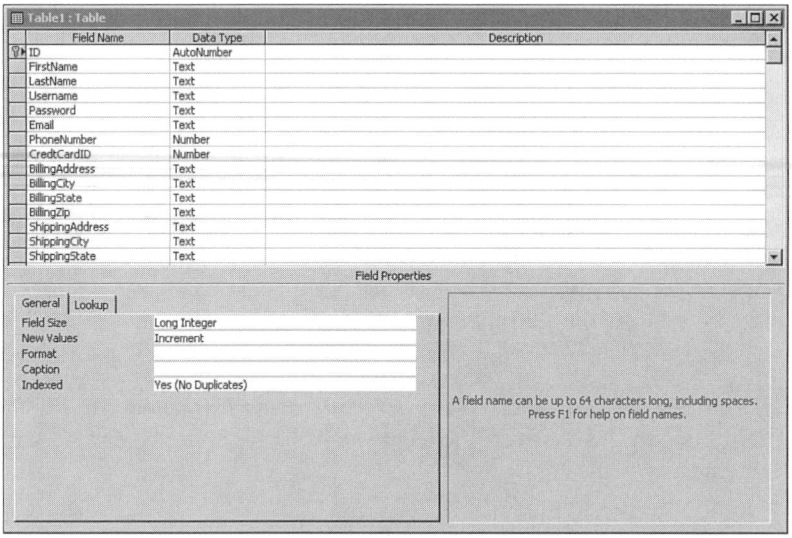

FIGURE 26.13   Create the customers table with the appropriate information and corresponding data type.

With the customers table now created, you are ready to save the file. From the File menu, select Save. In the dialog box, type **Customers** and click OK. Figure 26.14 shows the Save As dialog box.

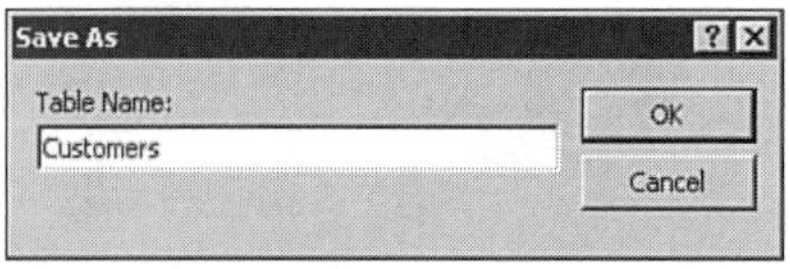

FIGURE 26.14   Type **Customers** and click OK.

Now that you have created all the columns, you're presented with the datasheet view. Use the datasheet view to fill up the table with as many rows of information as you like. Figure 26.15 displays the datasheet view.

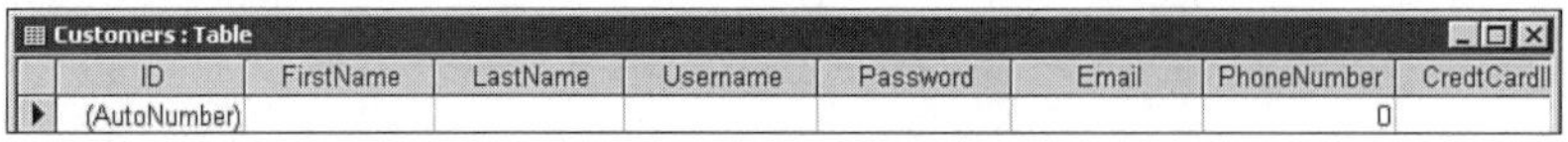

FIGURE 26.15   Use the datasheet view to fill up the table with rows of data.

You are now ready to create the next table.

The CreditCards Table

The creditcards table will be used initially to store a valid credit card number for a particular customer. You will be able to determine which credit card belongs to which customer through a relationship. The creditcards table contains the following information:

Field Name	Data Type
CustomerID	AutoNumber
CreditCardType	Text
CreditCardExpiration	Text

The Inventory Table

The inventory table will be used to maintain quantities for specific products. The inventory table contains the following information:

Field Name	Data Type
InventoryID	AutoNumber
ProductID	Number
Quantity	Number

The Orders Table

The orders table will be used as a temporary repository to keep items that a customer is planning on purchasing. After the order is completed, you can retrieve all that information and move it into the transactions table, completing the order. The orders table contains the following information:

Field Name	Data Type
CustomerID	Number
OrderNumber	Number
ProductID	Number
Quantity	Number

The Products Table

The products table will be used to store all the products that we will be selling in the Web store. The products table contains the following information:

Field Name	Data Type
ProductID	AutoNumber
ProductName	Text
ProductDescription	Memo

The Transactions Table

The transactions table is used to keep a log or history of all transactions that have been processed in the Web store. Generally it is good practice to keep a running record of all transactions in case you want to determine what items certain customers are buying, how many, and the amount that certain customers are spending at the Web store. The transactions table contains the following information:

Field Name	Data Type
TransactionID	AutoNumber
ProductID	Number
CustomerID	Number
DatePurchased	Date/Time

When you are completely finished creating your tables, your database view should look similar in design to Figure 26.16.

FIGURE 26.16   A display of all of the tables within the Web store database.

Creating Relationships Between the Tables

Now that you've created all the tables and columns within the database, you are ready to begin creating the relationships. Remember, relationships are what make the database efficient and keep you from duplicating data within individual tables. To begin establishing relationships between tables, follow these steps:

1. From the Tools menu, select Relationships.

2. When you are prompted with the Show Table dialog box, add every table by selecting the first table, holding down the Shift key, and then selecting the last table. Click Add.

3. Choose Close.

You are now ready to establish relationships between the tables. First, establish a relationship for the customers and orders tables. Notice that the customers table contains a CustomerID Primary Key and the orders table contains a CustomerID Foreign Key. The reason is that one customer can have many orders, so a one-to-many relationship must be created. The only way that can be accomplished is through the use of a foreign key. Access does not allow direct insertion of foreign keys; they are given when establishing a relationship between a primary key in one table and a field with the same data type and value in another table.

To create the relationship, simply drag the CustomerID field from the customers table into the CustomerID field in the orders table. You will be presented with the Edit Relationships dialog box, as shown in Figure 26.17.

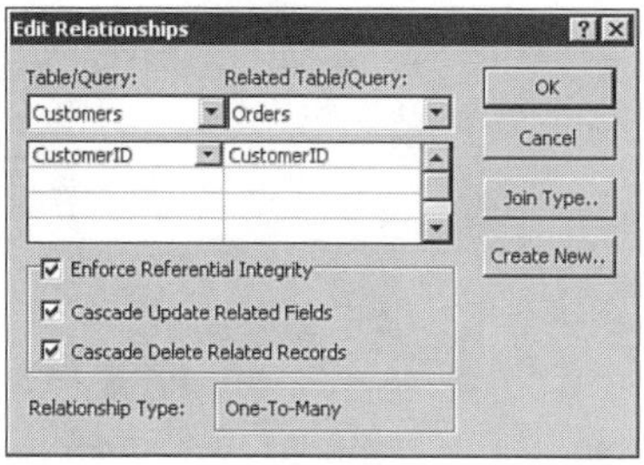

FIGURE 26.17 The Relationships Editor allows quick modification for relationships between tables.

Notice that the two fields are displayed directly underneath their corresponding tables.

Because this is a one-to-many relationship, you need to select Enforce Referential Integrity along with Cascade Update Related Fields and Cascade Delete Related Fields. This is done for referential integrity. If a customer is deleted from the Web store database, you would want all their orders deleted as well; otherwise, the database would be cluttered with redundant and, at times, unnecessary data. Notice the Relationship Type states that the relationship is indeed a one-to-many relationship. Select OK. The table that follows describes the relationships between tables:

Tables	Keys	Referential Integrity
Customers/Orders	CustomerID	Yes
Customers/CreditCards	CustomerID	Yes
Customers/Transactions	CustomerID	No
Orders/Transactions	ProductID	No
Orders/Products	ProductID	No
Products/Inventory	ProductID	Yes

When all the relationships have been established, the diagram should look similar to Figure 26.18.

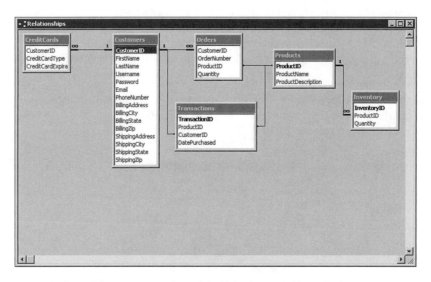

FIGURE 26.18   The Relationships window should look much like a diagram with connected lines showing relationships between tables.

A few points to consider after you have finished creating all of the relationships are the following:

- Remember that orders and credit cards will have a many relationship to the one customer. This is so because one customer can have many orders as well as credit cards on file. Also, referential integrity is enforced because if you delete a customer from the Web store database, you also want that customer's orders and credit cards on file to be deleted as well.

- A one-to-one relationship exists from customers to transactions. This is the case because the transactions table serves as a simple history of all transactions. Nothing should ever be deleted from this table.

- The products table has a one-to-one relationship with the transactions table as well as the orders table because both the orders and the transactions tables share information that the product table contains.

- A one-to-one relationship exists between the products table and the inventory table because a product can only have one quantity associated with it. You enforce referential integrity because if you delete a product, you also want the quantity from the inventory table deleted.

> **NOTE**
>
> Keep in mind that one-to-many relationships have icons at the end points of the relationship lines. A small "1" will appear next to the table with the one relationship and a small infinity symbol will appear, symbolizing the table with the many relationship.

Summary

This chapter has introduced you to some simple, yet important, concepts—mainly data storage. You learned about the skeleton of a database, which is composed of tables, columns, and rows, and about crucial concepts that can aid in performance, maintenance, and efficiency. The next chapter, "SQL Primer," goes beyond data storage and introduces you to the language used in data access—SQL.

26

CHAPTER **27**

SQL Primer

by Zak Ruvalcaba

The Structured Query Language

Up to this point you have become very familiar with just how easy it is to create a data store and establish a connection to it using Dreamweaver MX. As you progress through the coming chapters, you will see how easy it is to use Dreamweaver MX to extract information from that data store.

> **NOTE**
>
> A data store is a generic term given to information that is housed within any number of files, including Excel spreadsheets, databases, and even simple text files like XML.

Although Dreamweaver MX provides a simple process for the extraction of data from your database, you may quickly find your application growing far beyond the scope of simple data extraction. The kind of application you eventually build will have a direct impact on how complex your use of a data-access language will be. Dreamweaver MX provides a simple and easy-to-use process for commonly used data extraction and filtering tasks, but if you truly want to get the most out of your application, you should become familiar with the topics discussed within this chapter.

This chapter focuses on the language of today's database. Structured Query Language (SQL, pronounced "sequel") was established in the 1970s as a way of interacting with current database technologies and the tables that made them up. With roughly 30 keywords, SQL quickly became the language standard for simple and complex database operations. The keywords that you construct, also known as *statements,* range from a simple few to a complex string of subqueries and joins. Although this chapter cannot begin to cover all there is to know on the subject, it can provide you with an introduction to beginning and advanced SQL statements, clauses, joins, subqueries, and action queries.

Basic SQL

Just as your savings account would be useless without a valid ID or bank card to get to that money, information contained within a database is useless data unless you have the means of extracting it. SQL is the language that does just that; it allows for quick and complex access to the data contained within your database through the use of queries. Queries pose the questions and return the results to your application, usually in the form of a recordset.

> **CAUTION**
>
> Don't think of SQL as simply a way of extracting information. The SQL language can become complex, allowing not only queries from a database, but adding, modifying, and deleting infor-mation from a database as well.

Consider trying to extract information from the product table of the Web store example. If you set up the table correctly, it should resemble the table that follows:

Field Name	Date Type
ProductID	AutoNumber
ProductName	Text
ProductDescription	Memo

You could also list products within rows that could look like the following:

ProductID	ProductName	ProductDescription
1	Black Hawk Down	DVD
2	Black Hawk Down	VHS
3	Black Hawk Down	CD Soundtrack
4	The Natural	DVD
5	Pulp Fiction	DVD
6	Armageddon	DVD
7	Armageddon	VHS
8	Heat	DVD

Consider some important aspects about the following table, columns, and data contained within the eight rows. The products table contains three columns, a ProductID with an AutoNumber that increments a value whenever an item is added, a ProductName that contains a Text data type allowing for a simple title of the product, and a column for ProductDescription with a Memo data type. The last data type could be either Text or Memo. The reason for the Memo data type is simply as a precautionary measure in case the person who is doing the data entry for the product table wants to add a full paragraph description of the product being added. The last thing to consider is the data contained within the table. We are simply storing a list of DVDs, VHS tapes, and CD soundtracks that are to be sold within the Web store application.

The Select Statement

The foundation to all SQL queries is the Select statement. Made up of two keywords, the Select statement provides a means for retrieving the data from the database. In its simplest form, the Select statement is written using the following:

- **Select**   The Select keyword is used to identify the statement or action you are attempting to perform on the database. Other keywords include Insert, Delete, and Update.

- *** or Field Names**   The asterisk or names of the fields tell the statement which columns you want to extract data from.

- **From**   The From keyword identifies which table to extract the data from. The From keyword is required with all Select statements.

- **Table Name(s)**   The table name or names from which you want to extract the data.

The following example would extract all records from your products table:

```
Select * From Products
```

The preceding statement uses two keywords, the Select keyword and the From keyword to extract all records from the products table. Note the use of the "*" after the Select keyword. Rather than typing out every column name within our table in the statement, the "*" could be included instead. The following line would produce similar results:

```
Select ProductID, ProductName, ProductDescription From Products
```

The following table would produce the results of your statement:

ProductID	ProductName	ProductDescription
1	Black Hawk Down	DVD
2	Black Hawk Down	VHS
3	Black Hawk Down	CD Soundtrack

27

ProductID	ProductName	ProductDescription
4	The Natural	DVD
5	Pulp Fiction	DVD
6	Armageddon	DVD
7	Armageddon	VHS
8	Heat	DVD

Selecting Certain Fields

If you did not want to select all the fields within the database table, you could modify the field names to include only the fields that you wanted.

```
Select ProductID, ProductName From Products
```

Notice that the preceding statement would retrieve the data only from the ProductID and the ProductName fields. The results would produce the following:

ProductID	ProductName
1	Black Hawk Down
2	Black Hawk Down
3	Black Hawk Down
4	The Natural
5	Pulp Fiction
6	Armageddon
7	Armageddon
8	Heat

You could also modify the statement in an effort to retrieve the same information in a different order. For example, switching the field names by placing ProductName in front of ProductID would give the following result:

ProductName	ProductID
Black Hawk Down	1
Black Hawk Down	2
Black Hawk Down	3
The Natural	4
Pulp Fiction	5
Armageddon	6
Armageddon	7
Heat	8

Selecting Unique Data

The information within the productstable contains duplicate values. Although we know that *Black Hawk Down* has three formats, it does not change the fact that it is listed within ProductName three times. If someone wanted to know just the titles of the movies that were in the database, it would retrieve two values twice and in the case of the title *Black Hawk Down*, it would produce three results. The Distinct keyword could be used before the field name to extract only unique instances of data contained within the table column.

```
Select Distinct ProductName From Products
```

The preceding statement would produce the following result:

ProductName
Black Hawk Down
The Natural
Pulp Fiction
Armageddon
Heat

The Insert Statement

Collecting information from your users is not uncommon and in most cases, it is a necessity. With the Web store, although you would never want a user to add information to the products table, you would want them to register on your site so that they could begin shopping. When registering, you would want your users to create new accounts which would, in turn, create new records in the customers table.

To illustrate this point, take the customers table and observe some of the fields that make it up:

Field Name	Date Type
CustomerID	AutoNumber
FirstName	Text
LastName	Text
Username	Text
Password	Text
Email	Text
PhoneNumber	Number
BillingAddress	Text
BillingCity	Text
BillingState	Text
BillingZip	Text

27

You could easily generate a new record using the following statement:

```
Insert Into Customers (FirstName, LastName, Username, Password, Email,
PhoneNumber, BillingAddress, BillingCity, BillingState, BillingZip)
Values ('Zak', 'Ruvalcaba', 'zruvalcaba', 'password', 'zak@modulemedia.com',
'5555555555', '555 Sample St.', 'San Diego', 'Ca', '92069')
```

The preceding statement would insert all the values that you specified into the proper columns within the customers table. The Insert keyword generally uses:

- **Insert**   The Insert keyword is used to identify the statement or action you are attempting to perform on the database. Other keywords included Select, Delete, and Update.

- **Into**   The Into keyword specifies that you are inserting something into a specific table.

- **Table Name**   The table name that you want to insert the values into.

- **Values**   The actual values that are to be inserted.

You could also use the Select statement within the Insert statement to literally copy information from one table to the other, which is very similar to what you will be doing with the transactions table.

```
Insert Into Transactions (FirstName, LastName, Email) Select FirstName, LastName,
➥Email
From Customers
```

The Update Statement

The Update statement is used to define changes within your database tables. Database information is not static; rather, it is constantly changing depending on user feedback or input. The Update statement requires certain keywords, operators, and usually a Where clause to modify the specific record, for instance:

```
Update Customers Set LastName = "Smith" Where CustomerID = '2'
```

This statement would effectively change the last name of the customer whose ID matches 2.

> **NOTE**
>
> Operators enable you to connect certain portions of your statement, whereas clauses allow for more refined queries and searches. Both are discussed later in the chapter.

The Delete Statement

The Delete statement can be used to remove unneeded records from the database. The Delete statement can be used to delete all records, specific records, or records that meet certain criteria.

```
Delete From Customers
```

The preceding statement would effectively remove all the customers from the customers table.

```
Delete From Customer Where CustomerID = '2'
```

This statement would remove only the record with the CustomerID of 2.

```
Delete From Customer Where LastName = 'Smith'
```

This statement would remove all records that contain the last name of Smith.

Expression

If you are the least bit familiar with programming languages, you know that expressions are anything that, when calculated, result in a value. For instance, $1 + 1 = 2$ is an example of an expression. Expressions in SQL work much the same way. Consider the following data from the customers table:

CustomerID	FirstName	LastName
1	Zak	Ruvalcaba
2	David	Levinson
3	Matthew	Pizzi
4	Jessica	Ruvalcaba

You could use a simple Select statement to display the information exactly as it appears in the preceding table, or you could write an expression that concatenates the FirstName and LastName fields. The query would look like this:

```
Select CustomerID, FirstName & LastName As Name From Customers
```

Notice the "&" operator. The "&" operator is used to concatenate or join together two fields into one virtual field using the As keyword. The results would display as follows:

CustomerID	Name
1	ZakRuvalcaba
2	DavidLevinson
3	MatthewPizzi
4	JessicaRuvalcaba

27

Notice that there is no space between the first and last names. To add a space, you need to add a literal string value:

```
Select CustomerID, FirstName & ' ' & LastName As Name From Customers
```

Adding the space results in spaces between the first and last names:

CustomerID	Name
1	Zak Ruvalcaba
2	David Levinson
3	Matthew Pizzi
4	Jessica Ruvalcaba

Operators

In the previous section, you were introduced to the use of the "&" operator. Operators are used in programming languages to aid in the evaluation of expressions. The following table lists operators that you should be familiar with:

*	The multiplication operator is used when multiplying fields or values.
/	The divide operator is used when dividing fields or values.
–	The minus operator is used when subtracting fields or values.
>	The greater-than operator is used in Where clauses to determine whether a first value is greater than the second, such as `Select * From Customers Where CustomerID > 10`. The result would return all the CustomerIDs after 10.
<	The less-than operator is used in Where clauses to determine whether a first value is less than the second, such as `Select * From Customers Where CustomerID < 10`. The result would return CustomerIDs 1–9.
>=	The greater than or equal to operator is used in Where clauses to determine whether a first value is greater than or equal to the second, such as `Select * From Customers Where CustomerID >= 10`. The result would return CustomerIDs 1–10.
<=	The less than or equal to operator is used in Where clauses to determine whether a first value is less than or equal to the second, such as `Select * From Customers Where CustomerID <= 10`. The result would return all the CustomerIDs starting from 10.
<>, !=	Used to check whether a value is not equal to a second.
AND	Used with the Where clause in the Select statement. The AND operator returns a second value, such as `Select * From Customers Where CustomerID = 1 AND CustomerID = 2`.

OR   Used with the Where clause in the Select statement. The OR operator can be used when a certain condition needs to be met or when you can settle for a second, such as `Select * From Customers Where CustomerID = 1 OR CustomerID > 2`.

LIKE   The LIKE operator is used with Where clauses when a wildcard needs to be performed, such as `Select * From Customers Where LastName LIKE 'Smi%'`, which would return all customers whose last names start with "Smi."

NOT   Typically used in conjunction with the LIKE operator, the NOT operator is used when a value is not going to be LIKE the value of a second, such as `Select * From Customers Where LastName NOT LIKE 'Smi%'`.

_   The underscore operator is used with Where clauses and is performed when you do not know the second value, such as `Select * From Customers Where BillingState LIKE 'A_'`, which would return all customers' states that begin with A, such as AK, AL, AR, AZ, and so on.

%   The multiple character operator is similar to the underscore operator except that it allows for multiple characters, whereas the underscore operator allows only for two.

Functions

Aside from using operators to manually construct expressions, SQL provides built-in functions that you can use.

> **TIP**
>
> Functions are small blocks of code that can perform operations and return a value.

Functions are available simply by making a call to them and passing the value and/or values that you want it to operate on.

Date and Time Functions

Date and Time functions allow for manipulations using dates and times that are stored within your database. The following code:

```
Select * From Transactions Where DatePurchased Like '6/30/2002'
```

Would produce the following results:

TransactionID	ProductID	CustomerID	DatePurchased
24	3	2	6/30/02

If you wanted to find all the transactions from the previous month, you could use the DateAdd function:

```
Select * From Transactions Where DatePurchased > DateAdd(m, -1, Date())
```

Assuming that the current date was 6/30/02, the results would be

TransactionID	ProductID	CustomerID	DatePurchased
24	3	2	6/15/02
15	26	2	6/3/02
3	17	15	6/2/02

You will also notice that the DateAdd function accepts parameters.

TIP

Parameters are values that you pass into the function so that it knows what to do or how to return the value.

These parameters include the following:

- How much time will be added to the date. Typically, you would want to use one of three values: m for month, w for week, and d for day.

- How much time to add or subtract—in this case, one month will be subtracted.

- The date that you want to use. In this case, we are calling another function—the system date. By using date(), you are effectively reading the date and time from the computer and passing it in as a value.

- There are many other Date and Time functions. Too many, in fact, to cover in this small section. Date and Time functions are among the widely used functions in SQL and are worth the research.

CAUTION

If you are using a database other the SQL Server or Access, the function names that you use may differ. For instance, the DateAdd function is a Microsoft database function. Check with your documentation to determine the functions that are available with your database.

The Count Function

One of the most obvious functions available is the Count function. The Count function is used when a count of records needs to be performed. Consider the following table of data from the orders table:

CustomerID	OrderNumber	ProductID	Quantity
24	33423325	2	4
15	26234556	2	2
3	17456326	15	7

Use the following to count the amount of orders that you have taken in a day from the orders table:

```
Select Count(Quantity) As NumberOfPayments From Orders
```

The statement would result in the following:

NumberOfPayments

3

Notice that you pass in the field name as a parameter in the Count function. The parameter is evaluated and a value is returned into a virtual field named NumberOfPayments.

The Sum Function

Unlike the Count function that returns a value from a calculation on the number of fields, the Sum function performs a calculation on data within those fields. If, for instance, you needed to know the total number of items you sold, you could modify the statement to read:

```
Select Sum(Quantity) As Total From Orders
```

The statement would produce the following results:

Total

13

Rather than simply doing a count on the records, the sum is calculated based on the values within them.

The Avg Function

The Avg function returns the average of values within specific fields. If you modified the statement to read:

```
Select Avg(Quantity) As Average From Orders
```

27

The following would result:

Total

4.333

The Min and Max Functions

The Min and Max functions enable you to find the smallest and largest values of a specific record. To get the minimum quantity ordered, you could write

```
Select Min(Quantity) As Minimum From Orders
```

which would produce

Minimum

2

To receive the maximum value of a record in the database, try

```
Select Max(Quantity) As Maximum From Orders
```

which would produce

Maximum

7

Arithmetic Functions

Aside from using Sum, Min, Max, and Avg, a few other arithmetic functions can help you when calculating fields within your database. They are as follows:

ABS   Returns the absolute value.

CEIL   Returns the smallest integer value not greater than the value.

FLOOR   Returns the largest integer value not greater than the value.

COS   Returns the cosine of the value where the value is the radians.

COSH   Returns the hyperbolic cosine of the value where the value is the radians.

SIN   Returns the sine of the value where the value is the radians.

SINH   Returns the hyperbolic sine of the value where the value is the radians.

TAN   Returns the tangent of the value where the value is the radians.

TANH   Returns the hyperbolic tangent of the value where the value is the radians.

EXP   Returns the mathematical constant e by the provided value.

MOD   Returns the remainder of a value divided by a second.

SIGN   Returns the sign of the argument as –1, 0, or 1, depending on whether the value is negative, zero, or positive.

SQRT   Returns the non-negative square root of a value.

POWER   Returns the result of a value raised to the power of a second value.

LN   Returns the natural logarithm of a value.

LOG   Returns the logarithm of a value in the base of a second value.

String Functions

String functions are similar to other functions, except they work with literal text values rather than numerical values.

CHR   Converts an ASCII value to its string equivalent.

CONCAT   Concatenates (merges) two string into one.

INITCAP   Returns the first letter of each word capitalized.

UPPER   Returns the value in all uppercase.

LOWER   Returns the value in all lowercase.

LPAD   Returns a value padded on the left based on the numerical value you specify.

RPAD   Returns a value padded on the right based on the numerical value you specify.

LTRIM   Returns a value with the leftmost characters that match the number of characters that you specify omitted.

RTRIM   Returns a value with the rightmost characters that match the number of characters that you specify omitted.

REPLACE   Use the Replace function to change a portion of the string with a value that you specify. Replace takes three values (string, target, replacement string).

SUBSTR   Returns the substring of a value that begins at pos and is ten characters long. Substr takes three values (string, position, length).

LENGTH   Returns length of string in characters.

27

Clauses

Clauses are portions of SQL that allow for further refinement of the query or additional work that needs to be accomplished by the SQL statement. Clause covered in this section are

- The Where clause
- The Order By clause
- The Group By clause
- The Having clause

The Where Clause

The Where clause is used in conjunction with the Select statement to deliver a more refined search based on individual field criteria. This example could be used to extract a specific customer based on a last name:

```
Select * From Customers Where LastName = 'Smith'
```

Notice that the select is made only when a certain criteria is true. If a record with the LastName of "Smith" did not exist, it wouldn't return anything. You could refine your search even further by using the "And" operator:

```
Select * From Customers Where LastName = "Smith" And FirstName = "John"
```

The Order By Clause

The Order By Clause provides you with a quick way of sorting the results of your query in either ascending or descending order. Consider the following table of information:

CustomerID	FirstName	LastName	Email
1	Zak	Ruvalcaba	zak@modulemedia.com
2	Matthew	Pizzi	matt@sample.com
3	David	Levinson	david@sample2.com

If you selected all the records by using a simple Select All statement (Select *), it would return the results based on the CustomerID. Using the Select statement with an Order By clause would allow you to sort based on a different field name:

```
Select * From Customers Order By LastName
```

The preceding statement would return results in the following order:

CustomerID	FirstName	LastName	Email
3	David	Levinson	david@sample2.com
2	Matthew	Pizzi	matt@sample.com
1	Zak	Ruvalcaba	zak@modulemedia.com

You could also add the ASC or DESC designation to the end of the statement if you wanted a different criteria.

> **TIP**
>
> The ASC designation is the default order. If you exclude this from the end of your statement, it will assume that you want the results to appear in ascending order.

You could also order by multiple columns by adding a comma after the field name and entering a second field name:

```
Select * From Customers Order By LastName, FirstName
```

The Group By Clause

When a query statement includes a Group By clause, the Select statement for that query can list functions while operating on groups of data values in other columns. For example, data within the orders table could look similar to the following table:

CustomerID	OrderNumber	ProductID	Quantity
1	234234	2	2
1	044594	4	4
4	323244	35	4
7	352644	22	2
7	768894	4	2
7	562645	35	1

If you wanted to retrieve the amount of orders that were received for a particular day, you could run the following query:

```
Select Count(Quantity) As QuantityOfItems From Orders
```

The result would return:

QuantityOfItems

6

You could use the Group By clause in this instance to group the orders by CustomerID. Running the following statement:

```
Select CustomerID, Count(Quantity) As QuantityOfItems From Orders
Group By CustomerID
```

The result would be

CustomerID	QuantityOfItems
1	2
4	1
7	3

The result is based on the fact that customer 1 made two orders, customer 4 made 1 order, and customer 7 made 3 orders.

The Having Clause

The Having clause works similar to the Where clause except that you use the Having clause immediately after the Group By clause. Like the Where clause, the Having clause filters results based on criteria that you specify.

```
Select CustomerID, Count(Quantity) As QuantityOfItems From Orders
Group By CustomerID Having CustomerID Like '1'
```

The result is similar to the table in the Group By clause except that it returns the one result that we specified.

CustomerID	QuantityOfItems
1	2

Joins

Up to this point you have focused primarily on extracting data from a single table. Depending on how advanced your database becomes, at times you might want to extract data from multiple tables at once. If that is the case, you will need to use joins. Although there are several types of joins, two types will be covered here:

- Inner Joins
- Outer Joins

Inner Joins

Of the different types of joins, inner joins are by far the most popular. Inner joins allow you to see all the records of two tables that have a relation established for one another. Remember, the customers table and the creditcards table had a relationship established. The two tables are similar to the following:

CustomerID	FirstName	LastName
2	Zak	Ruvalcaba
4	Matthew	Pizzi

CustomerID	CreditCardType	CreditCardExpiration
2	Visa	5555555555555555
4	MasterCard	3333444455553333

Assume that you wanted to extract the information from the customers table for CustomerID 2. Before inner joins, you would have to perform two Select statements:

```
Select * From Customers Where CustomerID = 2
```

And

```
Select * From CreditCards Where CustomerID = 2
```

You can begin to see how tedious this could get, not to mention that it is completely inefficient. To solve this problem, an inner joins could be performed:

```
Select Customers.CustomerID, Customers.FirstName, Customers.LastName,
CreditCards.CustomerID, CreditCards.CreditCardType, CreditCards.CreditCardExpiration
From Customers Inner Join CreditCards On Customers.CustomerID = CreditCards.Cus-
tomerID
```

The joins would effectively produce one virtual table with the following results:

CustomerID	FirstName	LastName	CreditCardType	CreditCardExpiration
2	Zak	Ruvalcaba	Visa	5555555555555555
4	Matthew	Pizzi	MasterCard	3333444455553333

You will notice that the preceding table now becomes more efficient and manageable. Notice that rather than referencing the names of the tables, you used TableName.Field notation. This is crucial when using joins; otherwise, you would end up with two CustomerIDs without a direct reference to its corresponding table.

Outer Joins

Outer joins enable rows to be returned from a join in which one of the tables does not contain matching rows for the other table. Suppose you have two tables that contain the following information:

27

CustomerID	FirstName	AddressID
2	Zak	45634
4	Matthew	34754
5	Jessica	
10	David	97895

AddressID	Address
45634	555 Sample St., San Diego
34754	343 Chestnut Rd., San Diego
97895	523 Main St., San Diego

If you were to use an inner join on the preceding tables, such as:

```
Select Customers.FirstName, Customers.AddressID, Address.AddressID,
Address.Address From Customers Inner Join Address On
Customers.AddressID = Address.AddressID
```

It would return the following results:

FirstName	AddressID	Address
Zak	45634	555 Sample St., San Diego
Matthew	34754	343 Chestnut Rd., San Diego
David	97895	523 Main St., San Diego

Notice that the record that did not contain an AddressID was excluded. If an outer join were performed, such as:

```
Select Customers.FirstName, Customers.AddressID, Address.AddressID,
Address.Address From Customers Outer Join Address On
Customers.AddressID = Address.AddressID
```

The results would be slightly different:

FirstName	AddressID	Address
Zak	45634	555 Sample St., San Diego
Matthew	34754	343 Chestnut Rd., San Diego
David	97895	523 Main St., San Diego
Jessica		

Subqueries

Sometimes it may not be possible to retrieve the results that you need from a simple Select statement. At times, you might need to create a Select statement and compare the results to that of another statement. In that case, you would want to use subqueries. A subquery is a query that is nested inside another query. There are two types of subqueries that you can use:

- The In Operator
- The Embedded Select Statement

The In Operator

The In operator is used in a Select statement primarily to specify a list of values to be used with a primary query. A classic example is if you wanted to find all your customers who lived in California. You could write a Select statement using the In operator to accomplish that:

```
Select * From Customers Where CustomerState In ("Ca")
```

This statement would effectively return all the customers who live in the state of California, assuming you had a field for state.

The Embedded Select Statement

An Embedded Select statement is used when you want to perform a query within the where clause of a primary query. Suppose you wanted to see a list of customers who have completed orders for the week.

```
Select * From Customers Where CustomerID In
(Select Distinct CustomerID From Orders)
```

Using Access to Generate Queries

Queries lay the foundation for data extraction from databases. You have seen how to create simple and complex queries by hand and you now have a firm grasp as to how they are constructed with clauses, operators, conditions, and expressions. Unfortunately, like most programming and authoring languages, perfection takes time and practice. Fortunately for you, there is an easier way.

Rather than manually writing all your statements, you could rely on Access to create them for you. If you've been experimenting with Access on your own, you'll notice the Queries tab on the left column. Queries can be constructed and saved for reuse in the future with the query designer. Figure 27.1 shows the query designer.

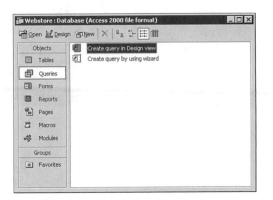

FIGURE 27.1   The query designer streamlines the way queries are created.

Generating Queries in Design View

The easiest and quickest way to generate queries is by creating them in design view. To create a simple select query, follow these steps:

1. Select the Query tab from the objects column.

2. Select Create Query in design view.

3. You can select the tables you want to include in your query from the Show Table dialog box, as shown in Figure 27.2. Select the customers table and click Add.

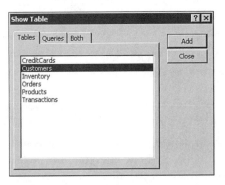

FIGURE 27.2   The Show Table dialog box enables you to select the tables you want to include in your query.

4. After your table is added to the designer, you are free to select the fields to include in the statement, the table those fields reside in, how to sort the records, and various criteria to include. Select Customer.* from the Fields drop-down list because this query will select all the records from the customers table. Figure 27.3 shows the drop-down list from the fields table.

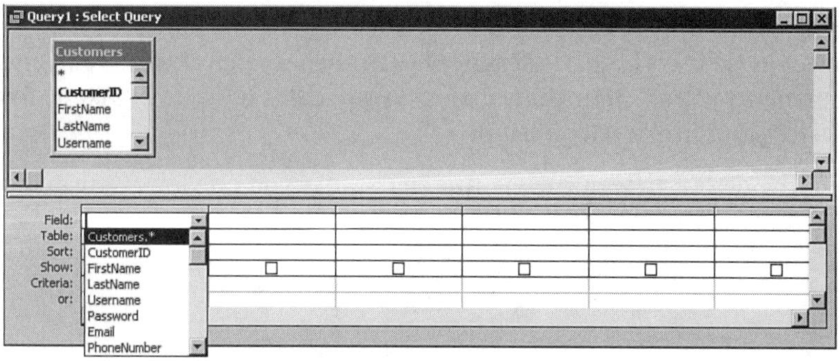

FIGURE 27.3   You can select which fields to include in your query.

> **NOTE**
>
> If you want to limit your query to two fields rather than the whole table, you can select one field from the fields drop-down list, move over to the right column, and select a different field.

5. After your query has been established, select SQL View from the View menu.

6. That's it! Figure 27.4 shows how you can copy and paste the SQL statement.

FIGURE 27.4   SQL View presents the SQL code that you can copy and paste into your application code.

7. Save your query with a name that is relevant to what it performs. Figure 27.5 shows the Save As dialog box.

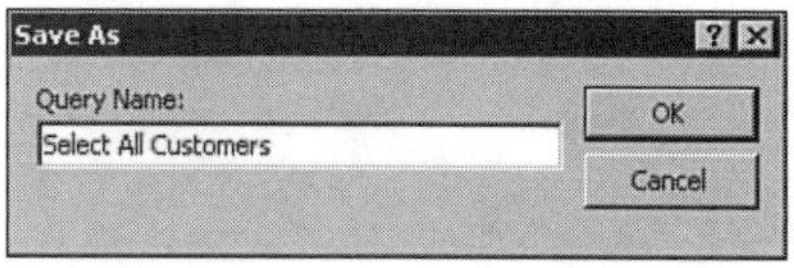

FIGURE 27.5   Save your query by selecting Save As from the File menu. Save your query with a name that is relevant to what the query does.

Generating Queries with Relationships

The true power in the Access query designer lies in the fact that it can even generate those complex statements with relationships that everyone hates to write by hand. To create another query that utilizes a relationship:

Right-click in the design view of the existing query that you previously created. Figure 27.6 shows the menu that will appear. Select Show Table.

FIGURE 27.6   You can continuously add tables by right-clicking in the designer.

Add the creditcards table. Notice the one-to-many relationship that is maintained between the two tables.

In the second column, select CreditCards.*. Figure 27.7 shows the view that you will be seeing.

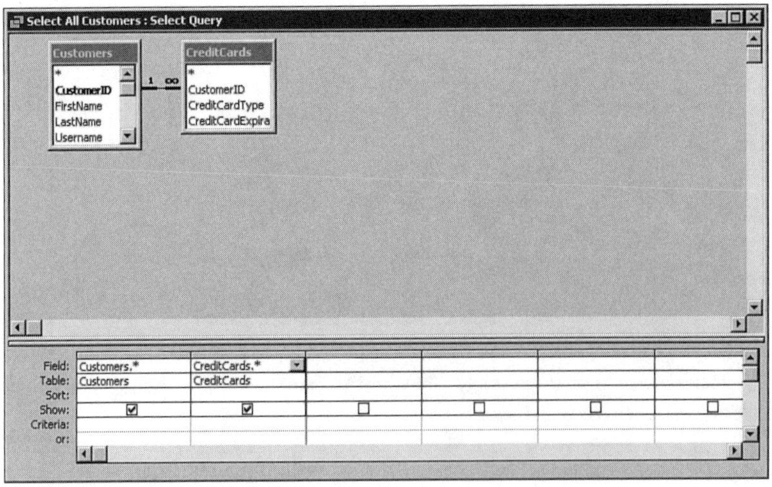

FIGURE 27.7   Select CreditCards.* to show all credit card fields.

Select SQL View from the View menu. Figure 27.8 shows the query that is generated.

FIGURE 27.8 The query designer streamlines the way queries are created.

Figure 27.9 shows the datasheet view available from the View menu. Notice the query includes all fields from both the customers table and the creditcards table.

BillingZip	ShippingAddres	ShippingCity	ShippingState	ShippingZip	CreditCards.C	CreditCardTy	CreditCardExpir

FIGURE 27.9 The query designer streamlines the way queries are created.

Summary

Data access is a crucial component to any application, and SQL provides the bridge and communication to that data. As you have seen, SQL not only returns simple results from individual tables, but it can produce complex data queries complete with filtering, sorting, expressions, and even nested statements. In the next chapter you'll begin putting the knowledge that you've learned about databases and the language that connects to those databases together into an application.

27

Working with Dynamic Data

by Zak Ruvalcaba

Building the Web Store Application Using ASP

Because you are reading this book, it is safe to assume that this is the chapter you have been waiting for. The power and capability to create dynamic Web applications utilizing any existing server model can amaze even the intermediate user. Rather than relying on traditional methods of displaying dynamic data, you will learn how to use Dreamweaver MX along with ASP to produce dynamic Web store functionality with relative ease and simplicity. Along with Dreamweaver MX's dynamic functionality, this section will cover the following areas of the Web Store application:

- Recordsets

- Paging

- Object Binding

- Region Repeaters

- Conditionals

If you have not done so already, you can download the support files for this chapter from www.dreamweavermxunleashed.com. The Web site contains all the support files for every chapter, including this one.

Creating the View Catalog Page

The View Catalog page of the Web store is the heart of the application. This is where users come to view the items that currently reside in the catalog and place any item that they choose in their shopping cart. Before you begin creating the application, take a look at the Web store database, which should reside within the Database folder of the project. Figure 28.1 shows the two tables that this chapter concerns itself with, the products and inventory tables.

FIGURE 28.1   The products and inventory tables are used in this chapter.

The products table contains the product information on what the Web store sells—DVDs. Figure 28.2 shows the titles and descriptions of the products the Web store sells.

ProductID	ProductName	ProductDescription
1	Abyss, The	DVD Widescreen
2	Air Force One	DVD Special Edition
3	Airplane	DVD Widescreen
4	Backdraft	DVD
5	Back To The Future	DVD Widescreen
6	Candyman	DVD
7	Cape Fear	DVD Special Edition
8	Dante's Peak	DVD
9	E.T.	DVD Widescreen
10	Fallen	DVD
11	Gattaca	DVD Widescreen
12	GI Jane	DVD
13	Major League	DVD
14	Mallrats	DVD Widescreen
15	Office Space	DVD
16	Raiders of the Lost Ark	DVD Special Edition
17	Saving Private Ryan	DVD Widescreen
18	Schindlers List	DVD
19	U-571	DVD Widescreen
20	Varsity Blues	DVD Widescreen
21	Young Guns	DVD Special Edition
(AutoNumber)		

Record: 22 of 22

FIGURE 28.2   The Web store sells DVD titles from current movie selections.

What the products table does not currently show are the images that will reside as thumbnails within the View Catalog page. This will be covered a bit later. Also, notice that Figure 28.3 shows the inventory table and the quantities for each item.

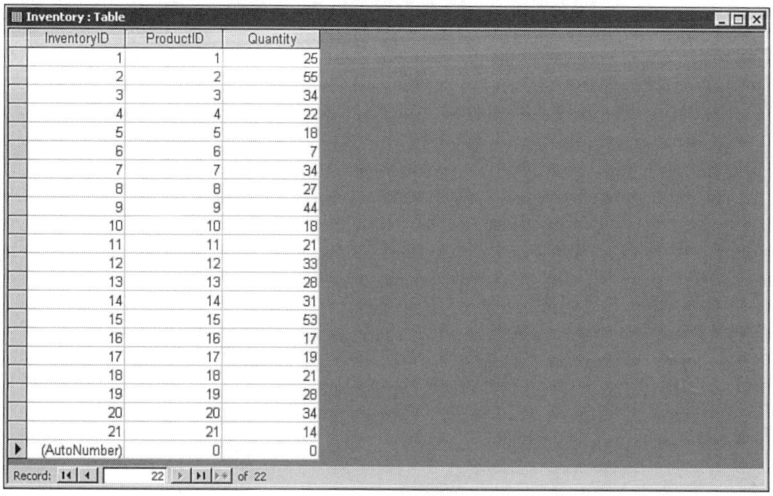

Inventory : Table

InventoryID	ProductID	Quantity
1	1	25
2	2	55
3	3	34
4	4	22
5	5	18
6	6	7
7	7	34
8	8	27
9	9	44
10	10	18
11	11	21
12	12	33
13	13	28
14	14	31
15	15	53
16	16	17
17	17	19
18	18	21
19	19	28
20	20	34
21	21	14
(AutoNumber)	0	0

Record: 22 of 22

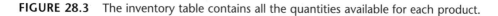

FIGURE 28.3 The inventory table contains all the quantities available for each product.

You may be asking yourself why there aren't any product names within the inventory table. Figure 28.4 shows the relationship between the products table and the inventory table. Remember, the relationship is created with the ProductID between the two tables; this is the reason for the ProductID within the inventory table rather than the simple ProductName.

NOTE

Technically the quantity field could reside within the products table. The reason for separating the products from the quantities is simplicity and scalability. If in the future you wanted to carry clothing, you could potentially have the same shirt in both blue and green. Because the shirt quantities would vary by color, a separate table to handle the quantities solves the dilemma.

Now that you've given the database a final overview, you are ready to begin extracting data from it. The next few sections cover

- Recordsets
- Dynamic Text
- Paging
- Conditionals

- Regions
- Commands

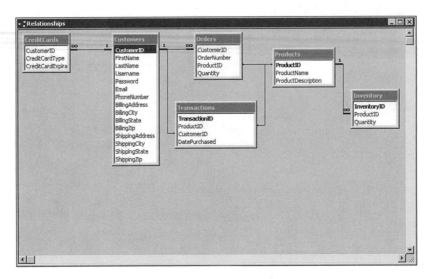

FIGURE 28.4   A relationship exists between the inventory table and products table based on the ProductID.

Creating a Recordset

By now you may be curious as to how the data within your database can be extracted into your application. Sure, you've learned a lot about SQL and are familiar with the commands to retrieve the information, but now what? SQL alone does not provide enough to be able to read from the database and write that data to the application; there's still a piece of the puzzle missing. That piece is the recordset. Recordsets act as an intermediary virtual table between the database and the application. You can write SQL commands to ask the questions of the database, also known as a query, but the information retrieved is stored within a recordset, allowing for programming logic to iterate through the recordset and ultimately present the data to the application in a structured way. Figure 28.5 illustrates this point.

Remember that the questions asked of the database are made in the form of queries, and queries are a process that usually involve SQL to structure how the question will be asked. In the case of the preceding example, the SQL commands could have a join to merge the two tables into one virtual table or recordset. The recordset is then browsed through by the application logic and presented to the user within a well-structured HTML document.

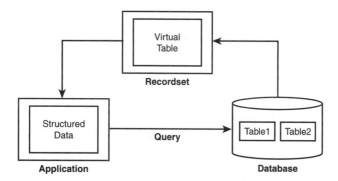

FIGURE 28.5 The application makes a call to the database which then returns data in the form of a recordset.

To demonstrate this point, you can create a simple recordset using Dreamweaver MX that will query the products table only. To create a recordset, follow the steps outlined next:

1. From the + icon in either the Bindings tab or the Server Behaviors tab, select Recordset (Query). Figure 28.6 shows the drop-down menu that you will see.

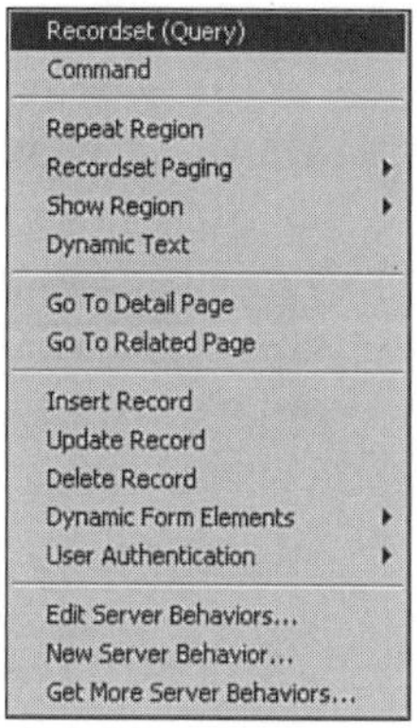

FIGURE 28.6 Select Recordset (Query) from either the Server Behaviors tab or the Bindings tab.

2. The Recordset dialog box appears. At this point, you can provide a name for the recordset.

3. Select the connection name from the dropdown list. If the name of your connection does not appear within the drop-down menu, it typically means that you did not define a connection. If that is the case, select Define to create the connection or refer back to Chapter 17, "Web Application Preparation," for more help on creating connections.

28

4. Pick the table within the database that you want to create a recordset for.

5. At this point, you can select All or Selected and choose only certain fields within the database that you want to include within the recordset.

6. You may also select optional Filters and Sorts. The results appear within Figure 28.7.

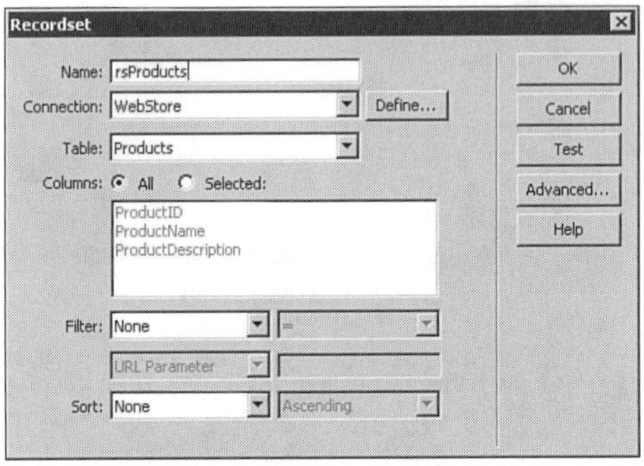

FIGURE 28.7   Fill out all the information within the recordset dialog box.

7. Select Test.

8. Figure 28.8 shows the returned recordset with all the data from the products table. Now that you know the recordset works, click OK.

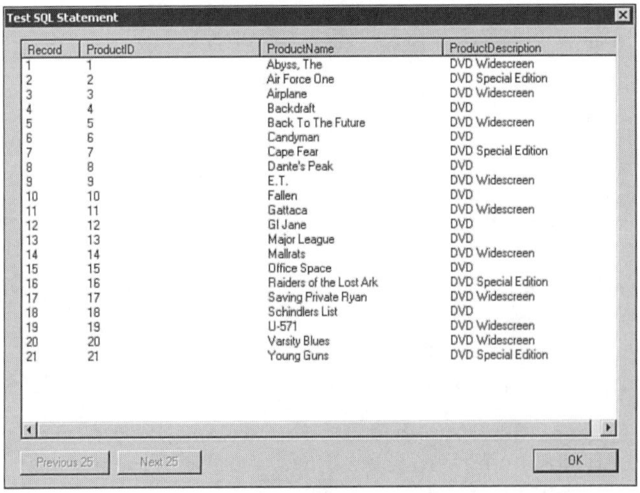

FIGURE 28.8   The test results show the recordset with populated data.

9. Select OK in the recordset dialog box. You will be returned to the authoring environ-ment, only this time you will have a new server behavior listed for the recordset. Figure 28.9 shows the Server Behavior panel with the new recordset behavior.

FIGURE 28.9   Creating a recordset displays the new behavior within the list.

Note that by selecting the Bindings tab and then expanding the recordset, you are able to view the field names contained within the recordset.

Creating an Advanced Recordset

Creating a simple recordset would serve your needs if you were merely performing a query of all or certain fields within the database. But what if you wanted to perform joins and merge two tables into one recordset? Unfortunately, the simple method would not do. Although creating advanced recordsets can become very complex, the trade-off is flexibil-ity, scalability, and power. Rather than creating multiple recordsets in which to store each and every table, you can join two or more tables into one recordset based on a common value. To create an advanced recordset for the products and inventory tables, follow these steps:

1. Now that you have a basic recordset already complete, why waste it? Double-click it within the Server Behaviors panel to open the Recordset dialog box again.

2. Click the Advanced button.

3. Figure 28.10 shows that the dialog box is relatively similar in design, except that you are able to enter SQL manually rather than allowing Dreamweaver MX to create it for you.

4. If you remember the lengthy code structure for creating SQL joins, begin typing. If you are like most people and like to rely on programs to do the work for you, open Access and create a new query in design view.

5. Add the products and inventory tables as shown in Figure 28.11.

6. Select Products.* from the products table and Inventory.* from the inventory table. Remember, the star signifies that all records will be extracted. Figure 28.12 shows the query designer.

28

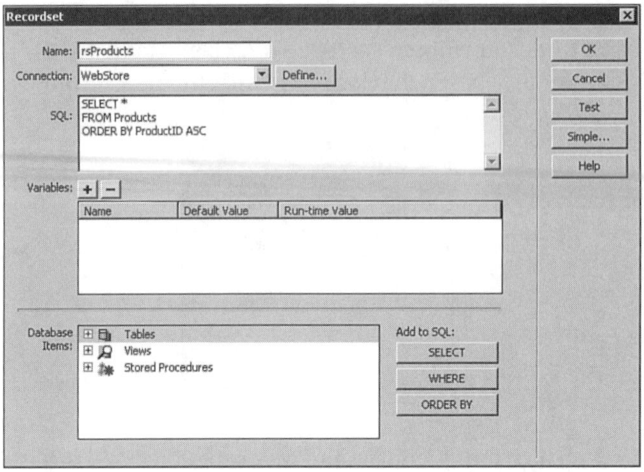

FIGURE 28.10   The Advanced Recordset tab enables you to manually type in the SQL code. This allows for greater flexibility.

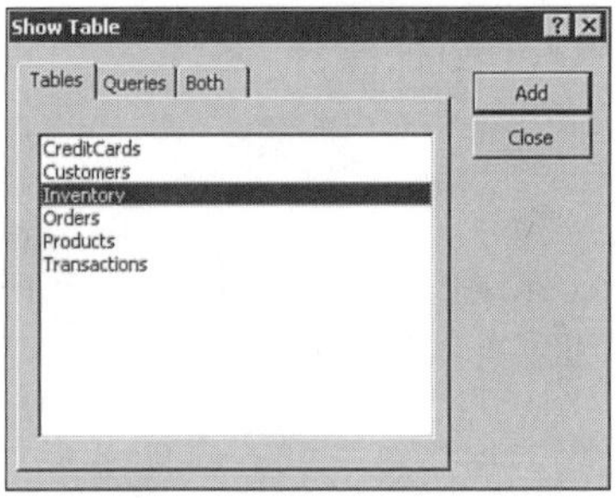

FIGURE 28.11   Add the products and inventory tables to the design view.

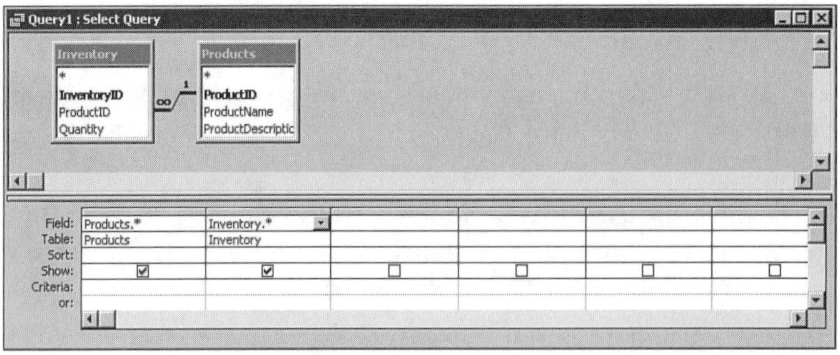

FIGURE 28.12   Select the fields from the tables that you want to include in your query.

7. To use the SQL code that was generated, select SQL View from the View menu. Figure 28.13 shows the SQL code that is generated.

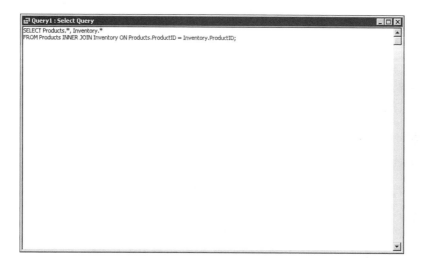

FIGURE 28.13   View the SQL code that is generated by selecting it from the View menu.

8. Copy the SQL code, save the query, and close Access.

9. You are now free to paste the code into the SQL box in the Advanced Recordset dialog box. Figure 28.14 shows the result.

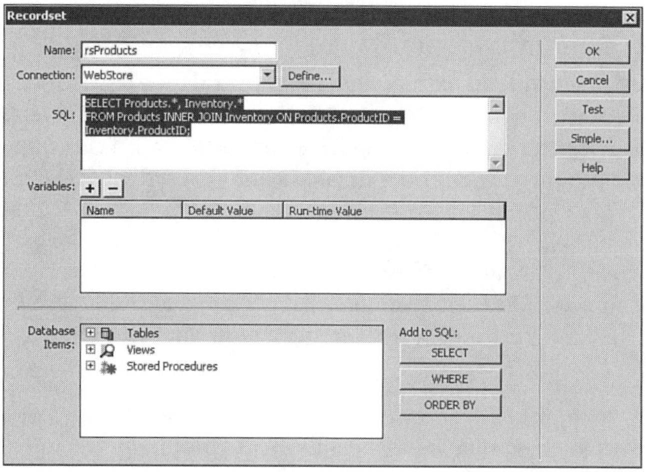

FIGURE 28.14   Paste the SQL code you created in Access into the SQL code box of the Advanced Recordset dialog box.

28

10. Figure 28.15 shows that when you select Test, you get all the results from both tables joined into one recordset view.

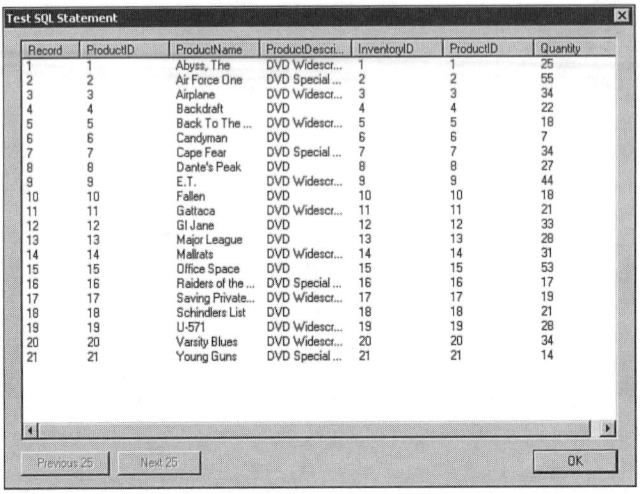

Record	ProductID	ProductName	ProductDescri...	InventoryID	ProductID	Quantity
1	1	Abyss, The	DVD Widescr...	1	1	25
2	2	Air Force One	DVD Special ...	2	2	55
3	3	Airplane	DVD Widescr...	3	3	34
4	4	Backdraft	DVD	4	4	22
5	5	Back To The ...	DVD Widescr...	5	5	18
6	6	Candyman	DVD	6	6	7
7	7	Cape Fear	DVD Special ...	7	7	34
8	8	Dante's Peak	DVD	8	8	27
9	9	E.T.	DVD Widescr...	9	9	44
10	10	Fallen	DVD	10	10	18
11	11	Gattaca	DVD Widescr...	11	11	21
12	12	GI Jane	DVD	12	12	33
13	13	Major League	DVD	13	13	28
14	14	Mallrats	DVD Widescr...	14	14	31
15	15	Office Space	DVD	15	15	53
16	16	Raiders of the ...	DVD Special ...	16	16	17
17	17	Saving Private...	DVD Widescr...	17	17	19
18	18	Schindlers List	DVD	18	18	21
19	19	U-571	DVD Widescr...	19	19	28
20	20	Varsity Blues	DVD Widescr...	20	20	34
21	21	Young Guns	DVD Special ...	21	21	14

FIGURE 28.15 Combine the contents of two tables into one recordset by using a join.

Whether you are creating simple or advanced recordsets within Dreamweaver MX, you can be assured that the process remains relatively simple. As you have seen, even complex joins can be achieved with ease. The next sections will introduce you to methods of extracting the data from the recordset into your application.

Working with Dynamic Elements

Now that you have been able to extract data from your data source, your next step is to structure it within your application somehow. Dreamweaver MX's Server Behavior and Binding panels provide the capabilities you need to get started producing dynamic elements that are centralized within the database but exposed via the application.

Dynamic Text

The first step to creating dynamic elements is making all your text as dynamic as possible. That is, allowing all your company's valuable information to reside within the database. To start creating dynamic text, begin by creating a table that will serve as the means of organizing the data output.

- Place a new table inside the viewcatalog.asp page by selecting Table from the Insert menu. This table should have only 1 row and 2 columns.
- Insert a nested table into the cell on the right with the specifications shown in Figure 28.16.

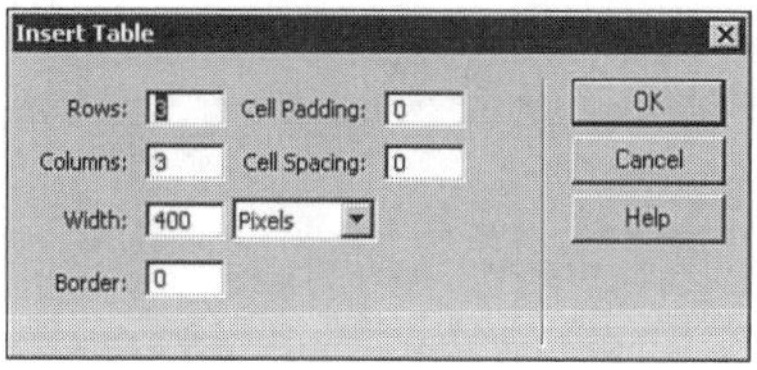

FIGURE 28.16   Insert a nested table.

- Merge the three cells on the right by clicking and selecting the Merge Cells command from the Table submenu, as shown in Figure 28.17.

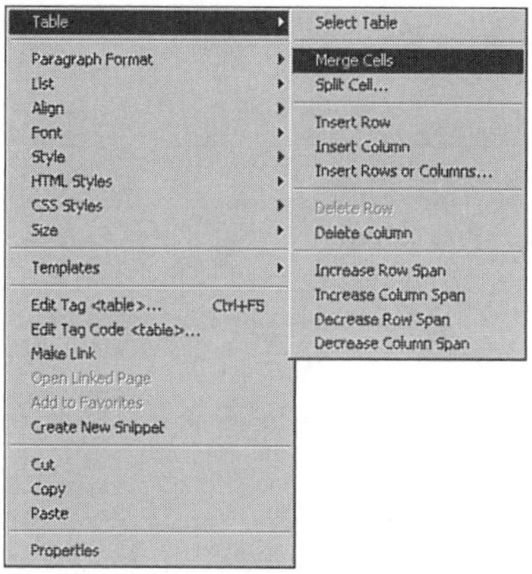

FIGURE 28.17   Merge the three cells on the right.

- Figure 28.18 shows the three data choices that you will place in the cells.

NOTE

I mentioned the addition of an image. Keep in mind that the image will be placed dynamically as well depending on which record you are currently on. This will be covered next.

NOTE

Notice that there is a text caption for cost. If you remember how the database was structured, there was no field for cost. This will be added in next and will demonstrate the use of the recordset refresh.

28

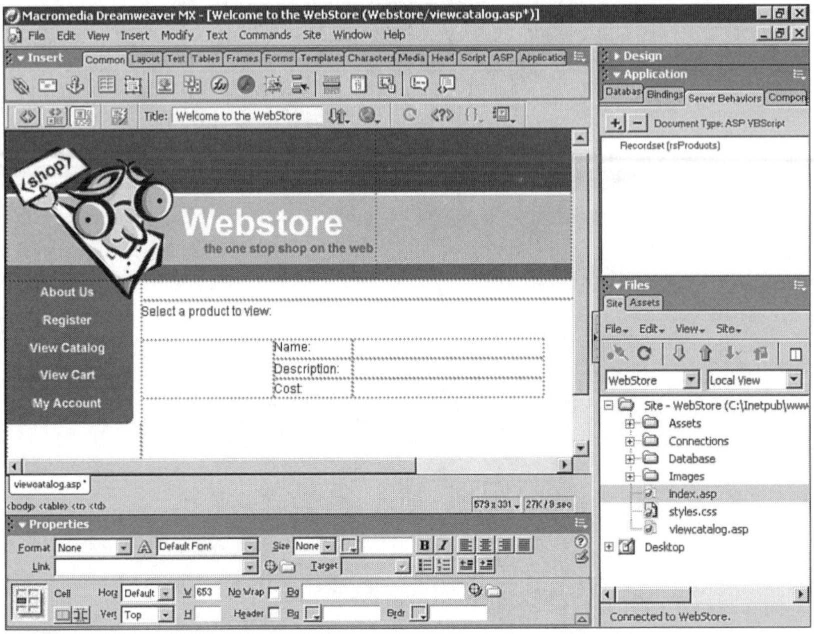

FIGURE 28.18   Place static text in the three fields to caption the dynamic text.

You've probably guessed by now that new fields have to be added into the database for cost of the products and for the image that relates to the DVD title. To do this, follow the steps outlined next:

1. Open the database file, which should reside in the Database folder of the application in Access.

2. Double-click to open the products table.

3. Switch to design view.

4. Add two new fields for ImagePath and ProductCost, as shown in Figure 28.19.

> **TIP**
>
> Access has no way of physically storing binary files. Instead, a path is inserted into the field, and later the application will use that path and dynamically change an `<img>` to coincide with the path in the database.

5. Go ahead and add the information for each field as shown in Figure 28.20. Notice that the image paths actually point to GIF images within the Thumbnails folder.

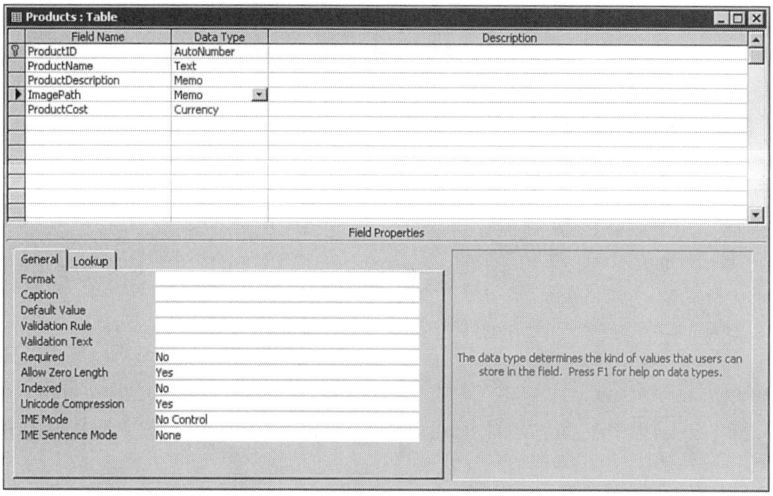

FIGURE 28.19 Add two new fields for ImagePath and ProductCost.

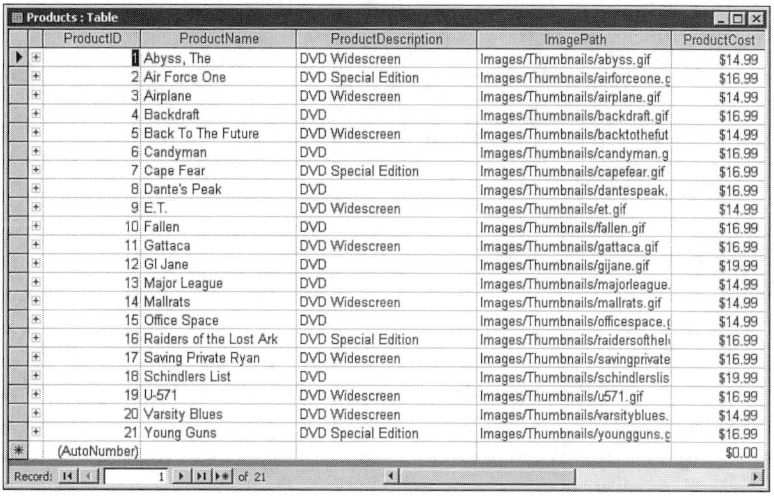

Products : Table

ProductID	ProductName	ProductDescription	ImagePath	ProductCost
1	Abyss, The	DVD Widescreen	Images/Thumbnails/abyss.gif	$14.99
2	Air Force One	DVD Special Edition	Images/Thumbnails/airforceone.g	$16.99
3	Airplane	DVD Widescreen	Images/Thumbnails/airplane.gif	$14.99
4	Backdraft	DVD	Images/Thumbnails/backdraft.gif	$16.99
5	Back To The Future	DVD Widescreen	Images/Thumbnails/backtothefut	$14.99
6	Candyman	DVD	Images/Thumbnails/candyman.g	$16.99
7	Cape Fear	DVD Special Edition	Images/Thumbnails/capefear.gif	$16.99
8	Dante's Peak	DVD	Images/Thumbnails/dantespeak.	$16.99
9	E.T.	DVD Widescreen	Images/Thumbnails/et.gif	$14.99
10	Fallen	DVD	Images/Thumbnails/fallen.gif	$16.99
11	Gattaca	DVD Widescreen	Images/Thumbnails/gattaca.gif	$16.99
12	GI Jane	DVD	Images/Thumbnails/gijane.gif	$19.99
13	Major League	DVD	Images/Thumbnails/majorleague.	$14.99
14	Mallrats	DVD Widescreen	Images/Thumbnails/mallrats.gif	$14.99
15	Office Space	DVD	Images/Thumbnails/officespace.g	$14.99
16	Raiders of the Lost Ark	DVD Special Edition	Images/Thumbnails/raidersofthel	$16.99
17	Saving Private Ryan	DVD Widescreen	Images/Thumbnails/savingprivate	$16.99
18	Schindlers List	DVD	Images/Thumbnails/schindlerslis	$19.99
19	U-571	DVD Widescreen	Images/Thumbnails/u571.gif	$16.99
20	Varsity Blues	DVD Widescreen	Images/Thumbnails/varsityblues.	$14.99
21	Young Guns	DVD Special Edition	Images/Thumbnails/youngguns.g	$16.99
(AutoNumber)				$0.00

Record: 1 of 21

FIGURE 28.20 Add all the relevant information for all the fields.

6. When you are finished, save the database and close Access.

That wasn't so bad! Whenever you want to add more information to the database, open it up and begin adding the necessary text. Now the problem becomes the recordset. Remember that you created a recordset based on the values that were previously in the database, not the recent changes. To correct this, select the Bindings tab and click the Refresh Recordset icon on the top right, as shown in Figure 28.21.

FIGURE 28.21 Refresh the recordset to update any changes made to the database.

With the Bindings panels still open, select the fields from within the recordset and drag them to their proper locations, as shown in Figure 28.22.

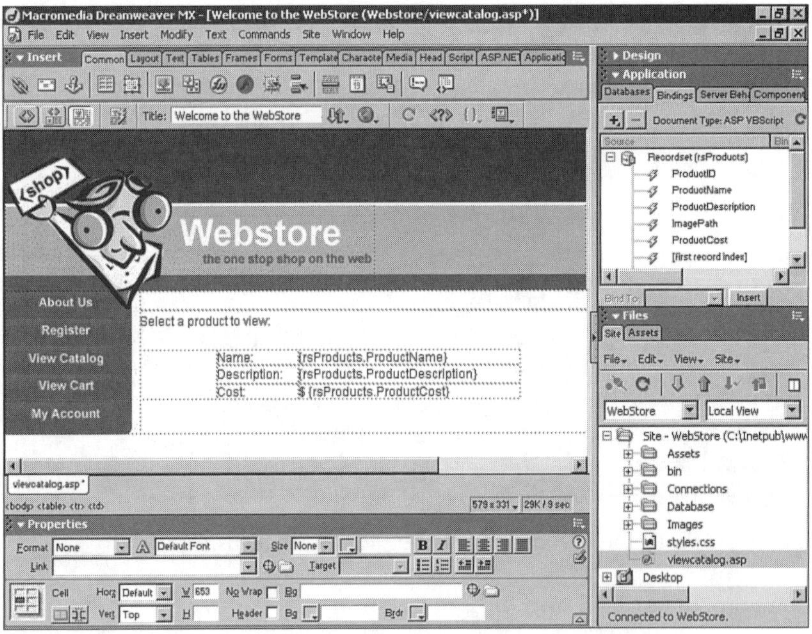

FIGURE 28.22 Drag the fields from the recordset into the proper cells.

Save the page and run it from the browser. Notice how the first record in the database is shown within the cells. Later you will learn about paging, which allows you to cycle through each record.

Dynamic Images

Now that you have created dynamic text within your application, you're ready to begin adding images. The images that will be added here will not be the typical static images that you have used throughout the book. To begin adding dynamic images, follow these steps:

1. Place your cursor in the cell designated for the image.

2. Select Image from the Insert menu.

3. Near the top of the Select Image Source dialog box, you can choose from the file system or from a data source. Select Data Source.

4. Figure 28.23 shows how you are able to select the ImagePath from the recordset. Select OK.

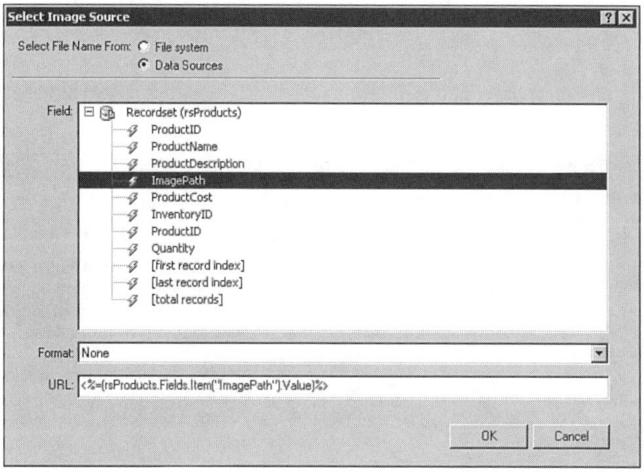

FIGURE 28.23   Insert an image dynamically by adding it from a data source rather than from the file system.

Figure 28.24 shows how the image icon has been inserted for you.

Save the file and view it in the browser. The image for the DVD should now appear as shown in Figure 28.25.

28

FIGURE 28.24   The image icon is used as a placeholder until the page is run.

FIGURE 28.25   The image is dynamically placed based on the path within the database.

Recordset Paging

Now that you've seen just how easy it is to place dynamic content within your site, you'll probably want to begin adding paging features. Paging exposes all records within a pagination system, not unlike those of a book. For every press of a button, your user can advance to the next record or, conversely, return to a previous record. Developers gain certain benefits from pagination, including

- **Load time**   Rather than the page having to process multiple records, it processes only one. Records are only loaded as users advance forward to another record.

- **Size constraints**   By paging through a recordset, screen real estate is ultimately gained. The records are loaded within a certain area of the page rather than all records showing down the page.

Dreamweaver MX's pagination behaviors include

- **Move to First Record**   Returns the user to the first record of the recordset.

- **Move to Previous Record**   Returns the user back one record.

- **Move to Next Record**   Advances the user one record forward.

- **Move to Last Record**   Advances the user to the last record in the recordset.

- **Move to Specific Record**   Advances or returns the user to a record that is specified by the developer or by a parameter passed by the user.

To begin adding pagination features to your site, follow these steps:

1. Place your cursor just below the table that includes all the dynamic data.

2. From the Recordset Paging submenu, select Move to Previous Record, as shown in Figure 28.26.

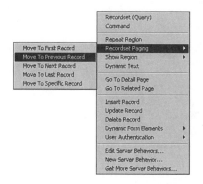

FIGURE 28.26   Add the Move To Previous Record behavior from the Recordset Paging submenu.

3. The Move To Previous Record dialog box will appear similar to Figure 28.27. Make sure that it will create the appropriate link and that it is being generated for the appropriate recordset. Select OK.

FIGURE 28.27   Confirm the settings from the Move To Previous Record dialog box.

4. Add a space and select Move to Next Record from the Recordset Paging submenu, as shown in Figure 28.26.

5. Save your file and test it in the browser. You should be able to navigate from the first record to the last record and back. Figure 28.28 shows the record *Air Force One* that appears after *The Abyss* as a result of clicking Next.

FIGURE 28.28   Selecting Next enables you to cycle through records.

Showing Specific Regions

Now that you have added the capability to cycle to the end of the recordset and back, consider the following problem: Users click Next until they get to the last record and then they are abruptly stopped. They keep clicking Next but nothing happens. The problem is that the users have reached the end of the recordset and they cannot go any further, but the user doesn't know that. Dreamweaver MX provided functionality in the form of a group of Show Region behaviors that alert users that they have reached the end of the recordset. The complete list of Show Region behaviors are as follows:

- **Show Region if Recordset Is Empty**   This behavior can be useful to alert a user that an empty result was returned from the database.

- **Show Region if Recordset Is Not Empty**   Use this behavior when you want to alert the user that results were indeed returned from the database.

- **Show Region if First Record**   If users are on the first record, you can alert them.

- **Show Region if Not First Record**   As users cycle through the records, you can provide a message. When they are on the first record, a message can be displayed.

- **Show Region if Last Record**   If users are on the last record, you can alert them.

- **Show Region if Not Last Record**   As the user cycles through the records, you can provide a message. When they are on the last record, a message can be displayed.

To add a Show Region behavior to your application, follow these steps:

1. Place the text **No more items to view** just below the table or where you want the text to appear.

2. With the text highlighted, select the server behavior Show Region if Last Record from the Show Region submenu, as shown in Figure 28.29.

3. Select the appropriate recordset from the dialog box and select OK.

4. Save the page and run it in a browser.

Figure 28.30 shows the message as it will appear when you reach the end of the recordset.

Using Repeat Region

Although recordset paging is the ideal model to strive for, at times you might want to display all the records in the database at once. The Repeat Region behavior enables you to create a pattern that repeats within the application. For instance, in the View Catalog Web store example, a table was created to display the content for the image, name, description, and cost. Using the Repeat Region server behavior, you are able to maintain that structure while repeating the contents for every record with the database. To create a repeatable region, follow the instructions outlined next:

1. Select the table for which you want to create the repeatable region.

2. Select Repeat Region from the Server Behaviors panel, as shown in Figure 28.31.

FIGURE 28.29   Add the Show Region server behavior to the text message you want displayed.

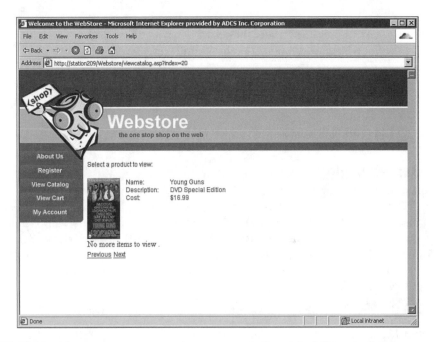

FIGURE 28.30   The message appears when you reach the end of the recordset.

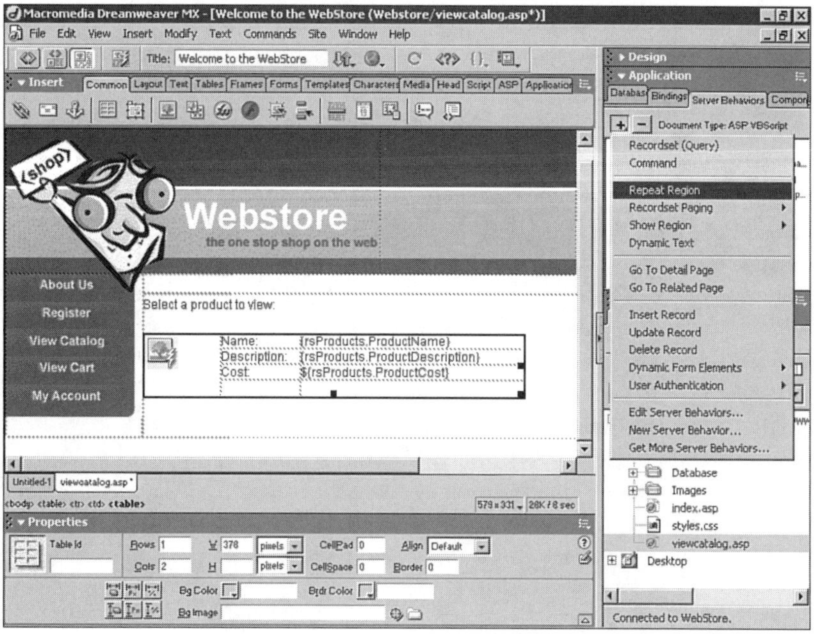

FIGURE 28.31   Select the table that you want to create the repeatable region for.

3. The Repeat Region dialog box allows you to enter choices regarding which recordset to create the repeat region for as well as how you want to display the results. The Repeat Region dialog box is shown in Figure 28.32.

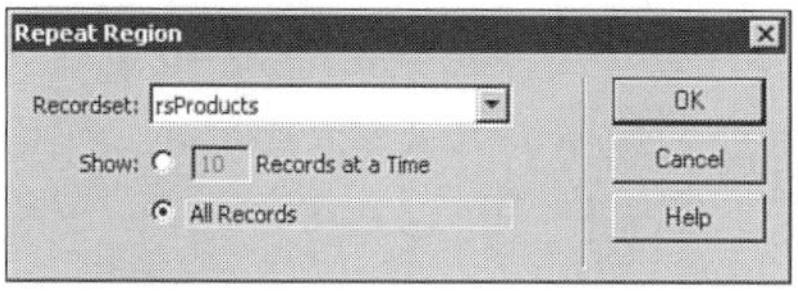

FIGURE 28.32   Select the options for show and recordset from the Repeat Region dialog box.

4. Save the file and run it in the browser.

Figure 28.33 shows all the records listed at once. You can scroll down the page to view all the DVDs that are contained within the products table.

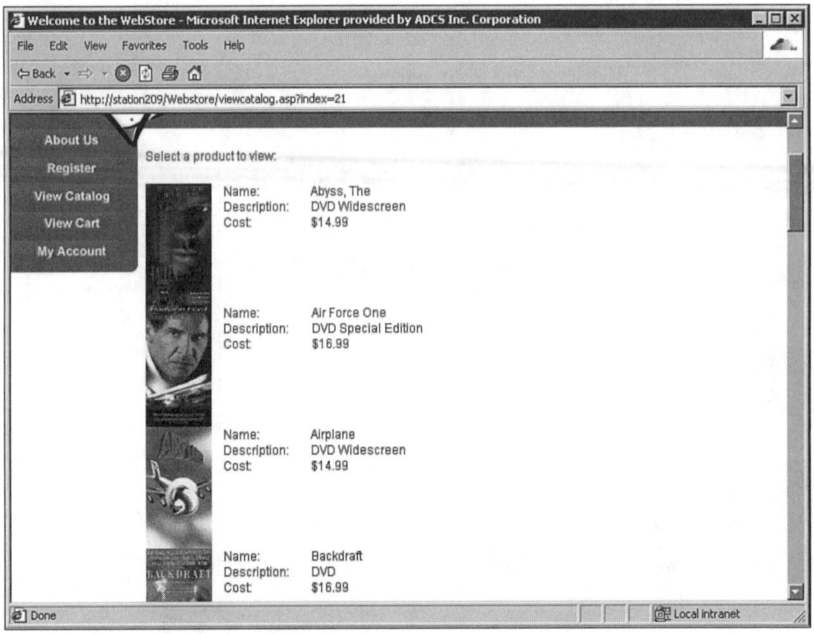

FIGURE 28.33   All the records are shown when you use the Repeat Region server behavior.

Building the Web Store Application Using ASP.NET

If you are reading this section, it is safe to say that you are curious about learning how to develop .NET applications in Dreamweaver MX or you are simply broadening your knowledge of the extensive functionality available in Dreamweaver MX.

When I first starting using UltraDev years back, I was amazed at the simplicity between the program and various server models that existed at the time, namely ASP, ColdFusion, and CGI. When I first started beta testing Visual Studio .NET and ASP.NET, I wondered if Macromedia would ever include the power of DataSets, DataGrids, and DataLists into its newest version of Dreamweaver, and if it did, how they would go about doing it. Now that Dreamweaver MX is out, I can tell you that I'm stunned at the integration between Dreamweaver MX, ASP.NET, and ADO.NET.

If you read the ASP section, most of this will be a review. What this section covers differently is the power in DataSets, DataLists, DataGrids, and the ASP.NET application development capabilities using Dreamweaver MX. This section covers the following topics:

- DataSets

- Paging

- Object Binding

- Region Repeaters
- Conditionals
- DataGrids
- DataLists

If you have not done so already, you can download the support files for this chapter from www.dreamweavermxunleashed.com. The Web site contains all the support files for every chapter, including this one.

Creating the View Catalog Page

The View Catalog page of the Web store is the heart of the application. This is where users will be able to come to view the items that currently reside in the catalog and place any item that they choose into their shopping cart. Before you begin creating the application, take a look at the Web store database, which should reside within the Database folder of the project. Figure 28.01, which is toward the beginning of the chapter, shows the two tables that this section concerns itself with—the products and inventory tables.

Figure 28.2 shows the products table. It contains the product information on what the Web store will sell—DVDs. It also contains the full path of the images, cost information, and a brief description of each item up for sale. Figure 28.3 shows the inventory table, which contains all the quantities for each item.

You may be asking yourself why there aren't any product names within the inventory table. Figure 28.4 shows the relationship between the products table and the inventory table. Remember, the relationship is created with the ProductID between the two tables; this is the reason for the ProductID within the inventory table rather than the simple ProductName.

> **NOTE**
>
> Technically the quantity field could reside within the products table. The reason for separating the products from the quantities is simplicity and scalability. If in the future you wanted to carry clothing, you could potentially have the same shirt in both blue and green. Because shirt quantities would vary, a separate table to handle the quantities solves the dilemma.

Now that you have an overview of the database, you are ready to begin extracting data from it. The next few sections will cover the following:

- DataSets
- Dynamic Elements
- Paging

28

- Conditionals

- Regions

- Commands

- DataGrids

- DataLists

Creating a New DataSet

If you are familiar with traditional data storage and retrieval models in ASP, you are familiar with the recordset. The recordset acts as a virtual table to store information that is retrieved from the database. DataSets are no different. To better understand DataSets is to better understand ADO.NET.

ADO.NET is a set of tools and namespaces that provide access to data stores regardless of the source. Three layers make up ADO.NET:

- **The Data Store**   The Data Store represents the physical location of your data. This can be an OLE database, a SQL database, or an XML file.

- **The Data Provider**   The Data Provider makes up the connection and the command that make up the virtual table that your data will be stored in.

- **The DataSet**   The DataSet is the virtual table and relationships that make up your data.

Now that you know the makeup of ADO.NET, you can begin to plug in all the different aspects that make up your application. Your data store consists of an OLE database in Access. In the previous chapter, you learned how to create a connection within an ASP.NET model. Now let's jump into creating the commands and working with DataSets. To begin creating a DataSet, open the viewcatalog.aspx file and follow these steps:

Begin creating the new DataSet by selecting DataSet from the Server Behaviors panel, as shown in Figure 28.34.

With the DataSet dialog box available, you are now able to select various options including the DataSet name, defining the connection, creating the command, and passing in any parameters if that is needed. Figure 28.35 shows the configuration for the View Catalog page. To create the command, you can either type it in manually, create it within Access and copy it over, or create it by interacting with the database items at the bottom of the dialog box and selecting the appropriate SQL buttons.

When you've finished configuring the command, you can test the DataSet by selecting the Test button. Figure 28.36 shows the results.

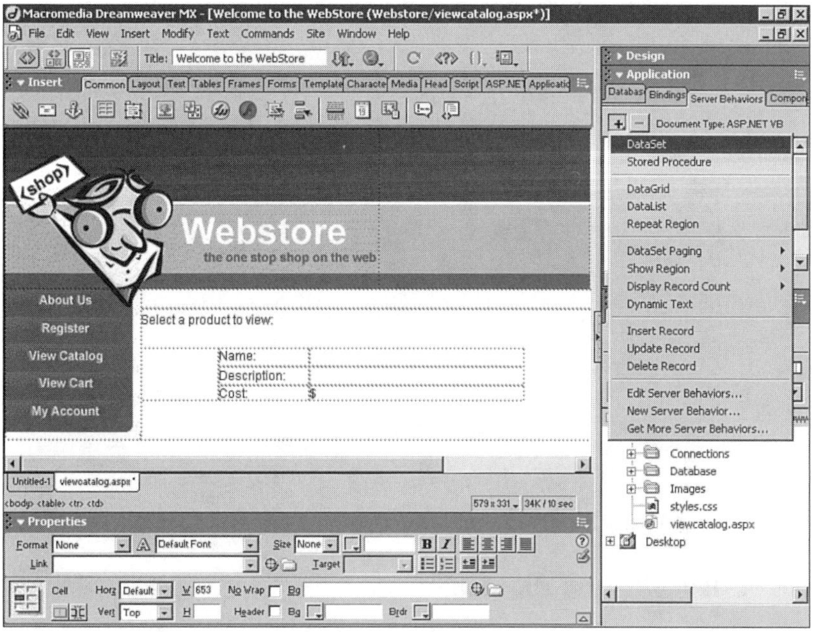

FIGURE 28.34   A new DataSet can be created by selecting it from the Server Behaviors panel.

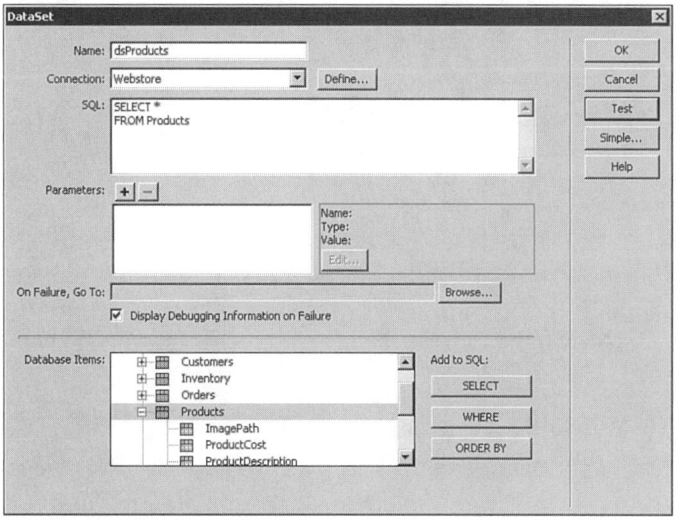

FIGURE 28.35   Configure your DataSet appropriately.

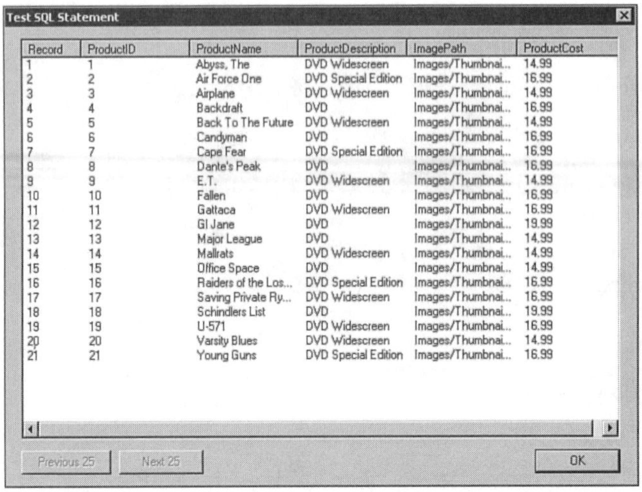

FIGURE 28.36   Testing the DataSet returns the complete list of items.

Click OK in the Test dialog box and click OK within the DataSet dialog box.

You can view all the fields within the DataSet by expanding it from the Bindings panel. Figure 28.37 shows the results of the Dataset.

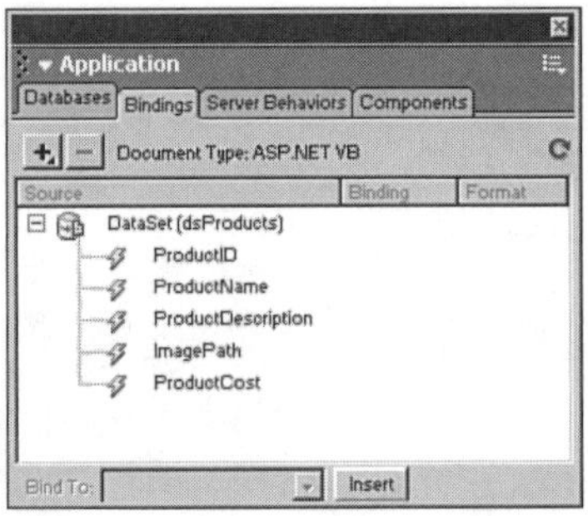

FIGURE 28.37   Expanding the DataSet enables you to see all the fields that it contains.

Working with Dynamic Elements

Now that you have a DataSet clearly defined, your next step is to get the information from the DataSet to your application. Dreamweaver MX's Server Behavior and Binding panels provide the capabilities you need to get started producing dynamic elements that are centralized within the database but exposed via the application.

Dynamic Text

The first step to creating a truly dynamic application is to make all your text elements as dynamic as possible. That is, allowing all your company's valuable information to reside within the database. To start creating dynamic text, begin by creating a table that will serve as the means of organizing the data output.

If you downloaded the support files for this section, you'll notice that the table structure has been created for you. You can begin creating dynamic text by following the steps outlined next:

1. Drag each item from the Bindings panel to its position within the table, as shown in Figure 28.38.

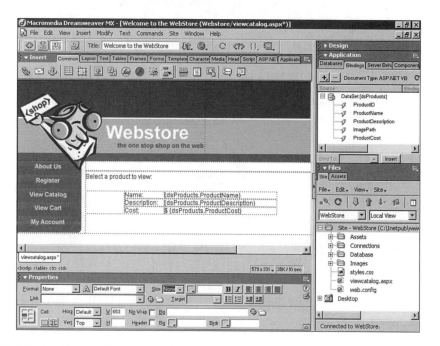

FIGURE 28.38   Drag each item into its respective position within the table.

2. Save the file and run it in the browser. Notice how the first record in the database is shown within the cells. The next section discusses paging, which will allow you to cycle through each record.

Dynamic Images

Now that you have created dynamic text within your application, you're ready to begin adding images. The images that will be added here will not be the typical static images that you have used throughout the book; rather, they will be dynamic. To begin adding dynamic images, follow these steps:

1. Place your cursor in the cell designated for the image.

2. Select Image from the Insert menu.

3. Near the top of the Select Image Source dialog box, you can select from the file system or from a data source. Select Data Source.

4. Figure 28.39 shows how you are able to select the ImagePath from the DataSet. Select OK.

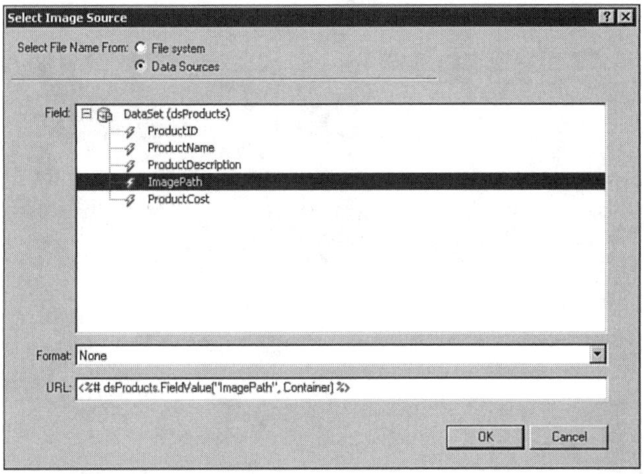

FIGURE 28.39   Select ImagePath from the DataSet to create a dynamic image.

5. An image icon will be inserted for you, signifying that a dynamic image exists.

6. Save the file and view it in the browser. The image for the DVD should now appear as shown in Figure 28.40.

DataSet Paging

Now that you've seen just how easy it is to place dynamic content within your site, you'll probably want to begin adding paging features. Paging exposes all records within a pagination system, not unlike those of a book. For every press of a button, your user can advance to the next record or, conversely, return to a previous record. Dreamweaver MX's pagination behaviors include the following:

- **Move to First Record**   Returns the user to the first record of the DataSet.

- **Move to Previous Record**   Returns the user back one record.

FIGURE 28.40   The image is dynamically placed based on the path specified within the database.

- **Move to Next Record**   Advances the user one record forward.
- **Move to Last Record**   Advances the user to the last record in the DataSet.

To begin adding pagination features to your site, follow these steps:

1. Place your cursor just below the table or near the location where you want to add the paging navigation bar.

2. Select Move to Previous Record from the DataSet Paging submenu of the Server Behaviors tab.

3. The Move to Previous Page dialog box appears, allowing you to choose the specific link to insert as well as the DataSet to cycle through. Select OK. The Previous link will show just below the table.

4. Repeat the action for the Next button. The result will be similar to Figure 28.41.

5. Save your page and run it in the browser. Notice how you are now able to advance and move backward through each record.

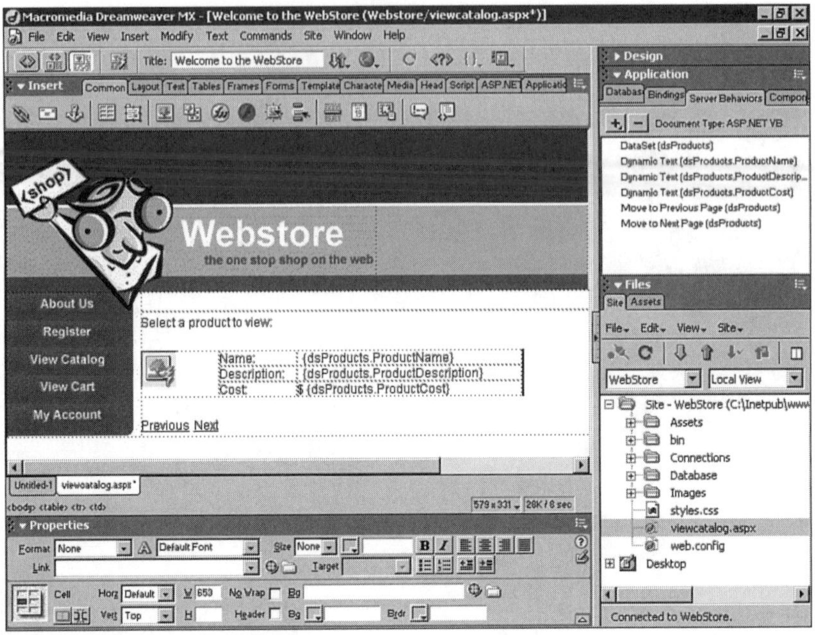

FIGURE 28.41   Page through your DataSet by adding paging behaviors to your site.

Using Repeat Region

Although DataSet paging is the ideal model to strive for, at times, you might want to display all the records in the database at once. The Repeat Region behavior enables you to create a pattern of repeatable instances within your application. For instance, in the View Catalog Web Store example, a table was created to display the content for the image, name, description, and cost. Using the Repeat Region server behavior, you are able to maintain that structure while repeating the contents for every record within the database. To create a repeatable region, follow the instructions outlined next:

1. Highlight the table that you want to create the repeatable region for.

2. Select Repeat Region from the Server Behaviors panel.

3. Select the recordset you want to repeat and select OK.

4. Save your work and run it in the browser. The result will look similar to Figure 28.42.

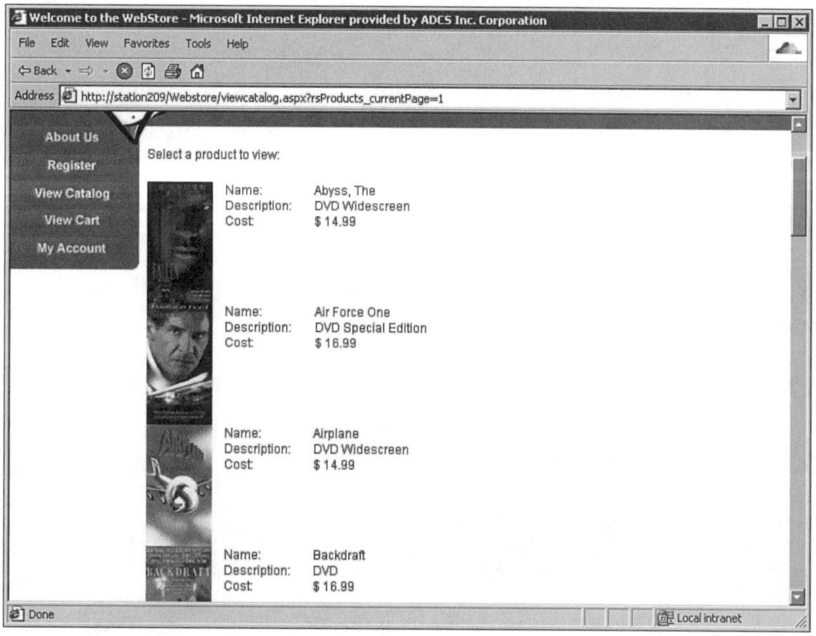

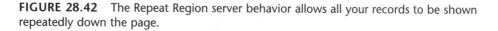

FIGURE 28.42 The Repeat Region server behavior allows all your records to be shown repeatedly down the page.

Display Record Count

As you allow users to cycle through your records, you may find that eventually you'll want to display some sort of message letting the user know what record they are on. This can be accomplished by simply displaying a numerical value for the record they've cycled to somewhere on the page. Dreamweaver MX includes a set of behaviors that allow you to do just that; they are known as Display Record Count. The Display Record Count server behaviors include the following:

- **Display Starting Record Number**   Displays the first record number of the DataSet.

- **Display Ending Record Number**   Displays the last record number of the DataSet.

- **Display Total Records**   Displays all the records of the DataSet. Typically this is a static number unless items are added to the database.

- **Display Current Page Number**   Displays the current record number of the DataSet. This number will change as the user pages through the records.

Like all the other behaviors that you have been working with, the Display Record Count behaviors can be inserted into your application very easily. To insert the Display Current Page Number behavior into the viewcatalog.aspx page, simply follow these steps:

1. Place your cursor somewhere on the page where the user is most likely to look for a record count. A good place is somewhere near the paging navigation bar.

2. Select the Display Current Page Number behavior from the Display Record Count submenu as shown in Figure 28.43.

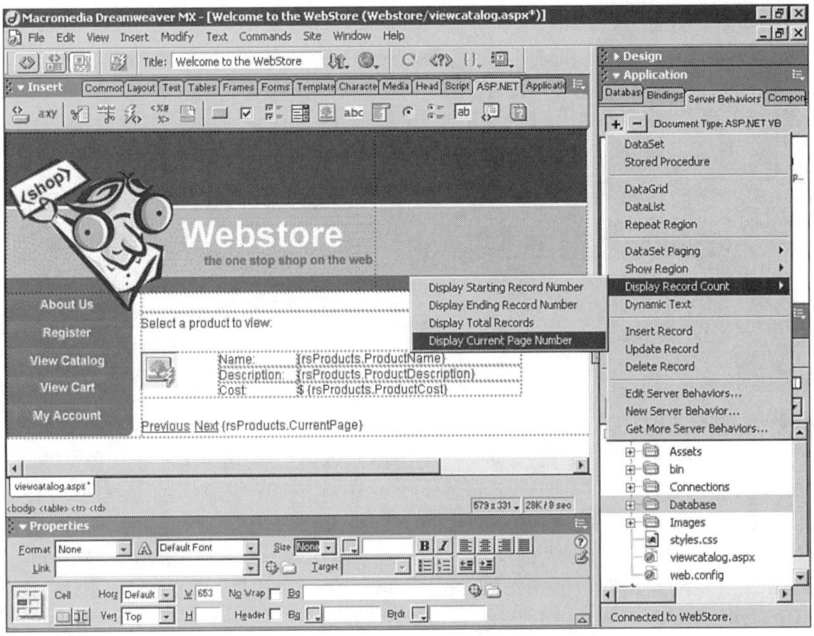

FIGURE 28.43   Insert the Display Current Record Count behavior.

- Save your work and run it in the browser. The results will be similar to Figure 28.44 in that the movie *The Abyss* is the first record and the number 1 is shown to the user next to the navigation bar.

FIGURE 28.44   The current record number will appear, indicating the number of the record the user is on.

Showing Specific Regions

Now that you have added the capability to cycle to the end of the DataSet and back, consider the following problem: Users click Next until they get to the last record and then they are abruptly stopped. They keep clicking Next but nothing happens. The problem is that the user has reached the end of the DataSet and they cannot go any further, but the user doesn't know that. Dreamweaver MX provides functionality in the form of a group of Show Region behaviors that alert users that they have reached the end of the DataSet. The complete list of Show Region behaviors are as follows:

- **Show if DataSet Is Empty**   This behavior can be useful to alert a user that an empty result was returned from the database.

- **Show if DataSet Is Not Empty**   Use this behavior when you want to alert the user that results were indeed returned from the database.

- **Show if First Page**   If the user is on the first record, you can show a message.

- **Show if Not First Page**   As the user cycles through the records, you can provide a message. When the user is on the first record, a message can be displayed.

- **Show if Last Page**   If the user is on the last record, you can provide a message.

- **Show if Not Last Page**   As the user cycles through the records, you can provide a message. When the user is on the last record, a message can be displayed.

To add a Show Region behavior to your application, follow these steps:

1. Place the text **This is the first item** just below the table or where you want the text to appear.

2. With the text highlighted, select the server behavior Show If First Page from the Show Region submenu, as shown in Figure 28.45.

3. Select the DataSet to use and click OK.

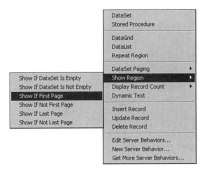

FIGURE 28.45   Add the Show Region behavior to the text message you want displayed.

4. Save the page and run it in a browser.

You will receive a message immediately when the page is loaded, because the record you are dealing with is indeed the first record. As you cycle through the records, the message will disappear.

Working with DataGrids

One of the most important and feature-rich controls included with Dreamweaver MX's ASP.NET integration is the DataGrid control. The DataGrid control, similar to the Repeat Region behavior and the DataSet Paging behaviors, enable you to display numerous records on the page while allowing pagination functionality. For instance, you could display every five records within the dataset while allowing paging to the next set of five records. As a footer, you could display a list of numbers that corresponded with every group of five records to display. As the user selects a new number, a new group of records is displayed. The DataGrid's flexibility does not end there; DataGrids also allow for column sorting, editing, and custom commands.

> **NOTE**
>
> Although this section provides a brief overview of the static features of the DataGrids, be aware that the DataGrid offers more than simple display functionality, most of which will be covered in more detail in the next chapter.

Some of the column types that are available with the DataGrid are listed next:

- **Simple Data Field**   The Simple Data Field is also known as the Bound Column in ASP.NET. This column lets you specify which data source field will be displayed and the data format that the field will use.

- **Free Form**   The Free Form column is also known as the Template Column in ASP.NET. The Free Form column lets you insert HTML text and server controls to create true custom designs.

- **Hyperlink**   The Hyperlink column lets you insert text that will be hyperlinked. The typical use for this is allowing users to view basic information but allowing them to link within a column to view more detailed information within a separate page.

- **Edit, Update, Cancel Buttons**   In ASP.NET, this column is called the Edit Command Column. The Edit, Update, and Cancel buttons allow you to perform in-place edits of your text without redirecting a user to another page. When this page is rendered, the Edit button is visible. When the user selects the Edit button, it is replaced by an editable control along with Update and Cancel buttons to update the text to the database.

- **Delete Buttons**   The Delete button enables users to delete the row that they select.

Adding a Simple DataGrid

Now that you know what a DataGrid is, let's create a simple DataGrid for the Web Store application. For the DataGrid, follow the steps outlined below:

1. Start with a new viewcatalog.aspx page.

2. Place the cursor just below the text and select the DataGrid behavior from the Server Behaviors panel, as shown in Figure 28.46.

3. The DataGrid dialog box appears. Select all the options including ID, the DataSet you are creating the DataGrid for, how many rows you want to show at any one time, navigation options, and the specific columns you want to show within the DataGrid. The results should look similar to Figure 28.47.

28

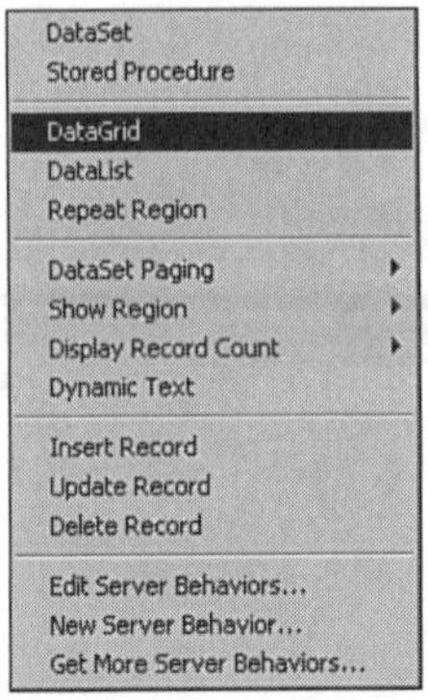

FIGURE 28.46   Select the DataGrid behavior.

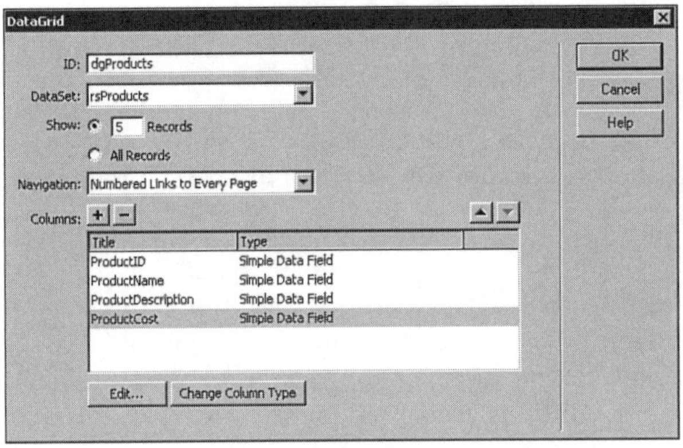

FIGURE 28.47   Enter all the information for the DataGrid.

4. Select OK.

5. The DataGrid will be inserted into your page, similar to Figure 28.48.

6. Save your file and run it in the browser. Figure 28.49 shows the results of what the DataGrid will look like after it is complete.

Notice that the column headers, alternating rows, and backgrounds have colors prespecified. In the following section, you learn how to change these.

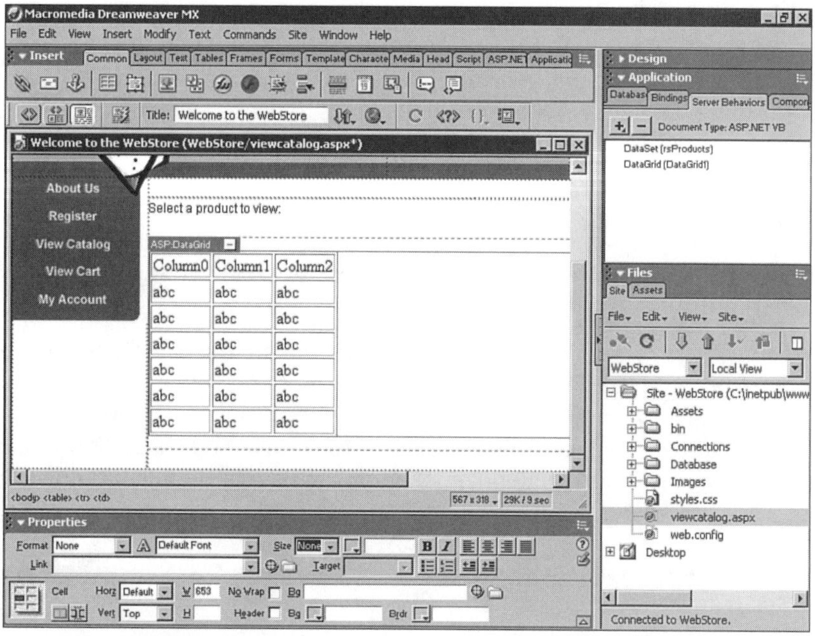

FIGURE 28.48   The DataGrid does not reveal any information until it is viewed within a Web browser.

FIGURE 28.49   The browser shows the result of the DataGrid.

Customizing the DataGrid's Color Scheme

If you got the DataGrid to work correctly, you'll notice right away that it contains a smooth default color scheme for the column headers, backgrounds, and alternating rows. Although the color scheme that Macromedia chooses to use as a default is tasteful, it does not match the color scheme of the Web Store application. To change the color scheme of the DataGrid, follow these steps:

1. Switch to code view of the viewcatalog.aspx page.

2. Navigate down the page until you find the tags for HeaderStyle, ItemStyle, AlternatingItemStyle, FootStyle, and PagerStyle.

3. The colors that you will be interested in modifying are the BackColor and ForeColor attributes of the HeaderStyle tag and the BackColor attribute of the AlternatingItemStyle tag. Locate those attributes and change the colors to #FFFFFF for ForeColor, #003366 for the BackColor of the HeaderStyle, and #99CC00 for the BackColor of the AlternatingItemStyle. If you are having trouble locating the attributes, see Figure 28.50.

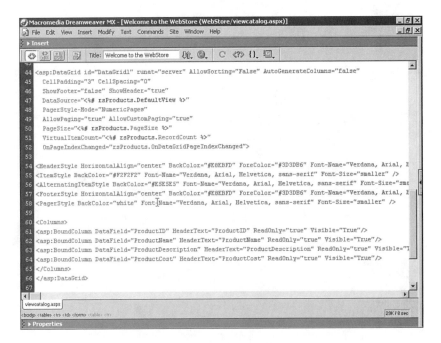

FIGURE 28.50   Change the color scheme for the HeaderStyle and AlternatingItemStyle tags.

4. Save your work and run the page in a browser. The results should look similar to Figure 28.51. Notice the color scheme now matches that of the Web store.

FIGURE 28.51 The color scheme will change to match the Web store's color scheme.

Hyperlinked Columns

As mentioned earlier, column types can be changed to different types, depending on what you are trying to accomplish. One of the several column types is that of a hyperlink. A hyperlinked column type allows the items that reside within that column to be hyperlinked to a different page. A good use for this is if you were creating a DataGrid for the simple reason of providing a brief description of a particular product. You could hyperlink the product name to allow the user to navigate to a page that provided a more detailed description of that product. To create a hyperlinked column, follow the steps outlined next:

1. Double-click the DataGrid behavior to open the DataGrid dialog again.

2. Select the ProductName column and choose Hyperlink from the Change Column Type button, as shown in Figure 28.52.

3. The Hyperlink column dialog box will appear, enabling you to specify the text that you want hyperlinked within the column you choose and the page you want that link to navigate to when you click it. The results of the dialog box should coincide with Figure 28.53.

28

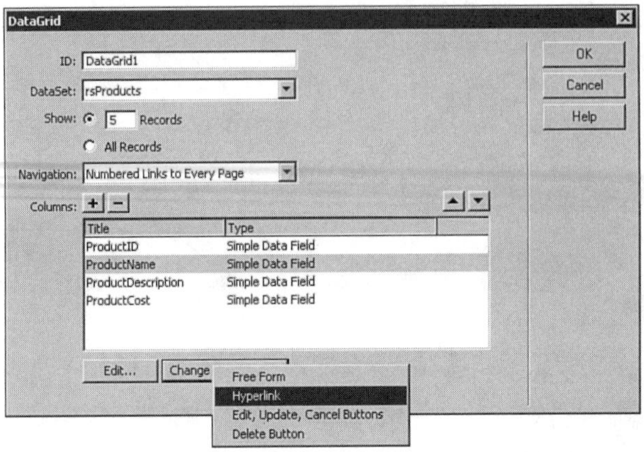

FIGURE 28.52   Change the column type of ProductName to Hyperlink.

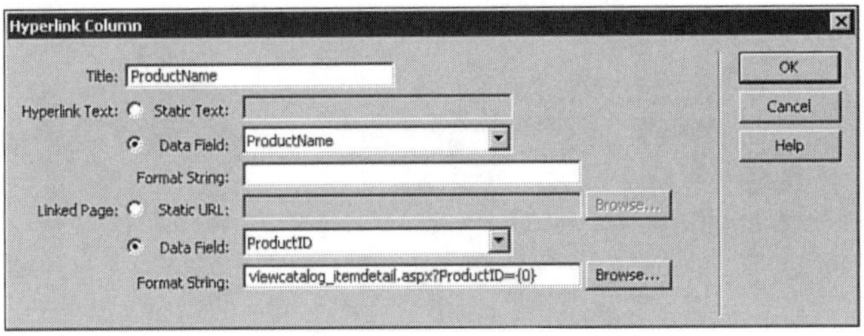

FIGURE 28.53   Change the options in the Hyperlink dialog box.

> **TIP**
>
> By selecting ProductID as the data field that will be linked, you are essentially passing a parameter along the querystring to the Details page. The Details page should be designed so that it takes that value and adjusts the page accordingly.

4. Select OK in the Hyperlink dialog box.

5. Select OK in the DataGrid dialog box.

6. Save your work and run it in the browser. The result should look similar to Figure 28.54.

7. Notice that the names within the ProductName column are now clickable. Clicking that item will link you to the itemdetails.aspx page that should be created for you and available for download at www.dreamweavermxunleashed.com.

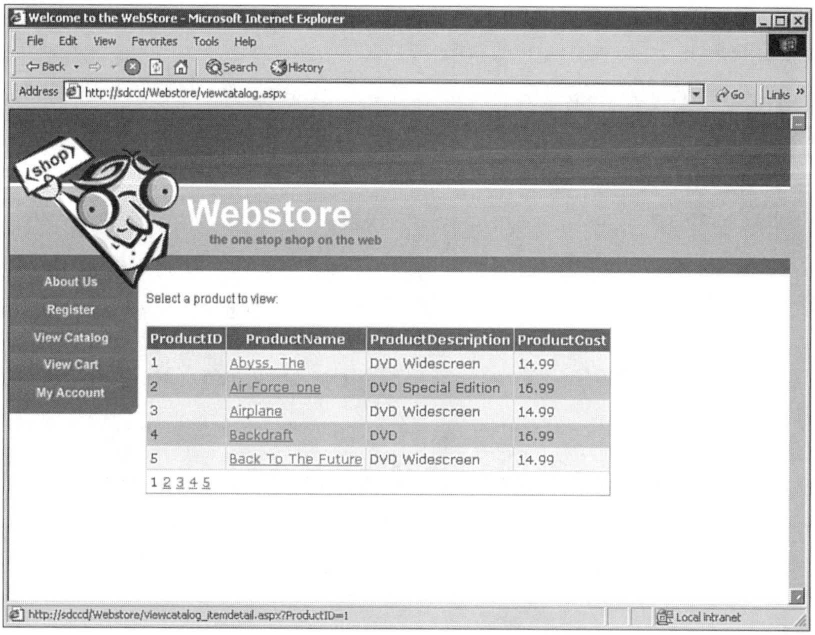

FIGURE 28.54   All the product names are now linked and ready to navigate to their appropriate page.

If you are curious to see what the itemdetails.aspx page looks like, open it to see that it is basically the old version of the viewcatalog.aspx page.

Working with DataLists

The DataList behavior functions much like the DataGrid behavior in that it allows for multiple items to be shown at once. Unlike the DataGrid behavior, however, the DataList behavior lacks the power and flexibility that you get with the DataGrid control. Like a DataGrid behavior, you can control the way your DataList is displayed by modifying its templates. The available templates are as follows:

- **Header**   The text and controls that will be rendered at the beginning of the list.

- **Item**   The text and controls that will be rendered once for each row.

- **Alternating Item**   Similar to the AlternatingItemStyle template for the DataGrid behavior, the Alternating Item template changes the background color of every other row within the DataList.

- **Edit Item**   The Edit Item template controls the look of the DataList row when it is in edit mode. Typically, edit mode consists of controls like the Text Box control.

28

- **Select Item**   The Select Item template controls the look of the DataList row when the user selects an item in the DataList.

- **Separator**   The elements to render between each item.

- **Footer**   The text and controls that will be rendered at the end of the list.

To add a DataList to your page, follow the steps outlined next:

1. Place your cursor where you want to insert the DataList and select DataList from the Server Behavior menu.

2. Figure 28.55 shows some of the options that you can add to your DataList, including ID, DataSet name, how many records to show at once, templates, and item organization.

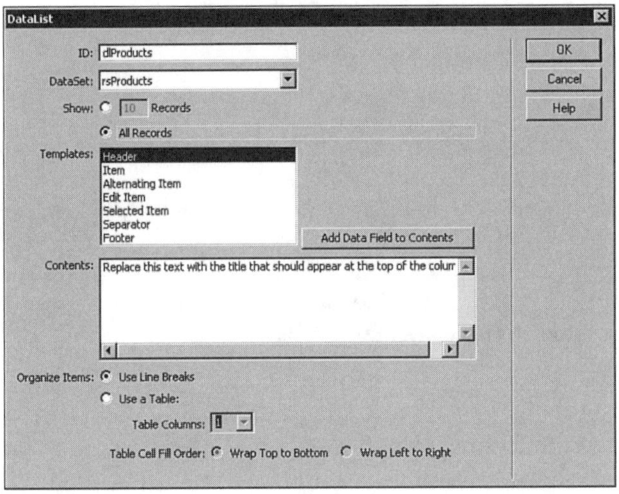

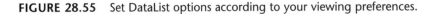

FIGURE 28.55   Set DataList options according to your viewing preferences.

3. Select the Header template and click the Add Data Field to Contents button. Figure 28.56 shows the dialog box that you will see.

4. Select OK. Figure 28.57 shows the code that is inserted into the contents of the template for the header.

5. Repeat the steps for the Item template, adding Product Name, Description, and Cost. Also note that you may add HTML markup to caption the dynamic text that will be brought in. The ends of each line have <br> tags inserted to create a line break between captions. Figure 28.58 shows the result.

6. Figure 28.59 shows how you can add a horizontal rule tag as the alternating item. This will add a separation between records.

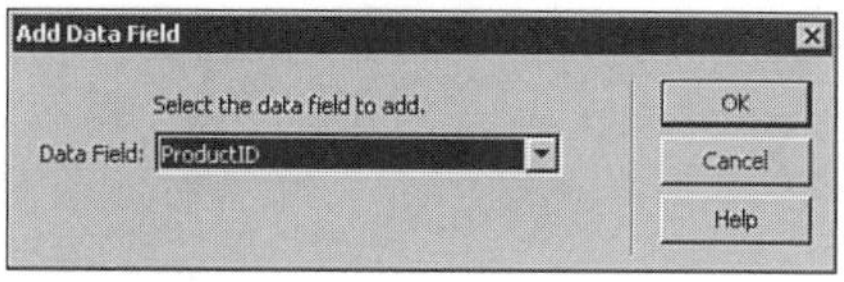

FIGURE 28.56   Select the DataField to view as the header.

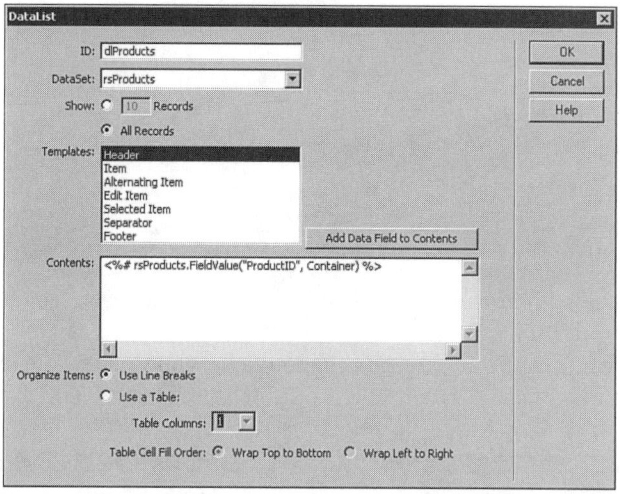

FIGURE 28.57   Code is inserted automatically for the Header template.

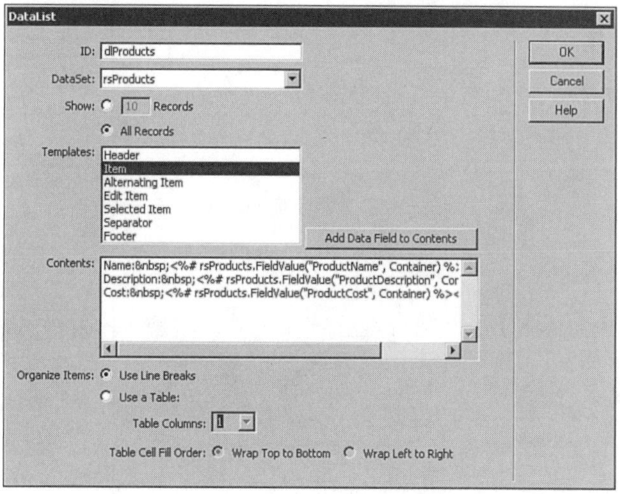

FIGURE 28.58   Add the product name, description, and cost to the Item template.

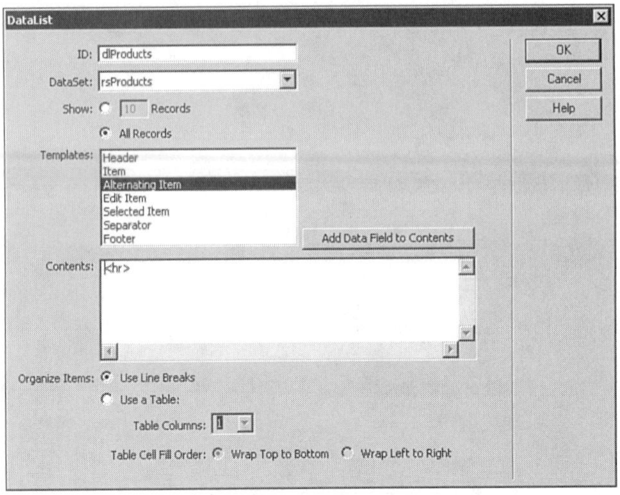

FIGURE 28.59   Add a horizontal rule to create a separation between records.

7. After you have finished modifying the templates, choose OK. The design view shows you a preliminary view of the results, as shown in Figure 28.60.

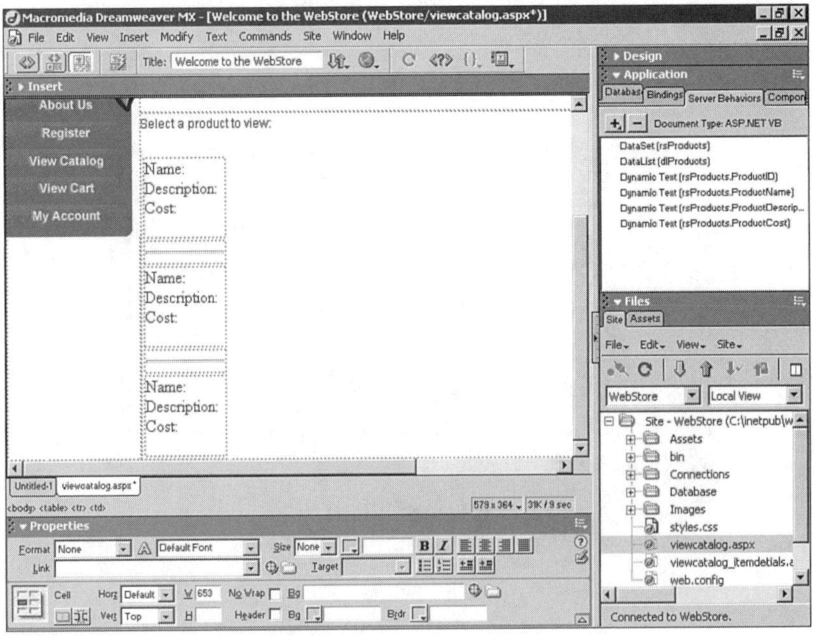

FIGURE 28.60   The design view shows you what the finished product will look like.

8. Save your work and run it in a browser. The results are shown in Figure 28.61.

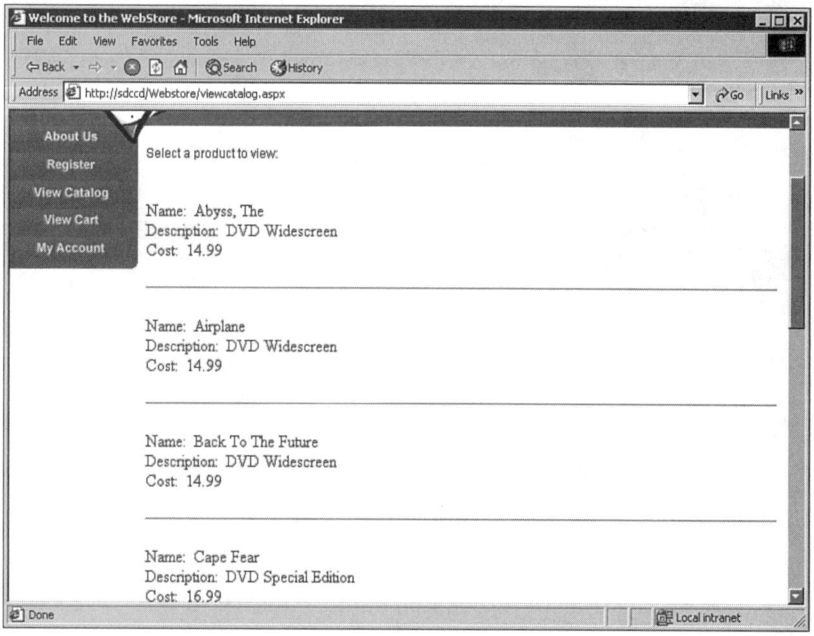

FIGURE 28.61   The DataList results in a customized list of records.

Live Data Mode

Although the Live Data Mode feature has been around since the first version of UltraDev, the new version of Live Data Mode is a bit more accessible than before. With the feature now available from the toolbar, Live Data Mode provides the capability to view dynamic data from within Dreamweaver MX's IDE without having to open a browser to see the results. The Live Data Mode feature is just a matter of clicking the icon to the right of the design view icon on the toolbar. Figure 28.62 shows the button depressed with dynamic content within the document window.

28

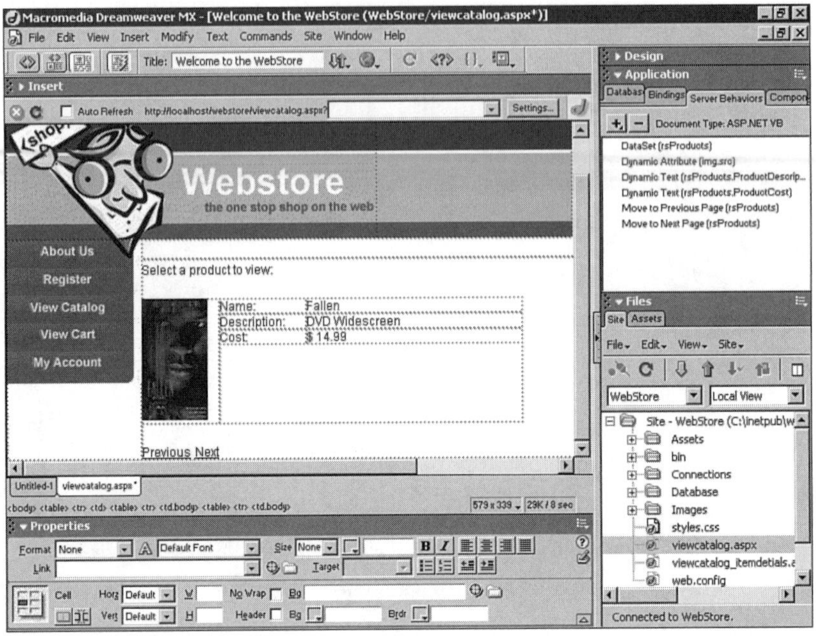

FIGURE 28.62   Select the Live Data Mode icon from the toolbar to view live content right in the document window.

Live Data Settings

Live Data Settings enable you to modify parameters and scripts that will be executed at runtime during Live Data Mode. For instance, if you switch to Live Data Mode, you'll notice that you can do little more than view the contents for that record. By modifying the setting for Live Data, you could essentially pass a parameter across the querystring to navigate to a different record. To modify Live Data Settings follow the instructions outlined next:

1. With Live Data Mode on, select Live Data Settings from the View menu. The Live Data Settings dialog box will appear.

2. Notice that you can modify the URL Request variable and value by selecting the + symbol.

3. Click it and enter the information shown in Figure 28.63.

> **NOTE**
>
> If this page was being viewed in the browser, dsProducts_currentPage would be the variable being sent across. Its value would change according to the page that you wanted to navigate to.

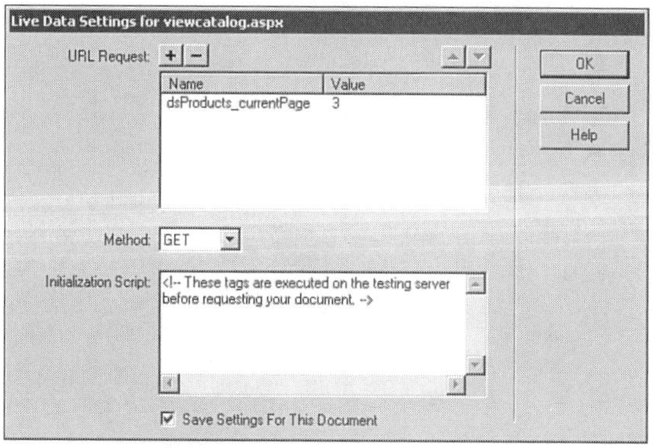

FIGURE 28.63   Live Data Settings allow you to modify variables and values that will be sent across the querystring.

   4. Select OK.

The result shows the movie information for *Airplane* because it is the third record.

> **TIP**
>
> You don't have to open the Live Data Settings dialog box every time you want to modify the URL Request. You can simply modify it in the Live Data Settings toolbar that appears just below the Object toolbar.

Summary

Producing dynamic content has traditionally been the goal of every developer. The ability to produce "placeholders" where text and images just seem to magically appear always seems to outweigh the static notion of typical Web sites. In the past, developers were required to know multiple languages and technologies to accomplish something as simple as a dynamic drop-down list. Dreamweaver MX provides the capability to produce dynamic content while maintaining its WYSIWYG functionality. Gone are the days of developers having to know everything about ASP, ADO, SQL, HTML, JavaScript, CSS, and so on. Although a bit of knowledge is still advantageous, creating dynamic content within Dreamweaver MX is still just a matter of dragging and dropping.

CHAPTER **29**

Modifying the Database

by Zak Ruvalcaba

One of the primary purposes for developing a dynamic Web application is not only to be able to view live data from your database, but also to modify, add, or delete the data within it. The last chapter exposed you to a key component of Web application development: dynamic data. Unfortunately, that knowledge will take you only as far as being able to modify the database when changes need to be made. To truly appreciate the power behind a fully dynamic application is to develop that application so that content constantly changes based on user or administrator input. This chapter focuses on creating forms in Dreamweaver MX that modify, add, or delete items within the database. It does not stop there, however, it also encompasses the world of e-business and shows how Dreamweaver MX is revolutionizing the creation of e-commerce applications through simplicity and ease of use.

As in previous chapters, the files used within this chapter are located at www.dreamweavermxunleashed.com.

Creating the Web Store New User Registration Page Using ASP

Like most Web applications, the Web store requires a page that allows visitors to register as new users and, ultimately based on certain permissions, be able to navigate the site, view items, and purchase items within the site based on those permissions or credentials. Although security is beyond the scope of this chapter, it is something to consider. It will become increasingly obvious that multiple users would end up sharing the same shopping cart unless they're distinguished by a unique identifier. Security will be covered with greater detail in Chapter 32, "Security and User Authentication."

A quick overview of the Web Store database reveals that you need to collect personal information and credit card information to process a visitor as a new user. Recall that the tables that make up customers' information lie within the customers and creditcards tables, as shown in Figure 29.1.

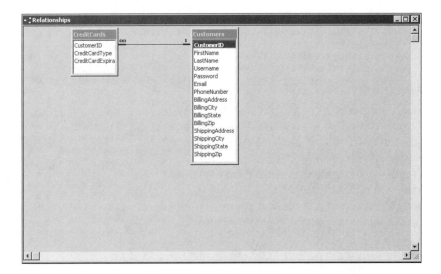

FIGURE 29.1   The customers and creditcards tables contain all the information for new users.

Upon further inspection of those tables, you'll notice that the following fields are necessary for new users to be created within the customers table:

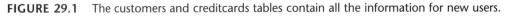

Field Name	Date Type
CustomerID	AutoNumber
FirstName	Text
LastName	Text
Username	Text
Password	Text
Email	Text
PhoneNumber	Number
BillingAddress	Text
BillingCity	Text
BillingState	Text
BillingZip	Text

Field Name	Date Type
ShippingAddress	Text
ShippingCity	Text
ShippingState	Text
ShippingZip	Text

The following information also needs to be collected within the creditcards table to associate a credit card with a particular customer.

Field Name	Date Type
CustomerID	Number
CreditCardType	Text
CreditCardExpiration	Text

Knowing the data that needs to reside within the database, you can now begin creating the New User Registration form to accommodate the data that will eventually be inserted.

Creating the New User Registration Form

Most applications, if not all, simulate the fields within a database with HTML form objects. Because form objects allow the user interaction with the Web application, they are the perfect channel for collecting information and subsequently inserting that information into the database. Before you can begin creating the New User Registration form, however, you must first create a table that will serve as the primary means for structuring the form objects in a cohesive and usable fashion. Begin creating the table by following the steps outlined next:

1. Begin creating the New User Registration form by creating a new page from a template. Select New from the File menu, navigate to the Templates tab, and select the WebStore template as shown in Figure 29.2.

> **CAUTION**
>
> If you have not obtained the chapter files from www.dreamweavermxunleashed.com, you will not have the template available.

2. Decide how many rows your table will contain. A quick count of all the necessary fields within the customers and creditcards tables reveals that you need about 16 rows. You may want to include a few to account for headers, dividers, and button elements. A safer number would be 26.

3. Place your cursor in the editable region, insert a new form by selecting it from the Insert menu. Now select Table from the Insert menu. Figure 29.3 shows the Insert Table dialog box with the appropriate data.

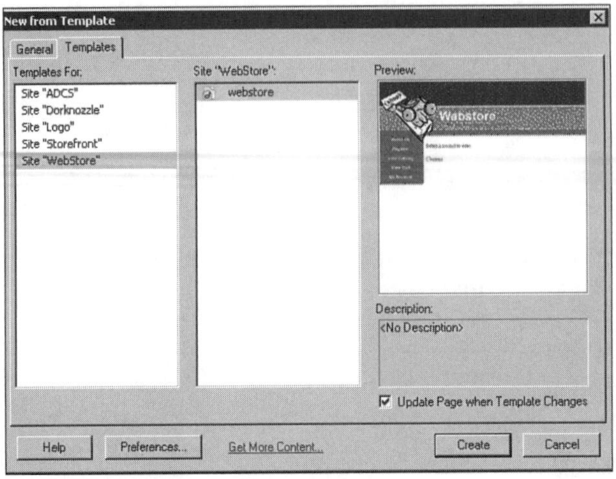

FIGURE 29.2   Create a new page from the WebStore template.

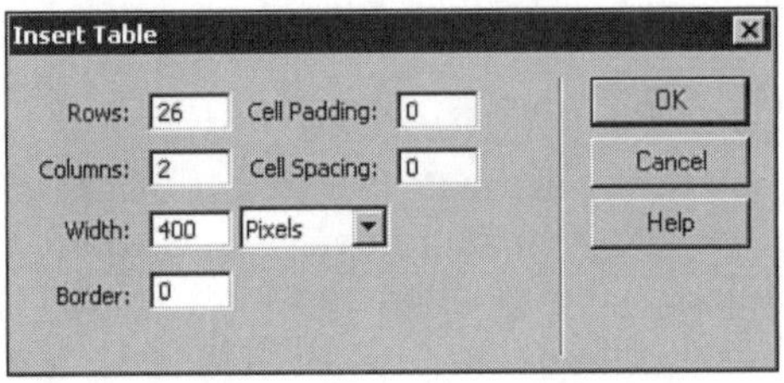

FIGURE 29.3   Create a new table by defining the rows, size, and so on.

4. Add all appropriate content for personal information, billing information, and shipping information. You can merge cells along the way to create the headers. The result is shown in Figure 29.4.

> **TIP**
>
> You can apply the "body" class from the Styles panel to make your text a bit more attractive.

5. You are now ready to begin adding all the form objects for the New User Registration form. The matrix below shows the fields, the appropriate form objects that should be inserted, and the names that should be given to each of the form objects.

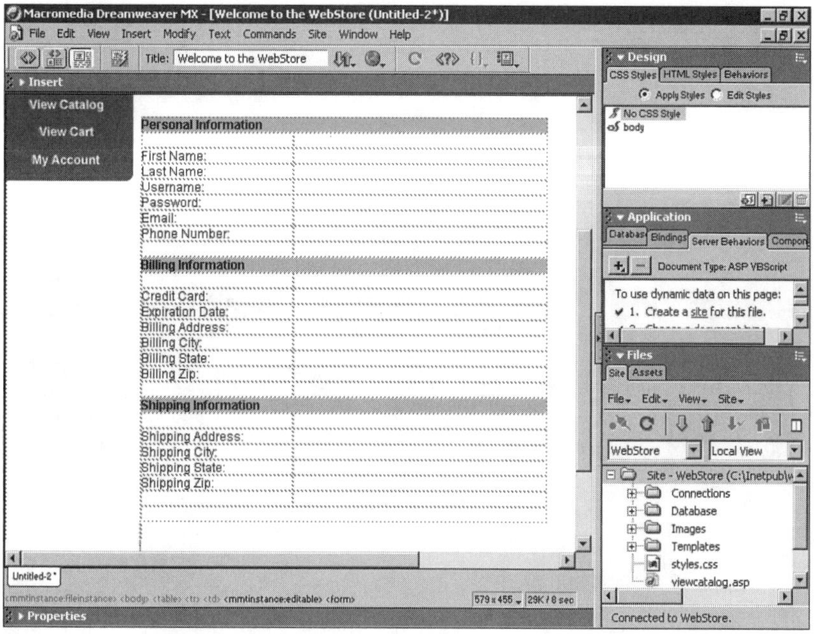

FIGURE 29.4   Add all appropriate content to the new table.

Field Name	Form Object	Name
First Name	Text Field	fname
Last Name	Text Field	lname
Username	Text Field	username
Password	Text Field	password
Email	Text Field	email
Phone Number	Text Field	phonenumber
Billing Address	Text Field	billingaddress
Billing City	Text Field	billingcity
Billing State	Text Field	billingstate
Billing Zip	Text Field	billingzip
Shipping Address	Text Field	shippingaddress
Shipping City	Text Field	shippingcity
Shipping State	Text Field	shippingstate
Shipping Zip	Text Field	shippingzip

29

Field Name	Form Object	Name
Credit Card Type	Menu	cctype
Credit Card Expiration	Menu	ccexpiration
	Submit Button	btnSubmit
	Reset Button	btnReset

The result of inserting all the form objects is shown in Figure 29.5.

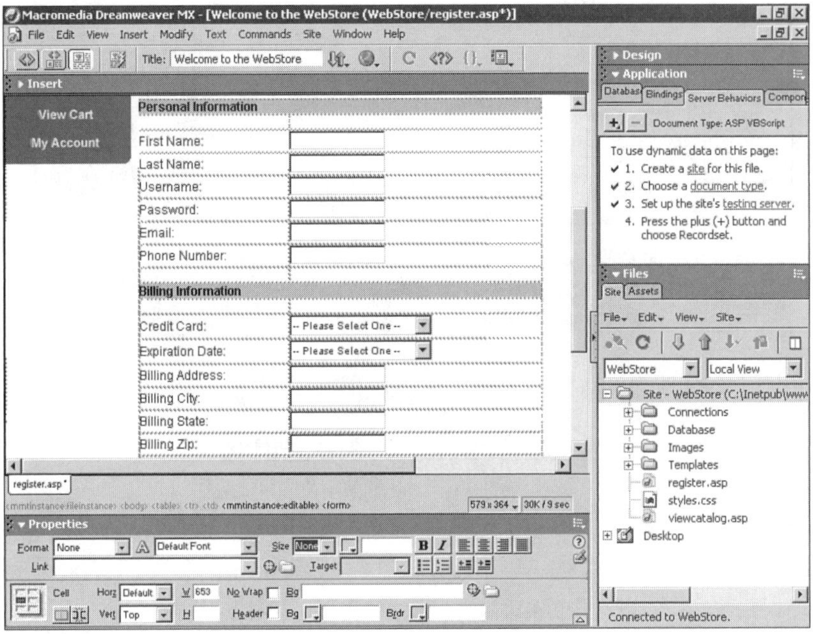

FIGURE 29.5   Insert all the form objects for the New User Registration.

TIP

Ideally you would want the credit card types to come from a separate table within the database called creditcardtypes and dynamically set the drop-down list based on the values within that table. For the sake of simplicity, you can hard-code the values in for the credit card type and expiration date.

---

6. Save the page as "register.asp" and run it within the browser. The result will look similar to Figure 29.6.

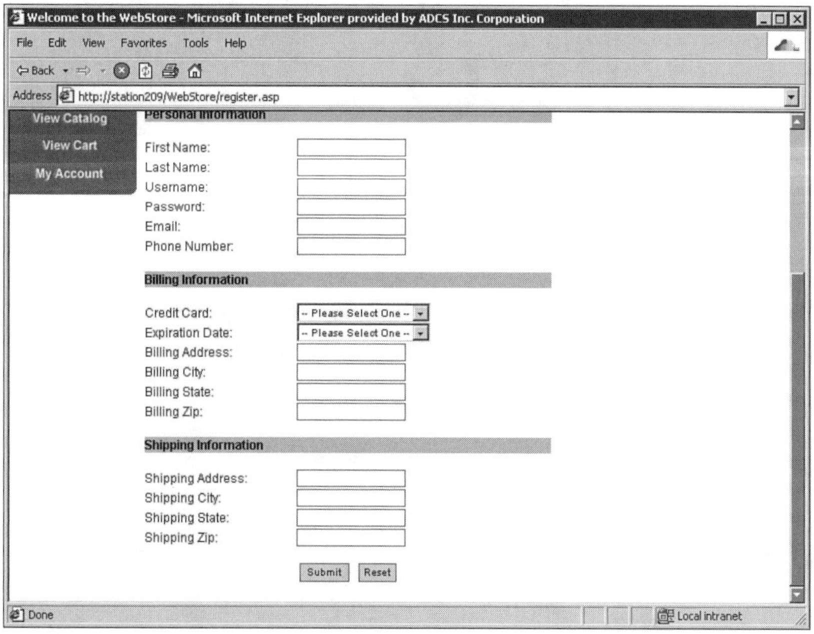

FIGURE 29.6   The New User Registration page allows the user to register for the Web store.

Inserting Records

Now that you have the New User Registration form created, you are ready to connect it to the database for insertion. Before you can begin adding any behaviors, you will want to create a new recordset for the customers and creditcards table. Remember, both the customers and creditcards tables exist as separate tables, so you will need to create a recordset that joins the two tables together. To create the recordset, follow the steps outlined next:

1. Open Access and create a New Query in design view.

2. Add the customers and creditcards tables as shown in Figure 29.7.

3. With the two tables added to the designer, select the fields that you want to include in the query. Figure 29.8 shows that you should include all the records for both the customers and creditcards tables. Remember, the "*" represents all fields.

4. To obtain the SQL code from the query that you have created, select SQL View from the View menu. Figure 29.9 shows the code that you can now copy.

29

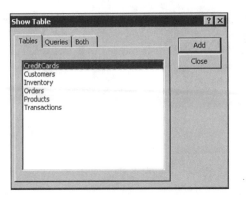

FIGURE 29.7   Add the customers and creditcards tables to the query designer.

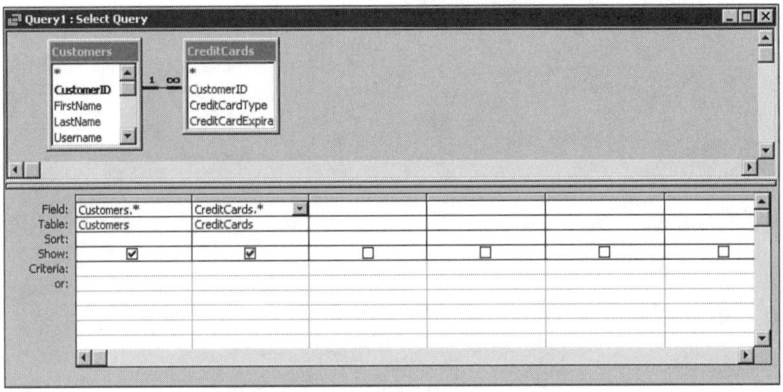

FIGURE 29.8   Select all the records for both tables.

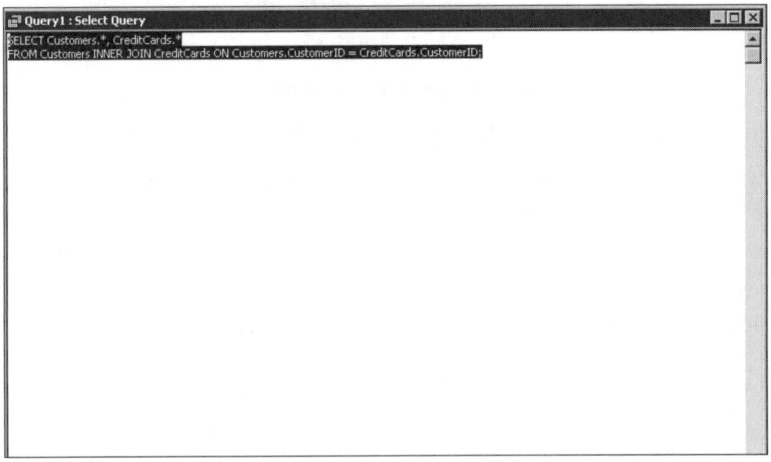

FIGURE 29.9   Copy the SQL code from the SQL View.

5. Save your query and close Access.

6. Return to the register.asp page and select Recordset from the Bindings panel. The Recordset dialog box appears.

7. Select the Advanced button and paste the code into the SQL box, as shown in Figure 29.10.

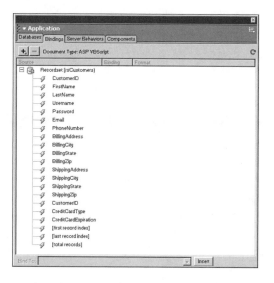

FIGURE 29.10   Paste the SQL code into the SQL box of the Advanced Recordset dialog box.

8. Select OK. The Bindings panel will now show the fields contained within the joined tables, as shown in Figure 29.11.

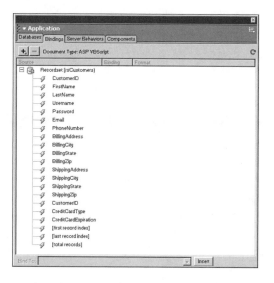

FIGURE 29.11   The recordset shows the fields from the joined tables.

Validating the Form

Now that you have the recordset created, you are ready to begin inserting the data into the database. But before you begin, make sure that you have valid data going in. The Validate Form behavior can be used to trap any errors on the client before a request is sent to the ASP application. For instance, because the PhoneNumber field within the customers table accepts only numeric values, you would not want to allow a user to insert anything but numbers into the Phone Number text field. The Validate Form behavior could allow you to check for invalid data and return an error message before the data is actually sent. To insert the behavior, follow the steps outlined next:

1. Select the Submit button and choose Validate Form from the Behaviors panel, as shown in Figure 29.12.

FIGURE 29.12   Insert the Validate Form behavior.

2. The Validate Form dialog box will appear. Choose Required for all the fields, Numbers for the Phone Number field, and E-mail Address for the E-mail field. The result is shown in Figure 29.13.

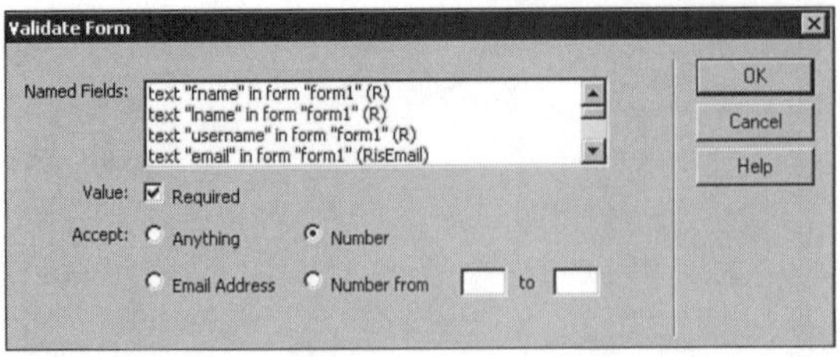

FIGURE 29.13   Select the appropriate options from the Validate Form dialog box.

3. Select OK.

4. Save your work and run it in the browser. Typing in incorrect data or forgetting to type in data in all fields results in an error message.

Inserting a New User into the Customers Table

Now that you can verify that the data being sent to the database is in fact legitimate, you can build the functionality for adding the data. Dreamweaver MX provides a server behavior in the Insert Record that allows for quick and intuitive insertions into the database. To insert the users record into the database, follow these steps:

1. Select Insert Record from the Server Behaviors panel, as shown in Figure 29.14.

FIGURE 29.14   Select the Insert Record server behavior.

2. The Insert Record dialog box appears. The Insert Record dialog box enables you to select a connection, a table to insert the data into, a page to redirect to after the data has been sent, the form to retrieve the values from, and a form elements selection box. The form elements selection box allows you to match up a form object with the corresponding field in the database. For the most part, Dreamweaver MX will find the match unless they are named differently, as is the case with fname and lname. If some do not match, select the appropriate match from the column drop-down list, as shown in Figure 29.15.

> **TIP**
>
> You may be wondering why the ccType and ccExpirationDate are ignored. These items were added to the new user registration form for demonstration purposes only. The database holds all the possible values for credit card and allows the user to choose which credit card they want to use upon checkout.

TIP

Confused about the difference between a form object and a form element? They're the same thing; they're just called form objects in the Insert menu and form elements in the Insert Record dialog box.

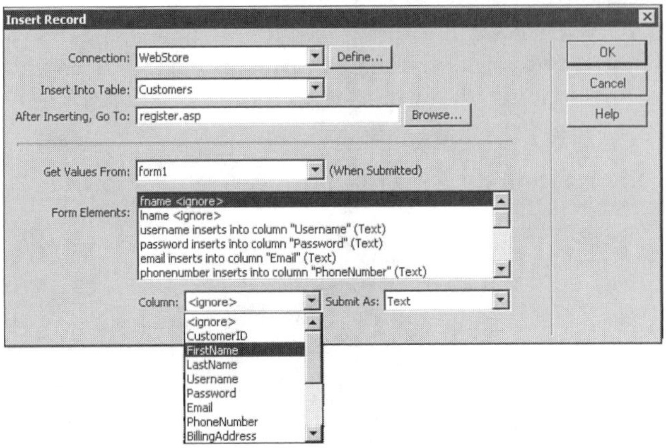

FIGURE 29.15 Match up the appropriate form object with its corresponding field in the database.

3. Select OK.
4. Save your work and run it in the browser. After you enter information into the fields and click Submit, it should redirect back to the same page.

TIP

You might want to create another page called confirm_newuser.asp. This page would alert users that their information has been successfully added. After you do that, you can change the redirect value within the Insert Record dialog box to that page.

5. Look at the customers tables within the database. Your values should appear as they do in Figure 29.16.

The Insert Record dialog box allows you to insert data into only one table. In the next section, you will modify the code to be able to insert data into both tables.

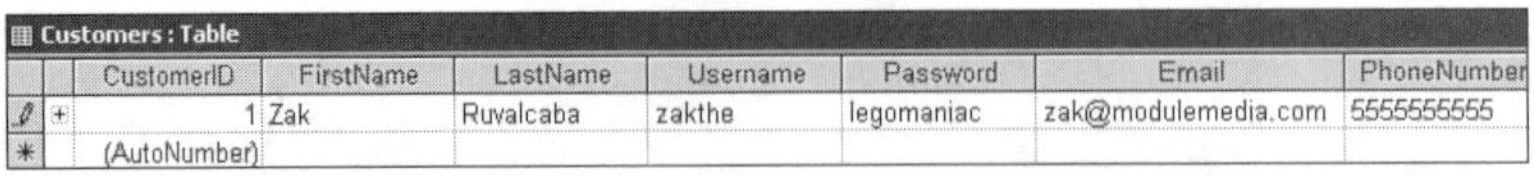
Customers : Table

CustomerID	FirstName	LastName	Username	Password	Email	PhoneNumber
1	Zak	Ruvalcaba	zakthe	legomaniac	zak@modulemedia.com	5555555555
(AutoNumber)						

FIGURE 29.16 The values from the form should go directly into the database.

Modifying the Code to Insert Data into Both Tables

Although Dreamweaver MX has many great features, it does not currently have the capability of inserting data into two tables at the same time. Although Macromedia does have a workaround for the problem, it does not currently have a solution that is usable within its framework.

NOTE

More information can be found about this problem from Macromedia's Web site at
`http://www.macromedia.com/support/ultradev/ts/documents/insert_mult_tables.htm`.

Currently the three choices for implementing multiple table insertions are as follows:

- Build separate pages to handle each table insert.

- Code the functionality by hand.

- Use stored procedures.

Because of the simplistic nature of the problem, we will code the functionality by hand. You can do this by rewriting the code that Dreamweaver MX creates for the recordset and subsequently adding your own Insert command to handle the insert to both tables.

1. Begin the process by removing the attached Insert Record server behavior.

2. Next switch to code view and scroll to the top of the page. You should see the same code as shown in Figure 29.17.

3. The code that you will be seeing creates and opens the recordset object. You can modify this code slightly to accommodate the multiple table insert. Replace the code you see with the following code:

```
Dim rsCustomers, objConn, cmdSQL
Set objConn = Server.CreateObject("ADODB.Connection")
Set rsCustomers = Server.CreateObject("ADODB.Recordset")

objConn = MM_Webstore_STRING
cmdSQL = "SELECT Customers.*, CreditCards.*
FROM Customers INNER JOIN CreditCards ON
Customers.CustomerID=CreditCards.CustomerID;"
rsCustomers.Open cmdSQL, objConn, 3, 3

If (Request.Form("btnSubmit") <> "") Then
rsCustomers.AddNew
rsCustomers ("FirstName") = Request.Form("fname")
rsCustomers ("LastName") = Request.Form("lname")
```

```
rsCustomers ("Username") = Request.Form("username")
rsCustomers ("Password") = Request.Form("password")
rsCustomers ("Email") = Request.Form("email")
rsCustomers ("PhoneNumber") = Request.Form("phonenumber")
rsCustomers ("BillingAddress") = Request.Form("billingaddress")
rsCustomers ("BillingCity") = Request.Form("billingcity")
rsCustomers ("BillingState") = Request.Form("billingstate")
rsCustomers ("BillingZip") = Request.Form("billingzip")
rsCustomers ("ShippingAddress") = Request.Form("shippingaddress")
rsCustomers ("ShippingCity") = Request.Form("shippingcity")
rsCustomers ("ShippingState") = Request.Form("shippingstate")
rsCustomers ("ShippingZip") = Request.Form("shippingzip")
rsCustomers ("CreditCardType") = Request.Form("cctype")
rsCustomers ("CreditCardExpiration") = Request.Form("ccexpiration")
rsCustomers.Update
End If
```

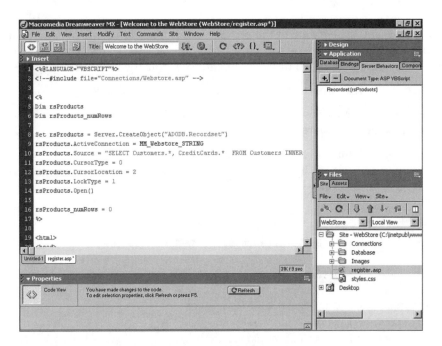

FIGURE 29.17   The recordset code can be modified to suit your needs.

4. Save your work and test it in the browser. Add the same information to all the form objects and click Submit. This time, rather than only the customers table receiving data, the creditcards table should receive data as well. Figure 29.18 shows the credit-cards table with data in it.

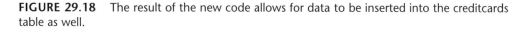

FIGURE 29.18   The result of the new code allows for data to be inserted into the creditcards table as well.

If you compare the original code to the code you just inserted, you can see that the only real differences lie in how the recordset was constructed, opened, and ultimately how the information was inserted.

Creating the My Account Page Using ASP

Now that you've added the functionality for your customers to insert their information into the database, you'll want to add more functionality to allow them to modify it. Suppose a customer moved to a new location and you shipped their product to their old address. You can imagine the confusion. Fortunately, Dreamweaver MX provides a behavior in the Update Record server behavior that enables you to develop a page for user administrative purposes.

Using dynamic form objects in conjunction with the Update Record server behavior, users will be able to see the information that resides in the database within editable form objects. After your customers edit the appropriate information, they need only to submit the form to update the information that lies within the database.

Creating the My Account Form

Because all the information will be placed into form objects, the My Account form will be constructed much the same way that the "register.asp" form was. To create the My Account form, follow these steps:

1. Create a new page from the WebStore template by selecting New from the File menu; then select the Advanced tab and select the WebStore template.

2. Change the Header editable region to My Account and replace the Content editable region by inserting a new form.

3. Change the action on the form to "myaccount.asp".

> **TIP**
>
> You can view the outline of the form by selecting the View Option button from the toolbar; then select Visual Aids and click Invisible Elements.

4. Copy the entire table from the register.asp page.

5. Paste the table into the form you just created within the My Account page. You will not need to change the names of any form objects.

6. Save the page as "myaccount.asp" and test it in the browser.

Working with Dynamic Form Elements

Now that you have the My Account form created, you will want to make all those form objects dynamic, meaning that when the page is loaded, text from the database automatically appears within them.

In the previous chapter, you learned how to create dynamic text by dragging an item from the recordset onto the page. Dynamic form objects are constructed much the same way in that you can drag an item from the recordset directly onto the form object that you want to bind that field to. Dynamic form objects can be created using one of three methods:

- Dragging a field from the recordset onto the form object.

- Using the Dynamic Form Elements server behaviors set.

- Select the form object and click the lightning bolt icon within the Properties Inspector to create a binding.

Either one of these three methods will do the job. Dragging an item from the recordset into the form object is probably the easiest and quickest way to accomplish the task, but for the sake of learning all the methods, try binding at least a few of the form objects using the process outlined next:

1. Insert a new row into your table just below Last Name. Create a new caption for Customer Number and add a new text field named CustomerID. This field will be used later so that Dreamweaver knows which record it has to update. You may also want to add the Disabled attribute to the tag so that users cannot change the value of this number.

2. Next, select Dynamic Text Field from the Dynamic Form Elements server behaviors submenu, as shown in Figure 29.19.

3. The Dynamic Text Field dialog box appears, allowing you to select the form object that you want dynamic. Select "fname" from the list and click the binding icon to set the value as shown in Figure 29.20.

4. After the Dynamic Data dialog box appears, you can select the field from the recordset that you want to bind the object to. You have the option to change the data type as well as the capability to modify the code if necessary. Select FirstName, as shown in Figure 29.21. Select OK.

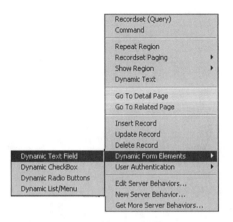

FIGURE 29.19   Select Dynamic Text Field from the Dynamic Form Elements submenu.

FIGURE 29.20   Select the binding icon to set the value of the dynamic form element.

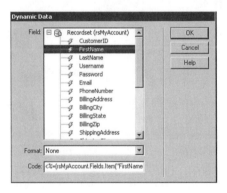

FIGURE 29.21   Select the field that you want to bind the object to and click OK.

5. The Dynamic Text Field dialog box will now have the value set. Select OK to complete the binding.

6. Figure 29.22 shows the text box with the appropriate field bound to it. Also notice that the properties inspector shows the bind within the Init Val field.

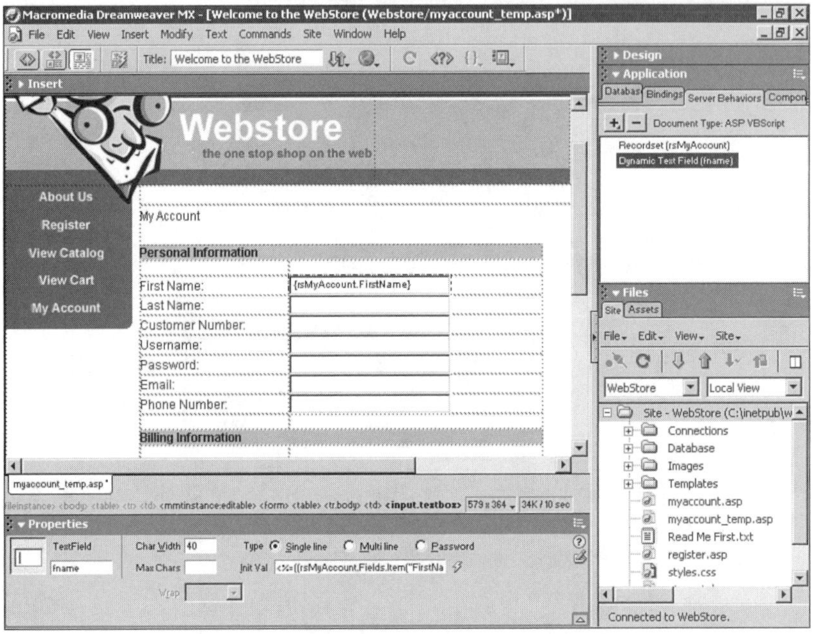

FIGURE 29.22   The field should now be bound to the appropriate form object.

7. Now that you have your first form object bound, you can create the rest of the form object bindings by using one of the three methods previously described. The only two form objects that you will not be binding are the Credit Card and Expiration Date form objects. Remember, these values are hard-coded in, and unless you want to create a separate table within the database, they will remain the same. When you are finished with the bindings, the result should look similar to Figure 29.23.

8. Save your work and run it in the browser. The result should look similar to Figure 29.24. Notice that all the data within the fields are bound according to the data that lies within the database.

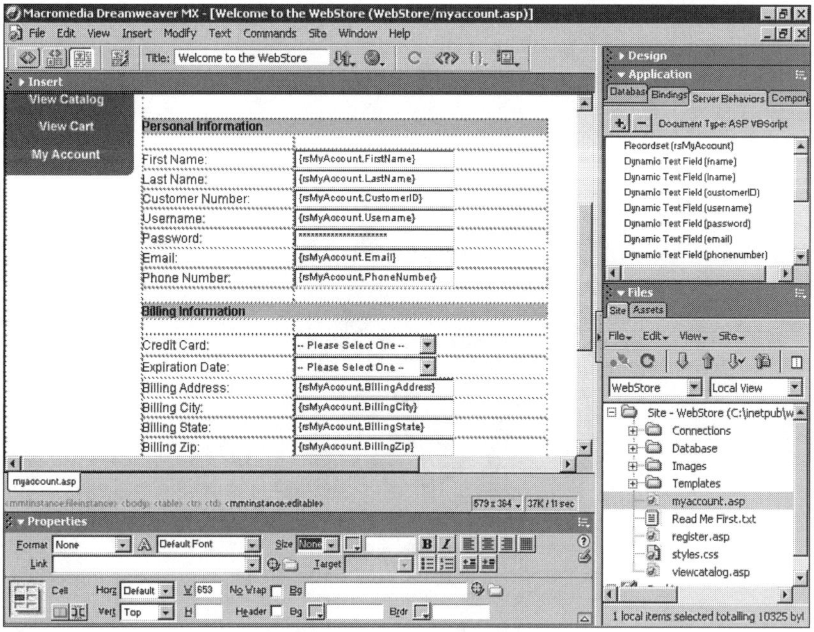

FIGURE 29.23   Bind all the form objects to complete the My Account page.

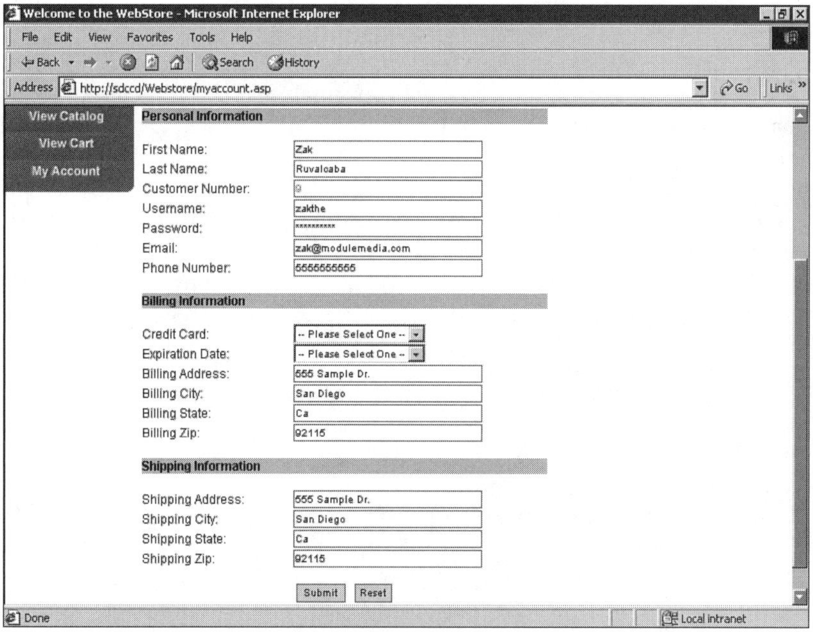

FIGURE 29.24   All the information within the database will show within the form objects.

Updating a User in the Customers Table

Now that you have the form created and all the objects are bound to the appropriate data fields, you are ready to add the functionality that enables users to modify their particular information. Remember the CustomerID text field you added into the form? This number will be used to track which customer is modifying information. If it weren't for this field containing the CustomerID, the Update Record server behavior would not be able to function properly. To add the Update Record functionality, follow the steps outlined next:

1. Select Update Record from the Server Behaviors panel, as shown in Figure 29.25.

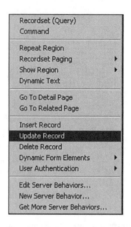

FIGURE 29.25   Insert the Update Record server behavior.

2. The Update Record dialog box enables you to select the connection, the table to update, the recordset to select the records from, the unique key column, and a URL to redirect to after the update takes place. The Update Record dialog box also enables you to match the form objects with the appropriate fields within the database. Remember to select "<ignore>" for the CustomerID. You are bound to receive an error if you try to update this field, as it is an automatically generated number within the database and is the reason you disabled the form object. Figure 29.26 shows the dialog box with all of the necessary modifications.

3. Save your work and test it in the browser. Figure 29.27 shows how you can change the original number, which was 5555555555, to 6666666666.

4. Click Submit.

Figure 29.28 shows the result of the change within the database.

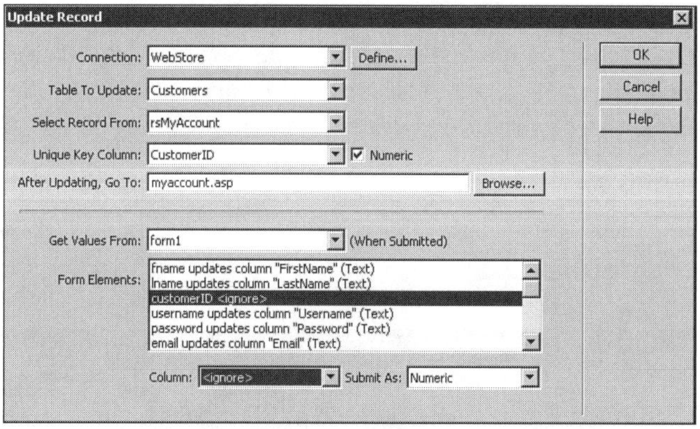

FIGURE 29.26   Complete the modification within the Update Record dialog box.

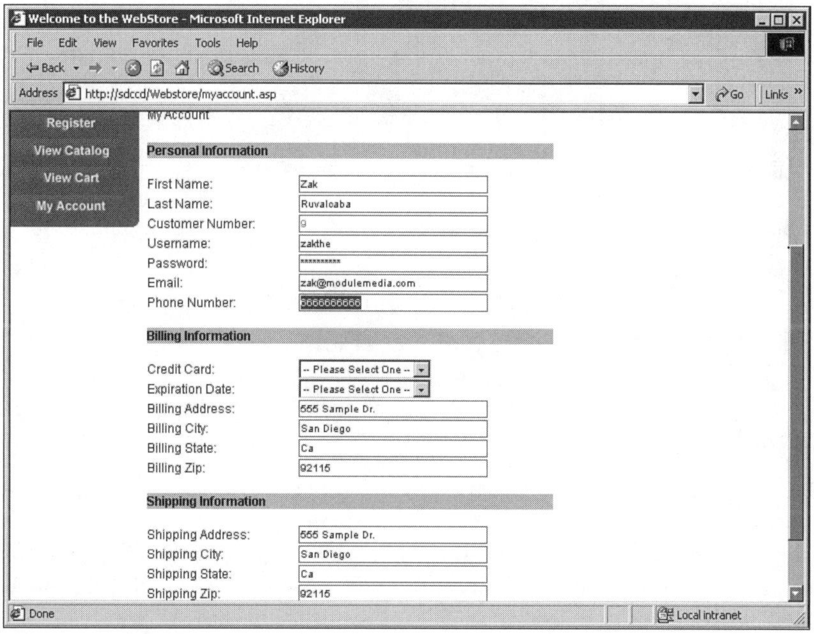

FIGURE 29.27   Change any of the form objects' default value.

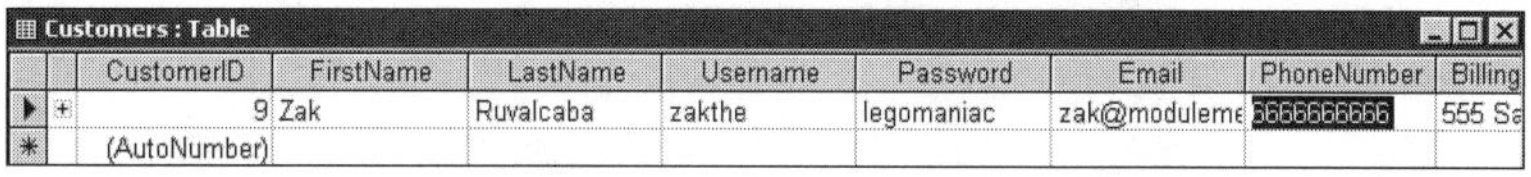

FIGURE 29.28   The PhoneNumber field within the database has been updated.

Modify the Code to Update Users' Information in Two Tables

Like the Insert Record server behavior, the Update Record server behavior supports only single table updates. Of course, like the Insert Record server behavior, the Update Record server behavior's code can be modified to accommodate multiple table updates.

1. Begin the process by removing the attached Update Record server behavior.

2. Switch to code view and scroll to the top of the page. You should see the same code as highlighted in Figure 29.29.

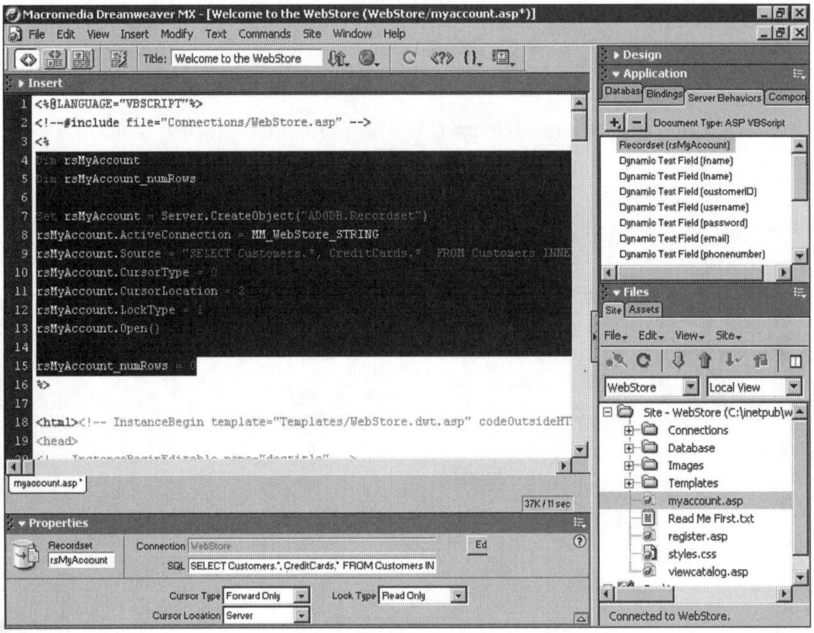

FIGURE 29.29   The recordset code can be modified to suit your needs.

3. The code that you will be seeing simply creates and opens the recordset object. You can modify this code slightly to accommodate the multiple table update. Add the following code:

```
Dim rsMyAccount, objConn, cmdSQL

Set objConn = Server.CreateObject("ADODB.Connection")
Set rsMyAccount = Server.CreateObject("ADODB.Recordset")

objConn = MM_Webstore_STRING
cmdSQL = "SELECT Customers.*, CreditCards.*
FROM Customers INNER JOIN CreditCards ON
Customers.CustomerID=CreditCards.CustomerID WHERE CustomerID=9;"
rsMyAccount.Open cmdSQL, objConn, 3, 3
```

```
If (Request.Form("btnSubmit") <> "") Then
rsMyAccount("FirstName") = Request.Form("fname")
rsMyAccount("LastName") = Request.Form("lname")
rsMyAccount("Username") = Request.Form("username")
rsMyAccount("Password") = Request.Form("password")
rsMyAccount("Email") = Request.Form("email")
rsMyAccount("PhoneNumber") = Request.Form("phonenumber")
rsMyAccount("BillingAddress") = Request.Form("billingaddress")
rsMyAccount("BillingCity") = Request.Form("billingcity")
rsMyAccount("BillingState") = Request.Form("billingstate")
rsMyAccount("BillingZip") = Request.Form("billingzip")
rsMyAccount("ShippingAddress") = Request.Form("shippingaddress")
rsMyAccount("ShippingCity") = Request.Form("shippingcity")
rsMyAccount("ShippingState") = Request.Form("shippingstate")
rsMyAccount("ShippingZip") = Request.Form("shippingzip")
rsMyAccount("CreditCardType") = Request.Form("cctype")
rsMyAccount("CreditCardExpiration") = Request.Form("ccexpiration")
rsMyAccount.Update
End If
```

4. Save your work and test it in the browser. Add the same information to all the form objects and click Submit. Figure 29.30 shows the changes made to the form objects.

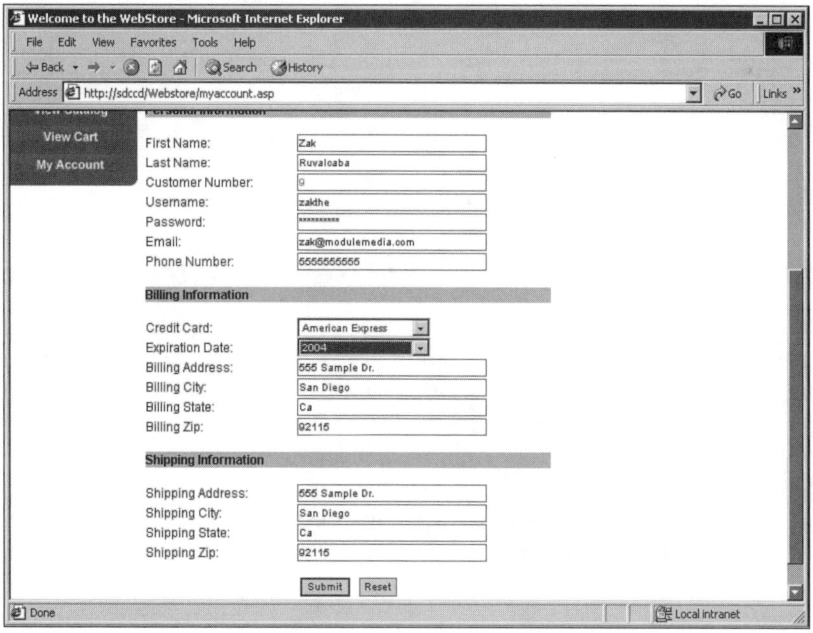

FIGURE 29.30 Change the form objects that you want to modify.

5. This time, rather than just the customers table receiving the modifications, the creditcards table does as well. Figure 29.31 shows the customers and creditcards tables with the modified data.

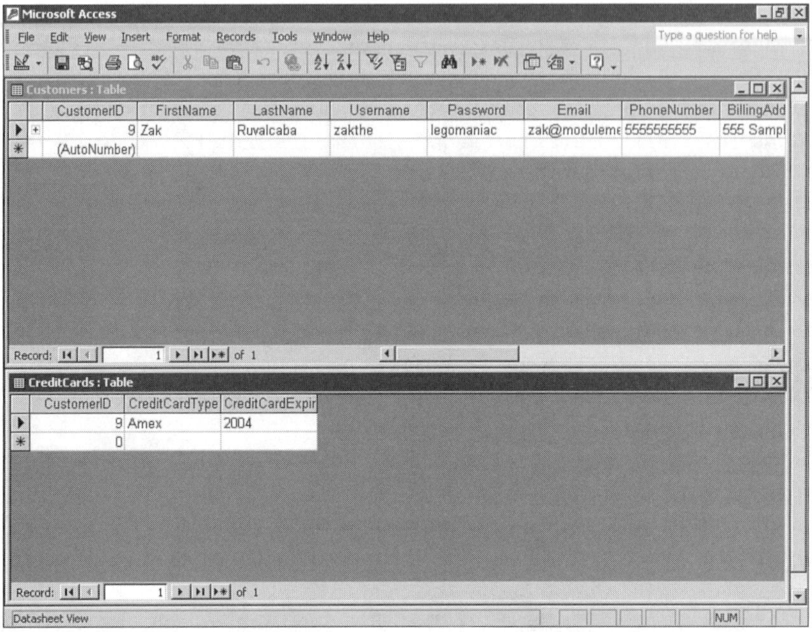

FIGURE 29.31   Both tables are updated with the appropriate information.

If you glance over the code that you customized for the Insert, you can see that the only real differences lie in the removal of the Add New statement, in renaming the recordset, and a filter was added to the SQL statement based on the ID to modify.

Building the Web Store New User Registration Page Using ASP.NET

Building the Web Store New User Registration page can be accomplished just as easily under the ASP.NET server model as it is with the ASP server model. In fact, there are subtle differences. Most of the differences between ASP.NET and ASP lie in the code, behaviors, and the interfaces that those behaviors implement. Of course, these changes will be pointed out when necessary. If you are specifically interested in ASP.NET and want to put aside the old technology in ASP, this section covers everything you need to know as it relates to Insert, Updates, and Deletes using ADO.NET within ASP.NET.

> **TIP**
>
> ADO.NET is Microsoft's next-generation technology for accessing data within relational and nonrelational databases.

Begin building the new pages by first taking a quick look at the Web Store database. The database reveals that you need to collect personal information and credit card information to process a visitor as a new user. Recall that the tables that make up customers' information lie within the customers and creditcards tables. Upon further inspection of those tables, you'll see that the following fields are necessary for new users to be created within the customers table:

Field Name	Date Type
CustomerID	AutoNumber
FirstName	Text
LastName	Text
Username	Text
Password	Text
Email	Text
PhoneNumber	Number
BillingAddress	Text
BillingCity	Text
BillingState	Text
BillingZip	Text
ShippingAddress	Text
ShippingCity	Text
ShippingState	Text
ShippingZip	Text

To associate a credit card with a particular customer, the following information also would need to be collected within the creditcards table.

Field Name	Date Type
CustomerID	AutoNumber
CreditCardType	Text
CreditCardExpiration	Text

Knowing the data that needs to reside within the database, you can now begin creating the New User Registration form to accommodate the data that will eventually be inserted.

Creating the New User Registration Form

Most ASP.NET driven Web applications simulate the fields within a database with Web controls. Because Web controls allow the user interaction with the Web application, they are the perfect channel for collecting information and subsequently inserting that information into the database. Before you can begin creating the New User Registration form, however, you must first create a table that will serve as the primary means for structuring the Web controls in a cohesive and usable fashion. Begin creating the table by following these steps:

1. Create a new page from a template. Select New from the File menu, navigate to the Templates tab, and select the WebStore template.

   > **WARNING**
   >
   > If you have not obtained the chapter files from www.dreamweavermxunleashed.com, you will not have the template available.

2. Place your cursor inside the editable region and insert a new form by selecting it from the Insert menu. This guarantees that the table you are about to insert gets placed directly into the form.

   > **TIP**
   >
   > Now switch to code view and insert the runat="server" into the form. Your ASP.NET page will not function correctly without this attribute. The result should look like this:
   >
   > `<form name="form1" runat="server"></form>`
   >
   > The method and action attributes are not required.

3. Now decide how many rows your table will contain. A quick count of all the necessary fields within the customers and creditcards tables reveals that you need about 16 rows. Place your cursor in the editable region containing the form tag and select Table from the Insert menu. Your values should be structured so that you have 26 rows, 2 columns, and a width of 400 pixels. Everything else should be set to 0.

4. Add all the appropriate content for personal information, billing information, and shipping information. You can merge cells along the way to create the headers. The result is shown in Figure 29.32.

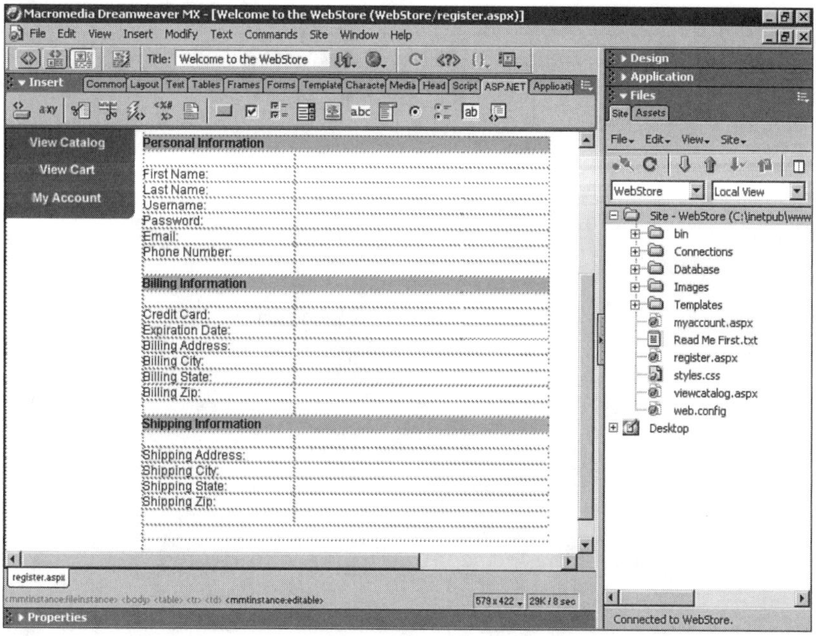

FIGURE 29.32   Add all the appropriate content to the new table.

TIP

You can apply the "body" class from the Styles panel to make your text a bit more attractive.

---

5. You are now ready to begin adding all the Web controls for the New User Registration form. You can insert all the controls either by selecting them from the Objects menu or by selecting ASP.NET Object from the Insert menu and selecting the appropriate control. The Tag Editor for the specific control enables you to customize all the attributes, including the ID, which is necessary for all Web controls to function properly. The matrix below shows the fields, the appropriate Web controls that should be inserted, and the IDs that should be given to each of the Web controls.

Field Name	Web Control	ID
First Name	Text Box	fname
Last Name	Text Box	lname
Username	Text Box	username
Password	Text Box	password
Email	Text Box	email
Phone Number	Text Box	phonenumber

Field Name	Web Control	ID
Billing Address	Text Box	billingaddress
Billing City	Text Box	billingcity
Billing State	Text Box	billingstate
Billing Zip	Text Box	billingzip
Shipping Address	Text Box	shippingaddress
Shipping City	Text Box	shippingcity
Shipping State	Text Box	shippingstate
Shipping Zip	Text Box	shippingzip
Credit Card Type	Menu	cctype
Credit Card Expiration	Menu	ccexpiration
Submit Button	btnSubmit	

6. The result of inserting all the Web controls is shown in Figure 29.33.

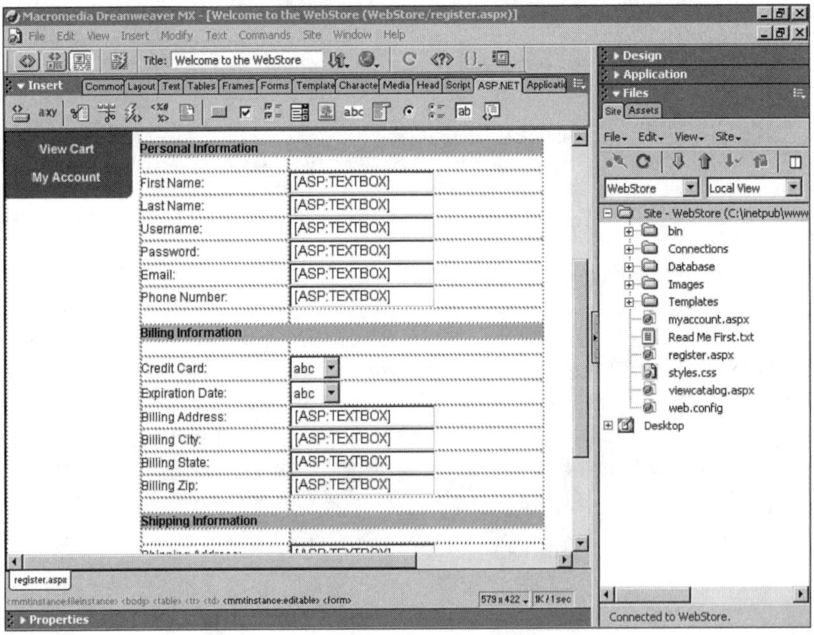

FIGURE 29.33 Insert all the Web controls for the New User Registration.

NOTE

Ideally you would want the credit card types to come from a separate table within the database called creditcardtypes and dynamically set the drop-down list based on the values within that table. For the sake of simplicity, you can hard-code the values in for the credit card type and expiration date.

7. Save the page as "register.aspx" and run it within the browser. The result will look similar to Figure 29.34.

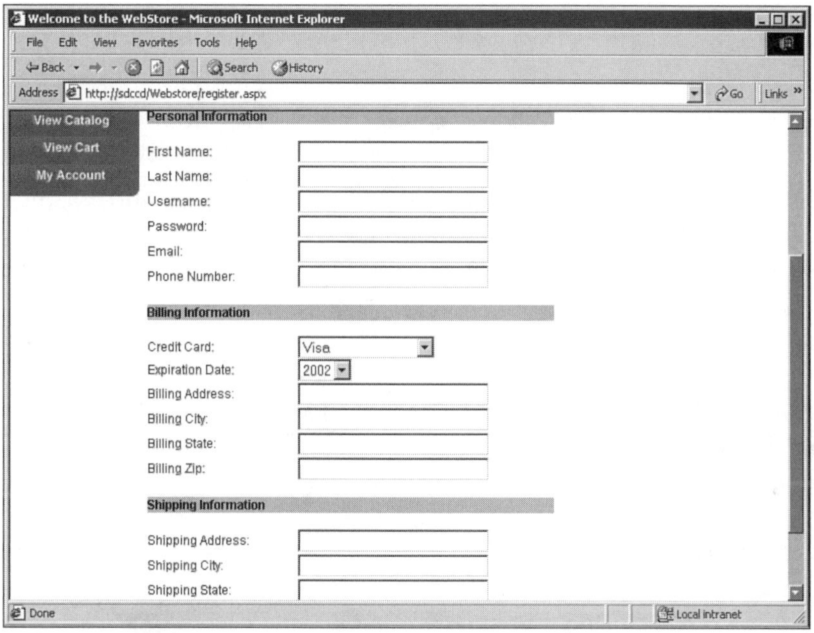

FIGURE 29.34   The New User Registration page allows the user to register for the Web store.

Save the page as "register.aspx" and run it within the browser. The result will look similar to Figure 29.34.

Validating the Form with Validation Controls

Now that you have the form created, you are ready to begin inserting the data into the database. But before you begin, you want to make sure that you have valid data going in. Validation controls can be used to trap any errors on the client before a request is sent to the ASP application. For instance, because the PhoneNumber field within the customers table accepts only numeric values, you would not want to allow a user to insert anything but numbers into the Phone Number text field. The use of Validation controls could allow you to check for invalid data and return an error message before the data is actually sent. There are numerous types of validation controls, including the following:

- **RequiredFieldValidator**   The RequiredFieldValidator is used to make a particular control a required entry.

- **CompareValidator**   The CompareValidator compares the value of a control with the value of another.

- **RangeValidator**   The RangeValidator checks to make sure that the value of a control falls between a certain range.

- **RegularExpressionValidator**   The RegularExpressionValidator checks for patterns using regular expressions.

- **ValidationSummary**   Display a list of errors within one alert box using ValidationSummary.

You can insert a RequiredFieldValidator control into your application by following these steps:

1. Switch to code view and navigate to the bottom of the page until you find the <asp:button> control. Enter the following attribute to turn validation on for the form: causesvalidation="True". The line of code should result in the following:

```
<asp:button id="btnSubmit" causesvalidation="True" Text="submit"
➡runat="server"></asp:button>
```

2. Switch back to design view and place your cursor next to the First Name text box control. Switch back to code view.

3. Select Tag from the Insert Menu. Navigate to ASP.NET Objects, select Validation Server Controls, and highlight RequiredFieldValidator, as shown in Figure 29.35. Choose Insert.

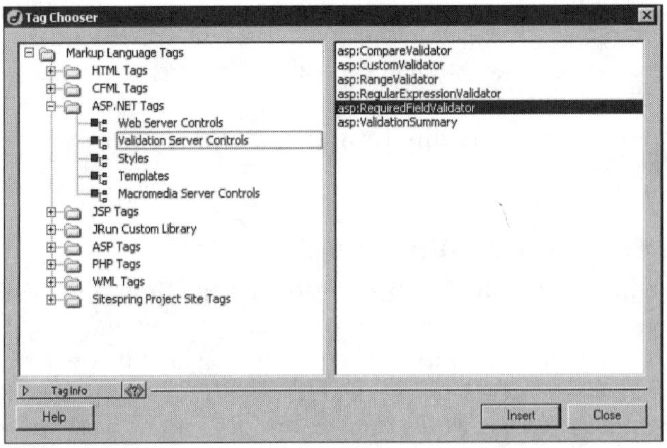

FIGURE 29.35   Insert the RequiredFieldValidator control.

4. Give your validation control an ID, the name of the control to validate, and a custom error message as shown in Figure 29.36. Choose OK.

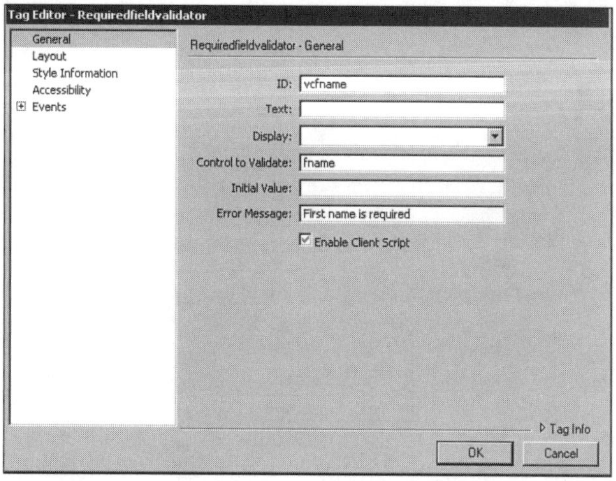

FIGURE 29.36   Enter all the appropriate information for your validation control.

5. Select Close. Your new validation control should now be inserted.

6. Save your work and run it in the browser. Not typing a value for First Name will result in an error message, as shown in Figure 29.37.

7. Repeat the process until all controls have a RequiredFieldValidator associated with them.

Inserting a New User

Now that your form is created and all your controls will be validated, you are ready to insert the data into the database. Dreamweaver MX provides a server behavior in the Insert Record that allows for quick and intuitive insertions into the database. To insert the user's record into the database, follow the steps outlined next:

1. Select Insert Record from the Server Behaviors panel.

2. The Insert Record dialog box appears. The Insert Record dialog box enables you to select a connection, a table, or a view to insert the data into, a page to redirect to after the data has been sent, the form to retrieve the values from, and a columns box allowing you to match up the appropriate Web control with its respective field. For the most part, Dreamweaver MX will find the match unless they are named differently, as is the case with fname and lname. If some do not match, select the appropriate match from the value drop-down list, as shown in Figure 29.38.

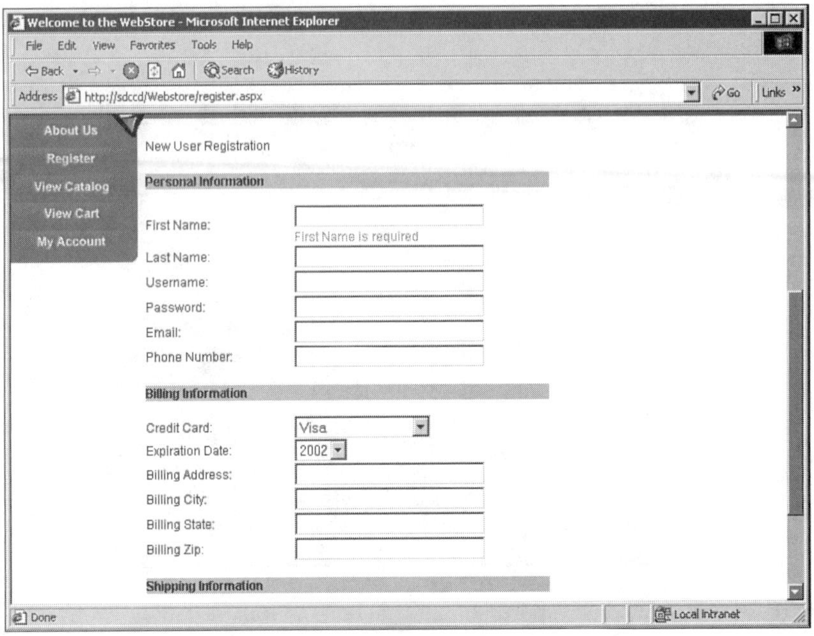

FIGURE 29.37 Forgetting to type in a value results in an error message.

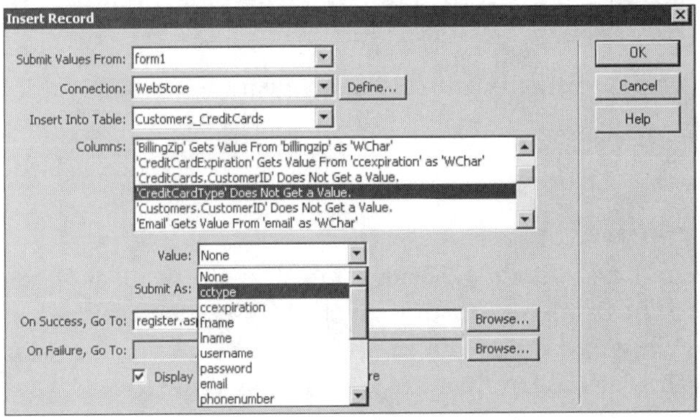

FIGURE 29.38 Match up the appropriate Web control with its corresponding field in the database.

NOTE

Unlike with the ASP server model, the Insert Record server behavior within the ASP.NET server model supports insertions into View. Remember the queries that you created and saved in Access that joined multiple tables? These are also known as views. Dreamweaver MX can use these views to insert data into multiple tables. The views appear within the Insert into Table drop-down list at the bottom. Notice that they are the same names as the saved queries within your Access database.

---

3. Select OK.

4. Save your work and run it in the browser. After you enter information into the fields and click Submit, it should redirect back to the same page.

> **TIP**
>
> You may want to create another page called "confirm_newuser.aspx". This page would alert users that their information has been successfully added. After you do that, you can change the redirect value within the Insert Record dialog box to that page.

5. Look at the customers and creditcards tables within the database. Your values should appear as they do in Figure 29.39.

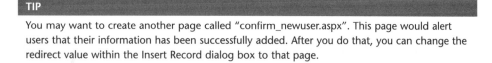

FIGURE 29.39   The values from the form should go directly into the database.

Creating the My Account Page Using ASP.NET

Now that you've added the functionality for your customers to insert their information into the database, you'll want to add more functionality to allow them to modify it. Suppose a customer moved to a new location and you shipped their product to their old address. You can imagine the confusion. Fortunately, Dreamweaver MX provides a behavior in the Update Record server behavior that enables you to develop a page for user administrative purposes.

Using dynamic Web controls in conjunction with the Update Record server behavior, users will be able to see the information that resides in the database within editable Web controls. After your customers edit the appropriate information, they need only to submit the form to update the information that lies within the database.

Creating the My Account Form

Because all the information will be placed into Web controls, the My Account form will be constructed much the same way that the register.aspx form was. To create the My Account form, follow the steps outlined next:

1. Create a new page from the WebStore template by selecting New from the File menu; then select the Advanced tab and select the WebStore template.

2. Change the Header editable region to My Account and replace the Content editable region by inserting a new form.

> **CAUTION**
>
> When inserting a new form, don't forget to go into the code and add a `runat="server"` attribute.

> **TIP**
>
> You can view the outline of the form by selecting the View Option button from the toolbar, selecting Visual Aids, and clicking Invisible Elements.

3. Copy the entire table from the "register.aspx" page.

4. Paste the table into the form you just created within the My Account page. You will not need to change the names of any Web controls.

5. Save the page as "myaccount.aspx" and test it in the browser.

Binding Form Elements

Now that you have the My Account form created, you will want to make all those Web controls dynamic, meaning that when the page is loaded, text from the database automatically appears within them.

In the previous chapter, you learned how to create dynamic text by dragging an item from the DataSet onto the page. Dynamic Web controls are constructed much the same way in that you can drag an item from the DataSet directly onto the form object that you want to bind that field to. You can start binding all your Web controls using the following process:

1. Create a new DataSet by selecting DataSet from the Bindings panel. When the DataSet dialog box appears, enter a new DataSet name, select the connection, and choose the Customers_CreditCards view for the table. Figure 29.40 shows the results.

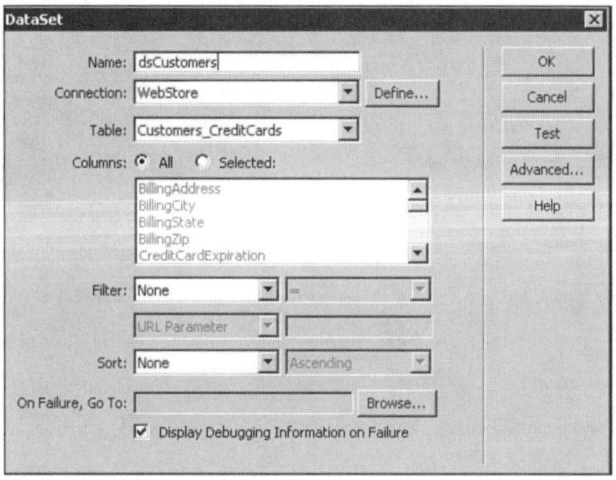

FIGURE 29.40   Enter all the appropriate information for your new DataSet.

2. Select OK. Figure 29.41 shows the Bindings panel with all the fields contained within your new DataSet.

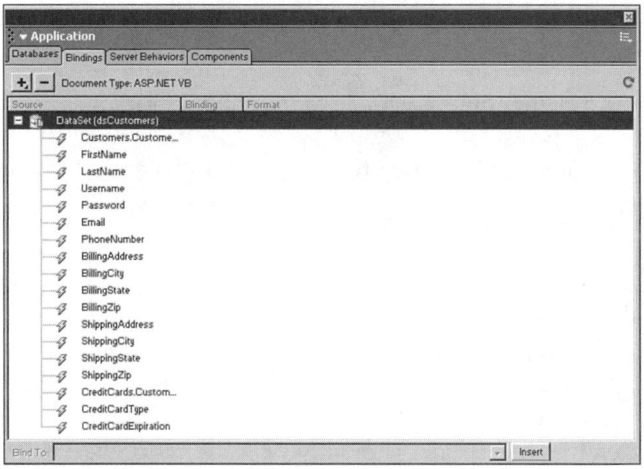

FIGURE 29.41   Expand the DataSet to view all the fields.

3. Insert a new row into your table just below Last Name. Create a new caption for Customer Number and add a new text box control with the ID CustomerID. This field will be used later so that Dreamweaver MX knows which record it has to update. You may also want to add the Disabled attribute to the tag so that users cannot change the value of this number.

4. Drag each field from the DataSet into its corresponding control. When you have all the controls bound, the result will look similar to Figure 29.42.

29

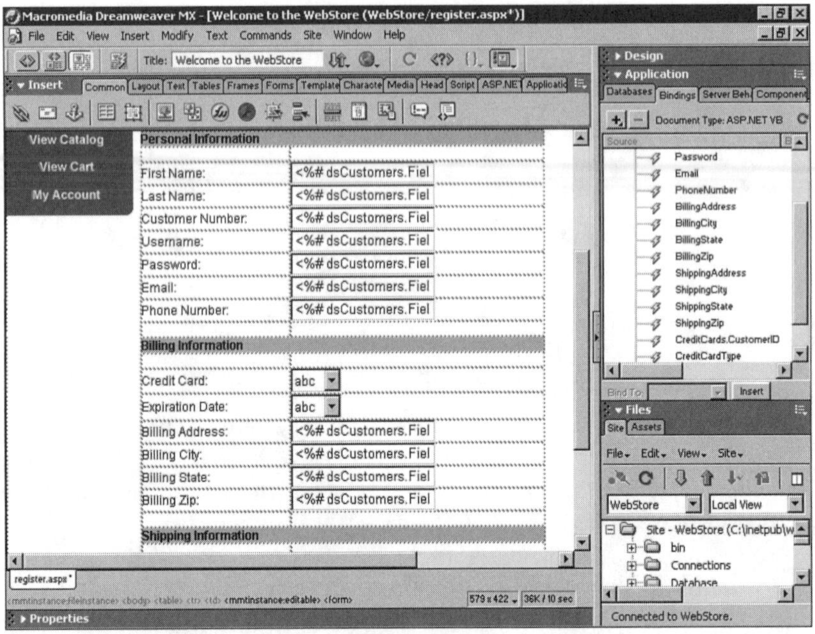

FIGURE 29.42 Bind all the controls with fields from the DataSet.

5. Save your work and run it in the browser. The result should look similar to Figure 29.43. Notice all the data within the fields is bound according to the data that lies within the database.

Updating an Existing User

Now that you have the form created and all the objects are bound to the appropriate data fields, you are ready to add the functionality that allows users to modify their particular information. Remember the CustomerID text field you added into the form? This number will be used to track which customer is modifying information. If it weren't for this field containing the CustomerID, the Update Record server behavior would not be able to function properly. To add the Update Record functionality, simply follow these steps:

1. Select Update Record from the Server Behaviors panel.

The Update Record dialog box allows you to select the connection, table or view to update, the form to select the object values from, the columns to update to, and a URL to redirect to after the update takes place. The Update Record dialog box also allows you to match the Web controls with the appropriate fields within the database. Figure 29.44 shows the dialog box with all the necessary modifications.

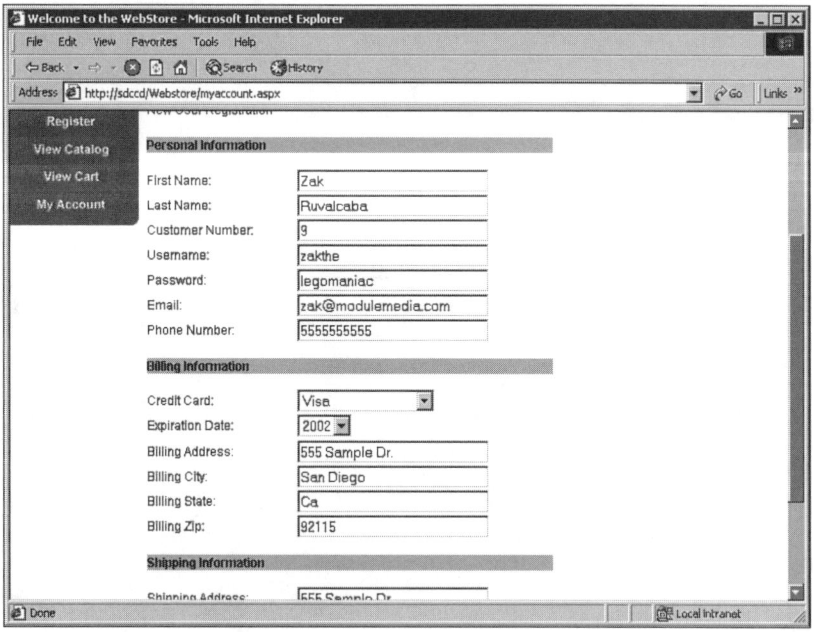

FIGURE 29.43 All the information within the database will show within the form objects.

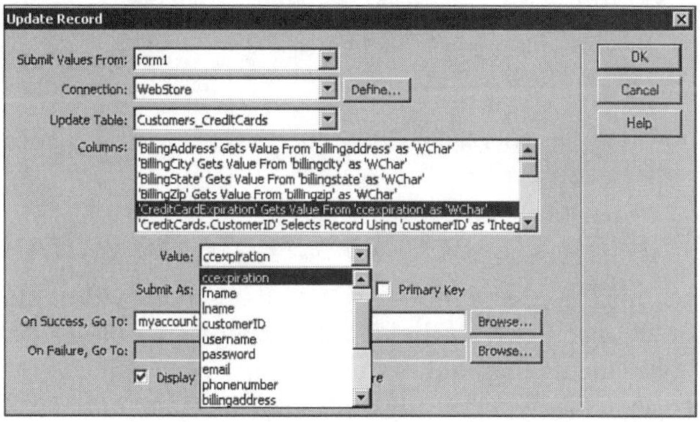

FIGURE 29.44 Complete the modifications within the Update Record dialog box.

2. Save your work and test it in the browser. Figure 29.45 shows how you can change the original phone number which was 5555555555 to 6666666666.

3. Click Submit.

Figure 29.46 shows the result of the change within the database.

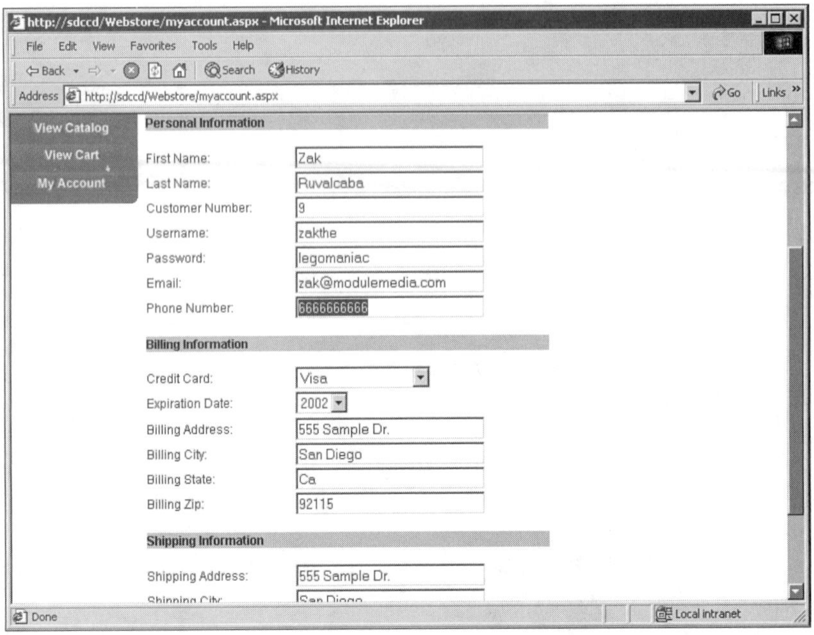

FIGURE 29.45   Change the default value for any of the form objects.

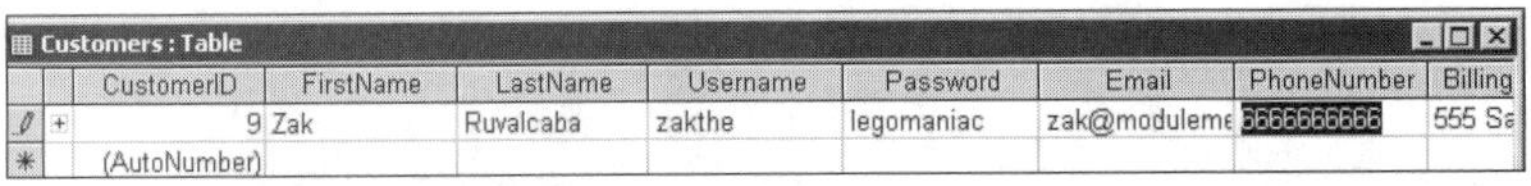

FIGURE 29.46   The PhoneNumber field within the database has been updated.

Using Application Objects to Create an Admin Page

Aimed at giving you quick access to sophisticated interactivity without having to rely on the various panels that encompass all the objects, application objects are basically predesigned Web components that you can use within your application. Application objects are easy to use; in fact, you already used some of them and may not have even known it. Application objects include the following:

- **Recordset**   Launches the Recordset dialog box that you would normally receive when selecting the Recordset server behavior from the Bindings panel.

- **Dynamic Table**   Enables you to quickly create and format a table complete with bound data from your recordset on-the-fly.

- **Dynamic Text**   Creates dynamic text from your recordset on-the-fly.

- **Recordset Navigation Bar**   Inserts First, Last, Previous, and Next pagination server behaviors complete with the Show Region behavior attached.

- **Recordset Navigation Status**   Displays a status message for which record the user is on while paging.

- **Repeated Region**   Creates a repeated region for a dynamic table.

- **Master Detail Page Set**   Arguably the most widely used application object, the master detail page set allows a developer to create a low detail page that links to a second more detailed page for a particular record.

- **Record Insertion Form**   Enables you to quickly build a form, complete with form objects that you specify, that when submitted, inserts into a table within the database.

- **Record Update Form**   Similar to the Record Insertion Form application objects, the Record Update Form enables you to build a form, complete with bound form objects, that allows your users to modify information within the database.

Dynamic Tables

You can quickly begin building an administration page for the Web store using some of the application objects that come prebundled with Dreamweaver MX. An admin page is a good way of keeping track and viewing products within your site, as well as deleting unnecessary items that you may not want.

> **NOTE**
>
> The admin page is built under an ASP server model. If you have not already done so, you may want to download the support files from www.dreamweavermxunleashed.com.

You can begin building the admin page by following the steps outlined next:

1. Create a new page by selecting New from the File menu. Select the Advanced tab and pick the WebStore template.

2. You now want to build a new query for your new recordset. Launch Access, select Create Query in Design View, and insert the products and inventory tables in the designer.

3. Rather than selecting all the records within the database, select ProductID, ProductName, and ProductCost from the products table and Quantity from the inventory table. The result is shown in Figure 29.47.

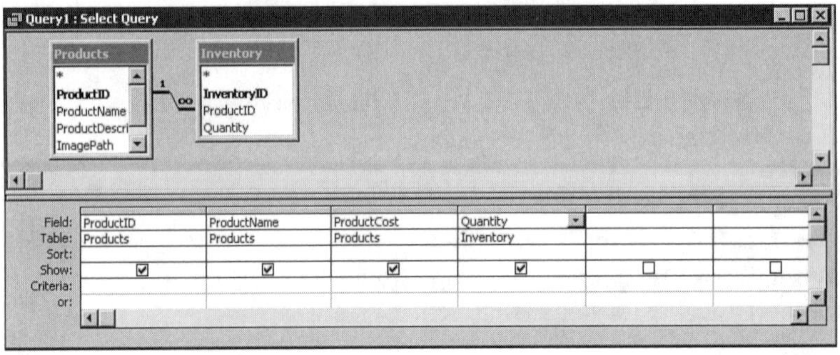

FIGURE 29.47   Begin generating a new query by selecting fields from the products and inventory tables.

4. Select SQL View from the View menu and copy the code. Save your query and close Access.

5. Create a new recordset by selecting it from the Application Objects submenu. Click the Advanced button and paste in the SQL code as shown in Figure 29.48.

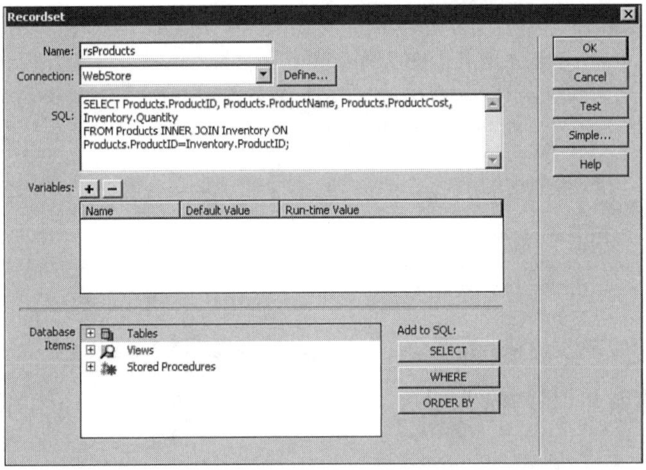

FIGURE 29.48   Paste the code into the SQL box.

6. Select OK.

7. Insert a new form into the page. This will come in handy later when you include delete functionality into the admin page.

8. Select Dynamic Table from the Application Objects submenu. The Dynamic Table dialog box appears. Figure 29.49 shows all the values that the table within the admin page will contain.

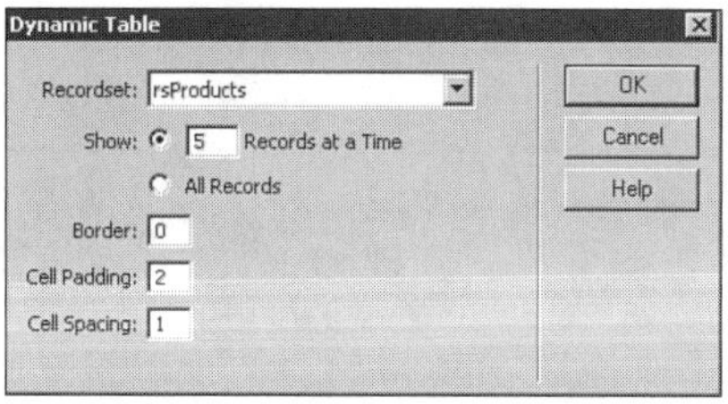

FIGURE 29.49   The Dynamic Table dialog box enables you to enter values for the creation of a table with dynamic text.

9. Select OK. The table is inserted into the workspace as shown in Figure 29.50. Make any necessary aesthetic adjustments.

FIGURE 29.50   The table shows the dynamic text within table cells.

10. Save your work as "admin.asp" and test it in the browser. The result will look similar to Figure 29.51.

29

FIGURE 29.51   Five records are shown within the table.

The Recordset Navigation Bar

Now that you have a dynamic table with data, you can use the recordset navigation bar object to include pagination. Rather than inserting four separate paging server behaviors along with four separate Show Region server behaviors, you can use the recordset navigation bar to accomplish the task in a few simple clicks. To insert a recordset navigation bar, follow these steps:

1. Place your cursor just below the dynamic table that you have just created and select Recordset Navigation Bar from the Application Objects submenu.

2. The Recordset Navigation Bar dialog box appears, enabling you to choose the recordset. You can also choose to use text or images as your navigational items. The result is shown in Figure 29.52.

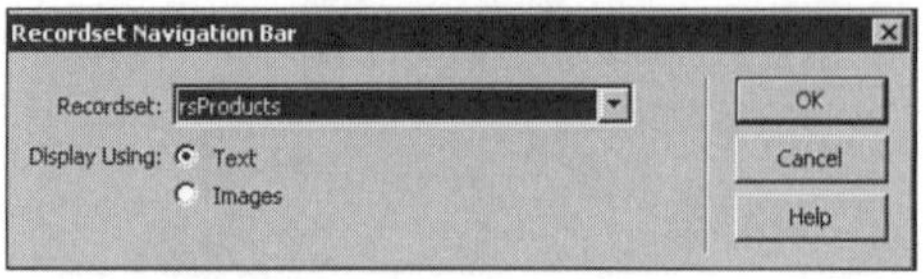

FIGURE 29.52   Choose the recordset to page through.

3. Figure 29.53 shows the navigation bar. Notice how all four navigational items are present. The Show Region server behaviors that are attached will cause these items to shift from being visible to invisible, depending on where you are within the record-set.

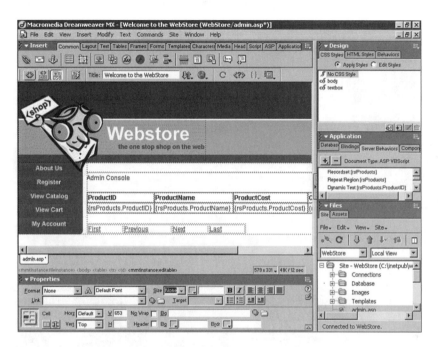

FIGURE 29.53   The navigational bar is inserted into your workspace.

4. Save your work and test it in the browser. The result will look similar to Figure 29.54. Notice that you are able to paginate five records at a time.

Deleting Records

Ordinarily you would not want to give your customers permission to delete their information. For the most part, that task should be left up to an administrator. Inserting a delete record functionality can be accomplished just as easily as the insert record or update record functionality was through the use of the Delete Record server behavior. The Delete Record server behavior enables you to add record deletion based on a form submit. To add the delete record functionality to the admin page, follow these steps:

1. Add a new column into the table by right-clicking in the productID column and selecting Insert Column from the Table submenu.

2. Insert a new button from the Form submenu directly into the new column, change the label to Delete, and the type to "None". The result is shown in Figure 29.55.

29

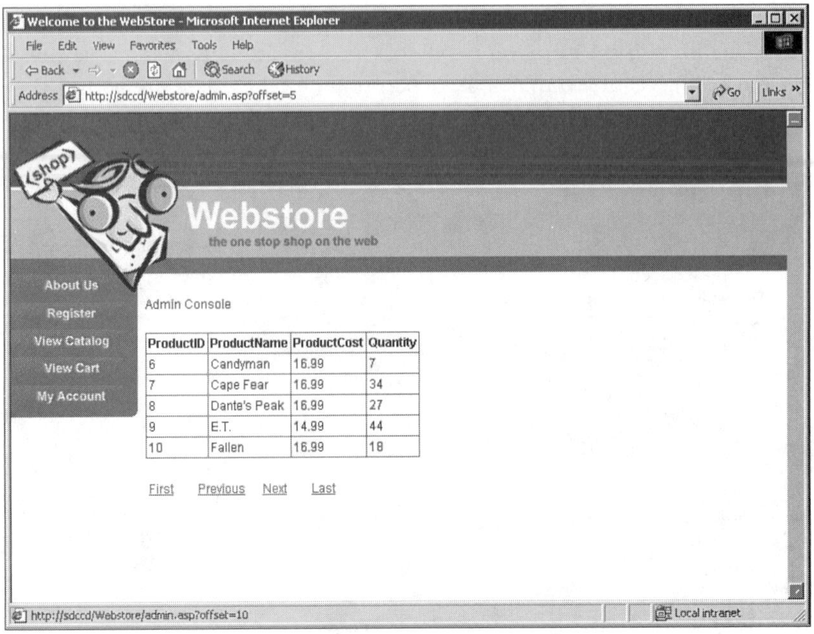

FIGURE 29.54   You are now able to paginate five records at a time.

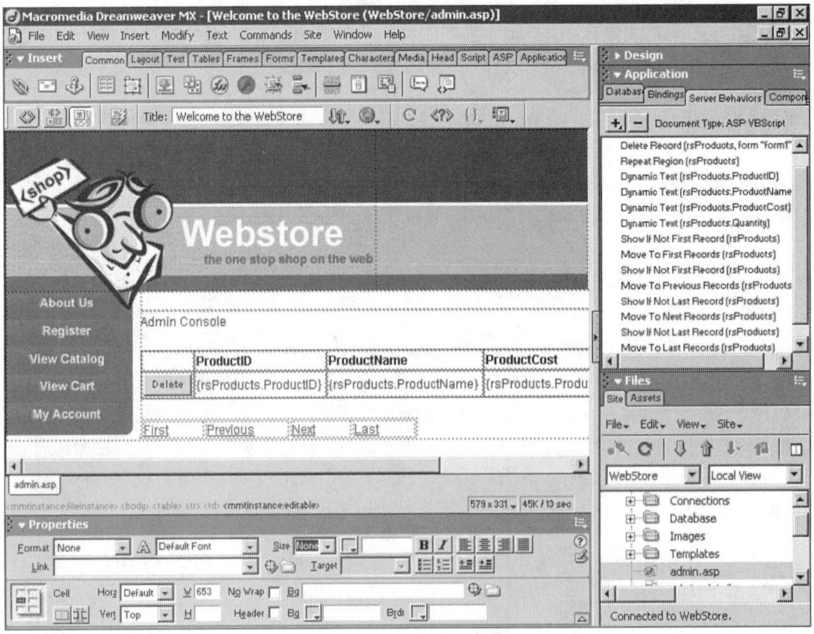

FIGURE 29.55   Insert a Submit button labeled Delete into the new column.

3. Select Delete Record from the Server Behaviors panel.

4. The Delete Record dialog box enables you to choose a connection, a table to delete from, the recordset to delete the item from, the unique key column, the form in which the data is contained, and a page to redirect to after the delete has been processed. The result is shown in Figure 29.56.

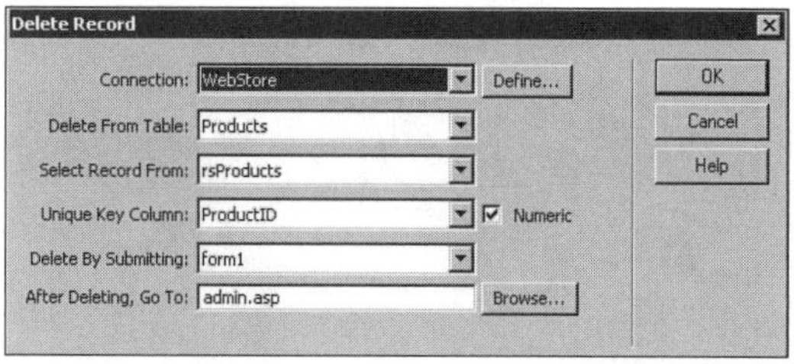

FIGURE 29.56   Insert the appropriate data into the Delete Record dialog box.

5. Save your work and test the admin page in the browser. Navigate a few records and select Delete.

6. Check the database to confirm the deletion.

Master Detail Page Set

The master detail page set application object is one of the most powerful objects built into Dreamweaver MX. The master detail page set enables you to create a single page with as many fields from the recordset as you like. You can make one of the items linkable to a detail page that exposes all the items for that record. The master detail page set is a great component to use when you do not want to expose all the fields within the recordset at once but instead, expose just a couple, allowing a user to see greater detail whenever the user wants by selecting a link. You can insert the master detail page set object by following the steps outlined next:

1. Remove all the other behaviors and recordset from the Server Behaviors panel.

2. Open Access and copy the SQL code from the previously created query that contained all the records from the products and inventory tables. Close Access.

3. Create a new recordset within Dreamweaver MX with the code that you just copied.

4. Place your cursor in the Content editable region and select the Master Detail Page Set from the Application Objects submenu.

5. The Insert Master Detail Page Set dialog box appears. The dialog box enables you to choose a Recordset, data to appear within the master page, the item you want linkable, the unique key to pass to the new page, how many records to show at a given time, the name of the detail page, and the fields to include within the detail page. The results are shown in Figure 29.57.

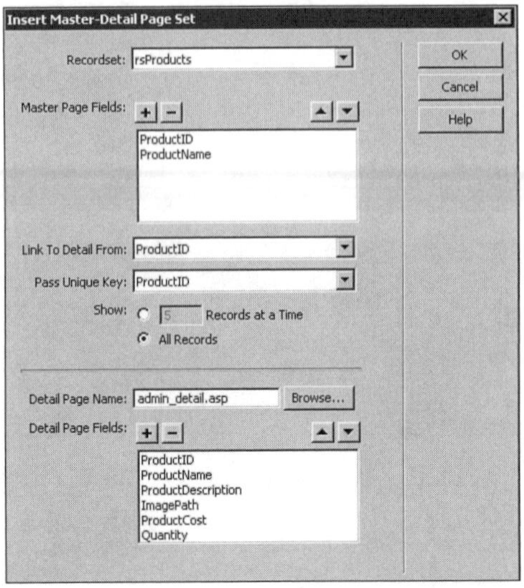

FIGURE 29.57   Insert the appropriate data within the Insert Master Detail Page Set dialog box.

6. Select OK. You will be taken immediately to the detail page as shown in Figure 29.58. Format the table accordingly. Save the page.

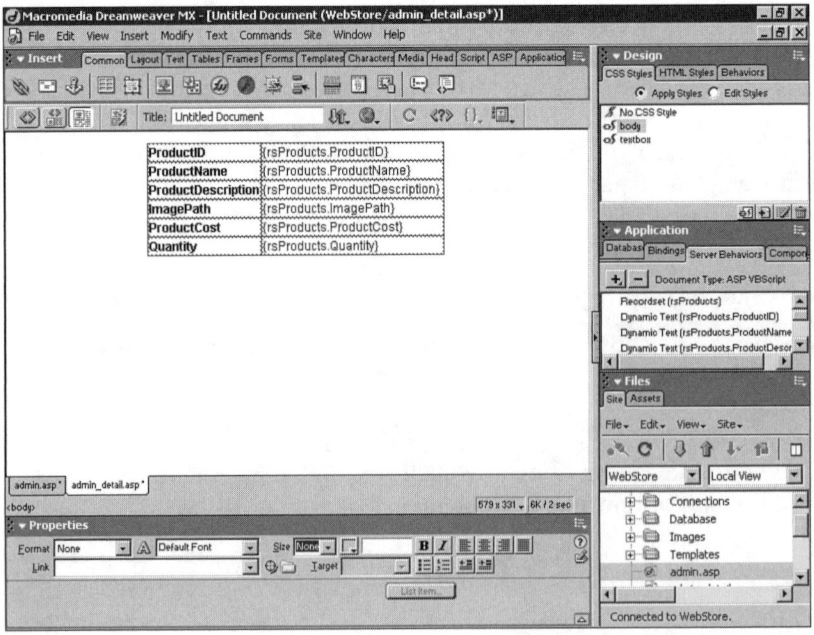

FIGURE 29.58   The detail page shows all the records that you specified to appear within it.

7. Switch back to the admin.asp page and format that page accordingly. Notice that a dynamic table along with a navigation bar and status are inserted for you. The result is shown in Figure 29.59.

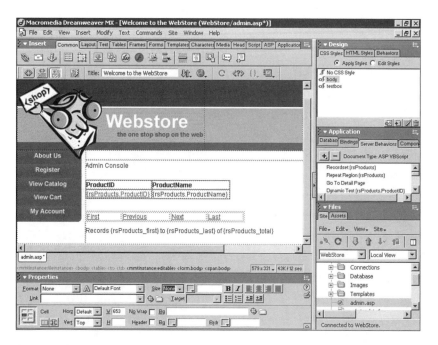

FIGURE 29.59 The Master page includes a dynamic table, a navigation bar, and the navigation status.

8. Save your work and test it in the browser. Selecting the ProductID will link you to the detail page for that specific item.

Summary

As you have progressed through the past two chapters, you have seen the amazing capabilities that Dreamweaver MX contains as far as reusable components that not only simplify development but make it much more enjoyable and fun. The next chapter will push past dynamic data and move into the world of e-commerce and Dreamweaver MX's support for it.

29

SQL Search Page

by Zak Ruvalcaba

As you have seen, a database exists for the sole purpose of storing data. Tables exist to separate that data into well-structured and meaningful blocks of information that can be accessed at any time in an ordered manner. Most successful Web sites exist because the information within those sites is relatively easy to access. When you search for a book on Amazon.com, you expect to find it within seconds of being on the site. You type in a book name, click Search, and the results appear in a well-structured and elegant manner. If you visit eBay's Web site in an effort to find that treasure that someone may be auctioning off, you type in the name of the item you are looking for and select a form object, usually a Submit button, to perform the search. It's safe to say that in today's application service provider (ASP) dominated business model, most companies employ some mechanism for allowing their users quick access to the data that powers the company.

It's true that the Web took off with the inception of the modern search engine. Companies such as Yahoo, Excite, Google, and Lycos fueled the medium we know as the Web by making the information within the billions of Web sites on the Internet accessible. Employing basic, filtered, and advanced methods of searching, those companies and others powered the Internet to what we know it as today. This chapter focuses on the ability to integrate these access methods into your Web application, specifically providing your users with the capabilities to search for information that they may need within your site.

If you have not done so, you can download all the support files for this and other chapters from www.dreamweavermxunleashed.com.

SQL Search

Finding information within your database can be a simple or a complex process. Depending on the search criteria, you can give your users the capability to narrow down their searches as fine as a specific date range. Suppose you wanted to find all customers within your database that had a last name of Smith; you could create a simple query within Access that selected all the records within the customers table whose last name was equivalent to the name Smith. Your SQL statement could look similar to

```
SELECT LastName FROM Customers WHERE LastName = 'Smith'
```

The result would return all the matching records. Indeed, the database is filled with information that users may want access to including the following:

- **Customers**   As an admin, you could perform a search within your customers table to extract customer-specific information including last name, first name, city, state, and so on.

- **CreditCards**   Again, as an admin, you could perform a search within the credit cards table to extract all Visa credit cards. This could eventually enable you to create a statistical analysis of the credit card of choice for your customers.

- **Products**   Probably the most important container of information, the products table could be searched by a user to determine whether a certain product is being sold through your company.

- **Inventory**   A user could search the inventory table, which would return results along with the product search to guarantee that a specific item is in stock.

- **Orders**   As an admin, you could perform a search to determine how many items you sold for a specific day, week, or month. You could also return a statistical analysis of those results so that you could better understand your customers' ordering habits and possibly suggest products in the future.

As you can see, just within the Web Store database, there is plenty available to search on. Whether you are approaching the problem as an admin or a user, the database ultimately is a warehouse of information. How you choose to access that information is up to you.

A Basic SQL-Based Search

In Chapter 26, "Database Primer," you learned how to display dynamic data to the user. You created a query and ultimately integrated that query into your application using a server behavior that presented dynamic data. The problem with that approach is that it's hard-coded, meaning that the data the user would end up seeing would always remain the same. What if your users didn't want to see what you were presenting to them? Fortunately for you, you could allow your users to perform a search within your site based on criteria that they specify through the use of form objects, recordsets, and variables. Before we jump ahead, let's dissect a common approach to creating search functionality. Figure 30.1 shows the Amazon Web site and the search form you would use to request a book.

FIGURE 30.1   Most Web sites employ some means of allowing their users to search for information.

Consider now that you had a database with a list of book titles. The user of the Web site types in a book name; the value of that text box is dynamically appended to a WHERE or a LIKE clause within a SQL statement. The database is then queried and the results are presented to the user in a well-structured manner. You can create your own basic SQL-based search page by following the steps outlined next:

> **NOTE**
>
> If you have not done so already, create a new project folder within the wwwroot directory of the Inetpub folder. Within your project folder, create a database file to use with this section. Also, make sure that the necessary steps have been taken to define that site within Dreamweaver MX.

1. Create a new page either within Notepad or Dreamweaver and enter the following HTML code:

```
<html>
<head>
<title>Search Page</title>
</head>

<body>
<form action="search_results.asp" method="post">
<input type="text" name="txtSearch">
<input type="submit" value="Submit">
</form>
</body>
</html>
```

2. Save the page as search.asp inside a folder within the Inetpub\wwwroot directory.

3. Create a new page for the search results named search_results.asp and enter the following code:

```
<%
Dim txtSearch, objConn, objRS, sqltext

txtSearch = Request.Form("txtSearch")

set objConn = Server.CreateObject("ADODB.Connection")
set objRS = Server.CreateObject("ADODB.RecordSet")

objConn.Open "Provider=Microsoft.Jet.OLEDB.4.0;" & _
"Data Source=C:\Inetpub\wwwroot\Search\WebStore.mdb;" & _
"Persist Security Info=False"

sqltext = "SELECT * FROM Products WHERE ProductName=" &txtSearch
objRS.Open sqltext, objConn, 3, 3
%>
<html>
<head>
<title>Search Page</title>
</head>

<body>
<%= objRS("ID") %><br>
<%= objRS("ProductName") %>
```

```
<%= objRS("ProductDescription") %>
</body>
</html>
<%
objRS.Close
objConn.Close
Set objConn = Nothing
Set objRS = Nothing
%>
```

4. Save your work and test it in the browser.

This simple application performs a search on the products table based on the ProductName that you specify within the search.asp page.

> **WARNING**
>
> Don't forget to place a copy of the Web Store database within the new folder that you created. This code assumes that you called that folder Search.

Stepping over the code reveals that the only real change to the code lies in the SQL statement. Notice the SQL statement contains a WHERE clause with the value of the previous form object appended to it. Request.Form("txtSearch") grabs that value and places it into the txtSearch variable.

> **NOTE**
>
> The search pages form method was created using POST. You could change the method to GET and produce the same result. Rather than using Request.Form, you would use Request.QueryString. The downside is that the value is exposed within the querystring.

Creating the Web Store Search Page

Now that you have a basic understanding as to how tables are queried based on user input, let's take a look at how the search functionality can be integrated into the Web Store application. You can begin creating a search page following the steps outlined next:

1. Create a new page by selecting New from the File menu. Select the Advanced tab and choose the WebStore template.

2. Save the page as search.asp.

3. Change the Header editable region to read Search and place a new form within the Content editable region.

30

4. Insert a text box form object into the form named txtSearch. Point the action to the search_results.asp page, which will be created next. Select POST as the method.

5. Insert a submit form object into the form named btnSearch. The result is shown in Figure 30.2.

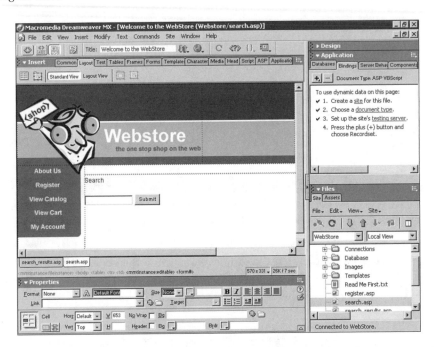

FIGURE 30.2   Create a new search page by adding the necessary form objects.

6. Save your work and test it in the browser. The result is shown in Figure 30.3.

Creating the Web Store Search Results Page

Now that the search page has been created, you'll want some way of collecting the value of the user input and actually processing the search. This page is where all the work is done. The search results page must contain the following components for the search to be processed correctly:

- Recordset of the table being searched on

- Proper variables to capture the users' input

- Dynamic text to display to the user the result of the search

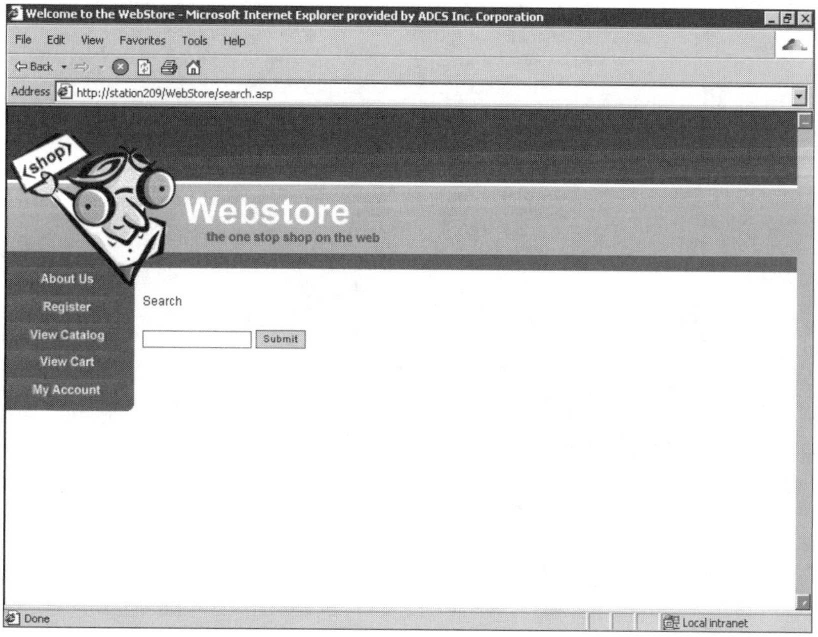

FIGURE 30.3   Place a value into the form and submit to send the value to the search results page.

Remember, a recordset will always be used to capture the results of the table information. To create a new recordset for the search results page, follow the steps outlined next:

1. Create a new page by selecting New from the File menu. Select the Advanced tab and choose the WebStore template.

2. Save the page as search_results.asp.

3. Select Recordset from the Bindings panel and switch to the advanced view.

4. Name the recordset **rsSearch** and select the Web Store connection.

5. You can build your SQL query either by typing the code into the box directly or by selecting the appropriate fields within the Database Items selection box, as shown in Figure 30.4.

6. Notice that the value appended to the WHERE clause specifically looks for the DVD *Fallen*.

7. Select Test. The results, as shown in Figure 30.5, show the data for the movie *Fallen*.

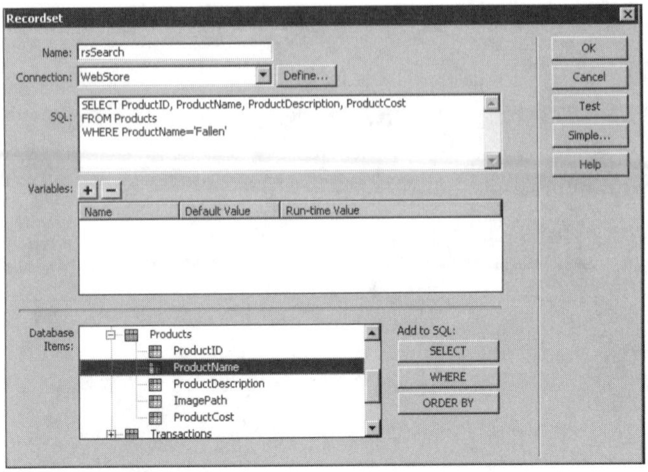

FIGURE 30.4   Create the query to extract a single record from the database.

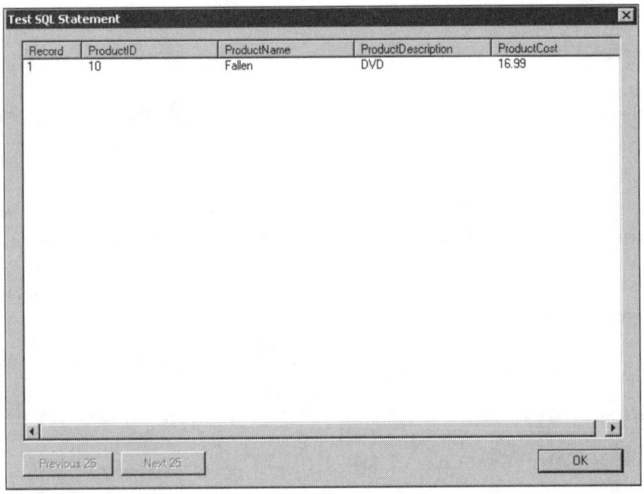

FIGURE 30.5   The results for the movie *Fallen* are shown in the test dialog box.

Although the query seems to work perfectly, it's still not dynamic to the user. The movie *Fallen* will always appear as the searched item. The next section will introduce you to working with variables, allowing you to capture the users' input, making the search much more dynamic.

Working with Variables

Up to this point, we have not discussed variables. Variables within Dreamweaver MX's Recordset dialog box allow you to capture user information from sessions, form requests, cookies, and application variables. They enable you to work dynamically, by passing values from one page to another. If you take the search page as an example, a user will submit the input via a form object to the search_results.asp page. Within the search_results.asp page, a piece of functionality needs to be added to allow for the capture of that input so that it can be automatically concatenated to the SQL statements' WHERE clause. That functionality is a variable. Variables within Dreamweaver enable you to capture the data being sent from a previous page and store it for later use. Variables contain three properties:

- **Name**   The physical name of the variable

- **Default Value**   A value to be assigned to the variable so that its value is never empty

- **Runtime Value**   The value to assign the variable

You can set up a variable to capture the user's input from the search page by following the steps outlined below:

1. Open the rsSearch recordset.

2. Add a variable to the variables list by selecting the plus (+) icon. The variable should contain the following properties:

Name	Default Value	Runtime Value
Search	abc	Request.Form("txtSearch")

3. Remember, to capture requests made from a form object, you use request.form followed by the name of the form object within quotes.

4. Modify the SQL statement so that you are using the keyword LIKE followed by the name of the variable, as shown in Figure 30.6.

5. Select OK. Figure 30.7 shows that the recordset looks the same as it normally would without the addition of a variable.

6. Continue to add all the dynamic text to the page, dragging the fields from the recordset onto their respective positions within the page. You may want to add captions for the field names.

7. Drag the Total Records field into the header so users are aware of how many records the search produced. Figure 30.8 shows the result of the dynamic text.

30

FIGURE 30.6   Add a variable and modify the SQL statement to accept the newly created variable name.

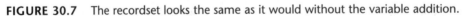

FIGURE 30.7   The recordset looks the same as it would without the variable addition.

8. Save your work and test it in the browser. Figure 30.9 shows the result of the input *Fallen*.

The results are made possible because of the variable. The variable captured the results of the request sent by the form's "post" submission. The variable was then appended to the SQL statement, which caused the dynamic search for the object's value.

FIGURE 30.8   Add the fields from the recordset as dynamic text.

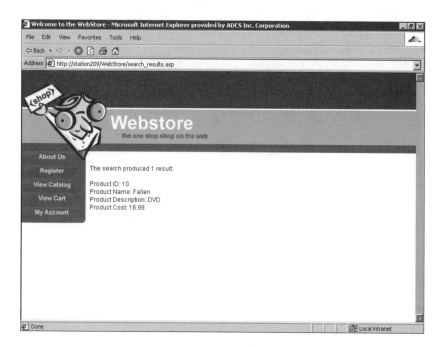

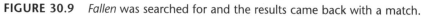

FIGURE 30.9   *Fallen* was searched for and the results came back with a match.

Repeating Regions

Now that your application has search capabilities, you may want to allow the user to search for more than one item. For now, a user can search based on a DVD name. Fortunately for us, there's only one DVD that matches the name searched for. But what if the user decided to search based on the description of the DVD? If you look over the data that is contained within that field, you'll notice that the search can contain DVD, DVD Widescreen, and DVD Special Edition. You could easily create a repeating region that would effectively handle the situation by listing all the records that match that search criteria rather than one. To create a repeating region for your data, follow the steps outlined next:

1. Add a line break after product cost and highlight the section of text including the dynamic data.

2. Select Repeat Region from the Server Behavior panel.

3. Figure 30.10 shows the dialog box that enables you to display all records within the recordset.

FIGURE 30.10   Add a repeat region server behavior to the page.

4. Next, open the recordset and change the WHERE clause to filter by ProductDescription, as shown in Figure 30.11.

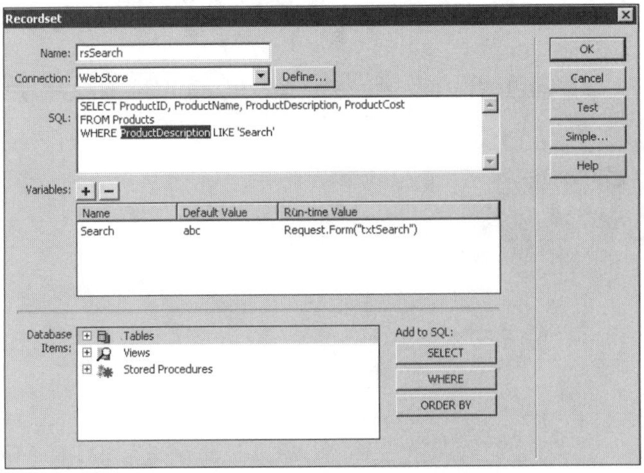

FIGURE 30.11   Change the recordset to filter by ProductDescription.

5. Select OK.

6. Save your work and test it in the browser. Figure 30.12 shows the result of including DVD Special Edition as the search value in the search.asp page.

FIGURE 30.12 The repeat region server behavior opens the door for your users by allowing them to search for data within the database that may have more than one result.

Alternative Text

Currently, as users search for data within the database, they are presented with results in a structured format. But suppose users enter a value to search by and the recordset cannot return a match? Currently, the message returns The search produced 0 results. You can see how counterintuitive this message is to the user, not to mention that it isn't very user friendly. Using the Show Region server behavior set, you could present users with an alternative text message alerting them of the failed search result and allow them to link back to the search.asp page to try their search again. To insert the alternative text into your search result page, follow the steps outlined next:

1. Insert a new line break just after the Show Region.

2. Insert the text **Sorry, no results match that search** and create a link for Try Again. Make Try Again link back to the search.asp page.

3. Highlight all the text and select the Show Region If Recordset Is Empty server behavior from the Show Region submenu, as shown in Figure 30.13.

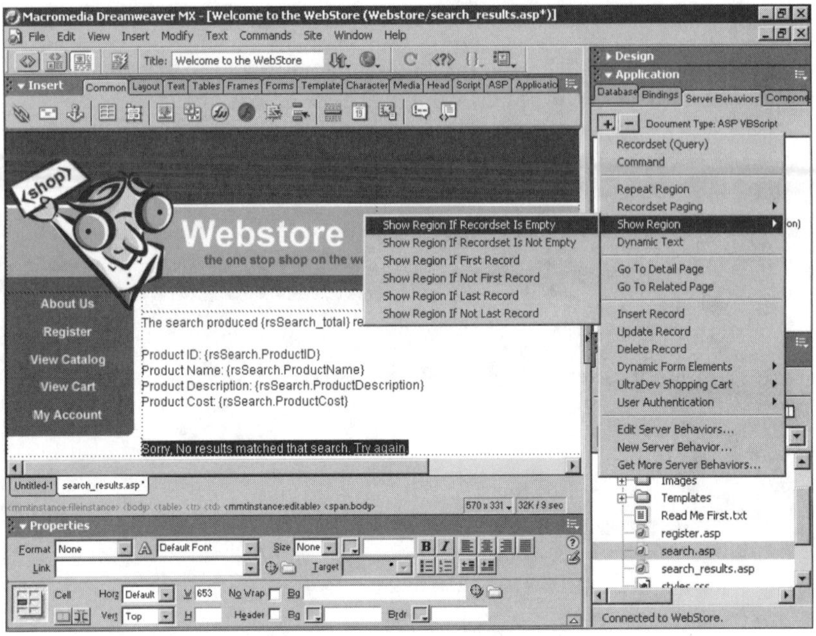

FIGURE 30.13   Insert the Show Region if Recordset Is Empty server behavior.

4. The Show Region dialog box will appear. Select the appropriate recordset (rsSearch) and click OK.

5. Save your work and test it within the browser.

6. In the search.asp page, type in something that you know it will not find, like **VHS**. Click Search. Your message will appear along with the link that allows you to link back to the search page, as shown in Figure 30.14.

Linking to a Detail Page by Passing a Parameter

Now that users know that the information they want exists within the database, you may want to add functionality that gives a little more detail about the product and allows them to purchase it. In the previous chapters you learned that a detail page is created to give more detail about a specific piece of data within your Web site. It doesn't have to be that simple; in fact, a detail page can be any page that you simply link to from a master page by passing a parameter. The detail page, in accordance with the parameter being passed either by the URL or by form post will change dynamically. In our search results example, you'll want to list the items that the user requested and provide the user with a way to link to that item within the viewcatalog.asp page, allowing them to purchase it. To create the detail page functionality, follow these steps:

1. Select the dynamic text for ProductName and select the Go To Detail Page server behavior, as shown in Figure 30.15.

FIGURE 30.14 If the recordset comes up empty, you are presented with the custom message.

2. The Go To Detail Page dialog box appears. The dialog box allows you to select the item that you are creating the link for. In this case, because you already had the item selected, the field is populated for you. The dialog box also enables you to select the page that will serve as the detail page, the name of the parameter to pass, the recordset name, the field to use as the value to the parameter, and an option for how to send the parameter across. Figure 30.16 shows the configuration that you should be using.

3. Select OK.

4. Save your work and test it in the browser. Perform the same search that you did before. This time notice that the dynamic product names are linked. Figure 30.17 shows how you are able to select the product name.

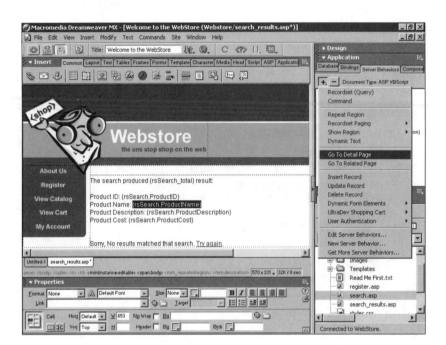

FIGURE 30.15   Insert the Go To Detail Page server behavior.

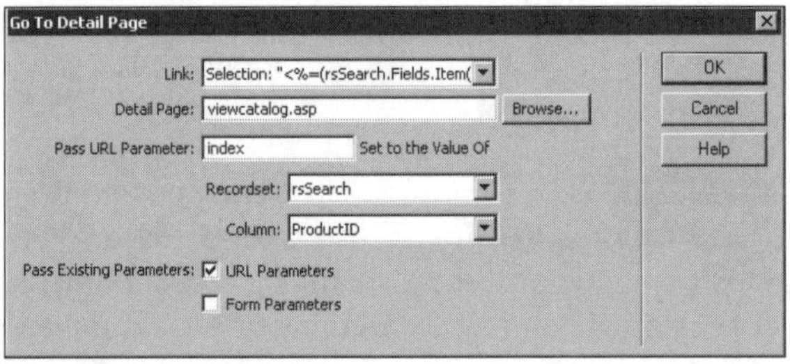

FIGURE 30.16   Apply all the appropriate settings to the Go To Detail Page dialog box.

5. Select the link. Figure 30.18 shows how you are redirected to the appropriate page.

Globalizing the Search Functionality

Now that most of the search functionality has been added to the Web store, you're ready to globalize it. What exactly does globalizing mean? Globalization is the term given to items or functionality that can be accessed from anywhere at any time. Currently, the search functionality can be accessed only from the search.asp page. What you want is for that functionality to be accessible from every page; that way, when a user has an immediate need to search for a particular item, it can be done no matter what page the user is on.

Accomplishing this task is as simple as copying the information that currently resides within the search.asp page and integrating it into the template, allowing for every page within the Web store to use the search functionality. To globalize the search functionality, follow these steps:

1. Open the template file that currently resides within the Templates folder.

FIGURE 30.17   Select the product name to link to a detail page.

2. You can either copy the code that exists within the search.asp page or insert a new form, text field, and button, as shown in Figure 30.19. Align the objects to the right of the page.

3. Select code/design view just to make sure all the code is formatted correctly. The result is shown in Figure 30.20.

4. Save the page. You should be asked to update all the pages that use the template, as shown in Figure 30.21.

5. The Update Pages dialog box will appear, alerting you of the files that Dreamweaver MX has updated, as shown in Figure 30.22.

FIGURE 30.18   The user is linked to the appropriate detail page.

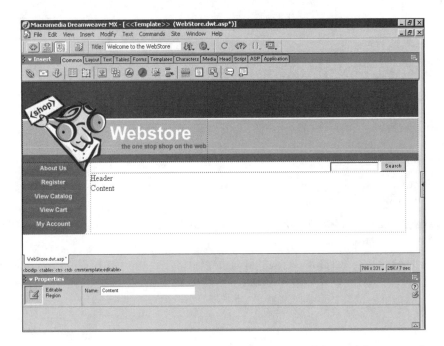

FIGURE 30.19   Insert the form objects into the top table row of the WebStore template.

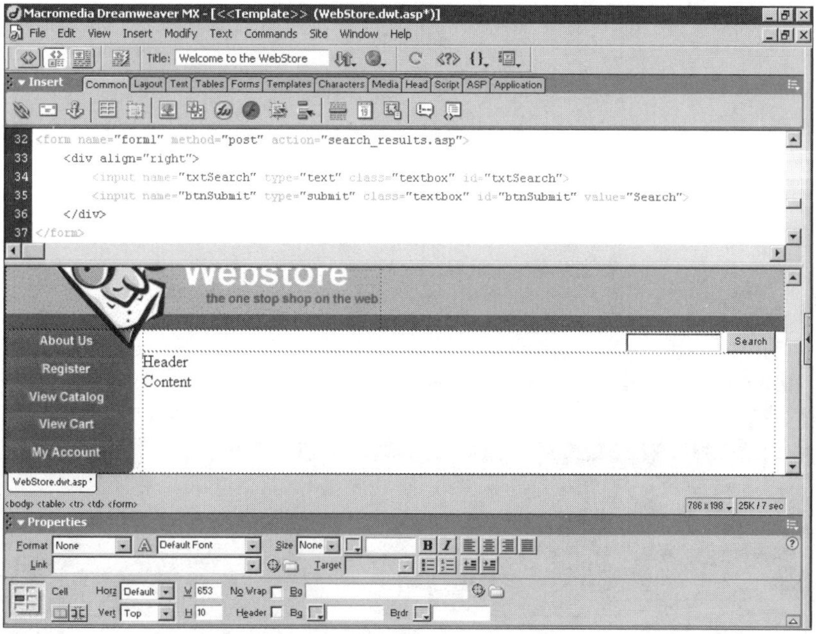

FIGURE 30.20 Format the code so that all the form objects are named appropriately and the form points to the search_results.asp page.

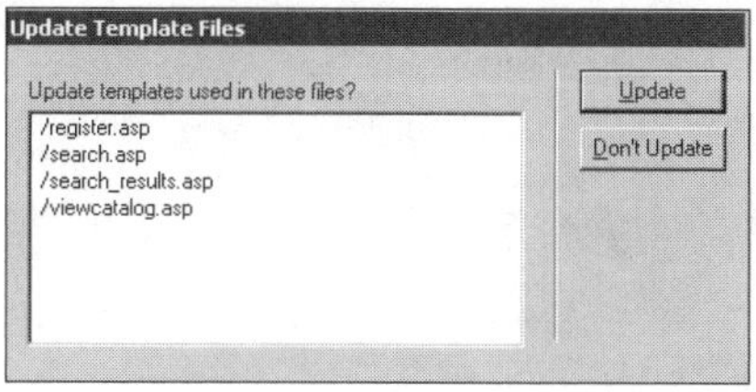

FIGURE 30.21 The Update Template Files dialog box allows you to update all pages that use the master template.

6. Select Close.

7. Save your work and test it in the browser. Figure 30.23 shows that no matter what page you visit, the search will appear. Try typing in the value **DVD Special Edition**.

8. Select Search. The results should appear the same as they did from the search.asp page.

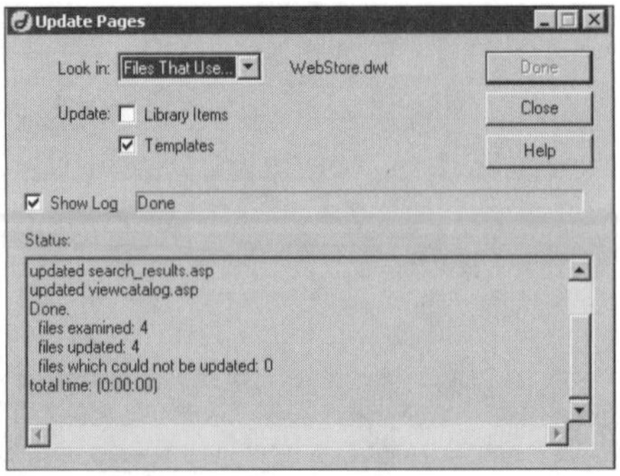

FIGURE 30.22   The Update Pages dialog box alerts you of the files that have been updated.

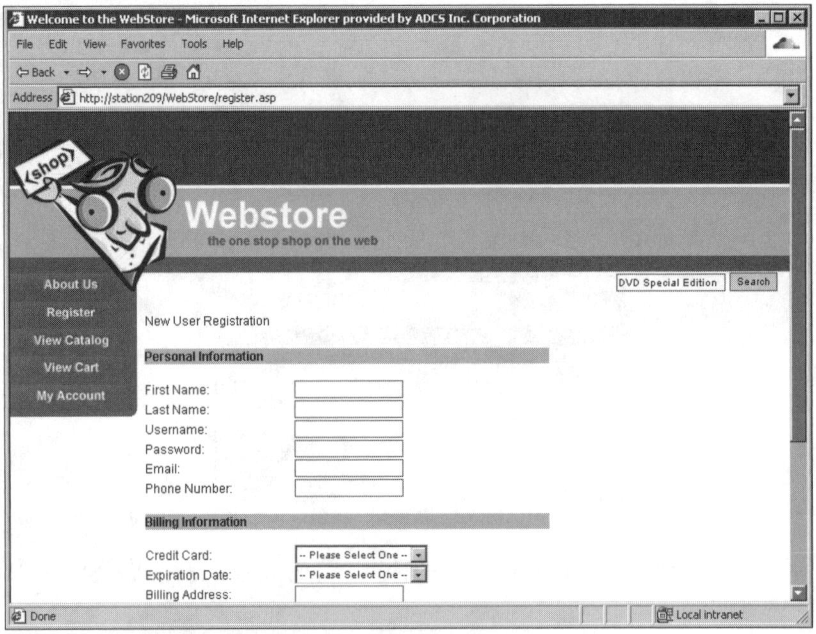

FIGURE 30.23   The search form appears on every page.

Creating the Advanced Search Page

The last step in creating a full-featured search engine within the Web store is to give the users as many options to select items within your Web application as possible. Currently a user must search using a keyword that currently exists within the database. Unfortunately, the user is able to select based on only one table within the database. Suppose the user wanted to select either DVD, DVD Widescreen, or DVD Special Edition from the

ProductDescription field and choose a DVD name from the ProductName field. The current configuration would make it impossible. Just a few changes to the template and some modifications to the recordset will round out the search functionality for the Web Store application. Begin adding the advanced search functionality by following the steps outlined next:

1. Open the template file from the Templates directory.

2. Add a new link for Advanced Search and point it to search.asp, as shown in Figure 30.24.

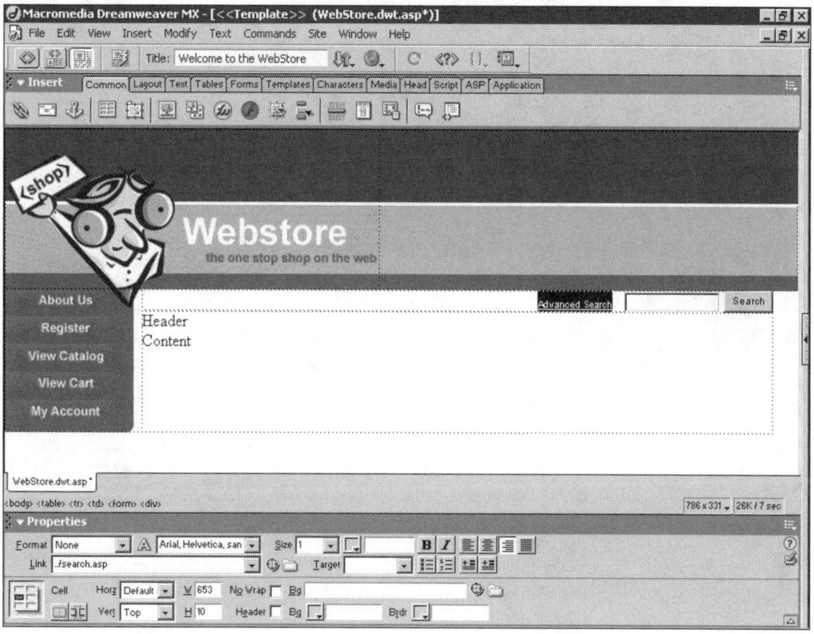

FIGURE 30.24   Add a new link for an advanced search.

3. Save the template and update all files that use the template.

4. Open search.asp. Change the header to Advanced Search and add a drop-down menu that will allow your users to search based on DVD, DVD Widescreen, and DVD Special Edition. The values are shown in Figure 30.25. Name the form object **selType**.

5. Figure 30.26 shows the result of adding the form values to the search.asp page.

30

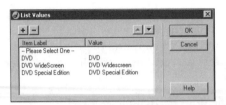

FIGURE 30.25   Add list values for three separate items within the product description table.

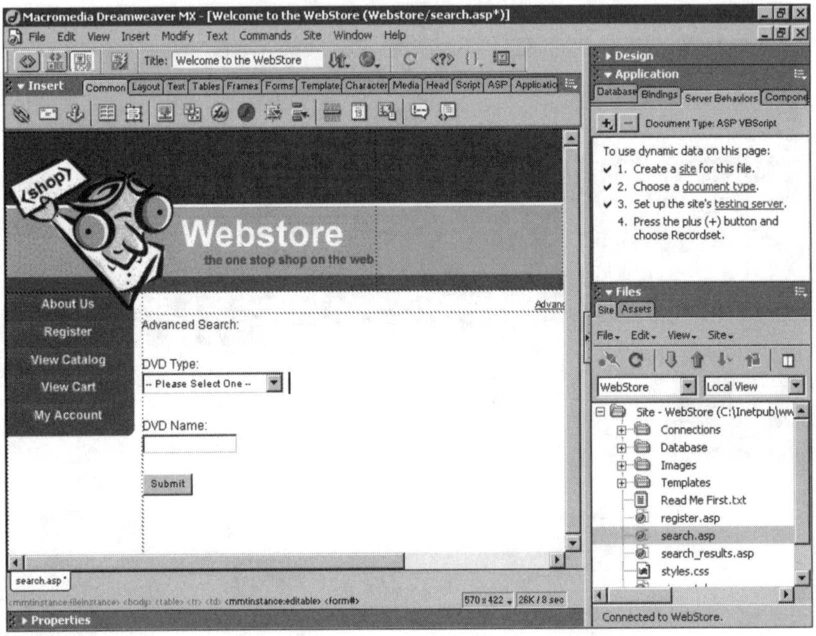

[figure: Macromedia Dreamweaver MX screenshot — Welcome to the WebStore (Webstore/search.asp*)]

FIGURE 30.26   Add new form objects to handle the advanced search.

6. Save your work. Open search_results.asp.

7. Open the recordset and make the changes as shown in Figure 30.27. Notice that a new variable was added to handle the request sent from the drop-down menu.

NOTE

The keyword AND filters the search by two criteria: txtSearch will handle the product name and selType will handle which kind of DVD the item will be.

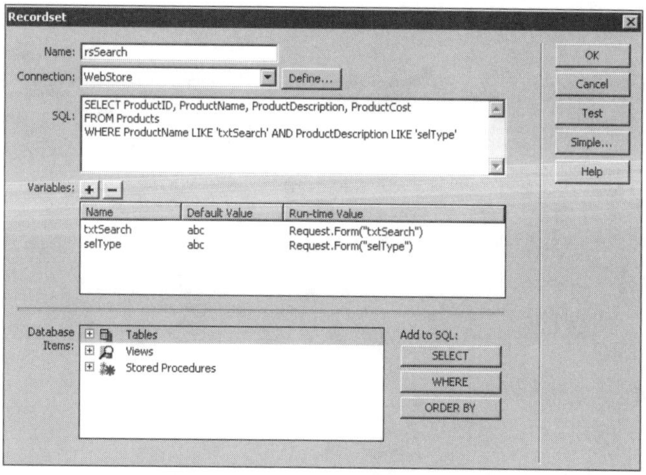

FIGURE 30.27   Make the appropriate changes to the recordset.

Figure 30.28 shows an item being searched on from the search.asp page. Remember that this page can be accessed by linking from the Advanced Search link at the top of any page in the application.

FIGURE 30.28   Enter values for the new search.

30

Figure 30.29 shows the results of the search.

FIGURE 30.29   *Cape Fear* is the result of the search.

> **TIP**
>
> You could narrow down the search results even further by using wildcards. A wildcard is signified by the "%" sign and allows for a keyword to be searched on that contains the letters that you specify. For instance, changing the SQL statement to read WHERE ProductName LIKE '%ll%' would return the results for *Mallrats* and *Fallen* because they both contain two l's. You can narrow your searches to be as complex as you want them; using wildcards is one way of accomplishing the task.

Creating the Web Store Search Functionality Using ASP.NET

Similar to the ASP server model, the search functionality can be created using ASP.NET. Unfortunately, with the ASP.NET server model comes a certain lack of functionality that will have to be hard coded in. For instance, using the ASP server model, you simply set the form action to point to the file that would do all the form processing. Because of PostBack, ASP.NET must be set up a bit differently.

> **TIP**
>
> PostBack refers to the process of submitting a form to itself. In a traditional ASP environment, a page is typically submitted to a second page that handles the processing for the first page. ASP.NET posts back to itself, handles the processing, and then uses a response.redirect to switch the user to a new page.

Begin creating the ASP.NET search page by following the steps outlined next:

1. Create a new page by selecting New from the File menu, switch to the Advanced tab, and select the WebStore template.

> **WARNING**
>
> For the page to be treated as an ASP.NET page by Dreamweaver MX, the document type must be set to ASP.NET VB/C#, and the testing server must be set up under an ASP.NET environment.

2. Immediately save the page as search.aspx. Insert the text **Search** where the Header editable region is.

3. Insert a new text box control as well as a button control where the Content editable region is. Because the Dreamweaver MX Properties Inspector will not recognize the objects, you will have to switch to code view and make the necessary changes, as shown in Figure 30.30. Be sure to name the controls appropriately.

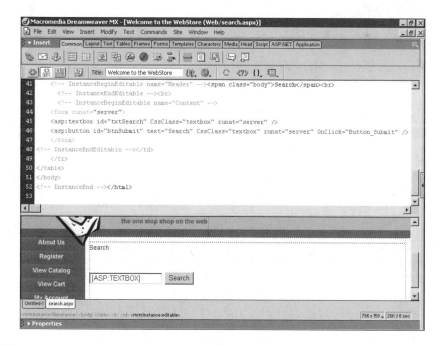

FIGURE 30.30   Create the new form and Web controls within the new page.

4. After you've created the new click event for the new button control, navigate to the top of the page and insert a new subroutine to handle the processing for the text box controls' input value. Notice how the text value of the text box control is concatenated to the URL within the response.redirect method, as shown in Figure 30.31.

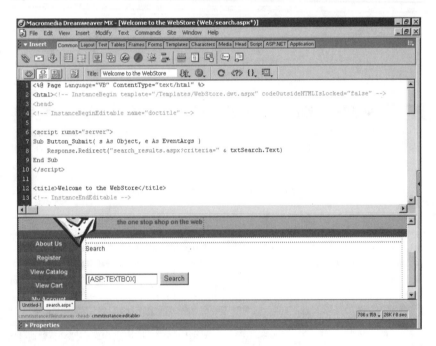

FIGURE 30.31   Create a new subroutine that redirects the users to a new page—in the process, appending the value to the querystring as a new parameter.

5. Save your work and close the page.

6. Create a new page by selecting New from the File menu, switch to the Advanced tab, and select the WebStore template.

7. Immediately save the page as search_results.aspx. Enter the text **Results** in the Header editable region. Create four new captions within the Content editable region, as shown in Figure 30.32. Eventually, these captions will display dynamic text.

8. Insert a new DataSet by selecting it from the Bindings panel. Switch to advanced view and build the SQL statement either by using the database items or by manually typing it in. Figure 30.33 shows the result of building the SQL statement.

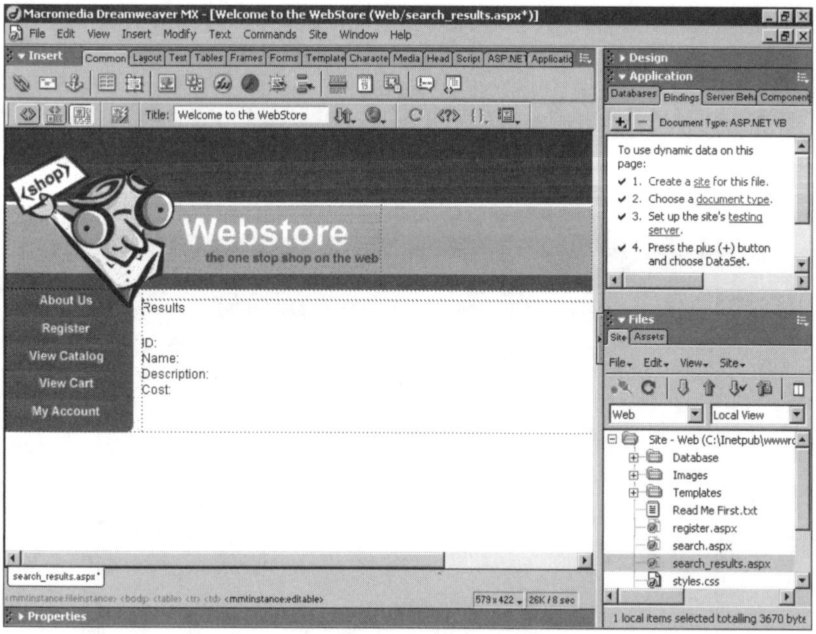

FIGURE 30.32   Insert captions to display what will eventually be dynamic text.

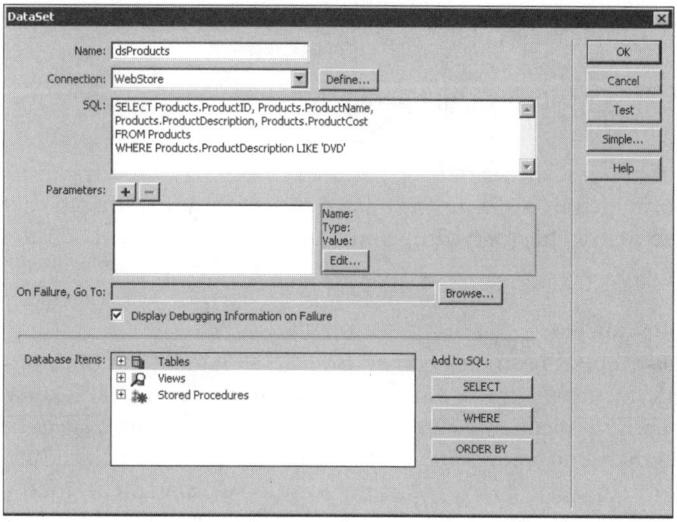

FIGURE 30.33   Build a new SQL statement to handle the keyword search.

9. Notice the use of the LIKE keyword. In this case, assume that a user is performing a search based on the keyword "DVD." The SQL statement will look within the ProductDescription table for a word that is "like" DVD. Figure 30.34 shows the result of testing the SQL statement. Try testing the statement by changing the value to DVD Widescreen and then DVD Special Edition. The result should change every time.

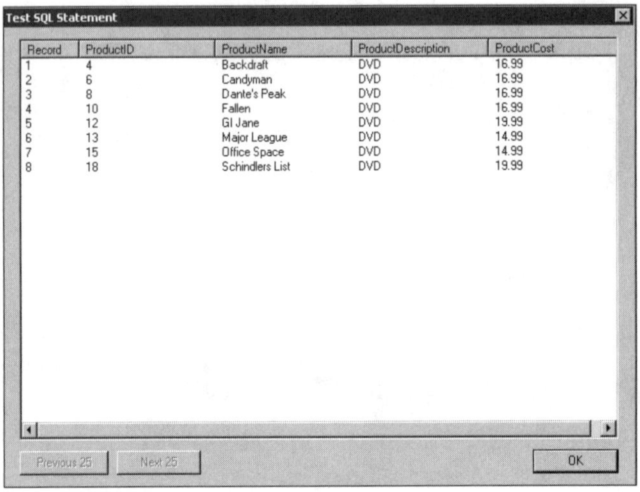

Test SQL Statement

Record	ProductID	ProductName	ProductDescription	ProductCost
1	4	Backdraft	DVD	16.99
2	6	Candyman	DVD	16.99
3	8	Dante's Peak	DVD	16.99
4	10	Fallen	DVD	16.99
5	12	GI Jane	DVD	19.99
6	13	Major League	DVD	14.99
7	15	Office Space	DVD	14.99
8	18	Schindlers List	DVD	19.99

Previous 25   Next 25   OK

FIGURE 30.34 Test the results of the new query.

10. Select OK, close the DataSet, and save your work.

Unfortunately, if you test the search page in the browser, your result will show little more than one record filtered by DVD. In the next section, you learn how to capture the value that is being sent across the querystring and dynamically concatenate it to the SQL statement as a parameter.

Working with Parameters

Now that the DataSet has been created and the SQL statement has been generated, you'll want to dynamically change the value that appears just after the LIKE keyword. Essentially what will happen is that value will become a parameter, meaning that rather than using a variable to store the value being sent across, a parameter will be passed into the SQL statement dynamically. To create a new parameter for the SQL statement, follow these steps:

1. Open the DataSet from within the search_results.aspx page.

2. Change the value just after the LIKE keyword to a question mark (?). This signifies that it will accept a new parameter.

3. Select the plus (+) icon from the Parameters dialog box. The Add Parameter dialog box will appear. Give the parameter a name such as "criteria," select the Char data type, and select the Build button to create the code that will capture the value being sent across the querystring.

4. Figure 30.35 shows the Build Value dialog box indicating the type of parameter being sent, the name of the parameter, and a default value in case the value being sent across is empty.

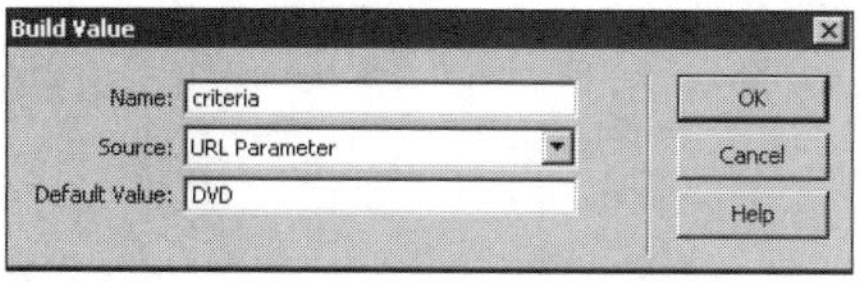

FIGURE 30.35   Enter values for the parameter within the Build Value dialog box.

5. Select OK. Figure 30.36 shows the results of the code that is generated and inserted into the Value dialog box for you.

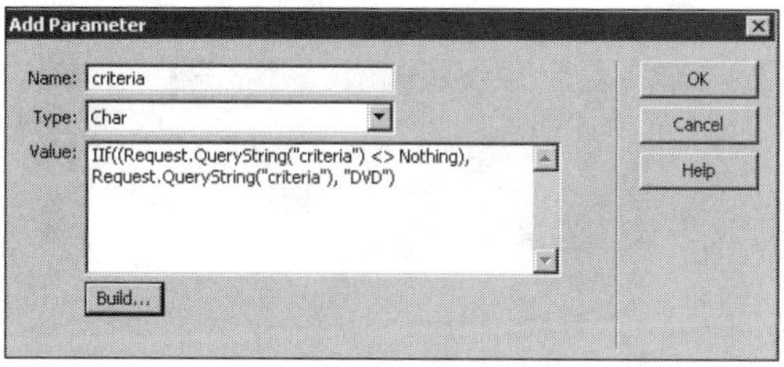

FIGURE 30.36   The code that will be used to capture the value is automatically generated for you.

6. Select OK. Figure 30.37 shows the result of the new parameter that was created. You can edit the parameter at any time by selecting the Edit button.

7. You can test the parameter by selecting the Test button. The Test Value dialog box will appear as shown in Figure 30.38, allowing you to enter a value for the new parameter. Enter **DVD**.

8. Figure 30.39 shows the result of the query based on the "DVD" filter criteria. Test the parameter's functionality by entering **DVD Widescreen** and **DVD Special Edition** within the Test Value dialog box.

30

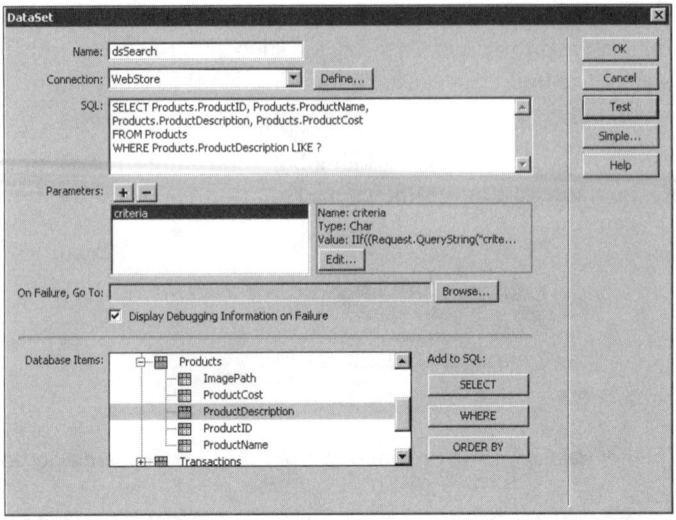

FIGURE 30.37 Create a new subroutine that redirects users to a new page, in the process, appending the value to the querystring as a new parameter.

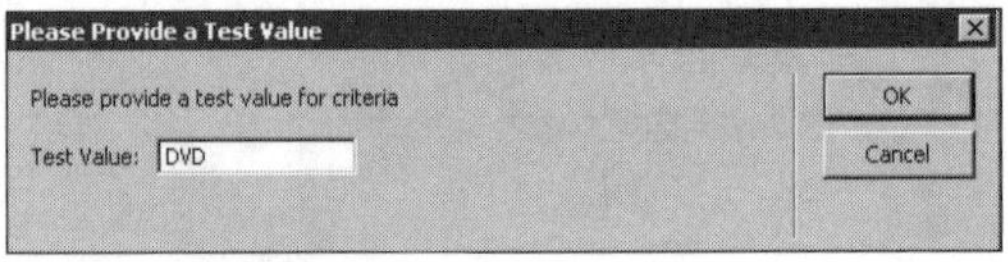

FIGURE 30.38 Enter a new value to test the new parameter.

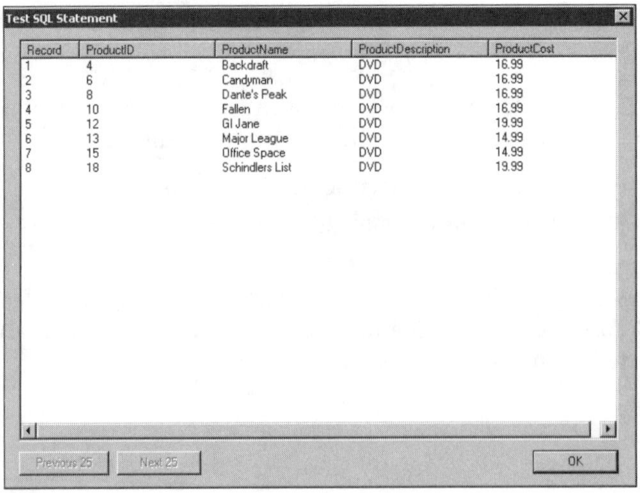

Record	ProductID	ProductName	ProductDescription	ProductCost
1	4	Backdraft	DVD	16.99
2	6	Candyman	DVD	16.99
3	8	Dante's Peak	DVD	16.99
4	10	Fallen	DVD	16.99
5	12	GI Jane	DVD	19.99
6	13	Major League	DVD	14.99
7	15	Office Space	DVD	14.99
8	18	Schindlers List	DVD	19.99

FIGURE 30.39 The results of the query display are shown.

9. Now that the DataSet is complete, you can create dynamic text within the page by dragging the fields into their respective positions, as shown in Figure 30.40.

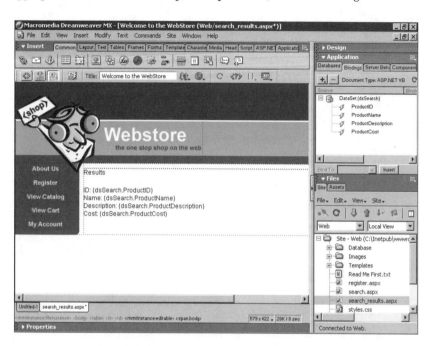

FIGURE 30.40   Drag the fields of the DataSet into the page, next to the captions that you created earlier.

10. Save your work and test it in the browser. Enter a value into the text box, such as DVD, DVD Widescreen, or DVD Special Edition. The result will be shown after you click Submit. Figure 30.41 shows how the value was passed across from page to page within the querystring under the name "criteria."

Repeating Regions
If you test the search functionality, you will realize that although roughly 10 records matched the criteria for DVD, only one showed up. The problem lies in the fact that the DataSet that is returned with the data is not exposing at once everything that it contains. Using the Repeat Region server behavior, you could effectively force the DataSet to show all its values in an elegant list. To create a repeating region for your search results, simply follow the steps outlined next:

1. Insert a new line break just after the last item (Product Cost).

2. Highlight all the text and select the Repeat Region server behavior.

3. Select OK from the Repeat Region dialog box.

30

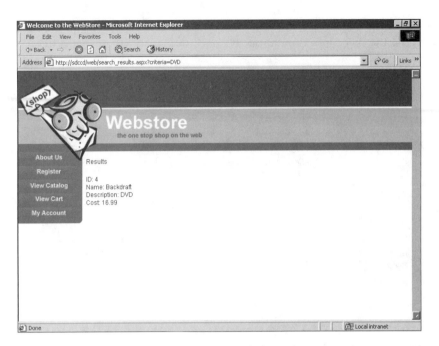

FIGURE 30.41   The parameter and value are passed along the querystring.

4. A new template of invisible elements will appear around the text.

5. Save your work and test it in the browser.

Figure 30.42 shows how all the records are exposed, rather than just one.

Alternative Text

Currently, as users search for data within the database, they are presented with results in a structured format. But suppose a user enters a value to search by and the DataSet cannot return a match? Using the Show Region server behavior set, you could present an alternative text message, alerting the user of the failed search result and enabling the user to link back to the search.aspx page to try the search again. To insert the alternative text into your search results page, follow these steps:

1. Insert a new line break just after the Show Region.

2. Insert the text **Your search produced no results** and create a link for Try Again. Make Try Again link back to the search.aspx page.

3. Highlight all the text and select the Show if DataSet Is Empty server behavior from the Show Region submenu, as shown in Figure 30.43.

FIGURE 30.42   The repeating region exposes all records within the DataSet.

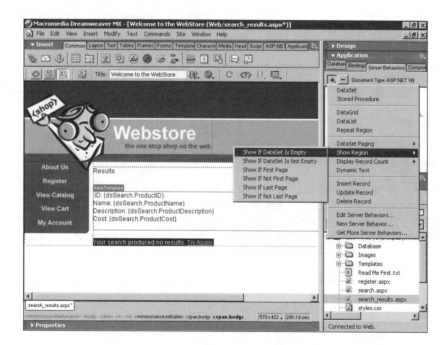

FIGURE 30.43   Insert the Show if DataSet Is Empty server behavior.

4. The Show Region dialog box will appear. Select the appropriate recordset (rsSearch) and click OK.

5. Save your work and test it within the browser.

6. In the search.aspx page, type in something that you know it will not find, like **VHS**. Click Search. Your message will appear along with the link that allows you to link back to the search page, as shown in Figure 30.44.

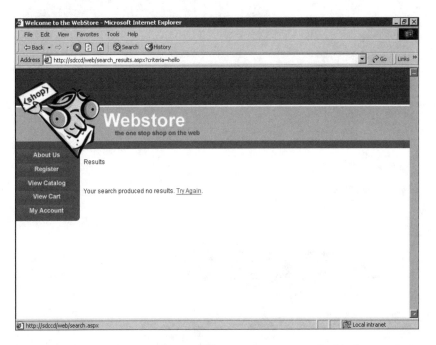

FIGURE 30.44   If the DataSet comes up empty, you are presented with the custom message.

Summary

By now you should have a solid understanding of querying databases, inserting and modifying databases, shopping cart technologies, and more recently, creating a globalized search for your application. Although it seems as though a lot was accomplished thus far, the next chapter will tie everything together in defining how your users will access your site.

31

Adding Shopping Cart Functionality

by Zak Ruvalcaba

Welcome to the chapter that covers the heart of all dynamic Web applications: the shopping cart. Most dynamic Web applications are created for the sole purpose of making money on the Web. Let's face it, why go through all the work of creating a dynamic Web application if you don't plan to make money through it? Sure, companies employ dynamic intranet sites and granted, there are still some, although very few, free Web applications that you can use. In the real world, however, dynamic Web applications are created in an attempt to make money by selling merchandise on the Web. Providing the capability to add items to a virtual shopping cart as you browse through a Web site is still very much a business that commands good money. Companies such as VeriSign, PayPal, WebAssist, and LinkPoint charge to provide developers with the capability to add this virtual shopping cart functionality to their own Web sites. Fortunately for you, Dreamweaver again comes through with the UltraDev Shopping Cart behavior, providing you, the developer, with yet another simple solution that would otherwise cost a few hundred dollars.

This chapter discusses creating an online shopping cart for the Web Store application. The topics covered in this chapter include

- A shopping cart definition
- An overview of the UltraDev Shopping Cart

- Installing the UltraDev Shopping Cart

- Building the Web Store shopping cart

If you have not already done so, you can download all the files for this and other chapters from www.dreamweavermxunleashed.com.

Creating the Web Store Shopping Cart

This chapter focuses on the UltraDev Shopping Cart behavior. Although the name may sound deceptive, it is still very much a part of the Dreamweaver MX framework. Not only is it still supported under Dreamweaver MX, but it functions as well under UltraDev 4 as it does with Dreamweaver MX. The next few sections will provide you with a brief description of shopping cart technologies, an overview of the Shopping Cart behavior, and finally, integrating the Shopping Cart behavior with the Web Store application.

What Is a Shopping Cart?

The term shopping cart has been thrown around for a few years now. But what exactly is a shopping cart? We know a shopping cart to be the basket on wheels that you push around at a grocery store. Think about why you use the grocery store shopping cart. You go to your local grocery store, you push around the cart and add items from shelves as you see fit. When your shopping cart is full or you decide that you are finished shopping, you push your shopping cart all the way to the front of the store to the checkout counter. At the checkout counter, you proceed by providing your debit card, cash, or check to the cashier, finish the transaction, and off you go. Sound familiar? The Web is no different; rather than a physical shopping cart, you are provided with a virtual shopping cart, which is little more than a cookie, user session, or temporary array. A virtual table, if you will, then takes items that users request from the database and stores them into a temporary location (cookie, session, array) until you are ready to check out. If you decide that you want another item or more of the same item, you keep adding to the cart. Similar to the grocery store checkout counters, virtual checkouts enable you to enter your credit card information for purchase, but rather than your physically walking away with the items, they are conveniently mailed to your doorstep.

Most people think of shopping carts in the terms of the preceding example. But in fact, the same methodology is used in Web sites such as Microsoft's Clip Art Gallery, MP3.com, or Photodisc. These Web sites use the same idea of a shopping cart, but rather than purchasing the items within your shopping cart, you simply download them. Think of online shopping carts as a virtual table that stores information that the user requests for downloading or purchasing.

The UltraDev Shopping Cart

The UltraDev Shopping Cart is the perfect example of Dreamweaver MX's flexibility and extensibility. It shows how one man can create a single set of behaviors that virtually eliminates dozens of hours of development time. Written purely in JavaScript by Rick Crawford, the UltraDev Shopping Cart consists of some powerful behaviors that enable you to create and manipulate merchandise within your Web application. Aside from the UltraDev Shopping Cart behavior, the UltraDev Shopping Cart behavior set consists of the following behaviors:

- **Add to Cart Via Form**   Enables the user to select a form object within a page to manually insert an item into the shopping cart.

- **Add to Cart Via Link**   Enables the user to select a link within a page to manually insert an item into the shopping cart.

- **Repeat Cart Region**   Similar to the Repeat Region behavior, the Repeat Cart Region repeats a table with multiple contents.

- **Update Cart**   Updates items within the cart via a form object contained within the shopping cart page.

- **Save Cart to Table**   Enables the user to save the order to a database table so that an administrator can later look through orders received for a particular day and mail merchandise out accordingly. This is where the orders table will come into play.

- **Get Unique ID from Table**   Enables the cart to dynamically retrieve a unique ID from a database table.

- **Empty Cart**   Selecting a link within the page empties the cart of its contents.

- **Redirect if Empty**   Redirects the user to a different page if the shopping cart is empty.

The UltraDev Shopping Cart's functionality begins with the UltraDev Shopping Cart behavior. Very similar to a recordset, the UltraDev Shopping Cart allows for dynamic text binding within form objects, tables, and so on. The UltraDev Shopping Cart behavior is created in either the Server Behaviors or the Bindings panel, again similar to the recordset. Shopping cart items appear within the drop-down, available from the (+) icon, along with the capability to bind the number of items within the cart, the sum of the quantity of all items within the cart, and the sum of the prices of all of the items within the cart.

> **NOTE**
>
> The good part about the UltraDev Shopping Cart is it's free. The bad part about the Ultradev Shopping Cart is that it was written for the first release of UltraDev and not Dreamweaver MX. To get some of the features to work correctly with Dreamweaver MX, modification to the code will be limited but required. The newest version of the UltraDev Shopping Cart, the UltraDev Shopping Cart II, works with newer versions of Dreamweaver and includes more functionality, but it costs money.

Now that you have a firm understanding of what constitutes the UltraDev Shopping Cart, let's go over the installation process.

Installing the UltraDev Shopping Cart

Like most, if not all Dreamweaver MX extensions, you can obtain the UltraDev Shopping Cart extension for free from the Macromedia Dreamweaver Exchange (`http://dynamic.macromedia.com/bin/MM/exchange/main.jsp?product=ultradev`). To obtain and install the necessary files, follow the steps outlined next:

1. Navigate to the Dreamweaver UltraDev Exchange. If you have not done so by now, you will be required to obtain a Macromedia user ID and password. After you obtain the proper user ID and password, you will be asked to log in. Successful login will redirect you to a personalized page, as shown in Figure 31.1.

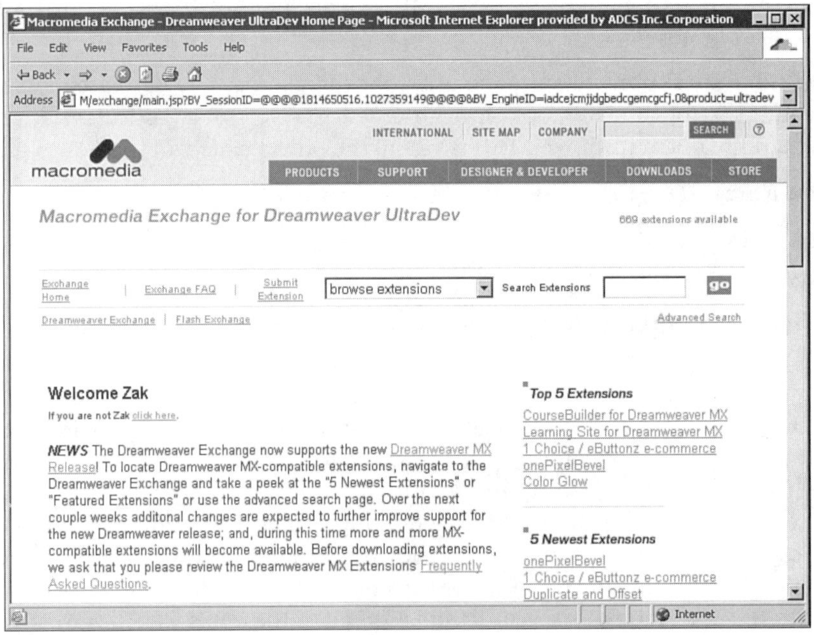

FIGURE 31.1 Log in with your user ID and password to access the personalized site.

2. Select the e-commerce extensions from the drop-down menu. Halfway down the second page, you will see the selection for the UltraDev Shopping Cart as well as the UltraDev Shopping Cart II. Download the UltraDev Shopping Cart by selecting the link as shown in Figure 31.2.

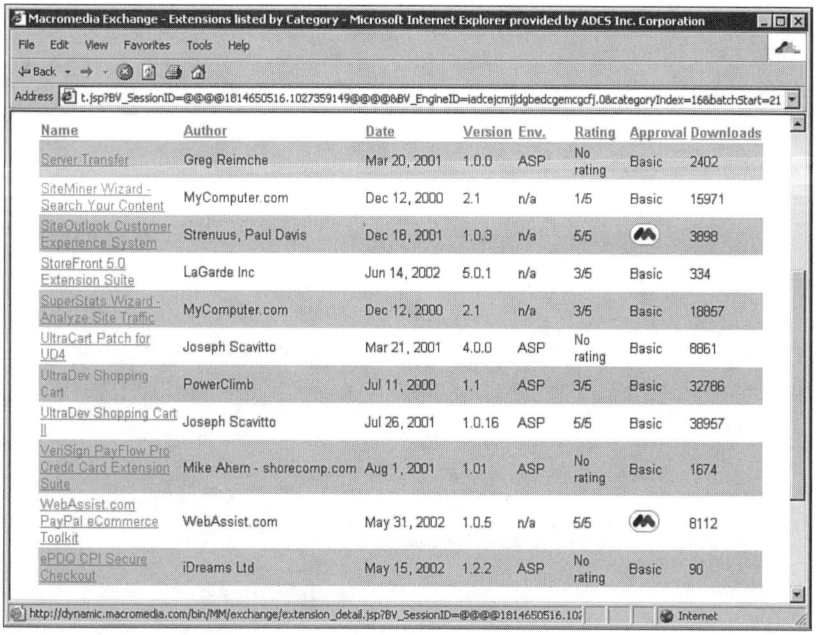

FIGURE 31.2 Select the UltraDev Shopping Cart extension.

TIP

To eliminate any coding errors, you should download and install the UltraCart Patch for UD4 available just above the UltraDev Shopping Cart. This guarantees that the UltraDev Shopping Cart will run smoothly.

3. After you select the appropriate extension, you will be presented with a choice for the type of computer you are using. Select PC, as shown in Figure 31.3.

4. After the Save As dialog box appears, navigate to the Downloaded Extensions folder within your Dreamweaver MX program folder and click Save, as shown in Figure 31.4.

5. Your last step is to find that MXP file within the Downloaded Extensions folder. Double-click it to install it, using the Macromedia Extension Manager as shown in Figure 31.5.

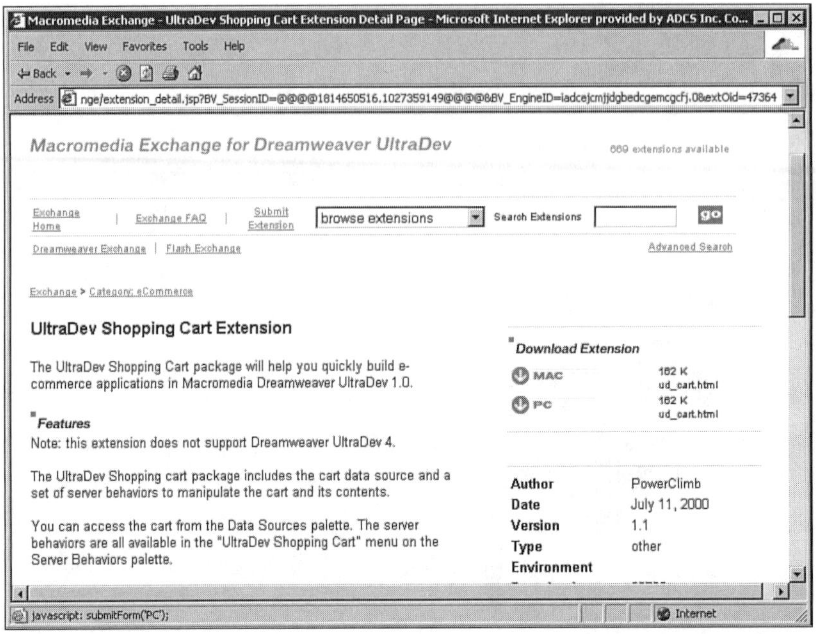

FIGURE 31.3   Select the extension based on the type of computer you are using.

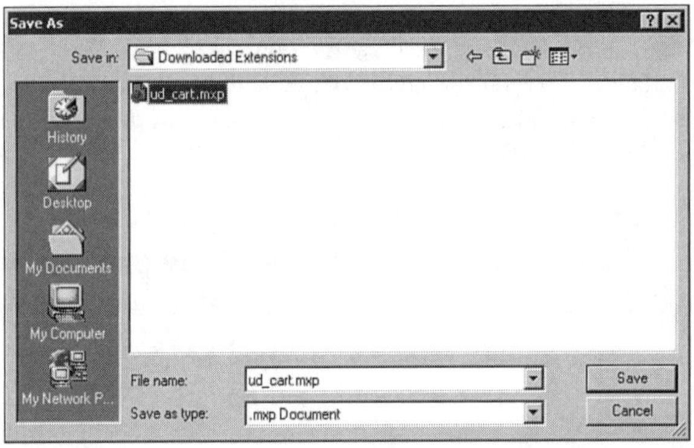

FIGURE 31.4   Save the extension to your Downloaded Extensions folder within Dreamweaver MX.

Integrating the Shopping Cart with the Web Store

Now that the UltraDev Shopping Cart has been installed, you can access it from either the Server Behaviors panel or the Bindings panel. The next few sections will go over the UltraDev Shopping Cart in more detail as it relates to the Web Store application. You can begin by opening Dreamweaver MX if you have not already done so. Choose the plus sign (+) icon from either the Server Behaviors panel or the Bindings panel to reveal the UltraDev Shopping Cart, as shown in Figure 31.6.

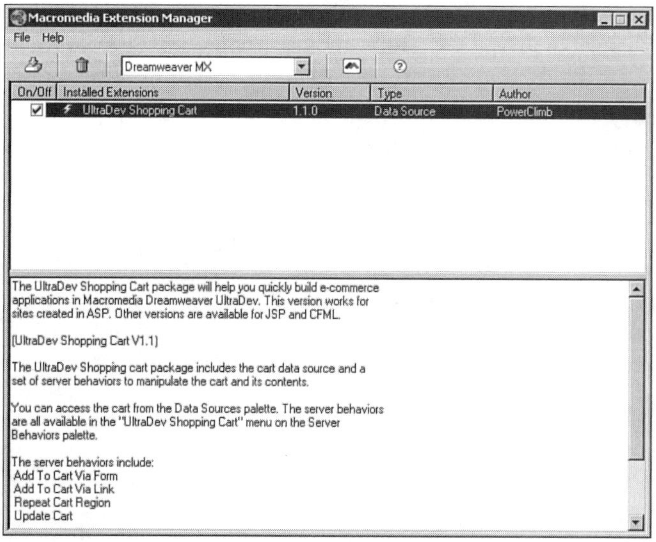

FIGURE 31.5   Install the Shopping Cart extension by double-clicking the MXP file, which is located in the Downloaded Extensions folder.

FIGURE 31.6   Select the plus sign (+) icon to reveal the newly installed UltraDev Shopping Cart.

Building the Web Store Shopping Cart

Oddly enough, the Web store shopping cart will be built starting with the viewcart.asp page. The reason for this is simple: first to demonstrate how the UltraDev Shopping Cart behavior is utilized and second because it is the only page that will use the binding features within it. You can begin building the Web store shopping cart by following the steps outlined next:

1. Create a new page by selecting New from the File menu. Navigate to the Advanced tab and select the WebStore template.

2. Immediately save the page as viewcart.asp.

3. Add the Shopping Cart behavior by selecting the UltraDev Shopping Cart from the Bindings panel. The UltraDev Shopping Cart dialog box appears. The UltraDev Shopping Cart dialog box enables you to configure the following options:

   - **Cart Name**   You can give your shopping cart any name that you want. Like a recordset, it's best to name the cart something relevant to your site.

   - **Cookie Expiration**   To store the information that users place within their carts, a cookie is written to the user's computer. You can set the number of days to store the cookie or select 0 for none. For the time being, select 0. This guarantees that when the browser is closed, the user's information will not be stored. It is important to note that by setting the number of days to store the cookie, you are essentially allowing users to come back and still have the same items inside their carts. The cart will not be empty until either the user physically empties it or the cookie expires.

   - **Shopping Cart Columns**   You can define the columns that the cart will use to store data. By default, ProductID, Quantity, Price, and Total cannot be deleted. These are functions that are used by the Shopping Cart behavior.

   - **Column Name**   You can edit the name of any column that you add.

   - **Compute By**   You can set how the UltraDev Shopping Cart will compute certain columns. For instance, the Total field multiplies the Price by the Quantity column to obtain a result. You can set these computations by hand using this selection.

4. When you are finished configuring the dialog box, the result should look similar to Figure 31.7.

5. Notice that the names of the columns match the Products table almost exactly. These columns will eventually be read from the dynamic text that is inserted within the viewcatalog.asp page.

6. Now that you have created the shopping cart, you are ready to begin building the table that will display the dynamic data. Insert the text **View Cart** in place of the Header editable region.

7. Insert a table with three rows and five columns. Insert the captions Product #, Name, Quantity, Price, and Total. Select all the captions and make them bold. The result is shown in Figure 31.8.

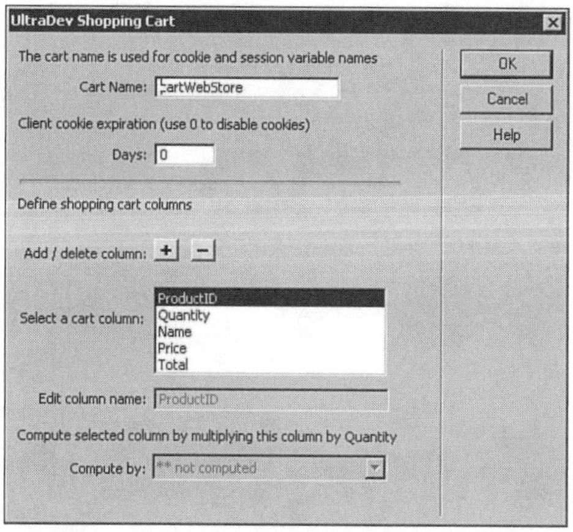

FIGURE 31.7   Configure your cart accordingly.

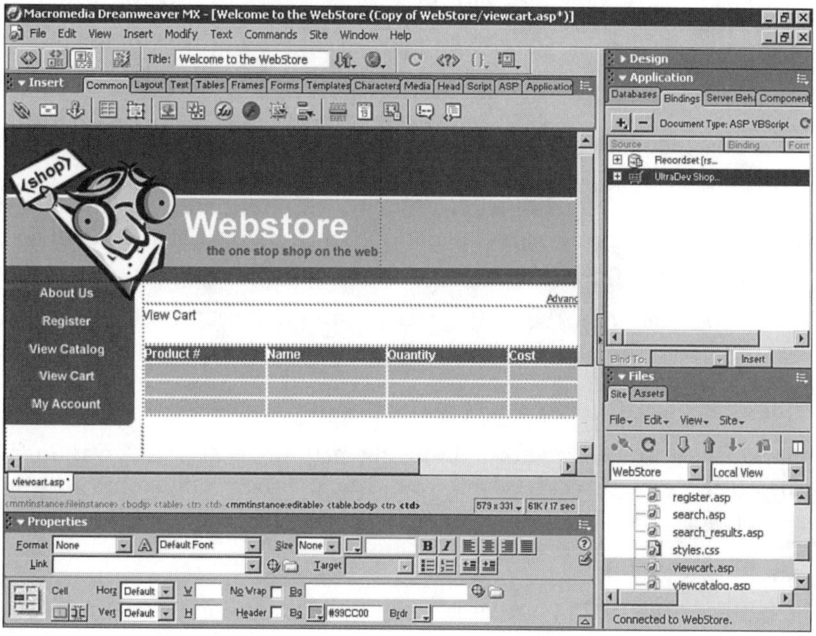

FIGURE 31.8   Create a new table that will display the items within the cart.

8. You are now free to drag the columns from the shopping cart into the appropriate table cells, as shown in Figure 31.9.

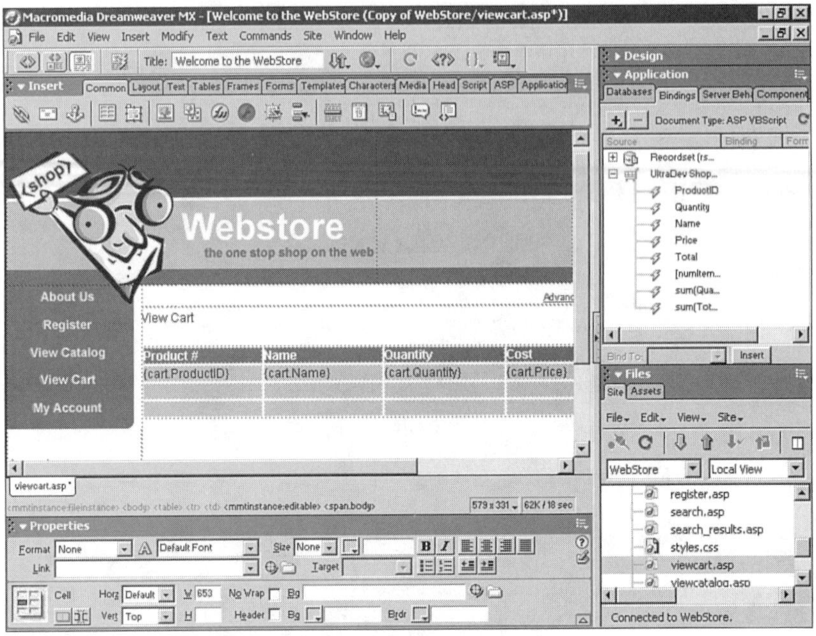

FIGURE 31.9   Drag the shopping cart columns into the appropriate cells within the table.

9. To calculate the grand total of all of the items within the cart, merge the two bottom-right cells, add the caption Grand Total, and drag the sum[total] column into the table cell. The result is shown in Figure 31.10.

10. You can also format how the total appears within that cell by selecting the drop-down arrow from the sum[Total] column within the shopping cart. Select Currency, as shown in Figure 31.11.

Although it doesn't seem like much was done, the majority of the work was, in fact, accomplished. The next few sections walk you through other options that are available within the shopping cart.

Repeating Cart Regions

Similar to bindings fields within a recordset, the UltraDev Shopping Cart will display only the first item added unless you allow for regions to repeat. You can insert the Repeat Cart Region to accomplish this task. To insert the Repeat Cart Region behavior, follow these steps:

1. Select the entire second row of the table within the viewcart.asp page and select the Repeat Cart Region behavior from the UltraDev Shopping Cart submenu, as shown in Figure 31.12.

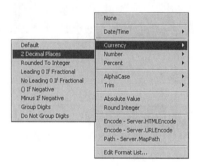

FIGURE 31.10 Create a cell for the grand total and drag the column from the shopping cart into it.

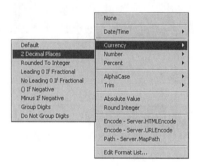

FIGURE 31.11 Format the text within the cell to a currency data type.

2. With the Repeat Cart Region behavior inserted, it may be a good idea to switch over to code/design view to make sure that the For...Next Loop was inserted correctly. These two lines of code loop through all the items within the cart, dynamically creating rows until there are no more items left to display. The code should resemble the code in Figure 31.13.

FIGURE 31.12   Insert the Repeat Cart Region to allow for records to repeat.

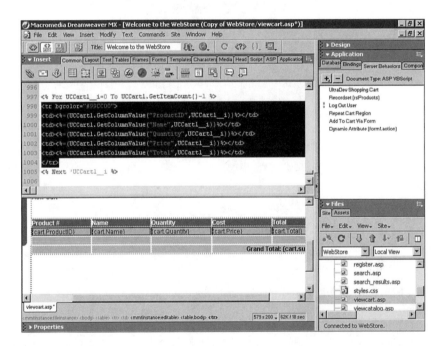

FIGURE 31.13   Check the code to make sure the loop was added correctly.

Emptying the Cart

As you may have guessed, after users begin filling their carts with items, it may become necessary to enable them to remove those items. Fortunately, by using the Empty Cart behavior, you can provide this functionality to your users. To insert the Empty Cart behavior, follow the steps outlined next:

1. Place your cursor in the second cell of the last row and insert a link with the text Empty Cart.

2. Select the Empty Cart behavior from the UltraDev Shopping Cart submenu, as shown in Figure 31.14.

FIGURE 31.14   Insert the Empty Cart behavior.

3. The Empty Cart dialog box appears. The link should be prepopulated for you because you selected it prior to inserting the behavior. You can also specify a redirect URL. For now, simply redirect the user to the viewcatalog.asp page. You can also include a parameter to be passed on to the querystring to alert the user that the cart is empty.

4. Select OK.

Making Quantities Editable

You've probably noticed that the quantities are currently hard coded, meaning that when the user adds an item to the cart, it automatically inserts a single item. You can allow users to modify how many items they would like in their carts by changing a text box value. Rather than binding the quantity column to the table cell, you can add a text box to allow users to modify the value on their own. Then by clicking an Update Cart button, users can change the quantities within the cart. You can add this functionality by following the steps outlined next:

1. Insert a new form button into the first cell of the last row. Give it the label Update Cart. Make sure that the button is set to Submit. The result is shown in Figure 31.15.

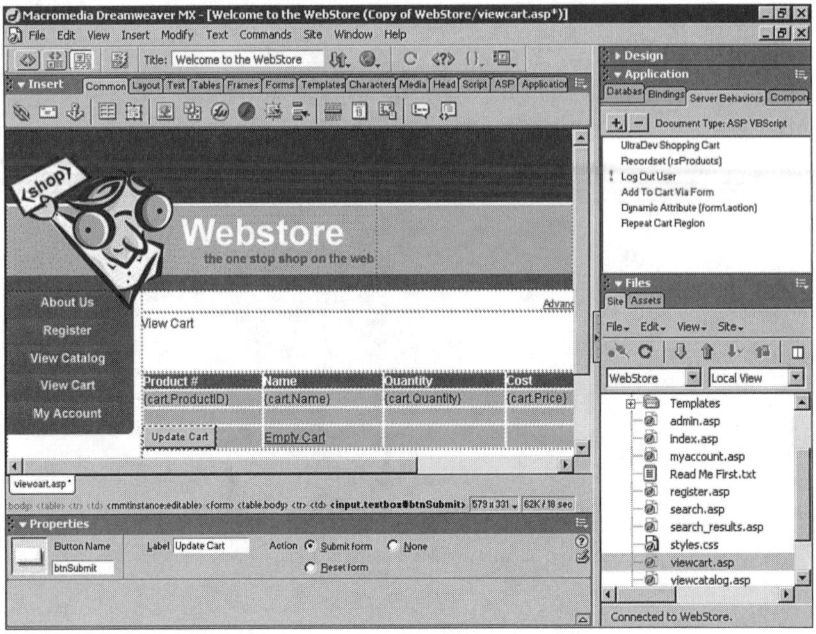

FIGURE 31.15   Insert a new button to update the quantities.

2. The next step is create the text field that will display the quantities and ultimately allow the user to make edits. Remove the text binding from within the Quantity column and insert a new text field form object. Name it Quantity.

3. Bind the Quantity column to the text field object, as shown in Figure 31.16.

4. The Update Cart behavior will now take care of the update. You can select the Update Cart behavior from the UltraDev Shopping Cart submenu, as shown in Figure 31.17.

5. The Update Cart behavior enables you to specify the form and form object to use for the cart update. You can also specify the URL to redirect to after the update takes place. You can add a parameter to alert the user of the update. The result is shown in Figure 31.18.

6. The last step is to add code that grabs the parameter and displays a message to the user. Add the text **The text has been updated** just below the table and insert the code similar to Figure 31.19.

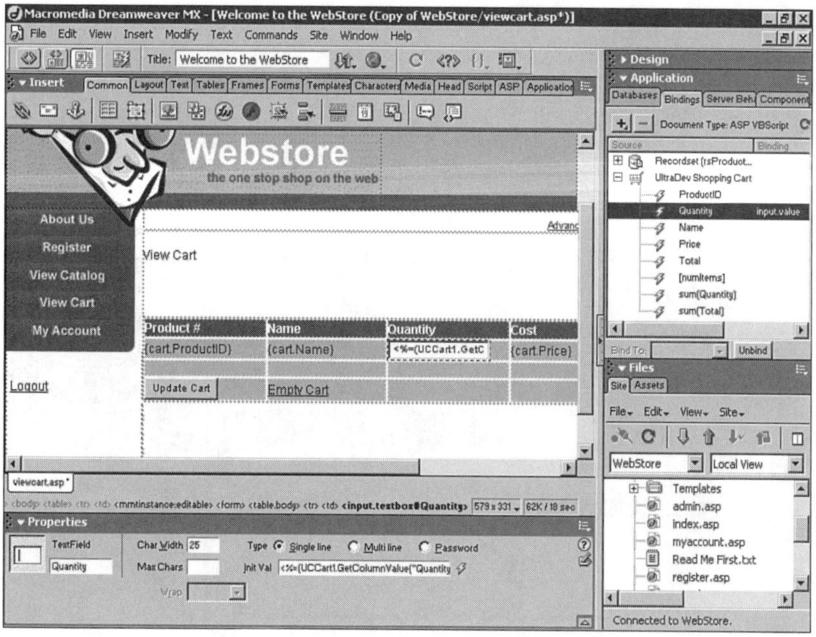

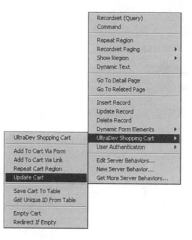

FIGURE 31.16   Bind the Quantity shopping cart column to the new text box.

FIGURE 31.17   Select the Update Cart behavior.

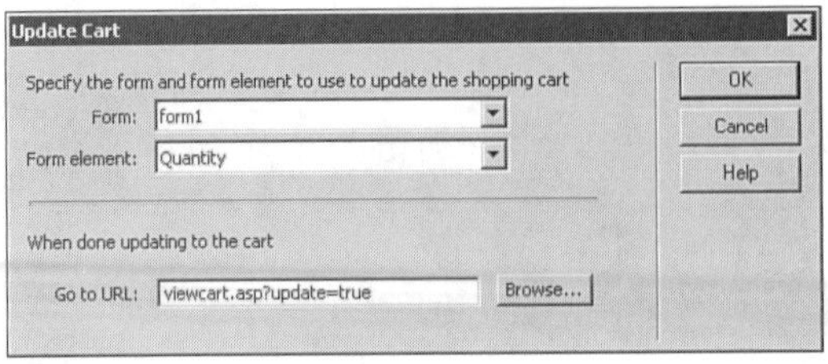

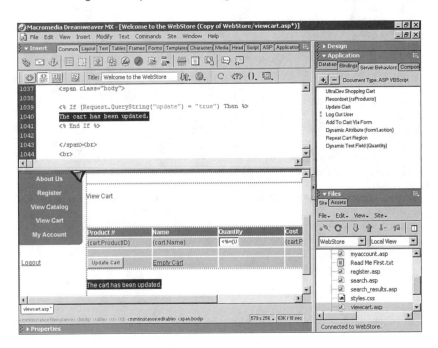

FIGURE 31.18   Configure the Update Cart dialog box to handle your update.

FIGURE 31.19   Add the code to handle the custom error message.

The viewcart.asp page should be completely finished. You will now be able to see all the items as the users insert them, clear the cart if necessary, and update items within the cart. The next step will focus in on the most important part of the chapter: adding items to the cart.

Adding Items to the Cart

So far you've learned how to display the items that the cart contains. But you can't stop there. You need to be able to add items to the cart before you can actually view them. This section introduces you to the Add to Cart Via Form behavior contained within the UltraDev Shopping Cart submenu.

As previously mentioned, there are two ways of adding items to the cart: Add to Cart Via Form and Add to Cart Via Link. Because both do virtually the same thing, this section will focus primarily on the Add to Cart Via Form behavior. To add an item to the cart, follow these steps:

1. Before you can begin adding items to the cart, you need to create a simple image field that will submit the contents of the dynamic text elements. Add two more rows to the table just below Cost.

2. Add a new image field pointing the source to the addtocart.gif located within the images directory. The result is shown in Figure 31.20. Remember, the image field acts the same as the Submit button form object.

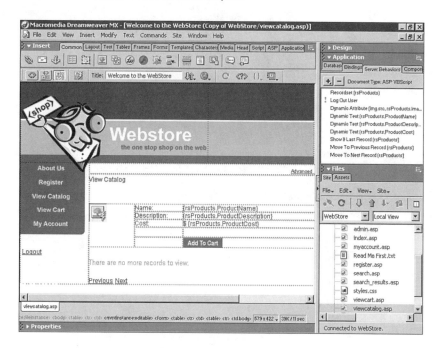

FIGURE 31.20   Insert a new image field to handle the form submission.

3. Add the Add to Cart Via Form server behavior by selecting it from the UltraDev Shopping Cart submenu, as shown in Figure 31.21.

4. The Add to Cart Via Form dialog box appears. The dialog box enables you to configure all the data items that will be sent into the cart. You are able to select the form that the data is coming from, all the cart columns and their corresponding data elements within the recordset, the actual recordset to use, and the URL to redirect to after the Add takes place. The important feature within this dialog box is within the cart columns. You want to make sure to match up the appropriate cart columns with

the appropriate data elements within the recordset. The exception is the Quantity column. You can use a numeric literal 1, guaranteeing that only one item will be inserted at a time. Remember, quantity edits are handled within the viewcart.asp page. The following table illustrates the data elements that you should point your cart columns to:

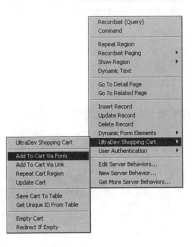

FIGURE 31.21 Add the Add to Cart Via Form.

Cart Column	Data Element	Value
ProductID	Recset Col	ProductID
Quantity	Literal	1
Name	Recset Col	ProductName
Price	Recset Col	ProductCost

5. The result of the dialog box will look similar to Figure 31.22.

6. Select OK.

7. Save your work and test it within the browser. Log in to the site and navigate to View Catalog.

8. Find a DVD to place into your cart and select the Add to Cart button. Figure 31.23 shows the result of the added item.

9. Select the View Catalog link again and try adding a different item. Figure 31.24 shows how a different item is added but the cart remembers the previous addition.

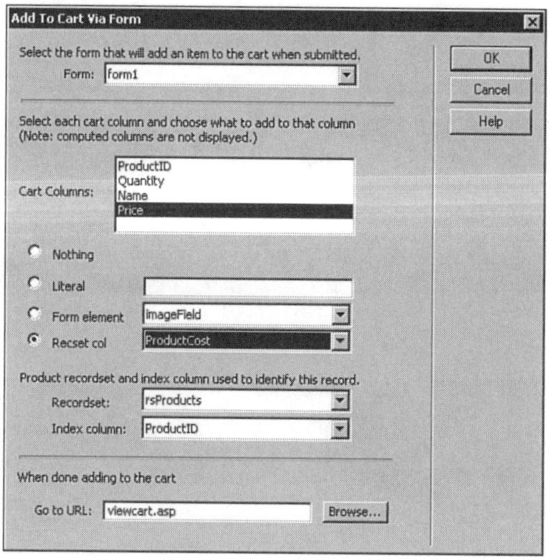

FIGURE 31.22   Configure the Add to Cart Via Form dialog box, matching the appropriate cart columns with their respective data elements.

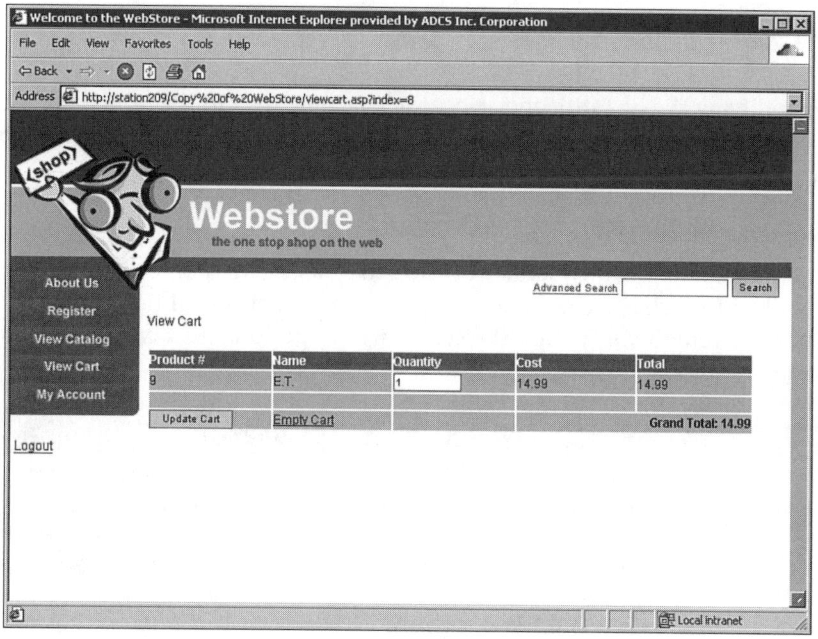

FIGURE 31.23   Adding an item displays it within the view cart page.

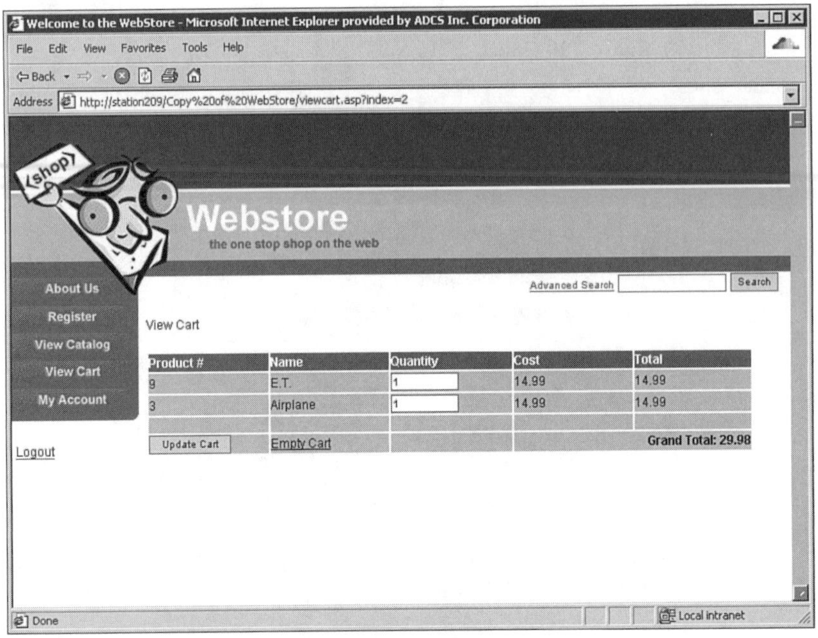

FIGURE 31.24   Adding another item lists it within the cart page.

10. Try modifying the quantity and select the Update Cart button. Notice how the grand total changes to compensate for the added quantity. Figure 31.25 shows the result.

Checking Out the Customer

Now that the customer has a good idea of what to order, the customer may want to continue with the purchase. This section covers creating a checkout page so that a particular customer can verify items within the cart as well as personal and credit card information.

NOTE

You will notice that throughout this section, there is no place for a customer to enter credit card information. The reason for this is twofold. First, we store the credit card information when the user registers, and second, tying the cart to a third-party payment host is beyond the scope of this book and is therefore not covered. This example assumes that the responsibility of running the credit card will rely on the merchant after the order has been processed. It's important to point out, though, that a truly dynamic site would integrate some third-party online payment service such as VeriSign or PayPal for electronic payment deductions.

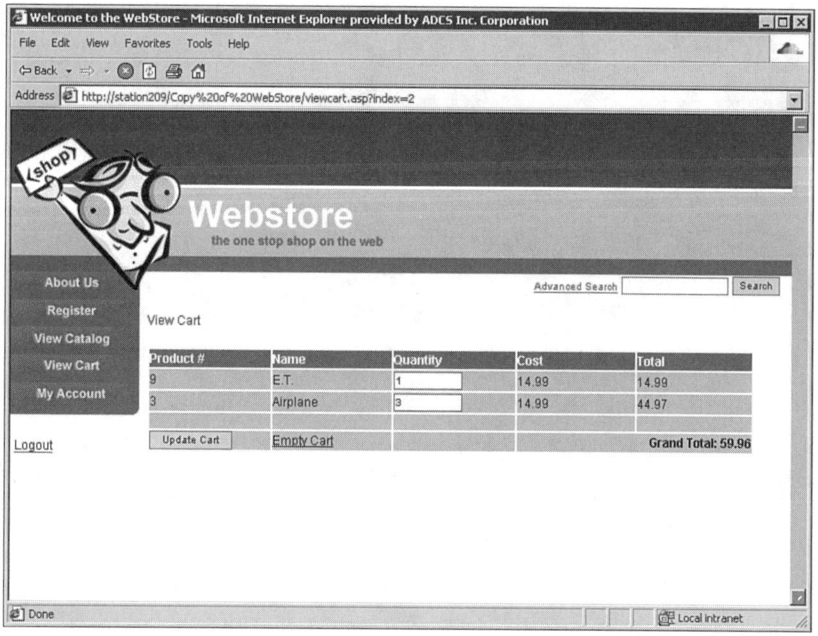

FIGURE 31.25   Modify the quantity to change the grand total.

Creating the Checkout Page

It's always a good idea to provide a quick synopsis of the user's information as well as a detailed overview of all the items that the user is purchasing. You may also want to provide randomly generated numbers that users can reference whenever they contact your customer support department. Another benefit to creating a checkout page is the capability for the user to track and print out the summary as an invoice. You can create the checkout page for the Web Store application by following these steps:

1. You can use the same viewcart.asp page by selecting Save As and saving the file as checkout.asp.

2. With checkout.asp open, add a new table with five rows and two columns with the captions Customer ID, Name, Shipping Address, Billing Address, and Credit Card. You may also want to add two more rows above that new table with the caption Order Number.

3. Remove the Update Cart button, Quantity text field, Empty Cart link, and all associated behaviors. Rebind the quantity column as a dynamic text element.

4. Create two more rows under the Cart table and place a new form Submit button aligned to the right. The result is shown in Figure 31.26.

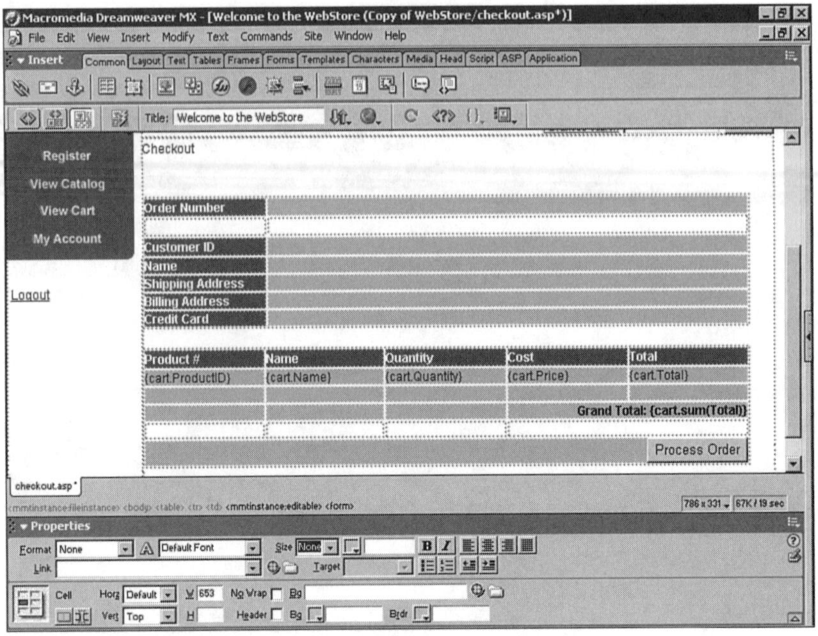

FIGURE 31.26   Create the new checkout.asp page by inserting table rows and a form Submit button.

5. Switch back to the viewcart.asp page and add two more rows just below the grand total. Add a Check Out link pointing to the checkout.asp page in the last cell. Align it right. The result is shown in Figure 31.27.

The next few steps outline creating a new recordset to retrieve the Customers information, as well as a customized way to create a randomized order number.

Obtaining the Customer ID

Probably the most crucial piece of the puzzle is the session variable that was created when the user logged in. The reason for this is simple. So far you've been adding items to your cart and modifying quantities without any concern for who these items will be for. If the user decided to purchase the items that they've added to their cart, how would the application know, or you the merchant know, who to send the final merchandise to? Retrieving and setting that information into the checkout page allows us to process that information and eventually update that customer into the orders table. Before we jump ahead of ourselves, let's look at how to retrieve the user's information into the checkout page:

1. First, create a new recordset in simple mode. Name the new recordset rsCustomer, define the table as the Customer_CreditCards view, and create a new filter for Username and set that equal to the session variable MM_Username. The result is shown in Figure 31.28.

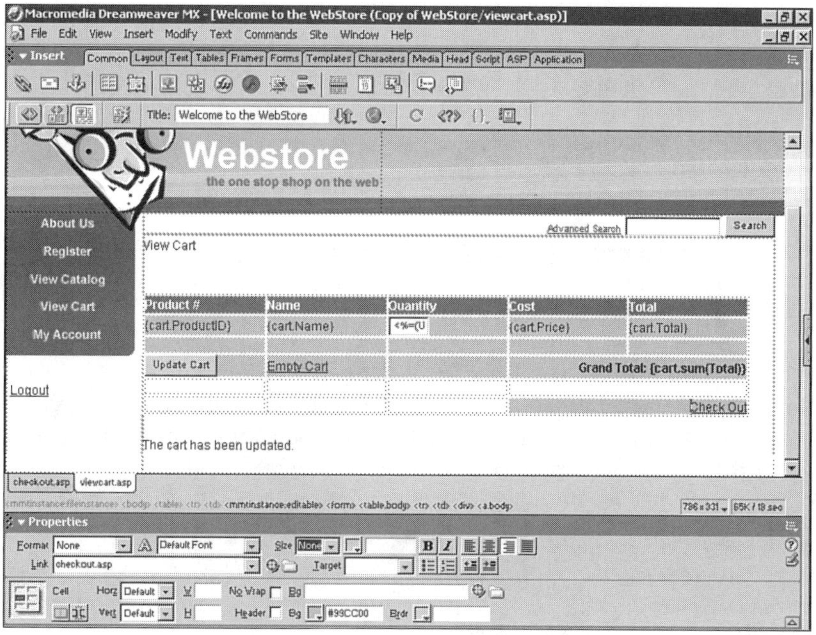

FIGURE 31.27   Add a new link that points to the checkout.asp page.

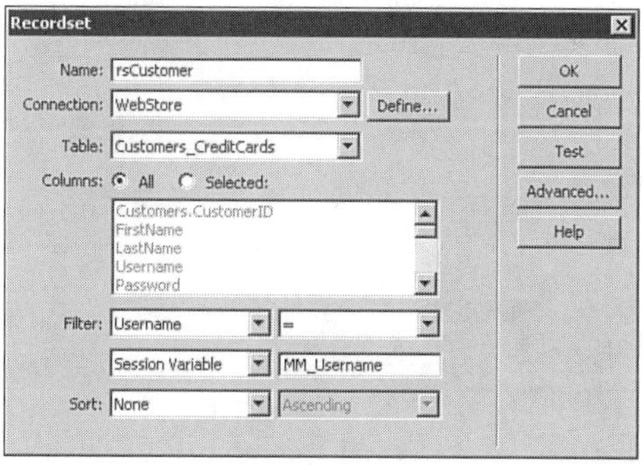

FIGURE 31.28   Create a new recordset for the customer.

TIP

Remember the queries you set up within the database? Those queries, also known as views, can be selected from the Table drop-down list. They replace having to type in all that SQL code within the Advanced screen.

2. Select the Test button. The Test Value dialog box will appear. Because you know that the username will be set to the only record within the database, enter it into the text field as shown in Figure 31.29. Select OK.

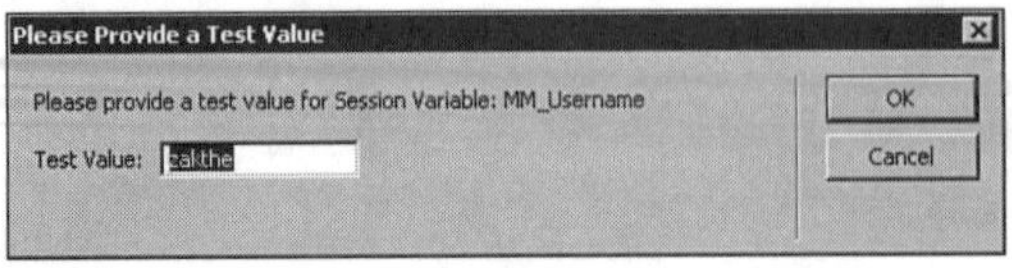

FIGURE 31.29   Enter a test value into the text field.

3. The results are shown in the Test SQL Statement window. Remember, the recordset will retrieve all the information exactly as you see it within Figure 31.30. The filter you created creates the WHERE clause with the value of the username and matches it up with the appropriate value within the database table. Select OK.

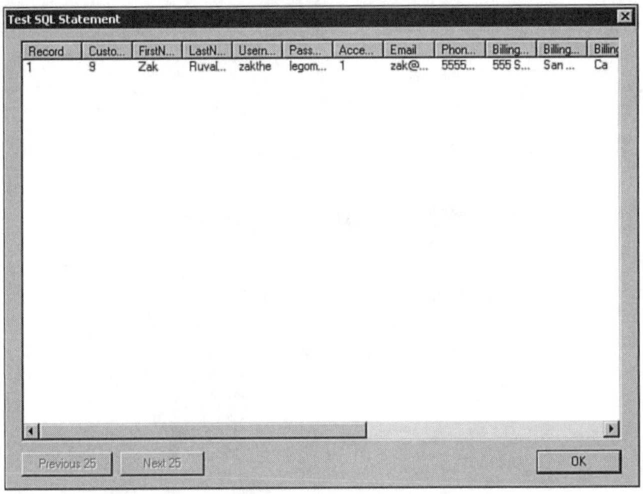

FIGURE 31.30   The results show exactly what the recordset will filter.

4. Select OK to create the new customer recordset.

5. With the recordset created, you are now ready to drag all the appropriate items into their respective fields within the table. The result will look similar to Figure 31.31.

Generating an Order Number

The creation of a randomly generated order number is always a good idea. This gives you a unique way of distinguishing the vast numbers of orders that you will eventually receive. It also provides a way for users to reference their orders if they ever need to contact you with a question or concern. You can create a randomly generated number by inserting some simple ASP code into your page. To do so, follow these steps:

1. Place your cursor inside the cell that will display the order number and switch to code view.

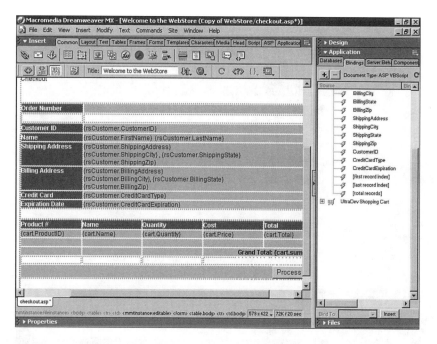

FIGURE 31.31   Drag all the data elements into their respective positions within the table.

2. Insert the code as it appears within Figure 31.32.

You can test the randomized code by launching the Web store in the browser. Navigate to the view catalog page and select an item. Next, click Check Out, as shown in Figure 31.33.

Figure 31.34 shows how the randomize function displays a five-digit number. Click Refresh to randomize to a new number.

Writing to the Orders Table

The last order of business is to save all the information that the merchant needs into the orders table. Remember that to make the application seamless, you would want to integrate some third-party merchant software. For simplicity's sake, you are going to write all the information to the database, allowing the merchant to extract the data as they see fit. A quick review of the orders table, shown in Figure 31.35, shows the data that you need to account for.

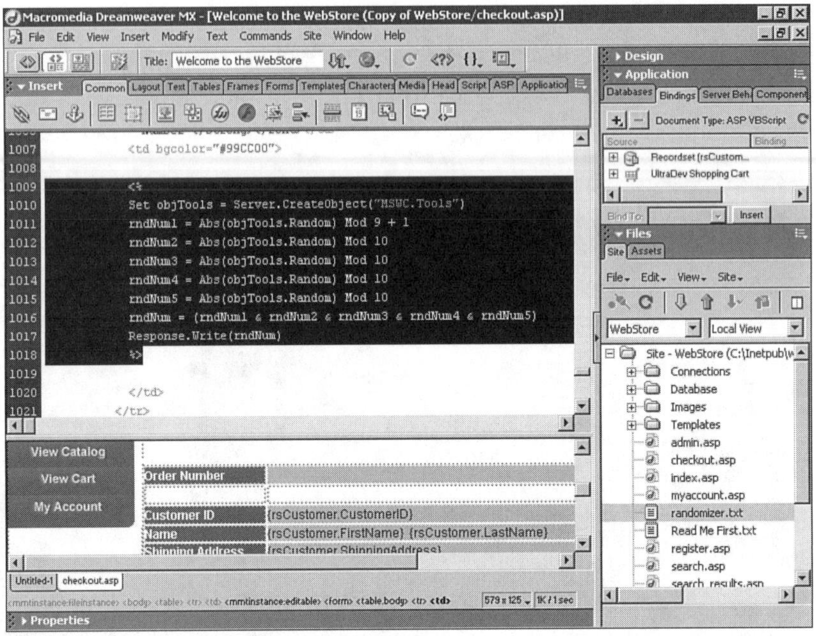

FIGURE 31.32   Insert the randomizer code to create an order number.

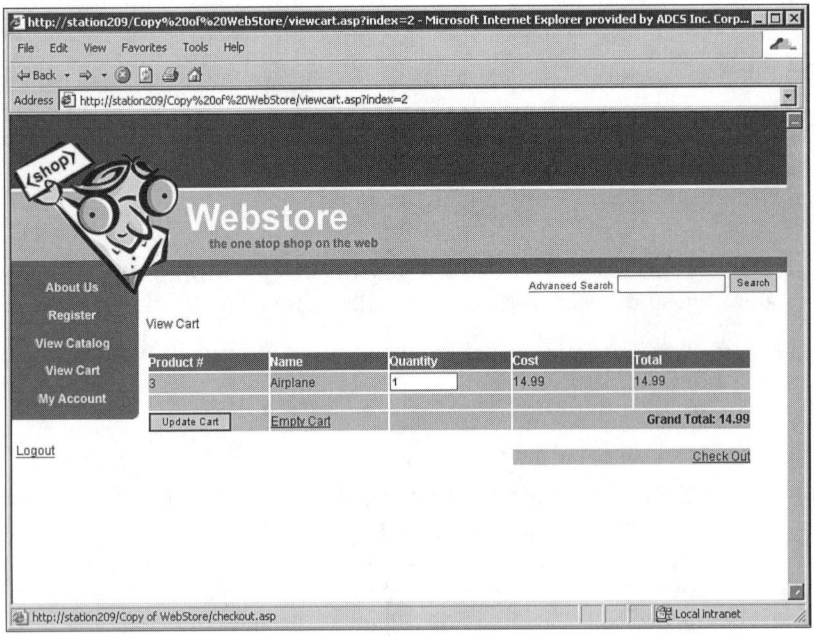

FIGURE 31.33   Select the checkout link to navigate to the checkout.asp page.

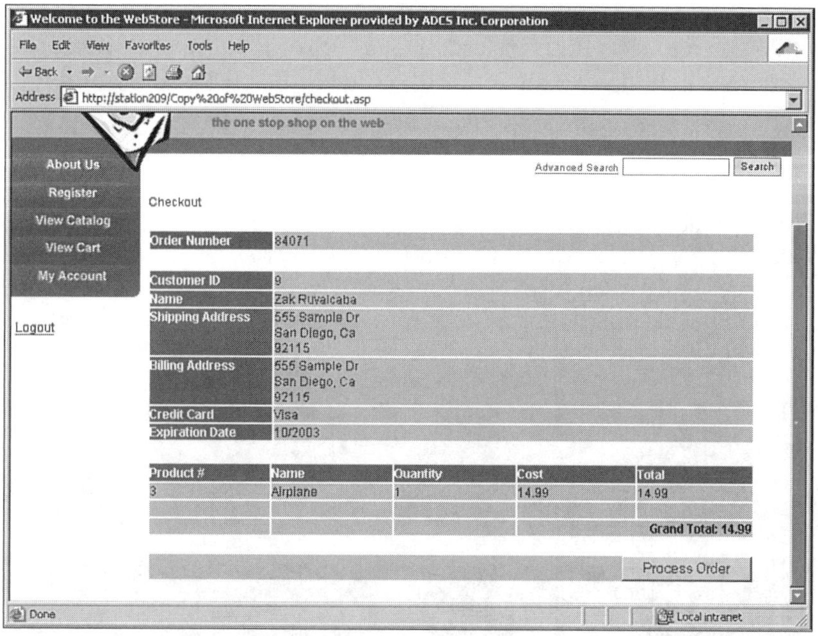

FIGURE 31.34 The randomize code displays a five-digit randomized number.

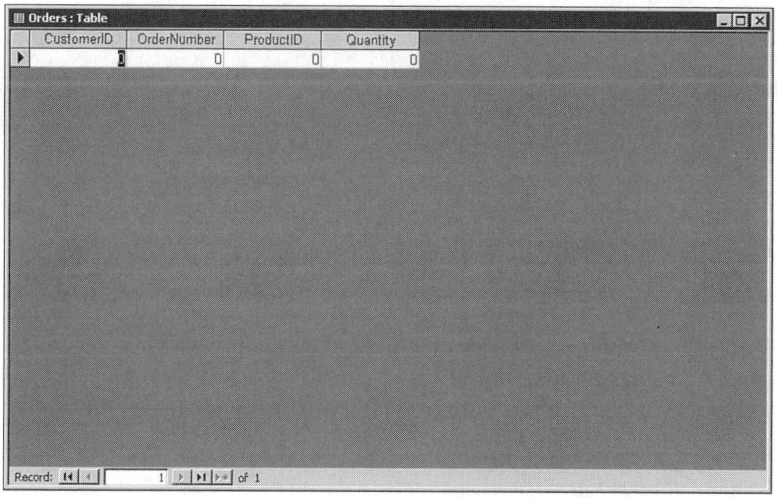

FIGURE 31.35 The orders table contains an ID from all the necessary tables.

You may be wondering why you are not including fields for all the information that is contained within the checkout.asp page. The beauty in relationships is that it lets you account for the rest of the data items within a given page through the use of the unique

ID. Later, when you want to extract all the information from a given table, you look it up by the ID that is contained within the orders table. This will make more sense toward the end of the section. To begin to write to the orders table, follow the steps outlined next:

1. Review how the information will be written to the orders table. You will use the Insert Record behavior, but remember that the Insert Record behavior requires form objects with data within them to extract. You can solve this problem by inserting hidden form fields next to all the data items within the checkout.asp page. You will need hidden form fields for the CustomerID, ProductID, Quantity, and OrderNumber fields. Insert new hidden form fields by placing your cursor next to the data item and selecting Hidden Field from the Form Objects submenu of the Insert menu. The result is shown in Figure 31.36.

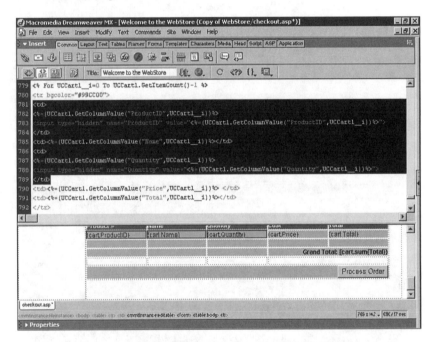

FIGURE 31.36   Insert hidden form fields for Quantity and Product ID.

2. Copy the two values and place them within the value attribute of the hidden fields.

```
<%= (UCCart1.GetColumnValue("ProductID",UCCart1_i)) %>
<%= (UCCart1.GetColumnValue("Quantity",UCCart1_i)) %>
```

3. This guarantees that the values are written not only to the table cells, but into the hidden form fields as well. Repeat the same steps for the Order Number and Customer ID. The result is shown in Figure 31.37.

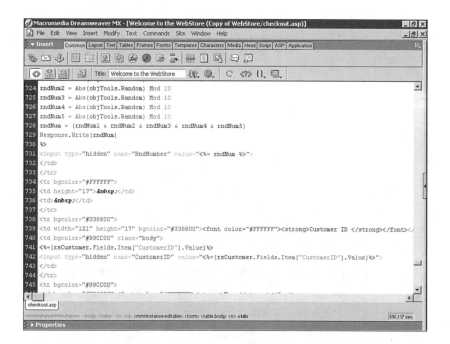

FIGURE 31.37   Insert hidden form fields for Customer ID and Order Number.

4. This time, copy the following items into the value attribute of the hidden form fields:

```
<%= rndNum %>
<%= (rsCustomer.Fields.Item("CustomerID").value) %>
```

5. Now that the form fields are inserted, you can create your Insert Record behavior.

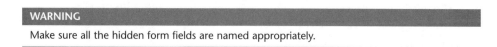

WARNING

Make sure all the hidden form fields are named appropriately.

6. Select Insert Record from the Server Behaviors drop-down menu, as shown in Figure 31.38.

7. The Insert Record dialog box will appear. Notice how only the hidden form fields appear within the Form Elements box. Match up the appropriate form objects with their respective field name within the orders table, as shown in Figure 31.39.

FIGURE 31.38   Insert the Insert Record server behavior.

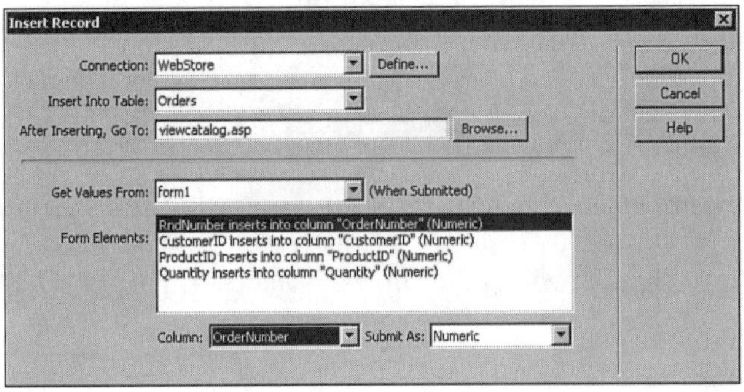

FIGURE 31.39   Modify the Form Elements box to match up the form objects with the record-set field names.

8. Save your work and test it in the browser. Make sure you log in; otherwise, the Customer won't be read correctly within the checkout.asp page.

9. Select an item from the viewcatalog.asp page. Click Checkout and select the Process Order button. You will be redirected back to the viewcatalog.asp page.

Figure 31.40 shows that if you open the orders table within Access, the appropriate information was indeed written.

If you open the customers table, you will find that the user was in fact the user whose CustomerID appears within the CustomerID column. If you open the products table, you will notice that the DVD selected is the DVD that appears within the orders table. Later, if you need to query the tables for the products and customers, you can filter the results based on the IDs that appear within the orders table.

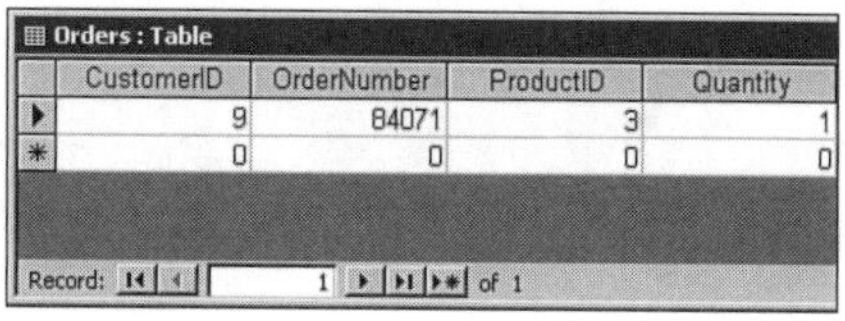

FIGURE 31.40   All the appropriate data was written to the orders table.

Summary

E-commerce is by all means an exciting, yet convoluted, topic. Depending on who you talk to, various theories and methodologies exist for how to handle transactions globally online. Fortunately for you, Dreamweaver MX provides rich extensions that alleviate the heartache that accompanies the subject.

Security and User Authentication

by Zak Ruvalcaba

One of the hottest topics going today is security. You can find Web sites, articles, ads, and books related to the subject. Many companies, consultants, and organizations are dedicated to helping you protect you and/or your company's vital asset—data. It's not a downside by any stretch of the imagination; in fact, major online news sites, portals, and even government agencies have been invaded in one form or another, all the while employing some measure of security. Although this chapter cannot begin to cover all there is to know regarding the subject, it can help you better understand the basic framework to securing your Web applications.

If you have not done so already, you can download the files for this and other chapters from `www.dreamweavermxunleashed.com`.

Securing the Web Store

The security umbrella encompasses many facets of information technology, including Web development. Make sure users go where they need to go and see what they're allowed to see within your application. Make sure everyone who visits your site logs in before they can view any pages and if they are not logged in, make sure that they don't just happen to type in the URL to a section of the application specifically meant for an administrator. Although different solutions exist for various applications that you may create—for instance, IIS could provide certain pages to users who have been authenticated by NT user groups within an intranet environment—this chapter focuses on simple form/script-based authentication.

Dreamweaver MX has a solution for securing the Web Store application in its user authentication server behaviors. In combination with some simple coding techniques, this chapter will enable you to accomplish the following tasks:

- Create a login page
- Restrict users based on username, password, and access level
- Log out users
- Create custom error messages
- Check for duplicate usernames
- Secure your ASP.NET application

Creating a Login Page

The first step to securing any Web application is to create a login page for your users. Obviously there would be no point in creating an admin page, for instance, if just anyone could use it. Ideally what you want is an application that allows your users to register and navigate through the site based on access rights that you specify. What benefit does this provide? You could assume that you would want everyone to come to your site and purchase items without the tedious task of becoming a registered user. The question becomes whether your users are repeat customers. If they are, they may be typing in all their personal information more than once, essentially ending up with more work than simply registering once the first time around. Another benefit is that you can store all your users' shipping and billing information, giving them a streamlined experience as they purchase items. As a developer, you may want to generate e-mails to your registered users, alerting them of specials and bargains. There are many benefits and reasons for maintaining registered users, and after they are registered, you will want them to access the site via a secure location, typically accessed through a login page.

You've seen login pages before; eBay, for instance, asks you to log in to their site before you bid on an item. You can see the correlation if you wanted to actually purchase something. How would the application know which shopping cart to place the item into? A login page enables you not only to maintain registered users, but to create sessions for the users' experience while they're on your site. That way, if a customer wants to purchase something, that item would be stored within that user's cart, belonging to that particular session. You can create a login page for the Web Store application by following the steps outlined next:

1. Create a new page by selecting New from the File menu. Choose the Advanced tab and select the Login template.

2. Within the content editable region, create a new form. Within the form, create a new table with four rows and three columns.

3. Below the new table, add a new link to the register.asp page; call it New User.

4. Create two new text box form objects, naming them username and password.

5. Add a Submit button object and change the label to read Login. The result is shown in Figure 32.1.

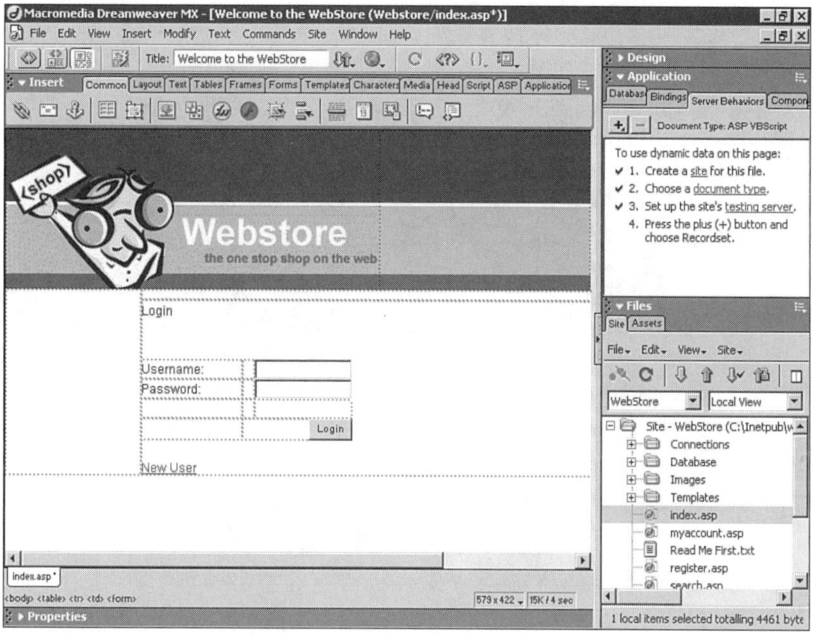

FIGURE 32.1   Create an outline for a login page.

1. You are now ready to insert the Log In User server behavior. Select the Log In User behavior from the User Authentication submenu, as shown in Figure 32.2.

2. The Log In User dialog box enables you to specify options for the client-side form and fields to match the form objects within the database, to redirect URLs for a successful connection and failed logins, and to specify an access restriction option. Although you will explore more of these options throughout the chapter, for now match up your settings with Figure 32.3.

FIGURE 32.2   Select the Log In User server behavior.

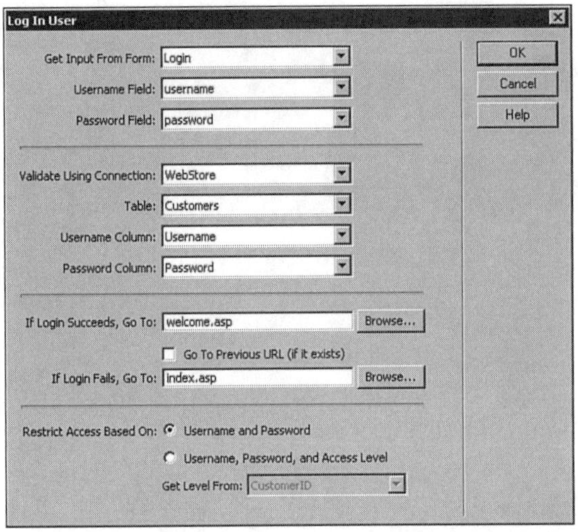

FIGURE 32.3   Add the appropriate settings for the Log In User dialog box.

3. Save the page as index.asp so that this will always be the first page that your users come to.

> **NOTE**
>
> If you have not done so already, you can configure IIS to accept index.asp as a default page. You can do this by right-clicking the Web site within IIS, selecting Properties, and choosing the Documents header.

4. Before you test the login page, check the customers table within the database to make sure that you have a valid username and password, as shown in Figure 32.4.

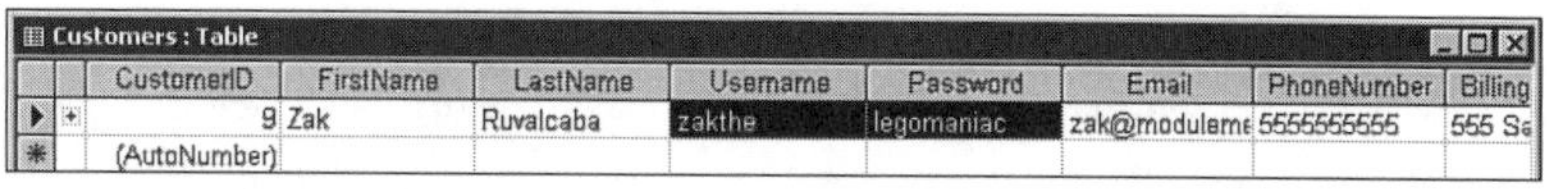

FIGURE 32.4   Check to make sure you have a valid username and password before attempting to log in.

5. Now that you know the username and password, try logging in. If you entered it correctly, you will be redirected to welcome.asp. If you entered it incorrectly, the page will simply redirect back to itself.

The great thing about the Log In User server behavior is that a session variable is automatically created for the user, called

```
Session("MM_Username")
```

This session can be used within other pages, either through server behaviors, code, or a combination of both to determine whether the user is logged in. You can even write out the user's name within the welcome message in the welcome.asp page. You can accomplish this by inserting the following code where the welcome message appears:

```
<span class="body">
Welcome to the WebStore <%= Session("MM_Username") %>
</span>
```

Now that you have a general understanding as to how the login page is created and what the basic framework is for creating a secure environment, jump to the next step: restricting users.

Restricting Access Based on Username, Password, and Access Level

Your next step in securing your Web application is to restrict those users who do not meet criteria specified by you. You can specify that criteria by setting an access level that will eventually be used to track users as they navigate through your site. The reason for this is simple—you want to make sure that your users do not accidentally navigate onto a page that they are not supposed to see, such as the admin.asp page. The last thing you want is for ordinary users to delete products from your store's database. You can create access levels for your users by following these steps:

1. Open the customers table in design view.

2. Right-click the e-mail field and select Insert Rows, as shown in Figure 32.5.

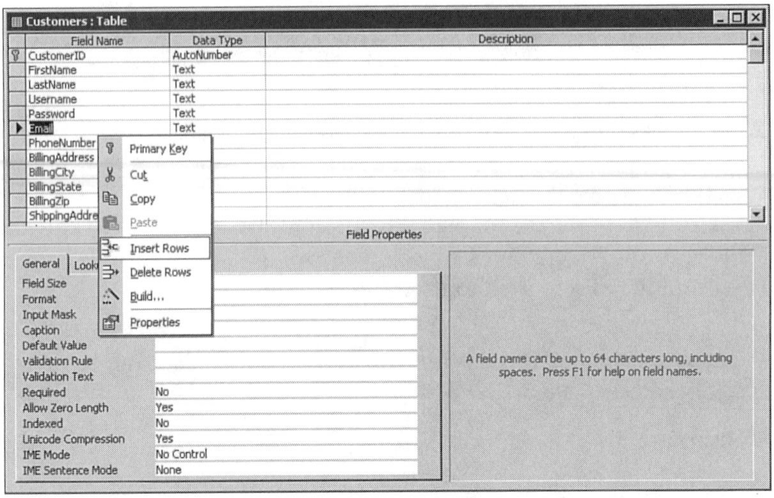

FIGURE 32.5   Insert a new row for the access level field.

3. Call the new field AccessLevel and give it a numeric data type, as shown in Figure 32.6.

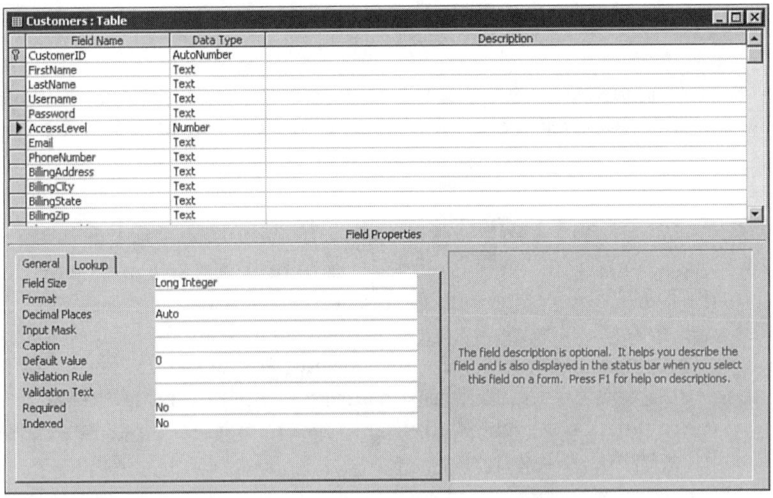

FIGURE 32.6   Call the new field **AccessLevel** and give it a numeric data type.

4. Switch to datasheet view and give the only user within the table an access level of 1, as shown in Figure 32.7. The following table describes the levels of users and how they will be tracked within the application:

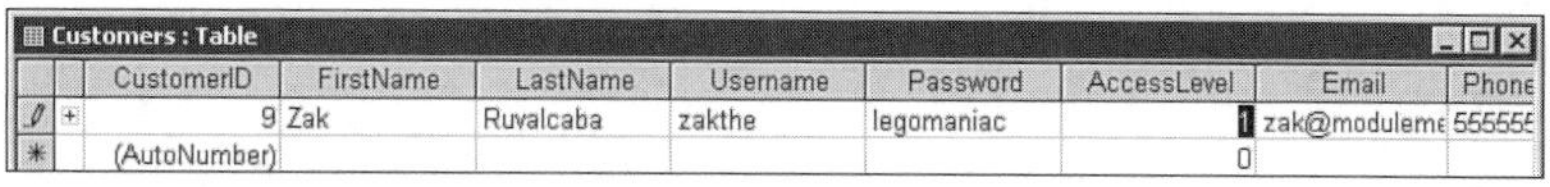

FIGURE 32.7   Give the administrator an access level of 1.

Level	Type	Description
1	Admin	Rights to the entire site
2	User	Rights to all excluding admin.asp

NOTE

If you have not done so already, you can change the name from Zak Ruvalcaba to your name within the customers table.

NOTE

You may want to add another fictitious user with an access level of 2. This will come in handy later in the chapter when you want to check the access level functionality. Don't forget to give the fictitious user a username and password, because you will need to log in using that name.

5. Reopen the Log In User server behavior and change the Restrict Access Based On to Username, Password, and Access Level. Change Get Level From to the new Access Level field, as shown in Figure 32.8.

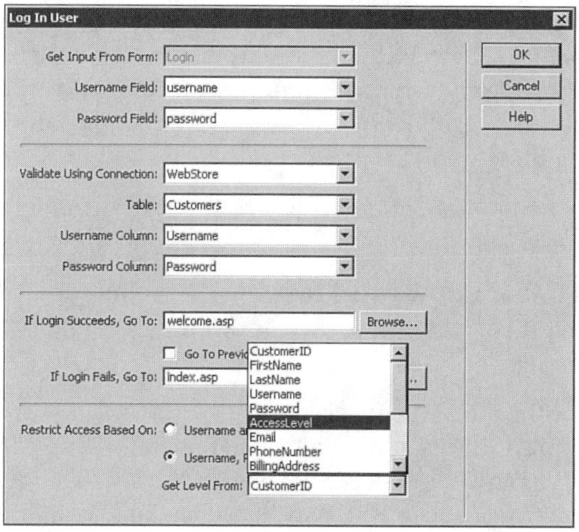

FIGURE 32.8   Change the login criteria to Username, Password, and Access Level.

Although you will not see any changes when you log in, know that a session variable is set for the access level named

```
Session("MM_UserAuthorization")
```

As you will see in the following sections, you can program against this variable to check whether a user has the appropriate access level to access a particular page. For now, you may want to see the variable in action. You can change the welcome page code to display the user access level as well. The following code illustrates this point:

```
<span class="body">
Welcome to the WebStore <%= Session("MM_Username") %><br>
Your access level is: <%= Session("MM_UserAuthorization") %><br>
You are classified as an:
<% If (Session("MM_UserAuthorization") = 1) Then %>
Administrator
<% Else %>
User
<% End If %>
</span>
```

Essentially, the code determines whether a user has an access level of 1. If the user does, it will provide a message stating that the user is an administrator. If the session is anything but 1, it will provide a message classifying them as a user.

Custom Error Messages

Although there are many error messages that you can present to the user, one that needs to be taken care of right away is the failed login error message. Currently, if a user logs in with an inappropriate username and password, the browser simply redirects to the same page and does nothing. Ideally, what you want is a custom error message that alerts the user of a failed login message, allowing them to try again. You can create a simple error message by following these steps:

1. Add two new rows to the login table just below the button form object that you created previously.

2. Add the text **That is not a valid login** in the second row. Change the font to a red color so that it appears as if it is an error message. Figure 32.9 shows the result of your additions.

3. The next step will be to somehow capture an error response from the login failure. You can accomplish this by setting a URL parameter within the Log In User dialog box. Open the Log In User dialog box and add the string "?valid=false" just after index.asp within the If Login Fails, Go To: dialog box, as shown in Figure 32.10.

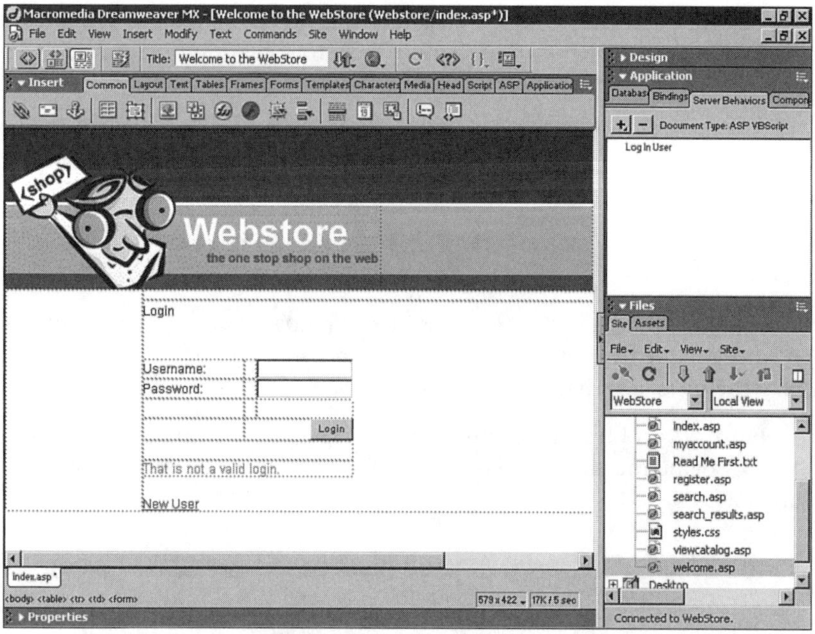

FIGURE 32.9   Add an error message to your login page.

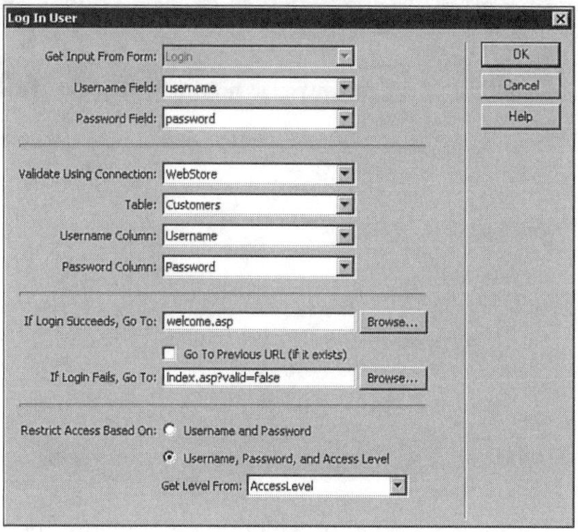

FIGURE 32.10   Add a parameter to the URL string for the failure response.

4. You'll now want to write some code to capture that parameter. Highlight the error message that you created in step 2 and switch to code/design view. Add the following code:

```
<% If (Request.QueryString("valid") = "false") Then %>
<font color="#FF0000" size="2" face="Arial">
That is not a valid login.
</font>
<% End If %>
```

5. This code will essentially check to see whether a parameter is being sent across the querystring named `valid`. If there is, and that parameter has a value of false, it will display the message, That is not a valid login.

6. Save your work and test the result in the browser. Try putting in bogus information and click Login. You should be presented with the error message shown in Figure 32.11.

FIGURE 32.11   Purposely enter wrong information to see the error message.

Check to See if User Is Logged In

Although you may think that your application is completely secure, it is, in fact, still completely vulnerable. What's to stop a user from simply typing in the URL to your application plus welcome.asp, completely bypassing your login page? You should never expect your users to use the login page simply because it's there. Most browsers even try to guess the URL you are typing by autofilling the complete URL. If users accidentally selected the welcome.asp page, they could easily bypass the login page and jump directly into the site, thus failing to create a session for the user and ultimately causing errors. You can avoid this problem by simply detecting whether the user's session exists. Because the user session is created at login, if the user tries to bypass the login screen, the application could detect that and redirect the user back. You can add the Restrict Access server behavior by following the steps outlined next:

1. Open the welcome.asp page.

2. Select the Restrict Access to Page server behavior from the User Authentication submenu, as shown in Figure 32.12.

FIGURE 32.12   Select the Restrict Access to Page server behavior.

3. The Restrict Access dialog box enables you to set user levels that are allowed to enter this page as well as a redirect URL for the failure. Select Define.

4. The Define Access Levels dialog box enables you to customize and configure access levels that are allowed to view your page. Select the + icon and add the values 1 and 2 as shown in Figure 32.13. Remember, this is a basic welcome page, so you want to allow both types of users in.

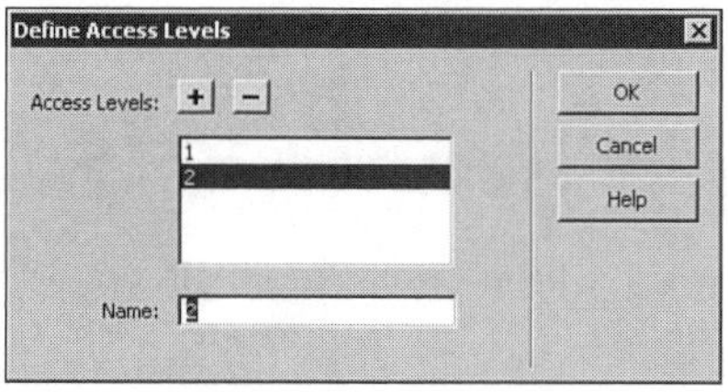

FIGURE 32.13   The Define Access Levels dialog box enables you to set access levels that are allowed to view that particular page.

5. Select OK.

6. Now add a parameter to the failure URL so that you can create a custom error message within the login page. The result is shown in Figure 32.14.

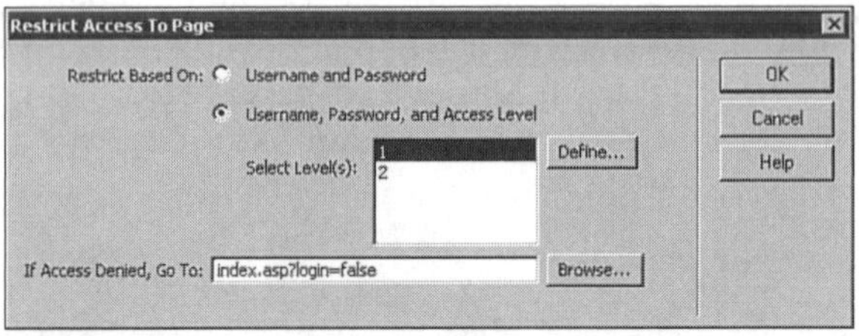

FIGURE 32.14   Add a parameter to the end of the querystring so that you can create a custom error message on the login page.

7. On the login page, create a new error message just below the previous error message that you created. Give the error message the text **You must be logged in** as shown in Figure 32.15.

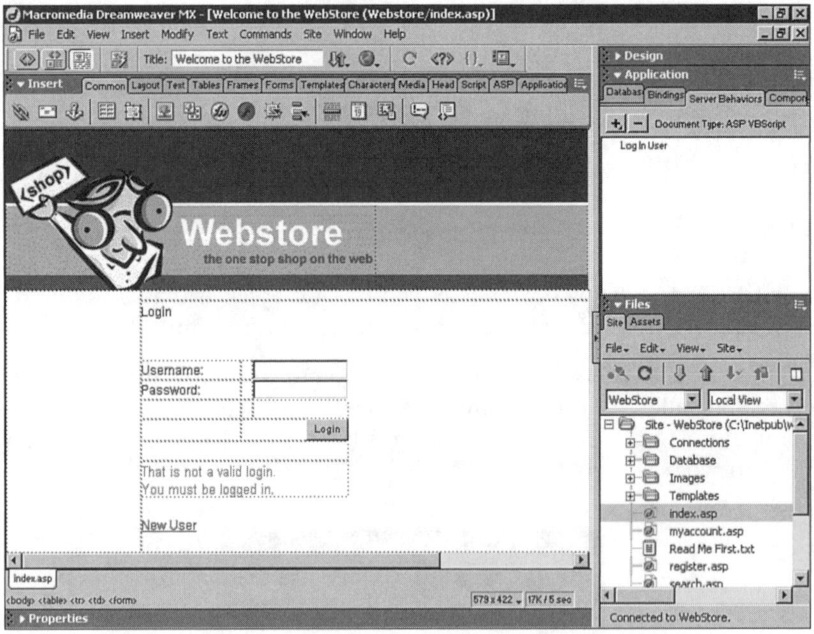

FIGURE 32.15   Create a new error message for the login requirement.

8. Switch to code/design view and type in the following code:

```
<% If (Request.QueryString("login") = "false") Then %>
<font color="#FF0000" size="2" face="Arial">
You must be logged in.
</font>
<% End If %>
```

9. Save your work.

This time, make sure all the browsers are closed. This will effectively terminate all sessions. Reopen the browser and try to go straight to the welcome.asp page without logging in first. You will be automatically redirected back to the login page and the custom error message will be displayed as shown in Figure 32.16.

FIGURE 32.16   If you try to bypass the login, you are redirected and presented with an error message.

You'll want to add this functionality to all the pages within the Web Store application. When you get to the admin.asp page, change the access level from 1 and 2 to just 1. This way, only a person with an access level of 1 can enter the admin.asp site.

Logging Out Users

Just as you require your users to log in, you will want them to log out as well. Logging out guarantees that the users' session variables are instantly terminated, forcing them to log in again. For the most part, users will simply close the browser, terminating the session, but if users continue to browse online, it may be a good idea to alert them to log out first. Session variables, by default, remain active for 20 minutes, so if users fail to log out, their sessions would remain active even though they're navigating another Web site. To create the logout functionality for the Web Store application, follow the steps outlined next:

1. Open the WebStore template located in the Templates directory within the Site Management window.

2. Place your cursor just after the My Account link and insert two line breaks (Shift+Enter). Insert a nonbreaking space (Ctrl+Shift+Space).

3. Type the test **Logout**.

4. With the text highlighted, select the Log Out User server behavior located within the User Authentication submenu of the Server Behaviors panel, as shown in Figure 32.17.

FIGURE 32.17   Insert the Log Out User server behavior.

5. The Log Out User dialog box appears, enabling you to specify criteria for the logout, including whether the logout will take place when the user clicks a button, a link, or when the page loads. You also can specify a page to redirect to after the user selects the button. By default, if the link is selected before you select the server behavior, the code should appear within the drop-down menu of Link Clicked, as shown in Figure 32.18.

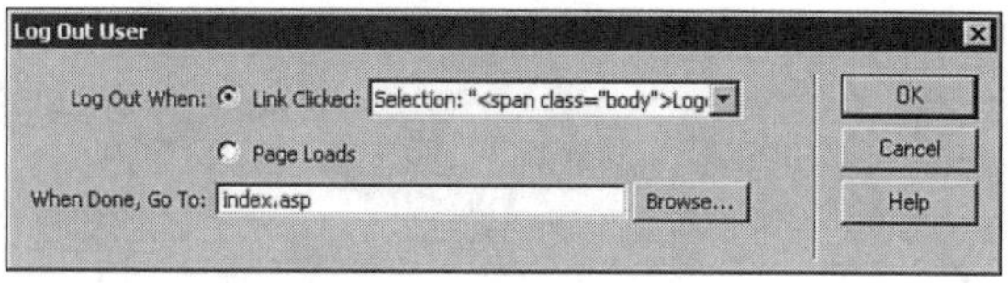

FIGURE 32.18   Specify the logout criteria within the Log Out User dialog box.

6. Select OK.

7. Save the page and update all pages that share the template.

8. Test the result in the browser. Log in and navigate through the site. Try clicking the logout link. Although it will appear as if nothing happened, in fact, your session was terminated. Try typing in welcome.asp in the address bar, and you should be redirected back to the login page with the error message displayed.

The following code gets inserted into the page:

```
Session.Contents.Remove("MM_Username")
Session.Contents.Remove("MM_UserAuthorization")
```

This code, utilizing the session object, physically removes the two session variables named MM_Username, which is the session variable that stores the username, and MM_UserAuthorization, which is the session variable that stores the access level.

Revamping the New User Registration Page

Now that most of the site has some sort of security integration, the last order of business is to make the register.asp page available only to new users. If a user has already registered, that user won't visit the page, but for users who have never been to the site, the New User Registration page must be made available and easy to find. You've added a link from the login page that jumps directly to the register.asp page; the only problem is that you still have buttons to the left of that page that link to the other Web store pages. A new user should not be given the opportunity to navigate to any portions of the site. You can change this by following the steps outlined next:

1. Open the register.asp page and cut the entire table that displays the captions and form objects. Make sure you cut the form in the process.

2. Open the Login template by selecting New from the File menu, navigating to the Advanced tab, and finding the Login template.

3. Paste the table into the Content editable region.

4. Immediately resave the page as register.asp, overwriting the previous version. The result is shown in Figure 32.19.

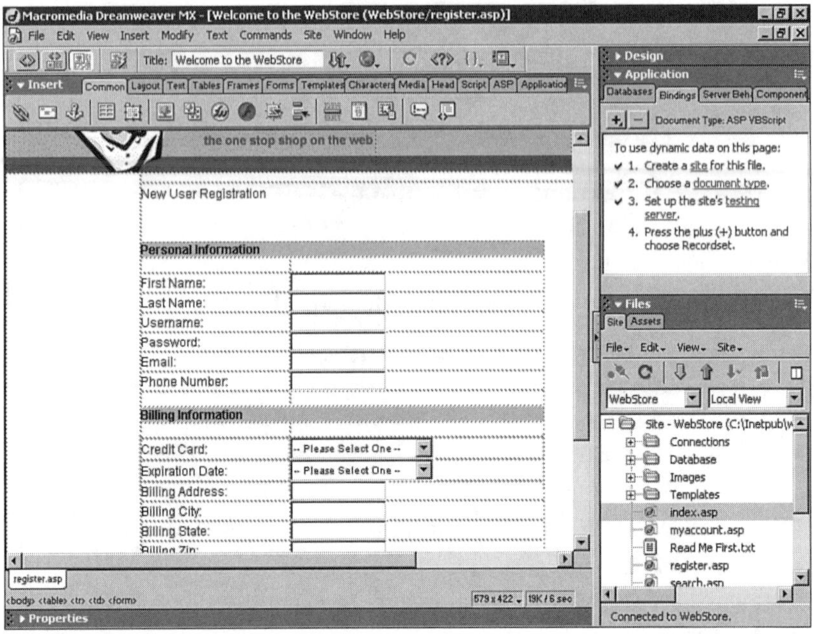

FIGURE 32.19   Paste the table of captions and form objects into a new register.asp page.

5. You may have to redefine the recordset and create the Insert Record server behavior. This time when you create the Insert Record server behavior, make sure you add a parameter on the querystring for the redirect URL. Later in the chapter, you will capture that parameter and welcome the user to the login page. The result is shown in Figure 32.20.

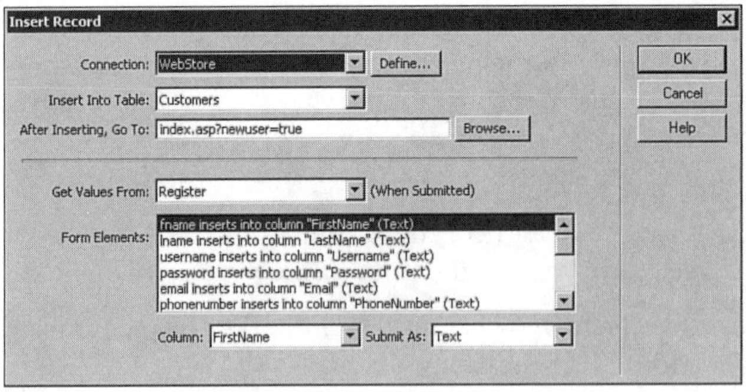

FIGURE 32.20   Add a parameter to the redirect URL.

Avoiding Duplicate Usernames

The last security-related server behavior is the Check New Username server behavior. The Check New Username server behavior enables you to check the username of the person that is registering on your site to make sure that a duplicate does not exist within the database. This is done to avoid confusion when people register within your site. Have you ever tried obtaining a username with AOL? It's almost impossible because most of the usernames are taken. AOL employs these same methods to avoid conflicts between users. You can check for duplicate usernames within your site by following these steps:

1. Within the new register.asp page, select the Check New Username server behavior available from the User Authentication submenu in the Server Behaviors panel, as shown in Figure 32.21.

FIGURE 32.21   Insert the Check New Username server behavior.

2. The Check New Username dialog box appears, allowing you to specify the field within the database to compare the value to. The Check New Username dialog box also enables you to specify a page to redirect to if there is a duplicate username. Figure 32.22 shows how you can append a parameter to the querystring so that you can create a custom error message for the user.

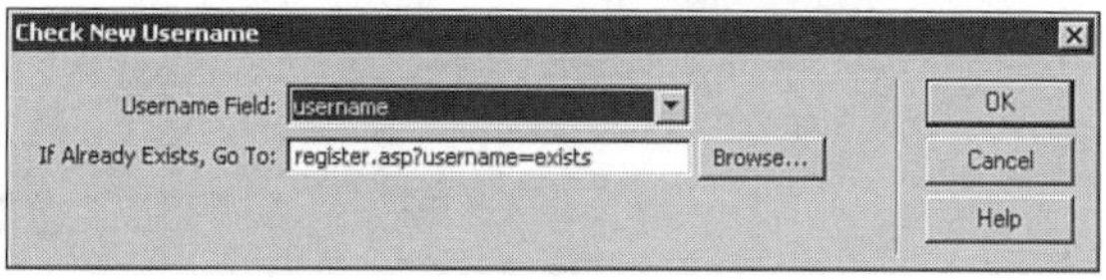

FIGURE 32.22   Specify the username field within the database as well as a parameter so that you can create a custom error message to the user if the proposed username does happen to be a duplicate.

3. You can create the custom error message by placing your cursor next to the username text field and inserting a new line break (Shift+Enter). Type the text **Username exists, try a different one** as shown in Figure 32.23.

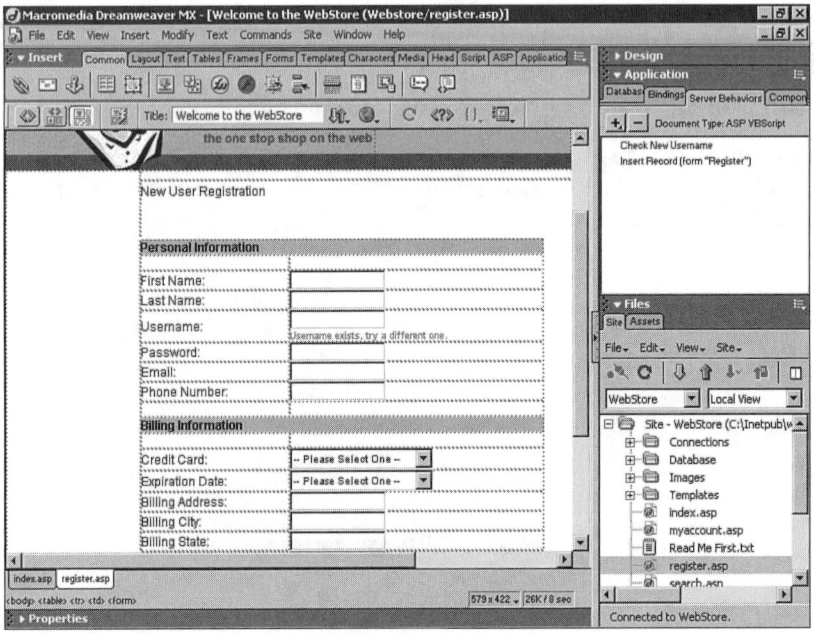

FIGURE 32.23   Create a custom error message to handle the duplicate username.

4. Now you'll want to capture the parameter that will be sent across if there does happen to be a duplicate username. Remember that parameter is "username" and the value is "exists". To handle this, wrap the text you wrote with the following code:

```
<% If (Request.QueryString("username") = "exists") Then %>
<font color="#FF0000" size="1" face="Arial">
Username exists, try a different one.
</font>
<% End If %>
```

5. The results will look similar to Figure 32.24.

6. Save your work.

Now that the user can pick a new username, he will be able to register on your site. The last thing you might want to do is add a custom message to users, welcoming them to your site and thanking them for registering. You can do this by opening index.asp and inserting the following code where the Header editable region currently resides:

```
<% If (Request.QueryString("newuser") = "true") Then %>
<span class="body">Welcome New User</span>
<% Else %>
<span class="body">Login</span>
<% End If %>
```

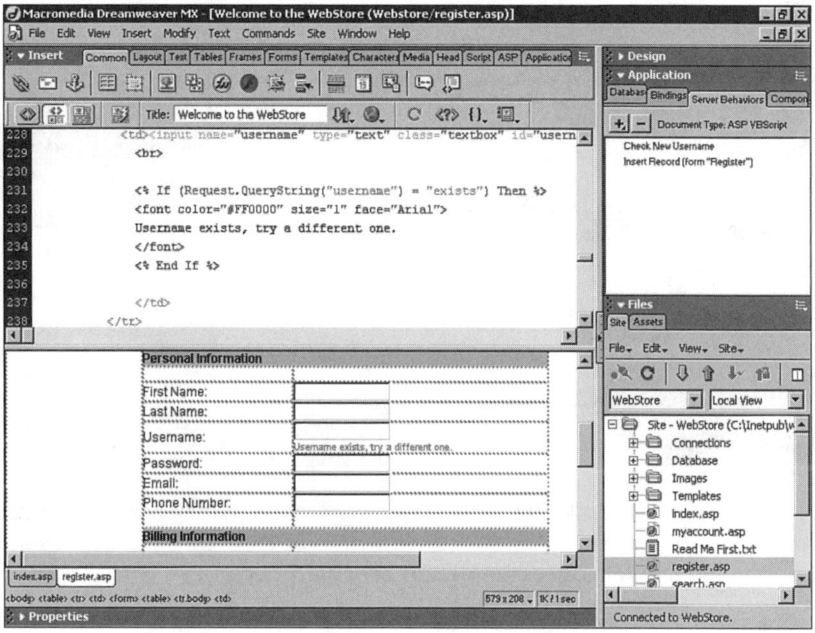

FIGURE 32.24 Add the code to handle the parameter being sent across.

The result is shown in Figure 32.25.

This code effectively checks for parameters coming across the querystring. It displays the text Welcome New User if it detects the parameter newuser with a value true and displays the text Login if it doesn't detect anything.

Setting Access Levels

Now that you are checking access levels throughout every page, you'll probably want some functionality in place that actually sets the access level when the user registers. Rather than manually going into the database each time a person registers, you could simply set a hidden field equal to a certain number, in this case 2, and have that automatically update the database. To add the functionality that sets the access level, follow these steps:

1. Within the register.asp page, insert a new hidden field by selecting Form Objects from the Insert menu and choosing Hidden Field.

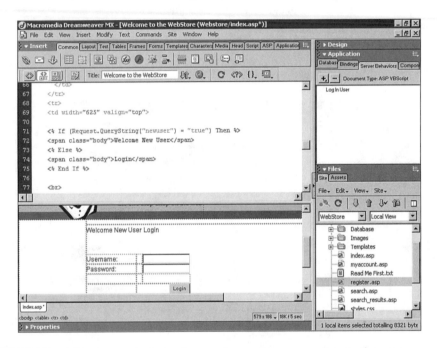

FIGURE 32.25   Add some code to create a custom welcome message to the user.

2. Name the hidden field **accesslevel** and give it a value of **2**.

3. Reopen the Insert Record server behavior.

4. Find the access level form object from the Form Elements selection box, find the AccessLevel column, and change the datatype to Numeric, as shown in Figure 32.26.

5. Save your work and test it in the browser. Create a new user. When you are finished, check the database to make sure all the appropriate information was added.

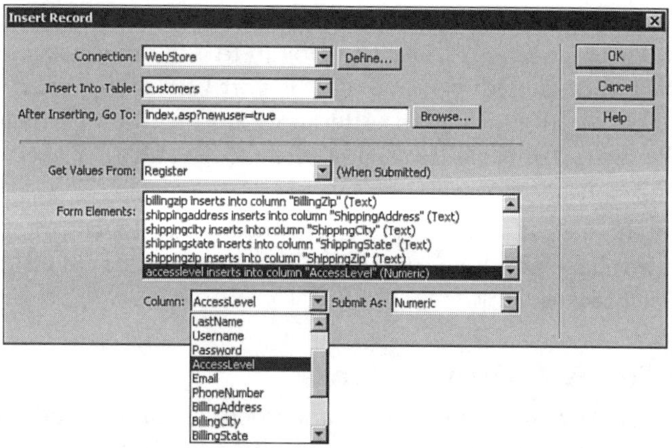

FIGURE 32.26   Connect the access level hidden field to the appropriate field within the database.

Securing ASP.NET Applications

Just as with the ASP server model, you can take advantage of user authentication using ASP.NET. Unlike ASP, the ASP.NET server model offers more robust options when it comes to storing user information. Traditionally with ASP, usernames and passwords are stored in a data store such as an XML file or database. Performing data retrieval from an XML file using the MSXML DOM was tedious at best, providing few other options than to use a database for user validation storage. Although these options are still available using the ASP.NET server model, retrieving and reading XML data is far simpler than traditional methods. Three user authentication methods are available using the ASP.NET server model:

- **Windows Authentication**   Windows authentication uses IIS in conjunction with operating system-level permissions to allow or deny users access to your Web application.

- **Forms Authentication**   Offering the most flexibility, forms authentication allows for the most control and customization for the developer. Using forms authentication, you now have the capability to rely on traditional methods of validation (XML file, database, hard-coded) as well as new methods (Web.Config, cookies) or a combination of both.

- **Passport Authentication**   By far the newest addition to user validation methods, passport authentication is the centralized authentication service provided through the .NET initiative by Microsoft. Because users rely on their MSN or Hotmail emails as their passport, developers need never worry about storing credential information on their own servers. When users log in to a site that has passport authentication enabled, they are redirected to the passport Web site where they enter their passport and password information. After users' information is validated, they are automatically redirected back the original site.

Although there are three great authentication methods, we will focus in on one: forms authentication. If you have not done so already, you can download the support files from www.dreamweavermxunleashed.com.

Working with Forms Authentication

Forms authentication is by far the most popular authentication method because of its flexibility to the user. An advantage of forms authentication lies in the fact that you are able to store usernames and passwords in virtually any data store, such as the Web.Config file, XML file, a database, or a combination of the three.

Forms authentication is cookie based. An authentication ticket is stored within a user cookie; after forms authentication is enabled for an entire directory, pages within that directory are unable to be accessed without the proper authentication ticket. Without the proper ticket, a user can be automatically redirected to the original page, forced to log in again. You will want to be familiar with four classes within the System.Web.Security namespace when you're working with user authentication:

- **FormsAuthentication**   Contains several methods for working with forms authentication.

- **FormsAuthenticationTicket**   Makes up the authentication ticket that is stored in the user's cookie.

- **FormsIdentity**   Represents the user's identity authenticated with forms authentication.

- **FormsAuthenticationModule**   The module used for forms authentication.

Now that you have a basic idea of the classes you will be using for your login page, let's see how a basic login page is constructed. There are three steps that need to be taken before forms authentication will work within your application:

1. Configure the authentication mode for the application within the Web.Config file.

2. Configure the authorization section to allow or deny certain users within the Web.Config file.

3. Create the login page that your users will use.

The first step is to configure the authentication mode for the application. This can be accomplished by opening the Web.Config file and adding the following lines of code:

```
<system.web>
<authentication mode="Forms" />
</system.web>
```

The result is shown in Figure 32.27.

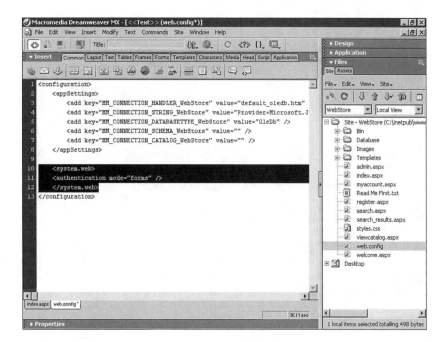

FIGURE 32.27   Modify the authentication mode for the application.

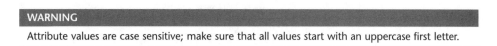

WARNING

Attribute values are case sensitive; make sure that all values start with an uppercase first letter.

Remember, there are four possibilities for mode: Forms, Windows, Passport, and None. Next, set the authorization mode by adding the following lines of code:

```
<authorization>
<deny users"?" />
</authorization>
```

The result is shown in Figure 32.28.

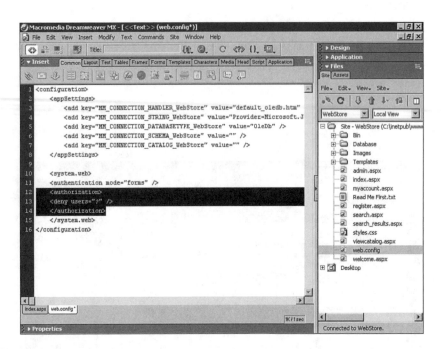

FIGURE 32.28   Set the authorization mode for the application.

The question mark (?) symbol represents all anonymous users. If a user tries to access a certain page and does not have the appropriate authentication ticket, the user is redirected back to the login page. You can also allow users to access certain directories within your application by adding a separate Web.Config file with the following code:

```
<authorization>
<allow users"?" />
</authorization>
```

The last step is to create the actual login page. You can create the login page for the Web Store application by following these steps:

1. Create a new page by selecting New from the File menu. Choose the Advanced tab and select the Login template.

2. Within the Content editable region, create a new form with a Runat="Server" attribute. Within the form, create a new table with four rows and three columns.

3. Below the new table add a new link to the register.aspx page and call it **New User**.

4. Create two new text box Web controls, naming them **username** and **password**.

5. Add a new button Web control and add the text **Login**. The result is shown in Figure 32.29. Be sure to add the commandname="Submit_Click" attribute to the tag. This will call the "Submit_Click" subroutine.

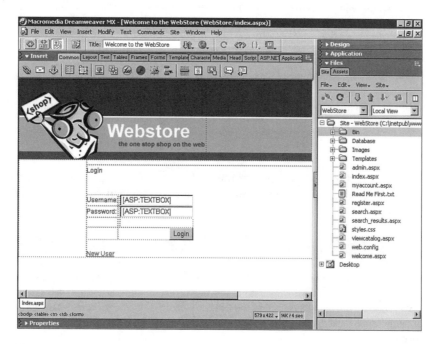

FIGURE 32.29   Create a login page.

6. You are now ready to insert the code that will make the login page work. Within the <head> tag of the new login page, add the following code:

```
<script runat="Server">
Sub Submit_Click(s As Object, e As EventArgs)
If IsValid Then
If (Username.Text = "zakthe" And Password.Text) = "legomaniac" Then
FormsAuthentication.RedirectFromLoginPage(Username.Text, True)
End If
End If
End Sub
</script>
```

7. Save your work as login.aspx and test it in the browser.

NOTE

Remember, by default if the authentication ticket does not exist on the users machine, the application will redirect to login.aspx. For this reason, the login page must be called login.aspx rather than index.aspx, which was the case when using the ASP server model.

In the preceding code, two lines make everything happen. The first:

```
If (Username.Text = "zakthe" And Password.Text) = "legomaniac" Then
```

checks to see if the values of the two text boxes are "zakthe" and "legomaniac". If they are correct, the next line is read:

```
FormsAuthentication.RedirectFromLoginPage(Username.Text, True)
```

This line calls the RedirectFromLoginPage method passing in two parameters. The first parameter is the username and the second parameter is a Boolean value indicating whether a cookie should be created.

TIP

If you are having unsuccessful results with the login page, make sure that you have created an application within IIS for the Web store. Because authentication within ASP.NET relies on an application-based model, it will not work if it has not been created. You can set the Web store to be an application by opening IIS, selecting the Default Web Sites directory, finding the Web Store application, right-clicking and selecting Properties, and clicking the Create button to create an application.

WARNING

If you are receiving an error upon successful login, you may have to change the welcome.aspx page to read default.aspx. By default, that is the page that the application will redirect to.

The login page you have just built is the simplest form you can possibly implement. The next sections will enable you to further customize the form and credential-storing means.

Configuring Forms Authentication

In the previous section, you learned how to create a basic login page. You also learned how to modify the Web.Config file by enabling the form authentication mode. In this section you will explore the forms authentication section within the Web.Config file in greater detail.

Aside from the basic authentication mode, the authentication section within the Web.Config file accepts a form element. The form element accepts the following attributes:

- **loginUrl**   The page that the user is redirected to when authentication is necessary. By default this is login.aspx but using this attribute, you can modify the file name to be index.aspx, as was the case with the ASP server model example.

- **name**   The name of the cookie to be stored on the user's machine. By default the name is set to ".ASPXAUTH".

- **timeout**   The amount of time in minutes before the cookie expires. By default this value is set to 30 minutes.

- **path**   The path used by the cookie. By default this value is set to "/".

- **protection**   The way the cookie data is protected. Values range from All, None, Encryption, and Validation. The default value is All.

An example of your newly modified Web.Config file could look similar to the following:

```
<configuration>
<system.Web>
<authentication mode="Forms">
<forms
name=".LoginCookie"
loginUrl="login.aspx"
protection="All"
timeout="40"
path="/" />
</authentication>
</system.Web>
</configuration>
```

Configuring Forms Authorization

As is the case with the authentication section of the Web.Config file, the authorization section can be modified to accept or deny certain users within your application. You can make fine-tuned decisions regarding who will and who will not be accepted into your application. For instance, the following code allows all anonymous users except for "mpizzi" and "zruvalcaba".

```
<configuration>
<system.Web>
<authorization>
<allow users="?" />
<deny users="mpizzi,zruvalcaba" />
</authorization>
</system.Web>
</configuration>
```

32

You can also control how users navigate through your site by modifying the verbs attribute to accept or deny HTTP Post or Get. For example the following code enables anyone to access pages using POST or GET but prevents "mpizzi" and "zruvalcaba" from using POST.

```
<configuration>
<system.Web>
<authorization>
<allow verbs="POST" users="*" />
<allow verbs="GET" users="*" />
<deny verbs="POST" users="mpizzi,zruvalcaba" />
</authorization>
</system.Web>
</configuration>
```

Web.Config File Authentication

The great thing about the Web.Config file is that it is flexible enough to allow you to store usernames and passwords within it. Although you will not want to store all the usernames and passwords for your users within the Web.Config file, you can store a few. The following code added to the forms element of the Web.Config file sets credentials for two users:

```
<configuration>
<system.Web>
<authentication mode="Forms" />
<forms>
<credentials passwordFormat="Clear" >
<user name="zakthe" password="legomaniac" />
<user name="mpizzi" password="pizza" />
</credentials>
</forms>
<authorization>
<deny users="?" />
</authorization>
</system.Web>
</configuration>
```

You can now modify the code that lies within the head of your login page to validate the usernames and passwords within the Web.Config file. The result will resemble the following:

```
<script runat="Server">
Sub Submit_Click(s As Object, e As EventArgs)
If IsValid Then
If FormsAuthentication.Authenticate(Username.Text, Password.Text) Then
```

```
FormsAuthentication.RedirectFromLoginPage(Username.Text, True)
End If
End If
End Sub
</script>
```

Database Authentication

Arguably the most flexible method of storing usernames and passwords is through the use
of a database table. This section discusses the use of a database table to validate user information. Before you begin, make sure that you modify the Web.Config file back to its original state. The result should resemble the following:

```
<system.web>
<authentication mode="Forms" />
<authorization>
<deny users"?" />
</authorization>
</system.web>
```

The next step is to retrieve and validate against the customers that are stored within the
customers table of the WebStore database. You can add the following code to handle the
authentication within the login.aspx file:

```
<%@ Import Namespace="System.Data.OleDb" %>

<html>
<head>

<script runat="Server">
Sub Submit_Click(s As Object, e As EventArgs)
 If IsValid Then
  If (Authenticate(Username.Text, Password.Text) > 0) Then
   FormsAuthentication.RedirectFromLoginPage(Username.Text, False)
  End If
 End If
End Sub


Function Authenticate(strUsername As String, strPassword As String) As Integer
Dim objConn As OleDbConnection
Dim objCmd As OleDbCommand
Dim dbReader As OleDbDataReader
Dim intResult As Integer
objConn = New OleDbConnection("Provider=Microsoft.Jet.OLEDB.4.0;Data Source=C:\
➥Inetpub\wwwroot\WebStore\Database\Webstore.mdb")
```

```
objCmd = New OleDbCommand("SELECT Username, Password FROM
Customers", objConn)

objConn.Open()
dbReader = objCmd.ExecuteReader()
 While dbReader.Read()
  If (strUsername = dbReader("Username") And
    strPassword = dbReader("Password")) Then
   intResult = 1
   Return intResult
  Else
   intResult = 0
   Return intResult
 End If
End While
dbReader.Close()
objConn.Close()
End Function
</script>

</head>
</html>
```

Let's pick apart the code to help you better understand how the user is validated. The first subroutine

```
Sub Submit_Click(s As Object, e As EventArgs)
 If IsValid Then
  If (Authenticate(Username.Text, Password.Text) > 0) Then
   FormsAuthentication.RedirectFromLoginPage(Username.Text, False)
  End If
 End If
End Sub
```

processes the "authenticate" function, passing in the two parameters for username and password. The return value, which we'll go over in a bit, is checked to make sure that it is greater than 0. If the return value is greater than 0, the RedirectFromLoginPage method is called.

The authenticate function is what performs most of the work. The function accepts two string parameters, strUsername and strPassword, which you know come in as the two text box control values. The next lines of code:

```
Dim objConn As OleDbConnection
Dim objCmd As OleDbCommand
```

```
Dim dbReader As OleDbDataReader
Dim intResult As Integer
```

instantiate the OleDbConnection, OleDbCommand, and OleDbReader objects as well as the return values variable, which will end up being a simple 1 or 0 value. The next few lines of code:

```
objConn = New OleDbConnection("Provider=Microsoft.Jet.OLEDB.4.0;Data
Source=C:\Inetpub\wwwroot\WebStore\Database\Webstore.mdb")

objCmd = New OleDbCommand("SELECT Username, Password FROM
Customers", objConn)

objConn.Open()
dbReader = objCmd.ExecuteReader()
```

set the connection string to the connection object, create the new command passing in the SQL statement as well as the connection string, open the connection, and set the DataReader equal to the ExecuteReader method of the command object. The last few lines of code

```
While dbReader.Read()
  If (strUsername = dbReader("Username") And strPassword = dbReader("Password"))
➥Then
    intResult = 1
    Return intResult
  Else
    intResult = 0
    Return intResult
  End If
End While
dbReader.Close()
objConn.Close()
```

loop through the DataReader and compare the values of the two text box controls with the Username and Password fields within the database. If a match is returned, intResult is set to 1 and the result is returned. If a match is not returned, intResult is set to 0 and the result is returned. The last two lines close the connection and DataReader objects.

Customer Error Messages

You can create custom error messages within the login.aspx page by adding label controls to your page and manually setting those labels whenever there is an error message. For example, if a login failure occurred, rather than letting the page simply reload, you could add a simple Else clause to the If statement that processes the login. To add a custom error message to your login page, follow the steps outlined next:

32

Add two new rows to your login table.

Add a label control in the second row. Change the fore color, bold, and ID attributes accordingly. Your control may resemble the following:

```
<asp:label ID="lblError" ForeColor="Red" Font-Bold="True" Runat="Server" />
```

Change your subroutine so that it resembles the one that follows:

```
Sub Submit_Click(s As Object, e As EventArgs)
 If IsValid Then
  If (Authenticate(Username.Text, Password.Text) > 0) Then
   FormsAuthentication.RedirectFromLoginPage(Username.Text, False)
  Else
   lblError.Text = "Your login was invalid. Please try again."
  End If
 End If
End Sub
```

This time when a user enters the wrong credentials, the user will receive an error message rather than a simple page reload.

Logging Out Users

There may be instances in which your users will no longer want to navigate within your application. People feel more secure having the knowledge that they have successfully logged out. For this and for security purposes, you might want to have your users log out of your site. You can create log out functionality within your application by following these steps:

1. Open the WebStore template located in the Templates directory within the Site Management window.

2. Place your cursor just after the My Account link and insert two line breaks (Shift+Enter). Insert a nonbreaking space (Ctrl+Shift+Space).

3. Insert a new linkbutton Web control. The code should look similar to the following:

   ```
   <asp:linkButton ID="lbLogOut" CssClass="Body" Text="Log Out"
   OnClick="Logout_Click" Runat="Server" />
   ```

4. Add a subroutine to handle the Logout_Click event. The subroutine should contain the following code:

   ```
   Sub Logout_Click()
   FormsAuthentication.SignOut()
   End Sub
   ```

This will effectively logout the user by terminating the cookie and redirecting the user to the login page.

Summary

In this chapter, you examined ways of securing both your ASP and ASP.NET applications. You learned about all the behaviors available with Dreamweaver MX to completely secure your ASP applications. You also went one step further and examined ways of securing ASP.NET applications by utilizing some of the classes available through the security namespace.

32

PART VII

Appendixes

IN THIS PART

APPENDIX **A**

Accessibility

by Kynn Bartlett

There is an implicit promise in the name of the World Wide Web—the promise of an information network that can be used by everyone around the world. The Web succeeds at what it does because of its universality. A Web document is written in one or more Web languages designed to be cross-platform and interoperable with a wide variety of technologies.

Clearly, the Web is designed to open to a broad range of users, and that's where things start to get tricky! The average Web user of moderate means in North America or Europe has a decently fast computer, a full-color monitor, a keyboard, a mouse, speakers, and a high-speed modem or a faster connection. But that's just the average user—and people tend to be scattered all over the range of possibility, rarely conforming to the same capabilities. Welcome to designing on the Web!

In this appendix, I'll explain what Web accessibility standards are, how they benefit both you and your users with disabilities, and how you can use Dreamweaver MX to ensure that everyone can use your site.

Accessibility Standards

The way you design a Web site determines, to a very large extent, who is able to access that site. If you're concerned only about those with the latest version of your favorite browser and the fastest hardware and connection, there's no guarantee that you'll make a Web site that can be used by anyone who falls outside of those parameters.

There's a very large group of users who tend to fall outside of nearly everyone's target audience when developers design for the Web—users with disabilities. If you haven't thought about disabled Web users before, that's okay—don't beat yourself up for it. It's hard to imagine some of the problems faced by disabled computer users unless you've experienced them yourself, usually through observation.

Web users with visual disabilities are often stymied by Web pages that rely on images, color, or visual layout to convey the meaning of the site's content. Those with limited vision will have difficulties with low-contrast colors or small fonts. Deaf or hard-of-hearing users won't hear the sound tracks of multimedia. Users with limited physical dexterity might not be able to drop and drag or do other activities requiring a mouse. Pages with complex text that lack illustrations and summaries will be very difficult for users with cognitive disabilities.

The Web isn't always easy to use if you have special needs. Some users, such as those who are blind, can rely on special assistive technologies such as screen readers, Braille displays, or screen magnifiers for Web access. However, these tools will work with your site only if you've carefully built your sites to allow access.

TIP

To learn more about how people with disabilities access the Web, visit the site of the International Center for Disability Resources on the Internet, at `http://www.icdri.org/`.

The process of creating a site that can be used by anyone regardless of disability is called *accessibility*. To properly create a Web site that is accessible, you'll need to know all about assistive technology, about how people with disabilities use the Web, and about how HTML and other Web languages function in browsers. You'll also need to be an expert on accessibility's close cousin, *usability*, which is the study of how people use computers effectively.

Sound like a lot of work? Well, it is, believe me—but fortunately you won't have to do all that work yourself. The knowledge you need to have to construct accessible Web sites has been codified into *accessibility standards*—which function as a checklist of sorts, so that you simply have to follow these rules to produce a site with no barriers to access.

Dreamweaver MX makes it even easier for you to follow those standards, because they're built right into the software itself. By using Dreamweaver MX's accessibility features to create and check your work, you can greatly simplify the process of creating accessible Web sites.

Standards Resources

When it comes to the World Wide Web, there is one primary source for nearly all of the standards you'll use—the World Wide Web Consortium (W3C for short).

The W3C is an international association of some of the major players in the Web, from browser makers to research organizations. The official specifications for HTML, XML, cascading style sheets (CSS), and other key Web technologies were created by the W3C's working groups and released as recommendations for adoption on the Web.

> **TIP**
>
> The W3C's Web site is located at `http://www.w3.org/` and is the definitive source for Web specifications. However, most Web specifications are incredibly dry reading, and unless you're some sort of masochist, you won't want to dive right into them. A better idea is to start at the Web site of the Web Standards Project (`http://www.webstandards.org/`), a group of expert Web developers who promote standards compliance.

One branch of the W3C concerns itself exclusively with access by people with disabilities—the Web Accessibility Initiative (WAI). Just as the W3C has produced standards for the HTML language, so has the WAI produced standards for accessibility.

Web Content Accessibility Guidelines

For Web developers, the most important WAI standards are contained in the Web Content Accessibility Guidelines (WCAG), which are a set of guidelines, checkpoints, and associated techniques that describe how to ensure the accessibility of your Web site.

> **TIP**
>
> You can read the full WCAG recommendation and download a checklist for easy reference from the W3C's Web site at `http://www.w3.org/tr/wcag/`.

The WCAG recommendation lists 14 basic principles, or guidelines, which promote accessibility:

1. Provide equivalent alternatives to auditory and visual content.
2. Don't rely on color alone.
3. Use markup and style sheets and do so properly.
4. Clarify natural language usage.
5. Create tables that transform gracefully.
6. Ensure that pages featuring new technologies transform gracefully.
7. Ensure user control of time-sensitive content changes.
8. Ensure direct accessibility of embedded user interfaces.
9. Design for device independence.
10. Use interim solutions.

11. Use W3C technologies and guidelines.

12. Provide context and orientation information.

13. Provide clear navigation mechanisms.

14. Ensure that documents are clear and simple.

Each of these guidelines is supported by one or more checkpoints. For example, the checkpoints for guideline 2 ("Don't rely on color alone") are

- 2.1 Ensure that all information conveyed with color is also available without color, for example from context or markup.

- 2.2 Ensure that foreground and background color combinations provide sufficient contrast when viewed by someone having color deficits or when viewed on a black and white screen.

Each checkpoint is given a priority value. A priority of one means that the failure to follow that checkpoint will exclude members of your audience with specific disabilities. Priority two checkpoints are designed to reduce the difficulty of access by people with disabilities, and priority three checkpoints actively improve the quality of access for individuals with special needs.

In WAI terminology, if your site fulfills all the priority one checkpoints, it is said to be Single-A compliant with WCAG. Meeting all priority one and two checkpoints grants your site Double-A status; and successfully meeting all the checkpoints qualifies a site as Triple-A level.

WCAG compliance levels have been accepted by many public and private organizations as the minimum requirement for sites they control. For example, California community college Web sites must meet at least WCAG Double-A standards, and the HTML Writers Guild (`http://www.hwg.org/`) has adopted Single-A accessibility requirements for official Guild sites.

Section 508
In addition to being directly adopted, the WCAG standard has been used to create specialized Web accessibility policies. The most influential of these is the standard employed by the United States of America for most government Web sites.

The requirements for federal sites are described in Section 508, subsection 1194, of the 1998 amendments to the Rehabilitation Act. That's a mouthful to say at once, so everyone simply refers to a set of requirements as Section 508.

The aim of Section 508 is to ensure that government information technology is accessible to people with disabilities, both those working within federal agencies and those citizens who are using public Web resources.

The Section 508 requirements for Web sites are modeled after the priority one checkpoints in WCAG, with a few modifications. Specifically, Section 508 adds some new requirements and eliminates a few priority checkpoints, while generally rewriting from the technical recommendation language of the W3C to the form of bureaucratic regulation favored in government work.

> **TIP**
>
> The official Web site for Section 508 is `http://www.section508.gov/`—but as with other standards sites, you might find more gentle introductions elsewhere. Jim Thatcher's Web site at `http://www.jimthatcher.com/` contains indispensable advice on meeting 508 standards as well as Web accessibility in general, and it deserves a place in your bookmarks.

Which Standard to Follow?

It's been said that the great thing about standards is that there are so many to choose from. Despite the humor of this statement, there's still some truth to it—there's not one universal standard for accessibility but several, including Single-A WCAG, Double-A WCAG, Triple-A WCAG, and Section 508.

The overlap between Single-A WCAG checkpoints and Section 508 requirements remains very strong, however, so the techniques used to make a site accessible by one standard will generally ensure that the other standard is met.

The Double-A and Triple-A WCAG standards are harder to meet, because they go beyond basic accessibility and require that Web pages not be difficult to use.

In some cases, you may be able to choose which standard to follow. Most commercial and personal Web sites are unregulated, and thus you can select your level of compliance. Many commercial sites will aim for Single-A compliance, but Double-A compliance improves site access for disabled users or employees. Private organizations or corporations that provide services to people with disabilities will want to achieve Triple-A compliance.

As mentioned previously, public sector Web sites may have legal requirements for accessibility, depending on the location and type of public entity. For example, U.S. federal agencies such as the Department of Forestry are required to meet the Section 508 requirements, and universities in Australia must meet WCAG Double-A. Your organization's legal or disability officer can advise you on specific regulatory obligations that apply to your Web site.

Conform with Standards

Conforming with accessibility standards provides many benefits. Besides reducing your potential legal complications (especially if you are subject to specific requirements), it can also improve the overall usability of your site because the considerations needed for producing an accessible Web site will also lead to a site that is improved for everyone. For example, a transcript of an audio speech can benefit anyone accessing the Web from a quiet public library.

Accessible standards also encourage designs that can be used on a diversity of Web access devices, including set-top boxes, Internet appliances, and PDAs. The same techniques that guarantee access for non-visual browsers also improve access for users of text-only cell phones.

Creating an accessible Web site consists of ensuring that you've coded your site so that a broad audience can use it. Your audience will include not only traditional browsers and Web devices, but also specialized programs or hardware collectively called *assistive technology*. Examples of assistive technology include screenreaders, pointing devices, voice recognition software, screen magnifiers, Braille terminals, and onscreen keyboards.

Assistive technologies are usually very innovative and clever approaches to overcoming obstacles, but like any computer feature, they can work only with what they're given, in terms of information. If a Braille terminal encounters an image that isn't labeled property (with an alt attribute), there's no way it can tell automatically if the image is a spacer GIF, a simple decoration, an important piece of content necessary for understanding the page, or a banner ad. As the author of a Web page, you can provide this necessary information so that the assistive technologies can function properly.

Here's an example—the Web page shown in Listing A.1 was created in Dreamweaver MX as an example of a straightforward design that nonetheless has serious accessibility problems for users with disabilities.

LISTING A.1   An Inaccessible HTML Page Made in Dreamweaver MX

```
<!DOCTYPE HTML PUBLIC "-//W3C//DTD HTML 4.01 Transitional//EN">
<html>
<head>
<title>Re-Elect President Littletree!</title>
<meta http-equiv="Content-Type" content="text/html; charset=iso-8859-1">
</head>
<body>
<img src="littletree.gif" width="125" height="125" align="right">
<img src="votebanner.gif" width="350" height="72">
<p>Do your patriotic duty as a loyal citizen and re-elect President
   Littletree when you vote! Remember, only TERRORISTS would even think
   of voting for the opposition!</p>
<p><strong>Looking for an accessible voting place?</strong> All of the
   polling stations marked in <font color="#990000">RED</font> have special
   voting booths for the blind!</p>
<div align="center">
  <table border="3" cellpadding="3" cellspacing="3">
```

LISTING A.1   Continued

```
    <tr>
      <td>Gorelick Observatory</td>
      <td><font color="#990000">Turner Morgan Memorial Park</font></td>
    </tr>
    <tr>
      <td>Bradford Avenue Park</td>
      <td><font color="#990000">R. Francis Smith Middle School</font></td>
    </tr>
    <tr>
      <td><font color="#990000">T.A. Baker Senior Center</font></td>
      <td>Corner of Plotnik and Knott</td>
    </tr>
    <tr>
      <td>Wetmore Dam Park</td>
      <td><font color="#990000">Lee-Barnsley College</font></td>
    </tr>
  </table>
</div>
<p><strong>Littletree's Most Recent Speech:</strong>
   <a href="speech04.wav">Listen now! (308K wav)</a></p>
<hr>
<p align="center"><font size="2">
  <a href="mailto:web@reelectlittletree.com">web@reelectlittletree.com</a>
  </font></p>
</body>
</html>
```

What does this page look like? It's fairly simple; see Figure A.1 for how it displays in a browser. It certainly doesn't look inaccessible at first glance.

Note, however, that the red color used on the page doesn't reproduce well in a black-and-white screenshot. It's difficult to tell which polling locations are accessible to the blind. What would this site be like for blind users?

To test, we'll use a text browser named Lynx (http://lynx.browser.org/) and view the page. Lynx displays all Web pages without images or colors, just as plain text. This is a useful approximation of what blind users experience when accessing a Web page. Most users who can't see will use a screenreader program that reads out loud the text from a browser (such as Internet Explorer or even Lynx) or a Braille display with raisable dots. Both of these methods are roughly equal to the text display of Lynx.

Figure A.2 shows us some serious problems—the banner at the top isn't identified beyond [IMAGE], and the color markings are clearly lost.

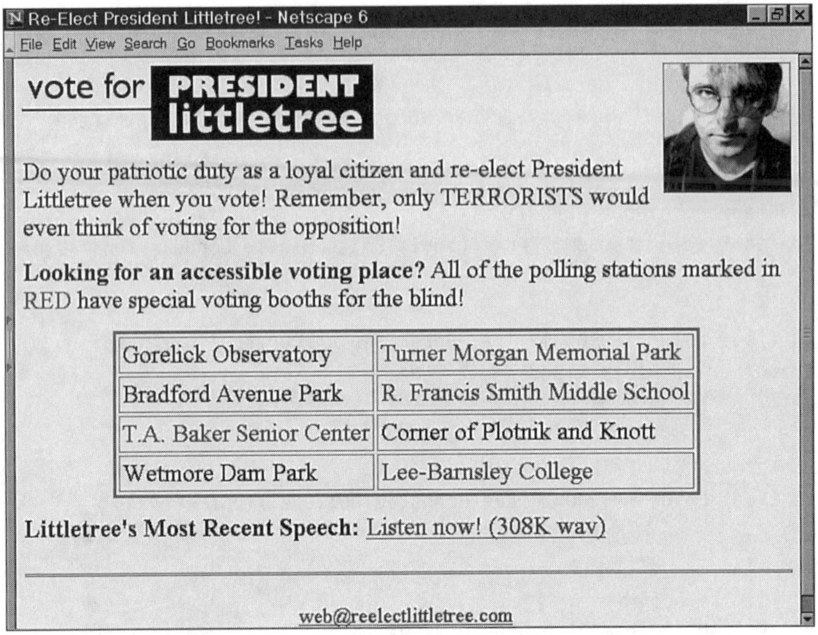

FIGURE A.1   This looks like a simple Web page on screen; how inaccessible could it be?

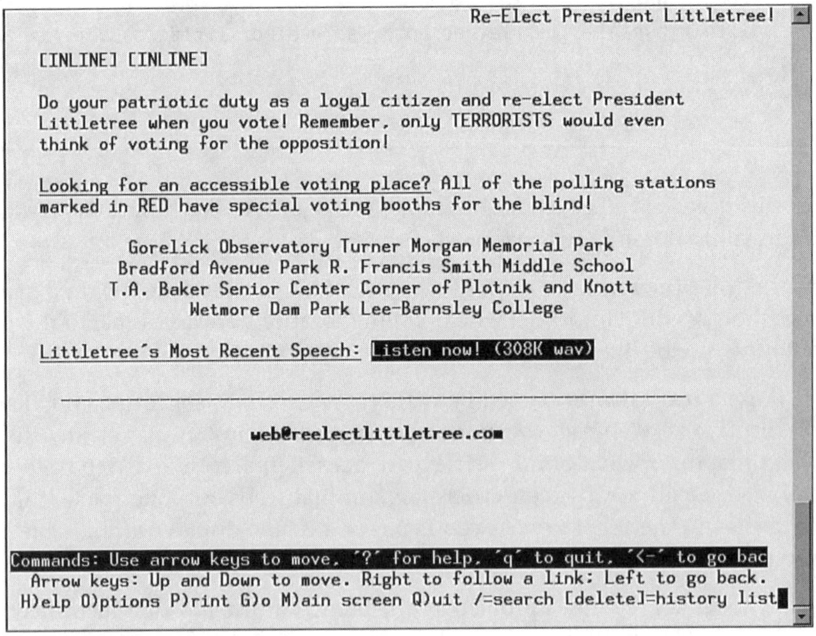

FIGURE A.2   The page is inaccessible when viewed in Lynx, a text browser.

A further problem exists but may not be immediately obvious—the speech link presents a problem to deaf users. Because the text of the speech is only available in a WAV file, anyone who is unable to hear sounds won't be able to know what this candidate stands for.

In Listing A.2, you can see a revised version of the page. This version was created by using the built-in accessibility check function in Dreamweaver MX, which is covered later in this appendix. The changes to the source code are shown in bold.

LISTING A.2   An Accessible Version of the Page in Listing A.1

```
<!DOCTYPE HTML PUBLIC "-//W3C//DTD HTML 4.01 Transitional//EN">
<html>
<head>
<title>Re-Elect President Littletree!</title>
<meta http-equiv="Content-Type" content="text/html; charset=iso-8859-1">
<style type="text/css">
  <!-- .access { color: red; }
      .footer { font-size: smaller; text-align: center; }
  -->
</style>
</head>
<body>
<img src="littletree.gif" width="125" height="125" align="right"
    alt="President N.K. Littletree" longdesc="littletree_longdesc.html">
<h1><img src="votebanner.gif" width="350" height="72"
        alt="Vote for President Littletree!"></h1>
<p>Do your patriotic duty as a loyal citizen and re-elect President
  Littletree when you vote! Remember, only TERRORISTS would even think
  of voting for the opposition!</p>
<p><strong>Looking for an accessible voting place?</strong> All of the
  polling stations followed by [Accessible] have special voting booths
  for the blind!</p>
<div align="center">
  <table border="3" cellpadding="3" cellspacing="3">
    <tr>
      <td>Gorelick Observatory</td>
      <td><span class="access">Turner Morgan Memorial Park</span>
            [Accessible]</td>
    </tr>
    <tr>
      <td>Bradford Avenue Park</td>
      <td><span class="access">R. Francis Smith Middle School</span>
            [Accessible]</td>
    </tr>
```

LISTING A.2   Continued

```
    <tr>
      <td><span class="access">T.A. Baker Senior Center</span> [Accessible]</td>
      <td>Corner of Plotnik and Knott</td>
    </tr>
    <tr>
      <td>Wetmore Dam Park</td>
      <td><span class="access">Lee-Barnsley College</span> [Accessible]</td>
    </tr>
  </table>
</div>
<p><strong>Littletree's Most Recent Speech:</strong>
  <a href="speech04.wav">Listen now! (308K wav)</a>
  <a href="speech04.html">Read the transcript!</a></p>
<hr>
<p class="footer">
  <a href="mailto:web@reelectlittletree.com">web@reelectlittletree.com</a>
  </p>
</body>
</html>
```

You'll notice that several new attributes such as alt and longdesc have been added. The word [Accessible] has been used to mark special voting sites, and a transcript link was placed after the audio file link. Also, <font> tags have been replaced with CSS styles.

The revised page is shown in Figure A.3 in Lynx; although the changes aren't dramatic, they are enough to allow a broader group of users (and voters!) to access the page.

Apply Standards to New Designs

It's always easiest to make a Web page or Web site accessible from the start and not have to spend time going back and redoing it from scratch. The effort of retrofitting is much harder than doing it right the first time.

Dreamweaver MX makes it easier to build accessible Web sites by providing accessible templates and by prompting you for necessary information when adding new HTML elements.

Accessible Design Templates

Dreamweaver MX comes with a default set of page designs; unfortunately, the basic page designs weren't created with accessibility in mind. Fortunately, an additional set of page designs were provided that include accessibility features such as <label> tags and variable font sizes, which allow you to set up an accessible page easily.

```
                                  Re-Elect President Littletree!  ▲
                                                                  ▒
   President N.M. Littletree

              Vote for President Littletree!

   Do your patriotic duty as a loyal citizen and re-elect President
   Littletree when you vote! Remember, only TERRORISTS would even
   think of voting for the opposition!

   Looking for an accessible voting place? All of the polling stations
   followed by [Accessible] have special voting booths for the blind!

      Gorelick Observatory Turner Morgan Memorial Park [Accessible]
    Bradford Avenue Park R. Francis Smith Middle School [Accessible]
    T.A. Baker Senior Center [Accessible] Corner of Plotnik and Knott
            Wetmore Dam Park Lee-Barnsley College [Accessible]

   Littletree's Most Recent Speech: Listen now! (308K wav) Read the
   transcript!


   ─────────────────────────────────────────────────────────

   web@reelectlittletree.com■                                     ▒
                                                                  ▼
  Commands: Use arrow keys to move, '?' for help, 'q' to quit, '<-' to go bac
   Arrow keys: Up and Down to move. Right to follow a link; Left to go back.
   H)elp O)ptions P)rint G)o M)ain screen Q)uit /=search [delete]=history list ▒
```

FIGURE A.3 Lynx now can view the page, as can many users with disabilities.

To use one of these templates, open a new file by going to File and selecting New. Select the category Page Design (Accessible) and you'll see a list of page types that can be used. Select one as shown in Figure A.4, open it up, and you're ready to start.

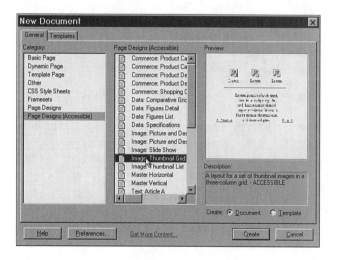

FIGURE A.4 Choose an accessible template as a starting point for a new Web page.

CAUTION

Merely using an accessible template does not guarantee that the final result will be accessible. You'll need to use the accessibility checker, described later in this appendix, and you should test your page carefully.

Accessibility Dialog Boxes

Dreamweaver MX also provides for a way to automatically be prompted for required accessibility information via dialog boxes. By default, these dialog boxes are turned off, but you can turn them on to ensure that you don't leave out any important attributes or tags.

Go to the Preferences menu and select Accessibility. You'll see the Options panel shown in Figure A.5.

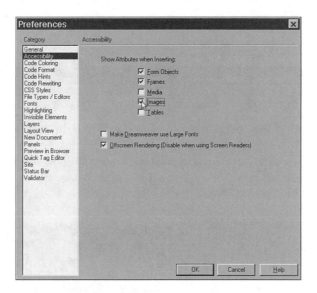

FIGURE A.5   Setting the accessibility options turns on accessibility dialog boxes.

Each of the five options—Images, Frames, Forms, Media, and Tables—turns on a different dialog box. When you insert one of those elements in your page, the dialog box will appear and prompt you for information. For example, if you try to add an image, you'll see the dialog box pictured in Figure A.6.

Each dialog box requests a different set of accessibility related attributes or information. These are shown in Table A.1.

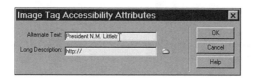

FIGURE A.6   The accessibility prompt for images requests *alt* and *longdesc* attributes.

TABLE A.1   Accessibility Dialog Boxes Are Activated by Setting Accessibility Options

Option (HTML Tag)	Accessibility Attributes
Image (`<img>`)	Alternative text (`alt`), Long Description (`longdesc`)
Frame (`<frame>`)	Frame Title (`title`)
Form (`<input>`, `<textarea>`)	Label (`<label>`), Style (nesting of `<label>`), Position (location of `<label>`), Access Key (`accesskey`), Tab Index (`tabindex`)
Media (`<object>`)	Title (`title`), Access Key (`accesskey`), Tab Index (`tabindex`)
Table (`<table>`)	Caption (`<caption>`), Align Caption (`<caption align>`), Summary (`summary`), Header (`scope`)

You're probably already familiar with the `alt` attribute; this is a text replacement for the image. An `alt` attribute isn't a description of the image, but a functional replacement for it. If the image has no function beyond decoration, the `alt` value should be `alt=""`. For little bullet icons, use `alt="*"`, not `alt="red circle"`. And definitely don't use the name of graphic, such as `alt="redbullt.jpg"`.

> **NOTE**
>
> Many people erroneously refer to "alt tags"—but `alt` is an attribute, and `<img>` is the tag. If you really want to bug the living daylights out of your least favorite HTML pedant, talk about "alt tags" constantly, but if you want to look like you're part of the markup intelligentsia, call it an `alt` attribute.

The `longdesc` attribute is used to provide a description of an image; unlike alt, `longdesc` is not a text value, but the URL of a page which describes the image in text. A `longdesc` should be used if the image contains information that isn't shown by the `alt` text, such as a chart or a graph. It can also be used to describe the contents of photographs or paintings.

The `title` attribute is a name or short description of a frame or object that is meant to be read to a human. A frame usually has a `name` attribute, but this is used by the browser to identify the frame and isn't necessarily written to make sense to the user. For example, `name="mnnav"` is confusing. The `title` should be clear and understandable and describe the function of the frame or object, such as `name="Main Navigation Panel"`.

The `accesskey` and `tabindex` attributes are used to enable improved keyboard navigation. The `accesskey` attribute designates a specific key that can be pressed in conjunction with the modifier key—usually the control or alt key—to activate a link or object. The numbers 1 through 0 work best for `accesskey` values. The `tabindex` key sets an order for tabbing through links and objects; pressing the Tab key advances you through the page in order of the `tabindex` attributes.

The `<label>` tag provides a text label for form controls, such as text fields or check boxes. You can determine the position of the label tags using the label settings on the dialog box. The `<label>` is important for screenreader users who need to know what each form field does when they can't rely on visual layout clues.

Tables have a number of attributes, such as `scope` and `summary`, that can be used to describe the relationship between the table header and the contents of the table cells. In addition, the `<caption>` tag can be used to add a caption to the table.

> **TIP**
>
> For more information on HTML tags and attributes used to make pages more accessible, be sure to visit the excellent accessibility tutorials at the Web Accessibility In Mind (WebAIM) site, `http://www.webaim.org/`.

Apply Standards to Existing Sites

As noted earlier, it's more efficient to build a site accessibly from the beginning. However, you may be dealing with older sites that need to be updated, or even sites you didn't design and have inherited responsibility for.

Dreamweaver MX assists you in bringing these existing pages up to compliance with the accessibility standards through accessibility reports which analyze your page, looking for specific problems. You can even run reports on all pages in one folder on your hard drive or on the entire Web site.

Check Accessibility

The accessibility report built in to Dreamweaver MX is set to check against both the WCAG and Section 508 standards. The WCAG standard is checked against only level Single-A accessibility; Double-A and Triple-A checkpoints aren't tested.

To check the accessibility of a page you're working on, first save the page. Then select the Check Page submenu from the File menu; the first choice is Check Accessibility, as shown in Figure A.7. Selecting this option will generate an accessibility report on your existing page.

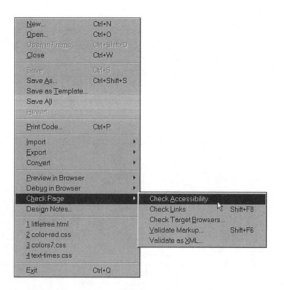

FIGURE A.7   The Check Accessibility function can be found in the File menu.

NOTE

The Check Accessibility function can be used only after you've saved the file you're working on. If you don't save before checking, the accessibility report won't reflect any recent changes.

An example of the output of an accessibility report can be seen in Figure A.8—this report was run on the Web page in Listing A.1, the uncorrected campaign page.

The accessibility check function runs an analysis of each part of your Web page, testing it against certain criteria called accessibility checks. For each one, it gives one of three results: pass, fail, or can't determine. If your page fails a check, you'll need to correct that to improve the accessibility of the page. A failed test is represented by a red X in the accessibility report.

WARNING

An automated checking program can do only so much; there's no perfect way to make software fix Web pages. It's possible for a page to pass every automated test and still be inaccessible. For this reason, you may want to read up on more accessibility techniques at the W3C's Web Accessibility Initiative site (http://www.w3.org/WAI/) and consider acquiring for your own testing purposes one of the programs used by people with disabilities.

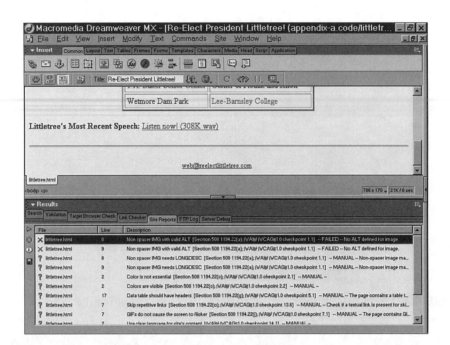

FIGURE A.8   The accessibility report identifies problems and potential problems.

Manual Checks

If the accessibility report has a question mark for the result of a test, that indicates that human judgment is necessary to determine if a test was passed. This is known as a *manual check*.

A good example of a manual check is the alt attribute for an image. The computer can tell if the <img> tag has an alt attribute, but it isn't able to determine whether the alt attribute is accurate. The purpose of the question mark is to tell you to evaluate the question your-self to determine if accessibility problems occur on the page.

Sitewide Accessibility Reports

To test a large number of Web pages, you don't have to individually load each one and run an accessibility report. Instead, you can simply use the Macromedia site report func-tion. This lets you select whether to run an accessibility report on the current page, the entire Web site you're working with, selected files in that site, or all the Web files in a folder.

To use the site reports, choose Reports from the Site menu. You'll see the choices shown in Figure A.9. Be sure to check the box for Accessibility and choose the appropriate files to test from the pull-down menu.

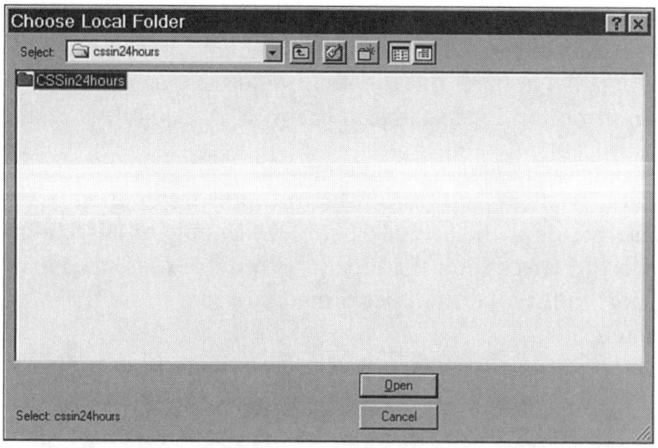

FIGURE A.9 You can test an entire site or a folder of HTML pages at once via the site reports function.

The accessibility report shown in Figure A.10 resulted from checking all the files within one folder.

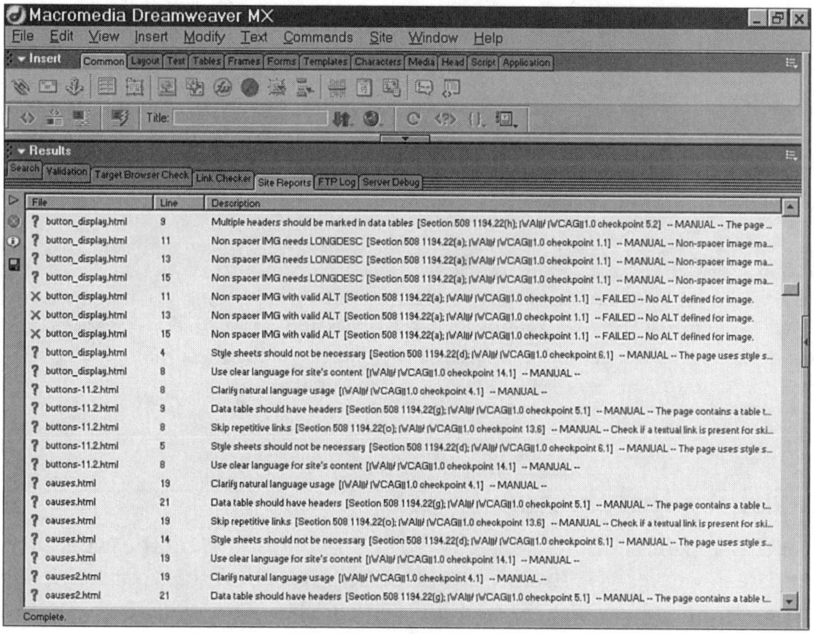

FIGURE A.10 The accessibility report for an entire Web site.

In addition to specifying the files to be checked, you can also set the report parameters to include or exclude certain accessibility checks. By default, the accessibility report checks both the WCAG Single-A standard and the Section 508 standard. To change this, highlight the accessibility report option by clicking on the word Accessibility, and then click the Report Settings button.

This calls up the choices shown in Figure A.11. You can toggle open the list of options by clicking the triangles beside each category. Using the Enable or Disable buttons, you can customize your report to check only the tests, or groups of tests, that matter to you. You can also set the report to list all checks performed, not just those that were failed or that need human judgment.

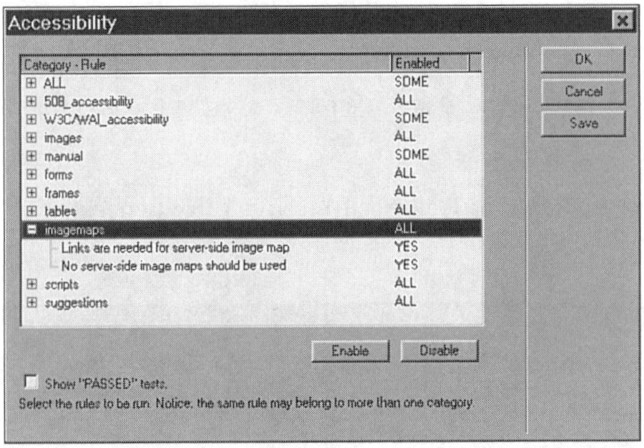

FIGURE A.11   You can turn off or on specific accessibility tests in the report options.

TIP

If you need more advanced accessibility evaluation and repair features, you may want to look at LIFT for Macromedia Dreamweaver, by UsableNet. This add-on for Dreamweaver MX sells for around $300 and can automate your accessibility upgrade process. For more details, see `http://www.usablenet.com/lift_dw/lift_dw.html` on the Web.

Accessibility Reference

The rest of this appendix is a reference to the checks performed by the accessibility checker in Dreamweaver MX. Each test is identified by a short title, but it's not always clear what each title means; the list that follows will clarify the meaning of the test titles.

NOTE

Dreamweaver MX comes with a built-in reference that is useful for understanding the accessibility reports, although the explanations can get a bit obscure and technical. To access the reference, open the Reference panel from the Window menu or highlight a report result and click the question mark button.

Image Tests

Images, because they're visual, can obviously present serious obstacles to users who can't see. There is also some danger that a strobing image could trigger seizures in photo-epileptic users. The tests that are run on images are shown in Table A.2.

TABLE A.2   Accessibility Checks Performed on Images

WCAG 1.0	Section 508	Accessibility Test
1.1	1194.22(a)	Spacer IMG with valid ALT
1.1	1194.22(a)	No LONGDESC for spacer IMG
1.1	1194.22(a)	Non spacer IMG with valid ALT
1.1	1194.22(a)	Non spacer IMG with equivalent ALT
1.1	1194.22(a)	Non spacer IMG with valid LONGDESC
1.1	1194.22(a)	Non spacer IMG needs LONGDESC
1.1	1194.22(a)	Image OBJECT with valid CONTENT
1.1	1194.22(a)	Image OBJECT with equivalent CONTENT
7.1	1194.22(j)	GIFs do not cause the screen to flicker

A spacer image is one that serves only to lay out the page and doesn't contain any useful information itself. Most of these are blank or transparent images. Any purely decorative image such as a spacer image should have an alt attribute value of alt="".

In the preceding table, some of these seem to be repeated with just a subtle change; for example, "Non spacer IMG with valid ALT" and "Non spacer IMG with equivalent ALT." A *valid* alt attribute is simply one that exists. If you leave off the alt attribute and give no value at all, it's not valid.

However, a valid alt attribute is not necessarily an *equivalent* alt attribute. Consider the top banner, which contained the text "Vote for President Littletree." If the alt value was alt="Vote", this would be a valid alt attribute, but it would not be an equivalent value.

An automatic program, such as the accessibility checker in Dreamweaver MX, can check to see if an alt attribute is valid—but only human judgment can determine if the value is equivalent. For this reason, there is a manual check that goes with some automatic checks. The longdesc attribute is another example—only a human can determine if there's additional information needed to convey the image content.

CAUTION

You may begin to think that images are the enemy of accessibility, and should be avoided. Nothing could be further from the truth! Images, when given appropriate `alt` and `longdesc` attributes, are not an accessibility problem. In fact, lack of images may introduce accessibility hurdles for some people, including those with problems reading because of cognitive disabilities. A good illustration really is worth a thousand words, so don't be afraid to use images—be afraid to not use them!

Imagemap Tests

Imagemaps share all the possible pitfalls that could accompany images and introduce several potential problems of their own. The special checks done on imagemaps are shown in Table A.3.

Table A.3   Accessibility Checks Performed on Imagemaps

WCAG 1.0	Section 508	Accessibility Test
1.1	1194.22(a)	AREA with valid ALT
1.1	1194.22(a)	AREA with equivalent ALT
1.2	1194.22(e)	Links are needed for server-side imagemap
9.1	1194.22(e)	No server-side image maps should be used

There are two types of imagemaps in HTML—client-side imagemaps that use <area> tags to define shapes, and server-side imagemaps that require a CGI script to determine the outcome of a map click.

Of the two, client-side maps are much more accessible because assistive technology programs can read the <area> tags and create a menu instead of an image with hotspots. However, each <area> must be marked with an appropriate `alt` attribute.

Server-side imagemaps present serious accessibility problems for users who can't see images, and thus whenever possible, they shouldn't be used. If you do use a server-side image map, you should make sure to provide equivalent text links for every hotspot on the imagemap.

Color and Style Tests

As shown in the campaign page example, the use of color can create accessibility problems when used carelessly. Contrast is important as well; blue links on light blue backgrounds are hard to see. Style sheets are almost always visual and may have many of the same problems as color when used to convey specific information. The checks for color and style sheets are shown on Table A.4.

TABLE A.4   Accessibility Checks Related to Colors and Style Sheets

WCAG 1.0	Section 508	Accessibility Test
2.1	1194.22(c)	Color is not essential
2.2	1194.22(c)	Colors are visible
6.1	1194.22(d)	Style sheets should not be necessary

Please keep in mind that neither of these are saying "don't use color" or "don't use CSS." In fact, you most assuredly should use both of them and use them regularly—color provides many usability and comprehension benefits, and style sheets are a boon to accessibility. These tests merely ask you to ensure that the vital information of the page isn't shown only in a style or color choice and is shown on the page in some other manner.

Form and Scripting Tests

Forms and scripts can present problems to assistive technology programs such as screenreaders. The checks done for forms and scripts are shown in Table A.5.

TABLE A.5   Accessibility Checks for Forms and Scripts

WCAG 1.0	Section 508	Accessibility Test
1.1	1194.22(a)	INPUT with valid ALT
1.1	1194.22(a)	INPUT with equivalent ALT
1.1	1194.22(a)	SCRIPT with valid NOSCRIPT
1.1	1194.22(a)	SCRIPT with equivalent NOSCRIPT
	1194.22(l)	Scripts are accessible
6.5		No JavaScript links are used
7.4	1194.22(p)	No auto refresh is used

The requirement for <input> tags to have alt attributes applies only to image Submit buttons—those <input> tags with type="image".

Scripts that have an effect such as presenting new content should have an equivalent <noscript> tag that either provides access to the content or links to a page or server-side program that has the same effect. Scripts that validate input or produce cosmetic effects such as mouseovers aren't required to have <noscript> tags.

Links that are purely JavaScript actions—or pull-down menus that change the current location without a Submit button being pressed—can be very difficult for assistive technologies and should be avoided. Also, pages that autorefresh based on <meta> tags can disrupt screenreaders; instead, use HTTP redirects in the server configuration or .htaccess file.

A

Table and Frame Tests

Tables and frames are very visual ways of presenting content in specific locations. When used injudiciously, they can introduce serious accessibility errors for people with visual disabilities, who may not be able to see the page at all or who may be using a screen magnifier and can't see the entire layout at once. The tests for tables and frames are listed in Table A.6.

TABLE A.6   Accessibility Checks Performed on Tables and Frames

WCAG 1.0	Section 508	Accessibility Test
5.1	1194.22(g)	Data table should have headers
5.1	1194.22(g)	Cell of data table should refer to headers
5.1	1194.22(g)	Data tables should be defined by TABLE tag
5.1	1194.22(g)	Multiple headers should be marked in data tables
12.1	1194.22(i)	FRAME with valid TITLE
12.1	1194.22(i)	IFRAME with valid TITLE

The tests listed for tables apply to *data tables*—tables that have been inserted to display tabular columns of information, such as a bus schedule. Web accessibility standards distinguish between data tables and *layout tables*, which are tables used to lay out Web pages in two dimensions on the screen. Only data tables require special coding for headers, and then only when the table is complex.

Frames that have `title` attributes can be identified by the browser by name. As mentioned earlier, a `title` attribute is meant to be a human-understandable name, such as `title="Navigation Frame"` or `title="Banner Ad Frame"`. Avoid naming your tables by their location; `alt="Left Frame"` is useless because it doesn't describe the function, just the location.

> **WARNING**
>
> Should you even use tables and frames for layout? Tables used to be a more serious accessibility problem when screenreaders would read across line by line, cutting cells in strange places. Current screenreaders have improved this, and all you have to do is make sure that your table cells make sense when read in the order they appear in the source code.
>
> Frames are more problematic—apart from potential accessibility hurdles, frames can introduce problems with bookmarking and usability. However, if labeled correctly, and if an appropriate <noframes> element is provided, frames can be made accessible as well.
>
> This doesn't mean that they're the best solution—often, a non-framed design with CSS for layout can accomplish as much as tables or frames and has even greater accessibility. Use tables and frames with care, if you decide to use them.

Multimedia and Applet Tests

Multimedia, as used here, refers both to video and audio; embedded objects can include Java applets, Flash animations, and more. The tests for these types of content are shown in Table A.7.

TABLE A.7 Accessibility Checks for Multimedia Files and Applets

WCAG 1.0	Section 508	Accessibility Test
1.1	1194.22(a)	Audio/video OBJECT with valid CONTENT
1.1	1194.22(a)	Audio/video OBJECT with equivalent CONTENT
1.1	1194.22(a)	OBJECT with valid CONTENT
1.1	1194.22(a)	OBJECT with equivalent CONTENT
1.4	1194.22(b)	Multimedia with synchronized alternative
1.3	1194.22(b)	Multimedia with equivalent audio description
1.1	1194.22(a)	Linked AUDIO with equivalent CONTENT
	1194.22(m)	Link to plug-in is present
1.1	1194.22(a)	APPLET with valid ALT
1.1	1194.22(a)	APPLET with valid CONTENT
1.1	1194.22(a)	APPLET with equivalent ALT

In general, the easiest way to deal with multimedia is to provide a text transcript of the information. In addition to the dialog, action and events must be described as well. A synchronized alternative is a text or audio version that plays at the same time as the video, such as a caption or an audio description. The synchronization is usually accomplished by using the Synchronized Multimedia Integration Language (SMIL).

> **TIP**
>
> To learn more about SMIL, visit the W3C's multimedia page at `http://www.w3.org/AudioVideo/` on the Web.

Other Accessibility Tests

Several other accessibility checks that are performed don't fall into separate categories, but nevertheless are very important for ensuring the accessibility of your site. These are shown in Table A.8.

TABLE A.8 Additional Accessibility Checks Performed by Dreamweaver MX

WCAG 1.0	Section 508	Accessibility Test
13.6	1194.22(o)	Skip repetitive links
7.1	1194.22(j)	Avoid causing the screen to flicker
14.1		Use clear language for site's content
4.1		Clarify natural language usage
		Proprietary tags are used
6.2	1194.22(k)	Text only equivalent page may be needed

Repetitive links are the pet peeves of many screenreader users. When a visual browser loads a Web page, a sighted user can instantly scan it in a glance, jumping to the content—usually in the middle of the page—and ignoring the navigation bars. Screenreader users don't have this luxury; they have to listen to all the links, on every page, again and again before reaching the content. For this reason, the Web accessibility standards suggest a Skip Navigation link at the top of the page that will take the user directly to the main content, bypassing the navigation bars.

In accessibility standards terminology, a natural language is any language that a human being speaks or writes. When part of a page is written in a different language, this could confuse screenreaders or automatic translation software; therefore, changes in natural language should be shown in the HTML tags. Use the `lang` attribute (and `xml:lang` in XHTML) to indicate changes in language, such as this:

```
<p>I counted to three:
  <span lang="es">Uno, dos, tres.</span>
</p>
```

If you've tried everything and you can't make a Web page accessible, you can make an equivalent page that is simpler and presents the same information in straightforward markup and language. This is often called a "text-only page," but in general, a text page isn't necessary! Nearly any page can be made accessible by adding a few extra tags and attributes.

Summary

By employing the techniques of accessible Web design, you can ensure that your users with disabilities won't be shut out from accessing your Web site. These techniques are described in the Web accessibility standards.

The World Wide Web Consortium's Web Content Accessibility Guidelines define the technical considerations for creating accessible Web sites. The WCAG checkpoints provide you with a blueprint for your accessible Web site and have been adopted (in modified form) by the United States government in the form of the Section 508 requirements.

Dreamweaver MX enables you to apply these accessibility standards to your new Web designs or to existing Web sites. Accessible templates and prompts for accessibility attributes let you design for accessibility from the start, and integrated site reports can spot accessibility problems in one HTML document or on an entire site. Complete reference to accessibility rules is available at any time through the Dreamweaver MX reference window.

Creating an accessible Web site shouldn't be an extra chore—it should be part and parcel of your good Web design practices. The special accessibility functions of Dreamweaver MX help make these important practices quick and easy to apply!

APPENDIX **B**

Server Behavior Builder

by Hugh Livingstone

Dreamweaver MX provides server behaviors to do the most common server-side processing tasks with the most popular application servers. Getting your Web page to interact with a database is easily done with Dreamweaver MX, and pretty much all the options you would want are covered.

However, there are bound to be occasions when there is something you want to do, but there is no server behavior available for you to do it. When this happens, you have a number of options.

- You can go to the Macromedia Exchange and download a server behavior to create the functionality you want.

- You can hand code the file to include the server-side code that's needed to do the job.

- You can build your own server behavior so that next time you want to do the same job, the code is already there for you or other members of your team.

This chapter describes each option in turn, discussing the pros and cons of each.

Downloading Extensions

Chapter 20, "Extending Dreamweaver MX," discussed extensions in some detail, but it concentrated on extensions that used client-side JavaScript. Server-side behaviors work in almost the same way.

Downloading an extension is great if you are not an experienced programmer, because all the code will have been written for you by someone who is experienced. All you have to do is download the extension, read the documentation, and then include it in your page. The disadvantage of extensions is that although many extensions are available to do a variety of common tasks, you may not be able to find one that does exactly what you want, in the way you want to do it.

Because you are downloading someone else's code, you are also putting yourself in the hands of another programmer. That programmer may not understand the task you want to do, so the code may not work quite the way you expect. When doing any coding on the server, security is a paramount concern, so always check that the behavior works properly, without exposing any details to the user that could be used for ill intent.

Although many extensions are free, some have to be paid for—but remember that you will probably spend less money on buying an extension that does the job than you would learning how to hand code one yourself.

Before You Download an Extension

Before downloading extensions, it's a good idea to first register at the Macromedia Exchange, the Web site where Dreamweaver Extensions are kept.

> **NOTE**
>
> Macromedia also has a section for Dreamweaver UltraDev. Dreamweaver UltraDev was the previous version of Dreamweaver that supported server-side scripting. Most UltraDev extensions will work in Dreamweaver MX, but do check the documentation that is supplied with the extension and test it out properly yourself. You should also read the Dreamweaver MX Extension FAQ that is displayed on the site.

Go to

```
http://www.macromedia.com/exchange/dreamweaver
```

You should see a Web page similar to Figure B.1. Follow the instructions to get a Macromedia ID. You'll need to supply an email address and password. After you are registered, you can download any extension you like. Extensions are grouped by application (Dreamweaver, Flash, ColdFusion, and so on) and within each application, they are grouped by function. You can also search for a particular extension name or function.

If you like the sound of an extension, read the reviews that other users have written to check whether the extension does what you want and without any problems. The extension author should also provide documentation about the extension—make sure you read this, too.

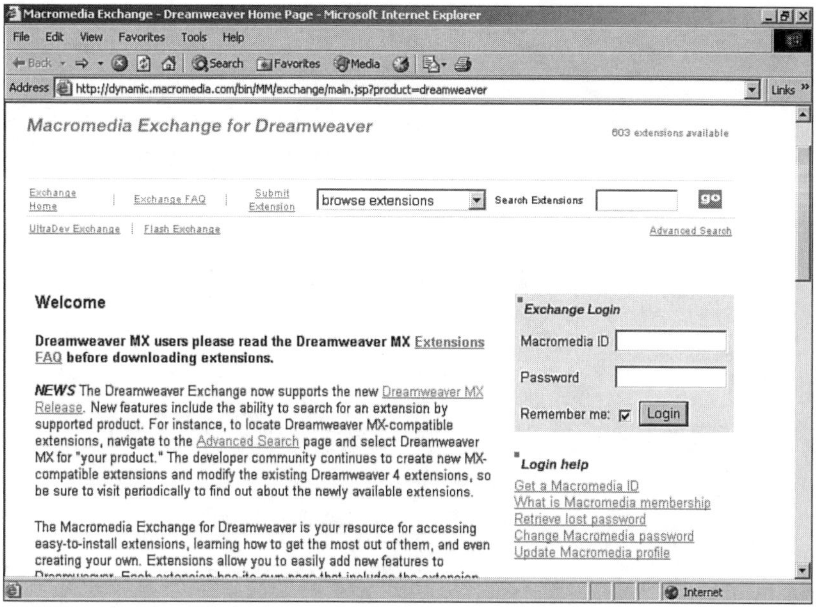

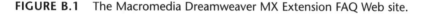

FIGURE B.1   The Macromedia Dreamweaver MX Extension FAQ Web site.

Using the Extension Manager

In Dreamweaver, select Help, Macromedia Exchange. You can also do the same thing by clicking the plus sign (+) button on the Server Behaviors panel and choosing Get More Server Behaviors. Both will take you to the Macromedia Dreamweaver Exchange site. After you have logged in, you can search for the type of extensions you want. You will probably be given quite a few choices to choose from. Figure B.2 shows the results from a search. Clicking each extension name gives you more details about it. Carefully choose the one that best fits your task. You may want to download a number of extensions to try them out.

After you have found an extension you want, download it. If given the choice in Windows, you should save the extension rather than open it. The best place to save the file (it will have the extension MXP) is in the Downloaded Extensions folder that Dreamweaver creates for you. It's usually at C:\Program Files\Macromedia\Dreamweaver MX\Downloaded Extensions for Windows, and hard drive : applications : Macromedia Dreamweaver MX : Downloaded Extensions on the Mac.

To install the extension within Dreamweaver, launch the Extension Manager by choosing Help, Manage Extensions. The Extension Manager appears, as shown in Figure B.3.

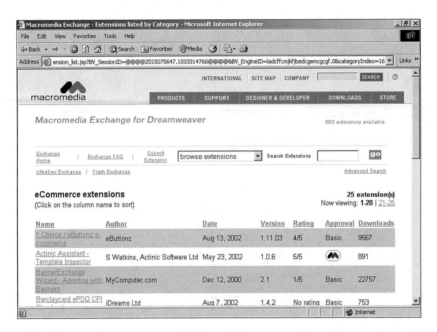

FIGURE B.2   Lots of extensions are available on the Macromedia Exchange. Go carefully through each one to choose the one that suits your task best.

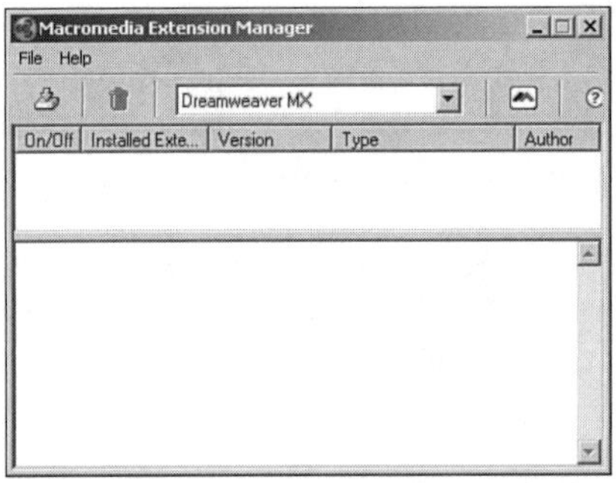

FIGURE B.3   The Extension Manager is the tool you use to install your extensions within Dreamweaver.

Choose File, Install Extension and select the MXP file you want to install. The extension will now be ready for use. When you click the plus button on the Server Behaviors panel, you will see the new behavior available.

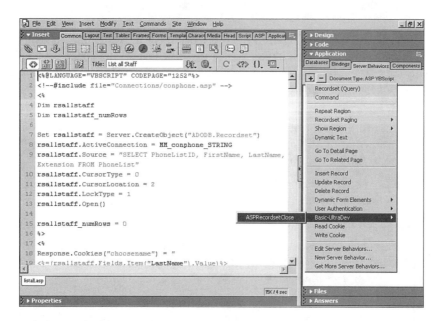

FIGURE B.4 After you have installed the extension, you can see it on the Add Server Behavior menu.

Hand Coding Your Own Server Behavior

If the functionality you want is going to be used only once on your site, you may want to simply hand code to do the job on that page. Although hand coding can be quick and familiar for programmers, the main drawback of hand coding is that you are producing a "one-off." The code you have written is not reusable by others. Even if you are an expert programmer for your chosen application server, there are probably others in your team who are not. When you use copy and paste to reuse code, you are depending that the code has been selected properly and that the parameters and variables you have used on one page are going to be valid on another page.

Resources for Learning Server-Side Programming

Throughout the rest of this chapter, it is assumed that you are familiar with the coding techniques for your chosen application server. You should already have some experience of writing dynamic pages by hand, without having to rely on Dreamweaver's behaviors. If you want to learn how to program your application server, following are some books and Web sites you could start with.

ColdFusion

If you are completely new to programming, ColdFusion is the best application server to start with. It is much easier to code than any of the others, using a tagging system similar to HTML. ColdFusion also deals with a lot of the low-level "plumbing," such as object management, for you; in other coding application servers you have to code this up yourself.

Dreamweaver has a lot of support for ColdFusion. Go to the Help menu and choose Using ColdFusion. You will find a lot of help there, including a tutorial. You can also read the ColdFusion documentation that is on the Dreamweaver MX CD. Look in the ColdFusion folder, and then in the ColdFusion Documents subfolder.

The best place on the Web to start for ColdFusion information is the Macromedia Web site (`http://www.macromedia.com`).

ASP and ASP.NET

The Microsoft developers network Web site (`http://msdn.Microsoft.com`) is the first place you should go. Other useful Web sites are 15 Seconds (`http://www.15seconds.com`) and 4 guys from Rolla (`http://www.4guysfromrolla.com`).

Many books are available for both ASP and ASP.NET, but if you are starting out you should look at the slightly more straightforward ASP first, before moving on to ASP.NET.

A good ASP book to start with is *Teach Yourself E-Commerce Programming with ASP in 21 Days*, by Stephen Walther, Steve Banick, and Jonathan Levine, published by Sams Publishing.

JSP

Learning JSP is a bit harder than other server-side technologies. It is usually assumed that you are already familiar with programming and that you already know ASP or Java. A good place to start is the Sun JSP documentation page at `http://java.sun.com/products/jsp/docs.html`.

PHP

A 10-part tutorial about PHP that is aimed at beginners is part of the Web Developer JavaScript Web site at Internet.com. It is called "Learning PHP: The What's and the Why's," by Elizabeth Fulghum. The rather obscure URL is

`http://webdeveloper.earthweb.com/webjs/article/0,,12721_900521,00.html`.

A site called "Learning PHP" has, unsurprisingly, a number of PHP tutorials on it. Go to

`http://www.phphelp.com`.

Support for Hand Coding in Dreamweaver

Much of the support for hand-coding in Dreamweaver is aimed at the HTML coder, but a lot of support is also available for ColdFusion, ASP.NET, and other server-side technologies. This makes Dreamweaver MX an excellent editor for ASP, JSP, and PHP.

Views and Other Editors

Dreamweaver has always let you see your code easily, and Dreamweaver MX extends this further. As you have already seen, three views can be chosen at the click of a button.

Design view gives you a visual page layout view. It renders the page in roughly the same way a Web browser would, but lets you see elements, such as comments, that would normally be invisible in the browser. The design view is the best choice when designing the page layout with HTML and CSS.

Code view shows you just the HTML, JavaScript, and server-side code in the page. Although you see every detail of the code, it's hard to imagine what the final page will look like. Code view has many options for customizing the workspace, which is covered in the next section.

Split view splits the screen in two so that you can see the code view at the top of the screen and the design view at the bottom. This view is great for seeing the interaction between the page code and how the page looks. However, I find the two views a little cramped for sustained work, and I use this view only for fiddling with the page design after I've done the main work.

Another view that you may prefer to use is the HomeSite/Coder-style workspace. This option is provided just after you install Dreamweaver, and most people forget about it. If you are used to using HomeSite, ColdFusion Studio, or another code-based editor, you may prefer the layout of this workspace, as shown in Figure B.5, with the panels docked on the left side. To get this workspace, choose Edit, Preferences, and then choose the General category. Next, click the button marked Change Workspace. Select the HomeSite/Coder-style workspace option (the nostalgic could also choose the Dreamweaver UltraDev workspace).

HomeSite+

If you just can't live without a code-only editor such as HomeSite, you can install HomeSite+, which is on the Dreamweaver installation CD. HomeSite+ combines HomeSite 5 and ColdFusion Studio 5 to give a code-only editor with lots of ColdFusion support. It is a simple, lean program that is perfect for quick code adjustments or for coding languages such as Perl and Java, which Dreamweaver does not support very well. HomeSite is a Windows-only program.

You are able to use both Dreamweaver and HomeSite+ for the same files. Changes you make in one program will be carried over into the other. In Dreamweaver, choose Edit, Edit with HomeSite. The first time you do this, the menu will read Edit with External Editor, and you will need to tell Dreamweaver where Homesite+.exe resides (usually in `C:\Program Files\Macromedia\HomeSite+`). If the file has not been saved, you are prompted to save it. After you have finished editing the file in HomeSite+, click the Dreamweaver button in the editor toolbar.

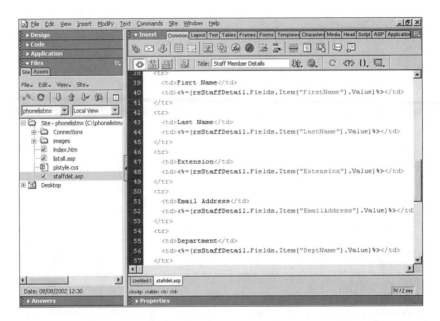

FIGURE B.5   The HomeSite/Coder-style workspace may be more comfortable to previous users of HomeSite or ColdFusion Studio.

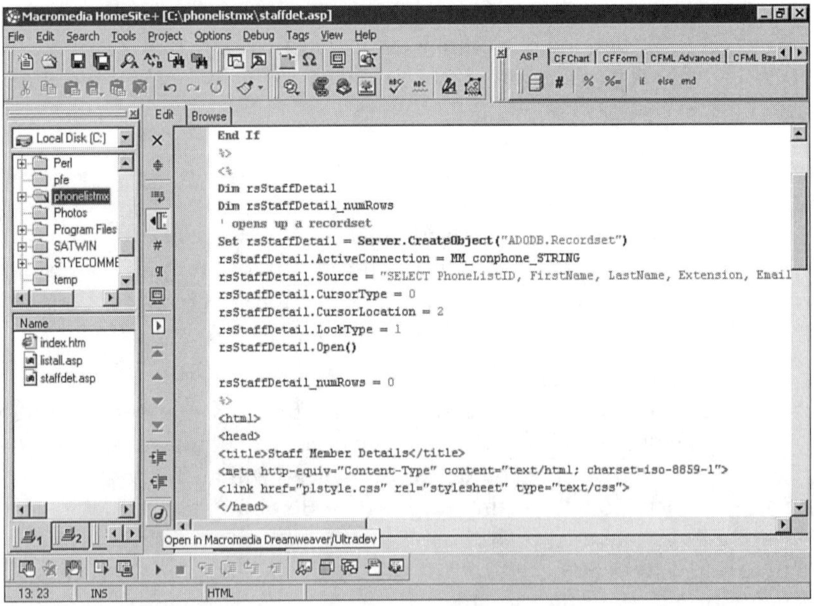

FIGURE B.6   HomeSite+ is a great code-only editor that integrates with Dreamweaver MX. You can install it from the Dreamweaver CD.

If you have another editor that you like to code in, you can set up Dreamweaver to integrate with that editor instead. Choose Edit, Preferences, and the File Types/Editors category. Next to the box marked External Editor, shown in Figure B.7, click the Browse button and choose the EXE file of your preferred code editor.

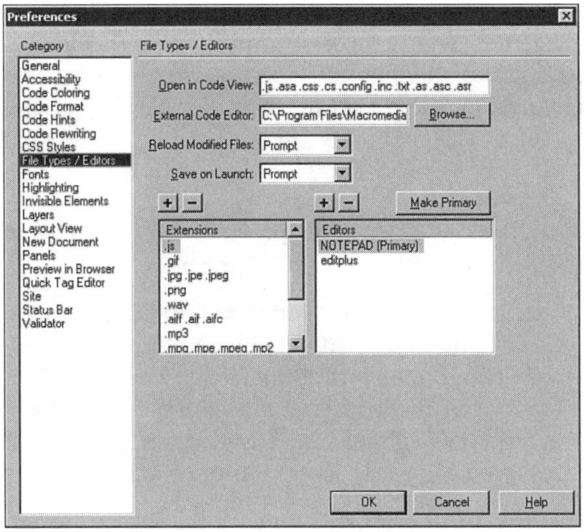

FIGURE B.7   You can choose your own favorite code editor to work alongside Dreamweaver MX.

Using Dreamweaver's Code View

For nearly all coding tasks, Dreamweaver's code view does the job as well as any code-only editor. You can set up a lot of your own preferences for how you like to work in code view. Select View, Code View Options. A small menu pops out for you to turn options on or off.

Word Wrap automatically wraps code onto the next line at column 76 (you can change this column in Preferences) but does not insert a newline or carriage-return character. This option is useful in conjunction with line numbering and when your screen is at a lower resolution.

Line Numbers displays line numbers along the left side of the code screen. A line with no number is wrapped from the previous line. It's a good idea to keep line numbering on. If your page has an error, the browser will often display the line number where the client-side or server-side code encountered a problem.

Highlight Invalid HTML means that Dreamweaver will highlight in yellow any HTML code it does not recognize. This option is useful if you are using a server-side technology Dreamweaver recognizes, but it can be a nuisance if you are editing any "unusual" files, such as Perl scripts. Highlighting usually goes on or off only after a refresh.

Syntax Coloring should invariably be left on—it's a great tool to help you spot mistakes in your code, such as not finishing off a string.

Auto Indent should also be left on—it means that when you press Return, the next line is indented the same as the previous line. It's important to indent your code to highlight *if blocks* and *loops*. It makes your code much easier to follow, both for yourself and others.

By choosing Edit, Preferences, you can also set other coding preferences. Most of these are fairly minor, and you can look them up in Dreamweaver's help files. The default options already set by Dreamweaver give the most flexibility for hosting pages on different systems and servers.

The Code Panel

As you are writing your code, the Code panel provides some great resources to help you. Expand it by clicking the arrow on the left side of the bar.

The Tag Inspector, on the left of the screen and shown in Figure B.8, provides you with a hierarchical view of the document. It's particularly useful for pages with complex layout, such as nested tables, or where there's lots of interactivity between your server-side code and HTML. As you click a tag in the Inspector, it becomes highlighted in the code, and as you move through the code view window, the corresponding tags will be highlighted in the Inspector. This means you can easily locate bits of code in long, complicated pages.

Underneath the tag list is a list of properties for each highlighted tag. You can edit or set tag properties here, and it will update the code.

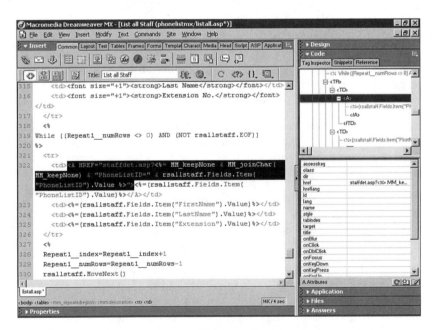

FIGURE B.8   The Tag Inspector interacts with the code view window so that you can easily locate particular tags and view their properties, as we are doing with this dynamic hyperlink.

Snippets

Code snippets are a new feature in Dreamweaver MX that have been inherited from ColdFusion Studio. Snippets are a bit like library items for code. Unlike library items, however, they do not automatically update, nor are they tied to a particular site.

Dreamweaver has some code snippets already built in. These are snippets of HTML and JavaScript to do common client-side tasks.

The Snippets panel, which is shown in Figure B.9, shows the selected snippet in the top window. Snippets are organized into folders in the window below.

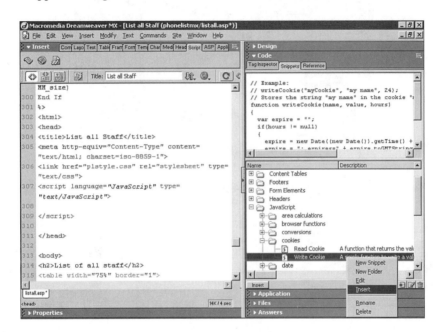

FIGURE B.9   Code Snippets let you reuse code. Dreamweaver already has some supplied snippets, such as this code to write a cookie with JavaScript.

To insert a code snippet, place the insertion cursor on the page where you want the snippet to go. Choose the snippet you want and right-click it (Control+click on the Mac). Then choose Insert from the pop-up menu.

To create your own snippets, you should first create a new folder for your own type of snippets. Right-click (Control+click on the Mac) in the Snippets window and choose New Folder. If the folder is created in the "wrong" place, you can drag it to the level you want. Highlight the code you want to use as the snippet and right-click (Control+click on the Mac) to choose Create New Snippet from the pop-up menu.

You will then be presented with the dialog box shown in Figure B.9 to fill in the snippet name and description. If you want the code to flow around a selected object, such as an image or table cell, select the Wrap Selection option, specifying which part of the code goes before the object and which after the object. If the code is a standalone block, such as the example in Figure B.10, choose the Insert Block option. You can also choose whether you see the snippet preview as code (most likely) or in design view.

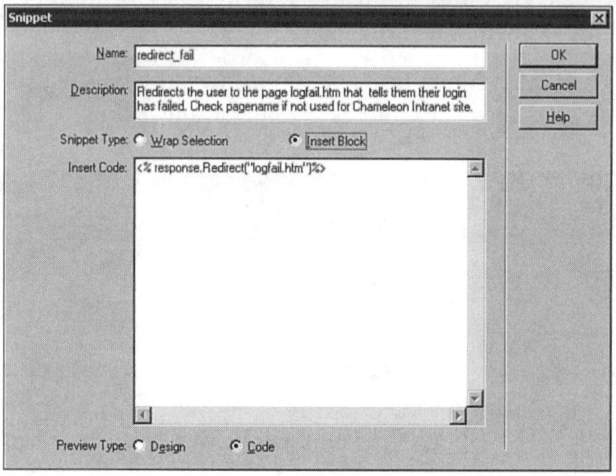

FIGURE B.10   When you insert a snippet, you also specify its attributes for other designers and you to see.

Reference
The right tab of the Code panel gives you access to a wealth of reference material. It includes reference books about HTML, CSS, Accessibility, JavaScript, ColdFusion, ASP and JSP. It's like having a bookshelf on your computer. To look up a tag, right-click (Control+click on the Mac) it when the Reference panel is open. The reference for that tag will be shown.

To browse the reference manually, choose the reference book you want to look at; below that, choose the tag or object and to its right the tag or object attribute that you want to learn about.

Tag Completion
For coders, one of the most exciting new features of Dreamweaver is code completion. With Code Hints, as Dreamweaver calls them, you get help about the particular tags and objects while you type them, as you can see in Figure B.11. This can really speed up coding by giving you the allowable attributes for an HTML or ColdFusion tag or the

available methods and properties of ASP and other application server objects. As long as you have code hints switched on, you will see lists of attributes, properties, or methods for supported tags and objects.

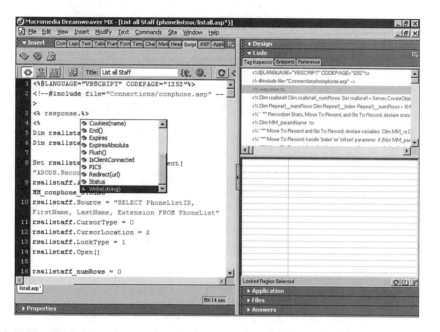

FIGURE B.11 Code Hints can really speed up your hand coding by showing you the allowable attributes, properties, or methods for a tag or object.

To turn Code Hints on, choose Edit, Preferences, and the Code Hints category. As you can see from Figure B.12, you can turn tag completion on or off and specify how long Dreamweaver will wait before dropping down the completion menu. You can also specify what types of hints you want Dreamweaver to supply—just turn them all on!

If you are an experienced programmer, hand-coding is very easy using Dreamweaver MX. Although UltraDev was considered a good tool for Visual Design, but with limited support for coding by hand, Dreamweaver MX includes lots of new tools that really help us to introduce our own code, to go beyond the built-in server behaviors. Dreamweaver MX now rivals many of the traditional development tools that have been used by Web and Database developers.

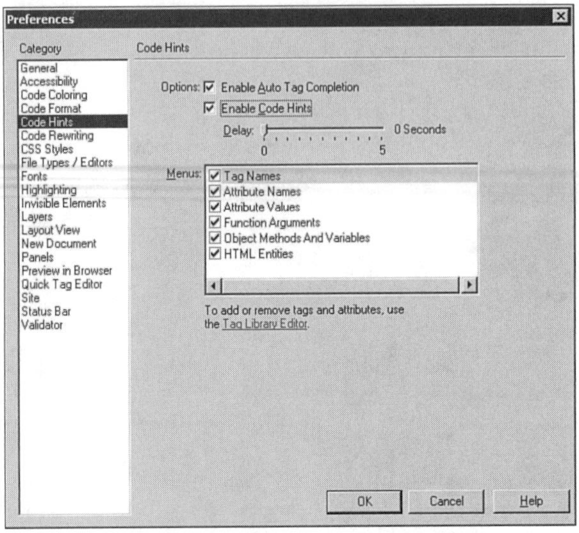

FIGURE B.12   Make sure Code Hints is turned on if you want to take advantage of this productivity bonus.

Server Behaviors

The built-in server behaviors are powerful because they allow nonprogrammers, or those with only a limited knowledge of server-side programming, to perform common functions such as displaying database records. They can be used by Web designers to visually design a page to produce simple Web applications. If they need to modify the page after design—maybe to reorder database columns or to add in more data—there is no need to hunt through and modify code; the server behavior can be easily changed.

Server behaviors are also useful to experienced programmers. So much of Web application coding is the repetition of common tasks, such as creating a recordset, opening it, and displaying the records. Server behaviors let you automate these common tasks with robust, standard code so that you can concentrate on the difficult parts.

Hand coding unique pages gets the job done, but unless you are a Web design team of one, and you are sure no one else will want to modify the page after you have finished with it, I would recommend adding a custom server behavior. Even if you are the sole developer, you can save yourself time in the long run by creating your own server behaviors.

Writing Server Behaviors

To write your own server behaviors is relatively simple, but you do need to be familiar with hand coding the functionality you want. You should first hand code the function you want to use and run the page to check that it works properly. After writing the behavior, you should use it again to check that all is well.

We are going to write two simple behaviors that read and write cookies, using VBScript for ASP. Even if you are not yet familiar with ASP, you should be able to follow along.

Writing a Cookie Behavior

Cookies are sent by the server to the client along with the requested page. If the cookie is given an expiration date, the client's browser will save the cookie on the client's machine so it can be referred to during future visits to the Web site. The client will send the cookie back to the server with each page request and form submission, and a server-side script can use this cookie value as part of the dynamic page-generation process. Although cookies are sent and processed by the server, you can also read and write cookies, using JavaScript, after the page has arrived at the client. Dreamweaver includes two code snippets to read and write cookies using JavaScript.

You are going to write your cookies from the server (using ASP), so you do not have to rely on the browser supporting JavaScript. The code is also much easier when done from the server side.

This behavior will save the value of a recordset column into a cookie on the user's machine. You will also write a behavior to read this cookie value, on subsequent pages or even site visits.

To start to write the behavior, open up the Application panel as shown in Figure B.13 and click the Server Behaviors tag. Click the plus button and choose New Server Behavior.

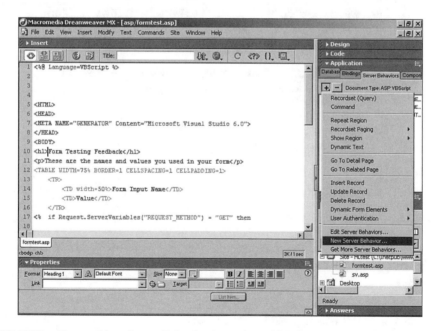

FIGURE B.13   Choose New Server Behavior from the Add Behavior menu to start writing your behavior.

You will now be presented with the New Server Behavior dialog box as shown in Figure B.14. Choose the document type you want to use (Dreamweaver should guess from the site you have open) and give the behavior a name. For this example, use Write Cookie (spaces are allowed here). Remember that other people are going to use the behavior, so make it descriptive of its function. This is a completely new behavior, so do not select the option box at the bottom of the box. click OK.

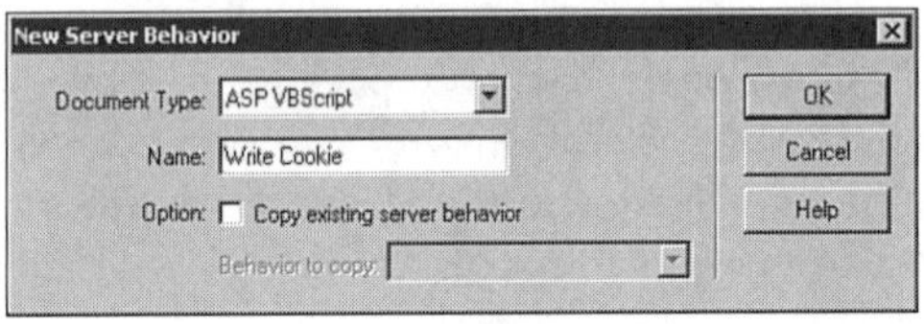

FIGURE B.14   Give your new behavior a descriptive name for others to use.

The next dialog box is shown in Figure B.14. This is where most of the work will be done. You will write blocks of code here and tell Dreamweaver where you want the code to be written on the page.

Add a code block by clicking the plus button on the top left. The suggested name is fine, so accept that.

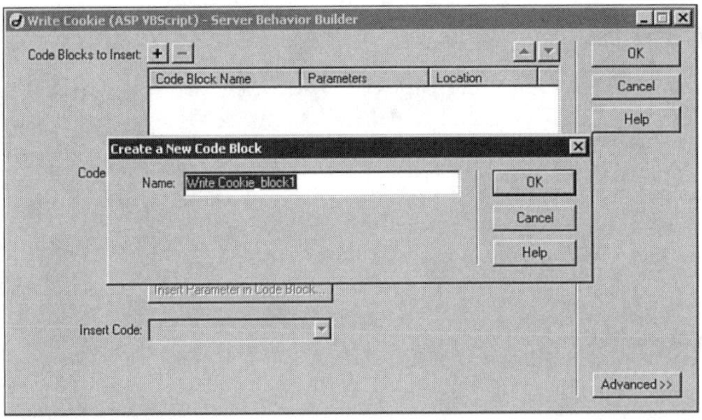

FIGURE B.15   Add a code block and give it a name.

The Code Block window asks you to replace the text with your own code. This is what you will do, inserting the ASP code that will write a cookie, as you can see from Figure B.15. The code is

```
<%Response.Cookies("cookiename") = "cookievalue"
Response.Cookies("cookiename").Expires = #12/31/2005# %>
```

This will write a cookie called "cookiename," with a value of "cookievalue" to the client, which will expire at the end of 2005. You can directly type the code in, if you are confident it will work, or copy and paste it from another file.

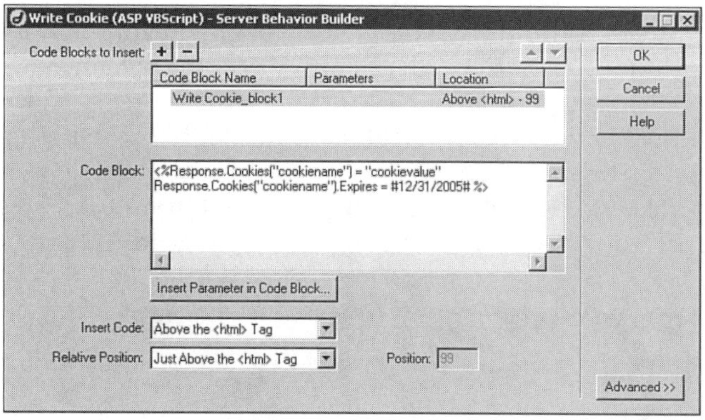

FIGURE B.16   Put the ASP code to write the cookie in the Code Block box.

Using Parameters

The code is correct and will write a cookie to the client, but the cookie will always be called cookiename and its value will always be cookievalue. You want to let the designers add their own cookie names and values. To do this, use Parameters.

To make the cookie name a choosable parameter, highlight the code cookiename. Click the Insert Parameter in Code Block button and enter a descriptive parameter name in the dialog box shown in Figure B.17. Remember that other designers will enter their own values for this parameter, so it should be clear what value they are setting. In this case, choose CookieName. Parameter names cannot have spaces.

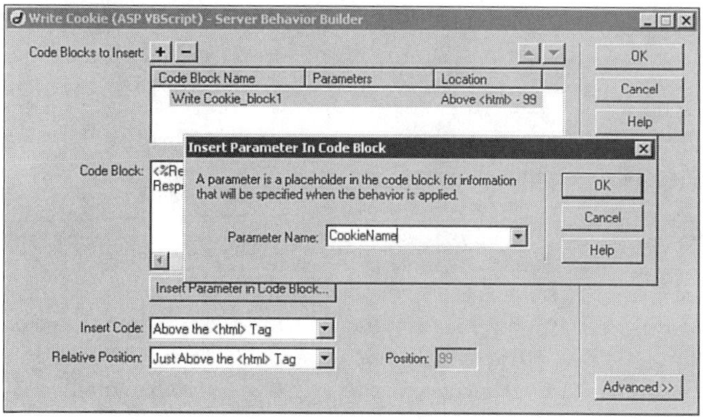

FIGURE B.17   Give the parameter a descriptive name—other Web designers will need to enter their own values.

Click the OK button to dismiss the dialog box. You will be asked if you want to replace all instances of the word "cookiename" with the new parameter; click Yes. If you now look at the code, you will see that `cookiename` has been replaced with `@@CookieName@@`. This indicates to Dreamweaver that a parameter goes here.

Now add another parameter for the cookie value. Again highlight the word cookievalue and click the Insert Parameter in Code Block button. Call the parameter CookieValue. If you examine the code, you will see that `cookievalue` has been replaced with `@@CookieValue@@`. Double-check that you still have the quotation marks in your code, as shown in Figure B.18. The expiration date is still "hard-coded" and set well into the future, which is perfectly acceptable—you don't want to confuse the designers with too many choices, or run the risk of them entering a date in the wrong format.

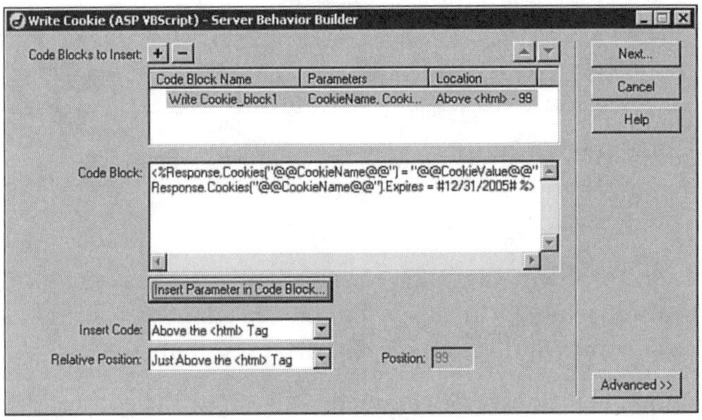

FIGURE B.18   Parameters are marked in the code with double At (@) symbols.

Code Placement

The next option to set is where you want Dreamweaver to put the code that the behavior will insert. Writing and reading cookies should be done at the beginning of a page and must be done before the browser is sent anything—even a doctype or <HTML> tag. This cookie value comes from a recordset, so it can be set only after the recordset has opened.

Choose Above the HTML Tag from the Insert Code menu, and the Relative Position will be Just After the Recordsets, as shown in Figure B.19.

NOTE

You can choose Custom Position and give the code block a weight. The code that opens a recordset has a weight of 50, so if you want the code to execute before the recordset opens, give it a weight of less than 50, and if the code depends on the recordset being open and therefore must execute after the open recordset code, give it a weight of more than 50.

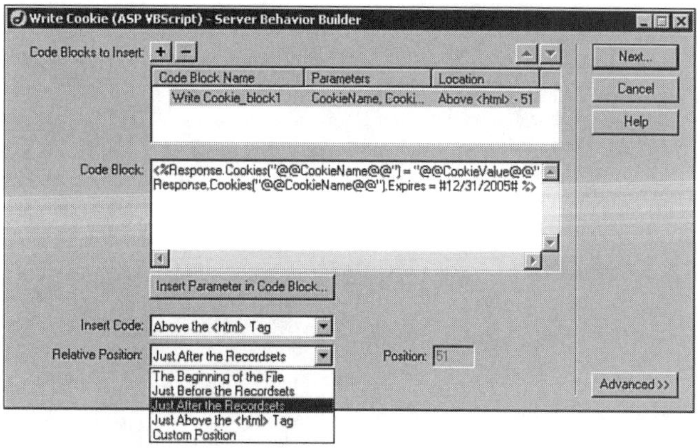

FIGURE B.19   You need to specify where the code will be inserted by Dreamweaver. The Insert Code menu specifies the approximate position, which can be set more precisely with the Relative Position menu.

After you have positioned the code block, click the Next button. This closes the Server Behavior Builder dialog box and opens the Generate Behavior dialog box. In this box, you can specify how designers will enter parameter values. After the designer chooses the server behavior, a dialog box will pop up, and it is here that you specify what it looks like. Each parameter can be entered with many types of interface controls.

With the up/down arrows at the top left of the list, you can change the order in which parameters are listed. Select a parameter name to move it. The arrow to the right of the name allows you to choose the type of interface control that will select the value. For the cookie name, use the default text box, and because you want to set the value from a recordset, the cookie value will use a Dynamic Text Field control.

As you can see from Figure B.20, you can choose from a wide variety of controls. You should choose the best control to minimize the possibility of invalid values being entered by designers through typing errors. After you have made your choice, click OK to dismiss the dialog box.

Using Your New Server Behavior

The new server behavior is now available in any ASP/VB Script site. If you now click the plus button on the Server Behavior tag, the drop-down menu shows the new server behavior, as you can see in Figure B.21.

If you choose the new behavior, you are presented with a dialog box to enter the cookie name into a text box and to choose the cookie value from a list of fields in the recordset, as you can see in Figure B.22.

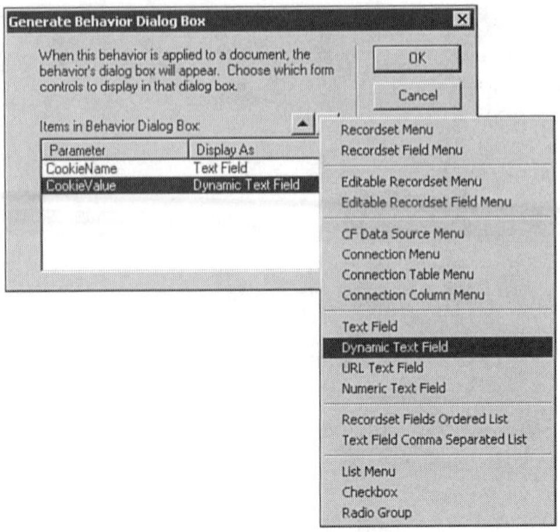

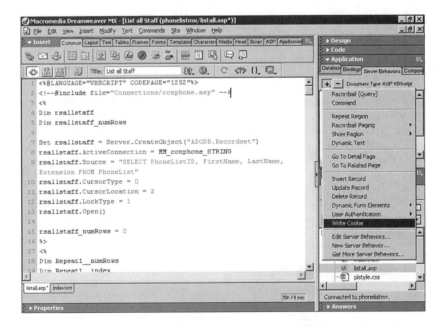

FIGURE B.20   You can choose the type of interface control that will be presented to designers when they enter parameter values.

FIGURE B.21   The new server behavior can be seen in the Add Behavior menu.

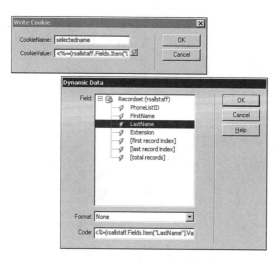

FIGURE B.22   The new server behavior lets designers enter their own cookie names and choose a field for the cookie value.

You should test that the behavior works on your page.

Another Server Behavior to Read the Cookie

To complete the cookie exercise, you need to read the cookies you have written. You can write a behavior that assigns the value of a cookie to a variable name chosen by the designer. This variable can be used for dynamically producing other page content.

You can enter Dreamweaver parameters directly into your code; remember that a parameter starts and finishes with double At signs. The code to read the cookie, including Dreamweaver parameters, is

```
<%@@variablename@@= request.cookies("@@CookieName@@")%>
```

Again, click the plus button on the Server Behavior tab and choose New Server Behavior. Call the new behavior **Read Cookie** and add a new code block. Enter the preceding code into the Code Block window, which automatically adds Dreamweaver parameters. The block should be positioned above the <HTML> Tag, and near the beginning of the file. The completed dialog box is shown in Figure B.23.

After you click Next, both parameter values should be entered using text boxes, as you can see from Figure B.24.

The second behavior—to read a cookie and assign its value to a variable—is complete. The new behavior should be tested out on a page.

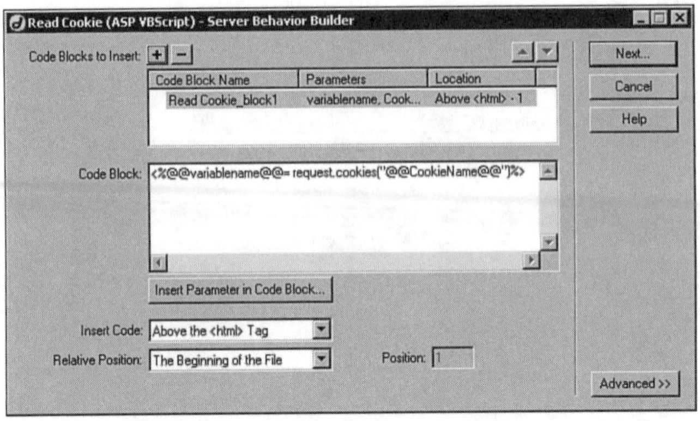

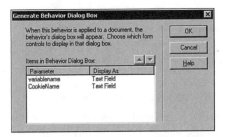

FIGURE B.23   Add the cookie-reading code to the Code Block window to continue writing the new behavior.

FIGURE B.24   The parameter values of the Read Cookie behavior will be entered by the designer using the default text boxes.

Editing and Removing Custom Behaviors

If the behavior does not work properly and needs to be edited, or if you want to remove the behavior completely, on the Add Behavior menu choose Edit Behavior.

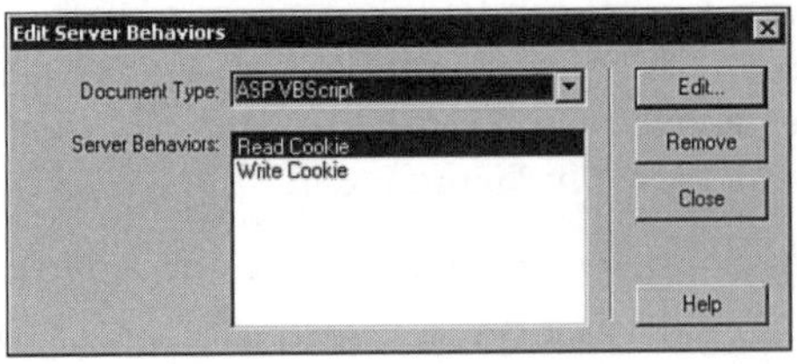

FIGURE B.25   Behaviors can be edited and removed by choosing Edit Behavior from the Add Behavior drop-down menu.

From this dialog box, you can remove the behavior with the Remove button, or Edit it using the Edit button that can be seen in Figure B.25. After you click the Edit button, you will receive a warning that you may corrupt the way the behavior is displayed by editing it.

Summary

In this chapter we moved beyond the preset server behaviors provided by Dreamweaver. Although you can do a lot with Dreamweaver "out of the box," inevitably you will want to perform some kind of customized behavior as you gain more experience designing dynamic sites.

Dreamweaver gives you many tools to help you hand code a new action on your site, and it gives you a lot of help along the way, with code hints and tag insertion tools. You also saw where you can go on the Web to get help on hand coding pages for various server models.

If you think you would want to reuse a custom behavior or you would like other members of your team to use it, you should write your own server behavior. With your own behaviors, you can get less-experienced users to include it on their pages, without their having to know the nitty-gritty of the code you have so carefully crafted.

As an example, you wrote customized server behaviors to read and write a cookie.

B

APPENDIX C

Integration with Flash MX

This appendix explores the possibilities of using Dreamweaver MX and integrating with Macromedia's Flash MX. Unfortunately, we won't have the space to cover things like Flash remoting in great detail; a few pages on the topic just wouldn't do it justice. But what we can look at is the possibilities of such technologies and get a basic understanding as to what the integration between these two applications can offer.

Writing ActionScript with Dreamweaver MX

Dreamweaver MX offers the capability to write ActionScript in its coding environment. This can often be beneficial for experts in ActionScript because it can provide a bigger workspace than the ActionScript panel in Flash. When you create ActionScript code outside of Flash, it's also easy to update. You can modify the Flash movie without ever opening Flash because in Flash you can create an include action.

For this next exercise, you'll have to download the puzzle.fla file from the companion Web site located at http://www.dreamweavermxunleashed.com.

Creating ActionScript Files in Dreamweaver MX

In this exercise you're going to create a puzzle. This exercise assumes you have a solid understanding of ActionScript, for I will not deconstruct the ActionScript code. After downloading the file, follow these steps to see how you can write ActionScript in Dreamweaver and apply it to objects in Flash.

1. Open the puzzle.fla file. Notice it's constructed of several pieces, as shown in Figure C.1.

FIGURE C.1   The file you are about to work with for this project is constructed of several puzzle-piece MovieClip objects.

2. Highlight one of the puzzle pieces and open the Actions panel. The keyboard short-cut is F9.

3. In the Actions panel, be sure to be in expert mode. In the top-right corner of the panel, click the submenu and choose Expert Mode, as shown in Figure C.2.

4. In the body of the panel, type `#include puzzle_script.as`.

5. Press Return (Mac) or Enter (Windows) to move the cursor down to the next line. On this second line, type `#include random.as`.

6. Highlight all the code and copy it by pressing Command+C (Mac) or Ctrl+C (Windows).

Normal Mode	⇧⌘N
✓ Expert Mode	⇧⌘E
Go to Line...	⌘,
Find...	⌘F
Find Again	⌘G
Replace...	⇧⌘H
Check Syntax	⌘T
Show Code Hint	^␣
Auto Format	⇧⌘F
Auto Format Options...	
Import From File...	⇧⌘I
Export As File...	⇧⌘X
Print...	
View Line Numbers	⇧⌘L
View Esc Shortcut Keys	
Preferences...	⌘U
Help	
Maximize Panel	
Close Panel	

FIGURE C.2   You can easily switch to expert mode by accessing the option from the drop-down menu.

7. You must highlight each of the puzzle pieces and apply these same actions. Do this until all the puzzle pieces contain this code.

   Right now this code does not add any functionality to your puzzle; what it does do, however, is refer to an external script file that you're about to create using Dreamweaver MX. To simplify this process, save this file in a new folder, called Puzzle, on your desktop. You'll also save the ActionScript files you're about to create in this folder as well so you don't have to worry about sourcing the correct paths. If everything is in the same directory, it will make explaining this example easier. In your own development, feel free to save files in whatever directories you choose; just make sure you source them properly in your code.

8. If you test the movie by pressing Command+Return (Mac) or Ctrl+Enter (Windows), you'll get a preview of what the file will look like. Again, the puzzle is not operational because you have to write the code for the include files in Dreamweaver.

9. Close out of the testing environment and hide or minimize Flash.

10. Open Dreamweaver MX. Create a new document by choosing File, New. This will open the New Document dialog box as shown in Figure C.3.

11. In the category section choose Other, and from the Other pane, choose ActionScript. Click the Create button to open a new ActionScript document.

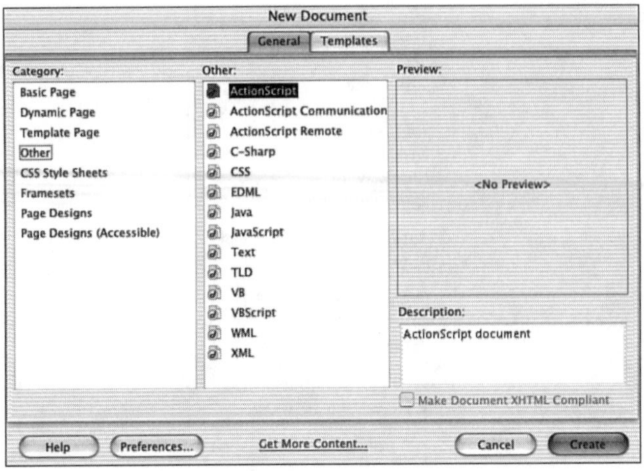

FIGURE C.3 The New Document dialog box offers several options for creating a variety of documents.

12. In the document, type the following code:

```
on (press) {
    xpos = this._x;
    ypos = this._y;
    if (finish != true) {
        _root.depthValue = _root.depthValue+1;
        this.SwapDepths (_root.depthValue);
        startDrag(this);
    }
}
on (release, release outside) {
    stopDrag();
    if (eval(this._droptarget) == eval ("_root."+this._name+"target")) {
        this._x = eval(this._droptarget)._x;
        this._y = eval(this._droptarget)._y;
        finish = true;
    } else {
        setProperty(this, _x, xpos);
        setProperty(this, _y, ypos);
    }
}
```

13. Save this document by choosing File, Save As to open the Save As dialog box. Save this file in the puzzle folder you created on the desktop and name it **puzzle_script.as**.

14. After saving the document, you should have an SWF file of the puzzle from testing it previously. Open the SWF file and notice that you now have the capability to drag the puzzle pieces into their desired locations. If you don't hit the appropriate location, the puzzle piece snaps back to the beginning location. Also notice that after the piece has been placed properly, you can no longer move the puzzle piece.

15. The last thing you should do to the puzzle is have the pieces randomly scatter when the puzzle first loads. All you have to do is write another ActionScript file. From the File menu, choose New to open the New Document dialog box. Choose Other for the category and ActionScript from the Other pane. This will create a new ActionScript document.

16. In the new document, type the following code to add the random scatter function–ality:

```
onClipEvent (load) {
    randomxpos = random(300);
    randomypos = random(300);
    setProperty(this, _x, randomxpos);
    setProperty(this, _y, randomypos);
}
```

This will add the random placement of each of the puzzle pieces on load.

17. Choose File, Save As to open the Save As dialog box to save this script. Name this file **random.as** and save it in the puzzle directory you created on the desktop earlier.

18. Open the SWF file and see that the pieces randomly display on the screen, as shown in Figure C.4.

You can tell by the power of these include files that you can edit and modify Flash SWF movies without ever opening Flash or even needing the FLA file. Again, this option may be more comfortable for experienced ActionScripters and coders who feel more comfortable in a larger, more spacious work environment.

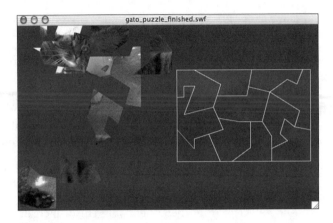

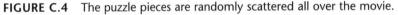

FIGURE C.4   The puzzle pieces are randomly scattered all over the movie.

Integration with Middleware

As you read in the previous chapters of this book, one of the great things about Dreamweaver is the robustness of the application development tools. With the new Macromedia MX product family line, the ease of Web application has been discovered in other applications aside from Dreamweaver, namely Flash MX.

Flash MX can be used to create Web applications with any middleware, whether it be ASP, PHP, or ColdFusion. You can develop these types of applications using such methods as loadVariables and getURL. It's not that these methods aren't adequate solutions, but there are more efficient, elegant options available for the new MX product family.

When Macromedia bought Allaire, they made a commitment to make ColdFusion the backbone of their Web application efforts. This shines through with Dreamweaver MX, Flash MX, and ColdFusion MX.

Flash MX and ColdFusion MX Integration

With the new versions of ColdFusion, Dreamweaver, and Flash comes tighter integration between these applications. There are no more workarounds to get Flash and ColdFusion to communicate with one another, and the new methods offer increased performance and reliability.

With these new products, Macromedia offers the next generation in the Web development process. Designers and developers can work together to create robust Flash applications. You can harness the power of Flash to offer an interesting and engaging front end and all the while offer a powerful and robust database back end.

With the MX versions of Flash and ColdFusion, Macromedia has brought the client and server closer together. All the communication is still performed through HTTP, but with added technology called AMF, or Action Message Format. AMF is part of the Macromedia Flash Remoting service. You're now able to access client ActionScript classes that will communicate with the Flash Gateway, the server-side component of the Flash Remoting Service. As mentioned earlier, in previous versions of Flash, most integration between ColdFusion and Flash was handled with the loadVariables, getURL actions, and the XML Object. These methods are still available for the Flash 6 Player and may be used with any type of middleware, but AMF is preferred when dealing with integers, arrays, recordsets, and structures.

What's truly exciting about these technologies is they push the envelope for Flash to be a truly viable Web authoring tool that goes far beyond vector-based animation and silly intros.

Flash MX Components

Flash MX components offer quick development tools for commonly created components. Furthermore, they offer the capability to create reusable code. You have the capability to access all different types of properties, parameters, and methods of these clips. You can find them in the Components panel by choosing Window, Components in Flash MX. This opens the Components panel, as pictured in Figure C.5.

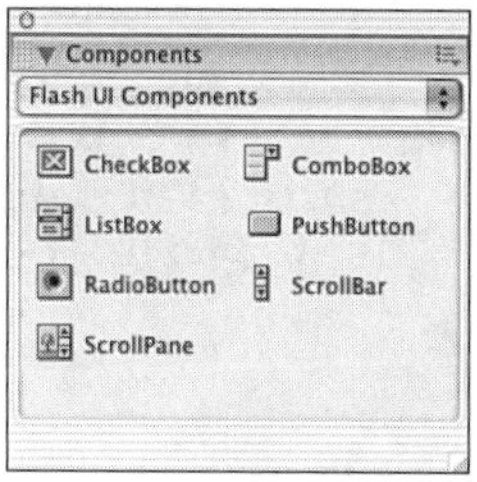

FIGURE C.5   The Components panel in Flash MX offers access to the components that ship with the product.

You can download additional components from the Macromedia Exchange (http://www.macromedia.com/exchange/flash), which is being constantly updated. The second set of components offers additional objects that are commonly created by developers.

You can install these components using the Macromedia Extension Manager, which must already be installed in your system, or you can install the Extension Manager by downloading it from the Macromedia Exchange site.

Not only do components save time for developers and designers alike, they also afford them the opportunity to work and collaborate with one another on various projects.

If you are looking into using components, you can also create your own, offering the ultimate in flexibility. Components offer a great amount of functionality, especially when integrating them with ColdFusion.

Previous Integration Methods

In previous versions of Flash, Macromedia introduced a way to communicate with applications servers over HTTP. These methods primarily included getURL and loadVariables. With Flash 5, Macromedia extended that functionality with the XML Object. Each method offers pro and cons, and all are still supported by the Flash 6 player.

getURL

The getURL method was first introduced in version 2 of Flash. However, the real functionality was realized in the Flash 4 player when the GET and POST options were added. This has always been a viable solution to send data to a server, but it calls for the Flash movie to redirect the browser to another page. This usually consists of a Flash movie sending variables to a non-Flash page, which, in turn, processes the data. This is also a one-way street because you can only send data from Flash with this method, but not retrieve it.

loadVariables

The loadVariables method was a great addition to the Flash 4 player. It provided the capability to use either the POST or GET method when sending data. The advantage of using loadVariables is that the Flash movie makes an HTTP request to the server without having to redirect the Flash movie. This is all handled behind the scenes. The issue with loadVariables is that the data needs to be URL encoded and sent in name/value pairs. This prevents sending and receiving complex data such as arrays, objects, and recordsets. There are ways to accomplish such complex structures to and from Flash, but this requires a good bit of ActionScript knowledge, and these ActionScript workarounds will require more overhead from the Flash player.

XML Object

The XML Object provides a great way to send and receive complex data structures to and from Flash. This was introduced in Flash 5 and works seamlessly with servers that transfer information using XML packets. Sending data using the XML object provides structure to your data as well as an increase in speed and reliability. The XML parsing and performance has improved substantially in the Flash 6 player. In version 5, an XML packet that contained many child nodes ran poorly, and the preferred method was to use XML packets that contained attributes instead of nodes. Now XML packets can contain many child nodes, and the performance gain is substantial. Although the performance has increased, you should still take into consideration how much data you are loading. It is still recommended that you break your data up into pieces if you're dealing with a good amount of information. This can reduce the strain in the Flash player and ultimately provide a better experience for the end user.

If you need to interact with different applications servers, you should be using the XML Object. If you find yourself in that situation, you may want to make the investment in learning more about the XML Object.

However, if you are looking to build robust Flash applications where Flash will serve solely as the front end, you should explore the new Macromedia Flash Remoting service components. In the next section, you'll learn a bit more about what Flash remoting has to offer.

Macromedia Flash Remoting Service

Macromedia Flash Remoting service serves as the layer of communication between Flash and the application server. Developers will now be able to interact with different applications servers such as ColdFusion MX, Java, and .NET. All communication will be handled through the new Action Message Format (AMF), which works well over HTTP. The server-side component of Macromedia Flash Remoting service, also known as the Flash Gateway, allows developers to make calls from Flash to the application server. New Macromedia Flash Remoting service classes are now available in ActionScript that allow Flash to communicate with the server through the Flash Gateway. These classes are known as NetServices and offer increased performance and functionality over the older methods previously discussed.

Summary

The capabilities of Flash and ColdFusion are constantly changing. However, this latest effort by Macromedia has closed the gap between creating Web applications in an HTML environment, much like you create with Dreamweaver, to creating robust Web applications with interesting and compelling interfaces loaded with interactivity and all that Flash has to offer.

Now is the most exciting time to be a Web developer, with endless possibilities with the tools of today, offering complex capabilities to build the Web sites of the future.

APPENDIX **D**

Language Resources

by Zak Ruvalcaba

Links

ASP

www.4guysfromrolla.com
Hands down the best Web site when it comes to ASP resources. Developed and maintained by Scott Mitchell, this Web site features everything from tutorials, sample scripts, articles, and so on.

www.asp101.com
A great resource for learning simple ASP. This site features sample scripts for everything including calendars, shopping carts, guest books, and the like. They're even migrating their site to serve the ASP.NET community.

msdn.microsoft.com/asp
Excellent Web resource for everything having to do with Web development, including ASP. This site features news, articles, headlines, tutorials, and resources on the topic. Because ASP is a Microsoft technology, this is probably your best resource site.

www.15seconds.com
Heavily toting Microsoft technologies, this site is a great reference for technologies, platforms, and languages such as Web Services, .NET, IIS, Data Access, Component Building, ADSI, ISAPI, Site Server, Scripting, and XML.

`www.w3schools.com`
A great online resource for learning anything about Web development. It offers great tutorials on various Web development topics, including ASP.

`www.aspalliance.com`
A good reference for the ASP developer featuring articles, product recommendations, tutorials, and so on.

`www.asptoday.com`
Another good reference for the ASP developer featuring articles, product recommendations, tutorials, and the like.

ASP.NET

`www.gotdotnet.com`
A great resource site providing information and links to various .NET topics, including ASP.NET, ADO.NET, Web Services, .NET Framework, the CLR, and the various languages built for the .NET environment.

`www.aspnextgen.com`
Also known as dotnetjunkies, this Web site features tons of software downloads, resources, links, samples, and articles on .NET topics.

`www.aspalliance.com/das/web.config.aspx`
Ever wonder what *all* of those tags do in the web.config file? Read this article.

`www.asp.net`
Microsoft's official ASP.NET Web site. If you're looking for good articles, tutorials, and free controls, this is your best bet.

`www.123aspx.com`
A great resource site providing information and links to various .NET topics including ASP.NET, ADO.NET, Web Services, .NET Framework, the CLR, and the various languages built for the .NET environment.

`msdn.microsoft.com/net/aspnet`
If you're into marketing hype and tech jargon, this is the site for you. If you want tutorials and code samples, visit `www.asp.net`. This site features everything you sort of wanted to know but didn't quite understand.

`www.411asp.net`
A good portal site to everything having to do with .NET, including ASP.NET.

ColdFusion

www.houseoffusion.com
A simple Web site devoted to ColdFusion. Includes articles and links to other ColdFusion resources.

www.forta.com/cf
Ben Forta, author of some of the most popular ColdFusion books, delivers his own Web site devoted to ColdFusion.

www.cfvault.com
A good reference for ColdFusion that contains news, articles, and links on the subject.

www.defusion.com
Another good reference for ColdFusion that contains news, articles, and links on the subject.

www.macromedia.com/software/coldfusion
The official Web site for ColdFusion MX. Find everything here from sample applications, tech notes, and so on.

Database

www.microsoft.com/sql
Official Web site for Microsoft's SQL Server.

www.microsoft.com/office/access
Official Web site for Microsoft's Access database.

www.oracle.com/ip/deploy/database
Official Web site for Oracle's line of database products.

www.mysql.com
Official Web site for MySQL.

www-4.ibm.com/software/data/db2
Official Web site for IBM's DB2.

Dreamweaver MX

www.massimocorner.com
Massimo Foti's Web site featuring tons of extensions for Dreamweaver, UltraDev, and MX.

www.ultradevextensions.com
Wayne Lambright's Dreamweaver and UltraDev tutorials and portals site for Dreamweaver and UltraDev users.

www.macromedia.com/support/dreamweaver/technotes.html
Complete tech notes for all current Dreamweaver MX issues.

`www.macromedia.com/software/dreamweaver`
Official Web site for Dreamweaver MX.

HTML

`www.htmlgoodies.com`
From the author of HTML Goodies comes the popular htmlgoodies.com. Packed full of, well, HTML goodies.

`www.webmonkey.com`
Also known as Webmonkey, this Web site is a great resource for beginners wanting to learn HTML, JavaScript, and more.

`www.w3.org/TR/html4`
The HTML 4.01 specification. You don't have to worry about this specification changing any time soon.

`www.hwg.org`
The HTML writers guild features great tutorials and resources regarding HTML.

`www.lynda.com`
A good source for training videos on most Web authoring platforms and languages, including HTML.

JavaScript

`www.javascript.com`
Tons of scripts and resources for JavaScript.

`www.echoecho.com`
My favorite Web site for JavaScript tips, tutorials, and browser statistics.

`www.javascriptsource.com`
One of the biggest resources for free scripts.

`www.javascriptkit.com`
Tons of scripts and resources for JavaScript.

`www.javascriptcity.com`
Tons of scripts and resources for JavaScript.

JSP

`www-3.ibm.com/software/webservers`
Main link for IBM's Websphere application server.

`java.sun.com/products/jsp`
Information from the source: SUN. This Web site is your best bet for information regarding JSP.

`jsptags.com/gettingstarted`
A very good introductory level Web site for those looking to get started with JSP.

`www.jspin.com`
Also known as the JSP Resource Index. This is another great Web site with many resources for JSP.

`www.macromedia.com/software/jrun`
The official Web site for Macromedia's JRun.

PHP

`www.php.net`
Everything you need to know about PHP. You can even download it here.

`www.phpbuilder.com`
Articles, news, headlines, and other great resources for PHP developers.

`php.resourceindex.com`
Great PHP resource site including definitions and documentation on PHP.

SQL

`www.w3schools.com/sql`
A great introduction to the Structured Query Language (SQL). Features great tutorials and vocabulary definitions.

`databases.about.com/cs/sql`
An awesome Web site devoted to SQL.

`www.aspalliance.com/habal/sql`
A great Web site with tutorials on SQL based primarily on its use with ASP.

Web Services

`www.w3.org/2002/ws`
The World Wide Web Consortium's Web site for Web Services features the Web Services Activity Statement, usage scenarios, architecture requirements, descriptions requirements, and so on. Be prepared to dig for information within this site.

`www.w3.org/TR/wsdl`
The Web Service Discovery Language working draft page as proposed by the W3C.

`www-106.ibm.com/developerworks/webservices`
IBM's Web Service Zone features great articles, tutorials, and discussions on the subject. A very Java-friendly site.

`www.webservices.org`
Web Services resource center with news, analysis, reviews, forums, FAQs, whitepapers, and software regarding the subject.

www.xmethods.net
This site is a "virtual laboratory" for developers, listing publicly available Web services and showcasing new ways this technology can be applied.

www.uddi.org
UDDI is the building block that will enable businesses to quickly, easily, and dynamically find and transact business with one another using their preferred applications. This Web site is a great start for learning more about UDDI: the Web Service registry.

XHTML

www.w3.org/TR/xhtml1
The current XHTML 1.0 specification straight from the source: the W3C.

www.xguru.com/tutorial/cat_index.asp?cat=2
A great resource for not only XHTML, but for XML, XSL, and XSLT.

www.xhtml.org
A plain and simple site that contains information regarding XHTML.

hotwired.lycos.com/webmonkey/00/50/index2a.html
The article that I always recommend when I'm too short on time to teach it myself.

XML

www.xml.com
This site prides itself in providing a community atmosphere where developers share ideas. It also provides development resources and solutions, and it features timely news, opinions, features, and tutorials.

www.xmldir.com
One of the largest resources for XML. This site also features extensive links to DTD, XSL, XSLT, ASP, and XML tutorials, parsers, editors, programming, basics, scripts, parsers, browsers, applications, java, and more.

www.w3.org/XML
The World Wide Web Consortium's Web site features details about the drafts issued by the XML Query, XML Schema, and XML Linking working groups. The site also features the working draft issued by the XML Core working group.

msdn.microsoft.com/xml
Excellent Web resource for everything having to do with Web development, including XML. This site features news, articles, headlines, tutorials, and resources on the topic.

www-106.ibm.com/developerworks/xml
IBM's developer works Web site provides a great resource for the development community. This site heavily focuses on Java and its coexisting relationship with XML.

General Resource Sites

`www.oreillynet.com`
Great site similar to Microsoft's MSDN. Features articles and How To's for dozens of technologies, languages, and platforms.

`www.w3schools.com`
A well-designed learning site featuring tutorials and learning modules for various scripting and authoring languages.

`msdn.microsoft.com`
The best resource site for Microsoft-related technologies. If you're looking for a site that is less on the technical side, this may not be the site for you.

Author Sites

`www.trainsimple.com`
Matthew Pizzi's corporate training Web site.

`www.modulemedia.com`
Zak Ruvalcaba's Internet consulting Web site.

Database Conversion

The process known as *upsizing* is the conversion of an Access database into a SQL Server database. You can upsize your database by following the steps outlined next:

1. Open the database you wish to upsize within Access and select Upsizing Wizard from the Database Utilities submenu of Tools, as shown in Figure D.1.

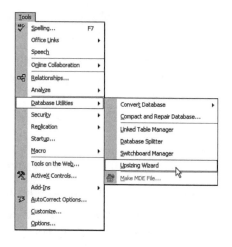

FIGURE D.1   Select the Upsizing Wizard option to begin converting your Access database to SQL Server.

2. The Upsizing Wizard dialog box appears. Select the network location of your SQL Server installation as well as the name for the database, as shown in Figure D.2.

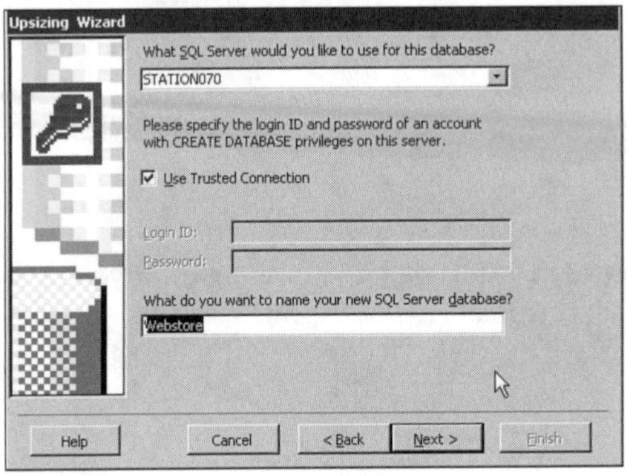

FIGURE D.2   Specify the name of the SQL Server installation and a name for the database.

3. Add all the tables that you want to convert into the new format, as shown in Figure D.3.

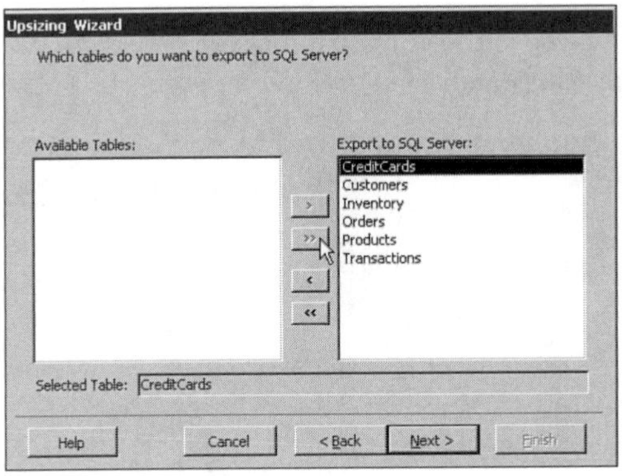

FIGURE D.3   Add the tables to be converted.

4. Specify all necessary table attributes including options for Indexes, Validation, and Table Relationships. It may be best to stick with the defaults as shown in Figure D.4.

5. Selecting Finish will begin the conversion process, as shown in Figure D.5.

6. Open your copy of SQL Server Enterprise Manager and view the newly converted database. The results should look similar to Figure D.6.

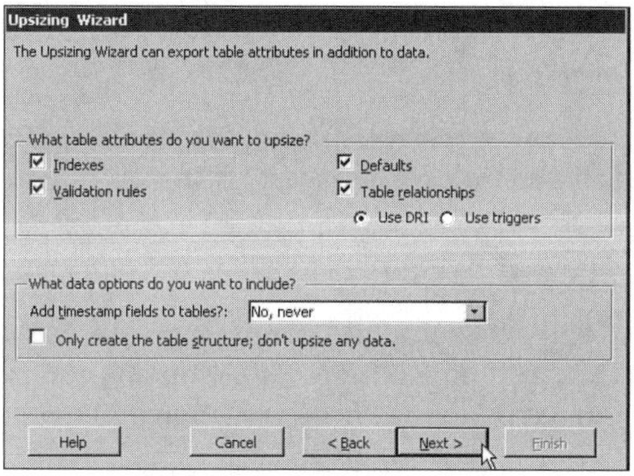

FIGURE D.4   Specify all the conversion options.

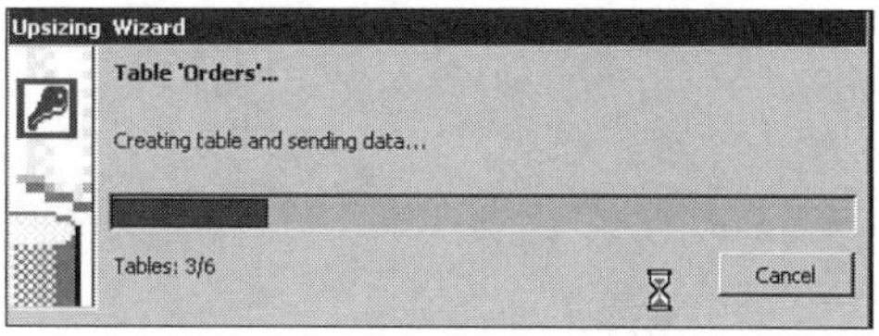

FIGURE D.5   Wait a few minutes while the conversion is in progress.

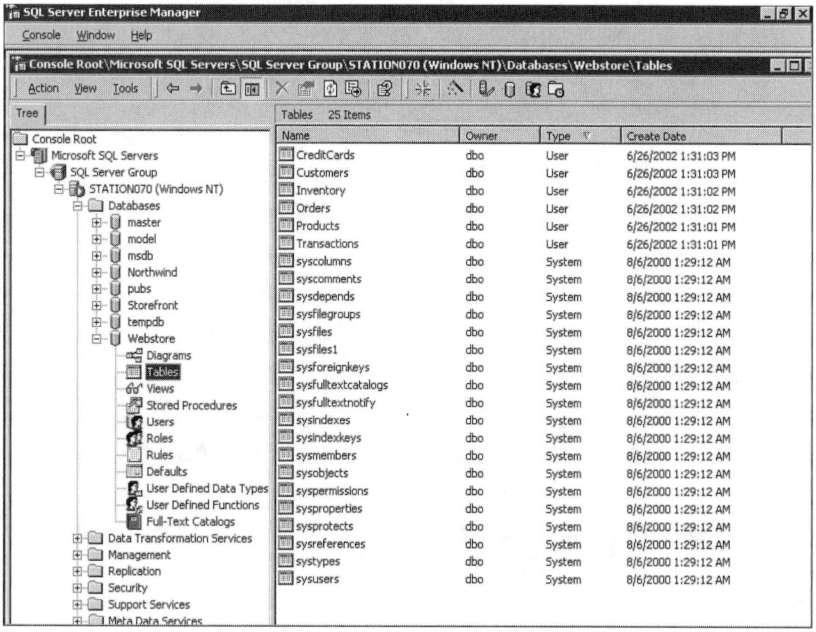

FIGURE D.6   Launch SQL Server Enterprise Manager and view the newly converted database.

Troubleshooting Dreamweaver MX Application Development Errors

www.macromedia.com/support/dreamweaver/technotes.html
Complete tech notes for all current Dreamweaver MX issues.

Web Service Proxy Class Issues

One of the issues I found while beta testing Dreamweaver MX was that the .NET SDK fails to create path variables that are required for compilation and class generation within Dreamweaver MX. Are you receiving the same error shown in Figure D.7?

FIGURE D.7   You can fix the proxy generation errors within the path variables.

To fix this program, follow the steps outlined next:

1. The first step is to locate the three files: vbc.exe, cvc.exe, and wsdl.exe. You can do this by performing a simple search within Windows. By default, the three files will be installed within these directories:

   ```
   C:\WINNT\Microsoft.NET\Framework\v1.0.3705\
   C:\Program Files\Microsoft Visual Studio .NET\FrameworkSDK\Bin
   ```

2. Check to make sure they are the same on your installation. After you have found the two locations, copy them; you will need to paste them in later.

3. The next step is to add these locations to the path variables by right-clicking the My Computer icon and selecting Properties.

4. Select the Advanced tab and click Environment Variables. Navigate to the Path Variables within the System Variables box, as shown in Figure D.8.

5. Choose Edit.

6. Append the locations to the end of the string, separating each path by a semicolon. Make sure not to add a semicolon to the end of the last path. The result is shown in Figure D.9.

7. Select OK. Close all the active windows and try to create a Web Service again. This time it will work.

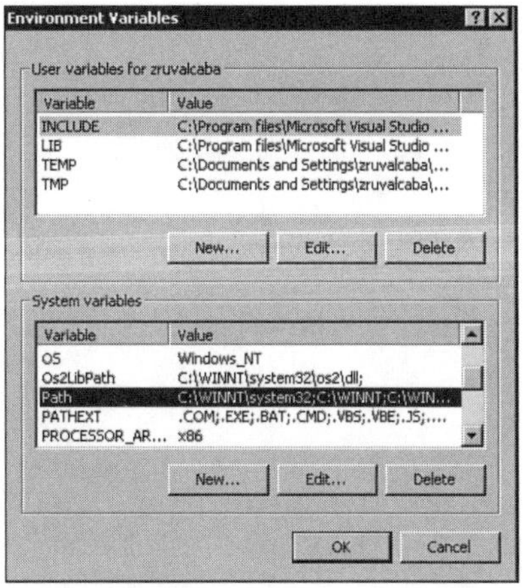

FIGURE D.8   Edit the Path variable.

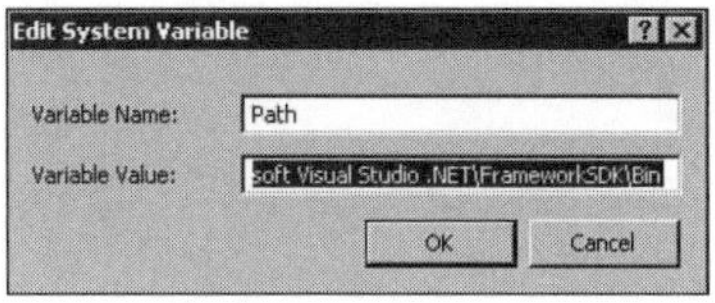

FIGURE D.9   Append the paths to the path variables string.

D

ColdFusion MX Tags and Beyond

By Hugh Livingstone

Dreamweaver MX is the first new version of Dreamweaver since Allaire (the software company that developed ColdFusion) merged with Macromedia. As a result, Dreamweaver incorporates some of the features of Allaire's ColdFusion Studio and has powerful support for ColdFusion. Of all the server-side technologies supported by Dreamweaver, there is no doubt that ColdFusion is most strongly represented.

This chapter assumes that you are familiar with ColdFusion already. The purpose here is not to teach you how to code ColdFusion pages, but how to use Dreamweaver to produce CF pages and code CFML. Nevertheless, if you have never used ColdFusion before, there should be enough here to whet your appetite and get you started exploring this simple, but powerful, server technology.

Introduction to ColdFusion

ColdFusion is an application server. In common with all application servers, it processes the server-side code instructions before returning the page to the client. Although traditional, static Web servers can respond only to requests for pages and return a static copy of the page to the client, with an application server you can

- Interact with a user through the use of forms to provide searching and other facilities on the site.

- Dynamically construct pages based on database results or other applications.

- Save customized information such as user preferences.

As explained in Chapter 21, "Working with CGI & Java Applets," the Web server and application server, such as ColdFusion, work together to process a page request from a user. This is what happens when the user requests a page from a Web site that uses ColdFusion.

1. The user requests a page by typing a URL into the browser or clicking a hyperlink.

2. The Web server receives the request. If the page requested is a static Web page—indicated by the extension HTM or HTML—the Web server simply sends a copy of this page to the client. This static page may still contain elements such as Flash movies or JavaScript that are processed on the client, but these elements are not the responsibility of the Web server.

3. If the page requested has the extension CFM, CFML, or CFC (for ColdFusion) the Web server passes the request on to the ColdFusion application server.

4. The application server runs the ColdFusion code to produce dynamically generated HTML. If the page contains HTML code (which most ColdFusion pages do) this is left untouched by ColdFusion.

5. After the code has been processed, the page is handed back to the Web server.

6. The Web server returns the page to the user.

This process is illustrated in Figure E.1.

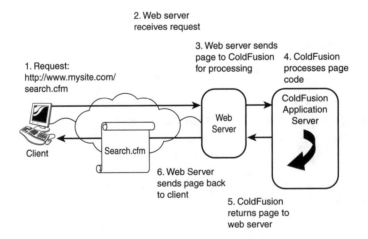

FIGURE E.1   Application servers such as ColdFusion work with the Web server to process dynamic pages.

This process is common to all application servers. With ColdFusion, the Web developer has a scripting environment that is much easier to code than other application servers, such as ASP.NET, ASP, JSP, or PHP—all of which are also supported by Dreamweaver.

ColdFusion uses a language called ColdFusion Markup Language (CFML) to code the server-side processing instructions. CFML is considerably easier to code than Visual Basic or JavaScript–like languages that other application servers use.

ColdFusion Markup Language (CFML) is a tag-based language, like HTML. CFML tags have start tags; usually they also have bodies and end tags and look very much like HTML. They provide a familiar way to code pages for Web designers.

CFML is made up of about 80 tags that provide a rich language for programming dynamic data-driven pages. CFML also encapsulates a lot of low-level programming detail within the CFML tags, so you do not have to instantiate low-level application objects or navigate through complex object interfaces, which most other application servers require you to do. With ColdFusion it is easy to

- Send emails from your Web application.
- Perform full-text searches through files in your Web site.
- Upload files to the server.
- Dynamically create charts in Web pages.

These tasks, quite complex in most application servers, can be done with just a few or even one CFML tag.

ColdFusion also contains the capability for you to write your own functions and create your own customized tags. ColdFusion has a scripting language similar to JavaScript, called CFScript, that can do this. If you really wanted to, you could use C++ or Java to customize your tags as well.

How to Get ColdFusion

A copy of ColdFusion Developer Edition comes on the Dreamweaver CD. This version of ColdFusion can be installed on your development machine to test out your ColdFusion pages. It allows access by only one user, which is all you need for developing and testing ColdFusion pages. If you want to host a Web site using ColdFusion, you need to purchase the full version of ColdFusion MX Server.

Alternatively, you could choose a Web host that already provides ColdFusion on its servers, but expect to pay a little more for this facility than you would for hosting ordinary HTML pages.

If you are developing a personal or noncommercial Web site, some Web hosts provide free ColdFusion hosting. They will probably put some restrictions on the type of files you can put on your site (no streaming videos, for example), and you won't get a personalized URL, but they are perfect for developing your ColdFusion skills and showing them off to the world. Free ColdFusion hosting is provided by CFM-Resources at

```
http://cfm-resources.com
```

Introduction to ColdFusion Markup Language

Most ColdFusion development is done by writing CFML for server-side processing, in conjunction with HTML for page layout and static elements. CFML is a full programming language, with tags to perform common programming tasks, such as the following:

- Create and manipulate variables.

- Write self-contained, reusable functions.

- Evaluate expressions to manipulate variable values.

- Use built-in functions for common data manipulation.

- Provide program flow control such as If Then branches.

- Repeat blocks of code using loops.

Tags

ColdFusion tags are not case sensitive and ignore whitespace, like HTML, but it is good practice (as it is with HTML) to stick to one case—it makes the code easier to understand and won't confuse you when you have to write case-sensitive languages such as JavaScript.

Some tags are single tags, like the HTML <img> tag. For example:

```
<cfset user = form.username>
```

This <cfset> tag sets a variable called user to the value of a form control called username.

Many other tags have opening and closing tags, with a tag body in between, as most HTML tags have. For example:

```
<cfoutput> Hello #user#!</cfoutput>
```

This <cfoutput> tag writes a message to the page containing the value of the variable called user.

Like HTML, CFML tags can also have attributes that give additional information about the use of the tag. For example

```
<cfoutput query="stafflist"> #firstname#</cfoutput>
```

This `<cfoutput>` tag also outputs a variable value, but this variable, `fullname`, comes from a database query named `stafflist`.

Examples of Simple CFML Tags in Use

Both Dreamweaver and ColdFusion provide lots of documentation about the use of ColdFusion. Later on in the appendix, you will see how to access information about all the ColdFusion tags available, but this section describes the use of relatively simple ColdFusion tags to demonstrate how to use ColdFusion in practice. Table E.1 lists a few of the common CFML tags.

TABLE E.1   Simple CFML Tags

CFML Tag	Description
<cfset>	Used to define a variable and give it a value.
<cfquery>...</cfquery>	Used to make a SQL query to a database and return a recordset.
<cfoutput>...</cfoutput>	Displays a query, variable value, or other operation in the Web page.
#variablename#	Surrounding a variable name or recordset fieldname with hash signs tells ColdFusion to output the value of the variable or field name.
<cfif>...</cfif>	Creates a conditional statement, so that one thing will be done if a condition is met, and something else will be done if the condition is not met.
<cfelse> and <cfelseif>	Used in conjunction with <cfif> so that a number of different conditions can be tested.
<!--- this is a comment --->	A CFML comment. It looks like an HTML comment, but it has three dashes, not two. CFML comments are not shown in the Web page, so they cannot be seen by the user if they View Source. Only the CFML designer can see them.

The following code listing, Listing E.1, shows these tags being used together. A database is queried, using a connection called conStaff, to retrieve selected fields from a table called tblStaff. The results of the query are listed on the page in a table, with the Managing Director shown in red, and the Finance Director shown in blue.

LISTING E.1   Example of Using Simple CFML Tags to Produce a Conditional Output from a Database

```
<cfquery name="rsall" datasource="conStaff">
SELECT firstname, lastname, title, phone FROM tblStaff
<!--- Selects all staff members from database --->
</cfquery>
<html>
<head>
<title>CFML Example</title>
</head>
```

LISTING E.1   Continued

```
<body>
<table width="50%" border="1">
  <tr bgcolor="#FFFFCC">
      <th>First Name</th>
      <th>Last Name</th>
      <th>Title</th>
      <th>Phone</th>
  </tr>
  <cfoutput query="rsall">
      <tr>
          <cfif #rsall.title# is "MD" >
<!--- apply special formatting to MD and FD --->
              <td><font color="red">#rsall.FirstName#</font></td>
              <td><font color="red">#rsall.LastName#</font></td>
          <cfelseif #rsall.title# is "FD" >
              <td><font color="blue">#rsall.FirstName#</font></td>
              <td><font color="blue">#rsall.LastName#</font></td>
          <cfelse>
              <td>#rsall.FirstName#</td>
              <td>#rsall.LastName#</td>
          </cfif>
          <td>#rsall.Title#</td>
          <td>#rsall.Phone#</td>
      </tr>
  </cfoutput>
</table>
</body>
</html>
```

As you can see from the listing, the CFML code is relatively simple and complements HTML very well.

Using Dreamweaver to Write CFML

ColdFusion is written in plain text, so you can use any text editor you like to write CFML—even Notepad or Simpletext. However most developers can write code much faster and easier with a dedicated development environment. With the release of Dreamweaver MX, Macromedia no longer produces ColdFusion Studio, which was the tool used by designers to help code their ColdFusion pages. Instead, many of the features of ColdFusion Studio have been incorporated into Dreamweaver MX. This makes Dreamweaver the primary development environment for ColdFusion pages, with the ease of use provided by its visual tools, such as server behaviors, combined with some very powerful tools for hand-coding.

If you are used to using HomeSite, ColdFusion Studio, or another code-based editor, you may prefer the layout of the HomeSite/Coder-style workspace, with the panels docked on the left side, as shown in Figure E.2. This view of your pages echoes the layout of ColdFusion studio in previous ColdFusion versions. To get this workspace, choose Edit, Preferences, and the General category. Then click the button marked Change Workspace. Select the HomeSite/Coder-style workspace option.

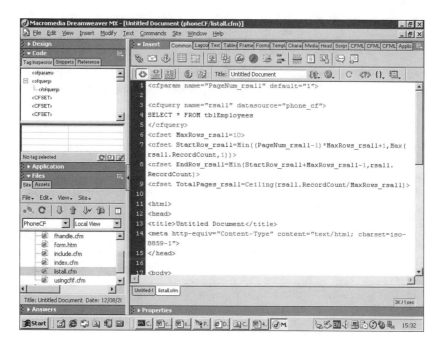

FIGURE E.2   The HomeSite/Coder-style workspace may be more comfortable to previous users of HomeSite or ColdFusion Studio.

If you still cannot bear to stop using ColdFusion Studio, take a look at HomeSite+. HomeSite+ is a code-only editor, combining HomeSite and ColdFusion studio with support for the latest ColdFusion MX features. A copy of HomeSite+ is included on the Dreamweaver MX CD. HomeSite+ is discussed in a little more detail in Appendix B, "Server Behavior Builder."

Most of us, however, will want to develop ColdFusion pages in Dreamweaver, and there are some great tools to help you do so.

Design View

One of the biggest frustrations for teams of Web developers is the interaction between Web designers and application developers. The Web designers may be given pages that don't fit in with the overall site appearance, but because so many elements depend on the output from server-side code, they are unable to envision what the page will finally look like.

The application developers will then complain that the designers have altered their code—making the page inoperable! With Dreamweaver, the designers and the developers can share a common environment, each seeing what the other is trying to achieve.

The design view, which most Web designers will do a lot of their work in, also shows the CFML on the page visually, so if Web designers are altering the visual layout of the page, they can see the CFML tags and avoid altering them, even if they don't understand them.

Using the design view also enables the application developers to code up the page appearance and layout very quickly. You can quickly produce prototypes of the pages for your boss, leaving the final page layout to the designers.

Server Behaviors

Using server behaviors lets Web designers build simple Web applications using only visual tools. Database query and result pages, navigating through pages of returned data, database updates and inserts, and user authentication can all be built without writing a single line of CFML code. The application developers can concentrate on the difficult functionality of the site and advanced features.

Using the server behaviors in Dreamweaver is a also great way to learn how to write CFML. The ColdFusion code written out by Dreamweaver is quite straightforward and easy to follow. Using the code produced by Dreamweaver, you can add, change, and take away bits of code, and then study the effect on the page.

Code View

When you need to develop pages that move beyond the server behaviors, you will mostly be using the code view. Code view shows you just the HTML, JavaScript and server-side code in the page. You see every detail of the code, but it's difficult to see how the final page will look. You can set up a lot of your own preferences of how you like to work in code view. Clicking the View Options button on the document toolbar pops up a small menu from which the options can be toggled on or off by selecting them, as seen in Figure E.3. You can also find these options by choosing the View menu, Code View options. These options are shown in Table E.2.

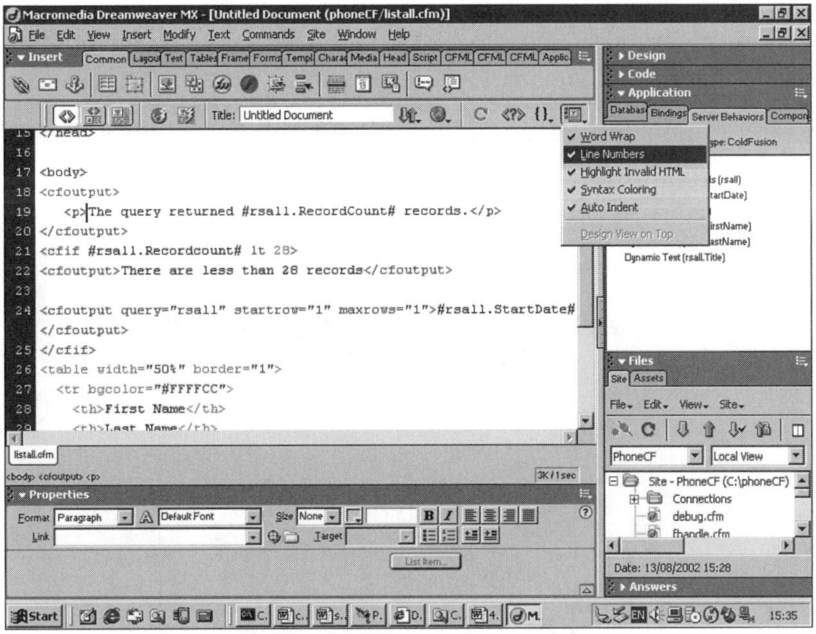

FIGURE E.3 You can change the options available to you in code view to help you hand code your CFML pages.

TABLE E.2 Code View Options

Option	Description
Word Wrap	Automatically wraps code onto the next line, but does not insert a new line or carriage return character.
Line Numbers	Displays line numbers along the left side of the code screen. A line with no number is wrapped from the previous line.
Highlight Invalid HTML	Highlights (in yellow) any HTML code Dreamweaver does not recognize.
Syntax Coloring	This colors your code so it is easier to differentiate between variables, strings, CFML tags, tag attributes, and so on. Very useful for spotting errors before running the page.
Auto Indent	If enabled, the next line is indented the same as the previous line. Otherwise, every new line starts at column 1.

Tag Chooser

The Tag Chooser is an invaluable guide to writing your own CFML. It helps you choose the correct CFML tag (there are more than 100 to choose from) and use the correct tag attributes.

Tag Chooser has most HTML and CFML tags built into it, tags for WML (Wireless Markup Language for WAP devices) plus other server technology tags such as ASP.NET and JSP. You can even add your own tags into the Tag Chooser library.

The Tag Chooser is used when writing your CFML pages. When you want to put in a tag that you may not know by heart or that you are not sure what the allowable attributes are, right-click (Control+click on the Mac) at the point you want the tag to be inserted. On the pop-up menu, choose Insert Tag, and as you can see in Figure E.4, the Tag Chooser appears.

FIGURE E.4   The Tag Chooser helps you code up your CFML tags correctly.

In Figure E.4 you can see that the left pane contains a list of the supported tag libraries—each library is associated with a particular technology. Click the small plus sign next to the CFML Tags folder icon. The folder expands to show you subgroups of CFML tags, such as Database Manipulation, Security, and so on.

Choose a subgroup, and in the right pane, all the tags associated with that group are listed, as you can see in Figure E.5. Some tags may be in more than one subgroup. Choose a tag, and if you want to find out what it does and how to use it, read the tag info pane underneath. If you cannot see a tag info pane, click the button marked Tag Info. This pane gives you information about the tag. Clicking the <?> button next to it makes the information appear in the Reference window of the Code Panel; it's the same information, but appears in a different place. If it seems that the tag is what you want, click the Insert button.

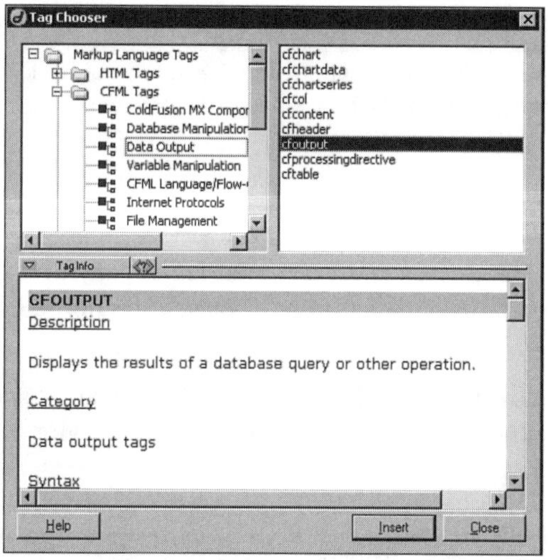

FIGURE E.5   The Tag Chooser groups tags by functionality and shows you information about the tag.

If the tag does not need any attributes (such as `<cfbreak>` to break out of a loop), it will be inserted, but the Tag Chooser will not close.

If the tag either requires or has optional attributes (such as `<cfquery>` to query a database), a dialog box will pop up, enabling you to enter the attribute values, as you can see in Figure E.6, which shows the Edit Attributes dialog box for a `<cfoutput>` tag.

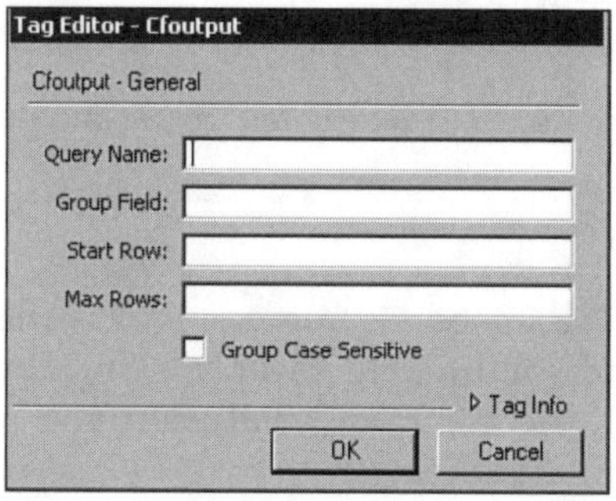

FIGURE E. 6   The Tag Chooser also enables you to easily enter tag attributes, if required.

After clicking OK, the tag is inserted, but the Tag Chooser does not disappear. This means that tags are sometimes put into the page behind the Tag Chooser window, without your realizing it. By the time you click the Close button to close the Tag Chooser, you find you have inserted 15 `<cfif>` tags!

> **WARNING**
>
> You can also insert tags by double-clicking the tag name. You may well do this by accident and not notice the tags being inserted behind the Tag Chooser window.

Editing Tags

Using the Tag Chooser, you can also edit tags that are already in your code. Right-click (Control+click on the Mac) inside a tag on your page and choose Edit Tag from the pop-up menu.

The Edit Attributes window from the Tag Chooser will appear, as shown in Figure E.7, enabling you to modify the attributes and therefore the behavior of the tag. Clicking OK updates the tag on the page.

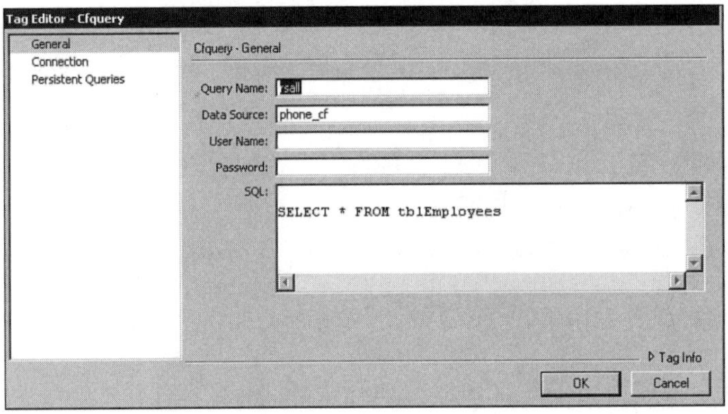

FIGURE E.7   Here we are editing a `<cfquery>` tag, modifying its attributes.

Insert Panels

Yet another way to use the Tag Chooser is from the Insert panel group. This panel of tool-bars, usually located at the top of the screen, will have slightly different panels depending on the server technology you are using. For ColdFusion, you get three extra panels; CFML Basic, CFML Flow, and CFML Advanced.

The CFML Basic panel, shown in Figure E.8, gives you buttons to insert common CFML tags for basic Web application design. As you move the mouse over each button, you see the tag that the button will insert. The CFML Flow panel lets you control program flow with tags such as `<cfif>` and `<cfelse>` and allows you to insert tags for error handling routines. The CFML Advanced panel gives you buttons to use ColdFusion utilities such as sending email and drawing charts.

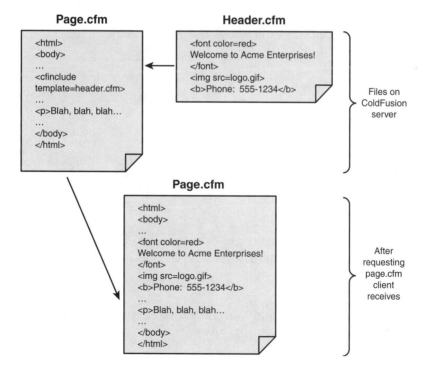

FIGURE E.8   The CFML Basic panel on the Insert bar. This gives buttons for inserting common CFML tags.

Clicking any of these buttons displays the Tag Chooser, open at the selected tag.

Include Pages with ColdFusion

When you use the `<cfinclude>` tag, the contents of a ColdFusion page can be included inside another ColdFusion page. This means that you need to write a certain task only once and include it in as many pages as you want. A common but basic use of include pages is to provide standard headers and footers for pages. Then, if the company details change or you want to update the design, the change needs to be made in only one file.

The process of inclusion is shown in Figure E.9. The `<cfinclude>` tag has a template attribute that specifies the file to include. The contents of this file are then inserted into the page at the point of the `<cfinclude>` tag. This content is treated the same as if it were in the calling page. The included content can be anything you like—HTML, CFML, or JavaScript, for instance. The included page will have access to all the variables in the calling page, so code can be run within it, referring to page specific values and parameters.

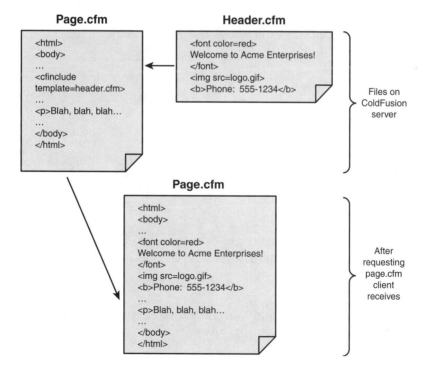

FIGURE E.9   How ColdFusion includes pages with the `<cfinclude>` tag.

To include a page, insert the <cfinclude> tag from the Tag Chooser, or click the button on the CFML Basic Insert panel. The Edit Tag dialog box will prompt you to enter the template attribute. Dreamweaver enables you to browse your site to choose this.

Hand Coding ColdFusion

If you need to use ColdFusion at an advanced level, you may need to move beyond CFML tags. Dreamweaver or any other application environment for that matter, will not write out the code for you. For advanced ColdFusion use, you may need to write code in CFScript.

CFScript provides the same and, in some cases, extended functionality that CFML tags do. CFScript has a syntax similar to JavaScript, and some programmers prefer to use CFScript rather than CFML tags because they are more used to coding in this fashion. CFScript gives the programmer some richer program-flow constructs, and usually CFScript code runs slightly faster than CFML; this may be a consideration on very busy Web sites. You can write some parts of the code using CFML tags and other parts in CFScript. CFML tags can use functions written in CFScript.

Dreamweaver will help you insert the <cfscript> tag and will color code your script to help you spot errors, but it will not prompt you to enter required parameters or arguments. For help writing CFScript, you will need to rely on the documentation, illustrated in Figure E.10, that comes with Dreamweaver. Choose Help, Using ColdFusion.

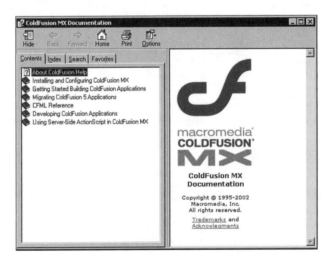

FIGURE E.10 Dreamweaver includes full documentation for ColdFusion.

Another source of documentation and help is the Dreamweaver CD itself. Look in the ColdFusion folder, ColdFusion Documents subfolder.

Code Snippets

Code snippets were a popular part of ColdFusion Studio and have been carried over into Dreamweaver MX. Snippets are a way to save small blocks of code so that they are always available to you, and other developers for use.

Snippets differ from server behaviors in that they do not present any interface to the designer for values and the like to be filled in. Server behaviors are best suited to common application tasks that may be undertaken by Web designers who are unfamiliar with ColdFusion code and who are unable, and do not want to, interact with CFML tags and script. You can build your own server behaviors, and Appendix B, "Server Behavior Builder" shows you how to, with an example.

Snippets are more likely to be used by application developers who do most of their work through hand coding. Snippets expose the developer to the code, and the developer will often perform minor modifications to the snippet to set correct variable names and values, for instance.

You could also think of snippets as like library items for code. Unlike library items, they do not automatically update or tie to a particular site.

To use snippets, expand the Code panel and select the Snippets tab. In the bottom pane is a series of folders into which snippets are organized. Each folder covers a particular technology or area of functionality. Dreamweaver has some code snippets already built in. These are snippets of HTML and JavaScript to do common client-side tasks. You can add your own snippets for ColdFusion.

If you expand a folder and select a code snippet, as we have done in Figure E.11, you will see the selected snippet in the top pane. HTML snippets are usually shown in a design view (showing what the HTML looks like in the browser), whereas JavaScript and other code snippets are shown in code view so that you can see the actual code.

Snippets can either be standalone blocks of code, or they may consist of code that wraps itself around an object. A section of code that redirects a page will probably be a standalone block of code, whereas code that modifies the behavior of a hyperlink will probably wrap itself around a hyperlink object.

Using Code Snippets

Code snippets are best used in code view. For JavaScript snippets, you will first need to insert the <script> tags. For a standalone block, place the insertion cursor on the page where you want it to go. For a wraparound snippet, select the object you want to wrap the code around. Choose the snippet you want and right-click it (Control+click on the Mac), as shown in Figure E.12. Then choose Insert from the pop-up menu.

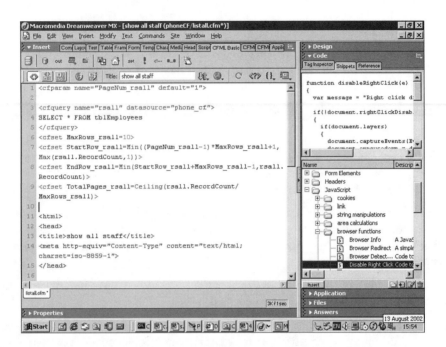

FIGURE E.11 Code Snippets let you reuse code. Some built-in snippets are already available, such as this JavaScript code to disable the right-click menu in the browser.

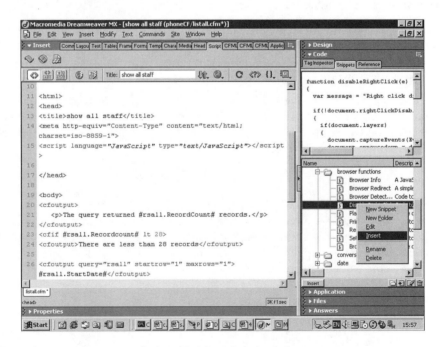

FIGURE E.12 Inserting a supplied JavaScript code snippet in your page.

Creating Your Own Code Snippets

To create your own snippets you should first create a new folder for your own type of snippets. Right-click (Control+click on the Mac) in the Snippets window and choose new folder. Give the snippet folder a descriptive name, remembering that other developers may well be using these snippets, too. If the folder is created in the "wrong" place, you can drag it to the level you want.

Right-click (Control+click on the Mac) on the folder and choose New Snippet from the pop-up menu. Alternatively, you may have already written the snippet code in the page—if so, highlight the code you want to use as the snippet and right-click (Control+click on the Mac) to choose Create New Snippet from the pop-up menu.

You will then be presented with the Snippet dialog box; fill in the snippet name and description. If you have highlighted existing code, the code box will already be filled in.

If you want the code to flow around a selected object, such as an image or table cell, select the Wrap Selection option, specifying which part of the code goes before the object and which after the object. If the code is a standalone block, choose the Insert Block option.

The Snippet dialog box is shown in Figure E.13. In this example, a block of CFML is used to display the age in a text input box if the age exists, but if the age field is empty, the words Age Unknown are displayed.

You can also choose whether you see the snippet preview as code (most likely) or in design view.

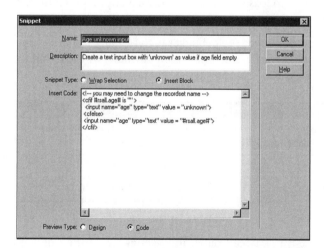

FIGURE E.13   Inserting a snippet, including a description for yourself and other designers.

Managing Snippets

To edit a snippet that exists, right-click (Control+click on the Mac) the snippet and choose Edit from the drop-down menu. The Snippet dialog box appears, and you can edit the code or change the description.

To move snippets into other folders, simply drag them to the folder you want.

Snippets are kept in files with the extension CSN. The folder structure of your Snippets panel is reflected in the folder that each file is kept in within the snippets subfolder of the Dreamweaver Configuration folder. This will usually be C:\Program Files\Macromedia\Dreamweaver MX\Configuration\Snippets in Windows, and Hard drive : Applications : Macromedia Dreamweaver MX : Configuration : Snippets, on the Mac.

You can exchange these snippet files with other developers in your organization, or even over the Web.

Debugging ColdFusion

One of the most powerful combinations of Dreamweaver and ColdFusion is the integrated debugger that Dreamweaver provides for ColdFusion pages. This feature is available only for ColdFusion and not for other server technologies.

When you use Dreamweaver, debugging information is displayed inside the Dreamweaver environment, allowing you quick access to the code that's causing problems. If you cannot see which part of your code is to blame, Dreamweaver provides a full set of page information to help you trace the problem.

The best way to find out about the debugger is to actually use it. We are going to construct a simple ColdFusion page with some deliberate mistakes in them and use the debugger to find, and fix, the errors.

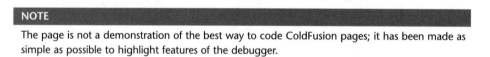

NOTE

The page is not a demonstration of the best way to code ColdFusion pages; it has been made as simple as possible to highlight features of the debugger.

Integrated debugging works only on Windows machines. On Macs you need to open the page in a separate browser window (Preview in Browser) and view the debugging information provided on that page at the bottom of the page.

The first step to take is to enable ColdFusion debugging, in the ColdFusion Administrator. Choose the Start button, Programs, Macromedia ColdFusion MX, Administrator. Internet Explorer starts, taking you to the login page, as shown in Figure E.14. You will have to enter the administrator's password that you set up while installing ColdFusion.

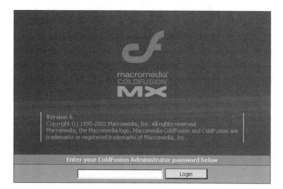

FIGURE E.14 Log in to the ColdFusion Administrator using the password you set during installation.

After entering the password, you will go to the ColdFusion Administrator's Home Page. This page is framed; click the Debugging Settings link in the left menu frame. You will be shown the debugging settings page, as you can see in Figure E.15. Select the Enable Debugging check box. All the other settings should be left as they are. When debugging is turned on, your pages will execute more slowly and show additional information in them. After your debugging session, you will probably want to turn debugging off by unchecking the Enable Debugging check box.

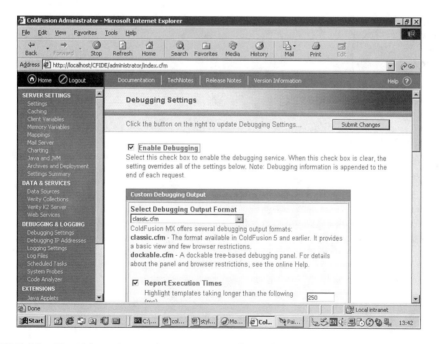

FIGURE E.15 The debugging options are set on the Debugging Settings page, selected from the menu frame on the left.

Next, create a page to debug. Listing E.2 is an example of a simple page that could be used for the debugging exercise. It uses the CompanyInfo database that is supplied with ColdFusion as a tutorial. The precise page details are not important. Listing E.2 contains an error in the SQL query—the table name is spelled incorrectly—the table should be called employee, but is mistakenly called employees, on line 2 of the listing.

LISTING E.2 Page with a SQL Error to Debug

```
<cfquery name="rsStaff" datasource="CompanyInfo">
SELECT * FROM Employees
</cfquery>
<html>
<head>
<title>Debugging ColdFusion</title>
<meta http-equiv="Content-Type" content="text/html; charset=iso-8859-1">
</head>

<body>
<cfoutput>
<p>There are #rsStaff.RecordCount# staff members listed </p>
</cfoutput>
<table width="100%" border="1">
  <tr>
    <th>ID Number</th>
    <th>First Name</th>
    <th>Last Name</th>
    <th>Start Date</th>
  </tr>
  <cfoutput query="rsStaff">
    <tr>
      <td>#rsStaff.Emp_ID#</td>
      <td>#rsStaff.FirstName#</td>
      <td>#rsStaff.LastName#</td>
        <cfif year(#rsstaff.StartDate# lt 1995>
                <td bgcolor="yellow">#rsStaff.StartDate#</td>
        <cfelse>
                <td>#rsStaff.StartDate#</td>
    </cfif>
        </tr>
  </cfoutput>
</table>

</body>
</html>
```

Click the Server Debug button on the document toolbar (it looks like a globe and lightning bolt). Dreamweaver will open up the page in an internal Internet Explorer browser window, showing the results of the page. Dreamweaver also opens a Results panel below the page, showing server debug information.

If your page has an error in it, as the page in Listing E.2 has, a debugging message will be shown on the page, giving information to help you locate the error.

In the Results panel, Dreamweaver shows lots of useful information for tracking down errors. If the page was called from another page—for example, a page that handles form results—all the pages the server processed to render the page are listed in the template stack folder. If the page has been run directly from Dreamweaver, as our example has, you will not see this folder.

Other information shown may include the SQL queries executed on the page, names of the server variables, and their values, if any. The panel also shows a summary of execution times.

The results of debugging the file in Listing E.2 are shown in Figure E.16. The page at the top of the screen includes a message to say that the database cannot find a table called "Employees." If you scroll down the Results pane, you will see a folder marked Exceptions. This gives a link to the file that created the error, followed by a line number.

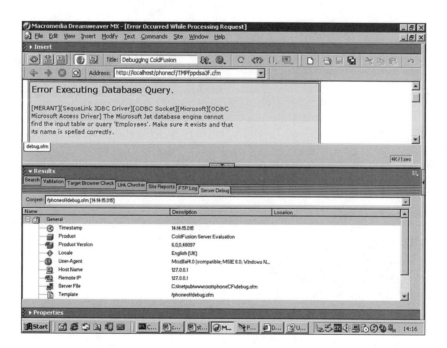

FIGURE E.16 Debugging information is shown on the page displayed in the top pane and in the Results panel below.

Clicking the link opens the file in code view and moves to that line number. Do not expect that this line will automatically contain the error. Sometimes the error occurs before the indicated line, but is only spotted a few lines further down. If you move up a few lines, you can fix the SQL query to spell the name of the table correctly as "Employee." If you click the Server Debug button again to rerun the file, it should run correctly. Take the opportunity to browse through the Results pane, examining the information shown.

The next debugging exercise is to spot a problem in the CFML code. Listing E.3 is almost the same as Listing E.2. The SQL query is now correct, but there is a missing bracket in the <cfif> tag on line 26.

LISTING E.3   Debugging a CFML Tag

```
<cfquery name="rsStaff" datasource="CompanyInfo">
SELECT * FROM Employees
</cfquery>
<html>
<head>
<title>Debugging ColdFusion</title>
<meta http-equiv="Content-Type" content="text/html; charset=iso-8859-1">
</head>

<body>
<cfoutput>
<p>There are #rsStaff.RecordCount# staff members listed </p>
</cfoutput>
<table width="100%" border="1">
  <tr>
    <th>ID Number</th>
    <th>First Name</th>
    <th>Last Name</th>
    <th>Start Date</th>
  </tr>
  <cfoutput query="rsStaff">
    <tr>
      <td>#rsStaff.Emp_ID#</td>
      <td>#rsStaff.FirstName#</td>
      <td>#rsStaff.LastName#</td>
        <cfif year(#rsstaff.StartDate# lt 1995
                <td bgcolor="yellow">#rsStaff.StartDate#</td>
        <cfelse>
                <td>#rsStaff.StartDate#</td>
      </cfif>
```

LISTING E.3   Continued

```
        </tr>
    </cfoutput>
</table>

</body>
</html>
```

Again, click the Server Debug button and view the page in the top window and the Results panel below. As you can see from Figure E.17, the Results panel indicates an exception at line 26. Clicking the line opens the page at line 26 in code view. You can carefully study this line and see where the error lies. Correct the error and debug again to check that all is well.

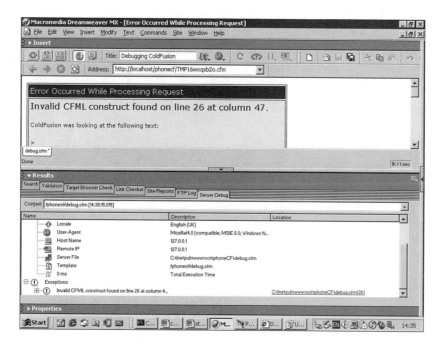

FIGURE E.17   The Results panel tells us where it thinks the error occurred on the page.

If you are running on a Mac, you do not get this debugging information within Dreamweaver. The debugging information is supplied by the ColdFusion Server (on the page which Windows users see in the top window of the debugging view) in a separate browser window for Macintosh users. This information, although not as well presented or as extensive as that provided in the debugging view, is quite adequate for you to spot errors on the page.

Summary

ColdFusion is a powerful, yet relatively easy to use, server-side technology. It is well supported by Dreamweaver MX, which has now been designated as the preferred development environment for ColdFusion by Macromedia.

ColdFusion uses tags that look like HTML to code up server-side functionality. These tags are known as ColdFusion Markup Language (CFML) and are supported by many other ColdFusion utilities, including a language-within-a-language called CFScript.

All the server behaviors in Dreamweaver support ColdFusion, making it easy to learn how to code your own ColdFusion pages. If you want to hand code your ColdFusion pages, Dreamweaver MX provides plenty of support. The Tag Chooser enables you to choose the correct tags, read about the right use of the tag, and insert the correct attributes.

Code snippets also provide a useful way to re-use your code or let other team members use it.

Finally, after you have constructed the page, Dreamweaver's integrated ColdFusion debugger lets you find, and quickly fix, any errors in the code.

Index

Symbols

A

How can we make this index more useful? Email us at indexes@samspublishing.com

array_pop function, 554

array_push function, 554

array_reverse function, 554

ASCII characters, 483

ASP (Active Server Pages), 501, 870

  commands, 380

  DSN connections, 411-412

  DSN-less connections, 416-418

  e-mails, sending, 519-521

  files, creating, 403-405

  integration, 508-509

  My Account page, 705

    dynamic form elements, 706-708

    My Account form, 705-706

    updating users, 710

  New User Registration page, 692-693

    form validation, 700-701

    multiple insertions, 703-705

    New User Registration form, 693-696

    records, adding, 697-699

    users, adding, 701-702

  objects, 501

    ADO, 504

    application, 503

    ASP integration, 509

    ASPError object, 505

    CDO, 504

    dictionary object, 505

    file system object, 504

    request, 502

    response, 502-503

    server, 503-504

    session, 503

  resources, 899-900

  Web application middleware, 380

  Web site, 899

Web Store application, 505, 643

  advanced recordsets, 649, 652

  document type, defining, 507

  dynamic images, 657-658

  dynamic text, 652-657

  new site, defining, 505-506

  pagination features, 659-660

  recordsets, 646-649

  repeat regions, 661-663

  specific regions, 660-661

  testing server, 508

  View Catalog page, 644-646

ASP 101 Web site, 899

ASP Alliance Web site, 900

ASP Today Web site, 900

ASP.NET, 509, 870

  .NET, 510-511

  .NET Framework, 511

  Base Classes, 512-513

  controls, 514

  e-mails, sending, 521-523

  integration, 518-519

  My Account page, 723

    form elements, 724-726

    My Account form, 724

    user updates, 726-727

  namespaces, 512-513

  New User Registration page, 714-716

    form validation, 719-721

    New User Registration form, 716-719

    users, adding, 721-723

  objects, 518

  pages, 513-514

  resources, 900

  security, 825. *See also* authentication, forms

  Web application middleware, 381

  Web site, 900

How can we make this index more useful? Email us at indexes@samspublishing.com

How can we make this index more useful? Email us at indexes@samspublishing.com

C

How can we make this index more useful? Email us at indexes@samspublishing.com

rows, 370, 599

security, 601-602

SQL Server, 382

stored procedures, 600

Sybase, 383

tables, 371, 596-598

changes, defining, 624

extracting data from multiple, 634

fields, selecting, 622

relationships, creating, 615-617

unique data, selecting, 623

triggers, 600-601

upsizing, 905-906

views, 601

Web store database, 607-609

creating, 608

creditcards table, 613

customers table, 609-612

data access, 608

data types, 607

inventory table, 613

orders table, 613

products table, 613

transactions table, 614

DataGrid dialog box, 677

DataGrids

adding, 677-678

ASP.NET, 676-677

color scheme, 680

DataList behavior, 683

DataLists, 683-684, 687

DataSet dialog box, 666, 724

DataSet Paging behaviors, 677

DataSets, 666

creating, 666-668

pagination, 670-671

repeat regions, 672

date & time, 107

Date command, 107

Date functions, 627-628

date/time data type, 610

DateAdd() function, 628

datetime column type, 568

DB2, 382, 901

DblRows table format, 145

DBMS (Database Management System), 595

debugging. *See also* **errors**

CFML tags, 932-933

ColdFusion, 928, 931-933

CFML tag, 932-933

SQL error, 930

JSP, 545-546

SQL errors, 930

declarations

CSS syntax, 241

JSP, 534

default fonts, 96

default images folder, 56

default layers, 281-282

default value property, 747

Define Access Levels dialog box, 815

defined functions, 454

definition lists, 101

Defusion Web site, 901

Delete Buttons (DataGrids), 677

Delete Record behavior, 733

Delete Record dialog box, 735

Delete statement, 625

deleting

assets, 231

columns, 140-141

database records, 625

favorites, 231

How can we make this index more useful? Email us at indexes@samspublishing.com

server-side behaviors

downloading, 865

Extension Manager, 867-868

pre-downloading, 866

sharing, 467

submission, 467, 472

extensions CSS properties, 255

external editors

adding, 348

Fireworks. *See* Fireworks

Photoshop, 362-363

selecting, 347-349

external links, 75

F

failed login error message, 812

Favorites

assets, 231-232

Assets panel, 217, 223

assets, adding, 230

fields

databases, 370

Java, 539

<fieldset> tag, 588

fieldsets, 167

file explorer, 11

file field, 167

file not found error, 492

file system object, 504

File tab (Optimize window), 353-354

File View Columns category (Advanced Definition dialog box), 63-66

FileMaker Pro, 384

files

ActionScript, 890-893

ASP, 403-405

behaviors, 453

dependent, 68

extensions, 867

Flash, 338-339

hiding, 60-61

HTML, 448

Image, 449

JavaScript, 449

js, 462

Macromedia Extension Installation, 469

maintaining, 72-73

menus.xml, 463-465

objects, 449

orphaned, 75

renaming, 73

Shockwave, 342-345

synchronizing, 68-69

transferring, 68

viewing, 63-66

Web.Config

ASP.NET configuration, 519

authentication, 832-833

filter property, 255

firewalls, 497

Fireworks

buttons, creating, 356-358

crop tool, 355

export area, 354

Export wizard, 354

GIFs, 352

HTML, inserting, 358-359

images, 350-351

JPEGs, 352

How can we make this index more useful? Email us at indexes@sampublishing.com

G

How can we make this index more useful? Email us at indexes@samspublishing.com

How can we make this index more useful? Email us at indexes@samspublishing.com

Insert List/Menu button, 161-162

Insert Master Detail Page Set dialog box, 735

Insert menu commands

Date, 107

Form, 151

Horizontal Rule, 108

Layer, 280

Insert Navigation Bar dialog box, 122

Insert panel, 12, 30-31

applications, 38-40

characters, 35

common objects, 32-33

forms, 34

frames, 34

framesets, creating, 182, 186

head objects, 37-38

layout, 33

media, 36-37

middleware, 40

scripts, 38

tables, 34

templates, 35

text, 33

Insert Panel group, 922-923

Insert Parameter in Code Block button, 881

Insert Radio Button, 159

Insert Radio Group button, 159

Insert Radio Group dialog box, 159

Insert Record dialog box, 702, 721

Insert Repeating Table dialog box, 210-211

Insert Rollover dialog box, 119

Insert Rows or Columns dialog box, 140

Insert statement, 623-624

Insert Table dialog box, 128

Insert Tabular Data command, 147

Insert Tabular Data dialog box, 147

Insert Tabular Data object, 33

Insert Text Area button, 157

Insert Text Field button, 154

inserting

accessibility, 24

assets

documents, 221-222

Favorites, 230

check boxes, 158

columns, 140

content, layers, 285

Datagrids, 677-678

drop-down menus, 161-162

external editors, 348

Flash files, 338-339

form objects, 153

forms, 151-153

images, 114-115

includes, 529

information, databases, 372-374

items, shopping carts, 788-792

keyframes, 311-312

layers, 280-282, 307-310

library items, 235

multiple data, tables, 703-705, 712-714

pagination features, 659-660

radio buttons, 158-159

records, databases, 562, 697-699

rows, 140

scrolling lists, 162-163

search engines, 497-498

Shockwave files, 342-345

submit buttons, 163-164

text fields, 154

How can we make this index more useful? Email us at indexes@samspublishing.com

J

How can we make this index more useful? Email us at indexes@samspublishing.com

How can we make this index more useful? Email us at indexes@samspublishing.com

N

O

How can we make this index more useful? Email us at indexes@samspublishing.com

How can we make this index more useful? Email us at indexes@samspublishing.com

How can we make this index more useful? Email us at indexes@samspublishing.com

V

How can we make this index more useful? Email us at indexes@samspublishing.com

How can we make this index more useful? Email us at indexes@samspublishing.com

X – Y - Z

Wouldn't it be great

if the world's leading technical publishers joined forces to deliver their best tech books in a common digital reference platform?

They have. Introducing
InformIT Online Books
powered by Safari.

POWERED BY Safari

InformIT Online Books

informit.com/onlinebooks

- **Specific answers to specific questions.**
InformIT Online Books' powerful search engine gives you relevance-ranked results in a matter of seconds.

- **Immediate results.**
With InformIt Online Books, you can select the book you want and view the chapter or section you need immediately.

- **Cut, paste, and annotate.**
Paste code to save time and eliminate typographical errors. Make notes on the material you find useful and choose whether or not to share them with your workgroup.

- **Customized for your enterprise.**
Customize a library for you, your department, or your entire organization. You pay only for what you need.

Get your first 14 days **FREE!**
InformIT Online Books is offering its members a 10-book subscription risk free for 14 days. Visit **http://www.informit.com/onlinebooks** for details.

Your Guide to Computer Technology

www.informit.com

Sams has partnered with **InformIT.com** to bring technical information to your desktop. Drawing on Sams authors and reviewers to provide additional information on topics you're interested in, **InformIT.com** has free, in-depth information you won't find anywhere else.

ARTICLES

Keep your edge with thousands of free articles, in-depth features, interviews, and information technology reference recommendations—all written by experts you know and trust.

POWERED BY

ONLINE BOOKS

Answers in an instant from **InformIT Online Books'** 600+ fully searchable online books. Sign up now and get your first 14 days **free**.

CATALOG

Review online sample chapters and author biographies to choose exactly the right book from a selection of more than 5,000 titles.

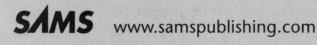

www.samspublishing.com